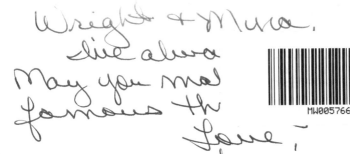

Wright + Mura,
live alwa
May you ma
famous th
Love,
Gayle

AFFIRMING YOU

ALECK ALEX

ALEXIS ALEC

Discovering the Biblical Meaning of Your Name

GAYLE CHANDLER

Source of Joy Publishers
Kernersville, NC

Published by Source of Joy Publishers
Kernersville, North Carolina
www.sourceofjoy.com

ISBN 10: 0-9818111-4-0
ISBN 13: 978-0-9818111-4-7

Library of Congress Control Number: 2008911384

First Source of Joy Publishers printing, January 2009

Introduction

You are holding in your hands a timeless resource. *Affirming You* will be pulled from your bookshelf on those special occasions when you want to positively declare the value of an individual. You will be expressing agreement with their Creator as to who they are created to be for His glory. This tool will give you entrance into the very heart of the person, regardless of age or level of maturity. The research within this book or that which you will do yourself will be a source of encouragement and affirmation.

The infallible truth of God's Word will speak life and purpose as it is expressed through the meaning of each name. Let the Lord use you to be the ultimate affirmer as you seize opportunities to let people know how very special they are.

To the four key men in my life:

My Heavenly Father
You have equipped me with vision and direction to bring honor back to
Your name with the extension of this ministry.

My Earthly Daddy: Alex Marvin "Buddy" Walker
Who always believed in me and expected the best of me
and was always there for me.

My Closest Friend: Jack Chandler
My husband—his loving support and encouragement
makes him the constant ultimate affirmer in my life.

My Treasured Grandson: Alec Chance Erickson
Who keeps me focused on leaving a rich inheritance to the
next generation—that of my heart.

Acknowledgements

A heart full of gratitude to:

Susan Whiteheart: my sister, the mastermind of the computer,
keeping me glued together.

Gwynn Savage: my sister who gave me much encouragement
and helped with research.

Kristen Eckstein: my guide through the whole publishing process.

Foreword

How parents agonize in choosing the name of a child-to-be! Naming books pile up, and Internet searches, and endless informal polls of friends and family. "What shall we name this longed-for child?" is the paramount question. Then suddenly, it comes—the perfect name! In her book, *Affirming You*, Gayle Chandler takes us on a journey that helps us discover the importance of names to God. A stunning picture comes to mind: Did God in His inimitable love, carefully and deliberately agonize to choose exactly the right name for each of us, His longed-for children? Did our Heavenly Parent whisper meaning into the hearts of our earthly parents—the meaning of who we were to be? This is a rich and wondrous look at the process and poignancy of naming, and of being named. Once you have read it, you will never again take a name lightly.

-*Karen Mains*

Director of *Hungry Souls,*
a division of *Mainstay Ministries*

About the Author

Gayle and her husband Jack pastored for almost thirty seven years. Together they have ministered in 26 countries. She has been very involved in all aspects of ministry, along with networking unity among area pastoral women from different denominations and directing children's camps. She has a passion to see people fulfill their God given identity and purpose. They have one daughter and one grandson and reside in Kernersville, North Carolina.

Chapter 1

As I would rock our baby daughter to sleep, I sang "Jesus, Jesus, there's just something about that name." This Gaither song was very popular at the time and a favorite when tucking in Lexi. Several times I would slowly stop rocking and singing, thinking she was asleep. Those little eyes would barely open and she would say "Dedus, Dedus." I knew I needed to rock and sing a little bit longer.

Jesus truly is the sweetest name I know! I have trained my spirit to call upon that Name in crisis or concern.

During an icy snow fall, I was returning to Indiana from speaking at a *Women's Aglow* meeting in Urbana, Illinois. While sliding off the interstate and into a deep ditch, I said "Jesus!" Immediately, a trustworthy couple stopped to help. Another time while on vacation, my husband and I flipped our thirty-one-foot travel trailer when a tire blew on the camper. As it fish-tailed out of control, I yelled "Jesus!" The camper flipped and was totaled, but our tow vehicle did not! On another occasion for a short season I was tormented with bad dreams. I woke Jack to pray. His first word was "Jesus." The torment left immediately.

No wonder that one-word prayer—Jesus—is so powerful, for it means Savior. Acts 2:21 says that everyone who calls on the name of the Lord will be saved. That one name calms a baby, rescues from tragedy, saves lives, and restores rest.

Philippians 2:9–11 in *The New International Version* says, "Therefore God exalted Him to the highest place and gave Him the name that is above every name, that at the name of Jesus every knee should bow, in heaven and earth and under the earth, and every tongue confess that Jesus Christ is Lord, to the glory of God the Father."

Picture His name over every single name ever named. The fullness of His authority is released as we connect with His character that is in each of His names. The more intimate I become with all the facets of His character, the more confident I am in walking in the authority He has given to me through my name.

When I first learned that my name *Gayle* means *source of joy*, I was disheartened. My parents' alcohol problems and eventual divorce, moving quite often, my poor grades in school, and my Mom's murder defined the opposite of joy for me.

The Lord made it clear to me that until I see Him as my *source of joy*, I will not be His *source of joy*. Unless His name is over my name, the opposite of my name will dominate. When I began defining Jesus as my source of joy, I began walking in the authority that joy is intended to bring.

That knowledge drove me to define joy based on God's Word, not by the world's standards or my emotions. The following is what He has taught me about my name, Gayle:

> Your heavenly Father has trusted you with a quality that releases healing, restores hope, and brings refreshing. You are one who takes the source of tears and defeat, and turns them into confident trust with rejoicing. As you experience and remain sensitive to the things that sorrow the heart of God, He will pour His oil of joy on and through you to restore hope to those who are mourning (Isaiah 61:1–3). Experiences of sorrow prepare for and enlarge your capacity for joy. The joy of the Lord will be your strength to endure the cross He has called you to bear. You are to fix your eyes on Jesus— the author and perfecter of your faith—Who for the joy set before Him endured the cross, scorning its shame, and sat down at the right hand of the throne of God (Hebrews 12:2). He will be faithful to give you a song in your "night" season (Psalm 42:8). God rejoices over you with gladness! (Zephaniah 3:17)

It took years to come to terms with the meaning of my first name, *Patricia*. It means *full of honor; noble one*. That did not seem to fit a life characterized by fear and intimidation. But as I experienced God as the one who is *full of honor—my noble one*—my fears were shattered. Yes, my palms still sweat and my knees shake when I am asked to speak publicly, but my inadequacies no longer rule me. Once again, my passion to be like my Lord overrides that which would destroy my identity.

Our names carry weight. They define who we are. They describe the character of God in which we are to extend. When we grasp the authority in

His name, we become His extension. I am responsible for the authority given me in my name through strength in His name. We enlarge His influence as we adopt His character. Life is centered around His reputation, not ours. One name should make God famous!

Proverbs 3:3–4 says, "Let love and faithfulness never leave you; bind them on the tablet of your heart. Then you will win favor and a *good name* in the sight of God and man." "A *good name* is more desirable than great riches; to be esteemed is better than silver or gold," Proverbs 22:1. Ecclesiastes 7:1 says, "A *good name* is better than fine perfume." (emphasis added) Are you getting His point that who you are far outweighs what you are?

A good name is characterized by choices that please God rather than man. We build a life that builds His honor and worth. This is done by focusing on eternal values over temporal ones. A good name is not merely a quality, but it is also expressed in action. The contrast is that "the name of the wicked will rot," Proverbs 10:7. The choice is ours!

During one of our visits to Israel, Jack bought me a necklace. It has the verse from Isaiah 49:16 written on it in Hebrew, "See, I have engraved you on the palms of My hands." The *New Living Translation* says, "See, I have written your name on My hand." There may have been thousands of Gayle's throughout the years, but He made room on His hand for mine! That is so awesome! He needed one more agent to bring His joy.

You will notice a picture on the cover of this book of large hands holding a small tree. This is an expression of our Heavenly Father holding our family tree. It is not an accident what family each of us was born into. Check out all of Psalm 139. In my family tree, I have four generations of "protector and helper of mankind; secure spirit" through my great-grandfather Aleck, my father Alex, my daughter Alexis, and my grandson Alec. Truly the Lord is carving His strong initials of a particular purpose He wants fulfilled through my family tree. We must trust the hand that created and formed us into His image to bring about abundant life to the legacy we each will leave.

In His hand I find refuge, protection, and provision to be all He made me to be. As I honor His name, He uses His hand to cleanse and erase all that brings dishonor to my name. His forgiveness and my surrender yield the pleasure I am created to bring Him.

The Lord can take the most vile, worthless name and restore value, purpose, and identity. I believe the Lord authorizes us to claim the positive traits of anyone's name that has injured us in any way. Saul of Tarsus had a terrible reputation as a chief persecutor. He made murderous threats against the Lord's disciples, even giving approval to Stephen's death. When God

9

humbled him at Damascus (which means *sackcloth weaver*), he was authorized by the Lord as His chosen instrument to carry His name before the Gentiles, their kings, and before the people of Israel. Saul was also called Paul. The name Paul means *little; dependent on God*. Who better could equip us to be totally dependent on God than Paul? He continues to serve as a dynamo of energy through his writings.

Who better could serve as an example of being a man after God's own heart than *beloved* David? What better choice could be made for the womb of our Savior than Mary, *myrrh; living fragrance*? The sweet aroma of myrrh is amplified through heat. Mary was chosen because she could walk through the fire and not be burned. Her humble surrender released His sweet fragrance.

As you read into the text, the definition of the name of Bible characters, you will better understand why they were chosen. In Genesis 5, from the Hebrew meanings we discover God's plan of redemption in the genealogy. The following list will show you the comparison:

Adam: *Man*
Seth: *Appointed*
Enosh: *Mortal*
Kenan: *Sorrow*
Mahalalel: *The blessed God*
Jared: *Shall come down*
Enoch: *Teaching*
Methuselah: *His death shall bring*
Lamech: *Despairing*
Noah: *Rest*

From this list, the following statement is derived:

Man appointed mortal sorrow. The blessed God shall come down teaching—His death shall bring the despairing rest.

You can now appreciate the timing of their birth and the fulfillment of their purposes for that season in history. The same is true with you.

The Lord says that He summons you by your name. You are His (Isaiah 43:1). He calls us neither by our title nor our occupation, but by our *name*! He desires to meet with us based on who we are. Even when it is all said and done, what matters is that our names are written in the Lamb's book of life (Revelation 21:27). Daniel 12:1 says, "He who overcomes will, like them, be dressed in white. I will never blot out his name before my Father and his angels."

Throughout the years I have summoned many people more closely to the Lord by giving them the meaning of their name. It began with sharing those definitions at baby dedications when we were in ministry serving as senior pastors. I have used this ministry at weddings, anniversaries, and funerals. I have given them as gifts to a cheerleader squad, a large day-care staff, and to family, neighbors, and friends. At the children's camp that I directed, I required that every child's name be researched.

One special opportunity I had was at a women's leadership conference. After sharing the meaning of each lady's name, the rest of the women declared positive traits they witnessed in agreement with her name's definition. Truly this tool gave way for them to build up one another in love.

Probably my favorite occasion to share names was at a slumber party. My dear friend, Betty Harris Connaway, invited her eight granddaughters over to prepare them to be brides. Besides all the fun, training, and food, I shared the meaning of each of their names. Of course the ages varied, as did their levels of understanding. But the tears of joy, words of encouragement, and warm hugs left lasting memories of affirmation of how special each of them will ever be.

Recently I was asked to speak at a funeral. Lillian's name meant *pure heart*. Not knowing the family very well, I began to research each of the names in her obituary. Much to my surprise, I found a common thread of God in three generations of *purity*. As I spoke, this was the challenge I gave that precious family: Pass on the legacy of being pure!

Joyce is a lady whom I worked with temporarily. I knew both of our names had to do with joy. That gave me direct access to her heart. Without knowing very much about the difficult season she was facing with her father's illness, God used me to be a source of joy and encouragement to her.

This tool has been effective at checkout lines, with waiters and waitresses, and anyone wearing a name-tag. If I have the name memorized, I seize the moment! Never once have I been rejected in sharing God's love through a person's name. It's as if I am releasing a prophetic mantle of God's purpose that is very welcomed. I never let my knowledge of whether they are a Christian or not change my approach. It has been an excellent witnessing tool!

I want to encourage you to fall in love with all the names of God. The better you know His names, the better you are equipped to minister to the variety of names that will cross your path. You can connect people with the very nature and character of God! The Lord revealed His different names at different stages in the Bible. He also allows us to connect with others in order to bring different character traits of the Lord at the very time they need it.

I love the story of Hagar. She was victimized and a castaway. God met her in her place of shame and hiding. He revealed Himself as *El Roi; the God who sees*. This knowledge energized Hagar to go back, raise Ishmael, and submit to authority.

Abraham was on Mount Moriah ready to sacrifice Isaac. As the knife was extended, the angel of the Lord said, "Don't do it! You passed the test! Look in the bush behind you and meet *Jehovah Jireh; your Provider!*" (my translation) As long as Abraham had served God, this was the first time he met that facet of Him!

Who we are should expose those in our lives to the specific Godly character quality we have been given. I also believe God brings people into our lives to do the same for us in our time of need and building.

It is so important to me that you catch the heart of this book. *Affirming You* is not just another baby name book. It is a timeless tool to help others know their identity based on the Word of God. My desire for you and me is that our name brings honor to the Lamb—for the fame of His name! Fall in love with the One—your Creator—who named you. Die without any regrets of bringing honor to His name through yours. After all, it is your name He will be looking for in the Lamb's Book of Life—be there!

Chapter 2

Who We Are, Not What We Are

"A good name is more desirable than great riches; to be esteemed is better than silver or gold," *New International Version*. In The Message it says, "A sterling reputation is better than striking it rich; a gracious spirit is better than money in the bank," Proverbs 22:1.

The Lord is telling us that our identity is in our name. He is placing more value on *who* we are rather than what we are. Our reputation is not measured by our occupation or title, but rather, our lives are described by fulfilling the meaning of our names.

For those belonging to Jesus, their names carry eternal value. "Even to them I will give in My house, and within My walls a place and a name better than that of sons and daughters; I will give them an everlasting name that will not be cut off," Isaiah 56:5. In contrast, the name of the wicked will be blotted out forever and ever (Psalm 9:5). It will be removed, wiped away, or obliterated. "The memory of the righteous will be a blessing, but the name of the wicked will rot," Proverbs 10:7.

God Puts Great Value on Names

Animals

Genesis 2:19–20 reveals how every living creature was named. "Now the Lord God had formed out of the ground all the beasts of the field and all the birds of the air. He brought them to the man to see what he would name them; and whatever the man called each living creature, that was its name. So the man gave names to all the livestock, the birds of the air, and all the beasts of the field."

Stars

"He (the Lord) determines the number of the stars and calls them each by name," Psalm 147:4.

People

There are 3,376 male and 181 female names in the Bible. "For this reason I kneel before the Father, from whom His whole family in heaven and on earth derives its name," Ephesians 3:14–15. We are even to greet one another by name (3 John 14).

All Names Come Under the Name of Jesus Christ!

The great Creator has a divine order to bring us to our fullest potential. It is simply prioritizing His name over ours. The following verses reveal some of His many names. As we confess the Lordship of Jesus Christ, our names bow in humble submission to His. This not only brings glorious protection, but great liberty to walk in the power of each of His mighty names.

1. "Therefore the Lord Himself will give you a sign: The virgin will be with child and will give birth to a son, and will call Him Immanuel," Isaiah 7:14.

2. "For unto us a child is born, to us a son is given, and the government will be on His shoulders. And He will be called Wonderful, Counselor, Mighty God, Everlasting Father, Prince of Peace," Isaiah 9:6.

3. "Therefore God exalted Him to the highest place and gave Him the name that is above every name, that at the name of Jesus every knee should bow, in heaven and on earth, and under the earth and every tongue confess that Jesus Christ is Lord to the glory of God the Father," Philippians 2:9–11.

The Process in Which to Study

The tools needed are:

1. A collection of a variety of name books, whether secular, religious, or ethnic. My favorites are those that give the literal meaning and suggested character quality.

2. A good dictionary and thesaurus.

3. An expository dictionary of the old and new testament words.

4. A *Strong's Concordance*.

5. Occasionally, an encyclopedia is needed.

6. A variety of Bible translations such as, *King James Version, New International Version, The Message, Amplified, New American Standard*, and the *New Living Translation*.

7. A variety of websites are also available.

Steps for Research:

1. **Choose the name**, clarify how it is spelled and pronounced, and whether it is a nickname (ie: Lexi for Alexis or Bill for William). Question whether it comes from being named after someone else such as Jenny for Virginia, Tori for Victoria, or Teri (a girl) named after Terry (a boy or girl). You may be looking for Kathy under the K's but find it under the C's with Catherine.

2. **Research the definition** from a variety of name books and/or online. List the meanings and their resources. Often one name will have a variety of meanings totally unrelated. The focus becomes balance. Choose the definition that is in the majority of the books for your word study. The meaning of the name may serve as the character quality.

3. **Create the character quality** if one is not given. My nephew's name is Dathan. The Dathan in the Bible was destroyed because of his rebellion (Numbers 16). The Biblical definition for Dathan is "their law; their decree;" in short meaning "not God's will, but their's be done." After much prayer, the Lord showed me the opposite is His plan: "following God's commands." When a name has a negative meaning God's plan is the opposite or positive meaning. Sometimes a name is defined by an **object** such as a lily, myrrh, laurel-leaves, or a rainbow. Or it can be defined by a **place** such as a gray fortress, pasture meadow from Scotland, a valley, from the dark water, or a steep hill. Or by an **occupation** like a candle maker, farmer, spear man, nurse, dweller at the crag, or a warrior. If a character quality is not given, you will need to research that object, place, or occupation. A character quality is a description of a distinctive trait or attribute; a person's moral behavior or an attribute of God displayed through an individual. It's a portrait of one's heart; a prophetic mantle defining who they are. This process is most important, for it is the estimation in which a person is held. Look for words that define the inner soul of a person. Keep it short—one to three words. Don't limit the word to just a noun, for it may be a verb or adjective. The last name of very dear friends of mine is Crow. Most of

my research on the crow (noun) was negative and disturbing. When I changed the focus to a verb, truth began to come. When one crows, it is a cry of pleasure and victory; one who awakens the morning!

4. Define key words from the definition and character quality. My name, *source of joy*, drove me to totally exhaust the word joy. I looked up every definition I could find and read every Bible verse concerning joy. Complete research requires you to break down antonyms and synonyms. Write down relating words and words that define the opposite.

5. Choose related scriptures. Some topics, such as grace, will have many to choose from while others, such as the word authority, will have very few. Select two key verses. Use some of the remaining references to weave into your summary.

6. Create a power-packed paragraph. This paragraph will affirm the Godly character qualities. Use a variety of words to drive home the meaning. It should also reveal issues to beware of. An example would be from "earnest devotee." I wrote, "You dispel division by bringing the very unity of God." The third element of the paragraph is showing the individual how he or she will be used of God for others. Instead of the negative or opposite destroying them, they break that very stronghold in others. Our names sharpen our sensitivity to specific needs in others.

Your name is brought to life through the name of Jesus in your spirit, not through your flesh. Satan tries to destroy us through the opposites of our names, but when redeemed they become the tools in which God uses us for His glory. It gives us entrance into the lives of others. Genesis 50:20 says, "You intended to harm me, but God intended it for good to accomplish what is now being done, the saving of many lives." The emphasis is not on *what* you are, but on *who* you are in Jesus—His character in and through you.

AARON

Light bringer; bringer of light

&

Psalm 27:1 *The Lord is my light and my salvation—whom shall I fear? The Lord is the stronghold of my life; of whom shall I be afraid.*

Proverbs 4:18 *The path of the righteous is like the first gleam of dawn, shining ever brighter till the full light of day.*

You are one who reflects the shining brightness of the countenance of Jesus. You are aggressive toward the fruitless deeds of darkness from the evil one, by exposing them to the light of Jesus. Everything exposed by light becomes visible, for it is the light that makes everything visible (Ephesians 5:11–14). This radiance that God has given you serves as a beacon to give guidance to those yet in darkness. Your life's mission is found in the following two verses: Isaiah 60:1–3 says, "Arise, shine, for your light has come, and the glory of the Lord rises upon you. See, darkness covers the earth, and thick darkness is over the peoples, but the Lord rises upon you and His glory appears over you. Nations will come to your light, and kings to the brightness of your dawn." And in Acts 13:47, "For this is what the Lord has commanded us: 'I have made you a light for the Gentiles, that you may bring salvation to the ends of the earth.'" Continue to shine as His star, leading many to righteousness (Daniel 12:3 and Philippians 2:15).

ABBY

My father's joy; source of joy

∞

Psalm 149:4–5 *For the Lord takes delight in His people; He crowns the humble with salvation. Let the saints rejoice in this honor and sing for joy on their beds.*

Psalm 45:7 *You love righteousness and hate wickedness; therefore God, your God, has set you above your companions by anointing you with the oil of joy.*

Psalm 16:11 says, "You have made known to me the path of life; You will fill me with joy in Your presence, with eternal pleasures at Your right hand." Your heavenly Father has trusted you with a quality that releases healing, restores hope, and brings refreshing. You are one who takes the source of tears and defeat, and turns them into confident trust with rejoicing. As you experience and remain sensitive to the things that sorrow the heart of God, He will pour His oil of joy on and through you to restore hope to those who are mourning (Isaiah 61:1–3). Experiences of sorrow prepare and enlarge your capacity for joy. The joy of the Lord will be your strength to endure the cross He has called you to bear. You are to fix your eyes on Jesus, the author and perfecter of your faith, who for the joy set before Him endured the cross, scorning its shame, and sat down at the right hand of the throne of God (Hebrews 12:2). He will be faithful to give you a song in your "night" season (Psalm 42:8). God rejoices over you with gladness! (Zephaniah 3:17)

ABIGAIL

My father's joy; source of joy

ℰℂ

Psalm 149:4–5 *For the Lord takes delight in His people; He crowns the humble with salvation. Let the saints rejoice in this honor and sing for joy on their beds.*

Psalm 45:7 *You love righteousness and hate wickedness; therefore God, your God, has set you above your companions by anointing you with the oil of joy.*

Psalm 16:11 says, "You have made known to me the path of life; You will fill me with joy in Your presence, with eternal pleasures at Your right hand." Your heavenly Father has trusted you with a quality that releases healing, restores hope, and brings refreshing. You are one who takes the source of tears and defeat, and turns them into confident trust with rejoicing. As you experience and remain sensitive to the things that sorrow the heart of God, He will pour His oil of joy on and through you to restore hope to those who are mourning (Isaiah 61:1–3). Experiences of sorrow prepare and enlarge your capacity for joy. The joy of the Lord will be your strength to endure the cross He has called you to bear. You are to fix your eyes on Jesus, the author and perfecter of your faith, who for the joy set before Him endured the cross, scorning its shame, and sat down at the right hand of the throne of God (Hebrews 12:2). He will be faithful to give you a song in your "night" season (Psalm 42:8). God rejoices over you with gladness! (Zephaniah 3:17)

ADAM

Man of earth; God's creation

ॐ

Ephesians 2:10 *For we are God's workmanship, created in Christ Jesus to do good works, which God prepared in advance for us to do.*

II Corinthians 5:17 *Therefore, if anyone is in Christ, he is a new creation; the old has gone, the new has come!*

Through you the Lord will bring Himself into existence: He will originate. How you deal with the past determines your future. Regardless of curses or blessings, failures or successes, you are God's platform for a "new thing." You cannot lean to your own understanding or reasoning. God Almighty created the heavens, the earth, and you in His image. Isaiah 42:9, "See, the former things have taken place, and new things I declare; before they spring into being I announce them to you." Isaiah 43:18–19, "Forget the former things; do not dwell on the past. See, I am doing a new thing! Now it springs up; do you not perceive it? I am making a way in the desert and streams in the wasteland." Isaiah 48:6b, "From now on I will tell you of new things, of hidden things unknown to you." Isaiah 65:17–19, "Behold, I will create new heavens and a new earth. The former things will not be remembered, nor will they come to mind. But be glad and rejoice forever in what I will create, for I will create Jerusalem to be a delight and its people a joy. I will rejoice over Jerusalem and take delight in My people; the sound of weeping and of crying will be heard in it no more." Because of your passion for the eternal over the temporal, you are used of God to remove what can be shaken—the created things—so that what cannot be shaken may remain (Hebrews 12:27). The more completely dependent you become on your Creator, the more productive your life will be for Him! I Peter 4:19, "So then, those who suffer according to God's will should commit themselves to their Creator and continue to do good." As you stay yielded and surrendered to God, the clay of your heart will stay tender. Only then can He mold you into the image of His Son, Jesus Christ. God will work His approval through you to those who feel ugly, worthless, and to those who have no hope.

ADDISON

Adam's descendent; God's creation

Ephesians 2:10 *For we are God's workmanship, created in Christ Jesus to do good works, which God prepared in advance for us to do.*

II Corinthians 5:17 *Therefore, if anyone is in Christ, he is a new creation; the old has gone, the new has come!*

Through you the Lord will bring Himself into existence: He will originate. How you deal with the past determines your future. Regardless of curses or blessings, failures or successes, you are God's platform for a "new thing." You cannot lean to your own understanding or reasoning. God Almighty created the heavens, the earth, and you in His image. Isaiah 42:9, "See, the former things have taken place, and new things I declare; before they spring into being I announce them to you." Isaiah 43:18–19, "Forget the former things; do not dwell on the past. See, I am doing a new thing! Now it springs up; do you not perceive it? I am making a way in the desert and streams in the wasteland." Isaiah 48:6b, "From now on I will tell you of new things, of hidden things unknown to you." Isaiah 65:17–19, "Behold, I will create new heavens and a new earth. The former things will not be remembered, nor will they come to mind. But be glad and rejoice forever in what I will create, for I will create Jerusalem to be a delight and its people a joy. I will rejoice over Jerusalem and take delight in My people; the sound of weeping and of crying will be heard in it no more." Because of your passion for the eternal over the temporal, you are used of God to remove what can be shaken—the created things—so that what cannot be shaken may remain (Hebrews 12:27). The more completely dependent you become on your Creator, the more productive your life will be for Him! I Peter 4:19, "So then, those who suffer according to God's will should commit themselves to their Creator and continue to do good." As you stay yielded and surrendered to God, the clay of your heart will stay tender. Only then can He mold you into the image of His Son, Jesus Christ. God will work His approval through you to those who feel ugly, worthless, and to those who have no hope.

ADRIAN

Black earth; creative heart

Colossians 1:16 *For by Him all things were created: things in heaven and on earth, visible and invisible, whether thrones or powers or rulers or authorities; all things were created by Him and for Him.*

Ephesians 2:10 *For we are God's workmanship, created in Christ Jesus to do good works, which God prepared in advance for us to do.*

Through you the Lord will bring Himself into existence; He will originate. How you deal with the past determines your future. Regardless of curses or blessings, failures or successes, you are God's platform for a "new thing." You cannot lean to your own understanding or reasoning. God Almighty created the heavens, the earth, and you in His image. Isaiah 42:9, "See, the former things have taken place, and new things I declare; before they spring into being I announce them to you." Isaiah 43:18–19, "Forget the former things; do not dwell on the past. See, I am doing a new thing! Now it springs up; do you not perceive it? I am making a way in the desert and streams in the wasteland." Isaiah 48:6b, "From now on I will tell you of new things, of hidden things unknown to you." Isaiah 65:17–19, "Behold, I will create new heavens and a new earth. The former things will not be remembered, nor will they come to mind. But be glad and rejoice forever in what I will create, for I will create Jerusalem to be a delight and its people a joy. I will rejoice over Jerusalem and take delight in My people; the sound of weeping and of crying will be heard in it no more." Because of your passion for the eternal over the temporal, you are used of God to remove what can be shaken—the created things—so that what cannot be shaken may remain (Hebrews 12:27). The more completely dependent you become on your Creator, the more productive your life will be for Him! I Peter 4:19, "So then, those who suffer according to God's will should commit themselves to their Creator and continue to do good." As you stay yielded and surrendered to God, the clay of your heart will stay tender. Only then can He mold you into the image of His Son, Jesus Christ. God will work His approval through you to those who feel ugly, worthless, and to those who have no hope.

ADRIANA

Black earth; creative heart

ঔ

Colossians 1:16 *For by Him all things were created: things in heaven and on earth, visible and invisible, whether thrones or powers or rulers or authorities; all things were created by Him and for Him.*

Ephesians 2:10 *For we are God's workmanship, created in Christ Jesus to do good works, which God prepared in advance for us to do.*

Through you the Lord will bring Himself into existence; He will originate. How you deal with the past determines your future. Regardless of curses or blessings, failures or successes, you are God's platform for a "new thing." You cannot lean to your own understanding or reasoning. God Almighty created the heavens, the earth, and you in His image. Isaiah 42:9, "See, the former things have taken place, and new things I declare; before they spring into being I announce them to you." Isaiah 43:18–19, "Forget the former things; do not dwell on the past. See, I am doing a new thing! Now it springs up; do you not perceive it? I am making a way in the desert and streams in the wasteland." Isaiah 48:6b, "From now on I will tell you of new things, of hidden things unknown to you." Isaiah 65:17–19, "Behold, I will create new heavens and a new earth. The former things will not be remembered, nor will they come to mind. But be glad and rejoice forever in what I will create, for I will create Jerusalem to be a delight and its people a joy. I will rejoice over Jerusalem and take delight in My people; the sound of weeping and of crying will be heard in it no more." Because of your passion for the eternal over the temporal, you are used of God to remove what can be shaken—the created things—so that what cannot be shaken may remain (Hebrews 12:27). The more completely dependent you become on your Creator, the more productive your life will be for Him! I Peter 4:19, "So then, those who suffer according to God's will should commit themselves to their Creator and continue to do good." As you stay yielded and surrendered to God, the clay of your heart will stay tender. Only then can He mold you into the image of His Son, Jesus Christ. God will work His approval through you to those who feel ugly, worthless, and to those who have no hope.

AIDEN

Fiery; enthusiastic

❧

Isaiah 62:1 *For Zion's sake I will not keep silent, for Jerusalem's sake I will not remain quiet, till her righteousness shines out like the dawn, her salvation like a blazing torch.*

II Timothy 1:6 *For this reason I remind you to fan into flame the gift of God, which is in you through the laying on of my hands.*

The way Jesus Christ served His heavenly Father is your only example to follow. The word "enthusiastic" means "possessed by God." Zeal for God's house consumed Jesus (John 2:17). Even to His parents He said, "Didn't you know I had to be in my Father's house?" Luke 2:49. "He put on righteousness as His breastplate, and the helmet of salvation on His head; He put on the garments of vengeance and wrapped Himself in zeal as in a cloak," Isaiah 59:17. Just as Jesus was determined and passionate, so are you. As you fervently worship God as the all-consuming fire (Hebrews 12:29), you will invade the strongholds of weariness in spirit, soul, and body. You bring balance to those dominated by their emotions. God's Word and His presence will keep His fire ignited in and through you. Guard against always putting out fires, but keep in mind that you must always start them! May you have an infusion of spiritual adrenaline.

AIMEE

Beloved one; beloved

ℰ

Deuteronomy 33:12 *Let the beloved of the Lord rest secure in Him, for He shields him all day long, and the one the Lord loves rests between His shoulders.*

I John 4:7 *Dear friends, let us love one another, for love comes from God. Everyone who loves has been born of God and knows God.*

You are highly valued, treasured, and precious to the Lord. You are an eye-witness of the very majesty of Jesus Christ. He received glory and honor from God the Father when the voice came to Him from the Majestic Glory, saying, "This is my Son, whom I love; with Him I am well pleased," II Peter 1:16–17. As you stay committed to Him, one day you will also hear those words. "We know and rely on the love of God for us. God is love, whoever lives in love lives in God and God in him," I John 4:16. You are expressive in worship because you are near to the heart of God. As you give respect, pleasure, and adoration to the Lord, He will give it back to you. You are aggressive to show the love of God to those who are disliked, abhorred, and hated. Rest secure in Him!

AL

Noble, brilliant; man of honor

෨

Isaiah 32:8 *But the noble man makes noble plans, and by noble deeds he stands.*

Luke 8:15 *But the seed on good soil stands for those with a noble and good heart, who hear the word, retain it, and by persevering produce a crop.*

Proverbs 18:12 says, "Before his downfall a man's heart is proud, but humility comes before honor." You are one who has a humble confidence in recognizing and expressing reverence, worship, adoration, trust, deference, tribute, admiration, and respect. This is the result of being secure in the truth of who you are in the Lord. Through humility, King Jesus made a way for you to be engrafted into His royalty. He made of Himself no reputation and took on the nature of a servant (Philippians 2:7) to affirm your value. Through self-denial, you prioritize excellence in virtue, truthfulness, and faithfulness. Because of the respect you have earned, you dismantle inferiority, disgrace, shame, and offenses. No one feels second-rate in your presence. The deeper that the Lord is your object of reverence, the greater your confidence will be in giving approval and worth. Because you are tall in spirit, your face is always turned upward.

ALANA

Beautiful; cheerful one

Proverbs 15:13 *A happy heart makes the face cheerful, but heartache crushes the spirit.*

Proverbs 17:22 *A cheerful heart is good medicine, but a crushed spirit dries up the bones.*

Your cheerful heart has a continual feast (Proverbs 15:15) and your cheerful look brings joy to the heart (Proverbs 15:30). Out of your deep love for God's Word, you are equipped to give approval, encouragement, and inspiration to the rejected, hopeless, and reluctant. You are very aware that Jesus Christ has overcome the world through His death and resurrection. In every situation you improve the outlook on the future. You cheer the despondent, downcast, and discouraged to victory. With the sorrows you allow God to heal in your own life, you are anointed to provide the oil of gladness to those who mourn (Isaiah 61:1–3). Your presence brings healing to the ugliest, most confused settings. God loves what a cheerful giver you are! (II Corinthians 9:7)

ALBERT

Noble, brilliant; man of honor

Isaiah 32:8 *But the noble man makes noble plans, and by noble deeds he stands.*

Luke 8:15 *But the seed on good soil stands for those with a noble and good heart, who hear the word, retain it, and by persevering produce a crop.*

Proverbs 18:12 says, "Before his downfall a man's heart is proud, but humility comes before honor." You are one who has a humble confidence in recognizing and expressing reverence, worship, adoration, trust, deference, tribute, admiration, and respect. This is the result of being secure in the truth of who you are in the Lord. Through humility, King Jesus made a way for you to be engrafted into His royalty. He made of Himself no reputation and took on the nature of a servant (Philippians 2:7) to affirm your value. Through self-denial, you prioritize excellence in virtue, truthfulness, and faithfulness. Because of the respect you have earned, you dismantle inferiority, disgrace, shame, and offenses. No one feels second-rate in your presence. The deeper that the Lord is your object of reverence, the greater your confidence will be in giving approval and worth. Because you are tall in spirit, your face is always turned upward.

ALEC

Protector and helper of mankind; secure spirit

જી

Deuteronomy 33:12 *Let the beloved of the Lord rest secure in Him, for He shields him all day long, and the one the Lord loves rests between His shoulders.*

Job 11:18 *You will be secure, because there is hope; you will look about you and take your rest in safety.*

Your life is bound securely in the bundle of the living by the Lord your God (I Samuel 25:29). You will not fear the terror of night, nor the arrow that flies by day (Psalm 91:5). You will have no fear of bad news; your heart is steadfast, trusting in the Lord (Psalm 112:7). You say with confidence that the Lord is your helper. God's sovereign protection frees you from doubt and harm. Because you find your shelter, assurance, stability, and strength in your personal relationship with the Lord, you are kept in a safe place. Lay with compassionate humility a firm foundation for others, providing them with solid security. As you stay hidden in the shadow of His wings (Psalm 61:4), you direct deliverance for the weak, insecure, unsheltered, and frail. You are to help others to become overcomers, victorious, confident, and secure—regardless of the risk and cost to you.

ALECK

Protector and helper of mankind; secure spirit

ல

Deuteronomy 33:12 *Let the beloved of the Lord rest secure in Him, for He shields him all day long, and the one the Lord loves rests between His shoulders.*

Job 11:18 *You will be secure, because there is hope; you will look about you and take your rest in safety.*

Your life is bound securely in the bundle of the living by the Lord your God (I Samuel 25:29). You will not fear the terror of night, nor the arrow that flies by day (Psalm 91:5). You will have no fear of bad news; your heart is steadfast, trusting in the Lord (Psalm 112:7). You say with confidence that the Lord is your helper. God's sovereign protection frees you from doubt and harm. Because you find your shelter, assurance, stability, and strength in your personal relationship with the Lord, you are kept in a safe place. Lay with compassionate humility a firm foundation for others, providing them with solid security. As you stay hidden in the shadow of His wings (Psalm 61:4), you direct deliverance for the weak, insecure, unsheltered, and frail. You are to help others to become overcomers, victorious, confident, and secure—regardless of the risk and cost to you.

ALETA

Little winged one; truth

&

Psalm 89:1–2 *I will sing of the Lord's great love forever; with my mouth I will make Your faithfulness known through all generations. I will declare that Your love stands firm forever, that You established Your faithfulness in heaven itself.*

Psalm 51:6 *Surely You desire truth in the inner parts; You teach me wisdom in the inmost place.*

John 14:6 *Jesus answered, "I am the way and the truth and the life. No one comes to the Father except through Me."*

"You know the truth and the truth has set you free," John 8:32. You are one who is aggressive toward lies and deception. Your purpose is to bring about truth through openness, revelation, authenticity, accuracy, and honesty. As God's messenger, you will have firmness in keeping and executing His promises and also your own. Your God-given wisdom will be based on God's Word alone. Zechariah 8:16 says, "These are the things you are to do: Speak the truth to each other, and render true and sound judgment in your courts." May true instruction be in your mouth and nothing false be found on your lips (Malachi 2:6).

ALEX

Protector and helper of mankind; secure spirit

ﬡ

Deuteronomy 33:12 *Let the beloved of the Lord rest secure in Him, for He shields him all day long, and the one the Lord loves rests between His shoulders.*

Job 11:18 *You will be secure, because there is hope; you will look about you and take your rest in safety.*

Your life is bound securely in the bundle of the living by the Lord your God (I Samuel 25:29). You will not fear the terror of night, nor the arrow that flies by day (Psalm 91:5). You will have no fear of bad news; your heart is steadfast, trusting in the Lord (Psalm 112:7). You say with confidence that the Lord is your helper. God's sovereign protection frees you from doubt and harm. Because you find your shelter, assurance, stability, and strength in your personal relationship with the Lord, you are kept in a safe place. Lay with compassionate humility a firm foundation for others, providing them with solid security. As you stay hidden in the shadow of His wings (Psalm 61:4), you direct deliverance for the weak, insecure, unsheltered, and frail. You are to help others to become overcomers, victorious, confident, and secure—regardless of the risk and cost to you.

ALEXANDER

Protector and helper of mankind; secure spirit

&

Deuteronomy 33:12 *Let the beloved of the Lord rest secure in Him, for He shields him all day long, and the one the Lord loves rests between His shoulders.*

Job 11:18 *You will be secure, because there is hope; you will look about you and take your rest in safety.*

Your life is bound securely in the bundle of the living by the Lord your God (I Samuel 25:29). You will not fear the terror of night, nor the arrow that flies by day (Psalm 91:5). You will have no fear of bad news; your heart is steadfast, trusting in the Lord (Psalm 112:7). You say with confidence that the Lord is your helper. God's sovereign protection frees you from doubt and harm. Because you find your shelter, assurance, stability, and strength in your personal relationship with the Lord, you are kept in a safe place. Lay with compassionate humility a firm foundation for others, providing them with solid security. As you stay hidden in the shadow of His wings (Psalm 61:4), you direct deliverance for the weak, insecure, unsheltered, and frail. You are to help others to become overcomers, victorious, confident, and secure—regardless of the risk and cost to you.

ALEXIS

Protector and helper of mankind; secure spirit

Deuteronomy 33:12 *Let the beloved of the Lord rest secure in Him, for He shields him all day long, and the one the Lord loves rests between His shoulders.*

Job 11:18 *You will be secure, because there is hope; you will look about you and take your rest in safety.*

Your life is bound securely in the bundle of the living by the Lord your God (I Samuel 25:29). You will not fear the terror of night, nor the arrow that flies by day (Psalm 91:5). You will have no fear of bad news; your heart is steadfast, trusting in the Lord (Psalm 112:7). You say with confidence that the Lord is your helper. God's sovereign protection frees you from doubt and harm. Because you find your shelter, assurance, stability, and strength in your personal relationship with the Lord, you are kept in a safe place. Lay with compassionate humility a firm foundation for others, providing them with solid security. As you stay hidden in the shadow of His wings (Psalm 61:4), you direct deliverance for the weak, insecure, unsheltered, and frail. You are to help others to become overcomers, victorious, confident, and secure—regardless of the risk and cost to you.

ALICE

Truthful one; truthful

❧

Psalm 89:1–2 *I will sing of the Lord's great love forever; with my mouth I will make Your faithfulness known through all generations. I will declare that Your love stands firm forever, that You established Your faithfulness in heaven itself.*

Psalm 51:6 *Surely You desire truth in the inner parts; You teach me wisdom in the inmost place.*

John 14:6 *Jesus answered, "I am the way and the truth and the life. No one comes to the Father except through Me."*

"You know the truth and the truth has set you free," John 8:32. You are one who is aggressive toward lies and deception. Your purpose is to bring about truth through openness, revelation, authenticity, accuracy, and honesty. As God's messenger, you will have firmness in keeping and executing His promises and also your own. Your God-given wisdom will be based on God's Word alone. Zechariah 8:16 says, "These are the things you are to do: Speak the truth to each other, and render true and sound judgment in your courts." May true instruction be in your mouth and nothing false be found on your lips (Malachi 2:6).

ALICIA

Truthful one; truthful

&

Psalm 89:1–2 *I will sing of the Lord's great love forever; with my mouth I will make Your faithfulness known through all generations. I will declare that Your love stands firm forever, that You established Your faithfulness in heaven itself.*

Psalm 51:6 *Surely You desire truth in the inner parts; You teach me wisdom in the inmost place.*

John 14:6 *Jesus answered, "I am the way and the truth and the life. No one comes to the Father except through Me."*

"You know the truth and the truth has set you free," John 8:32. You are one who is aggressive toward lies and deception. Your purpose is to bring about truth through openness, revelation, authenticity, accuracy, and honesty. As God's messenger, you will have firmness in keeping and executing His promises and also your own. Your God-given wisdom will be based on God's Word alone. Zechariah 8:16 says, "These are the things you are to do: Speak the truth to each other, and render true and sound judgment in your courts." May true instruction be in your mouth and nothing false be found on your lips (Malachi 2:6).

ALIDA

Wing; free spirit

&

Isaiah 61:1   The Spirit of the Sovereign Lord is on me, because the Lord has anointed me to preach good news to the poor. He has sent me to bind up the brokenhearted, to proclaim freedom for the captives and release from darkness for the prisoners.

Galatians 5:1   It is for freedom that Christ has set us free. Stand firm, then, and do not let yourselves be burdened again by a yoke of slavery.

There are no restrictions on your abandoned commitment to the Lord Jesus Christ. Knowing God's truth frees you from the bondage and care of sin and oppression (John 8:32). The free gift of God—Jesus Christ—exchanges offense for God's grace, condemnation for justification, shame for holiness and the spirit of the world for the Spirit of God. You are fearless as you loose those in bondage and give pardon to the imprisoned—all because the law of the Spirit of life set you free from the law of sin and death. Do not use your freedom to indulge the sinful nature; rather, serve one another in love (Galatians 5:13). Freely you have received; freely give (Matthew 10:8).

ALIYAH

Exalted; humble

❧

Micah 6:8 *He has showed you, O man, what is good. And what does the Lord require of you? To act justly and to love mercy and to walk humbly with your God.*

I Peter 5:6 *Humble yourselves, therefore, under God's mighty hand, that He may lift you up in due time.*

Prove to be trustworthy over little and God will make you ruler over much (Luke 19:17). The higher you lift the Lord, the more dependent you will be on Him. He increases; you decrease (John 3:30). Being exalted only comes from God—not from you or anyone else. It is for the purpose of enlarging His kingdom. Take no credit for the enormous favor God will give you. It is His grace that will give entrance to these doors of favor, as you choose His approval over man's. Philippians 2:3 says, "Do nothing out of selfish ambition or vain conceit, but in humility consider others better than yourselves." Humility and the fear of the Lord bring wealth, honor, and life (Proverbs 22:4).

ALLAN

Handsome; cheerful one

ॐ

Proverbs 15:13 *A happy heart makes the face cheerful, but heartache crushes the spirit.*

Proverbs 17:22 *A cheerful heart is good medicine, but a crushed spirit dries up the bones.*

Your cheerful heart has a continual feast (Proverbs 15:15) and your cheerful look brings joy to the heart (Proverbs 15:30). Out of your deep love for God's Word, you are equipped to give approval, encouragement, and inspiration to the rejected, hopeless, and reluctant. You are very aware that Jesus Christ has overcome the world through His death and resurrection. In every situation you improve the outlook on the future. You cheer the despondent, downcast, and discouraged to victory. With the sorrows you allow God to heal in your own life, you are anointed to provide the oil of gladness to those who mourn (Isaiah 61:1–3). Your presence brings healing to the ugliest, most confused settings. God loves what a cheerful giver you are! (II Corinthians 9:7)

ALLEE

Brilliant; illuminated

Psalm 27:1 *The Lord is my light and my salvation—whom shall I fear? The Lord is the stronghold of my life; of whom shall I be afraid.*

Proverbs 4:18 *The path of the righteous is like the first gleam of dawn, shining ever brighter till the full light of day.*

You are one who reflects the shining brightness of the countenance of Jesus. You are aggressive toward the fruitless deeds of darkness from the evil one, by exposing them to the light of Jesus. Everything exposed by light becomes visible, for it is the light that makes everything visible (Ephesians 5:11–14). This radiance that God has given you serves as a beacon to give guidance to those yet in darkness. Your life's mission is found in the following two verses: Isaiah 60:1–3 says, "Arise, shine, for your light has come, and the glory of the Lord rises upon you. See, darkness covers the earth, and thick darkness is over the peoples, but the Lord rises upon you and His glory appears over you. Nations will come to your light, and kings to the brightness of your dawn." And in Acts 13:47, "For this is what the Lord has commanded us: 'I have made you a light for the Gentiles, that you may bring salvation to the ends of the earth.'" Continue to shine as His star, leading many to righteousness (Daniel 12:3 and Philippians 2:15).

ALLEN

Handsome; cheerful one

ॐ

Proverbs 15:13 *A happy heart makes the face cheerful, but heartache crushes the spirit.*

Proverbs 17:22 *A cheerful heart is good medicine, but a crushed spirit dries up the bones.*

Your cheerful heart has a continual feast (Proverbs 15:15) and your cheerful look brings joy to the heart (Proverbs 15:30). Out of your deep love for God's Word, you are equipped to give approval, encouragement, and inspiration to the rejected, hopeless, and reluctant. You are very aware that Jesus Christ has overcome the world through His death and resurrection. In every situation you improve the outlook on the future. You cheer the despondent, downcast, and discouraged to victory. With the sorrows you allow God to heal in your own life, you are anointed to provide the oil of gladness to those who mourn (Isaiah 61:1–3). Your presence brings healing to the ugliest, most confused settings. God loves what a cheerful giver you are! (II Corinthians 9:7)

ALLIE

Brilliant; illuminated

&

Psalm 27:1 *The Lord is my light and my salvation—whom shall I fear? The Lord is the stronghold of my life; of whom shall I be afraid.*

Proverbs 4:18 *The path of the righteous is like the first gleam of dawn, shining ever brighter till the full light of day.*

You are one who reflects the shining brightness of the countenance of Jesus. You are aggressive toward the fruitless deeds of darkness from the evil one, by exposing them to the light of Jesus. Everything exposed by light becomes visible, for it is the light that makes everything visible (Ephesians 5:11–14). This radiance that God has given you serves as a beacon to give guidance to those yet in darkness. Your life's mission is found in the following two verses: Isaiah 60:1–3 says, "Arise, shine, for your light has come, and the glory of the Lord rises upon you. See, darkness covers the earth, and thick darkness is over the peoples, but the Lord rises upon you and His glory appears over you. Nations will come to your light, and kings to the brightness of your dawn." And in Acts 13:47, "For this is what the Lord has commanded us: 'I have made you a light for the Gentiles, that you may bring salvation to the ends of the earth.'" Continue to shine as His star, leading many to righteousness (Daniel 12:3 and Philippians 2:15).

ALLISON

Truthful; truthful one

ॐ

Psalm 89:1–2 *I will sing of the Lord's great love forever; with my mouth I will make Your faithfulness known through all generations. I will declare that Your love stands firm forever, that You established Your faithfulness in heaven itself.*

Psalm 51:6 *Surely You desire truth in the inner parts; You teach me wisdom in the inmost place.*

John 14:6 *Jesus answered, "I am the way and the truth and the life. No one comes to the Father except through Me."*

"You know the truth and the truth has set you free," John 8:32. You are one who is aggressive toward lies and deception. Your purpose is to bring about truth through openness, revelation, authenticity, accuracy, and honesty. As God's messenger, you will have firmness in keeping and executing His promises and also your own. Your God-given wisdom will be based on God's Word alone. Zechariah 8:16 says, "These are the things you are to do: Speak the truth to each other, and render true and sound judgment in your courts." May true instruction be in your mouth and nothing false be found on your lips (Malachi 2:6).

ALTA

High or lofty; noble spirit

∽

Isaiah 32:8 *But the noble man makes noble plans, and by noble deeds he stands.*

Luke 8:15 *But the seed on good soil stands for those with a noble and good heart, who hear the word, retain it, and by persevering produce a crop.*

Proverbs 18:12 says, "Before his downfall a man's heart is proud, but humility comes before honor." You are one who has a humble confidence in recognizing and expressing reverence, worship, adoration, trust, deference, tribute, admiration, and respect. This is the result of being secure in the truth of who you are in the Lord. Through humility, King Jesus made a way for you to be engrafted into His royalty. He made of Himself no reputation and took on the nature of a servant (Philippians 2:7) to affirm your value. Through self-denial, you prioritize excellence in virtue, truthfulness, and faithfulness. Because of the respect you have earned, you dismantle inferiority, disgrace, shame, and offenses. No one feels second-rate in your presence. The deeper that the Lord is your object of reverence, the greater your confidence will be in giving approval and worth. Because you are tall in spirit, your face is always turned upward.

ALYSSA

Truthful; truthful one

ॐ

Psalm 89:1–2 *I will sing of the Lord's great love forever; with my mouth I will make Your faithfulness known through all generations. I will declare that Your love stands firm forever, that You established Your faithfulness in heaven itself.*

Psalm 51:6 *Surely You desire truth in the inner parts; You teach me wisdom in the inmost place.*

John 14:6 *Jesus answered, "I am the way and the truth and the life. No one comes to the Father except through Me."*

"You know the truth and the truth has set you free," John 8:32. You are one who is aggressive toward lies and deception. Your purpose is to bring about truth through openness, revelation, authenticity, accuracy, and honesty. As God's messenger, you will have firmness in keeping and executing His promises and also your own. Your God-given wisdom will be based on God's Word alone. Zechariah 8:16 says, "These are the things you are to do: Speak the truth to each other, and render true and sound judgment in your courts." May true instruction be in your mouth and nothing false be found on your lips (Malachi 2:6).

AMANDA

Worthy of love; beloved

❧

Deuteronomy 33:12 *Let the beloved of the Lord rest secure in Him, for He shields him all day long, and the one the Lord loves rests between His shoulders.*

I John 4:7 *Dear friends, let us love one another, for love comes from God. Everyone who loves has been born of God and knows God.*

You are highly valued, treasured, and precious to the Lord. You are an eye-witness of the very majesty of Jesus Christ. He received glory and honor from God the Father when the voice came to Him from the Majestic Glory, saying, "This is my Son, whom I love; with Him I am well pleased," II Peter 1:16–17. As you stay committed to Him, one day you will also hear those words. "We know and rely on the love of God for us. God is love, whoever lives in love lives in God and God in him," I John 4:16. You are expressive in worship because you are near to the heart of God. As you give respect, pleasure, and adoration to the Lord, He will give it back to you. You are aggressive to show the love of God to those who are disliked, abhorred, and hated. Rest secure in Him!

AMBER

Jewel; precious one

Zephaniah 3:17 *The Lord your God is with you, He is mighty to save. He will take great delight in you, He will quiet you with His love, He will rejoice over you with singing.*

Ephesians 5:28–30 *In this same way, husbands ought to love their wives as their own bodies. He who loves his wife loves himself. After all, no one ever hated His own body, but he feeds and cares for it, just as Christ does the church - for we are members of His body.*

You are God's "treasured possession" (Deuteronomy 7:6). By giving the very life of His Son, God has committed to highly value you and take good care of you. He will treat you tenderly in tough times. You are to relate to others as Jesus relates to the Father and to us. Paul served as an example for you. I Thessalonians 2:7–8 says, "We were gentle among you, like a mother caring for her little children. We loved you so much that we were delighted to share with you not only the gospel of God but our lives as well, because you had become so dear to us." The warmth you experience being held close to His heart will enable you to melt the ice in others—the rejected and the castaways. Be free to be intimate with your Maker with trust and selfless submission.

AMELIA

Industrious one; diligent one

ℰℭ

Colossians 1:16 *For by Him all things were created: things in heaven and on earth, visible and invisible, whether thrones or powers or rulers or authorities; all things were created by Him and for Him.*

Ephesians 2:10 *For we are God's workmanship, created in Christ Jesus to do good works, which God prepared in advance for us to do.*

To be industrious means to be skillful, hardworking, zealous, and diligent. By persevering, you give careful attention to detail. There is not a lazy bone in your body. Through you the Lord will originate. How you deal with the past determines your future. Regardless of the curses or blessings, the failures or successes, you are God's platform for a "new thing." You cannot lean on your own understanding or reasoning. God Almighty created the heavens, the earth, and you in His image. So the more completely dependent you become on your Creator, the more productive your life will be for Him! I Peter 4:19, "So then, those who suffer according to God's will should commit themselves to their Creator and continue to do good."

AMOS

Bearer of a burden; compassionate spirit

෨

Hosea 11:4 *I led them with cords of human kindness, with ties of love; I lifted the yoke from their neck and bent down to feed them.*

Matthew 9:36 *When He saw the crowds, He had compassion on them, because they were harassed and helpless, like sheep without a shepherd.*

You are obedient, respectful, faithful, and bring pleasure to those whom you serve. Even with inconsiderate behavior, you are patient (I Peter 2:18). You are tender with the harsh, merciful with the intolerant, and sympathetic with the suffering. Because you cast your cares on the Lord, you are able to lift the burdens of others (Psalm 55:22). The reason you are so easily trusted is because of your humble nature. All glory and credit belong to God, not you. Your passion to help energizes you to meet the need regardless of what it is—guidance, relief, encouragement, or support. God allows you to see the root of the need rather than being sidetracked by all the symptoms. Sickness is healed, the hungry are fed, sight is restored, the unlovely are touched and the afflicted are delivered. You defend rather than offend, forgive rather than accuse, and you protect rather than abandon. You can depend on God's fresh supply daily. "Because of the Lord's great love we are not consumed, for His compassions never fail. They are new every morning; great is your faithfulness," Lamentations 3:22–23. Your compassion connects the heart of God to the heart of man.

AMY

Beloved one; beloved

℘

Deuteronomy 33:12 *Let the beloved of the Lord rest secure in Him, for He shields him all day long, and the one the Lord loves rests between His shoulders.*

I John 4:7 *Dear friends, let us love one another, for love comes from God. Everyone who loves has been born of God and knows God.*

You are highly valued, treasured, and precious to the Lord. You are an eye-witness of the very majesty of Jesus Christ. He received glory and honor from God the Father when the voice came to Him from the Majestic Glory, saying, "This is my Son, whom I love; with Him I am well pleased," II Peter 1:16–17. As you stay committed to Him, one day you will also hear those words. "We know and rely on the love of God for us. God is love, whoever lives in love lives in God and God in him," I John 4:16. You are expressive in worship because you are near to the heart of God. As you give respect, pleasure, and adoration to the Lord, He will give it back to you. You are aggressive to show the love of God to those who are disliked, abhorred, and hated. Rest secure in Him!

ANDRAE

Strong; manly

&

Proverbs 24:5 *A wise man has great power, and a man of knowledge increases strength.*

Ephesians 6:10 *Finally, be strong in the Lord and in His mighty power.*

You are one who has an un-compromised commitment to righteousness, respectability, honesty, character, excellence, value, worth, kindness, innocence, generosity, trustworthiness, faithfulness, justice, hope, and love. You can do everything through Him who gives you strength (Philippians 4:11–13). The Lord is the source of your strength because you turn back the battle at the gate (Isaiah 28:6). You renew your strength by your hope being in the Lord (Isaiah 40:31). Jesus says, "My grace is sufficient for you, for My power is made perfect in weaknesses. Therefore you will boast all the more gladly about your weaknesses, so that Christ's power may rest on you. That is why for Christ's sake, you delight in weaknesses, in insults, in hardships, in persecutions, and in difficulties. For when you are weak, then you are strong," II Corinthians 12:9–10. You are clothed with strength and dignity (Proverbs 31:25).

ANDREA

Womanly; Godly woman

Zephaniah 3:17 *The Lord your God is with you, He is mighty to save. He will take great delight in you, He will quiet you with His love, He will rejoice over you with singing.*

Ephesians 5:28–30 *In this same way, husbands ought to love their wives as their own bodies. He who loves his wife loves himself. After all, no one ever hated His own body, but he feeds and cares for it, just as Christ does the church - for we are members of His body.*

You are God's "treasured possession" (Deuteronomy 7:6). By giving the very life of His Son, God has committed to highly value you and take good care of you. He will treat you tenderly in tough times. You are to relate to others as Jesus relates to the Father and to us. Paul served as an example for you. I Thessalonians 2:7–8 says, "We were gentle among you, like a mother caring for her little children. We loved you so much that we were delighted to share with you not only the gospel of God but our lives as well, because you had become so dear to us." The warmth you experience being held close to His heart will enable you to melt the ice in others—the rejected and the castaways. Be free to be intimate with your Maker with trust and selfless submission.

ANDREW

Strong; manly

&

Proverbs 24:5 *A wise man has great power, and a man of knowledge increases strength.*

Ephesians 6:10 *Finally, be strong in the Lord and in His mighty power.*

You are one who has an un-compromised commitment to righteousness, respectability, honesty, character, excellence, value, worth, kindness, innocence, generosity, trustworthiness, faithfulness, justice, hope, and love. You can do everything through Him who gives you strength (Philippians 4:11–13). The Lord is the source of your strength because you turn back the battle at the gate (Isaiah 28:6). You renew your strength by your hope being in the Lord (Isaiah 40:31). Jesus says, "My grace is sufficient for you, for My power is made perfect in weaknesses. Therefore you will boast all the more gladly about your weaknesses, so that Christ's power may rest on you. That is why for Christ's sake, you delight in weaknesses, in insults, in hardships, in persecutions, and in difficulties. For when you are weak, then you are strong," II Corinthians 12:9–10. You are clothed with strength and dignity (Proverbs 31:25).

ANDY

Strong; manly

⮎

Proverbs 24:5 A wise man has great power, and a man of knowledge increases strength.

Ephesians 6:10 Finally, be strong in the Lord and in His mighty power.

You are one who has an un-compromised commitment to righteousness, respectability, honesty, character, excellence, value, worth, kindness, innocence, generosity, trustworthiness, faithfulness, justice, hope, and love. You can do everything through Him who gives you strength (Philippians 4:11–13). The Lord is the source of your strength because you turn back the battle at the gate (Isaiah 28:6). You renew your strength by your hope being in the Lord (Isaiah 40:31). Jesus says, "My grace is sufficient for you, for My power is made perfect in weaknesses. Therefore you will boast all the more gladly about your weaknesses, so that Christ's power may rest on you. That is why for Christ's sake, you delight in weaknesses, in insults, in hardships, in persecutions, and in difficulties. For when you are weak, then you are strong," II Corinthians 12:9–10. You are clothed with strength and dignity (Proverbs 31:25).

ANGEL

Messenger; bringer of truth

ଚ୰

Psalm 89:1–2 *I will sing of the Lord's great love forever; with my mouth I will make Your faithfulness known through all generations. I will declare that Your love stands firm forever, that You established Your faithfulness in heaven itself.*

Psalm 51:6 *Surely You desire truth in the inner parts; You teach me wisdom in the inmost place.*

John 14:6 *Jesus answered, "I am the way and the truth and the life. No one comes to the Father except through Me."*

"You know the truth and the truth has set you free," John 8:32. You are one who is aggressive toward lies and deception. Your purpose is to bring about truth through openness, revelation, authenticity, accuracy, and honesty. As God's messenger, you will have firmness in keeping and executing His promises and also your own. Your God-given wisdom will be based on God's Word alone. Zechariah 8:16 says, "These are the things you are to do: Speak the truth to each other, and render true and sound judgment in your courts." May true instruction be in your mouth and nothing false be found on your lips (Malachi 2:6).

ANGELA

Messenger; bringer of truth

❧

Psalm 89:1–2 *I will sing of the Lord's great love forever; with my mouth I will make Your faithfulness known through all generations. I will declare that Your love stands firm forever, that You established Your faithfulness in heaven itself.*

Psalm 51:6 *Surely You desire truth in the inner parts; You teach me wisdom in the inmost place.*

John 14:6 *Jesus answered, "I am the way and the truth and the life. No one comes to the Father except through Me."*

"You know the truth and the truth has set you free," John 8:32. You are one who is aggressive toward lies and deception. Your purpose is to bring about truth through openness, revelation, authenticity, accuracy, and honesty. As God's messenger, you will have firmness in keeping and executing His promises and also your own. Your God-given wisdom will be based on God's Word alone. Zechariah 8:16 says, "These are the things you are to do: Speak the truth to each other, and render true and sound judgment in your courts." May true instruction be in your mouth and nothing false be found on your lips (Malachi 2:6).

ANGELINA

Messenger; bringer of truth

Psalm 89:1–2 *I will sing of the Lord's great love forever; with my mouth I will make Your faithfulness known through all generations. I will declare that Your love stands firm forever, that You established Your faithfulness in heaven itself.*

Psalm 51:6 *Surely You desire truth in the inner parts; You teach me wisdom in the inmost place.*

John 14:6 *Jesus answered, "I am the way and the truth and the life. No one comes to the Father except through Me."*

"You know the truth and the truth has set you free," John 8:32. You are one who is aggressive toward lies and deception. Your purpose is to bring about truth through openness, revelation, authenticity, accuracy, and honesty. As God's messenger, you will have firmness in keeping and executing His promises and also your own. Your God-given wisdom will be based on God's Word alone. Zechariah 8:16 says, "These are the things you are to do: Speak the truth to each other, and render true and sound judgment in your courts." May true instruction be in your mouth and nothing false be found on your lips (Malachi 2:6).

ANITA

Graceful one; gracious one

ॐ

Romans 8:32 *He who did not spare His own Son, but gave Him up for us all—how will He not also, along with Him, graciously give us all things?*

I Corinthians 15:10 *But by the grace of God I am what I am, and His grace to me was not without effect.*

Ephesians 2:8 says, "For it is by grace you have been saved, through faith—and this is not from yourselves, it is the gift of God." You are one who brings about balance and harmony through mercy, forgiveness, approval, kindness, and patience—all with a grateful heart. This attitude of gratitude will rule in the midst of inconsiderate behavior. Your nature defies the law of the Pharisees, and is against being self-reliant, prejudice, and selfish. Being full of grace is devotion built through faithfulness and a willingness to quickly pardon. You are blessed with creativity in expressing God's greatest gift of grace—the life of His only Son, Jesus Christ. God says to you through Jeremiah 24:7, "I will give them a heart to know Me, that I am the Lord. They will be My people, and I will be their God, for they will return to Me with all their heart." Ezekiel 11:19 says, "I will give them an undivided heart and put a new spirit in them; I will remove from them their heart of stone and give them a heart of flesh." Accountability will keep your report accurate and your integrity irreproachable.

ANN

Graceful one; God's gracious gift

☙

Romans 8:32 *He who did not spare His own Son, but gave Him up for us all—how will He not also, along with Him, graciously give us all things?*

I Corinthians 15:10 *But by the grace of God I am what I am, and His grace to me was not without effect.*

Ephesians 2:8 says, "For it is by grace you have been saved, through faith—and this is not from yourselves, it is the gift of God." You are one who brings about balance and harmony through mercy, forgiveness, approval, kindness, and patience—all with a grateful heart. This attitude of gratitude will rule in the midst of inconsiderate behavior. Your nature defies the law of the Pharisees, and is against being self-reliant, prejudice, and selfish. Being full of grace is devotion built through faithfulness and a willingness to quickly pardon. You are blessed with creativity in expressing God's greatest gift of grace—the life of His only Son, Jesus Christ. God says to you through Jeremiah 24:7, "I will give them a heart to know Me, that I am the Lord. They will be My people, and I will be their God, for they will return to Me with all their heart." Ezekiel 11:19 says, "I will give them an undivided heart and put a new spirit in them; I will remove from them their heart of stone and give them a heart of flesh." Accountability will keep your report accurate and your integrity irreproachable.

ANNA

Graceful one; gracious one

※

Romans 8:32 *He who did not spare His own Son, but gave Him up for us all—how will He not also, along with Him, graciously give us all things?*

I Corinthians 15:10 *But by the grace of God I am what I am, and His grace to me was not without effect.*

Ephesians 2:8 says, "For it is by grace you have been saved, through faith—and this is not from yourselves, it is the gift of God." You are one who brings about balance and harmony through mercy, forgiveness, approval, kindness, and patience—all with a grateful heart. This attitude of gratitude will rule in the midst of inconsiderate behavior. Your nature defies the law of the Pharisees, and is against being self-reliant, prejudice, and selfish. Being full of grace is devotion built through faithfulness and a willingness to quickly pardon. You are blessed with creativity in expressing God's greatest gift of grace—the life of His only Son, Jesus Christ. God says to you through Jeremiah 24:7, "I will give them a heart to know Me, that I am the Lord. They will be My people, and I will be their God, for they will return to Me with all their heart." Ezekiel 11:19 says, "I will give them an undivided heart and put a new spirit in them; I will remove from them their heart of stone and give them a heart of flesh." Accountability will keep your report accurate and your integrity irreproachable.

ANNE

Graceful one; gracious one

 ❧

Romans 8:32 *He who did not spare His own Son, but gave Him up for us all—how will He not also, along with Him, graciously give us all things?*

I Corinthians 15:10 *But by the grace of God I am what I am, and His grace to me was not without effect.*

Ephesians 2:8 says, "For it is by grace you have been saved, through faith—and this is not from yourselves, it is the gift of God." You are one who brings about balance and harmony through mercy, forgiveness, approval, kindness, and patience—all with a grateful heart. This attitude of gratitude will rule in the midst of inconsiderate behavior. Your nature defies the law of the Pharisees, and is against being self-reliant, prejudice, and selfish. Being full of grace is devotion built through faithfulness and a willingness to quickly pardon. You are blessed with creativity in expressing God's greatest gift of grace—the life of His only Son, Jesus Christ. God says to you through Jeremiah 24:7, "I will give them a heart to know Me, that I am the Lord. They will be My people, and I will be their God, for they will return to Me with all their heart." Ezekiel 11:19 says, "I will give them an undivided heart and put a new spirit in them; I will remove from them their heart of stone and give them a heart of flesh." Accountability will keep your report accurate and your integrity irreproachable.

ANNETTE

Graceful one; gracious one

ॐ

Romans 8:32 *He who did not spare His own Son, but gave Him up for us all—how will He not also, along with Him, graciously give us all things?*

I Corinthians 15:10 *But by the grace of God I am what I am, and His grace to me was not without effect.*

Ephesians 2:8 says, "For it is by grace you have been saved, through faith—and this is not from yourselves, it is the gift of God." You are one who brings about balance and harmony through mercy, forgiveness, approval, kindness, and patience—all with a grateful heart. This attitude of gratitude will rule in the midst of inconsiderate behavior. Your nature defies the law of the Pharisees, and is against being self-reliant, prejudice, and selfish. Being full of grace is devotion built through faithfulness and a willingness to quickly pardon. You are blessed with creativity in expressing God's greatest gift of grace—the life of His only Son, Jesus Christ. God says to you through Jeremiah 24:7, "I will give them a heart to know Me, that I am the Lord. They will be My people, and I will be their God, for they will return to Me with all their heart." Ezekiel 11:19 says, "I will give them an undivided heart and put a new spirit in them; I will remove from them their heart of stone and give them a heart of flesh." Accountability will keep your report accurate and your integrity irreproachable.

ANNIE

Graceful one; gracious one

ඟ

Romans 8:32 *He who did not spare His own Son, but gave Him up for us all—how will He not also, along with Him, graciously give us all things?*

I Corinthians 15:10 *But by the grace of God I am what I am, and His grace to me was not without effect.*

Ephesians 2:8 says, "For it is by grace you have been saved, through faith—and this is not from yourselves, it is the gift of God." You are one who brings about balance and harmony through mercy, forgiveness, approval, kindness, and patience—all with a grateful heart. This attitude of gratitude will rule in the midst of inconsiderate behavior. Your nature defies the law of the Pharisees, and is against being self-reliant, prejudice, and selfish. Being full of grace is devotion built through faithfulness and a willingness to quickly pardon. You are blessed with creativity in expressing God's greatest gift of grace—the life of His only Son, Jesus Christ. God says to you through Jeremiah 24:7, "I will give them a heart to know Me, that I am the Lord. They will be My people, and I will be their God, for they will return to Me with all their heart." Ezekiel 11:19 says, "I will give them an undivided heart and put a new spirit in them; I will remove from them their heart of stone and give them a heart of flesh." Accountability will keep your report accurate and your integrity irreproachable.

ANTHONY

Inestimable; priceless one

⍩

Exodus 19:5 *Now if you obey me fully and keep my covenant, then out of all nations you will be My treasured possession.*

I Corinthians 6:20 *You were bought at a price. Therefore honor God with your body.*

With a humble confidence, you recognize that your undeserved worth is based on the spotless Lamb sacrificed for you. No greater love will you experience than from the One who laid down His life for you. You pour back your love to Him lavishly with no thought of the cost to you or your reputation. In fact, you are willing to give up everything you have to be His disciple (Luke 14:25–33). This debt of love causes you to give forethought to all your investments as to whether Christ gets all the glory. You will not gamble or be bribed because you know the incredible price paid for you. Therefore you bring value to the insignificant, meaning to the absurd, and worth to the wasted. Your high standard of excellence will bear eternal fruit because of your commitment to please God more than man. As a child of the King, through you castaways will be restored to heirs.

ANTONIO

Inestimable; priceless one

Exodus 19:5 *Now if you obey me fully and keep my covenant, then out of all nations you will be My treasured possession.*

I Corinthians 6:20 *You were bought at a price. Therefore honor God with your body.*

With a humble confidence, you recognize that your undeserved worth is based on the spotless Lamb sacrificed for you. No greater love will you experience than from the One who laid down His life for you. You pour back your love to Him lavishly with no thought of the cost to you or your reputation. In fact, you are willing to give up everything you have to be His disciple (Luke 14:25–33). This debt of love causes you to give forethought to all your investments as to whether Christ gets all the glory. You will not gamble or be bribed because you know the incredible price paid for you. Therefore you bring value to the insignificant, meaning to the absurd, and worth to the wasted. Your high standard of excellence will bear eternal fruit because of your commitment to please God more than man. As a child of the King, through you castaways will be restored to heirs.

APRIL

Opening; new in faith

&

Proverbs 2:7–8 He holds victory in store for the upright, He is a shield to those whose walk is blameless, for He guards the course of the just and protects the way of His faithful ones.

Hebrews 11:1 Now faith is being sure of what we hope for and certain of what we do not see.

Because you believe in Jesus Christ, you have eternal life (John 3:15). Faith must be accompanied by action in order to bring life (James 2:17). You are one who has made a commitment to God to be loyal, true, dependable, enduring, and steadfast. Your ultimate purpose is to please God in all you do, for you know without faith it is impossible (Hebrews 11:6). Everything is possible for him who believes (Mark 9:23). You are confident that every one of His promises to you will be fulfilled. Your loyalty is shown by a steadfast devotion of an unquestioning kind. This is why you are especially sensitive to betrayal. This allows God to restore hope, security, purpose, and His faithfulness in those whom He has given you to serve. Your commitment is with singleness of heart and ready obedience. You are kept in perfect peace because your mind is steadfast and you trust in your God (Isaiah 26:3).

ARIANNA

Silver; utterly pure

&

I Timothy 5:22 *...do not share in the sins of others. Keep yourself pure.*

I Peter 1:22 *Now that you have purified yourselves by obeying the truth so that you have sincere love for your brothers, love one another deeply, from the heart.*

Through the process of heat, trials, and refinement, purity is established. Your nature defies being stubborn, judgmental, and haughty. The commandment of the Lord is clear—giving insight to life (Psalm 19:8). You bring wholeness to the dirty, defiled, contaminated, polluted, double-minded, and raped. Your willingness to be transparent is the venue through which He makes His Word clear, simple, and unadulterated. Your choice to be pure enables you to see God (Matthew 5:8) and to know Him as King and Friend (Proverbs 22:11). It also allows your words to be pleasant (Proverbs 15:26) and causes you to ascend to the holy place of the Lord, where you receive blessings and righteousness from the God of salvation (Psalm 24:3–5). Proverbs 20:11 says, "Even a child is known by his actions, by whether his conduct is pure and right."

ARIEL

Lion of God; courageous

❧

Deuteronomy 31:6 *Be strong and courageous. Do not be afraid or terrified because of them, for the Lord your God goes with you; He will never leave you nor forsake you.*

Joshua 1:7 *Be strong and very courageous. Be careful to obey all the law My servant Moses gave you; do not turn from it to the right or to the left, that you may be successful wherever you go.*

You are equipped with mental and moral strength to venture, persevere, and withstand danger, fear, and difficulty. You have the firmness of mind to take a firm stand. You meet strain with fortitude and resilience, even when opposed or threatened. You have firm determination to achieve God's purpose in your life. With stubborn persistence and unwillingness to admit defeat, you base all victory on the finished work of the cross of Jesus. The Victor will use you to remove obstacles and invade darkness and death in order to bring the lost to a decision for Jesus. God's divine presence in and through you will bind fear and lead people to their God-given inheritance.

ARLEEN

A pledge; faithful one

&

Proverbs 2:7–8 *He holds victory in store for the upright, He is a shield to those whose walk is blameless, for He guards the course of the just and protects the way of His faithful ones.*

Psalm 15:1–5 *Lord, who may dwell in Your sanctuary? Who may live on Your holy hill? He whose walk is blameless and who does what is righteous, who speaks the truth from his heart and has no slander on his tongue, who does his neighbor no wrong and casts no slur on his fellow man, who despises a vile man but honors those who fear the Lord, who keeps his oath even when it hurts, who lends his money without usury and does not accept a bribe against the innocent. He who does these things will never be shaken.*

You are one who has made a commitment to God to be loyal, true, dependable, enduring, and steadfast. You unmask anything fake with the reality of God's Word. You are aggressive towards lies and deception to bring about truth. You are especially sensitive to betrayal, so that God can restore hope, security, purpose, and His faithfulness in those whom He has given you to serve. "Be faithful, even to the point of death, and I will give you a crown of life," Revelation 2:10. Anticipate the Master saying to you, "Well done, good and faithful servant! You have been faithful with a few things; I will put you in charge of many things. Come and share your Master's happiness!" (Matthew 25:21) "The one who calls you is faithful and he will do it," I Thessalonians 5:24.

ARLENE

A pledge; faithful one

❧

Proverbs 2:7–8 *He holds victory in store for the upright, He is a shield to those whose walk is blameless, for He guards the course of the just and protects the way of His faithful ones.*

Psalm 15:1–5 *Lord, who may dwell in Your sanctuary? Who may live on Your holy hill? He whose walk is blameless and who does what is righteous, who speaks the truth from his heart and has no slander on his tongue, who does his neighbor no wrong and casts no slur on his fellow man, who despises a vile man but honors those who fear the Lord, who keeps his oath even when it hurts, who lends his money without usury and does not accept a bribe against the innocent. He who does these things will never be shaken.*

You are one who has made a commitment to God to be loyal, true, dependable, enduring, and steadfast. You unmask anything fake with the reality of God's Word. You are aggressive towards lies and deception to bring about truth. You are especially sensitive to betrayal, so that God can restore hope, security, purpose, and His faithfulness in those whom He has given you to serve. "Be faithful, even to the point of death, and I will give you a crown of life," Revelation 2:10. Anticipate the Master saying to you, "Well done, good and faithful servant! You have been faithful with a few things; I will put you in charge of many things. Come and share your Master's happiness!" (Matthew 25:21) "The one who calls you is faithful and he will do it," I Thessalonians 5:24.

ARLETA

A pledge; faithful one

৪৩

Proverbs 2:7–8 *He holds victory in store for the upright, He is a shield to those whose walk is blameless, for He guards the course of the just and protects the way of His faithful ones.*

Psalm 15:1–5 *Lord, who may dwell in Your sanctuary? Who may live on Your holy hill? He whose walk is blameless and who does what is righteous, who speaks the truth from his heart and has no slander on his tongue, who does his neighbor no wrong and casts no slur on his fellow man, who despises a vile man but honors those who fear the Lord, who keeps his oath even when it hurts, who lends his money without usury and does not accept a bribe against the innocent. He who does these things will never be shaken.*

You are one who has made a commitment to God to be loyal, true, dependable, enduring, and steadfast. You unmask anything fake with the reality of God's Word. You are aggressive towards lies and deception to bring about truth. You are especially sensitive to betrayal, so that God can restore hope, security, purpose, and His faithfulness in those whom He has given you to serve. "Be faithful, even to the point of death, and I will give you a crown of life," Revelation 2:10. Anticipate the Master saying to you, "Well done, good and faithful servant! You have been faithful with a few things; I will put you in charge of many things. Come and share your Master's happiness!" (Matthew 25:21) "The one who calls you is faithful and he will do it," I Thessalonians 5:24.

ARTHUR

Noble one; man of integrity

&

Psalm 41:12 *In my integrity You uphold me and set me in Your presence forever.*

Proverbs 11:3 *The integrity of the upright guides them, but the unfaithful are destroyed by their duplicity.*

Spiritual deafness results from unheeded warnings, calloused hearts, rebellious disobedience, and stubborn unfaithfulness. This is prevented by being quick to hear, teachable, and having faith in God's Word. Security comes from knowing God's ears are attentive to your cry—before you call, He answers. Discernment and righteous judgment produce integrity. Integrity results in yielding weakness to God's power, based on a blameless walk. Proverbs 10:9 says, "The man of integrity walks securely, but he who takes crooked paths will be found out." You are one who has an uncompromised commitment to righteousness, respectability, honesty, character, excellence, innocence, generosity, trustworthiness, faithfulness, justice, hope, and love. Be truthful with others, as well as yourself. Be the same in public as you are in private. Titus 2:7–8 says, "In everything set them an example by doing what is good. In your teaching show integrity, seriousness and soundness of speech that cannot be condemned, so that those who oppose you may be ashamed because they have nothing bad to say about us."

ARTIE

Noble one; man of integrity

&

Psalm 41:12 *In my integrity You uphold me and set me in Your presence forever.*

Proverbs 11:3 *The integrity of the upright guides them, but the unfaithful are destroyed by their duplicity.*

Spiritual deafness results from unheeded warnings, calloused hearts, rebellious disobedience, and stubborn unfaithfulness. This is prevented by being quick to hear, teachable, and having faith in God's Word. Security comes from knowing God's ears are attentive to your cry—before you call, He answers. Discernment and righteous judgment produce integrity. Integrity results in yielding weakness to God's power, based on a blameless walk. Proverbs 10:9 says, "The man of integrity walks securely, but he who takes crooked paths will be found out." You are one who has an uncompromised commitment to righteousness, respectability, honesty, character, excellence, innocence, generosity, trustworthiness, faithfulness, justice, hope, and love. Be truthful with others, as well as yourself. Be the same in public as you are in private. Titus 2:7–8 says, "In everything set them an example by doing what is good. In your teaching show integrity, seriousness and soundness of speech that cannot be condemned, so that those who oppose you may be ashamed because they have nothing bad to say about us."

ASHLEE

From the ash tree meadow; agreement

8⌒⌀

Ecclesiastes 4:12   *Though one may be overpowered, two can defend themselves. A cord of three strands is not quickly broken.*

I Corinthians 1:10   *I appeal to you, brothers, in the name of our Lord Jesus Christ, that all of you agree with one another so that there may be no divisions among you and that you may be perfectly united in mind and thought.*

You are one who has chosen to separate yourself from wickedness, darkness, unbelief, idolatry, and uncleanness in order to be yoked together with your Heavenly Father. He will live and walk with you. He will be your God and you will be His son (II Corinthians 6:14–18). This inseparable union results in:

Psalm 133—anointing and God's blessings;

I Corinthians 12—no jealousy over different giftings in God's body;

Romans 6:5—identity with Christ's death and resurrection;

Philippians 2:1–5—having Christ's attitude—one in spirit and purpose;

Colossians 2:2–3—complete understanding of Christ's wisdom;

Ephesians 2:19–22—being a dwelling where God lives by His Spirit;

Ephesians 4:16—spiritual maturity.

You will have a greater sensitivity for ministry to relationships that are separated, severed, deserted, or abandoned. As Christ's team player, you will gladly take the risk to touch these types of people, in order that they may be one with Him in harmony. You will serve as a link to bring closeness.

ASHLEY

From the ash tree meadow; agreement

&

Ecclesiastes 4:12 *Though one may be overpowered, two can defend themselves. A cord of three strands is not quickly broken.*

I Corinthians 1:10 *I appeal to you, brothers, in the name of our Lord Jesus Christ, that all of you agree with one another so that there may be no divisions among you and that you may be perfectly united in mind and thought.*

You are one who has chosen to separate yourself from wickedness, darkness, unbelief, idolatry, and uncleanness in order to be yoked together with your Heavenly Father. He will live and walk with you. He will be your God and you will be His son (II Corinthians 6:14–18). This inseparable union results in:

Psalm 133—anointing and God's blessings;

I Corinthians 12—no jealousy over different giftings in God's body;

Romans 6:5—identity with Christ's death and resurrection;

Philippians 2:1–5—having Christ's attitude—one in spirit and purpose;

Colossians 2:2–3—complete understanding of Christ's wisdom;

Ephesians 2:19–22—being a dwelling where God lives by His Spirit;

Ephesians 4:16—spiritual maturity.

You will have a greater sensitivity for ministry to relationships that are separated, severed, deserted, or abandoned. As Christ's team player, you will gladly take the risk to touch these types of people, in order that they may be one with Him in harmony. You will serve as a link to bring closeness.

ASHLYN

From the ash tree meadow; agreement

❦

Ecclesiastes 4:12 *Though one may be overpowered, two can defend themselves. A cord of three strands is not quickly broken.*

I Corinthians 1:10 *I appeal to you, brothers, in the name of our Lord Jesus Christ, that all of you agree with one another so that there may be no divisions among you and that you may be perfectly united in mind and thought.*

You are one who has chosen to separate yourself from wickedness, darkness, unbelief, idolatry, and uncleanness in order to be yoked together with your Heavenly Father. He will live and walk with you. He will be your God and you will be His son (II Corinthians 6:14–18). This inseparable union results in:

Psalm 133—anointing and God's blessings;

I Corinthians 12—no jealousy over different giftings in God's body;

Romans 6:5—identity with Christ's death and resurrection;

Philippians 2:1–5—having Christ's attitude—one in spirit and purpose;

Colossians 2:2–3—complete understanding of Christ's wisdom;

Ephesians 2:19–22—being a dwelling where God lives by His Spirit;

Ephesians 4:16—spiritual maturity.

You will have a greater sensitivity for ministry to relationships that are separated, severed, deserted, or abandoned. As Christ's team player, you will gladly take the risk to touch these types of people, in order that they may be one with Him in harmony. You will serve as a link to bring closeness.

AUBREY

Counselor of elves; noble one

Isaiah 32:8 *But the noble man makes noble plans, and by noble deeds he stands.*

Luke 8:15 *But the seed on good soil stands for those with a noble and good heart, who hear the word, retain it, and by persevering produce a crop.*

Proverbs 18:12 says, "Before his downfall a man's heart is proud, but humility comes before honor." You are one who has a humble confidence in recognizing and expressing reverence, worship, adoration, trust, deference, tribute, admiration, and respect. This is the result of being secure in the truth of who you are in the Lord. Through humility, King Jesus made a way for you to be engrafted into His royalty. He made of Himself no reputation and took on the nature of a servant (Philippians 2:7) to affirm your value. Through self-denial, you prioritize excellence in virtue, truthfulness, and faithfulness. Because of the respect you have earned, you dismantle inferiority, disgrace, shame, and offenses. No one feels second-rate in your presence. The deeper that the Lord is your object of reverence, the greater your confidence will be in giving approval and worth. Because you are tall in spirit, your face is always turned upward.

AUDREY

Noble strength; noble and strong

Isaiah 32:8 *But the noble man makes noble plans, and by noble deeds he stands.*

Luke 8:15 *But the seed on good soil stands for those with a noble and good heart, who hear the word, retain it, and by persevering produce a crop.*

Proverbs 18:12 says, "Before his downfall a man's heart is proud, but humility comes before honor." You are one who has a humble confidence in recognizing and expressing reverence, worship, adoration, trust, deference, tribute, admiration, and respect. This is the result of being secure in the truth of who you are in the Lord. Through humility, King Jesus made a way for you to be engrafted into His royalty. He made of Himself no reputation and took on the nature of a servant (Philippians 2:7) to affirm your value. Through self-denial, you prioritize excellence in virtue, truthfulness, and faithfulness. Because of the respect you have earned, you dismantle inferiority, disgrace, shame, and offenses. No one feels second-rate in your presence. The deeper that the Lord is your object of reverence, the greater your confidence will be in giving approval and worth. Because you are tall in spirit, your face is always turned upward.

AUSTIN

Worthy of reverence; noble heart

ᘓ

Isaiah 32:8 *But the noble man makes noble plans, and by noble deeds he stands.*

Luke 8:15 *But the seed on good soil stands for those with a noble and good heart, who hear the word, retain it, and by persevering produce a crop.*

Proverbs 18:12 says, "Before his downfall a man's heart is proud, but humility comes before honor." You are one who has a humble confidence in recognizing and expressing reverence, worship, adoration, trust, deference, tribute, admiration, and respect. This is the result of being secure in the truth of who you are in the Lord. Through humility, King Jesus made a way for you to be engrafted into His royalty. He made of Himself no reputation and took on the nature of a servant (Philippians 2:7) to affirm your value. Through self-denial, you prioritize excellence in virtue, truthfulness, and faithfulness. Because of the respect you have earned, you dismantle inferiority, disgrace, shame, and offenses. No one feels second-rate in your presence. The deeper that the Lord is your object of reverence, the greater your confidence will be in giving approval and worth. Because you are tall in spirit, your face is always turned upward.

AUTUMN

The fall season; reaper

୧୧

Hosea 10:12 *Sow for yourselves righteousness, reap the fruit of unfailing love, and break up your unplowed ground; for it is time to seek the Lord, until He comes and showers righteousness on you.*

Galatians 6:8 *The one who sows to please his sinful nature will reap destruction; the one who sows to please the Spirit, from the Spirit will reap eternal life.*

The Lord would have you know that "the very hairs of your head are all numbered, so do not be afraid; you are worth more than many sparrows to Him" (Luke 12:7). "Cast all your anxieties on Him because He cares for you," I Peter 5:7. With this total dependence on the Lord, you will obtain a great harvest for His kingdom. Psalm 126:5–6 says, "Those who sow in tears will reap with songs of joy. He who goes out weeping, carrying seed to sow, will return with songs of joy, carrying sheaves with him." As a caring one, you are cautious in avoiding mistakes and very attentive to details. His compassion flowing to and through you equips you to show concern for the neglected and the indifferent. The complacent will be challenged to release their burdens and worries to the burden bearer, Jesus Christ. The Good Shepherd will continue to nurture you as you nurture others.

AVA

Birdlike; bearer of good news

&

Psalm 37:39 *The salvation of the righteous comes from the Lord; He is their stronghold in time of trouble.*

Isaiah 12:2 *Surely God is my salvation; I will trust and not be afraid. The Lord, the Lord, is my strength and my song; He has become my salvation.*

The salvation of God is the light of His Son revealed in every crevice of your life. Where you are vulnerable, insecure, unstable, and weak, the Lord will rescue, deliver, and protect. The Lord desires to preserve you from being false, deceptive, misleading, and exaggerating. With your dependence on God for your salvation, you will ever want to be real and honest, with nothing to hide. God uses you to lay Jesus Christ as the foundation in the lives of others. He is the only way! (Acts 4:12) You are His hands to rescue, release, and pardon. You have one message—the message of the cross—which is the power of God!

AVERY

Self counsel; a good counselor

❧

James 3:17 *But the wisdom that comes from heaven is first of all pure; then peace-loving, considerate, submissive, full of mercy and good fruit, impartial and sincere.*

Proverbs 9:10 *The fear of the Lord is the beginning of wisdom, and knowledge of the Holy One is understanding.*

You are a person of moral excellence. You exemplify right living put into practice. The Lord has not only equipped you with skills for living correctly, but also the ability to impart that to others. The Spirit of truth will guide you into all truth, allowing you to have insight into the true nature of things (John 16:13). Out of your reverential respect for the Lord, you have wisdom to give guidance and direction. You are a safe sounding board who steers those who are hungry for knowledge of the Holy One in the right direction. You need only to ask for the wisdom you lack, and God will give it to you generously (James 1:5). Having spiritual discernment is having the ability to separate the difference between God's wisdom and the world's and the ability to make the right choice—regardless. Luke 21:15 says, "For I will give you words and wisdom that none of your adversaries will be able to resist or contradict."

BAILEY

Bailiff; stewardship

❧

Matthew 25:21 *His master replied, "Well done, good and faithful servant! You have been faithful with a few things; I will put you in charge of many things. Come and share your master's happiness!"*

Titus 1:3 *And at His appointed season He brought His word to light through the preaching entrusted to me by the command of God our Savior.*

You have a clear understanding that everything you are and all you possess are from God and belong to God. He has loaned everything to you and made you responsible to care for and use it for His glory. God has entrusted you to manage His affairs with accountability and integrity—without hiding anything and without manipulation. Obeying His commands allows you to give direction and oversight to those without goals and to show order to those in confusion. The Bible will be your greatest possession of stewardship. You are a servant to the body of Christ—the church—by the commission God gave you to present His Word in its fullness (Colossians 1:25). Your goal is not to please men, but God, who tests your heart (I Thessalonians 2:4). You are regarded as a servant of Christ, entrusted with the secret things of God. This trust requires you to prove yourself faithful (I Corinthians 4:1–2). You should use whatever gift you have received to serve others, faithfully administering God's grace in its various forms (I Peter 4:10). As you allow God to govern, coach, and guide your life, He will authorize you to be that for others.

BARBARA

Stranger; coming with joy

&

Psalm 149:4–5 *For the Lord takes delight in His people; He crowns the humble with salvation. Let the saints rejoice in this honor and sing for joy on their beds.*

Psalm 45:7 *You love righteousness and hate wickedness; therefore God, your God, has set you above your companions by anointing you with the oil of joy.*

Psalm 16:11 says, "You have made known to me the path of life; You will fill me with joy in Your presence, with eternal pleasures at Your right hand." Your heavenly Father has trusted you with a quality that releases healing, restores hope, and brings refreshing. You are one who takes the source of tears and defeat, and turns them into confident trust with rejoicing. As you experience and remain sensitive to the things that sorrow the heart of God, He will pour His oil of joy on and through you to restore hope to those who are mourning (Isaiah 61:1–3). Experiences of sorrow prepare and enlarge your capacity for joy. The joy of the Lord will be your strength to endure the cross He has called you to bear. You are to fix your eyes on Jesus, the author and perfecter of your faith, who for the joy set before Him endured the cross, scorning its shame, and sat down at the right hand of the throne of God (Hebrews 12:2). He will be faithful to give you a song in your "night" season (Psalm 42:8). God rejoices over you with gladness! (Zephaniah 3:17)

BARBIE

Stranger; coming with joy

౪

Psalm 149:4–5 *For the Lord takes delight in His people; He crowns the humble with salvation. Let the saints rejoice in this honor and sing for joy on their beds.*

Psalm 45:7 *You love righteousness and hate wickedness; therefore God, your God, has set you above your companions by anointing you with the oil of joy.*

Psalm 16:11 says, "You have made known to me the path of life; You will fill me with joy in Your presence, with eternal pleasures at Your right hand." Your heavenly Father has trusted you with a quality that releases healing, restores hope, and brings refreshing. You are one who takes the source of tears and defeat, and turns them into confident trust with rejoicing. As you experience and remain sensitive to the things that sorrow the heart of God, He will pour His oil of joy on and through you to restore hope to those who are mourning (Isaiah 61:1–3). Experiences of sorrow prepare and enlarge your capacity for joy. The joy of the Lord will be your strength to endure the cross He has called you to bear. You are to fix your eyes on Jesus, the author and perfecter of your faith, who for the joy set before Him endured the cross, scorning its shame, and sat down at the right hand of the throne of God (Hebrews 12:2). He will be faithful to give you a song in your "night" season (Psalm 42:8). God rejoices over you with gladness! (Zephaniah 3:17)

BELLA

Beautiful; beautiful one

ℰℐ

Isaiah 61:1–3 *The Spirit of the Sovereign Lord is on me, because the Lord has anointed me to preach good news to the poor. He has sent me to bind up the brokenhearted, to proclaim freedom for the captives and release from darkness for the prisoners, to proclaim the year of the Lord's favor and the day of vengeance of our God, to comfort all who mourn, and provide for those who grieve in Zion—to bestow on them a crown of beauty instead of ashes, the oil of gladness instead of mourning, and a garment of praise instead of a spirit of despair. They will be called oaks of righteousness, a planting of the Lord for the display of His splendor.*

Psalm 27:4 *One thing I ask of the Lord, this is what I seek: that I may dwell in the house of the Lord all the days of my life, to gaze upon the beauty of the Lord and to seek Him in His temple.*

The Lord desires to give you a private audience with Himself. This intimacy will allow you to reflect Him in all you are, all you do, and in all you say. You are one who radiates the beauty of the Lord with calm assurance of being pleasing, flawless, clean, and pure before Him. You are one who is marked by honesty without being prejudice or impartial. You are able to minister to the victim as well as the victimizer. You are not offended at the ashes of people's lives because you know how God turns them to His beauty. This is accomplished by the cleansing power of the blood of the Lamb— Jesus Christ. Because you prioritize eternal over temporal, you are not side-tracked on the external, whether it be ugly or beautiful. God has gifted you with the ability to see His beauty—regardless.

BEN

Son of the right hand; favored son

❧

Exodus 33:13 *If you are pleased with me, teach me Your ways so I may know You and continue to find favor with You. Remember that this nation is Your people.*

Proverbs 3:3–4 *Let love and faithfulness never leave you; bind them around your neck, write them on the tablet of your heart. Then you win favor and a good name in the sight of God and man.*

Proverbs 16:15 says, "When a king's face brightens, it means life; his favor is like a rain cloud in spring." The key to favor is your commitment to God's love and faithfulness—always being aware that you are nothing without Him. But with Him, you are everything. As you daily wait on Him, abundant life is yours (Proverbs 8:34–35). As with Esther, you will have entrance to those in authority over you to be endued with power and resources. As your ways please the Lord, He will make even your enemies live at peace with you (Proverbs 16:7). The knowledge of God's approval keeps you focused on speaking the Word of God with authority, wherein you are not pleasing man, but God (I Thessalonians 2:4). You are energized and strengthened in your affirming of others—in doing good (Hebrews 13:16). The security you have as God's child gives you a willingness to contribute to the success and welfare of others, with no jealousy or partiality, but with humility, meekness, and gentleness.

BENJAMIN

Son of the right hand; favored son

&

Exodus 33:13 *If you are pleased with me, teach me Your ways so I may know You and continue to find favor with You. Remember that this nation is Your people.*

Proverbs 3:3–4 *Let love and faithfulness never leave you; bind them around your neck, write them on the tablet of your heart. Then you win favor and a good name in the sight of God and man.*

Proverbs 16:15 says, "When a king's face brightens, it means life; his favor is like a rain cloud in spring." The key to favor is your commitment to God's love and faithfulness—always being aware that you are nothing without Him. But with Him, you are everything. As you daily wait on Him, abundant life is yours (Proverbs 8:34–35). As with Esther, you will have entrance to those in authority over you to be endued with power and resources. As your ways please the Lord, He will make even your enemies live at peace with you (Proverbs 16:7). The knowledge of God's approval keeps you focused on speaking the Word of God with authority, wherein you are not pleasing man, but God (I Thessalonians 2:4). You are energized and strengthened in your affirming of others—in doing good (Hebrews 13:16). The security you have as God's child gives you a willingness to contribute to the success and welfare of others, with no jealousy or partiality, but with humility, meekness, and gentleness.

BESSIE

Consecrated to God

৪১

Romans 12:1 *Therefore, I urge you brothers, in view of God's mercy, to offer your bodies as living sacrifices, holy and pleasing to God—this is your spiritual act of worship.*

Philippians 3:7–8 *But whatever was to my profit I now consider loss for the sake of Christ. What is more, I consider everything a loss compared to the surpassing greatness of knowing Christ Jesus my Lord, for whose sake I have lost all things. I consider them rubbish, that I may gain Christ.*

Before you were born, God set you apart and appointed you as a prophet to the nations (Jeremiah 1:5). You are to be devoted irrevocably to the worship of God. He will pour out His anointing upon you as you are faithful to follow Him wholeheartedly (Psalm 119:34). You are one who has made a commitment to be loyal, true, dependable, enduring, and steadfast. You unmask anything fake with the reality of God's Word. You are aggressive towards lies and deception in order to bring about truth. You are especially sensitive to betrayal, so that God can restore hope, security, purpose, and His faithfulness in those whom He has given you to serve. Let your eyes keep to God's ways (Proverbs 23:26).

BETH

Consecrated to God; consecrated one

ೞ

Romans 12:1 *Therefore, I urge you brothers, in view of God's mercy, to offer your bodies as living sacrifices, holy and pleasing to God—this is your spiritual act of worship.*

Philippians 3:7–8 *But whatever was to my profit I now consider loss for the sake of Christ. What is more, I consider everything a loss compared to the surpassing greatness of knowing Christ Jesus my Lord, for whose sake I have lost all things. I consider them rubbish, that I may gain Christ.*

Before you were born, God set you apart and appointed you as a prophet to the nations (Jeremiah 1:5). You are to be devoted irrevocably to the worship of God. He will pour out His anointing upon you as you are faithful to follow Him wholeheartedly (Psalm 119:34). You are one who has made a commitment to be loyal, true, dependable, enduring, and steadfast. You unmask anything fake with the reality of God's Word. You are aggressive towards lies and deception in order to bring about truth. You are especially sensitive to betrayal, so that God can restore hope, security, purpose, and His faithfulness in those whom He has given you to serve. Let your eyes keep to God's ways (Proverbs 23:26).

BETHANY

House of God; abiding place of God

&

Psalm 23:6 *Surely goodness and love will follow me all the days of my life, and I will dwell in the house of the Lord forever.*

Psalm 16:8 *I have set the Lord always before me. Because He is at my right hand, I will not be shaken.*

Psalm 63:7 *I sing in the shadow of Thy wings.*

Abide means to stay, dwell, submit, and to endure. The Lord has promised to strengthen your heart because you are fully committed to Him (II Chronicles 16:9). Do not think it strange that the closer you get to Him, the darker it will become. It is like one focusing in the dark room of a photographer—you will be the first to see the by-products of the "negatives"—the good out of the bad! In the holy of holies, where He dwells, there is no natural form of light—just His glory. It is in that shadow where He will birth the songs and reveal the hidden treasures of His heart. You are one whose intimate friendship with the Lord will bring reconciliation to the offended, distressed, and troubled.

BETTY

Consecrated to God

Romans 12:1 *Therefore, I urge you brothers, in view of God's mercy, to offer your bodies as living sacrifices, holy and pleasing to God—this is your spiritual act of worship.*

Philippians 3:7–8 *But whatever was to my profit I now consider loss for the sake of Christ. What is more, I consider everything a loss compared to the surpassing greatness of knowing Christ Jesus my Lord, for whose sake I have lost all things. I consider them rubbish, that I may gain Christ.*

Before you were born, God set you apart and appointed you as a prophet to the nations (Jeremiah 1:5). You are to be devoted irrevocably to the worship of God. He will pour out His anointing upon you as you are faithful to follow Him wholeheartedly (Psalm 119:34). You are one who has made a commitment to be loyal, true, dependable, enduring, and steadfast. You unmask anything fake with the reality of God's Word. You are aggressive towards lies and deception in order to bring about truth. You are especially sensitive to betrayal, so that God can restore hope, security, purpose, and His faithfulness in those whom He has given you to serve. Let your eyes keep to God's ways (Proverbs 23:26).

BEV

Dweller at the beaver meadow; diligent spirit

❧

Colossians 1:16 *For by Him all things were created: things in heaven and on earth, visible and invisible, whether thrones or powers or rulers or authorities; all things were created by Him and for Him.*

Ephesians 2:10 *For we are God's workmanship, created in Christ Jesus to do good works, which God prepared in advance for us to do.*

To be industrious means to be skillful, hardworking, zealous, and diligent. By persevering, you give careful attention to detail. There is not a lazy bone in your body. Through you the Lord will originate. How you deal with the past determines your future. Regardless of the curses or blessings, the failures or successes, you are God's platform for a "new thing." You cannot lean on your own understanding or reasoning. God Almighty created the heavens, the earth, and you in His image. So the more completely dependent you become on your Creator, the more productive your life will be for Him! I Peter 4:19, "So then, those who suffer according to God's will should commit themselves to their Creator and continue to do good."

BEVERLY

Dweller at the beaver meadow; diligent spirit

Colossians 1:16 *For by Him all things were created: things in heaven and on earth, visible and invisible, whether thrones or powers or rulers or authorities; all things were created by Him and for Him.*

Ephesians 2:10 *For we are God's workmanship, created in Christ Jesus to do good works, which God prepared in advance for us to do.*

To be industrious means to be skillful, hardworking, zealous, and diligent. By persevering, you give careful attention to detail. There is not a lazy bone in your body. Through you the Lord will originate. How you deal with the past determines your future. Regardless of the curses or blessings, the failures or successes, you are God's platform for a "new thing." You cannot lean on your own understanding or reasoning. God Almighty created the heavens, the earth, and you in His image. So the more completely dependent you become on your Creator, the more productive your life will be for Him! I Peter 4:19, "So then, those who suffer according to God's will should commit themselves to their Creator and continue to do good."

BILL

Resolute protector; great protector

ৼ

Job 11:18 *You will be secure, because there is hope; you will look about you and take your rest in safety.*

Psalm 32:7 *You are my hiding place; You will protect me from trouble and surround me with songs of deliverance.*

Psalm 27:5 *For in the day of trouble He will keep me safe in His dwelling; He will hide me in the shelter of His tabernacle and set me high upon a rock.*

You are securely wrapped up and protected by Jesus Christ, who frees you from doubt and harm. Because you find your shelter, assurance, stability, and strength in your personal relationship with the Lord, you are kept in a safe place. You are confident that the Lord will fight for you; you need only be still (Exodus 14:14). As you stand firm on God's solid foundation (II Timothy 2:19) and stay hidden in the shadow of His wings (Psalm 61:4), you will provide deliverance for the weak, insecure, unsheltered, and frail. Instead of being defensive, you are a defender of injustice done to all mankind. You let discretion protect you (Proverbs 2:11). You will shield others from the enemy's destruction with love (I Corinthians 13:7) and the power of God's name (John 17:11). You display God's compassion through your humility. What you let him be in you, you will be to others.

BILLIE

Resolute protector; great protector

❦

Job 11:18 *You will be secure, because there is hope; you will look about you and take your rest in safety.*

Psalm 32:7 *You are my hiding place; You will protect me from trouble and surround me with songs of deliverance.*

Psalm 27:5 *For in the day of trouble He will keep me safe in His dwelling; He will hide me in the shelter of His tabernacle and set me high upon a rock.*

You are securely wrapped up and protected by Jesus Christ, who frees you from doubt and harm. Because you find your shelter, assurance, stability, and strength in your personal relationship with the Lord, you are kept in a safe place. You are confident that the Lord will fight for you; you need only be still (Exodus 14:14). As you stand firm on God's solid foundation (II Timothy 2:19) and stay hidden in the shadow of His wings (Psalm 61:4), you will provide deliverance for the weak, insecure, unsheltered, and frail. Instead of being defensive, you are a defender of injustice done to all mankind. You let discretion protect you (Proverbs 2:11). You will shield others from the enemy's destruction with love (I Corinthians 13:7) and the power of God's name (John 17:11). You display God's compassion through your humility. What you let him be in you, you will be to others.

BILLY

Resolute protector; great protector

&

Job 11:18 *You will be secure, because there is hope; you will look about you and take your rest in safety.*

Psalm 32:7 *You are my hiding place; You will protect me from trouble and surround me with songs of deliverance.*

Psalm 27:5 *For in the day of trouble He will keep me safe in His dwelling; He will hide me in the shelter of His tabernacle and set me high upon a rock.*

You are securely wrapped up and protected by Jesus Christ, who frees you from doubt and harm. Because you find your shelter, assurance, stability, and strength in your personal relationship with the Lord, you are kept in a safe place. You are confident that the Lord will fight for you; you need only be still (Exodus 14:14). As you stand firm on God's solid foundation (II Timothy 2:19) and stay hidden in the shadow of His wings (Psalm 61:4), you will provide deliverance for the weak, insecure, unsheltered, and frail. Instead of being defensive, you are a defender of injustice done to all mankind. You let discretion protect you (Proverbs 2:11). You will shield others from the enemy's destruction with love (I Corinthians 13:7) and the power of God's name (John 17:11). You display God's compassion through your humility. What you let him be in you, you will be to others.

BLAKE

Attractive; cheerful one

ℰℐ

Proverbs 15:13 *A happy heart makes the face cheerful, but heartache crushes the spirit.*

Proverbs 17:22 *A cheerful heart is good medicine, but a crushed spirit dries up the bones.*

Your cheerful heart has a continual feast (Proverbs 15:15) and your cheerful look brings joy to the heart (Proverbs 15:30). Out of your deep love for God's Word, you are equipped to give approval, encouragement, and inspiration to the rejected, hopeless, and reluctant. You are very aware that Jesus Christ has overcome the world through His death and resurrection. In every situation you improve the outlook on the future. You cheer the despondent, downcast, and discouraged to victory. With the sorrows you allow God to heal in your own life, you are anointed to provide the oil of gladness to those who mourn (Isaiah 61:1–3). Your presence brings healing to the ugliest, most confused settings. God loves what a cheerful giver you are! (II Corinthians 9:7)

BLYTHE

Happy, cheerful; full of joy

℘

Psalm 149:4–5 *For the Lord takes delight in His people; He crowns the humble with salvation. Let the saints rejoice in this honor and sing for joy on their beds.*

Psalm 45:7 *You love righteousness and hate wickedness; therefore God, your God, has set you above your companions by anointing you with the oil of joy.*

Psalm 16:11 says, "You have made known to me the path of life; You will fill me with joy in Your presence, with eternal pleasures at Your right hand." Your heavenly Father has trusted you with a quality that releases healing, restores hope, and brings refreshing. You are one who takes the source of tears and defeat, and turns them into confident trust with rejoicing. As you experience and remain sensitive to the things that sorrow the heart of God, He will pour His oil of joy on and through you to restore hope to those who are mourning (Isaiah 61:1–3). Experiences of sorrow prepare and enlarge your capacity for joy. The joy of the Lord will be your strength to endure the cross He has called you to bear. You are to fix your eyes on Jesus, the author and perfecter of your faith, who for the joy set before Him endured the cross, scorning its shame, and sat down at the right hand of the throne of God (Hebrews 12:2). He will be faithful to give you a song in your "night" season (Psalm 42:8). God rejoices over you with gladness! (Zephaniah 3:17)

BOB

Shining with fame; excellent worth

℘

II Corinthians 8:7 *But just as you excel in everything—in faith, in speech, in knowledge, in complete earnestness and in your love for us—see that you also excel in this grace of giving.*

Philippians 4:8 *Finally, brothers, whatever is true, whatever is noble, whatever is right, whatever is pure, whatever is lovely, whatever is admirable—if anything is excellent or praiseworthy—think about such things.*

Excellent worth is comprised in your worship of God. Revelation 5:12 says, "Worthy is the Lamb, who was slain, to receive power and wealth and wisdom and strength and honor and glory and praise!" "All this also comes from the Lord Almighty, wonderful in counsel and magnificent in wisdom," Isaiah 28:29. God has given you an eye for quality, demonstrating His excellence of character and conduct. You go beyond human capacity with faith that transcends all understanding. Your faith is of greater worth than gold (I Peter 1:7). In quality, skill, and achievement, you go the extra mile. This is all about giving, not getting; serving, not controlling. Perfectionism leads to legalism. Excellence releases freedom. You are to show the insignificant and the wasted the more excellent way of God's love (I Corinthians 12:31 and chapter 13) and kindness (2 Peter 1:5–7). You are to excel in gifts that build up the church (I Corinthians 14:12). God uses you to restore genuine value, purpose, and productivity. Devoting yourself to doing what is good will lead to what is excellent and profitable for everyone (Titus 3:8). Your gentle and quiet spirit is of great worth in God's eyes (I Peter 3:4).

BONNIE

Sweet and good; a good heart

Proverbs 16:24 *Pleasant words are a honeycomb, sweet to the soul and healing to the bones.*

Psalm 119:103 *How sweet are Your words to my taste, sweeter than honey to my mouth!*

The Word of God is described as being "sweeter than honey from the honeycomb" in Psalm 19:10. It is symbolic of wisdom that is sweet to the soul, giving you a future hope that will not be cut off (Proverbs 24:13–14). Proverbs 27:7 says, "He who is full loathes honey, but to the hungry even what is bitter tastes sweet." The Lord has blessed you with the ability to see the good in everything. Even when bitter things come into your life, you are able to allow Him to turn it for His good because you hunger for more of Him. His fruit, the fruit of the Spirit, is sweet to your taste (Song of Solomon 2:3). As you are saturated with God's Word, your own words will be welcoming, agreeable, and pleasing. You are anointed to bring approval to those drinking the "bitter cup," giving them hope that will not be cut off. Because you have "tasted that the Lord is good," you will nurture spiritual hunger in new believers for the Word of God.

BRAD

From the broad meadow; abundant provider

Psalm 1:1–3 *Blessed is the man who does not walk in the counsel of the wicked or stand in the way of sinners or sit in the seat of mockers. But his delight is in the law of the Lord, and on His law he meditates day and night. He is like a tree planted by the streams of water, which yields its fruit in season and whose leaf does not wither. Whatever he does prospers.*

Joshua 1:8 *Do not let this book of the law depart from your mouth; meditate on it day and night, so that you may be careful to do everything written in it. Then you will be prosperous and successful.*

You are one who knows that your success is not based on luck or good fortune. It is because you are willing to loose your life for Christ's sake in order to find it (Matthew 10:39). You let the word of Christ dwell in you richly (Colossians 3:16). You allow the Lord to stretch and strengthen you in order to enlarge your borders of influence and maturity (Isaiah 54:1–3). You welcome the cutting and pruning that makes way for increase to bear fruit, more fruit, and much fruit (John 15). You enter a covenant with the Lord of obedience, seeking Him diligently and wholeheartedly (II Chronicles 31:21), which causes you to prosper in everything you do (Deuteronomy 29:9). You are content in need and in plenty (Philippians 4:11–12) because prosperity is not a love of money (I Timothy 6:6–10), power, popularity, or possessions. In spite of failure, disappointment, loss, and defeat, you let nothing separate you from the love of God (Romans 8:37–39). Instead of being blind to the hungry, you will feed them. Instead of abhorring the naked, you will clothe them. Instead of ignoring the poor and fatherless, you will be God's hand of provision. You will offer provisions of hope, courage, and strength not to give up, but rather to start again and to make it to the finish line. You are a faithful steward helping them exchange their temporal for His eternal (Philippians 4:19). As your mantle is to build up, develop, and cause to succeed, know that "no weapon formed against you will prosper," Isaiah 54:17. Your goal is to hear the Master say, "Well done, good and faithful servant! You have been faithful with a few things, I will put you in charge of many things. Come share your Master's happiness!" (Matthew 25:21) May you prosper in all things and be in health, just as your soul prospers (3 John 2).

BRADEN

From the broad meadow; delivered

❧

Psalm 130:7–8 *O Israel, put your hope in the Lord, for with the Lord is unfailing love and with Him is full redemption. He Himself will redeem Israel from all their sins.*

Galatians 3:13–14 *Christ redeemed us from the curse of the law by becoming a curse for us, for it is written: "Cursed is everyone who is hung on a tree." He redeemed us in order that the blessing given to Abraham might come to the Gentiles through Christ Jesus, so that by faith we might receive the promise of the Spirit.*

You are of incredible worth to God! Through His rich grace and by the blood of His Son, your sins are forgiven. You were supposed to be beaten and executed for your sin, but Jesus Christ walked up to you and said, "I'll take it for you." Nothing you could ever do would equal the price paid for you in full by your Savior (I Peter 1:18–19). God will never lower His standards, but He will with outstretched arms reach to your depths—to every trap set for you—in order to buy you back to make you His child and heir (Exodus 6:6 and Galatians 4:4). His arm will never be too short to ransom you, nor does He lack the strength to rescue you (Isaiah 50:2). He rescued you, not from the presence of evil, but from the absence of righteousness. Because you know that the foot of the cross is level for all, you take prompt action in freeing others from danger and destruction. You have a passion to release those held captive, restore those who have given up, and to rescue those who have been abandoned. Through you, the lost will be connected to their Deliverer. You are an advocate for truth with great joy (Isaiah 35). The liberty God has given you, you will give to others because you know your Redeemer lives (Job 19:25). Your life is a living "thank you" to your Savior.

BRADLEY

From the broad meadow; abundant provider

❧

Psalm 1:1–3 *Blessed is the man who does not walk in the counsel of the wicked or stand in the way of sinners or sit in the seat of mockers. But his delight is in the law of the Lord, and on His law he meditates day and night. He is like a tree planted by the streams of water, which yields its fruit in season and whose leaf does not wither. Whatever he does prospers.*

Joshua 1:8 *Do not let this book of the law depart from your mouth; meditate on it day and night, so that you may be careful to do everything written in it. Then you will be prosperous and successful.*

You are one who knows that your success is not based on luck or good fortune. It is because you are willing to loose your life for Christ's sake in order to find it (Matthew 10:39). You let the word of Christ dwell in you richly (Colossians 3:16). You allow the Lord to stretch and strengthen you in order to enlarge your borders of influence and maturity (Isaiah 54:1–3). You welcome the cutting and pruning that makes way for increase to bear fruit, more fruit, and much fruit (John 15). You enter a covenant with the Lord of obedience, seeking Him diligently and wholeheartedly (II Chronicles 31:21), which causes you to prosper in everything you do (Deuteronomy 29:9). You are content in need and in plenty (Philippians 4:11–12) because prosperity is not a love of money (I Timothy 6:6–10), power, popularity, or possessions. In spite of failure, disappointment, loss, and defeat, you let nothing separate you from the love of God (Romans 8:37–39). Instead of being blind to the hungry, you will feed them. Instead of abhorring the naked, you will clothe them. Instead of ignoring the poor and fatherless, you will be God's hand of provision. You will offer provisions of hope, courage, and strength not to give up, but rather to start again and to make it to the finish line. You are a faithful steward helping them exchange their temporal for His eternal (Philippians 4:19). As your mantle is to build up, develop, and cause to succeed, know that "no weapon formed against you will prosper," Isaiah 54:17. Your goal is to hear the Master say, "Well done, good and faithful servant! You have been faithful with a few things, I will put you in charge of many things. Come share your Master's happiness!" (Matthew 25:21) May you prosper in all things and be in health, just as your soul prospers (3 John 2).

BRADY

From the broad meadow; abundant provider

ℰℐ

Psalm 1:1–3 *Blessed is the man who does not walk in the counsel of the wicked or stand in the way of sinners or sit in the seat of mockers. But his delight is in the law of the Lord, and on His law he meditates day and night. He is like a tree planted by the streams of water, which yields its fruit in season and whose leaf does not wither. Whatever he does prospers.*

Joshua 1:8 *Do not let this book of the law depart from your mouth; meditate on it day and night, so that you may be careful to do everything written in it. Then you will be prosperous and successful.*

You are one who knows that your success is not based on luck or good fortune. It is because you are willing to loose your life for Christ's sake in order to find it (Matthew 10:39). You let the word of Christ dwell in you richly (Colossians 3:16). You allow the Lord to stretch and strengthen you in order to enlarge your borders of influence and maturity (Isaiah 54:1–3). You welcome the cutting and pruning that makes way for increase to bear fruit, more fruit, and much fruit (John 15). You enter a covenant with the Lord of obedience, seeking Him diligently and wholeheartedly (II Chronicles 31:21), which causes you to prosper in everything you do (Deuteronomy 29:9). You are content in need and in plenty (Philippians 4:11–12) because prosperity is not a love of money (I Timothy 6:6–10), power, popularity, or possessions. In spite of failure, disappointment, loss, and defeat, you let nothing separate you from the love of God (Romans 8:37–39). Instead of being blind to the hungry, you will feed them. Instead of abhorring the naked, you will clothe them. Instead of ignoring the poor and fatherless, you will be God's hand of provision. You will offer provisions of hope, courage, and strength not to give up, but rather to start again and to make it to the finish line. You are a faithful steward helping them exchange their temporal for His eternal (Philippians 4:19). As your mantle is to build up, develop, and cause to succeed, know that "no weapon formed against you will prosper," Isaiah 54:17. Your goal is to hear the Master say, "Well done, good and faithful servant! You have been faithful with a few things, I will put you in charge of many things. Come share your Master's happiness!" (Matthew 25:21) May you prosper in all things and be in health, just as your soul prospers (3 John 2).

BRANDON

From the beacon hill; strong in victory

I John 5:4 *Everyone born of God overcomes the world. This is the victory that has overcome the world, even our faith.*

II Corinthians 2:14 *But thanks be to God, who always leads us in triumphal procession in Christ and through us spreads everywhere the fragrance of the knowledge of Him.*

Because of your faith in Jesus Christ, you will ever be aggressive towards the enemy's tools of defeat, failure, and victimization. You will push back Satan and overcome all his power. Jesus has given you authority to trample on snakes and scorpions and to overcome all the power of the enemy; nothing will harm you (Luke 10:19). Even in the severest of afflictions—such as hardship, persecution, famine, nakedness, danger, or sword—you are more than a conqueror through Christ who loves you (Romans 8:35–37). "Everyone born of God overcomes the world. This is the victory that has overcome the world, even our faith," I John 5:4. "Take heart, Jesus has overcome the world," John 16:33.

BRAYDEN

From the broad meadow; delivered

Psalm 130:7–8 *O Israel, put your hope in the Lord, for with the Lord is unfailing love and with Him is full redemption. He Himself will redeem Israel from all their sins.*

Galatians 3:13–14 *Christ redeemed us from the curse of the law by becoming a curse for us, for it is written: "Cursed is everyone who is hung on a tree." He redeemed us in order that the blessing given to Abraham might come to the Gentiles through Christ Jesus, so that by faith we might receive the promise of the Spirit.*

You are of incredible worth to God! Through His rich grace and by the blood of His Son, your sins are forgiven. You were supposed to be beaten and executed for your sin, but Jesus Christ walked up to you and said, "I'll take it for you." Nothing you could ever do would equal the price paid for you in full by your Savior (I Peter 1:18–19). God will never lower His standards, but He will with outstretched arms reach to your depths—to every trap set for you—in order to buy you back to make you His child and heir (Exodus 6:6 and Galatians 4:4). His arm will never be too short to ransom you, nor does He lack the strength to rescue you (Isaiah 50:2). He rescued you, not from the presence of evil, but from the absence of righteousness. Because you know that the foot of the cross is level for all, you take prompt action in freeing others from danger and destruction. You have a passion to release those held captive, restore those who have given up, and to rescue those who have been abandoned. Through you, the lost will be connected to their Deliverer. You are an advocate for truth with great joy (Isaiah 35). The liberty God has given you, you will give to others because you know your Redeemer lives (Job 19:25). Your life is a living "thank you" to your Savior.

BRENDA

Fiery; enthusiastic

❧

Isaiah 62:1 *For Zion's sake I will not keep silent, for Jerusalem's sake I will not remain quiet, till her righteousness shines out like the dawn, her salvation like a blazing torch.*

II Timothy 1:6 *For this reason I remind you to fan into flame the gift of God, which is in you through the laying on of my hands.*

The way Jesus Christ served His heavenly Father is your only example to follow. The word "enthusiastic" means "possessed by God." Zeal for God's house consumed Jesus (John 2:17). Even to His parents He said, "Didn't you know I had to be in my Father's house?" Luke 2:49. "He put on righteousness as His breastplate, and the helmet of salvation on His head; He put on the garments of vengeance and wrapped Himself in zeal as in a cloak," Isaiah 59:17. Just as Jesus was determined and passionate, so are you. As you fervently worship God as the all-consuming fire (Hebrews 12:29), you will invade the strongholds of weariness in spirit, soul, and body. You bring balance to those dominated by their emotions. God's Word and His presence will keep His fire ignited in and through you. Guard against always putting out fires, but keep in mind that you must always start them! May you have an infusion of spiritual adrenaline.

BRENDAN

Raven; brave

৵

Joshua 1:7 *Be strong and very courageous. Be careful to obey all the law My servant Moses gave you; do not turn from it to the right or to the left, that you may be successful wherever you go.*

Philippians 1:27b–28 *I will know that you stand firm in one spirit, contending as one man for the faith of the gospel without being frightened in any way by those who oppose you. This is a sign to them that they will be destroyed, but that you will be saved—and that by God.*

The brave are courageous, heroic, resolute, without dread, and bold. Cowards are fearful, timid, and fainthearted. They see victory in size rather than in faith. Running, hiding, escape mechanisms, and desertion are their game plan. They are dominated by the fear of man. You are dominated by your respectful fear of God. In stubborn faith, you say, "Nothing can hinder the Lord, nothing is impossible with Him." Your confidence lies in God's abiding presence and His great strength. God has mantled you as His encourager, invading strongholds of doubt and fear. Speak the Word of God boldly (Acts 4:31). The Lord trusts you to champion His cause by advancing the kingdom of heaven in all that you do.

BRENT

Steep hill; rising above

❧

Psalm 1:1–3 *Blessed is the man who does not walk in the counsel of the wicked or stand in the way of sinners or sit in the seat of mockers. But his delight is in the law of the Lord, and on His law he meditates day and night. He is like a tree planted by the streams of water, which yields its fruit in season and whose leaf does not wither. Whatever he does prospers.*

Joshua 1:8 *Do not let this book of the law depart from your mouth; meditate on it day and night, so that you may be careful to do everything written in it. Then you will be prosperous and successful.*

You are one who knows that your success is not based on luck or good fortune. It is because you are willing to loose your life for Christ's sake in order to find it (Matthew 10:39). You let the word of Christ dwell in you richly (Colossians 3:16). You allow the Lord to stretch and strengthen you in order to enlarge your borders of influence and maturity (Isaiah 54:1–3). You welcome the cutting and pruning that makes way for increase to bear fruit, more fruit, and much fruit (John 15). You enter a covenant with the Lord of obedience, seeking Him diligently and wholeheartedly (II Chronicles 31:21), which causes you to prosper in everything you do (Deuteronomy 29:9). You are content in need and in plenty (Philippians 4:11–12) because prosperity is not a love of money (I Timothy 6:6–10), power, popularity, or possessions. In spite of failure, disappointment, loss, and defeat, you let nothing separate you from the love of God (Romans 8:37–39). Instead of being blind to the hungry, you will feed them. Instead of abhorring the naked, you will clothe them. Instead of ignoring the poor and fatherless, you will be God's hand of provision. You will offer provisions of hope, courage, and strength not to give up, but rather to start again and to make it to the finish line. You are a faithful steward helping them exchange their temporal for His eternal (Philippians 4:19). As your mantle is to build up, develop, and cause to succeed, know that "no weapon formed against you will prosper," Isaiah 54:17. Your goal is to hear the Master say, "Well done, good and faithful servant! You have been faithful with a few things, I will put you in charge of many things. Come share your Master's happiness!" (Matthew 25:21) May you prosper in all things and be in health, just as your soul prospers (3 John 2).

BRETT

Gifted; gift of the Lord

&

James 1:17 *Every good and perfect gift is from above, coming down from the Father of the heavenly lights, who does not change like shifting shadows.*

I Samuel 16:7 *But the Lord said to Samuel, "Do not consider his appearance or his height, for I have rejected him. The Lord does not look at the things man looks at. Man looks at the outward appearance, but the Lord looks at the heart."*

You are God's tribute to Himself, His personal reward. Your life defines God's manners, with priorities on giving rather than receiving. You are to fan into flame the gift of God (II Timothy 1:6). Through you He will display His favor, encouragement and kindness even to the undeserved and hated. As you look beyond faults and see needs, you are God's channel through which His unselfish love flows and is revealed. Discipline your attention to the Giver, not to the gift, nor its wrappings. Give diligence to preserving a humble, submitted heart in full surrender to the Lord. Proverbs 18:16 says, "A gift opens the way for the giver and ushers him into the presence of the great."

BRIAN

Strength, virtue; strong in virtue

☙

Proverbs 24:5 *A wise man has great power, and a man of knowledge increases strength.*

Ephesians 6:10 *Finally, be strong in the Lord and in His mighty power.*

You are one who has an un-compromised commitment to righteousness, respectability, honesty, character, excellence, value, worth, kindness, innocence, generosity, trustworthiness, faithfulness, justice, hope, and love. You can do everything through Him who gives you strength (Philippians 4:11–13). The Lord is the source of your strength because you turn back the battle at the gate (Isaiah 28:6). You renew your strength by your hope being in the Lord (Isaiah 40:31). Jesus says, "My grace is sufficient for you, for My power is made perfect in weaknesses. Therefore you will boast all the more gladly about your weaknesses, so that Christ's power may rest on you. That is why for Christ's sake, you delight in weaknesses, in insults, in hardships, in persecutions, and in difficulties. For when you are weak, then you are strong," II Corinthians 12:9–10. You are clothed with strength and dignity (Proverbs 31:25).

BRIANNA

Strength, honor; strong in virtue

Proverbs 24:5 *A wise man has great power, and a man of knowledge increases strength.*

Ephesians 6:10 *Finally, be strong in the Lord and in His mighty power.*

You are one who has an un-compromised commitment to righteousness, respectability, honesty, character, excellence, value, worth, kindness, innocence, generosity, trustworthiness, faithfulness, justice, hope, and love. You can do everything through Him who gives you strength (Philippians 4:11–13). The Lord is the source of your strength because you turn back the battle at the gate (Isaiah 28:6). You renew your strength by your hope being in the Lord (Isaiah 40:31). Jesus says, "My grace is sufficient for you, for My power is made perfect in weaknesses. Therefore you will boast all the more gladly about your weaknesses, so that Christ's power may rest on you. That is why for Christ's sake, you delight in weaknesses, in insults, in hardships, in persecutions, and in difficulties. For when you are weak, then you are strong," II Corinthians 12:9–10. You are clothed with strength and dignity (Proverbs 31:25).

BRIANNE

Strength, honor; strong in virtue

સ્જ

Proverbs 24:5 *A wise man has great power, and a man of knowledge increases strength.*

Ephesians 6:10 *Finally, be strong in the Lord and in His mighty power.*

You are one who has an un-compromised commitment to righteousness, respectability, honesty, character, excellence, value, worth, kindness, innocence, generosity, trustworthiness, faithfulness, justice, hope, and love. You can do everything through Him who gives you strength (Philippians 4:11–13). The Lord is the source of your strength because you turn back the battle at the gate (Isaiah 28:6). You renew your strength by your hope being in the Lord (Isaiah 40:31). Jesus says, "My grace is sufficient for you, for My power is made perfect in weaknesses. Therefore you will boast all the more gladly about your weaknesses, so that Christ's power may rest on you. That is why for Christ's sake, you delight in weaknesses, in insults, in hardships, in persecutions, and in difficulties. For when you are weak, then you are strong," II Corinthians 12:9–10. You are clothed with strength and dignity (Proverbs 31:25).

BRICE

Quick one; quick to excel

ౚ

II Corinthians 8:7 *But just as you excel in everything—in faith, in speech, in knowledge, in complete earnestness and in your love for us—see that you also excel in this grace of giving.*

Philippians 4:8 *Finally, brothers, whatever is true, whatever is noble, whatever is right, whatever is pure, whatever is lovely, whatever is admirable—if anything is excellent or praiseworthy—think about such things.*

Excellent worth is comprised in your worship of God. Revelation 5:12 says, "Worthy is the Lamb, who was slain, to receive power and wealth and wisdom and strength and honor and glory and praise!" "All this also comes from the Lord Almighty, wonderful in counsel and magnificent in wisdom," Isaiah 28:29. God has given you an eye for quality, demonstrating His excellence of character and conduct. You go beyond human capacity with faith that transcends all understanding. Your faith is of greater worth than gold (I Peter 1:7). In quality, skill, and achievement, you go the extra mile. This is all about giving, not getting; serving, not controlling. Perfectionism leads to legalism. Excellence releases freedom. You are to show the insignificant and the wasted the more excellent way of God's love (I Corinthians 12:31 and chapter 13) and kindness (2 Peter 1:5-7). You are to excel in gifts that build up the church (I Corinthians 14:12). God uses you to restore genuine value, purpose, and productivity. Devoting yourself to doing what is good will lead to what is excellent and profitable for everyone (Titus 3:8). Your gentle and quiet spirit is of great worth in God's eyes (I Peter 3:4).

BRIDGET

Strength, power; strong one

ℰↄ

Proverbs 24:5 *A wise man has great power, and a man of knowledge increases strength.*

Ephesians 6:10 *Finally, be strong in the Lord and in His mighty power.*

You are one who has an un-compromised commitment to righteousness, respectability, honesty, character, excellence, value, worth, kindness, innocence, generosity, trustworthiness, faithfulness, justice, hope, and love. You can do everything through Him who gives you strength (Philippians 4:11–13). The Lord is the source of your strength because you turn back the battle at the gate (Isaiah 28:6). You renew your strength by your hope being in the Lord (Isaiah 40:31). Jesus says, "My grace is sufficient for you, for My power is made perfect in weaknesses. Therefore you will boast all the more gladly about your weaknesses, so that Christ's power may rest on you. That is why for Christ's sake, you delight in weaknesses, in insults, in hardships, in persecutions, and in difficulties. For when you are weak, then you are strong," II Corinthians 12:9–10. You are clothed with strength and dignity (Proverbs 31:25).

BRINLEIGH

Passionate; passionate one

Isaiah 62:1 *For Zion's sake I will not keep silent, for Jerusalem's sake I will not remain quiet, till her righteousness shines out like the dawn, her salvation like a blazing torch.*

II Timothy 1:6 *For this reason I remind you to fan into flame the gift of God, which is in you through the laying on of my hands.*

The way Jesus Christ served His heavenly Father is your only example to follow. The word "enthusiastic" means "possessed by God." Zeal for God's house consumed Jesus (John 2:17). Even to His parents He said, "Didn't you know I had to be in my Father's house?" Luke 2:49. "He put on righteousness as His breastplate, and the helmet of salvation on His head; He put on the garments of vengeance and wrapped Himself in zeal as in a cloak," Isaiah 59:17. Just as Jesus was determined and passionate, so are you. As you fervently worship God as the all-consuming fire (Hebrews 12:29), you will invade the strongholds of weariness in spirit, soul, and body. You bring balance to those dominated by their emotions. God's Word and His presence will keep His fire ignited in and through you. Guard against always putting out fires, but keep in mind that you must always start them! May you have an infusion of spiritual adrenaline.

BRITTANY

From Britain; strong

ॐ

Proverbs 24:5 *A wise man has great power, and a man of knowledge increases strength.*

Ephesians 6:10 *Finally, be strong in the Lord and in His mighty power.*

You are one who has an un-compromised commitment to righteousness, respectability, honesty, character, excellence, value, worth, kindness, innocence, generosity, trustworthiness, faithfulness, justice, hope, and love. You can do everything through Him who gives you strength (Philippians 4:11–13). The Lord is the source of your strength because you turn back the battle at the gate (Isaiah 28:6). You renew your strength by your hope being in the Lord (Isaiah 40:31). Jesus says, "My grace is sufficient for you, for My power is made perfect in weaknesses. Therefore you will boast all the more gladly about your weaknesses, so that Christ's power may rest on you. That is why for Christ's sake, you delight in weaknesses, in insults, in hardships, in persecutions, and in difficulties. For when you are weak, then you are strong," II Corinthians 12:9–10. You are clothed with strength and dignity (Proverbs 31:25).

BRITTNEY

From Britain; strong

ॐ

Proverbs 24:5 *A wise man has great power, and a man of knowledge increases strength.*

Ephesians 6:10 *Finally, be strong in the Lord and in His mighty power.*

You are one who has an un-compromised commitment to righteousness, respectability, honesty, character, excellence, value, worth, kindness, innocence, generosity, trustworthiness, faithfulness, justice, hope, and love. You can do everything through Him who gives you strength (Philippians 4:11–13). The Lord is the source of your strength because you turn back the battle at the gate (Isaiah 28:6). You renew your strength by your hope being in the Lord (Isaiah 40:31). Jesus says, "My grace is sufficient for you, for My power is made perfect in weaknesses. Therefore you will boast all the more gladly about your weaknesses, so that Christ's power may rest on you. That is why for Christ's sake, you delight in weaknesses, in insults, in hardships, in persecutions, and in difficulties. For when you are weak, then you are strong," II Corinthians 12:9–10. You are clothed with strength and dignity (Proverbs 31:25).

BRODY

Ditch; established by God

ॐ

Deuteronomy 33:27 *The eternal God is your refuge, and underneath are the everlasting arms. He will drive out your enemy before you, saying, "Destroy him!"*

Isaiah 46:4 *Even to your old age and gray hairs I am He, I am He who will sustain you. I have made you and I will carry you; I will sustain you and I will rescue you.*

A support holds up a structure with a firm foundation. God gives you help and approval through blessing, comfort, encouragement, friendship, loyalty, and protection. When you face tough times, God will carry you on eagles' wings and hold you close to Himself (Exodus 19:4). He will stoop to whatever level you are to make you great (Psalm 18:35). Not only are you upheld by His righteous right hand (Isaiah 41:10), but you uphold others. You serve as a mainstay to strengthen and uphold; to build up and reinforce. This endurance brings wholeness to all those you touch. II Timothy 2:19 says, "Nevertheless, God's solid foundation stands firm, sealed with this inscription: 'The Lord knows those who are His,'" and, "Everyone who confesses the name of the Lord must turn away from wickedness."

BROOKE

Brook; refreshing one

❧

Acts 3:19 *Repent, then, and turn to God, so that your sins may be wiped out, that times of refreshing may come from the Lord.*

II Timothy 1:16 *May the Lord show mercy to the household of Onesiphorus, because he often refreshed me and was not ashamed of my chains.*

You are one who restores strength because of knowing your own weakness. One who revives life because of dying to self. One who renews supply because of being emptied of self. One who reconciles offenses because your wisdom is from Christ. To bring this refreshing, you must know the all-sufficient one—El-Shaddai—in all your insufficiencies. As you learn to rest in His presence (Exodus 33:14), you will be a channel for His revival. Psalm 42:1–2 says, "As the deer pants for streams of water, so my soul pants for you, O God. My soul thirsts for God, for the living God. When can I go and meet with God?" To be His brook or His stream you must dwell in His stream. Stay thirsty for God's living water (John 7:37–38).

BROOKLYN

Brook; refreshing one

୧୦

Acts 3:19 *Repent, then, and turn to God, so that your sins may be wiped out, that times of refreshing may come from the Lord.*

II Timothy 1:16 *May the Lord show mercy to the household of Onesiphorus, because he often refreshed me and was not ashamed of my chains.*

You are one who restores strength because of knowing your own weakness. One who revives life because of dying to self. One who renews supply because of being emptied of self. One who reconciles offenses because your wisdom is from Christ. To bring this refreshing, you must know the all-sufficient one—El-Shaddai—in all your insufficiencies. As you learn to rest in His presence (Exodus 33:14), you will be a channel for His revival. Psalm 42:1–2 says, "As the deer pants for streams of water, so my soul pants for you, O God. My soul thirsts for God, for the living God. When can I go and meet with God?" To be His brook or His stream you must dwell in His stream. Stay thirsty for God's living water (John 7:37–38).

BRYAN

Strength, virtue; strong in virtue

એ

Proverbs 24:5 *A wise man has great power, and a man of knowledge increases strength.*

Ephesians 6:10 *Finally, be strong in the Lord and in His mighty power.*

You are one who has an un-compromised commitment to righteousness, respectability, honesty, character, excellence, value, worth, kindness, innocence, generosity, trustworthiness, faithfulness, justice, hope, and love. You can do everything through Him who gives you strength (Philippians 4:11–13). The Lord is the source of your strength because you turn back the battle at the gate (Isaiah 28:6). You renew your strength by your hope being in the Lord (Isaiah 40:31). Jesus says, "My grace is sufficient for you, for My power is made perfect in weaknesses. Therefore you will boast all the more gladly about your weaknesses, so that Christ's power may rest on you. That is why for Christ's sake, you delight in weaknesses, in insults, in hardships, in persecutions, and in difficulties. For when you are weak, then you are strong," II Corinthians 12:9–10. You are clothed with strength and dignity (Proverbs 31:25).

BRYCE

Quick one; quick to excel

&

II Corinthians 8:7 *But just as you excel in everything—in faith, in speech, in knowledge, in complete earnestness and in your love for us—see that you also excel in this grace of giving.*

Philippians 4:8 *Finally, brothers, whatever is true, whatever is noble, whatever is right, whatever is pure, whatever is lovely, whatever is admirable—if anything is excellent or praiseworthy—think about such things.*

Excellent worth is comprised in your worship of God. Revelation 5:12 says, "Worthy is the Lamb, who was slain, to receive power and wealth and wisdom and strength and honor and glory and praise!" "All this also comes from the Lord Almighty, wonderful in counsel and magnificent in wisdom," Isaiah 28:29. God has given you an eye for quality, demonstrating His excellence of character and conduct. You go beyond human capacity with faith that transcends all understanding. Your faith is of greater worth than gold (I Peter 1:7). In quality, skill, and achievement, you go the extra mile. This is all about giving, not getting; serving, not controlling. Perfectionism leads to legalism. Excellence releases freedom. You are to show the insignificant and the wasted the more excellent way of God's love (I Corinthians 12:31 and chapter 13) and kindness (2 Peter 1:5-7). You are to excel in gifts that build up the church (I Corinthians 14:12). God uses you to restore genuine value, purpose, and productivity. Devoting yourself to doing what is good will lead to what is excellent and profitable for everyone (Titus 3:8). Your gentle and quiet spirit is of great worth in God's eyes (I Peter 3:4).

BRYNNA

Defender; defender of mankind

Deuteronomy 33:12 *Let the beloved of the Lord rest secure in Him, for He shields him all day long, and the one the Lord loves rests between His shoulders.*

Job 11:18 *You will be secure, because there is hope; you will look about you and take your rest in safety.*

Your life is bound securely in the bundle of the living by the Lord your God (1 Samuel 25:29). You will not fear the terror of night, nor the arrow that flies by day (Psalm 91:5). You will have no fear of bad news; your heart is steadfast, trusting in the Lord (Psalm 112:7). You say with confidence that the Lord is your helper. God's sovereign protection frees you from doubt and harm. Because you find your shelter, assurance, stability, and strength in your personal relationship with the Lord, you are kept in a safe place. Lay with compassionate humility a firm foundation for others, providing them with solid security. As you stay hidden in the shadow of His wings (Psalm 61:4), you direct deliverance for the weak, insecure, unsheltered, and frail. You are to help others to become overcomers, victorious, confident, and secure—regardless of the risk and cost to you.

BUDDY

Famous friend; friendly spirit

&

Proverbs 17:17 *A friend loves at all times, and a brother is born for adversity.*

Ecclesiastes 4:9–10 *Two are better than one, because they have a good return for their work: if one falls down his friend can help him up. But pity the man who falls and has no one to help him up!*

Christ was the preeminent example of friendship. John 15:13–14 says, "Greater love has no man than this, that he lay down his life for his friends. You are my friends if you do what I command." With open arms, He gave all. Your mantle is to be God's man of peace. This is achieved by being understanding, loyal, faithful, and true. Proverbs 18:24 says, "A man of many companions may come to ruin, but there is a friend who sticks closer than a brother." It comes natural for you to be hospitable, generous, helpful, and good-humored. Your influence is based on your ability to be approachable, trusted, and respectful. Strangers who are lonely, outcast, or abandoned will find refuge with your "welcome" sign written on your heart. You are loving, as well as being loved—everyone's neighbor; everyone's buddy. Psalm 119:63 says, "I am a friend to all who fear You, to all who follow Your precepts." Proverbs 22:11 says, "He who loves a pure heart and whose speech is gracious will have the King for his friend."

BUTCH

Butcher; industrious

&

Colossians 1:16 *For by Him all things were created: things in heaven and on earth, visible and invisible, whether thrones or powers or rulers or authorities; all things were created by Him and for Him.*

Ephesians 2:10 *For we are God's workmanship, created in Christ Jesus to do good works, which God prepared in advance for us to do.*

To be industrious means to be skillful, hardworking, zealous, and diligent. By persevering, you give careful attention to detail. There is not a lazy bone in your body. Through you the Lord will originate. How you deal with the past determines your future. Regardless of the curses or blessings, the failures or successes, you are God's platform for a "new thing." You cannot lean on your own understanding or reasoning. God Almighty created the heavens, the earth, and you in His image. So the more completely dependent you become on your Creator, the more productive your life will be for Him! I Peter 4:19, "So then, those who suffer according to God's will should commit themselves to their Creator and continue to do good."

BYRON

Bear; full of strength

ℰϽ

Proverbs 24:5 *A wise man has great power, and a man of knowledge increases strength.*

Ephesians 6:10 *Finally, be strong in the Lord and in His mighty power.*

You are one who has an un-compromised commitment to righteousness, respectability, honesty, character, excellence, value, worth, kindness, innocence, generosity, trustworthiness, faithfulness, justice, hope, and love. You can do everything through Him who gives you strength (Philippians 4:11–13). The Lord is the source of your strength because you turn back the battle at the gate (Isaiah 28:6). You renew your strength by your hope being in the Lord (Isaiah 40:31). Jesus says, "My grace is sufficient for you, for My power is made perfect in weaknesses. Therefore you will boast all the more gladly about your weaknesses, so that Christ's power may rest on you. That is why for Christ's sake, you delight in weaknesses, in insults, in hardships, in persecutions, and in difficulties. For when you are weak, then you are strong," II Corinthians 12:9–10. You are clothed with strength and dignity (Proverbs 31:25).

CADEN

Companion; friend

&

Proverbs 17:17 *A friend loves at all times, and a brother is born for adversity.*

Ecclesiastes 4:9–10 *Two are better than one, because they have a good return for their work: if one falls down his friend can help him up. But pity the man who falls and has no one to help him up!*

Christ was the preeminent example of friendship. John 15:13–14 says, "Greater love has no man than this, that he lay down his life for his friends. You are my friends if you do what I command." With open arms, He gave all. Your mantle is to be God's man of peace. This is achieved by being understanding, loyal, faithful, and true. Proverbs 18:24 says, "A man of many companions may come to ruin, but there is a friend who sticks closer than a brother." It comes natural for you to be hospitable, generous, helpful, and good-humored. Your influence is based on your ability to be approachable, trusted, and respectful. Strangers who are lonely, outcast, or abandoned will find refuge with your "welcome" sign written on your heart. You are loving, as well as being loved—everyone's neighbor; everyone's buddy. Psalm 119:63 says, "I am a friend to all who fear You, to all who follow Your precepts." Proverbs 22:11 says, "He who loves a pure heart and whose speech is gracious will have the King for his friend."

CALEB

Whole-hearted; faithful

❧

Proverbs 2:7–8 *He holds victory in store for the upright, He is a shield to those whose walk is blameless, for He guards the course of the just and protects the way of His faithful ones.*

Psalm 15:1–5 *Lord, who may dwell in Your sanctuary? Who may live on Your holy hill? He whose walk is blameless and who does what is righteous, who speaks the truth from his heart and has no slander on his tongue, who does his neighbor no wrong and casts no slur on his fellow man, who despises a vile man but honors those who fear the Lord, who keeps his oath even when it hurts, who lends his money without usury and does not accept a bribe against the innocent. He who does these things will never be shaken.*

You are one who has made a commitment to God to be loyal, true, dependable, enduring, and steadfast. You unmask anything fake with the reality of God's Word. You are aggressive towards lies and deception to bring about truth. You are especially sensitive to betrayal, so that God can restore hope, security, purpose, and His faithfulness in those whom He has given you to serve. "Be faithful, even to the point of death, and I will give you a crown of life," Revelation 2:10. Anticipate the Master saying to you, "Well done, good and faithful servant! You have been faithful with a few things; I will put you in charge of many things. Come and share your Master's happiness!" (Matthew 25:21) "The one who calls you is faithful and he will do it," I Thessalonians 5:24.

CALLIE

Singing lark; cheerful one

ଐ

Proverbs 15:13 *A happy heart makes the face cheerful, but heartache crushes the spirit.*

Proverbs 17:22 *A cheerful heart is good medicine, but a crushed spirit dries up the bones.*

Your cheerful heart has a continual feast (Proverbs 15:15) and your cheerful look brings joy to the heart (Proverbs 15:30). Out of your deep love for God's Word, you are equipped to give approval, encouragement, and inspiration to the rejected, hopeless, and reluctant. You are very aware that Jesus Christ has overcome the world through His death and resurrection. In every situation you improve the outlook on the future. You cheer the despondent, downcast, and discouraged to victory. With the sorrows you allow God to heal in your own life, you are anointed to provide the oil of gladness to those who mourn (Isaiah 61:1–3). Your presence brings healing to the ugliest, most confused settings. God loves what a cheerful giver you are! (II Corinthians 9:7)

CAMERON

Crooked nose; man of distinction

༄

I Kings 3:9 *So give Your servant a discerning heart to govern Your people and to distinguish between right and wrong. For who is able to govern this great people of Yours?*

Hebrews 5:14 *But solid food is for the mature, who by constant use have trained themselves to distinguish good from evil.*

The sense of smell is the strongest of the five senses. In scripture it is equaled to discernment. It is marked by perception, justice, and insight, along with the ability to investigate and examine based on the absolute truth of scripture. Distinction is defined by the act of noticing differences, discretion, sensitivity, and the ability to distinguish good from evil. You are one who takes the crooked, dishonest corruptions of life and gives clear direction on God's straight path, from pollution to purpose. God has equipped you to remove the obstacles of dullness, indifference, and insignificance. He uses you as His shelter from the wind, His refuge from the storm, His streams of water in the desert, and His great rock in a thirsty land (Isaiah 32:1–8). This brings hearing to the deaf, sight to the blind, and understanding to the mind. This discernment will require disciplining your mind to be set on what the Spirit desires, which is justice and freedom. Stay away from what the carnal nature desires, which is judgment and criticism. You live His life, not yours. You think His thoughts, not yours. You speak His words, not yours. Intimacy with the Lord in His Word and in prayer will prevent you from being offended by the "crooked," so that your focus will be on how He discerns. He is the ultimate man of distinction.

CAMRON

Crooked nose; man of distinction

ૹ

I Kings 3:9 *So give Your servant a discerning heart to govern Your people and to distinguish between right and wrong. For who is able to govern this great people of Yours?*

Hebrews 5:14 *But solid food is for the mature, who by constant use have trained themselves to distinguish good from evil.*

The sense of smell is the strongest of the five senses. In scripture it is equaled to discernment. It is marked by perception, justice, and insight, along with the ability to investigate and examine based on the absolute truth of scripture. Distinction is defined by the act of noticing differences, discretion, sensitivity, and the ability to distinguish good from evil. You are one who takes the crooked, dishonest corruptions of life and gives clear direction on God's straight path, from pollution to purpose. God has equipped you to remove the obstacles of dullness, indifference, and insignificance. He uses you as His shelter from the wind, His refuge from the storm, His streams of water in the desert, and His great rock in a thirsty land (Isaiah 32:1–8). This brings hearing to the deaf, sight to the blind, and understanding to the mind. This discernment will require disciplining your mind to be set on what the Spirit desires, which is justice and freedom. Stay away from what the carnal nature desires, which is judgment and criticism. You live His life, not yours. You think His thoughts, not yours. You speak His words, not yours. Intimacy with the Lord in His Word and in prayer will prevent you from being offended by the "crooked," so that your focus will be on how He discerns. He is the ultimate man of distinction.

CANDICE

Glittering, glowing white; bright one

Psalm 27:1 *The Lord is my light and my salvation—whom shall I fear? The Lord is the stronghold of my life; of whom shall I be afraid.*

Proverbs 4:18 *The path of the righteous is like the first gleam of dawn, shining ever brighter till the full light of day.*

You are one who reflects the shining brightness of the countenance of Jesus. You are aggressive toward the fruitless deeds of darkness from the evil one, by exposing them to the light of Jesus. Everything exposed by light becomes visible, for it is the light that makes everything visible (Ephesians 5:11–14). This radiance that God has given you serves as a beacon to give guidance to those yet in darkness. Your life's mission is found in the following two verses: Isaiah 60:1–3 says, "Arise, shine, for your light has come, and the glory of the Lord rises upon you. See, darkness covers the earth, and thick darkness is over the peoples, but the Lord rises upon you and His glory appears over you. Nations will come to your light, and kings to the brightness of your dawn." And in Acts 13:47, "For this is what the Lord has commanded us: 'I have made you a light for the Gentiles, that you may bring salvation to the ends of the earth.'" Continue to shine as His star, leading many to righteousness (Daniel 12:3 and Philippians 2:15).

CANDY

Glittering, glowing white; bright one

ॐ

Psalm 27:1 *The Lord is my light and my salvation - whom shall I fear? The Lord is the stronghold of my life; of whom shall I be afraid.*

Proverbs 4:18 *The path of the righteous is like the first gleam of dawn, shining ever brighter till the full light of day.*

You are one who reflects the shining brightness of the countenance of Jesus. You are aggressive toward the fruitless deeds of darkness from the evil one, by exposing them to the light of Jesus. Everything exposed by light becomes visible, for it is the light that makes everything visible (Ephesians 5:11–14). This radiance that God has given you serves as a beacon to give guidance to those yet in darkness. Your life's mission is found in the following two verses: Isaiah 60:1–3 says, "Arise, shine, for your light has come, and the glory of the Lord rises upon you. See, darkness covers the earth, and thick darkness is over the peoples, but the Lord rises upon you and His glory appears over you. Nations will come to your light, and kings to the brightness of your dawn." And in Acts 13:47, "For this is what the Lord has commanded us: 'I have made you a light for the Gentiles, that you may bring salvation to the ends of the earth.'" Continue to shine as His star, leading many to righteousness (Daniel 12:3 and Philippians 2:15).

CARL

Farm; strong; manly

ℰ

Proverbs 24:5 *A wise man has great power, and a man of knowledge increases strength.*

Ephesians 6:10 *Finally, be strong in the Lord and in His mighty power.*

You are one who has an un-compromised commitment to righteousness, respectability, honesty, character, excellence, value, worth, kindness, innocence, generosity, trustworthiness, faithfulness, justice, hope, and love. You can do everything through Him who gives you strength (Philippians 4:11–13). The Lord is the source of your strength because you turn back the battle at the gate (Isaiah 28:6). You renew your strength by your hope being in the Lord (Isaiah 40:31). Jesus says, "My grace is sufficient for you, for My power is made perfect in weaknesses. Therefore you will boast all the more gladly about your weaknesses, so that Christ's power may rest on you. That is why for Christ's sake, you delight in weaknesses, in insults, in hardships, in persecutions, and in difficulties. For when you are weak, then you are strong," II Corinthians 12:9–10. You are clothed with strength and dignity (Proverbs 31:25).

CARLENE

Little womanly one; refreshing joy

&

Psalm 149:4–5 *For the Lord takes delight in His people; He crowns the humble with salvation. Let the saints rejoice in this honor and sing for joy on their beds.*

Psalm 45:7 *You love righteousness and hate wickedness; therefore God, your God, has set you above your companions by anointing you with the oil of joy.*

Psalm 16:11 says, "You have made known to me the path of life; You will fill me with joy in Your presence, with eternal pleasures at Your right hand." Your heavenly Father has trusted you with a quality that releases healing, restores hope, and brings refreshing. You are one who takes the source of tears and defeat, and turns them into confident trust with rejoicing. As you experience and remain sensitive to the things that sorrow the heart of God, He will pour His oil of joy on and through you to restore hope to those who are mourning (Isaiah 61:1–3). Experiences of sorrow prepare and enlarge your capacity for joy. The joy of the Lord will be your strength to endure the cross He has called you to bear. You are to fix your eyes on Jesus, the author and perfecter of your faith, who for the joy set before Him endured the cross, scorning its shame, and sat down at the right hand of the throne of God (Hebrews 12:2). He will be faithful to give you a song in your "night" season (Psalm 42:8). God rejoices over you with gladness! (Zephaniah 3:17)

CARMEN

Song; song of joy

❦

Psalm 149:4–5 *For the Lord takes delight in His people; He crowns the humble with salvation. Let the saints rejoice in this honor and sing for joy on their beds.*

Psalm 45:7 *You love righteousness and hate wickedness; therefore God, your God, has set you above your companions by anointing you with the oil of joy.*

Psalm 16:11 says, "You have made known to me the path of life; You will fill me with joy in Your presence, with eternal pleasures at Your right hand." Your heavenly Father has trusted you with a quality that releases healing, restores hope, and brings refreshing. You are one who takes the source of tears and defeat, and turns them into confident trust with rejoicing. As you experience and remain sensitive to the things that sorrow the heart of God, He will pour His oil of joy on and through you to restore hope to those who are mourning (Isaiah 61:1–3). Experiences of sorrow prepare and enlarge your capacity for joy. The joy of the Lord will be your strength to endure the cross He has called you to bear. You are to fix your eyes on Jesus, the author and perfecter of your faith, who for the joy set before Him endured the cross, scorning its shame, and sat down at the right hand of the throne of God (Hebrews 12:2). He will be faithful to give you a song in your "night" season (Psalm 42:8). God rejoices over you with gladness! (Zephaniah 3:17)

CARMIE

Song; song of joy

ℰↄ

Psalm 149:4–5 *For the Lord takes delight in His people; He crowns the humble with salvation. Let the saints rejoice in this honor and sing for joy on their beds.*

Psalm 45:7 *You love righteousness and hate wickedness; therefore God, your God, has set you above your companions by anointing you with the oil of joy.*

Psalm 16:11 says, "You have made known to me the path of life; You will fill me with joy in Your presence, with eternal pleasures at Your right hand." Your heavenly Father has trusted you with a quality that releases healing, restores hope, and brings refreshing. You are one who takes the source of tears and defeat, and turns them into confident trust with rejoicing. As you experience and remain sensitive to the things that sorrow the heart of God, He will pour His oil of joy on and through you to restore hope to those who are mourning (Isaiah 61:1–3). Experiences of sorrow prepare and enlarge your capacity for joy. The joy of the Lord will be your strength to endure the cross He has called you to bear. You are to fix your eyes on Jesus, the author and perfecter of your faith, who for the joy set before Him endured the cross, scorning its shame, and sat down at the right hand of the throne of God (Hebrews 12:2). He will be faithful to give you a song in your "night" season (Psalm 42:8). God rejoices over you with gladness! (Zephaniah 3:17)

CAROL

Womanly; song of joy

❧

Psalm 149:4–5 *For the Lord takes delight in His people; He crowns the humble with salvation. Let the saints rejoice in this honor and sing for joy on their beds.*

Psalm 45:7 *You love righteousness and hate wickedness; therefore God, your God, has set you above your companions by anointing you with the oil of joy.*

Psalm 16:11 says, "You have made known to me the path of life; You will fill me with joy in Your presence, with eternal pleasures at Your right hand." Your heavenly Father has trusted you with a quality that releases healing, restores hope, and brings refreshing. You are one who takes the source of tears and defeat, and turns them into confident trust with rejoicing. As you experience and remain sensitive to the things that sorrow the heart of God, He will pour His oil of joy on and through you to restore hope to those who are mourning (Isaiah 61:1–3). Experiences of sorrow prepare and enlarge your capacity for joy. The joy of the Lord will be your strength to endure the cross He has called you to bear. You are to fix your eyes on Jesus, the author and perfecter of your faith, who for the joy set before Him endured the cross, scorning its shame, and sat down at the right hand of the throne of God (Hebrews 12:2). He will be faithful to give you a song in your "night" season (Psalm 42:8). God rejoices over you with gladness! (Zephaniah 3:17)

CAROLINE

Little womanly one; refreshing joy

ৎ১

Psalm 149:4–5 *For the Lord takes delight in His people; He crowns the humble with salvation. Let the saints rejoice in this honor and sing for joy on their beds.*

Psalm 45:7 *You love righteousness and hate wickedness; therefore God, your God, has set you above your companions by anointing you with the oil of joy.*

Psalm 16:11 says, "You have made known to me the path of life; You will fill me with joy in Your presence, with eternal pleasures at Your right hand." Your heavenly Father has trusted you with a quality that releases healing, restores hope, and brings refreshing. You are one who takes the source of tears and defeat, and turns them into confident trust with rejoicing. As you experience and remain sensitive to the things that sorrow the heart of God, He will pour His oil of joy on and through you to restore hope to those who are mourning (Isaiah 61:1–3). Experiences of sorrow prepare and enlarge your capacity for joy. The joy of the Lord will be your strength to endure the cross He has called you to bear. You are to fix your eyes on Jesus, the author and perfecter of your faith, who for the joy set before Him endured the cross, scorning its shame, and sat down at the right hand of the throne of God (Hebrews 12:2). He will be faithful to give you a song in your "night" season (Psalm 42:8). God rejoices over you with gladness! (Zephaniah 3:17)

CAROLYN

Womanly; song of joy

⬥

Psalm 149:4–5 *For the Lord takes delight in His people; He crowns the humble with salvation. Let the saints rejoice in this honor and sing for joy on their beds.*

Psalm 45:7 *You love righteousness and hate wickedness; therefore God, your God, has set you above your companions by anointing you with the oil of joy.*

Psalm 16:11 says, "You have made known to me the path of life; You will fill me with joy in Your presence, with eternal pleasures at Your right hand." Your heavenly Father has trusted you with a quality that releases healing, restores hope, and brings refreshing. You are one who takes the source of tears and defeat, and turns them into confident trust with rejoicing. As you experience and remain sensitive to the things that sorrow the heart of God, He will pour His oil of joy on and through you to restore hope to those who are mourning (Isaiah 61:1–3). Experiences of sorrow prepare and enlarge your capacity for joy. The joy of the Lord will be your strength to endure the cross He has called you to bear. You are to fix your eyes on Jesus, the author and perfecter of your faith, who for the joy set before Him endured the cross, scorning its shame, and sat down at the right hand of the throne of God (Hebrews 12:2). He will be faithful to give you a song in your "night" season (Psalm 42:8). God rejoices over you with gladness! (Zephaniah 3:17)

CARRIE

Strong, womanly; strong woman

გა

Proverbs 24:5 *A wise man has great power, and a man of knowledge increases strength.*

Ephesians 6:10 *Finally, be strong in the Lord and in His mighty power.*

You are one who has an un-compromised commitment to righteousness, respectability, honesty, character, excellence, value, worth, kindness, innocence, generosity, trustworthiness, faithfulness, justice, hope, and love. You can do everything through Him who gives you strength (Philippians 4:11–13). The Lord is the source of your strength because you turn back the battle at the gate (Isaiah 28:6). You renew your strength by your hope being in the Lord (Isaiah 40:31). Jesus says, "My grace is sufficient for you, for My power is made perfect in weaknesses. Therefore you will boast all the more gladly about your weaknesses, so that Christ's power may rest on you. That is why for Christ's sake, you delight in weaknesses, in insults, in hardships, in persecutions, and in difficulties. For when you are weak, then you are strong," II Corinthians 12:9–10. You are clothed with strength and dignity (Proverbs 31:25).

CARSON

Dweller by the marsh; firm foundation

❧

Deuteronomy 33:27 *The eternal God is your refuge, and underneath are the everlasting arms. He will drive out your enemy before you, saying, "Destroy him!"*

Isaiah 46:4 *Even to your old age and gray hairs I am He, I am He who will sustain you. I have made you and I will carry you; I will sustain you and I will rescue you.*

A support holds up a structure with a firm foundation. God gives you help and approval through blessing, comfort, encouragement, friendship, loyalty, and protection. When you face tough times, God will carry you on eagles' wings and hold you close to Himself (Exodus 19:4). He will stoop to whatever level you are to make you great (Psalm 18:35). Not only are you upheld by His righteous right hand (Isaiah 41:10), but you uphold others. You serve as a mainstay to strengthen and uphold; to build up and reinforce. This endurance brings wholeness to all those you touch. II Timothy 2:19 says, "Nevertheless, God's solid foundation stands firm, sealed with this inscription:'The Lord knows those who are His,'" and, "Everyone who confesses the name of the Lord must turn away from wickedness."

CARTER

Maker of carts; industrious spirit

&

Colossians 1:16 *For by Him all things were created: things in heaven and on earth, visible and invisible, whether thrones or powers or rulers or authorities; all things were created by Him and for Him.*

Ephesians 2:10 *For we are God's workmanship, created in Christ Jesus to do good works, which God prepared in advance for us to do.*

To be industrious means to be skillful, hardworking, zealous, and diligent. By persevering, you give careful attention to detail. There is not a lazy bone in your body. Through you the Lord will originate. How you deal with the past determines your future. Regardless of the curses or blessings, the failures or successes, you are God's platform for a "new thing." You cannot lean on your own understanding or reasoning. God Almighty created the heavens, the earth, and you in His image. So the more completely dependent you become on your Creator, the more productive your life will be for Him! I Peter 4:19, "So then, those who suffer according to God's will should commit themselves to their Creator and continue to do good."

CASSIDY

Clever; full of wisdom

ଚ୨

James 3:17 *But the wisdom that comes from heaven is first of all pure; then peace-loving, considerate, submissive, full of mercy and good fruit, impartial and sincere.*

Proverbs 9:10 *The fear of the Lord is the beginning of wisdom, and knowledge of the Holy One is understanding.*

You are a person of moral excellence. You exemplify right living put into practice. The Lord has not only equipped you with skills for living correctly, but also the ability to impart that to others. The Spirit of truth will guide you into all truth, allowing you to have insight into the true nature of things (John 16:13). Out of your reverential respect for the Lord, you have wisdom to give guidance and direction. You are a safe sounding board who steers those who are hungry for knowledge of the Holy One in the right direction. You need only to ask for the wisdom you lack, and God will give it to you generously (James 1:5). Having spiritual discernment is having the ability to separate the difference between God's wisdom and the world's and the ability to make the right choice—regardless. Luke 21:15 says, "For I will give you words and wisdom that none of your adversaries will be able to resist or contradict."

CATHERINE

Pure one

I Timothy 5:22 *...do not share in the sins of others. Keep yourself pure.*

I Peter 1:22 *Now that you have purified yourselves by obeying the truth so that you have sincere love for your brothers, love one another deeply, from the heart.*

Through the process of heat, trials, and refinement, purity is established. Your nature defies being stubborn, judgmental, and haughty. The commandment of the Lord is clear—giving insight to life (Psalm 19:8). You bring wholeness to the dirty, defiled, contaminated, polluted, double-minded, and raped. Your willingness to be transparent is the venue through which He makes His Word clear, simple, and unadulterated. Your choice to be pure enables you to see God (Matthew 5:8) and to know Him as King and Friend (Proverbs 22:11). It also allows your words to be pleasant (Proverbs 15:26) and causes you to ascend to the holy place of the Lord, where you receive blessings and righteousness from the God of salvation (Psalm 24:3–5). Proverbs 20:11 says, "Even a child is known by his actions, by whether his conduct is pure and right."

CATHY

Pure one

I Timothy 5:22 *...do not share in the sins of others. Keep yourself pure.*

I Peter 1:22 *Now that you have purified yourselves by obeying the truth so that you have sincere love for your brothers, love one another deeply, from the heart.*

Through the process of heat, trials, and refinement, purity is established. Your nature defies being stubborn, judgmental, and haughty. The commandment of the Lord is clear—giving insight to life (Psalm 19:8). You bring wholeness to the dirty, defiled, contaminated, polluted, double-minded, and raped. Your willingness to be transparent is the venue through which He makes His Word clear, simple, and unadulterated. Your choice to be pure enables you to see God (Matthew 5:8) and to know Him as King and Friend (Proverbs 22:11). It also allows your words to be pleasant (Proverbs 15:26) and causes you to ascend to the holy place of the Lord, where you receive blessings and righteousness from the God of salvation (Psalm 24:3–5). Proverbs 20:11 says, "Even a child is known by his actions, by whether his conduct is pure and right."

CECIL

Blind; humble spirit

❧

Micah 6:8 *He has showed you, O man, what is good. And what does the Lord require of you? To act justly and to love mercy and to walk humbly with your God.*

I Peter 5:6 *Humble yourselves, therefore, under God's mighty hand, that He may lift you up in due time.*

Prove to be trustworthy over little and God will make you ruler over much (Luke 19:17). The higher you lift the Lord, the more dependent you will be on Him. He increases; you decrease (John 3:30). Being exalted only comes from God—not from you or anyone else. It is for the purpose of enlarging His kingdom. Take no credit for the enormous favor God will give you. It is His grace that will give entrance to these doors of favor, as you choose His approval over man's. Philippians 2:3 says, "Do nothing out of selfish ambition or vain conceit, but in humility consider others better than yourselves." Humility and the fear of the Lord bring wealth, honor, and life (Proverbs 22:4).

CELIA

Blind; humble spirit

&

Micah 6:8 *He has showed you, O man, what is good. And what does the Lord require of you? To act justly and to love mercy and to walk humbly with your God.*

I Peter 5:6 *Humble yourselves, therefore, under God's mighty hand, that He may lift you up in due time.*

Prove to be trustworthy over little and God will make you ruler over much (Luke 19:17). The higher you lift the Lord, the more dependent you will be on Him. He increases; you decrease (John 3:30). Being exalted only comes from God—not from you or anyone else. It is for the purpose of enlarging His kingdom. Take no credit for the enormous favor God will give you. It is His grace that will give entrance to these doors of favor, as you choose His approval over man's. Philippians 2:3 says, "Do nothing out of selfish ambition or vain conceit, but in humility consider others better than yourselves." Humility and the fear of the Lord bring wealth, honor, and life (Proverbs 22:4).

CELINA

Peaceful; where God dwells

ॐ

Isaiah 26:3 *You will keep in perfect peace him whose mind is steadfast, because he trusts in You.*

Philippians 4:7 *And the peace of God, which transcends all understanding, will guard your hearts and your minds in Christ Jesus.*

Your life defines peace. You will have a content and calm composure in the midst of distress, disturbance, or agitation. As you follow the Prince of Peace, you will be secure in who you are in Christ. The discipline of keeping your mind on Christ, loving God's law, and being controlled by the Holy Spirit will keep you in perfect peace. God's peace will serve as an umpire to determine whether you are safe or out of God's will (Colossians 3:15). Do not think it strange when you are in battles, fights, and quarrels, because God wants to use you to bring harmony, order, unity, agreement, quietness, and calmness to the adverse situation. You are one whose intimate friendship with the Lord brings reconciliation to the offended, distressed, and troubled. "In repentance and rest is your salvation, in quietness and trust is your strength," Isaiah 30:15. Your refreshing comes as you renew your mind daily in the Word of God. "Great peace have they who love Your law, and nothing can make them stumble," Psalm 119:165.

CELINE

Peaceful; where God dwells

ℰℂ

Isaiah 26:3 *You will keep in perfect peace him whose mind is steadfast, because he trusts in You.*

Philippians 4:7 *And the peace of God, which transcends all understanding, will guard your hearts and your minds in Christ Jesus.*

Your life defines peace. You will have a content and calm composure in the midst of distress, disturbance, or agitation. As you follow the Prince of Peace, you will be secure in who you are in Christ. The discipline of keeping your mind on Christ, loving God's law, and being controlled by the Holy Spirit will keep you in perfect peace. God's peace will serve as an umpire to determine whether you are safe or out of God's will (Colossians 3:15). Do not think it strange when you are in battles, fights, and quarrels, because God wants to use you to bring harmony, order, unity, agreement, quietness, and calmness to the adverse situation. You are one whose intimate friendship with the Lord brings reconciliation to the offended, distressed, and troubled. "In repentance and rest is your salvation, in quietness and trust is your strength," Isaiah 30:15. Your refreshing comes as you renew your mind daily in the Word of God. "Great peace have they who love Your law, and nothing can make them stumble," Psalm 119:165.

CHAD

Warlike; defender

❧

Proverbs 31:8–9 *Speak up for those who cannot speak for themselves, for the rights of all who are destitute. Speak up and judge fairly; defend the rights of the poor and needy.*

II Timothy 2:3–4 *Endure hardship with us like a good soldier of Christ Jesus. No one serving as a soldier gets involved in civilian affairs—he wants to please his commanding officer.*

As God's warlike defender, you are His example of a champion, soldier, and hero. The ultimate war is a contest with death and when Christ said, "It is finished" on the cross, He declared victory over death, hell, and the grave. You are called to be used of God as one who protects by warding off attacks, calling for justice, and providing shelter. When God is all this to you, you will be that vindication for others. Your ultimate purpose is to be one who stands in the gap (Ezekiel 22:30); to be a defender of the weak. This includes those who are easily influenced, the confused, lowly, faint, frail, fragile, and the frightened. Your primary spiritual warfare will be that of intercession—reaching, meeting, and entreating God for His favor.

CHANCE

A king's secretary; a learned man

&

Proverbs 22:11 *He who loves a pure heart and whose speech is gracious will have the king for his friend.*

Proverbs 3:3 *Let love and faithfulness never leave you; bind them around your neck, write them on the tablet of your heart.*

Deuteronomy 29:29 says, "The secret things belong to the Lord our God, but the things revealed belong to us and to our children forever, that we may follow all the words of this law." God's covenant to you is that He will put His law in your mind and write it on your heart. He will be yours and you will be His (Jeremiah 31:33). You are a letter from Christ—a living epistle—not written with ink, but with the Spirit of the living God (II Corinthians 3:3). You must invest in hiding God's Word in your heart (Psalm 119:11) to make your own words have eternal credibility. Only as you apply God's wisdom to your own heart will He entrust you with the secrets of His. This intimate friendship with the King will allow you the privilege of clearly recording His revelation (John 15:15, I Corinthians 2:9–10, and Amos 3:7). Habakkuk 2:2–3 says, "Write down the revelation and make it plain on tablets so that a herald may run with it. For the revelation awaits an appointed time; it speaks of the end and will not prove false. Though it linger, wait for it; it will certainly come and will not delay."

CHANCELLOR

A king's secretary: a learned man

෫ධ

Proverbs 22:11 *He who loves a pure heart and whose speech is gracious will have the king for his friend.*

Proverbs 3:3 *Let love and faithfulness never leave you; bind them around your neck, write them on the tablet of your heart.*

Deuteronomy 29:29 says, "The secret things belong to the Lord our God, but the things revealed belong to us and to our children forever, that we may follow all the words of this law." God's covenant to you is that He will put His law in your mind and write it on your heart. He will be yours and you will be His (Jeremiah 31:33). You are a letter from Christ—a living epistle—not written with ink, but with the Spirit of the living God (II Corinthians 3:3). You must invest in hiding God's Word in your heart (Psalm 119:11) to make your own words have eternal credibility. Only as you apply God's wisdom to your own heart will He entrust you with the secrets of His. This intimate friendship with the King will allow you the privilege of clearly recording His revelation (John 15:15, I Corinthians 2:9–10, and Amos 3:7). Habakkuk 2:2–3 says, "Write down the revelation and make it plain on tablets so that a herald may run with it. For the revelation awaits an appointed time; it speaks of the end and will not prove false. Though it linger, wait for it; it will certainly come and will not delay."

CHANDLER

Candle maker; bearer of light

Psalm 27:1 *The Lord is my light and my salvation—whom shall I fear? The Lord is the stronghold of my life; of whom shall I be afraid.*

Proverbs 4:18 *The path of the righteous is like the first gleam of dawn, shining ever brighter till the full light of day.*

You are one who reflects the shining brightness of the countenance of Jesus. You are aggressive toward the fruitless deeds of darkness from the evil one, by exposing them to the light of Jesus. Everything exposed by light becomes visible, for it is the light that makes everything visible (Ephesians 5:11–14). This radiance that God has given you serves as a beacon to give guidance to those yet in darkness. Your life's mission is found in the following two verses: Isaiah 60:1–3 says, "Arise, shine, for your light has come, and the glory of the Lord rises upon you. See, darkness covers the earth, and thick darkness is over the peoples, but the Lord rises upon you and His glory appears over you. Nations will come to your light, and kings to the brightness of your dawn." And in Acts 13:47, "For this is what the Lord has commanded us: 'I have made you a light for the Gentiles, that you may bring salvation to the ends of the earth.'" Continue to shine as His star, leading many to righteousness (Daniel 12:3 and Philippians 2:15).

CHARLENE

Little womanly one; womanly

ॐ

Zephaniah 3:17 *The Lord your God is with you, He is mighty to save. He will take great delight in you, He will quiet you with His love, He will rejoice over you with singing.*

Ephesians 5:28–30 *In this same way, husbands ought to love their wives as their own bodies. He who loves his wife loves himself. After all, no one ever hated His own body, but he feeds and cares for it, just as Christ does the church - for we are members of His body.*

You are God's "treasured possession" (Deuteronomy 7:6). By giving the very life of His Son, God has committed to highly value you and take good care of you. He will treat you tenderly in tough times. You are to relate to others as Jesus relates to the Father and to us. Paul served as an example for you. I Thessalonians 2:7–8 says, "We were gentle among you, like a mother caring for her little children. We loved you so much that we were delighted to share with you not only the gospel of God but our lives as well, because you had become so dear to us." The warmth you experience being held close to His heart will enable you to melt the ice in others—the rejected and the castaways. Be free to be intimate with your Maker with trust and selfless submission.

CHARLES

Strong; manly

Proverbs 24:5 *A wise man has great power, and a man of knowledge increases strength.*

Ephesians 6:10 *Finally, be strong in the Lord and in His mighty power.*

You are one who has an un-compromised commitment to righteousness, respectability, honesty, character, excellence, value, worth, kindness, innocence, generosity, trustworthiness, faithfulness, justice, hope, and love. You can do everything through Him who gives you strength (Philippians 4:11–13). The Lord is the source of your strength because you turn back the battle at the gate (Isaiah 28:6). You renew your strength by your hope being in the Lord (Isaiah 40:31). Jesus says, "My grace is sufficient for you, for My power is made perfect in weaknesses. Therefore you will boast all the more gladly about your weaknesses, so that Christ's power may rest on you. That is why for Christ's sake, you delight in weaknesses, in insults, in hardships, in persecutions, and in difficulties. For when you are weak, then you are strong," II Corinthians 12:9–10. You are clothed with strength and dignity (Proverbs 31:25).

CHARLOTTE

Little womanly one; joy to the Lord

❧

Psalm 149:4–5 *For the Lord takes delight in His people; He crowns the humble with salvation. Let the saints rejoice in this honor and sing for joy on their beds.*

Psalm 45:7 *You love righteousness and hate wickedness; therefore God, your God, has set you above your companions by anointing you with the oil of joy.*

Psalm 16:11 says, "You have made known to me the path of life; You will fill me with joy in Your presence, with eternal pleasures at Your right hand." Your heavenly Father has trusted you with a quality that releases healing, restores hope, and brings refreshing. You are one who takes the source of tears and defeat, and turns them into confident trust with rejoicing. As you experience and remain sensitive to the things that sorrow the heart of God, He will pour His oil of joy on and through you to restore hope to those who are mourning (Isaiah 61:1–3). Experiences of sorrow prepare and enlarge your capacity for joy. The joy of the Lord will be your strength to endure the cross He has called you to bear. You are to fix your eyes on Jesus, the author and perfecter of your faith, who for the joy set before Him endured the cross, scorning its shame, and sat down at the right hand of the throne of God (Hebrews 12:2). He will be faithful to give you a song in your "night" season (Psalm 42:8). God rejoices over you with gladness! (Zephaniah 3:17)

CHARMAY

Song; song of joy

&

Psalm 149:4–5 *For the Lord takes delight in His people; He crowns the humble with salvation. Let the saints rejoice in this honor and sing for joy on their beds.*

Psalm 45:7 *You love righteousness and hate wickedness; therefore God, your God, has set you above your companions by anointing you with the oil of joy.*

Psalm 16:11 says, "You have made known to me the path of life; You will fill me with joy in Your presence, with eternal pleasures at Your right hand." Your heavenly Father has trusted you with a quality that releases healing, restores hope, and brings refreshing. You are one who takes the source of tears and defeat, and turns them into confident trust with rejoicing. As you experience and remain sensitive to the things that sorrow the heart of God, He will pour His oil of joy on and through you to restore hope to those who are mourning (Isaiah 61:1–3). Experiences of sorrow prepare and enlarge your capacity for joy. The joy of the Lord will be your strength to endure the cross He has called you to bear. You are to fix your eyes on Jesus, the author and perfecter of your faith, who for the joy set before Him endured the cross, scorning its shame, and sat down at the right hand of the throne of God (Hebrews 12:2). He will be faithful to give you a song in your "night" season (Psalm 42:8). God rejoices over you with gladness! (Zephaniah 3:17)

CHASE

Hunter; seeking one

Hosea 10:12 *Sow for yourselves righteousness, reap the fruit of unfailing love, and break up your unplowed ground; for it is time to seek the Lord, until He comes and showers righteousness on you.*

Deuteronomy 4:29 *But if from there you seek the Lord your God, you will find Him if you look for Him with all your heart and with all your soul.*

The Lord has divine attraction for you. He captures you with His love. He delights in you seeking His face. As the bee feeds on pollen and nectar, you feed on God's Word. The bees carry pollen from blossom to blossom, enabling flowering plants to produce seeds. You perform the same tasks through prayer and intercession. They perform a dance to give direction for rich food; you do that through worship. In self-denial, you keep your hands clean and your heart pure (Proverbs 24:3–6). With your diligent pursuit of the Lord, you bring order and have the ability to cause others to search for that same intimacy with Him. To the aimless, you give direction to stay the course. To the complacent, you ignite hunger through prayer and worship. Honey is the byproduct of your life!

CHELSEA

Seaport; protector of mankind

∞

Deuteronomy 33:12 *Let the beloved of the Lord rest secure in Him, for He shields him all day long, and the one the Lord loves rests between His shoulders.*

Job 11:18 *You will be secure, because there is hope; you will look about you and take your rest in safety.*

Your life is bound securely in the bundle of the living by the Lord your God (I Samuel 25:29). You will not fear the terror of night, nor the arrow that flies by day (Psalm 91:5). You will have no fear of bad news; your heart is steadfast, trusting in the Lord (Psalm 112:7). You say with confidence that the Lord is your helper. God's sovereign protection frees you from doubt and harm. Because you find your shelter, assurance, stability, and strength in your personal relationship with the Lord, you are kept in a safe place. Lay with compassionate humility a firm foundation for others, providing them with solid security. As you stay hidden in the shadow of His wings (Psalm 61:4), you direct deliverance for the weak, insecure, unsheltered, and frail. You are to help others to become overcomers, victorious, confident, and secure—regardless of the risk and cost to you.

CHELSEY

Seaport; protector of mankind

∞

Deuteronomy 33:12 *Let the beloved of the Lord rest secure in Him, for He shields him all day long, and the one the Lord loves rests between His shoulders.*

Job 11:18 *You will be secure, because there is hope; you will look about you and take your rest in safety.*

Your life is bound securely in the bundle of the living by the Lord your God (I Samuel 25:29). You will not fear the terror of night, nor the arrow that flies by day (Psalm 91:5). You will have no fear of bad news; your heart is steadfast, trusting in the Lord (Psalm 112:7). You say with confidence that the Lord is your helper. God's sovereign protection frees you from doubt and harm. Because you find your shelter, assurance, stability, and strength in your personal relationship with the Lord, you are kept in a safe place. Lay with compassionate humility a firm foundation for others, providing them with solid security. As you stay hidden in the shadow of His wings (Psalm 61:4), you direct deliverance for the weak, insecure, unsheltered, and frail. You are to help others to become overcomers, victorious, confident, and secure—regardless of the risk and cost to you.

CHERISE

Dear beloved one; cherished one

&

Zephaniah 3:17 *The Lord your God is with you, He is mighty to save. He will take great delight in you, He will quiet you with His love, He will rejoice over you with singing.*

Ephesians 5:28–30 *In this same way, husbands ought to love their wives as their own bodies. He who loves his wife loves himself. After all, no one ever hated His own body, but he feeds and cares for it, just as Christ does the church - for we are members of His body.*

You are God's "treasured possession" (Deuteronomy 7:6). By giving the very life of His Son, God has committed to highly value you and take good care of you. He will treat you tenderly in tough times. You are to relate to others as Jesus relates to the Father and to us. Paul served as an example for you. I Thessalonians 2:7–8 says, "We were gentle among you, like a mother caring for her little children. We loved you so much that we were delighted to share with you not only the gospel of God but our lives as well, because you had become so dear to us." The warmth you experience being held close to His heart will enable you to melt the ice in others—the rejected and the castaways. Be free to be intimate with your Maker with trust and selfless submission.

CHLOE

Young blade of grass; full of life

ॐ

John 14:6 *Jesus answered, I am the way and the truth and the life. No one comes to the Father except through Me.*

Deuteronomy 30:19–20 *This day I call heaven and earth as witnesses against you that I have set before you life and death, blessings and curses. Now choose life, so that you and your children may live and that you may love the Lord your God, listen to His voice, and hold fast to Him. For the Lord is your life, and He will give you many years in the land He swore to give to your fathers, Abraham, Isaac, and Jacob.*

Your life's purpose is to serve God, seek His kingdom, do the Father's will, finish the divine task, complete the course joyfully, and attain Christ-likeness. You throw a life-line to those with a death sentence—those who are weary, disgusted, bitter, empty, barren, oppressed, and isolated. With your focus kept on eternal rather than temporal values, you will bring Christ's resurrection power to hearts in the grave. The very gates of hell cannot prevail and be strong enough to stand up under the direct attack of the church. Colossians 3:1–4 says, "Since, then, you have been raised with Christ, set your hearts on things above, not on earthly things. For you died, and your life is now hidden with Christ in God. When Christ, who is your life, appears, then you also will appear with Him in glory." I Samuel 25:29 says, "Your life will be bound securely in the bundle of the living by the Lord your God. But the lives of your enemies He will hurl away as from the pocket of a sling." Psalm 27:1 says, "The Lord is the stronghold of your life—of whom shall you be afraid?" Enjoy life to the fullest! (John 10:10)

CHONDA

One who is passionate; passionate one

ꙮ

Isaiah 62:1 *For Zion's sake I will not keep silent, for Jerusalem's sake I will not remain quiet, till her righteousness shines out like the dawn, her salvation like a blazing torch.*

II Timothy 1:6 *For this reason I remind you to fan into flame the gift of God, which is in you through the laying on of my hands.*

The way Jesus Christ served His heavenly Father is your only example to follow. The word "enthusiastic" means "possessed by God." Zeal for God's house consumed Jesus (John 2:17). Even to His parents He said, "Didn't you know I had to be in my Father's house?" Luke 2:49. "He put on righteousness as His breastplate, and the helmet of salvation on His head; He put on the garments of vengeance and wrapped Himself in zeal as in a cloak," Isaiah 59:17. Just as Jesus was determined and passionate, so are you. As you fervently worship God as the all-consuming fire (Hebrews 12:29), you will invade the strongholds of weariness in spirit, soul, and body. You bring balance to those dominated by their emotions. God's Word and His presence will keep His fire ignited in and through you. Guard against always putting out fires, but keep in mind that you must always start them! May you have an infusion of spiritual adrenaline.

CHRIS

Christ bearer; follower of Christ

&

I Chronicles 28:9 *And you, my son Solomon, acknowledge the God of your father, and serve Him with wholehearted devotion and with a willing mind, for the Lord searches every heart and understands every motive behind the thoughts. If you seek Him, He will be found by you; but if you forsake Him, He will reject you forever.*

I Corinthians 15:58 *Therefore, my dear brothers, stand firm. Let nothing move you. Always give yourselves fully to the work of the Lord, because you know that your labor is not in vain.*

Your very being lives to be in constant harmony with your Creator—that the both of your hearts beat as one. Therefore, you are continually yielding every area to the likeness of Christ with strong discipline as you follow Him. You have a devoted allegiance to Christ and His teachings. Your character is one of devotion, dedication, consecration, loyalty, and faithfulness. You are called to help the fallen take a stand and to remove shame and fear. You dispel division by bringing the very unity of God. As you seek and trust in Him with all your heart, leaning not to your own understanding, He will protect you from being blind-sided by the enemy of your soul. Be known as one who loves God with all your heart, soul, mind, and strength. You are one whom God has chosen to be an example of His Son, Jesus Christ.

CHRISTIAN

Believer in Christ; follower of Christ

ॐ

I Chronicles 28:9   *And you, my son Solomon, acknowledge the God of your father, and serve Him with wholehearted devotion and with a willing mind, for the Lord searches every heart and understands every motive behind the thoughts. If you seek Him, He will be found by you; but if you forsake Him, He will reject you forever.*

I Corinthians 15:58 *Therefore, my dear brothers, stand firm. Let nothing move you. Always give yourselves fully to the work of the Lord, because you know that your labor is not in vain.*

Your very being lives to be in constant harmony with your Creator— that the both of your hearts beat as one. Therefore, you are continually yielding every area to the likeness of Christ with strong discipline as you follow Him. You have a devoted allegiance to Christ and His teachings. Your character is one of devotion, dedication, consecration, loyalty, and faithfulness. You are called to help the fallen take a stand and to remove shame and fear. You dispel division by bringing the very unity of God. As you seek and trust in Him with all your heart, leaning not to your own understanding, He will protect you from being blind-sided by the enemy of your soul. Be known as one who loves God with all your heart, soul, mind, and strength. You are one whom God has chosen to be an example of His Son, Jesus Christ.

CHRISTINA

Believer in Christ; follower of Christ

ᙏ

I Chronicles 28:9 *And you, my son Solomon, acknowledge the God of your father, and serve Him with wholehearted devotion and with a willing mind, for the Lord searches every heart and understands every motive behind the thoughts. If you seek Him, He will be found by you; but if you forsake Him, He will reject you forever.*

I Corinthians 15:58 *Therefore, my dear brothers, stand firm. Let nothing move you. Always give yourselves fully to the work of the Lord, because you know that your labor is not in vain.*

Your very being lives to be in constant harmony with your Creator—that the both of your hearts beat as one. Therefore, you are continually yielding every area to the likeness of Christ with strong discipline as you follow Him. You have a devoted allegiance to Christ and His teachings. Your character is one of devotion, dedication, consecration, loyalty, and faithfulness. You are called to help the fallen take a stand and to remove shame and fear. You dispel division by bringing the very unity of God. As you seek and trust in Him with all your heart, leaning not to your own understanding, He will protect you from being blind-sided by the enemy of your soul. Be known as one who loves God with all your heart, soul, mind, and strength. You are one whom God has chosen to be an example of His Son, Jesus Christ.

CHRISTINE

Believer in Christ; follower of Christ

જી

I Chronicles 28:9   *And you, my son Solomon, acknowledge the God of your father, and serve Him with wholehearted devotion and with a willing mind, for the Lord searches every heart and understands every motive behind the thoughts. If you seek Him, He will be found by you; but if you forsake Him, He will reject you forever.*

I Corinthians 15:58   *Therefore, my dear brothers, stand firm. Let nothing move you. Always give yourselves fully to the work of the Lord, because you know that your labor is not in vain.*

Your very being lives to be in constant harmony with your Creator—that the both of your hearts beat as one. Therefore, you are continually yielding every area to the likeness of Christ with strong discipline as you follow Him. You have a devoted allegiance to Christ and His teachings. Your character is one of devotion, dedication, consecration, loyalty, and faithfulness. You are called to help the fallen take a stand and to remove shame and fear. You dispel division by bringing the very unity of God. As you seek and trust in Him with all your heart, leaning not to your own understanding, He will protect you from being blind-sided by the enemy of your soul. Be known as one who loves God with all your heart, soul, mind, and strength. You are one whom God has chosen to be an example of His Son, Jesus Christ.

CHRISTOPHER

Christ bearer; follower of Christ

I Chronicles 28:9   *And you, my son Solomon, acknowledge the God of your father, and serve Him with wholehearted devotion and with a willing mind, for the Lord searches every heart and understands every motive behind the thoughts. If you seek Him, He will be found by you; but if you forsake Him, He will reject you forever.*

I Corinthians 15:58   *Therefore, my dear brothers, stand firm. Let nothing move you. Always give yourselves fully to the work of the Lord, because you know that your labor is not in vain.*

Your very being lives to be in constant harmony with your Creator—that the both of your hearts beat as one. Therefore, you are continually yielding every area to the likeness of Christ with strong discipline as you follow Him. You have a devoted allegiance to Christ and His teachings. Your character is one of devotion, dedication, consecration, loyalty, and faithfulness. You are called to help the fallen take a stand and to remove shame and fear. You dispel division by bringing the very unity of God. As you seek and trust in Him with all your heart, leaning not to your own understanding, He will protect you from being blind-sided by the enemy of your soul. Be known as one who loves God with all your heart, soul, mind, and strength. You are one whom God has chosen to be an example of His Son, Jesus Christ.

CHRISTY

Believer in Christ; follower of Christ

&

I Chronicles 28:9 *And you, my son Solomon, acknowledge the God of your father, and serve Him with wholehearted devotion and with a willing mind, for the Lord searches every heart and understands every motive behind the thoughts. If you seek Him, He will be found by you; but if you forsake Him, He will reject you forever.*

I Corinthians 15:58 *Therefore, my dear brothers, stand firm. Let nothing move you. Always give yourselves fully to the work of the Lord, because you know that your labor is not in vain.*

Your very being lives to be in constant harmony with your Creator—that the both of your hearts beat as one. Therefore, you are continually yielding every area to the likeness of Christ with strong discipline as you follow Him. You have a devoted allegiance to Christ and His teachings. Your character is one of devotion, dedication, consecration, loyalty, and faithfulness. You are called to help the fallen take a stand and to remove shame and fear. You dispel division by bringing the very unity of God. As you seek and trust in Him with all your heart, leaning not to your own understanding, He will protect you from being blind-sided by the enemy of your soul. Be known as one who loves God with all your heart, soul, mind, and strength. You are one whom God has chosen to be an example of His Son, Jesus Christ.

CHUCK

Strong; manly

∞

Proverbs 24:5 *A wise man has great power, and a man of knowledge increases strength.*

Ephesians 6:10 *Finally, be strong in the Lord and in His mighty power.*

You are one who has an un-compromised commitment to righteousness, respectability, honesty, character, excellence, value, worth, kindness, innocence, generosity, trustworthiness, faithfulness, justice, hope, and love. You can do everything through Him who gives you strength (Philippians 4:11–13). The Lord is the source of your strength because you turn back the battle at the gate (Isaiah 28:6). You renew your strength by your hope being in the Lord (Isaiah 40:31). Jesus says, "My grace is sufficient for you, for My power is made perfect in weaknesses. Therefore you will boast all the more gladly about your weaknesses, so that Christ's power may rest on you. That is why for Christ's sake, you delight in weaknesses, in insults, in hardships, in persecutions, and in difficulties. For when you are weak, then you are strong," II Corinthians 12:9–10. You are clothed with strength and dignity (Proverbs 31:25).

CIARA

Black; pure one

☙

I Timothy 5:22 *...do not share in the sins of others. Keep yourself pure.*

I Peter 1:22 *Now that you have purified yourselves by obeying the truth so that you have sincere love for your brothers, love one another deeply, from the heart.*

Through the process of heat, trials, and refinement, purity is established. Your nature defies being stubborn, judgmental, and haughty. The commandment of the Lord is clear—giving insight to life (Psalm 19:8). You bring wholeness to the dirty, defiled, contaminated, polluted, double-minded, and raped. Your willingness to be transparent is the venue through which He makes His Word clear, simple, and unadulterated. Your choice to be pure enables you to see God (Matthew 5:8) and to know Him as King and Friend (Proverbs 22:11). It also allows your words to be pleasant (Proverbs 15:26) and causes you to ascend to the holy place of the Lord, where you receive blessings and righteousness from the God of salvation (Psalm 24:3–5). Proverbs 20:11 says, "Even a child is known by his actions, by whether his conduct is pure and right."

CINDY

The moon; reflector of light

❧

Psalm 27:1 *The Lord is my light and my salvation—whom shall I fear? The Lord is the stronghold of my life; of whom shall I be afraid.*

Proverbs 4:18 *The path of the righteous is like the first gleam of dawn, shining ever brighter till the full light of day.*

You are one who reflects the shining brightness of the countenance of Jesus. You are aggressive toward the fruitless deeds of darkness from the evil one, by exposing them to the light of Jesus. Everything exposed by light becomes visible, for it is the light that makes everything visible (Ephesians 5:11–14). This radiance that God has given you serves as a beacon to give guidance to those yet in darkness. Your life's mission is found in the following two verses: Isaiah 60:1–3 says, "Arise, shine, for your light has come, and the glory of the Lord rises upon you. See, darkness covers the earth, and thick darkness is over the peoples, but the Lord rises upon you and His glory appears over you. Nations will come to your light, and kings to the brightness of your dawn." And in Acts 13:47, "For this is what the Lord has commanded us: 'I have made you a light for the Gentiles, that you may bring salvation to the ends of the earth.'" Continue to shine as His star, leading many to righteousness (Daniel 12:3 and Philippians 2:15).

CLAIRE

Clear, bright; reflector of light

&

Psalm 27:1 *The Lord is my light and my salvation—whom shall I fear? The Lord is the stronghold of my life; of whom shall I be afraid.*

Proverbs 4:18 *The path of the righteous is like the first gleam of dawn, shining ever brighter till the full light of day.*

You are one who reflects the shining brightness of the countenance of Jesus. You are aggressive toward the fruitless deeds of darkness from the evil one, by exposing them to the light of Jesus. Everything exposed by light becomes visible, for it is the light that makes everything visible (Ephesians 5:11–14). This radiance that God has given you serves as a beacon to give guidance to those yet in darkness. Your life's mission is found in the following two verses: Isaiah 60:1–3 says, "Arise, shine, for your light has come, and the glory of the Lord rises upon you. See, darkness covers the earth, and thick darkness is over the peoples, but the Lord rises upon you and His glory appears over you. Nations will come to your light, and kings to the brightness of your dawn." And in Acts 13:47, "For this is what the Lord has commanded us: 'I have made you a light for the Gentiles, that you may bring salvation to the ends of the earth.'" Continue to shine as His star, leading many to righteousness (Daniel 12:3 and Philippians 2:15).

CLAUDETTE

Lame one; full of humility

ℰ

Micah 6:8 *He has showed you, O man, what is good. And what does the Lord require of you? To act justly and to love mercy and to walk humbly with your God.*

I Peter 5:6 *Humble yourselves, therefore, under God's mighty hand, that He may lift you up in due time.*

Prove to be trustworthy over little and God will make you ruler over much (Luke 19:17). The higher you lift the Lord, the more dependent you will be on Him. He increases; you decrease (John 3:30). Being exalted only comes from God—not from you or anyone else. It is for the purpose of enlarging His kingdom. Take no credit for the enormous favor God will give you. It is His grace that will give entrance to these doors of favor, as you choose His approval over man's. Philippians 2:3 says, "Do nothing out of selfish ambition or vain conceit, but in humility consider others better than yourselves." Humility and the fear of the Lord bring wealth, honor, and life (Proverbs 22:4).

CLAUDIA

Lame one; full of humility

Micah 6:8 *He has showed you, O man, what is good. And what does the Lord require of you? To act justly and to love mercy and to walk humbly with your God.*

I Peter 5:6 *Humble yourselves, therefore, under God's mighty hand, that He may lift you up in due time.*

Prove to be trustworthy over little and God will make you ruler over much (Luke 19:17). The higher you lift the Lord, the more dependent you will be on Him. He increases; you decrease (John 3:30). Being exalted only comes from God—not from you or anyone else. It is for the purpose of enlarging His kingdom. Take no credit for the enormous favor God will give you. It is His grace that will give entrance to these doors of favor, as you choose His approval over man's. Philippians 2:3 says, "Do nothing out of selfish ambition or vain conceit, but in humility consider others better than yourselves." Humility and the fear of the Lord bring wealth, honor, and life (Proverbs 22:4).

CLAY

Town at a clay sight; in God's mold

ॐ

Colossians 1:16 *For by Him all things were created: things in heaven and on earth, visible and invisible, whether thrones or powers or rulers or authorities; all things were created by Him and for Him.*

Ephesians 2:10 *For we are God's workmanship, created in Christ Jesus to do good works, which God prepared in advance for us to do.*

Through you the Lord will bring Himself into existence; He will originate. How you deal with the past determines your future. Regardless of curses or blessings, failures or successes, you are God's platform for a "new thing." You cannot lean to your own understanding or reasoning. God Almighty created the heavens, the earth, and you in His image. Isaiah 42:9, "See, the former things have taken place, and new things I declare; before they spring into being I announce them to you." Isaiah 43:18–19, "Forget the former things; do not dwell on the past. See, I am doing a new thing! Now it springs up; do you not perceive it? I am making a way in the desert and streams in the wasteland." Isaiah 48:6b, "From now on I will tell you of new things, of hidden things unknown to you." Isaiah 65:17–19, "Behold, I will create new heavens and a new earth. The former things will not be remembered, nor will they come to mind. But be glad and rejoice forever in what I will create, for I will create Jerusalem to be a delight and its people a joy. I will rejoice over Jerusalem and take delight in My people; the sound of weeping and of crying will be heard in it no more." Because of your passion for the eternal over the temporal, you are used of God to remove what can be shaken—the created things—so that what cannot be shaken may remain (Hebrews 12:27). The more completely dependent you become on your Creator, the more productive your life will be for Him! I Peter 4:19, "So then, those who suffer according to God's will should commit themselves to their Creator and continue to do good." As you stay yielded and surrendered to God, the clay of your heart will stay tender. Only then can He mold you into the image of His Son, Jesus Christ. God will work His approval through you to those who feel ugly, worthless, and to those who have no hope.

CLIFF

From the cliff-ford; vigilant

✒

Isaiah 62:6 *I have posted watchmen on your walls, O Jerusalem; they will never be silent day or night. You who call on the Lord give yourselves no rest.*

I Corinthians 16:13–14 *Be on your guard; stand firm in the faith; be men of courage; be strong. Do everything in love.*

The Lord has appointed you as His watchman. You must hear His voice and give warning for Him (Ezekiel 3:17). You must be watchful, alert, prepared, actively observant, and on guard. You have quick intelligence and a readiness to take prompt action—whether alerting to danger or opportunities. You are spiritually wide awake and aware of all surrounding circumstances. This is accomplished by your devoted prayer life and your being watchful and thankful (Colossians 4:2). You are able to keep your head in all situations (II Timothy 4:5). You are self-controlled and alert, able to resist the devil and stand firm in your faith (I Peter 5:8–9). You exercise self-restraint that governs all passions and desires. This enables you to be conformed to the mind of Christ. You must stay ready for the Lord's return (Luke 12:35–40).

CLIFFORD

From the cliff-ford; vigilant

&

Isaiah 62:6 *I have posted watchmen on your walls, O Jerusalem; they will never be silent day or night. You who call on the Lord give yourselves no rest.*

I Corinthians 16:13–14 *Be on your guard; stand firm in the faith; be men of courage; be strong. Do everything in love.*

The Lord has appointed you as His watchman. You must hear His voice and give warning for Him (Ezekiel 3:17). You must be watchful, alert, prepared, actively observant, and on guard. You have quick intelligence and a readiness to take prompt action—whether alerting to danger or opportunities. You are spiritually wide awake and aware of all surrounding circumstances. This is accomplished by your devoted prayer life and your being watchful and thankful (Colossians 4:2). You are able to keep your head in all situations (II Timothy 4:5). You are self-controlled and alert, able to resist the devil and stand firm in your faith (I Peter 5:8–9). You exercise self-restraint that governs all passions and desires. This enables you to be conformed to the mind of Christ. You must stay ready for the Lord's return (Luke 12:35–40).

CLOE

Young blade of grass; full of life

৪৩

John 14:6 *Jesus answered, I am the way and the truth and the life. No one comes to the Father except through Me.*

Deuteronomy 30:19–20 *This day I call heaven and earth as witnesses against you that I have set before you life and death, blessings and curses. Now choose life, so that you and your children may live and that you may love the Lord your God, listen to His voice, and hold fast to Him. For the Lord is your life, and He will give you many years in the land He swore to give to your fathers, Abraham, Isaac, and Jacob.*

Your life's purpose is to serve God, seek His kingdom, do the Father's will, finish the divine task, complete the course joyfully, and attain Christ-likeness. You throw a life-line to those with a death sentence—those who are weary, disgusted, bitter, empty, barren, oppressed, and isolated. With your focus kept on eternal rather than temporal values, you will bring Christ's resurrection power to hearts in the grave. The very gates of hell cannot prevail and be strong enough to stand up under the direct attack of the church. Colossians 3:1–4 says, "Since, then, you have been raised with Christ, set your hearts on things above, not on earthly things. For you died, and your life is now hidden with Christ in God. When Christ, who is your life, appears, then you also will appear with Him in glory." I Samuel 25:29 says, "Your life will be bound securely in the bundle of the living by the Lord your God. But the lives of your enemies He will hurl away as from the pocket of a sling." Psalm 27:1 says, "The Lord is the stronghold of your life—of whom shall you be afraid?" Enjoy life to the fullest! (John 10:10)

CLYDE

Of good report; integrity

༄

Psalm 41:12 *In my integrity You uphold me and set me in Your presence forever.*

Proverbs 11:3 *The integrity of the upright guides them, but the unfaithful are destroyed by their duplicity.*

Spiritual deafness results from unheeded warnings, calloused hearts, rebellious disobedience, and stubborn unfaithfulness. This is prevented by being quick to hear, teachable, and having faith in God's Word. Security comes from knowing God's ears are attentive to your cry—before you call, He answers. Discernment and righteous judgment produce integrity. Integrity results in yielding weakness to God's power, based on a blameless walk. Proverbs 10:9 says, "The man of integrity walks securely, but he who takes crooked paths will be found out." You are one who has an uncompromised commitment to righteousness, respectability, honesty, character, excellence, innocence, generosity, trustworthiness, faithfulness, justice, hope, and love. Be truthful with others, as well as yourself. Be the same in public as you are in private. Titus 2:7–8 says, "In everything set them an example by doing what is good. In your teaching show integrity, seriousness and soundness of speech that cannot be condemned, so that those who oppose you may be ashamed because they have nothing bad to say about us."

CODY

Ally

ℰℐ

I Corinthians 1:10 *I appeal to you, brothers, in the name of our Lord Jesus Christ, that all of you agree with one another so that there may be no divisions among you and that you may be perfectly united in mind and thought.*

Ephesians 4:3 *Make every effort to keep the unity of the Spirit through the bond of peace.*

As an ally, you network a coming together for a common purpose. You connect people to one another to work in harmony—even in time of war. Your effectiveness is based on your friendship with Christ (John 15:13–14), who taught you to lay down your life for Him and others. You are a friend to all who fear God and follow His rules (Psalm 119:63). Being unequally yoked with unbelievers in any way is not an option (II Corinthians 6:14–18). The Lord will destroy whatever success you attain if you make alliance with one who is guilty of wickedness (II Chronicles 20). You put the power of agreement at such a high premium that you avoid strife (Proverbs 20:30), quarrels, resentment (II Timothy 2:24), and all forms of being prejudiced. As with Moses, God wants to speak to you face to face. As with Abraham, God wants to call you His friend. As with Nehemiah, God wants you to carry out great works (Nehemiah 4:16–17). He has equipped you to bring unity of purpose through strong relationship building. Your lifetime portion of scripture is in Philippians 2:1–2, "If you have any encouragement from being united with Christ, if any comfort from His love, if any fellowship with the Spirit, if any tenderness and compassion, then make my joy complete by being like-minded, having the same love, being one in spirit and purpose."

COLBY

Dark farm; bright one

&

Psalm 27:1 *The Lord is my light and my salvation—whom shall I fear? The Lord is the stronghold of my life; of whom shall I be afraid.*

Proverbs 4:18 *The path of the righteous is like the first gleam of dawn, shining ever brighter till the full light of day.*

You are one who reflects the shining brightness of the countenance of Jesus. You are aggressive toward the fruitless deeds of darkness from the evil one, by exposing them to the light of Jesus. Everything exposed by light becomes visible, for it is the light that makes everything visible (Ephesians 5:11–14). This radiance that God has given you serves as a beacon to give guidance to those yet in darkness. Your life's mission is found in the following two verses: Isaiah 60:1–3 says, "Arise, shine, for your light has come, and the glory of the Lord rises upon you. See, darkness covers the earth, and thick darkness is over the peoples, but the Lord rises upon you and His glory appears over you. Nations will come to your light, and kings to the brightness of your dawn." And in Acts 13:47, "For this is what the Lord has commanded us: 'I have made you a light for the Gentiles, that you may bring salvation to the ends of the earth.'" Continue to shine as His star, leading many to righteousness (Daniel 12:3 and Philippians 2:15).

COLE

Victory of the people; victorious spirit

☡

I John 5:4 *Everyone born of God overcomes the world. This is the victory that has overcome the world, even our faith.*

II Corinthians 2:14 *But thanks be to God, who always leads us in triumphal procession in Christ and through us spreads everywhere the fragrance of the knowledge of Him.*

Because of your faith in Jesus Christ, you will ever be aggressive towards the enemy's tools of defeat, failure, and victimization. You will push back Satan and overcome all his power. Jesus has given you authority to trample on snakes and scorpions and to overcome all the power of the enemy; nothing will harm you (Luke 10:19). Even in the severest of afflictions—such as hardship, persecution, famine, nakedness, danger, or sword—you are more than a conqueror through Christ who loves you (Romans 8:35–37). "Everyone born of God overcomes the world. This is the victory that has overcome the world, even our faith," I John 5:4. "Take heart, Jesus has overcome the world," John 16:33.

COLIN

Victory of the people; victorious spirit

ઠ

I John 5:4 *Everyone born of God overcomes the world. This is the victory that has overcome the world, even our faith.*

II Corinthians 2:14 *But thanks be to God, who always leads us in triumphal procession in Christ and through us spreads everywhere the fragrance of the knowledge of Him.*

Because of your faith in Jesus Christ, you will ever be aggressive towards the enemy's tools of defeat, failure, and victimization. You will push back Satan and overcome all his power. Jesus has given you authority to trample on snakes and scorpions and to overcome all the power of the enemy; nothing will harm you (Luke 10:19). Even in the severest of afflictions—such as hardship, persecution, famine, nakedness, danger, or sword—you are more than a conqueror through Christ who loves you (Romans 8:35–37). "Everyone born of God overcomes the world. This is the victory that has overcome the world, even our faith," I John 5:4. "Take heart, Jesus has overcome the world," John 16:33.

COLTON

Dark; full of light

&

Psalm 27:1 *The Lord is my light and my salvation—whom shall I fear? The Lord is the stronghold of my life; of whom shall I be afraid.*

Proverbs 4:18 *The path of the righteous is like the first gleam of dawn, shining ever brighter till the full light of day.*

You are one who reflects the shining brightness of the countenance of Jesus. You are aggressive toward the fruitless deeds of darkness from the evil one, by exposing them to the light of Jesus. Everything exposed by light becomes visible, for it is the light that makes everything visible (Ephesians 5:11–14). This radiance that God has given you serves as a beacon to give guidance to those yet in darkness. Your life's mission is found in the following two verses: Isaiah 60:1–3 says, "Arise, shine, for your light has come, and the glory of the Lord rises upon you. See, darkness covers the earth, and thick darkness is over the peoples, but the Lord rises upon you and His glory appears over you. Nations will come to your light, and kings to the brightness of your dawn." And in Acts 13:47, "For this is what the Lord has commanded us: 'I have made you a light for the Gentiles, that you may bring salvation to the ends of the earth.'" Continue to shine as His star, leading many to righteousness (Daniel 12:3 and Philippians 2:15).

CONNIE

Firmness, constancy; earnest devotee

જી

Psalm 63:1, 5, 8   *My soul thirsts for You. My soul will be satisfied. My soul clings to you.*

I Corinthians 15:58   *Therefore, my dear brothers, stand firm. Let nothing move you. Always give yourselves fully to the work of the Lord, because you know that your labor is not in vain.*

Your very being lives to be in constant harmony with your Creator; that both of your hearts beat as one. Therefore, you are continually yielding every area to the likeness of Christ with strong discipline. You have a devoted allegiance to Christ and his teachings. Your character is one of devotion, dedication, consecration, loyalty, and faithfulness. You are called to help the fallen take a stand, and to remove shame and fear. You dispel division by bringing the very unity of God. As you seek and trust in Him with all your heart, leaning not to your own understanding, He will protect you from being blind-sided by the enemy of your soul. Be known as one who loves God with all your heart, soul, mind, and strength.

CONNOR

Able to counsel; full of wisdom

ॐ

James 3:17 *But the wisdom that comes from heaven is first of all pure; then peace-loving, considerate, submissive, full of mercy and good fruit, impartial and sincere.*

Proverbs 9:10 *The fear of the Lord is the beginning of wisdom, and knowledge of the Holy One is understanding.*

You are a person of moral excellence. You exemplify right living put into practice. The Lord has not only equipped you with skills for living correctly, but also the ability to impart that to others. The Spirit of truth will guide you into all truth, allowing you to have insight into the true nature of things (John 16:13). Out of your reverential respect for the Lord, you have wisdom to give guidance and direction. You are a safe sounding board who steers those who are hungry for knowledge of the Holy One in the right direction. You need only to ask for the wisdom you lack, and God will give it to you generously (James 1:5). Having spiritual discernment is having the ability to separate the difference between God's wisdom and the world's and the ability to make the right choice—regardless. Luke 21:15 says, "For I will give you words and wisdom that none of your adversaries will be able to resist or contradict."

CONRAD

Able to counsel; full of wisdom

&

James 3:17 *But the wisdom that comes from heaven is first of all pure; then peace-loving, considerate, submissive, full of mercy and good fruit, impartial and sincere.*

Proverbs 9:10 *The fear of the Lord is the beginning of wisdom, and knowledge of the Holy One is understanding.*

You are a person of moral excellence. You exemplify right living put into practice. The Lord has not only equipped you with skills for living correctly, but also the ability to impart that to others. The Spirit of truth will guide you into all truth, allowing you to have insight into the true nature of things (John 16:13). Out of your reverential respect for the Lord, you have wisdom to give guidance and direction. You are a safe sounding board who steers those who are hungry for knowledge of the Holy One in the right direction. You need only to ask for the wisdom you lack, and God will give it to you generously (James 1:5). Having spiritual discernment is having the ability to separate the difference between God's wisdom and the world's and the ability to make the right choice—regardless. Luke 21:15 says, "For I will give you words and wisdom that none of your adversaries will be able to resist or contradict."

CONSTANCE

Firmness, constancy; earnest devotee

છ

Psalm 63:1, 5, 8   *My soul thirsts for You. My soul will be satisfied. My soul clings to you.*

I Corinthians 15:58   *Therefore, my dear brothers, stand firm. Let nothing move you. Always give yourselves fully to the work of the Lord, because you know that your labor is not in vain.*

Your very being lives to be in constant harmony with your Creator; that both of your hearts beat as one. Therefore, you are continually yielding every area to the likeness of Christ with strong discipline. You have a devoted allegiance to Christ and his teachings. Your character is one of devotion, dedication, consecration, loyalty, and faithfulness. You are called to help the fallen take a stand, and to remove shame and fear. You dispel division by bringing the very unity of God. As you seek and trust in Him with all your heart, leaning not to your own understanding, He will protect you from being blind-sided by the enemy of your soul. Be known as one who loves God with all your heart, soul, mind, and strength.

COOPER

Barrel maker; helper

ॐ

Hosea 11:4 *I led them with cords of human kindness, with ties of love; I lifted the yoke from their neck and bent down to feed them.*

Matthew 9:36 *When He saw the crowds, He had compassion on them, because they were harassed and helpless, like sheep without a shepherd.*

You are obedient, respectful, faithful, and bring pleasure to those whom you serve. Even with inconsiderate behavior, you are patient (I Peter 2:18). You are tender with the harsh, merciful with the intolerant, and sympathetic with the suffering. Because you cast your cares on the Lord, you are able to lift the burdens of others (Psalm 55:22). The reason you are so easily trusted is because of your humble nature. All glory and credit belong to God, not you. Your passion to help energizes you to meet the need regardless of what it is—guidance, relief, encouragement, or support. God allows you to see the root of the need rather than being sidetracked by all the symptoms. Sickness is healed, the hungry are fed, sight is restored, the unlovely are touched and the afflicted are delivered. You defend rather than offend, forgive rather than accuse, and you protect rather than abandon. You can depend on God's fresh supply daily. "Because of the Lord's great love we are not consumed, for His compassions never fail. They are new every morning; great is your faithfulness," Lamentations 3:22–23. Your compassion connects the heart of God to the heart of man.

CORA

Dweller by a hollow; prosperous one

ℰↄ

Psalm 1:1–3 Blessed is the man who does not walk in the counsel of the wicked or stand in the way of sinners or sit in the seat of mockers. But his delight is in the law of the Lord, and on His law he meditates day and night. He is like a tree planted by the streams of water, which yields its fruit in season and whose leaf does not wither. Whatever he does prospers.

Joshua 1:8 Do not let this book of the law depart from your mouth; meditate on it day and night, so that you may be careful to do everything written in it. Then you will be prosperous and successful.

You are one who knows that your success is not based on luck or good fortune. It is because you are willing to loose your life for Christ's sake in order to find it (Matthew 10:39). You let the word of Christ dwell in you richly (Colossians 3:16). You allow the Lord to stretch and strengthen you in order to enlarge your borders of influence and maturity (Isaiah 54:1–3). You welcome the cutting and pruning that makes way for increase to bear fruit, more fruit, and much fruit (John 15). You enter a covenant with the Lord of obedience, seeking Him diligently and wholeheartedly (II Chronicles 31:21), which causes you to prosper in everything you do (Deuteronomy 29:9). You are content in need and in plenty (Philippians 4:11–12) because prosperity is not a love of money (I Timothy 6:6–10), power, popularity, or possessions. In spite of failure, disappointment, loss, and defeat, you let nothing separate you from the love of God (Romans 8:37–39). Instead of being blind to the hungry, you will feed them. Instead of abhorring the naked, you will clothe them. Instead of ignoring the poor and fatherless, you will be God's hand of provision. You will offer provisions of hope, courage, and strength not to give up, but rather to start again and to make it to the finish line. You are a faithful steward helping them exchange their temporal for His eternal (Philippians 4:19). As your mantle is to build up, develop, and cause to succeed, know that "no weapon formed against you will prosper," Isaiah 54:17. Your goal is to hear the Master say, "Well done, good and faithful servant! You have been faithful with a few things, I will put you in charge of many things. Come share your Master's happiness!" (Matthew 25:21) May you prosper in all things and be in health, just as your soul prospers (3 John 2).

COREY

Dweller by a hollow; prosperous one

∞

Psalm 1:1–3 *Blessed is the man who does not walk in the counsel of the wicked or stand in the way of sinners or sit in the seat of mockers. But his delight is in the law of the Lord, and on His law he meditates day and night. He is like a tree planted by the streams of water, which yields its fruit in season and whose leaf does not wither. Whatever he does prospers.*

Joshua 1:8 *Do not let this book of the law depart from your mouth; meditate on it day and night, so that you may be careful to do everything written in it. Then you will be prosperous and successful.*

You are one who knows that your success is not based on luck or good fortune. It is because you are willing to loose your life for Christ's sake in order to find it (Matthew 10:39). You let the word of Christ dwell in you richly (Colossians 3:16). You allow the Lord to stretch and strengthen you in order to enlarge your borders of influence and maturity (Isaiah 54:1–3). You welcome the cutting and pruning that makes way for increase to bear fruit, more fruit, and much fruit (John 15). You enter a covenant with the Lord of obedience, seeking Him diligently and wholeheartedly (II Chronicles 31:21), which causes you to prosper in everything you do (Deuteronomy 29:9). You are content in need and in plenty (Philippians 4:11–12) because prosperity is not a love of money (I Timothy 6:6–10), power, popularity, or possessions. In spite of failure, disappointment, loss, and defeat, you let nothing separate you from the love of God (Romans 8:37–39). Instead of being blind to the hungry, you will feed them. Instead of abhorring the naked, you will clothe them. Instead of ignoring the poor and fatherless, you will be God's hand of provision. You will offer provisions of hope, courage, and strength not to give up, but rather to start again and to make it to the finish line. You are a faithful steward helping them exchange their temporal for His eternal (Philippians 4:19). As your mantle is to build up, develop, and cause to succeed, know that "no weapon formed against you will prosper," Isaiah 54:17. Your goal is to hear the Master say, "Well done, good and faithful servant! You have been faithful with a few things, I will put you in charge of many things. Come share your Master's happiness!" (Matthew 25:21) May you prosper in all things and be in health, just as your soul prospers (3 John 2).

CORINA

Dweller by a hollow; prosperous one

&

Psalm 1:1–3 Blessed is the man who does not walk in the counsel of the wicked or stand in the way of sinners or sit in the seat of mockers. But his delight is in the law of the Lord, and on His law he meditates day and night. He is like a tree planted by the streams of water, which yields its fruit in season and whose leaf does not wither. Whatever he does prospers.

Joshua 1:8 Do not let this book of the law depart from your mouth; meditate on it day and night, so that you may be careful to do everything written in it. Then you will be prosperous and successful.

You are one who knows that your success is not based on luck or good fortune. It is because you are willing to loose your life for Christ's sake in order to find it (Matthew 10:39). You let the word of Christ dwell in you richly (Colossians 3:16). You allow the Lord to stretch and strengthen you in order to enlarge your borders of influence and maturity (Isaiah 54:1–3). You welcome the cutting and pruning that makes way for increase to bear fruit, more fruit, and much fruit (John 15). You enter a covenant with the Lord of obedience, seeking Him diligently and wholeheartedly (II Chronicles 31:21), which causes you to prosper in everything you do (Deuteronomy 29:9). You are content in need and in plenty (Philippians 4:11–12) because prosperity is not a love of money (I Timothy 6:6–10), power, popularity, or possessions. In spite of failure, disappointment, loss, and defeat, you let nothing separate you from the love of God (Romans 8:37–39). Instead of being blind to the hungry, you will feed them. Instead of abhorring the naked, you will clothe them. Instead of ignoring the poor and fatherless, you will be God's hand of provision. You will offer provisions of hope, courage, and strength not to give up, but rather to start again and to make it to the finish line. You are a faithful steward helping them exchange their temporal for His eternal (Philippians 4:19). As your mantle is to build up, develop, and cause to succeed, know that "no weapon formed against you will prosper," Isaiah 54:17. Your goal is to hear the Master say, "Well done, good and faithful servant! You have been faithful with a few things, I will put you in charge of many things. Come share your Master's happiness!" (Matthew 25:21) May you prosper in all things and be in health, just as your soul prospers (3 John 2).

CORRIE

Dweller by a hollow; prosperous one

Psalm 1:1–3 Blessed is the man who does not walk in the counsel of the wicked or stand in the way of sinners or sit in the seat of mockers. But his delight is in the law of the Lord, and on His law he meditates day and night. He is like a tree planted by the streams of water, which yields its fruit in season and whose leaf does not wither. Whatever he does prospers.

Joshua 1:8 Do not let this book of the law depart from your mouth; meditate on it day and night, so that you may be careful to do everything written in it. Then you will be prosperous and successful.

You are one who knows that your success is not based on luck or good fortune. It is because you are willing to loose your life for Christ's sake in order to find it (Matthew 10:39). You let the word of Christ dwell in you richly (Colossians 3:16). You allow the Lord to stretch and strengthen you in order to enlarge your borders of influence and maturity (Isaiah 54:1–3). You welcome the cutting and pruning that makes way for increase to bear fruit, more fruit, and much fruit (John 15). You enter a covenant with the Lord of obedience, seeking Him diligently and wholeheartedly (II Chronicles 31:21), which causes you to prosper in everything you do (Deuteronomy 29:9). You are content in need and in plenty (Philippians 4:11–12) because prosperity is not a love of money (I Timothy 6:6–10), power, popularity, or possessions. In spite of failure, disappointment, loss, and defeat, you let nothing separate you from the love of God (Romans 8:37–39). Instead of being blind to the hungry, you will feed them. Instead of abhorring the naked, you will clothe them. Instead of ignoring the poor and fatherless, you will be God's hand of provision. You will offer provisions of hope, courage, and strength not to give up, but rather to start again and to make it to the finish line. You are a faithful steward helping them exchange their temporal for His eternal (Philippians 4:19). As your mantle is to build up, develop, and cause to succeed, know that "no weapon formed against you will prosper," Isaiah 54:17. Your goal is to hear the Master say, "Well done, good and faithful servant! You have been faithful with a few things, I will put you in charge of many things. Come share your Master's happiness!" (Matthew 25:21) May you prosper in all things and be in health, just as your soul prospers (3 John 2).

CORY

Dweller by a hollow; prosperous one

ॐ

Psalm 1:1–3 Blessed is the man who does not walk in the counsel of the wicked or stand in the way of sinners or sit in the seat of mockers. But his delight is in the law of the Lord, and on His law he meditates day and night. He is like a tree planted by the streams of water, which yields its fruit in season and whose leaf does not wither. Whatever he does prospers.

Joshua 1:8 Do not let this book of the law depart from your mouth; meditate on it day and night, so that you may be careful to do everything written in it. Then you will be prosperous and successful.

You are one who knows that your success is not based on luck or good fortune. It is because you are willing to loose your life for Christ's sake in order to find it (Matthew 10:39). You let the word of Christ dwell in you richly (Colossians 3:16). You allow the Lord to stretch and strengthen you in order to enlarge your borders of influence and maturity (Isaiah 54:1–3). You welcome the cutting and pruning that makes way for increase to bear fruit, more fruit, and much fruit (John 15). You enter a covenant with the Lord of obedience, seeking Him diligently and wholeheartedly (II Chronicles 31:21), which causes you to prosper in everything you do (Deuteronomy 29:9). You are content in need and in plenty (Philippians 4:11–12) because prosperity is not a love of money (I Timothy 6:6–10), power, popularity, or possessions. In spite of failure, disappointment, loss, and defeat, you let nothing separate you from the love of God (Romans 8:37–39). Instead of being blind to the hungry, you will feed them. Instead of abhorring the naked, you will clothe them. Instead of ignoring the poor and fatherless, you will be God's hand of provision. You will offer provisions of hope, courage, and strength not to give up, but rather to start again and to make it to the finish line. You are a faithful steward helping them exchange their temporal for His eternal (Philippians 4:19). As your mantle is to build up, develop, and cause to succeed, know that "no weapon formed against you will prosper," Isaiah 54:17. Your goal is to hear the Master say, "Well done, good and faithful servant! You have been faithful with a few things, I will put you in charge of many things. Come share your Master's happiness!" (Matthew 25:21) May you prosper in all things and be in health, just as your soul prospers (3 John 2).

COURTNEY

Dweller in the court; giver of love

&

John 3:16 *For God so loved the world that He gave His one and only Son, that whoever believes in Him shall not perish but have everlasting life.*

Ephesians 3:17–19 *I pray that you, being rooted and established in love, may have power, together with all the saints, to grasp how wide and long and deep is the love of Christ, and to know this love that surpasses knowledge—that you may be filled to the measure of all the fullness of God.*

A giver is one who yields without restraint or control. You set apart people or things for a particular purpose or use. You put things into the possession of another for his use, by a commitment of trust. You attribute, ascribe, distribute, and communicate. The opposite of a giver of love is one who withholds, takes back, yields under pressure, retreats, resists, remains rigid, and betrays. This person holds resentment, rejection, avoidance, disapproval, bitterness, prejudice, selfishness, and hatred.

Love is devotion, affection, and involvement, which is based on admiration, respect, and appreciation. Love attaches, cleaves to, and sticks fast to anyone in order to build up and please. Love has an unselfish concern that freely accepts another in loyalty and seeks his good. When love is given, it becomes the channel through which God can befriend a person. The supreme expression of love is the self-sacrifice of our Lord on Calvary. I John 4:10 says, "This is love: not that we loved God, but that He loved us and sent His Son an atoning sacrifice for our sins." The character of love is expressed in patience and kindness—not envy, boasting, pride, rudeness, self-seeking, is not easily angered, keeps no records of wrongs, does not delight in evil, but rejoices in the truth. It always perseveres. Love never fails (I Corinthians 13:4–8).

CRAIG

Dwell by the crag; strong, enduring

&

Proverbs 24:5 *A wise man has great power, and a man of knowledge increases strength.*

Ephesians 6:10 *Finally, be strong in the Lord and in His mighty power.*

You are one who has an un-compromised commitment to righteousness, respectability, honesty, character, excellence, value, worth, kindness, innocence, generosity, trustworthiness, faithfulness, justice, hope, and love. You can do everything through Him who gives you strength (Philippians 4:11–13). The Lord is the source of your strength because you turn back the battle at the gate (Isaiah 28:6). You renew your strength by your hope being in the Lord (Isaiah 40:31). Jesus says, "My grace is sufficient for you, for My power is made perfect in weaknesses. Therefore you will boast all the more gladly about your weaknesses, so that Christ's power may rest on you. That is why for Christ's sake, you delight in weaknesses, in insults, in hardships, in persecutions, and in difficulties. For when you are weak, then you are strong," II Corinthians 12:9–10. You are clothed with strength and dignity (Proverbs 31:25).

CRYSTAL

Transparent; purity

જી

I Timothy 5:22 *...do not share in the sins of others. Keep yourself pure.*

I Peter 1:22 *Now that you have purified yourselves by obeying the truth so that you have sincere love for your brothers, love one another deeply, from the heart.*

Through the process of heat, trials, and refinement, purity is established. Your nature defies being stubborn, judgmental, and haughty. The commandment of the Lord is clear—giving insight to life (Psalm 19:8). You bring wholeness to the dirty, defiled, contaminated, polluted, double-minded, and raped. Your willingness to be transparent is the venue through which He makes His Word clear, simple, and unadulterated. Your choice to be pure enables you to see God (Matthew 5:8) and to know Him as King and Friend (Proverbs 22:11). It also allows your words to be pleasant (Proverbs 15:26) and causes you to ascend to the holy place of the Lord, where you receive blessings and righteousness from the God of salvation (Psalm 24:3–5). Proverbs 20:11 says, "Even a child is known by his actions, by whether his conduct is pure and right."

CURTIS

Courteous one

&

Titus 3:4–5 *But when the kindness and love of God our Savior appeared, He saved us, not because of righteous things we had done, but because of His mercy.*

I Peter 3:8–9 *Finally, all of you, live in harmony with one another; be sympathetic, love as brothers, be compassionate and humble. Do not repay evil with evil or insult with insult, but with blessing, because to this you were called so that you may inherit a blessing.*

God first, others next, and you last. With a servant's heart and a humble mind, you extend the gracious approval of the Lord. This graciousness springs from an inherit thoughtfulness and consideration. Through you, God defines good manners and politeness. You are hospitable to the shipwrecked (Acts 28:7) and you bring divine connection for needs to be provided (Acts 27:3). Because you are attentive to details, the broken are dealt with gently. The rejected are shown kindness and the humble are given honor. Your conversation is always full of grace and seasoned with salt (Colossians 4:6). The behavior of the rude and impolite are corrected because you will not be misled. You know that bad company corrupts good character (I Corinthians 15:33). You show respect to all because of your willingness to value the opinion of another and overlook an offense (Proverbs 19:11). Like Jesus, you are a friend of the publicans and sinners (Luke 7:34).

CYBIL

Future gazing; prophetic

ॐ

Isaiah 62:6 *I have posted watchmen on your walls, O Jerusalem; they will never be silent day or night. You who call on the Lord give yourselves no rest.*

I Corinthians 16:13–14 *Be on your guard; stand firm in the faith; be men of courage; be strong. Do everything in love.*

The Lord has appointed you as His watchman. You must hear His voice and give warning for Him (Ezekiel 3:17). You must be watchful, alert, prepared, actively observant, and on guard. You have quick intelligence and a readiness to take prompt action—whether alerting to danger or opportunities. You are spiritually wide awake and aware of all surrounding circumstances. This is accomplished by your devoted prayer life and your being watchful and thankful (Colossians 4:2). You are able to keep your head in all situations (II Timothy 4:5). You are self-controlled and alert, able to resist the devil and stand firm in your faith (I Peter 5:8–9). You exercise self-restraint that governs all passions and desires. This enables you to be conformed to the mind of Christ. You must stay ready for the Lord's return (Luke 12:35–40).

CYNTHIA

The moon; reflector of light

&

Psalm 27:1 *The Lord is my light and my salvation—whom shall I fear? The Lord is the stronghold of my life; of whom shall I be afraid.*

Proverbs 4:18 *The path of the righteous is like the first gleam of dawn, shining ever brighter till the full light of day.*

You are one who reflects the shining brightness of the countenance of Jesus. You are aggressive toward the fruitless deeds of darkness from the evil one, by exposing them to the light of Jesus. Everything exposed by light becomes visible, for it is the light that makes everything visible (Ephesians 5:11–14). This radiance that God has given you serves as a beacon to give guidance to those yet in darkness. Your life's mission is found in the following two verses: Isaiah 60:1–3 says, "Arise, shine, for your light has come, and the glory of the Lord rises upon you. See, darkness covers the earth, and thick darkness is over the peoples, but the Lord rises upon you and His glory appears over you. Nations will come to your light, and kings to the brightness of your dawn." And in Acts 13:47, "For this is what the Lord has commanded us: 'I have made you a light for the Gentiles, that you may bring salvation to the ends of the earth.'" Continue to shine as His star, leading many to righteousness (Daniel 12:3 and Philippians 2:15).

DAISY

Eye of the day; full of life

❦

John 14:6 *Jesus answered, I am the way and the truth and the life. No one comes to the Father except through Me.*

Deuteronomy 30:19–20 *This day I call heaven and earth as witnesses against you that I have set before you life and death, blessings and curses. Now choose life, so that you and your children may live and that you may love the Lord your God, listen to His voice, and hold fast to Him. For the Lord is your life, and He will give you many years in the land He swore to give to your fathers, Abraham, Isaac, and Jacob.*

Your life's purpose is to serve God, seek His kingdom, do the Father's will, finish the divine task, complete the course joyfully, and attain Christ-likeness. You throw a life-line to those with a death sentence—those who are weary, disgusted, bitter, empty, barren, oppressed, and isolated. With your focus kept on eternal rather than temporal values, you will bring Christ's resurrection power to hearts in the grave. The very gates of hell cannot prevail and be strong enough to stand up under the direct attack of the church. Colossians 3:1–4 says, "Since, then, you have been raised with Christ, set your hearts on things above, not on earthly things. For you died, and your life is now hidden with Christ in God. When Christ, who is your life, appears, then you also will appear with Him in glory." I Samuel 25:29 says, "Your life will be bound securely in the bundle of the living by the Lord your God. But the lives of your enemies He will hurl away as from the pocket of a sling." Psalm 27:1 says, "The Lord is the stronghold of your life—of whom shall you be afraid?" Enjoy life to the fullest! (John 10:10)

DAKOTA

Ally

૭

I Corinthians 1:10 *I appeal to you, brothers, in the name of our Lord Jesus Christ, that all of you agree with one another so that there may be no divisions among you and that you may be perfectly united in mind and thought.*

Ephesians 4:3 *Make every effort to keep the unity of the Spirit through the bond of peace.*

As an ally, you network a coming together for a common purpose. You connect people to one another to work in harmony—even in time of war. Your effectiveness is based on your friendship with Christ (John 15:13–14), who taught you to lay down your life for Him and others. You are a friend to all who fear God and follow His rules (Psalm 119:63). Being unequally yoked with unbelievers in any way is not an option (II Corinthians 6:14–18). The Lord will destroy whatever success you attain if you make alliance with one who is guilty of wickedness (II Chronicles 20). You put the power of agreement at such a high premium that you avoid strife (Proverbs 20:30), quarrels, resentment (II Timothy 2:24), and all forms of being prejudiced. As with Moses, God wants to speak to you face to face. As with Abraham, God wants to call you His friend. As with Nehemiah, God wants you to carry out great works (Nehemiah 4:16–17). He has equipped you to bring unity of purpose through strong relationship building. Your lifetime portion of scripture is in Philippians 2:1–2, "If you have any encouragement from being united with Christ, if any comfort from His love, if any fellowship with the Spirit, if any tenderness and compassion, then make my joy complete by being like-minded, having the same love, being one in spirit and purpose."

DALE

Dweller in the valley; courageous

❧

Deuteronomy 31:6 *Be strong and courageous. Do not be afraid or terrified because of them, for the Lord your God goes with you; He will never leave you nor forsake you.*

Joshua 1:7 *Be strong and very courageous. Be careful to obey all the law My servant Moses gave you; do not turn from it to the right or to the left, that you may be successful wherever you go.*

You are equipped with mental and moral strength to venture, persevere, and withstand danger, fear, and difficulty. You have the firmness of mind to take a firm stand. You meet strain with fortitude and resilience, even when opposed or threatened. You have firm determination to achieve God's purpose in your life. With stubborn persistence and unwillingness to admit defeat, you base all victory on the finished work of the cross of Jesus. The Victor will use you to remove obstacles and invade darkness and death in order to bring the lost to a decision for Jesus. God's divine presence in and through you will bind fear and lead people to their God-given inheritance.

DALLAS

Wise; full of wisdom

&

James 3:17 *But the wisdom that comes from heaven is first of all pure; then peace-loving, considerate, submissive, full of mercy and good fruit, impartial and sincere.*

Proverbs 9:10 *The fear of the Lord is the beginning of wisdom, and knowledge of the Holy One is understanding.*

You are a person of moral excellence. You exemplify right living put into practice. The Lord has not only equipped you with skills for living correctly, but also the ability to impart that to others. The Spirit of truth will guide you into all truth, allowing you to have insight into the true nature of things (John 16:13). Out of your reverential respect for the Lord, you have wisdom to give guidance and direction. You are a safe sounding board who steers those who are hungry for knowledge of the Holy One in the right direction. You need only to ask for the wisdom you lack, and God will give it to you generously (James 1:5). Having spiritual discernment is having the ability to separate the difference between God's wisdom and the world's and the ability to make the right choice—regardless. Luke 21:15 says, "For I will give you words and wisdom that none of your adversaries will be able to resist or contradict."

DAN

God is my judge; God is judge

❧

Psalm 96:10–13 *Say among the nations, "The Lord reigns." The world is firmly established, it cannot be moved; He will judge the peoples with equity. Let the heavens rejoice, let the earth be glad; let the sea resound, and all that is in it; let the fields be jubilant, and everything in them. Then all the trees of the forest will sing for joy; they will sing before the Lord, for He comes, He comes to judge the earth. He will judge the world in righteousness and the peoples in His truth.*

II Timothy 4:1–5 *In the presence of God and of Christ Jesus, who will judge the living and the dead, and in view of His appearing and His kingdom, I give you this charge: Preach the Word; be prepared in season and out of season; correct, rebuke and encourage—with great patience and great instructions. For the time will come when men will not put up with sound doctrine. Instead, to suit their own desires, they will gather around them a great number of teachers to say what their itching ears want to hear. They will turn their ears away from the truth and turn aside to myths. But you, keep your head in all situations, endure hardship, do the work of an evangelist, discharge all the duties of your ministry.*

God Almighty is your Governor, Ruler, and Authority. He has the first and last word. He calls the shots, makes the decisions, and pronounces the sentence. He gives you discernment to know what His purpose is for your life. By his Word, you will know right from wrong and guilt from innocence. You will not yield to distrust, dishonesty, compromise, or to pleasing man more than God. He will be Supreme. Job 27:2–6 defines the stand you will take should God ever need to vindicate your integrity. Judges 2:18 says, "Whenever the Lord raised up a judge for them, He was with the judge and saved them out of the hands of their enemies as long as the judge lived; for the Lord had compassion on them as they groaned under those who oppressed and afflicted them." God gives deliverance and freedom from injustice. He will use you to do the same.

DANA

A dane; industrious spirit

Colossians 1:16 *For by Him all things were created: things in heaven and on earth, visible and invisible, whether thrones or powers or rulers or authorities; all things were created by Him and for Him.*

Ephesians 2:10 *For we are God's workmanship, created in Christ Jesus to do good works, which God prepared in advance for us to do.*

To be industrious means to be skillful, hardworking, zealous, and diligent. By persevering, you give careful attention to detail. There is not a lazy bone in your body. Through you the Lord will originate. How you deal with the past determines your future. Regardless of the curses or blessings, the failures or successes, you are God's platform for a "new thing." You cannot lean on your own understanding or reasoning. God Almighty created the heavens, the earth, and you in His image. So the more completely dependent you become on your Creator, the more productive your life will be for Him! I Peter 4:19, "So then, those who suffer according to God's will should commit themselves to their Creator and continue to do good."

DANIEL

God is my judge; God is judge

&

Psalm 96:10–13 *Say among the nations, "The Lord reigns." The world is firmly established, it cannot be moved; He will judge the peoples with equity. Let the heavens rejoice, let the earth be glad; let the sea resound, and all that is in it; let the fields be jubilant, and everything in them. Then all the trees of the forest will sing for joy; they will sing before the Lord, for He comes, He comes to judge the earth. He will judge the world in righteousness and the peoples in His truth.*

II Timothy 4:1–5 *In the presence of God and of Christ Jesus, who will judge the living and the dead, and in view of His appearing and His kingdom, I give you this charge: Preach the Word; be prepared in season and out of season; correct, rebuke and encourage—with great patience and great instructions. For the time will come when men will not put up with sound doctrine. Instead, to suit their own desires, they will gather around them a great number of teachers to say what their itching ears want to hear. They will turn their ears away from the truth and turn aside to myths. But you, keep your head in all situations, endure hardship, do the work of an evangelist, discharge all the duties of your ministry.*

God Almighty is your Governor, Ruler, and Authority. He has the first and last word. He calls the shots, makes the decisions, and pronounces the sentence. He gives you discernment to know what His purpose is for your life. By his Word, you will know right from wrong and guilt from innocence. You will not yield to distrust, dishonesty, compromise, or to pleasing man more than God. He will be Supreme. Job 27:2-6 defines the stand you will take should God ever need to vindicate your integrity. Judges 2:18 says, "Whenever the Lord raised up a judge for them, He was with the judge and saved them out of the hands of their enemies as long as the judge lived; for the Lord had compassion on them as they groaned under those who oppressed and afflicted them." God gives deliverance and freedom from injustice. He will use you to do the same.

DANIELLE

God is my judge; God is judge

❧

Psalm 96:10–13 *Say among the nations, "The Lord reigns." The world is firmly established, it cannot be moved; He will judge the peoples with equity. Let the heavens rejoice, let the earth be glad; let the sea resound, and all that is in it; let the fields be jubilant, and everything in them. Then all the trees of the forest will sing for joy; they will sing before the Lord, for He comes, He comes to judge the earth. He will judge the world in righteousness and the peoples in His truth.*

II Timothy 4:1–5 *In the presence of God and of Christ Jesus, who will judge the living and the dead, and in view of His appearing and His kingdom, I give you this charge: Preach the Word; be prepared in season and out of season; correct, rebuke and encourage—with great patience and great instructions. For the time will come when men will not put up with sound doctrine. Instead, to suit their own desires, they will gather around them a great number of teachers to say what their itching ears want to hear. They will turn their ears away from the truth and turn aside to myths. But you, keep your head in all situations, endure hardship, do the work of an evangelist, discharge all the duties of your ministry.*

God Almighty is your Governor, Ruler, and Authority. He has the first and last word. He calls the shots, makes the decisions, and pronounces the sentence. He gives you discernment to know what His purpose is for your life. By his Word, you will know right from wrong and guilt from innocence. You will not yield to distrust, dishonesty, compromise, or to pleasing man more than God. He will be Supreme. Job 27:2–6 defines the stand you will take should God ever need to vindicate your integrity. Judges 2:18 says, "Whenever the Lord raised up a judge for them, He was with the judge and saved them out of the hands of their enemies as long as the judge lived; for the Lord had compassion on them as they groaned under those who oppressed and afflicted them." God gives deliverance and freedom from injustice. He will use you to do the same.

DARCY

Dark one; full of light

෪

Psalm 27:1 *The Lord is my light and my salvation—whom shall I fear? The Lord is the stronghold of my life; of whom shall I be afraid.*

Proverbs 4:18 *The path of the righteous is like the first gleam of dawn, shining ever brighter till the full light of day.*

You are one who reflects the shining brightness of the countenance of Jesus. You are aggressive toward the fruitless deeds of darkness from the evil one, by exposing them to the light of Jesus. Everything exposed by light becomes visible, for it is the light that makes everything visible (Ephesians 5:11–14). This radiance that God has given you serves as a beacon to give guidance to those yet in darkness. Your life's mission is found in the following two verses: Isaiah 60:1–3 says, "Arise, shine, for your light has come, and the glory of the Lord rises upon you. See, darkness covers the earth, and thick darkness is over the peoples, but the Lord rises upon you and His glory appears over you. Nations will come to your light, and kings to the brightness of your dawn." And in Acts 13:47, "For this is what the Lord has commanded us: 'I have made you a light for the Gentiles, that you may bring salvation to the ends of the earth.'" Continue to shine as His star, leading many to righteousness (Daniel 12:3 and Philippians 2:15).

DARLA

Little dear one; tenderly loved

❧

Deuteronomy 33:12 *Let the beloved of the Lord rest secure in Him, for He shields him all day long, and the one the Lord loves rests between His shoulders.*

I John 4:7 *Dear friends, let us love one another, for love comes from God. Everyone who loves has been born of God and knows God.*

You are highly valued, treasured, and precious to the Lord. You are an eye-witness of the very majesty of Jesus Christ. He received glory and honor from God the Father when the voice came to Him from the Majestic Glory, saying, "This is my Son, whom I love; with Him I am well pleased," II Peter 1:16–17. As you stay committed to Him, one day you will also hear those words. "We know and rely on the love of God for us. God is love, whoever lives in love lives in God and God in him," I John 4:16. You are expressive in worship because you are near to the heart of God. As you give respect, pleasure, and adoration to the Lord, He will give it back to you. You are aggressive to show the love of God to those who are disliked, abhorred, and hated. Rest secure in Him!

DARLENE

Little dear one; tenderly loved

Deuteronomy 33:12 *Let the beloved of the Lord rest secure in Him, for He shields him all day long, and the one the Lord loves rests between His shoulders.*

I John 4:7 *Dear friends, let us love one another, for love comes from God. Everyone who loves has been born of God and knows God.*

You are highly valued, treasured, and precious to the Lord. You are an eye-witness of the very majesty of Jesus Christ. He received glory and honor from God the Father when the voice came to Him from the Majestic Glory, saying, "This is my Son, whom I love; with Him I am well pleased," II Peter 1:16–17. As you stay committed to Him, one day you will also hear those words. "We know and rely on the love of God for us. God is love, whoever lives in love lives in God and God in him," I John 4:16. You are expressive in worship because you are near to the heart of God. As you give respect, pleasure, and adoration to the Lord, He will give it back to you. You are aggressive to show the love of God to those who are disliked, abhorred, and hated. Rest secure in Him!

DARRYL

Beloved one; beloved

℘

Deuteronomy 33:12 *Let the beloved of the Lord rest secure in Him, for He shields him all day long, and the one the Lord loves rests between His shoulders.*

I John 4:7 *Dear friends, let us love one another, for love comes from God. Everyone who loves has been born of God and knows God.*

You are highly valued, treasured, and precious to the Lord. You are an eye-witness of the very majesty of Jesus Christ. He received glory and honor from God the Father when the voice came to Him from the Majestic Glory, saying, "This is my Son, whom I love; with Him I am well pleased," II Peter 1:16–17. As you stay committed to Him, one day you will also hear those words. "We know and rely on the love of God for us. God is love, whoever lives in love lives in God and God in him," I John 4:16. You are expressive in worship because you are near to the heart of God. As you give respect, pleasure, and adoration to the Lord, He will give it back to you. You are aggressive to show the love of God to those who are disliked, abhorred, and hated. Rest secure in Him!

DATHAN

Their law, their decree; following God's commands

Deuteronomy 26:16–17 The Lord your God commands you this day to follow these decrees and laws; carefully observe them with all your heart and with all your soul. You have declared this day that the Lord is your God and that you will walk in His ways, that you will keep His decrees, commands and laws, and that you will obey Him.

I John 5:2–4 This is how we know that we love the children of God: by loving God and carrying out His commands. This is love for God: to obey His commands. And His commands are not burdensome, for everyone born of God overcomes the world. This is the victory that has overcome the world, even our faith.

The intense love you have for God motivates you to walk in His ways, obey His commands, hold fast to Him, and serve Him with all your heart and soul (Joshua 22:5). This releases you to prosper in all you do and wherever you go. You are constantly aware that the Lord knows your heart and understands every motive behind your thoughts (I Chronicles 28:9). Obedience and remaining faithful to Jesus requires patient endurance (Revelation 14:12). Your transparent heart allows nothing to be done in secret, for you have nothing to hide. Because Christ suffered for you, as you follow in His steps your life serves as an example of moral purity with uncompromised standards (I Peter 2:21). The reason you are a leader is because you are His follower. Instead of resisting authority, you define authority based on God's Word and the respect that you show. You will turn those who follow worthless idols and become worthless themselves to their excellent value in Jesus. You are all about recycling what the world considers "trash" into God's treasured possession.

Nothing is ever wasted—not one pain or one tear. The stubborn will surrender themselves to the Lord; the rebellious will yield themselves to the Lord; the destroyed will trust themselves to the Lord; the arrogant will humble themselves to the Lord; the confused will focus themselves upon the Lord. The world would say, "It's my way, or the highway." You say, "It's God's way or no way."

DAVE

Beloved one; beloved

ॐ

Deuteronomy 33:12 *Let the beloved of the Lord rest secure in Him, for He shields him all day long, and the one the Lord loves rests between His shoulders.*

I John 4:7 *Dear friends, let us love one another, for love comes from God. Everyone who loves has been born of God and knows God.*

You are highly valued, treasured, and precious to the Lord. You are an eye-witness of the very majesty of Jesus Christ. He received glory and honor from God the Father when the voice came to Him from the Majestic Glory, saying, "This is my Son, whom I love; with Him I am well pleased," II Peter 1:16–17. As you stay committed to Him, one day you will also hear those words. "We know and rely on the love of God for us. God is love, whoever lives in love lives in God and God in him," I John 4:16. You are expressive in worship because you are near to the heart of God. As you give respect, pleasure, and adoration to the Lord, He will give it back to you. You are aggressive to show the love of God to those who are disliked, abhorred, and hated. Rest secure in Him!

DAVID

Beloved one; beloved

&

Deuteronomy 33:12 *Let the beloved of the Lord rest secure in Him, for He shields him all day long, and the one the Lord loves rests between His shoulders.*

I John 4:7 *Dear friends, let us love one another, for love comes from God. Everyone who loves has been born of God and knows God.*

You are highly valued, treasured, and precious to the Lord. You are an eye-witness of the very majesty of Jesus Christ. He received glory and honor from God the Father when the voice came to Him from the Majestic Glory, saying, "This is my Son, whom I love; with Him I am well pleased," II Peter 1:16–17. As you stay committed to Him, one day you will also hear those words. "We know and rely on the love of God for us. God is love, whoever lives in love lives in God and God in him," I John 4:16. You are expressive in worship because you are near to the heart of God. As you give respect, pleasure, and adoration to the Lord, He will give it back to you. You are aggressive to show the love of God to those who are disliked, abhorred, and hated. Rest secure in Him!

DEAN

Dweller in the valley; courageous heart

Deuteronomy 31:6 *Be strong and courageous. Do not be afraid or terrified because of them, for the Lord your God goes with you; He will never leave you nor forsake you.*

Joshua 1:7 *Be strong and very courageous. Be careful to obey all the law My servant Moses gave you; do not turn from it to the right or to the left, that you may be successful wherever you go.*

You are equipped with mental and moral strength to venture, persevere, and withstand danger, fear, and difficulty. You have the firmness of mind to take a firm stand. You meet strain with fortitude and resilience, even when opposed or threatened. You have firm determination to achieve God's purpose in your life. With stubborn persistence and unwillingness to admit defeat, you base all victory on the finished work of the cross of Jesus. The Victor will use you to remove obstacles and invade darkness and death in order to bring the lost to a decision for Jesus. God's divine presence in and through you will bind fear and lead people to their God-given inheritance.

DEBBIE

The bee; seeking one

❧

Hosea 10:12 *Sow for yourselves righteousness, reap the fruit of unfailing love, and break up your unplowed ground; for it is time to seek the Lord, until He comes and showers righteousness on you.*

Deuteronomy 4:29 *But if from there you seek the Lord your God, you will find Him if you look for Him with all your heart and with all your soul.*

The Lord has divine attraction for you. He captures you with His love. He delights in you seeking His face. As the bee feeds on pollen and nectar, you feed on God's Word. The bees carry pollen from blossom to blossom, enabling flowering plants to produce seeds. You perform the same tasks through prayer and intercession. They perform a dance to give direction for rich food; you do that through worship. In self-denial, you keep your hands clean and your heart pure (Proverbs 24:3–6). With your diligent pursuit of the Lord, you bring order and have the ability to cause others to search for that same intimacy with Him. To the aimless, you give direction to stay the course. To the complacent, you ignite hunger through prayer and worship. Honey is the byproduct of your life!

DEBBY

The bee; seeking one

ॐ

Hosea 10:12 *Sow for yourselves righteousness, reap the fruit of unfailing love, and break up your unplowed ground; for it is time to seek the Lord, until He comes and showers righteousness on you.*

Deuteronomy 4:29 *But if from there you seek the Lord your God, you will find Him if you look for Him with all your heart and with all your soul.*

The Lord has divine attraction for you. He captures you with His love. He delights in you seeking His face. As the bee feeds on pollen and nectar, you feed on God's Word. The bees carry pollen from blossom to blossom, enabling flowering plants to produce seeds. You perform the same tasks through prayer and intercession. They perform a dance to give direction for rich food; you do that through worship. In self-denial, you keep your hands clean and your heart pure (Proverbs 24:3–6). With your diligent pursuit of the Lord, you bring order and have the ability to cause others to search for that same intimacy with Him. To the aimless, you give direction to stay the course. To the complacent, you ignite hunger through prayer and worship. Honey is the byproduct of your life!

DEBORAH

The bee; seeking one

ॐ

Hosea 10:12 *Sow for yourselves righteousness, reap the fruit of unfailing love, and break up your unplowed ground; for it is time to seek the Lord, until He comes and showers righteousness on you.*

Deuteronomy 4:29 *But if from there you seek the Lord your God, you will find Him if you look for Him with all your heart and with all your soul.*

The Lord has divine attraction for you. He captures you with His love. He delights in you seeking His face. As the bee feeds on pollen and nectar, you feed on God's Word. The bees carry pollen from blossom to blossom, enabling flowering plants to produce seeds. You perform the same tasks through prayer and intercession. They perform a dance to give direction for rich food; you do that through worship. In self-denial, you keep your hands clean and your heart pure (Proverbs 24:3–6). With your diligent pursuit of the Lord, you bring order and have the ability to cause others to search for that same intimacy with Him. To the aimless, you give direction to stay the course. To the complacent, you ignite hunger through prayer and worship. Honey is the byproduct of your life!

DEBRA

The bee; seeking one

&

Hosea 10:12 *Sow for yourselves righteousness, reap the fruit of unfailing love, and break up your unplowed ground; for it is time to seek the Lord, until He comes and showers righteousness on you.*

Deuteronomy 4:29 *But if from there you seek the Lord your God, you will find Him if you look for Him with all your heart and with all your soul.*

The Lord has divine attraction for you. He captures you with His love. He delights in you seeking His face. As the bee feeds on pollen and nectar, you feed on God's Word. The bees carry pollen from blossom to blossom, enabling flowering plants to produce seeds. You perform the same tasks through prayer and intercession. They perform a dance to give direction for rich food; you do that through worship. In self-denial, you keep your hands clean and your heart pure (Proverbs 24:3–6). With your diligent pursuit of the Lord, you bring order and have the ability to cause others to search for that same intimacy with Him. To the aimless, you give direction to stay the course. To the complacent, you ignite hunger through prayer and worship. Honey is the byproduct of your life!

DEE

Sorrows; compassionate spirit

৩

Hosea 11:4 *I led them with cords of human kindness, with ties of love; I lifted the yoke from their neck and bent down to feed them.*

Matthew 9:36 *When He saw the crowds, He had compassion on them, because they were harassed and helpless, like sheep without a shepherd.*

You are obedient, respectful, faithful, and bring pleasure to those whom you serve. Even with inconsiderate behavior, you are patient (I Peter 2:18). You are tender with the harsh, merciful with the intolerant, and sympathetic with the suffering. Because you cast your cares on the Lord, you are able to lift the burdens of others (Psalm 55:22). The reason you are so easily trusted is because of your humble nature. All glory and credit belong to God, not you. Your passion to help energizes you to meet the need regardless of what it is—guidance, relief, encouragement, or support. God allows you to see the root of the need rather than being sidetracked by all the symptoms. Sickness is healed, the hungry are fed, sight is restored, the unlovely are touched and the afflicted are delivered. You defend rather than offend, forgive rather than accuse, and you protect rather than abandon. You can depend on God's fresh supply daily. "Because of the Lord's great love we are not consumed, for His compassions never fail. They are new every morning; great is your faithfulness," Lamentations 3:22–23. Your compassion connects the heart of God to the heart of man.

DEELLA

Of nobility; noble one

❦

Isaiah 32:8 *But the noble man makes noble plans, and by noble deeds he stands.*

Luke 8:15 *But the seed on good soil stands for those with a noble and good heart, who hear the word, retain it, and by persevering produce a crop.*

Proverbs 18:12 says, "Before his downfall a man's heart is proud, but humility comes before honor." You are one who has a humble confidence in recognizing and expressing reverence, worship, adoration, trust, deference, tribute, admiration, and respect. This is the result of being secure in the truth of who you are in the Lord. Through humility, King Jesus made a way for you to be engrafted into His royalty. He made of Himself no reputation and took on the nature of a servant (Philippians 2:7) to affirm your value. Through self-denial, you prioritize excellence in virtue, truthfulness, and faithfulness. Because of the respect you have earned, you dismantle inferiority, disgrace, shame, and offenses. No one feels second-rate in your presence. The deeper that the Lord is your object of reverence, the greater your confidence will be in giving approval and worth. Because you are tall in spirit, your face is always turned upward.

DELORES

Sorrows; compassionate spirit

❧

Hosea 11:4 *I led them with cords of human kindness, with ties of love; I lifted the yoke from their neck and bent down to feed them.*

Matthew 9:36 *When He saw the crowds, He had compassion on them, because they were harassed and helpless, like sheep without a shepherd.*

You are obedient, respectful, faithful, and bring pleasure to those whom you serve. Even with inconsiderate behavior, you are patient (I Peter 2:18). You are tender with the harsh, merciful with the intolerant, and sympathetic with the suffering. Because you cast your cares on the Lord, you are able to lift the burdens of others (Psalm 55:22). The reason you are so easily trusted is because of your humble nature. All glory and credit belong to God, not you. Your passion to help energizes you to meet the need regardless of what it is—guidance, relief, encouragement, or support. God allows you to see the root of the need rather than being sidetracked by all the symptoms. Sickness is healed, the hungry are fed, sight is restored, the unlovely are touched and the afflicted are delivered. You defend rather than offend, forgive rather than accuse, and you protect rather than abandon. You can depend on God's fresh supply daily. "Because of the Lord's great love we are not consumed, for His compassions never fail. They are new every morning; great is your faithfulness," Lamentations 3:22–23. Your compassion connects the heart of God to the heart of man.

DENISE

God of wine; wise discerner

❧

James 3:17 *But the wisdom that comes from heaven is first of all pure; then peace-loving, considerate, submissive, full of mercy and good fruit, impartial and sincere.*

Proverbs 9:10 *The fear of the Lord is the beginning of wisdom, and knowledge of the Holy One is understanding.*

You are a person of moral excellence. You exemplify right living put into practice. The Lord has not only equipped you with skills for living correctly, but also the ability to impart that to others. The Spirit of truth will guide you into all truth, allowing you to have insight into the true nature of things (John 16:13). Out of your reverential respect for the Lord, you have wisdom to give guidance and direction. You are a safe sounding board who steers those who are hungry for knowledge of the Holy One in the right direction. You need only to ask for the wisdom you lack, and God will give it to you generously (James 1:5). Having spiritual discernment is having the ability to separate the difference between God's wisdom and the world's and the ability to make the right choice—regardless. Luke 21:15 says, "For I will give you words and wisdom that none of your adversaries will be able to resist or contradict."

DENNIS

God of wine; wise discerner

∞

James 3:17 *But the wisdom that comes from heaven is first of all pure; then peace-loving, considerate, submissive, full of mercy and good fruit, impartial and sincere.*

Proverbs 9:10 *The fear of the Lord is the beginning of wisdom, and knowledge of the Holy One is understanding.*

You are a person of moral excellence. You exemplify right living put into practice. The Lord has not only equipped you with skills for living correctly, but also the ability to impart that to others. The Spirit of truth will guide you into all truth, allowing you to have insight into the true nature of things (John 16:13). Out of your reverential respect for the Lord, you have wisdom to give guidance and direction. You are a safe sounding board who steers those who are hungry for knowledge of the Holy One in the right direction. You need only to ask for the wisdom you lack, and God will give it to you generously (James 1:5). Having spiritual discernment is having the ability to separate the difference between God's wisdom and the world's and the ability to make the right choice—regardless. Luke 21:15 says, "For I will give you words and wisdom that none of your adversaries will be able to resist or contradict."

DEREK

Ruler of the people; a just leader

❧

Deuteronomy 28:13 *The Lord will make you the head, not the tail. If you pay attention to the commands of the Lord your God that I give you this day and carefully follow them, you will always be at the top, never at the bottom.*

Mark 10:43–45 *...Whoever wants to become great among you must be your servant, and whoever wants to be first must be slave of all. For even the Son of Man did not come to be served, but to serve, and to give His life as a ransom for many.*

You have been set apart with vision and perspective to reproduce the likeness of Christ in others by reflecting His image. You are guided by principles and values worth dying for. You know how to balance transparency with being an example. You are one who is secure enough to be vulnerable. You do not lead to gather followers; you lead to develop leaders. You lead by honoring God with authority, influence, direction, foresight, and skill. Your credible choices set a precedence for favor. You earn trust by your willingness to confront and bring discipline in a Godly manner. You are strong enough to let your "yes" be "yes" and your "no" be "no," with no compromise or jealousy. Your strength is determined by your submitted and teachable servant's heart. The more you mature, the more humble, gentle, and meek you will become. With integrity you communicate love, affirmation, nurturing, and spiritual care. If you as a shepherd ever forget what it is like to be a sheep, you will become a hireling. Your highest aim is to honor and glorify God.

DERRICK

Ruler of the people; a just leader

&

Deuteronomy 28:13   *The Lord will make you the head, not the tail. If you pay attention to the commands of the Lord your God that I give you this day and carefully follow them, you will always be at the top, never at the bottom.*

Mark 10:43–45   *...Whoever wants to become great among you must be your servant, and whoever wants to be first must be slave of all. For even the Son of Man did not come to be served, but to serve, and to give His life as a ransom for many.*

You have been set apart with vision and perspective to reproduce the likeness of Christ in others by reflecting His image. You are guided by principles and values worth dying for. You know how to balance transparency with being an example. You are one who is secure enough to be vulnerable. You do not lead to gather followers; you lead to develop leaders. You lead by honoring God with authority, influence, direction, foresight, and skill. Your credible choices set a precedence for favor. You earn trust by your willingness to confront and bring discipline in a Godly manner. You are strong enough to let your "yes" be "yes" and your "no" be "no," with no compromise or jealousy. Your strength is determined by your submitted and teachable servant's heart. The more you mature, the more humble, gentle, and meek you will become. With integrity you communicate love, affirmation, nurturing, and spiritual care. If you as a shepherd ever forget what it is like to be a sheep, you will become a hireling. Your highest aim is to honor and glorify God.

DEVA

Divine; in God's glory

ፙ

Isaiah 58:8   *Then your light will break forth like the dawn, and your healing will quickly appear; then your righteousness will go before you, and the glory of the Lord will be your rear guard.*

Romans 8:17–18   *Now if we are children, then we are heirs—heirs of God and co-heirs with Christ, if indeed we share in His sufferings in order that we may also share in His glory. I consider that our present sufferings are not worth comparing with the glory that will be revealed in us.*

Isaiah 60:1 says, "Arise, shine, for your light has come, and the glory of the Lord rises upon you." You are God's consecrated, anointed one to show forth His brilliant beauty in your security of His creation of you. The current work of the Lord is revealed in and through you as you display His majesty, splendor, and honor in worship. Sharing in His glory results in the Holy Spirit ruling over the flesh. This equips you to confront shame, confusion, dishonor, and reproach (Psalm 4:2 and Philippians 3:19). You lift up heads that hang down (Psalm 3:3) and you defy spiritual deafness, pride, arrogance, idolatry, and self-righteousness. You are ever mindful of laying aside your reputation for His! Glory is God's character exhibited through His Son in grace, power, resurrection, and transfiguration. He is the source through which all splendor, perfection, and protection proceed. Your presence reveals His (I Chronicles 16:24–35).

DEVIN

A poet; a writer

&

Proverbs 22:11 *He who loves a pure heart and whose speech is gracious will have the king for his friend.*

Proverbs 3:3   *Let love and faithfulness never leave you; bind them around your neck, write them on the tablet of your heart.*

Deuteronomy 29:29 says, "The secret things belong to the Lord our God, but the things revealed belong to us and to our children forever, that we may follow all the words of this law." God's covenant to you is that He will put His law in your mind and write it on your heart. He will be yours and you will be His (Jeremiah 31:33). You are a letter from Christ—a living epistle—not written with ink, but with the Spirit of the living God (II Corinthians 3:3). You must invest in hiding God's Word in your heart (Psalm 119:11) to make your own words have eternal credibility. Only as you apply God's wisdom to your own heart will He entrust you with the secrets of His. This intimate friendship with the King will allow you the privilege of clearly recording His revelation (John 15:15, I Corinthians 2:9–10, and Amos 3:7). Habakkuk 2:2–3 says, "Write down the revelation and make it plain on tablets so that a herald may run with it. For the revelation awaits an appointed time; it speaks of the end and will not prove false. Though it linger, wait for it; it will certainly come and will not delay."

DEVON

A poet; a writer

ℰℭ

Proverbs 22:11 *He who loves a pure heart and whose speech is gracious will have the king for his friend.*

Proverbs 3:3 *Let love and faithfulness never leave you; bind them around your neck, write them on the tablet of your heart.*

Deuteronomy 29:29 says, "The secret things belong to the Lord our God, but the things revealed belong to us and to our children forever, that we may follow all the words of this law." God's covenant to you is that He will put His law in your mind and write it on your heart. He will be yours and you will be His (Jeremiah 31:33). You are a letter from Christ—a living epistle—not written with ink, but with the Spirit of the living God (II Corinthians 3:3). You must invest in hiding God's Word in your heart (Psalm 119:11) to make your own words have eternal credibility. Only as you apply God's wisdom to your own heart will He entrust you with the secrets of His. This intimate friendship with the King will allow you the privilege of clearly recording His revelation (John 15:15, I Corinthians 2:9–10, and Amos 3:7). Habakkuk 2:2–3 says, "Write down the revelation and make it plain on tablets so that a herald may run with it. For the revelation awaits an appointed time; it speaks of the end and will not prove false. Though it linger, wait for it; it will certainly come and will not delay."

DIANA

Divine one; in God's glory

೮౨

Isaiah 58:8   *Then your light will break forth like the dawn, and your healing will quickly appear; then your righteousness will go before you, and the glory of the Lord will be your rear guard.*

Romans 8:17-18   *Now if we are children, then we are heirs—heirs of God and co-heirs with Christ, if indeed we share in His sufferings in order that we may also share in His glory. I consider that our present sufferings are not worth comparing with the glory that will be revealed in us.*

Isaiah 60:1 says, "Arise, shine, for your light has come, and the glory of the Lord rises upon you." You are God's consecrated, anointed one to show forth His brilliant beauty in your security of His creation of you. The current work of the Lord is revealed in and through you as you display His majesty, splendor, and honor in worship. Sharing in His glory results in the Holy Spirit ruling over the flesh. This equips you to confront shame, confusion, dishonor, and reproach (Psalm 4:2 and Philippians 3:19). You lift up heads that hang down (Psalm 3:3) and you defy spiritual deafness, pride, arrogance, idolatry, and self-righteousness. You are ever mindful of laying aside your reputation for His! Glory is God's character exhibited through His Son in grace, power, resurrection, and transfiguration. He is the source through which all splendor, perfection, and protection proceed. Your presence reveals His (I Chronicles 16:24-35).

DIANE

Divine one; in God's glory

❧

Isaiah 58:8 *Then your light will break forth like the dawn, and your healing will quickly appear; then your righteousness will go before you, and the glory of the Lord will be your rear guard.*

Romans 8:17–18 *Now if we are children, then we are heirs—heirs of God and co-heirs with Christ, if indeed we share in His sufferings in order that we may also share in His glory. I consider that our present sufferings are not worth comparing with the glory that will be revealed in us.*

Isaiah 60:1 says, "Arise, shine, for your light has come, and the glory of the Lord rises upon you." You are God's consecrated, anointed one to show forth His brilliant beauty in your security of His creation of you. The current work of the Lord is revealed in and through you as you display His majesty, splendor, and honor in worship. Sharing in His glory results in the Holy Spirit ruling over the flesh. This equips you to confront shame, confusion, dishonor, and reproach (Psalm 4:2 and Philippians 3:19). You lift up heads that hang down (Psalm 3:3) and you defy spiritual deafness, pride, arrogance, idolatry, and self-righteousness. You are ever mindful of laying aside your reputation for His! Glory is God's character exhibited through His Son in grace, power, resurrection, and transfiguration. He is the source through which all splendor, perfection, and protection proceed. Your presence reveals His (I Chronicles 16:24–35).

DICK

Powerful ruler; brave, strong

☙

Deuteronomy 28:13   *The Lord will make you the head, not the tail. If you pay attention to the commands of the Lord your God that I give you this day and carefully follow them, you will always be at the top, never at the bottom.*

Mark 10:43–45   *...Whoever wants to become great among you must be your servant, and whoever wants to be first must be slave of all. For even the Son of Man did not come to be served, but to serve, and to give His life as a ransom for many.*

You have been set apart with vision and perspective to reproduce the likeness of Christ in others by reflecting His image. You are guided by principles and values worth dying for. You know how to balance transparency with being an example. You are one who is secure enough to be vulnerable. You do not lead to gather followers; you lead to develop leaders. You lead by honoring God with authority, influence, direction, foresight, and skill. Your credible choices set a precedence for favor. You earn trust by your willingness to confront and bring discipline in a Godly manner. You are strong enough to let your "yes" be "yes" and your "no" be "no," with no compromise or jealousy. Your strength is determined by your submitted and teachable servant's heart. The more you mature, the more humble, gentle, and meek you will become. With integrity you communicate love, affirmation, nurturing, and spiritual care. If you as a shepherd ever forget what it is like to be a sheep, you will become a hireling. Your highest aim is to honor and glorify God.

DILLAN

The sea; faithful

❧

Proverbs 2:7–8 *He holds victory in store for the upright, He is a shield to those whose walk is blameless, for He guards the course of the just and protects the way of His faithful ones.*

Psalm 15:1–5 *Lord, who may dwell in Your sanctuary? Who may live on Your holy hill? He whose walk is blameless and who does what is righteous, who speaks the truth from his heart and has no slander on his tongue, who does his neighbor no wrong and casts no slur on his fellow man, who despises a vile man but honors those who fear the Lord, who keeps his oath even when it hurts, who lends his money without usury and does not accept a bribe against the innocent. He who does these things will never be shaken.*

You are one who has made a commitment to God to be loyal, true, dependable, enduring, and steadfast. You unmask anything fake with the reality of God's Word. You are aggressive towards lies and deception to bring about truth. You are especially sensitive to betrayal, so that God can restore hope, security, purpose, and His faithfulness in those whom He has given you to serve. "Be faithful, even to the point of death, and I will give you a crown of life," Revelation 2:10. Anticipate the Master saying to you, "Well done, good and faithful servant! You have been faithful with a few things; I will put you in charge of many things. Come and share your Master's happiness!" (Matthew 25:21) "The one who calls you is faithful and he will do it," I Thessalonians 5:24.

DILLON

The sea; faithful

❧

Proverbs 2:7–8 *He holds victory in store for the upright, He is a shield to those whose walk is blameless, for He guards the course of the just and protects the way of His faithful ones.*

Psalm 15:1–5 *Lord, who may dwell in Your sanctuary? Who may live on Your holy hill? He whose walk is blameless and who does what is righteous, who speaks the truth from his heart and has no slander on his tongue, who does his neighbor no wrong and casts no slur on his fellow man, who despises a vile man but honors those who fear the Lord, who keeps his oath even when it hurts, who lends his money without usury and does not accept a bribe against the innocent. He who does these things will never be shaken.*

You are one who has made a commitment to God to be loyal, true, dependable, enduring, and steadfast. You unmask anything fake with the reality of God's Word. You are aggressive towards lies and deception to bring about truth. You are especially sensitive to betrayal, so that God can restore hope, security, purpose, and His faithfulness in those whom He has given you to serve. "Be faithful, even to the point of death, and I will give you a crown of life," Revelation 2:10. Anticipate the Master saying to you, "Well done, good and faithful servant! You have been faithful with a few things; I will put you in charge of many things. Come and share your Master's happiness!" (Matthew 25:21) "The one who calls you is faithful and he will do it," I Thessalonians 5:24.

DOMINIC

The Lords; God's possession

&

Romans 12:1 *Therefore, I urge you brothers, in view of God's mercy, to offer your bodies as living sacrifices, holy and pleasing to God—this is your spiritual act of worship.*

Philippians 3:7–8 *But whatever was to my profit I now consider loss for the sake of Christ. What is more, I consider everything a loss compared to the surpassing greatness of knowing Christ Jesus my Lord, for whose sake I have lost all things. I consider them rubbish, that I may gain Christ.*

Before you were born, God set you apart and appointed you as a prophet to the nations (Jeremiah 1:5). You are to be devoted irrevocably to the worship of God. He will pour out His anointing upon you as you are faithful to follow Him wholeheartedly (Psalm 119:34). You are one who has made a commitment to be loyal, true, dependable, enduring, and steadfast. You unmask anything fake with the reality of God's Word. You are aggressive towards lies and deception in order to bring about truth. You are especially sensitive to betrayal, so that God can restore hope, security, purpose, and His faithfulness in those whom He has given you to serve. Let your eyes keep to God's ways (Proverbs 23:26).

DON

World mighty; overcomer

୫୬

Revelation 2:7   *To him who overcomes, I will give the right to eat from the tree of life, which is in the paradise of God.*

Romans 8:37   *No, in all these things we are more than conquerors through Him who loved us.*

An overcomer is a winner, champion, and victor who subdues, triumphs, and prevails. That which is intended to overwhelm, overthrow, defeat, humiliate, and manipulate is placed in your hands to gain and acquire by force. You win by overcoming obstacles and opposition. You overthrow by bringing down the destructive power of the enemy. The domineering control intended to thwart one's destiny is brought in subjection to the Victor's power. As you age, so shall you be equipped with increased strength to subdue the enemy's strongholds (Deuteronomy 33:25). You will reverse the curse in everyone you touch by releasing the surpassing victory enabled only by the One who loves you. God uses you to raise the standard, go over and above the mark, seize the Promised Land, and to be more than a conqueror.

DONALD

World mighty; overcomer

&

Revelation 2:7   *To him who overcomes, I will give the right to eat from the tree of life, which is in the paradise of God.*

Romans 8:37   *No, in all these things we are more than conquerors through Him who loved us.*

An overcomer is a winner, champion, and victor who subdues, triumphs, and prevails. That which is intended to overwhelm, overthrow, defeat, humiliate, and manipulate is placed in your hands to gain and acquire by force. You win by overcoming obstacles and opposition. You overthrow by bringing down the destructive power of the enemy. The domineering control intended to thwart one's destiny is brought in subjection to the Victor's power. As you age, so shall you be equipped with increased strength to subdue the enemy's strongholds (Deuteronomy 33:25). You will reverse the curse in everyone you touch by releasing the surpassing victory enabled only by the One who loves you. God uses you to raise the standard, go over and above the mark, seize the Promised Land, and to be more than a conqueror.

DONNA

Lady; dignity of character

છ

Psalm 27:4   *One thing I ask of the Lord, this is what I seek: that I may dwell in the house of the Lord all the days of my life, to gaze upon the beauty of the Lord and to seek Him in His temple.*

Philippians 4:5   *Let your gentleness be evident to all. The Lord is near.*

You are one who radiates the beauty of the Lord with calm assurance of being pleasing, flawless, clean, and pure before Him. As one who is marked by honesty, you have no prejudice or impartiality. You are able to minister to the victim as well as the victimizer. This is accomplished by the cleansing power of the blood of the Lamb, Jesus Christ. Your dignity is shown as you give honor to the undeserved, show kindness to the harsh, and remain calm in the face of violence. God exchanges the consuming ashes of your life for a crown of beauty (Isaiah 61:3). God rewards you with His righteous hand.

DONOVAN

World mighty; overcomer

Revelation 2:7   *To him who overcomes, I will give the right to eat from the tree of life, which is in the paradise of God.*

Romans 8:37   *No, in all these things we are more than conquerors through Him who loved us.*

An overcomer is a winner, champion, and victor who subdues, triumphs, and prevails. That which is intended to overwhelm, overthrow, defeat, humiliate, and manipulate is placed in your hands to gain and acquire by force. You win by overcoming obstacles and opposition. You overthrow by bringing down the destructive power of the enemy. The domineering control intended to thwart one's destiny is brought in subjection to the Victor's power. As you age, so shall you be equipped with increased strength to subdue the enemy's strongholds (Deuteronomy 33:25). You will reverse the curse in everyone you touch by releasing the surpassing victory enabled only by the One who loves you. God uses you to raise the standard, go over and above the mark, seize the Promised Land, and to be more than a conqueror.

DORENE

Sullen; devoted heart

&

Psalm 63:1, 5, 8 *My soul thirsts for You. My soul will be satisfied. My soul clings to you.*

I Corinthians 15:58 *Therefore, my dear brothers, stand firm. Let nothing move you. Always give yourselves fully to the work of the Lord, because you know that your labor is not in vain.*

Your very being lives to be in constant harmony with your Creator; that both of your hearts beat as one. Therefore, you are continually yielding every area to the likeness of Christ with strong discipline. You have a devoted allegiance to Christ and his teachings. Your character is one of devotion, dedication, consecration, loyalty, and faithfulness. You are called to help the fallen take a stand, and to remove shame and fear. You dispel division by bringing the very unity of God. As you seek and trust in Him with all your heart, leaning not to your own understanding, He will protect you from being blindsided by the enemy of your soul. Be known as one who loves God with all your heart, soul, mind, and strength.

DORIS

Bountiful; excellent in virtue

&

James 3:17 *But the wisdom that comes from heaven is first of all pure; then peace-loving, considerate, submissive, full of mercy and good fruit, impartial and sincere.*

Proverbs 9:10 *The fear of the Lord is the beginning of wisdom, and knowledge of the Holy One is understanding.*

You are a person of moral excellence. You exemplify right living put into practice. The Lord has not only equipped you with skills for living correctly, but also the ability to impart that to others. The Spirit of truth will guide you into all truth, allowing you to have insight into the true nature of things (John 16:13). Out of your reverential respect for the Lord, you have wisdom to give guidance and direction. You are a safe sounding board who steers those who are hungry for knowledge of the Holy One in the right direction. You need only to ask for the wisdom you lack, and God will give it to you generously (James 1:5). Having spiritual discernment is having the ability to separate the difference between God's wisdom and the world's and the ability to make the right choice—regardless. Luke 21:15 says, "For I will give you words and wisdom that none of your adversaries will be able to resist or contradict."

DOROTHY

Gift of Jehovah; gift of God

∞

James 1:17 *Every good and perfect gift is from above, coming down from the Father of the heavenly lights, who does not change like shifting shadows.*

I Samuel 16:7 *But the Lord said to Samuel, "Do not consider his appearance or his height, for I have rejected him. The Lord does not look at the things man looks at. Man looks at the outward appearance, but the Lord looks at the heart."*

You are God's tribute to Himself, His personal reward. Your life defines God's manners, with priorities on giving rather than receiving. You are to fan into flame the gift of God (II Timothy 1:6). Through you He will display His favor, encouragement and kindness even to the undeserved and hated. As you look beyond faults and see needs, you are God's channel through which His unselfish love flows and is revealed. Discipline your attention to the Giver, not to the gift, nor its wrappings. Give diligence to preserving a humble, submitted heart in full surrender to the Lord. Proverbs 18:16 says, "A gift opens the way for the giver and ushers him into the presence of the great."

DORSEY

Free spirit; free spirit

&

Isaiah 61:1 *The Spirit of the Sovereign Lord is on me, because the Lord has anointed me to preach good news to the poor. He has sent me to bind up the brokenhearted, to proclaim freedom for the captives and release from darkness for the prisoners.*

Galatians 5:1 *It is for freedom that Christ has set us free. Stand firm, then, and do not let yourselves be burdened again by a yoke of slavery.*

There are no restrictions on your abandoned commitment to the Lord Jesus Christ. Knowing God's truth frees you from the bondage and care of sin and oppression (John 8:32). The free gift of God—Jesus Christ—exchanges offense for God's grace, condemnation for justification, shame for holiness and the spirit of the world for the Spirit of God. You are fearless as you loose those in bondage and give pardon to the imprisoned—all because the law of the Spirit of life set you free from the law of sin and death. Do not use your freedom to indulge the sinful nature; rather, serve one another in love (Galatians 5:13). Freely you have received; freely give (Matthew 10:8).

DOT

Gift of Jehovah; gift of God

∞

James 1:17 *Every good and perfect gift is from above, coming down from the Father of the heavenly lights, who does not change like shifting shadows.*

I Samuel 16:7 *But the Lord said to Samuel, "Do not consider his appearance or his height, for I have rejected him. The Lord does not look at the things man looks at. Man looks at the outward appearance, but the Lord looks at the heart."*

You are God's tribute to Himself, His personal reward. Your life defines God's manners, with priorities on giving rather than receiving. You are to fan into flame the gift of God (II Timothy 1:6). Through you He will display His favor, encouragement and kindness even to the undeserved and hated. As you look beyond faults and see needs, you are God's channel through which His unselfish love flows and is revealed. Discipline your attention to the Giver, not to the gift, nor its wrappings. Give diligence to preserving a humble, submitted heart in full surrender to the Lord. Proverbs 18:16 says, "A gift opens the way for the giver and ushers him into the presence of the great."

DOTTIE

Gift of Jehovah; gift of God

James 1:17   *Every good and perfect gift is from above, coming down from the Father of the heavenly lights, who does not change like shifting shadows.*

I Samuel 16:7   *But the Lord said to Samuel, "Do not consider his appearance or his height, for I have rejected him. The Lord does not look at the things man looks at. Man looks at the outward appearance, but the Lord looks at the heart."*

You are God's tribute to Himself, His personal reward. Your life defines God's manners, with priorities on giving rather than receiving. You are to fan into flame the gift of God (II Timothy 1:6). Through you He will display His favor, encouragement and kindness even to the undeserved and hated. As you look beyond faults and see needs, you are God's channel through which His unselfish love flows and is revealed. Discipline your attention to the Giver, not to the gift, nor its wrappings. Give diligence to preserving a humble, submitted heart in full surrender to the Lord. Proverbs 18:16 says, "A gift opens the way for the giver and ushers him into the presence of the great."

DOUG

From the dark water; seeker of light

Psalm 27:1 *The Lord is my light and my salvation—whom shall I fear? The Lord is the stronghold of my life; of whom shall I be afraid.*

Proverbs 4:18 *The path of the righteous is like the first gleam of dawn, shining ever brighter till the full light of day.*

You are one who reflects the shining brightness of the countenance of Jesus. You are aggressive toward the fruitless deeds of darkness from the evil one, by exposing them to the light of Jesus. Everything exposed by light becomes visible, for it is the light that makes everything visible (Ephesians 5:11–14). This radiance that God has given you serves as a beacon to give guidance to those yet in darkness. Your life's mission is found in the following two verses: Isaiah 60:1–3 says, "Arise, shine, for your light has come, and the glory of the Lord rises upon you. See, darkness covers the earth, and thick darkness is over the peoples, but the Lord rises upon you and His glory appears over you. Nations will come to your light, and kings to the brightness of your dawn." And in Acts 13:47, "For this is what the Lord has commanded us: 'I have made you a light for the Gentiles, that you may bring salvation to the ends of the earth.'" Continue to shine as His star, leading many to righteousness (Daniel 12:3 and Philippians 2:15).

DOUGLAS

From the dark water; seeker of light

ℰℒ

Psalm 27:1 *The Lord is my light and my salvation—whom shall I fear? The Lord is the stronghold of my life; of whom shall I be afraid.*

Proverbs 4:18 *The path of the righteous is like the first gleam of dawn, shining ever brighter till the full light of day.*

You are one who reflects the shining brightness of the countenance of Jesus. You are aggressive toward the fruitless deeds of darkness from the evil one, by exposing them to the light of Jesus. Everything exposed by light becomes visible, for it is the light that makes everything visible (Ephesians 5:11–14). This radiance that God has given you serves as a beacon to give guidance to those yet in darkness. Your life's mission is found in the following two verses: Isaiah 60:1–3 says, "Arise, shine, for your light has come, and the glory of the Lord rises upon you. See, darkness covers the earth, and thick darkness is over the peoples, but the Lord rises upon you and His glory appears over you. Nations will come to your light, and kings to the brightness of your dawn." And in Acts 13:47, "For this is what the Lord has commanded us: 'I have made you a light for the Gentiles, that you may bring salvation to the ends of the earth.'" Continue to shine as His star, leading many to righteousness (Daniel 12:3 and Philippians 2:15).

DREW

Strong; manly

ℰ

Proverbs 24:5 *A wise man has great power, and a man of knowledge increases strength.*

Ephesians 6:10 *Finally, be strong in the Lord and in His mighty power.*

You are one who has an un-compromised commitment to righteousness, respectability, honesty, character, excellence, value, worth, kindness, innocence, generosity, trustworthiness, faithfulness, justice, hope, and love. You can do everything through Him who gives you strength (Philippians 4:11–13). The Lord is the source of your strength because you turn back the battle at the gate (Isaiah 28:6). You renew your strength by your hope being in the Lord (Isaiah 40:31). Jesus says, "My grace is sufficient for you, for My power is made perfect in weaknesses. Therefore you will boast all the more gladly about your weaknesses, so that Christ's power may rest on you. That is why for Christ's sake, you delight in weaknesses, in insults, in hardships, in persecutions, and in difficulties. For when you are weak, then you are strong," II Corinthians 12:9–10. You are clothed with strength and dignity (Proverbs 31:25).

DUSTIN

Brave fighter; loyal heart

❧

Romans 12:9–10 *Love must be sincere. Hate what is evil; cling to what is good. Be devoted to one another in brotherly love. Honor one another above yourselves.*

Proverbs 2:7–8 *He holds victory in store for the upright, He is a shield to those whose walk is blameless, for He guards the course of the just and protects the way of His faithful ones.*

As one with a loyal spirit, the Lord has called you to be faithful, devoted, obedient, dependable, and true. You are noble in disarming the enemy's attacks of fear, selfishness, failure, betrayal, dishonesty, and faithlessness. You are unyielding and have a resolute confidence in your commitment to God's Word. With it, you will help others overcome being cowards, losers, quitters, or betrayers. Knowing God's loyalty to you will strengthen your loyalty to others. Isaiah 1:17 says, "Learn to do right! Seek justice, encourage the oppressed. Defend the cause of the fatherless, plead the case of the widow."

DUTCHESS

One of nobility; noble one

&

Isaiah 32:8 *But the noble man makes noble plans, and by noble deeds he stands.*

Luke 8:15 *But the seed on good soil stands for those with a noble and good heart, who hear the word, retain it, and by persevering produce a crop.*

Proverbs 18:12 says, "Before his downfall a man's heart is proud, but humility comes before honor." You are one who has a humble confidence in recognizing and expressing reverence, worship, adoration, trust, deference, tribute, admiration, and respect. This is the result of being secure in the truth of who you are in the Lord. Through humility, King Jesus made a way for you to be engrafted into His royalty. He made of Himself no reputation and took on the nature of a servant (Philippians 2:7) to affirm your value. Through self-denial, you prioritize excellence in virtue, truthfulness, and faithfulness. Because of the respect you have earned, you dismantle inferiority, disgrace, shame, and offenses. No one feels second-rate in your presence. The deeper that the Lord is your object of reverence, the greater your confidence will be in giving approval and worth. Because you are tall in spirit, your face is always turned upward.

DWIGHT

White; dweller in truth

❧

Psalm 89:1–2   *I will sing of the Lord's great love forever; with my mouth I will make Your faithfulness known through all generations. I will declare that Your love stands firm forever, that You established Your faithfulness in heaven itself.*

Psalm 51:6   *Surely You desire truth in the inner parts; You teach me wisdom in the inmost place.*

John 14:6   *Jesus answered, "I am the way and the truth and the life. No one comes to the Father except through Me."*

"You know the truth and the truth has set you free," John 8:32. You are one who is aggressive toward lies and deception. Your purpose is to bring about truth through openness, revelation, authenticity, accuracy, and honesty. As God's messenger, you will have firmness in keeping and executing His promises and also your own. Your God-given wisdom will be based on God's Word alone. Zechariah 8:16 says, "These are the things you are to do: Speak the truth to each other, and render true and sound judgment in your courts." May true instruction be in your mouth and nothing false be found on your lips (Malachi 2:6).

DYLAN

The sea; faithful

ॐ

Proverbs 2:7–8   *He holds victory in store for the upright, He is a shield to those whose walk is blameless, for He guards the course of the just and protects the way of His faithful ones.*

Psalm 15:1–5   *Lord, who may dwell in Your sanctuary? Who may live on Your holy hill? He whose walk is blameless and who does what is righteous, who speaks the truth from his heart and has no slander on his tongue, who does his neighbor no wrong and casts no slur on his fellow man, who despises a vile man but honors those who fear the Lord, who keeps his oath even when it hurts, who lends his money without usury and does not accept a bribe against the innocent. He who does these things will never be shaken.*

You are one who has made a commitment to God to be loyal, true, dependable, enduring, and steadfast. You unmask anything fake with the reality of God's Word. You are aggressive towards lies and deception to bring about truth. You are especially sensitive to betrayal, so that God can restore hope, security, purpose, and His faithfulness in those whom He has given you to serve. "Be faithful, even to the point of death, and I will give you a crown of life," Revelation 2:10. Anticipate the Master saying to you, "Well done, good and faithful servant! You have been faithful with a few things; I will put you in charge of many things. Come and share your Master's happiness!" (Matthew 25:21) "The one who calls you is faithful and he will do it," I Thessalonians 5:24.

EARL

Nobleman; man of honor

ଌ

Isaiah 32:8 *But the noble man makes noble plans, and by noble deeds he stands.*

Luke 8:15 *But the seed on good soil stands for those with a noble and good heart, who hear the word, retain it, and by persevering produce a crop.*

Proverbs 18:12 says, "Before his downfall a man's heart is proud, but humility comes before honor." You are one who has a humble confidence in recognizing and expressing reverence, worship, adoration, trust, deference, tribute, admiration, and respect. This is the result of being secure in the truth of who you are in the Lord. Through humility, King Jesus made a way for you to be engrafted into His royalty. He made of Himself no reputation and took on the nature of a servant (Philippians 2:7) to affirm your value. Through self-denial, you prioritize excellence in virtue, truthfulness, and faithfulness. Because of the respect you have earned, you dismantle inferiority, disgrace, shame, and offenses. No one feels second-rate in your presence. The deeper that the Lord is your object of reverence, the greater your confidence will be in giving approval and worth. Because you are tall in spirit, your face is always turned upward.

EASTER

Springlike; transformed heart

❦

Ezekiel 36:26–27 *I will give you a new heart and put a new spirit in you; I will remove from you your heart of stone and give you a heart of flesh. And I will put My spirit in you and move you to follow My decrees and be careful to keep My laws.*

Romans 12:2 *Do not conform any longer to the pattern of this world, but be transformed by the renewing of your mind. Then you will be able to test and approve what God's will is—His good, pleasing and perfect will.*

The cross of Jesus Christ is your ultimate source of transformation. He exchanged your sin for His righteousness, your death for His life, your darkness for His light, your earthly for His eternal, and your past for His future. You were lost, but now you are found. You were blind, but now you see. The old has now become new. II Corinthians 5:17 says, "Therefore, if anyone is in Christ, he is a new creation; the old has gone, the new has come!" A metamorphosis is your transformation from God through Christ. Your conversion by the blood of Jesus is the greatest miracle you will ever experience. This changeless God has traded your sorrow for His joy, your pain for His healing, your emptiness for His fullness, and your rejection for His forgiveness. He adopts, accepts, and loves you. Put to death what belongs to your earthly nature and be clothed with the likeness of Christ (Colossians 3:1–14). As you align your will with His and are continually renewed in the knowledge of God's Word, He will transform many lives through yours. For those living a lie you bring truth, for the dying you bring life, for the rejected you bring acceptance, and for the trapped you bring freedom. His resurrection power flows in and through you. You will continually be transformed into the Lord's likeness with ever-increasing glory (II Corinthians 3:18).

ED

Prosperous guardian

೭ℜ

Psalm 1:1–3 *Blessed is the man who does not walk in the counsel of the wicked or stand in the way of sinners or sit in the seat of mockers. But his delight is in the law of the Lord, and on His law he meditates day and night. He is like a tree planted by the streams of water, which yields its fruit in season and whose leaf does not wither. Whatever he does prospers.*

Joshua 1:8 *Do not let this book of the law depart from your mouth; meditate on it day and night, so that you may be careful to do everything written in it. Then you will be prosperous and successful.*

You are one who knows that your success is not based on luck or good fortune. It is because you are willing to loose your life for Christ's sake in order to find it (Matthew 10:39). You let the word of Christ dwell in you richly (Colossians 3:16). You allow the Lord to stretch and strengthen you in order to enlarge your borders of influence and maturity (Isaiah 54:1–3). You welcome the cutting and pruning that makes way for increase to bear fruit, more fruit, and much fruit (John 15). You enter a covenant with the Lord of obedience, seeking Him diligently and wholeheartedly (II Chronicles 31:21), which causes you to prosper in everything you do (Deuteronomy 29:9). You are content in need and in plenty (Philippians 4:11–12) because prosperity is not a love of money (I Timothy 6:6–10), power, popularity, or possessions. In spite of failure, disappointment, loss, and defeat, you let nothing separate you from the love of God (Romans 8:37–39). Instead of being blind to the hungry, you will feed them. Instead of abhorring the naked, you will clothe them. Instead of ignoring the poor and fatherless, you will be God's hand of provision. You will offer provisions of hope, courage, and strength not to give up, but rather to start again and to make it to the finish line. You are a faithful steward helping them exchange their temporal for His eternal (Philippians 4:19). As your mantle is to build up, develop, and cause to succeed, know that "no weapon formed against you will prosper," Isaiah 54:17. Your goal is to hear the Master say, "Well done, good and faithful servant! You have been faithful with a few things, I will put you in charge of many things. Come share your Master's happiness!" (Matthew 25:21) May you prosper in all things and be in health, just as your soul prospers (3 John 2).

EDWARD

Prosperous guardian

❧

Psalm 1:1–3 *Blessed is the man who does not walk in the counsel of the wicked or stand in the way of sinners or sit in the seat of mockers. But his delight is in the law of the Lord, and on His law he meditates day and night. He is like a tree planted by the streams of water, which yields its fruit in season and whose leaf does not wither. Whatever he does prospers.*

Joshua 1:8 *Do not let this book of the law depart from your mouth; meditate on it day and night, so that you may be careful to do everything written in it. Then you will be prosperous and successful.*

You are one who knows that your success is not based on luck or good fortune. It is because you are willing to loose your life for Christ's sake in order to find it (Matthew 10:39). You let the word of Christ dwell in you richly (Colossians 3:16). You allow the Lord to stretch and strengthen you in order to enlarge your borders of influence and maturity (Isaiah 54:1–3). You welcome the cutting and pruning that makes way for increase to bear fruit, more fruit, and much fruit (John 15). You enter a covenant with the Lord of obedience, seeking Him diligently and wholeheartedly (II Chronicles 31:21), which causes you to prosper in everything you do (Deuteronomy 29:9). You are content in need and in plenty (Philippians 4:11–12) because prosperity is not a love of money (I Timothy 6:6–10), power, popularity, or possessions. In spite of failure, disappointment, loss, and defeat, you let nothing separate you from the love of God (Romans 8:37–39). Instead of being blind to the hungry, you will feed them. Instead of abhorring the naked, you will clothe them. Instead of ignoring the poor and fatherless, you will be God's hand of provision. You will offer provisions of hope, courage, and strength not to give up, but rather to start again and to make it to the finish line. You are a faithful steward helping them exchange their temporal for His eternal (Philippians 4:19). As your mantle is to build up, develop, and cause to succeed, know that "no weapon formed against you will prosper," Isaiah 54:17. Your goal is to hear the Master say, "Well done, good and faithful servant! You have been faithful with a few things, I will put you in charge of many things. Come share your Master's happiness!" (Matthew 25:21) May you prosper in all things and be in health, just as your soul prospers (3 John 2).

EDWIN

Rich friend; friendly spirit

❧

Proverbs 17:17 *A friend loves at all times, and a brother is born for adversity.*

Ecclesiastes 4:9–10 *Two are better than one, because they have a good return for their work: if one falls down his friend can help him up. But pity the man who falls and has no one to help him up!*

Christ was the preeminent example of friendship. John 15:13–14 says, "Greater love has no man than this, that he lay down his life for his friends. You are my friends if you do what I command." With open arms, He gave all. Your mantle is to be God's man of peace. This is achieved by being understanding, loyal, faithful, and true. Proverbs 18:24 says, "A man of many companions may come to ruin, but there is a friend who sticks closer than a brother." It comes natural for you to be hospitable, generous, helpful, and good-humored. Your influence is based on your ability to be approachable, trusted, and respectful. Strangers who are lonely, outcast, or abandoned will find refuge with your "welcome" sign written on your heart. You are loving, as well as being loved—everyone's neighbor; everyone's buddy. Psalm 119:63 says, "I am a friend to all who fear You, to all who follow Your precepts." Proverbs 22:11 says, "He who loves a pure heart and whose speech is gracious will have the King for his friend."

ELAINE

The lily maid; bright one

Psalm 27:1   *The Lord is my light and my salvation—whom shall I fear? The Lord is the stronghold of my life; of whom shall I be afraid.*

Proverbs 4:18   *The path of the righteous is like the first gleam of dawn, shining ever brighter till the full light of day.*

You are one who reflects the shining brightness of the countenance of Jesus. You are aggressive toward the fruitless deeds of darkness from the evil one, by exposing them to the light of Jesus. Everything exposed by light becomes visible, for it is the light that makes everything visible (Ephesians 5:11–14). This radiance that God has given you serves as a beacon to give guidance to those yet in darkness. Your life's mission is found in the following two verses: Isaiah 60:1–3 says, "Arise, shine, for your light has come, and the glory of the Lord rises upon you. See, darkness covers the earth, and thick darkness is over the peoples, but the Lord rises upon you and His glory appears over you. Nations will come to your light, and kings to the brightness of your dawn." And in Acts 13:47, "For this is what the Lord has commanded us: 'I have made you a light for the Gentiles, that you may bring salvation to the ends of the earth.'" Continue to shine as His star, leading many to righteousness (Daniel 12:3 and Philippians 2:15).

ELEANOR

Light; bright one

Psalm 27:1 *The Lord is my light and my salvation—whom shall I fear? The Lord is the stronghold of my life; of whom shall I be afraid.*

Proverbs 4:18 *The path of the righteous is like the first gleam of dawn, shining ever brighter till the full light of day.*

You are one who reflects the shining brightness of the countenance of Jesus. You are aggressive toward the fruitless deeds of darkness from the evil one, by exposing them to the light of Jesus. Everything exposed by light becomes visible, for it is the light that makes everything visible (Ephesians 5:11–14). This radiance that God has given you serves as a beacon to give guidance to those yet in darkness. Your life's mission is found in the following two verses: Isaiah 60:1–3 says, "Arise, shine, for your light has come, and the glory of the Lord rises upon you. See, darkness covers the earth, and thick darkness is over the peoples, but the Lord rises upon you and His glory appears over you. Nations will come to your light, and kings to the brightness of your dawn." And in Acts 13:47, "For this is what the Lord has commanded us: 'I have made you a light for the Gentiles, that you may bring salvation to the ends of the earth.'" Continue to shine as His star, leading many to righteousness (Daniel 12:3 and Philippians 2:15).

ELI

My God is Jehovah; the Lord is my God

&

Proverbs 18:10 *The name of the Lord is a strong tower; the righteous run to it and are safe.*

James 5:17–18 *Elijah was a man just like us. He prayed earnestly that it would not rain, and it did not rain on the land for three and a half years. Again he prayed, and the heavens gave rain and the earth produced its crops.*

As a fearless reformer, Elijah confronted idolatry, rebuked kings, and pulled no punches in his mission to rescue Israel from its spiritual and moral decay. He was known as "the prophet of fire," a prototype of John the Baptist. Like him, you are confident to speak God's promises and pray earnestly until they are realized. You will experience the miraculous. In your place of solitude you learn that where God leads, He will always provide. Guard against physical and emotional exhaustion, self-pity, discouragement, despondency, despair, and isolation. Develop discernment to God's gentle whisper. As you stand in the gap, there is an anointing on you to transfer God's mantle to others in a double portion.

ELIANA

God has answered my prayers; promises accomplished

❧

Psalm 91:15 *He will call upon me, and I will answer Him; I will be with him in trouble, I will deliver him and honor him.*

II Peter 3:9 *The Lord is not slow in keeping His promise, as some understand slowness. He is patient with you, not wanting anyone to perish, but everyone to come to repentance.*

You, like Isaac, are a child of promise (Galatians 4:28). Hebrews 11:17–19 says, "By faith Abraham, when God tested him, offered Isaac as a sacrifice. He who had received the promises was about to sacrifice his one and only son, even though God had said to him, 'It is through Isaac that your offspring will be reckoned.' Abraham reasoned that God could raise the dead, and figuratively speaking, he did receive Isaac back from death." "If you belong to Christ, then you are Abraham's seed, and heirs according to the promise," Galatians 3:29. Abraham was fully persuaded that God had power to do what He had promised (Romans 4:21). You have inherited this same strong faith as you stay committed to God's Word and love Him (James 2:5). As God's fulfilled promise, you will not choose deception, denial, or to break any covenant you make. God will answer you because your motives are pure—without secret sin, indifference, stubbornness, instability, self-indulgence, and disobedience. You want God's will more than yours, regardless of the cost. Being given God's great and precious promises releases you to participate in His divine nature (II Peter 1:4).

ELIJAH

My God is Jehovah; the Lord is my God

⮂

Proverbs 18:10 *The name of the Lord is a strong tower; the righteous run to it and are safe.*

James 5:17–18 *Elijah was a man just like us. He prayed earnestly that it would not rain, and it did not rain on the land for three and a half years. Again he prayed, and the heavens gave rain and the earth produced its crops.*

As a fearless reformer, Elijah confronted idolatry, rebuked kings, and pulled no punches in his mission to rescue Israel from its spiritual and moral decay. He was known as "the prophet of fire," a prototype of John the Baptist. Like him, you are confident to speak God's promises and pray earnestly until they are realized. You will experience the miraculous. In your place of solitude you learn that where God leads, He will always provide. Guard against physical and emotional exhaustion, self-pity, discouragement, despondency, despair, and isolation. Develop discernment to God's gentle whisper. As you stand in the gap, there is an anointing on you to transfer God's mantle to others in a double portion.

ELIZABETH

Consecrated to God; consecrated one

Romans 12:1 *Therefore, I urge you brothers, in view of God's mercy, to offer your bodies as living sacrifices, holy and pleasing to God—this is your spiritual act of worship.*

Philippians 3:7–8 *But whatever was to my profit I now consider loss for the sake of Christ. What is more, I consider everything a loss compared to the surpassing greatness of knowing Christ Jesus my Lord, for whose sake I have lost all things. I consider them rubbish, that I may gain Christ.*

Before you were born, God set you apart and appointed you as a prophet to the nations (Jeremiah 1:5). You are to be devoted irrevocably to the worship of God. He will pour out His anointing upon you as you are faithful to follow Him wholeheartedly (Psalm 119:34). You are one who has made a commitment to be loyal, true, dependable, enduring, and steadfast. You unmask anything fake with the reality of God's Word. You are aggressive towards lies and deception in order to bring about truth. You are especially sensitive to betrayal, so that God can restore hope, security, purpose, and His faithfulness in those whom He has given you to serve. Let your eyes keep to God's ways (Proverbs 23:26).

ELLA

Bright one

Psalm 27:1 *The Lord is my light and my salvation—whom shall I fear? The Lord is the stronghold of my life; of whom shall I be afraid.*

Proverbs 4:18 *The path of the righteous is like the first gleam of dawn, shining ever brighter till the full light of day.*

You are one who reflects the shining brightness of the countenance of Jesus. You are aggressive toward the fruitless deeds of darkness from the evil one, by exposing them to the light of Jesus. Everything exposed by light becomes visible, for it is the light that makes everything visible (Ephesians 5:11–14). This radiance that God has given you serves as a beacon to give guidance to those yet in darkness. Your life's mission is found in the following two verses: Isaiah 60:1–3 says, "Arise, shine, for your light has come, and the glory of the Lord rises upon you. See, darkness covers the earth, and thick darkness is over the peoples, but the Lord rises upon you and His glory appears over you. Nations will come to your light, and kings to the brightness of your dawn." And in Acts 13:47, "For this is what the Lord has commanded us: 'I have made you a light for the Gentiles, that you may bring salvation to the ends of the earth.'" Continue to shine as His star, leading many to righteousness (Daniel 12:3 and Philippians 2:15).

ELLEN

Bright one

&

Psalm 27:1 *The Lord is my light and my salvation—whom shall I fear? The Lord is the stronghold of my life; of whom shall I be afraid.*

Proverbs 4:18 *The path of the righteous is like the first gleam of dawn, shining ever brighter till the full light of day.*

You are one who reflects the shining brightness of the countenance of Jesus. You are aggressive toward the fruitless deeds of darkness from the evil one, by exposing them to the light of Jesus. Everything exposed by light becomes visible, for it is the light that makes everything visible (Ephesians 5:11-14). This radiance that God has given you serves as a beacon to give guidance to those yet in darkness. Your life's mission is found in the following two verses: Isaiah 60:1-3 says, "Arise, shine, for your light has come, and the glory of the Lord rises upon you. See, darkness covers the earth, and thick darkness is over the peoples, but the Lord rises upon you and His glory appears over you. Nations will come to your light, and kings to the brightness of your dawn." And in Acts 13:47, "For this is what the Lord has commanded us: 'I have made you a light for the Gentiles, that you may bring salvation to the ends of the earth.'" Continue to shine as His star, leading many to righteousness (Daniel 12:3 and Philippians 2:15).

EMILY

Industrious; diligent one

જી

Colossians 1:16 *For by Him all things were created: things in heaven and on earth, visible and invisible, whether thrones or powers or rulers or authorities; all things were created by Him and for Him.*

Ephesians 2:10 *For we are God's workmanship, created in Christ Jesus to do good works, which God prepared in advance for us to do.*

To be industrious means to be skillful, hardworking, zealous, and diligent. By persevering, you give careful attention to detail. There is not a lazy bone in your body. Through you the Lord will originate. How you deal with the past determines your future. Regardless of the curses or blessings, the failures or successes, you are God's platform for a "new thing." You cannot lean on your own understanding or reasoning. God Almighty created the heavens, the earth, and you in His image. So the more completely dependent you become on your Creator, the more productive your life will be for Him! I Peter 4:19, "So then, those who suffer according to God's will should commit themselves to their Creator and continue to do good."

EMMA

Nurse; caring one

Isaiah 41:10   *So do not fear, for I am with you; do not be dismayed, for I am your God. I will strength you and help you; I will uphold you with My righteous right hand.*

I Corinthians 15:58   *Therefore, my dear brothers, stand firm. Let nothing move you. Always give yourselves fully to the work of the Lord, because you know that your labor in the Lord is not in vain.*

You say with confidence that the Lord is your helper. You are not afraid. What can man do to you (Hebrews 13:6)? This trust allows you the important role of being God's hands extended to your world. You serve with the strength He provides so that He gets all the credit (I Peter 4:11). Like the good Samaritan, you are moved with compassion to give practical help, providing sacrifice and kindness with unselfishness (Luke 10:25–37). You are eyes to the blind, feet to the lame, and the father to the needy (Job 29:15–16). You make the most of every opportunity to do good to all people (Galatians 6:10). As a caring one, you are cautious in avoiding mistakes and very attentive to details. His compassion flowing to and through you equips you to show concern for the neglected and indifferent. The complacent will be challenged to release their burdens and worries to the burden bearer, Jesus Christ. The Good Shepherd will continue to nurture you as you nurture others. Because you are devoted to the service of the Lord, you will hear, "Well done, good and faithful servant! You have been faithful with a few things; I will put you in charge of many things. Come and share your master's happiness!" (Matthew 25:23)

EMMANUEL

God with us; God's faithfulness

⅋

Proverbs 2:7–8   *He holds victory in store for the upright, He is a shield to those whose walk is blameless, for He guards the course of the just and protects the way of His faithful ones.*

Psalm 15:1–5   *Lord, who may dwell in Your sanctuary? Who may live on Your holy hill? He whose walk is blameless and who does what is righteous, who speaks the truth from his heart and has no slander on his tongue, who does his neighbor no wrong and casts no slur on his fellow man, who despises a vile man but honors those who fear the Lord, who keeps his oath even when it hurts, who lends his money without usury and does not accept a bribe against the innocent. He who does these things will never be shaken.*

You are one who has made a commitment to God to be loyal, true, dependable, enduring, and steadfast. You unmask anything fake with the reality of God's Word. You are aggressive towards lies and deception to bring about truth. You are especially sensitive to betrayal, so that God can restore hope, security, purpose, and His faithfulness in those whom He has given you to serve. "Be faithful, even to the point of death, and I will give you a crown of life," Revelation 2:10. Anticipate the Master saying to you, "Well done, good and faithful servant! You have been faithful with a few things; I will put you in charge of many things. Come and share your Master's happiness!" (Matthew 25:21) "The one who calls you is faithful and he will do it," I Thessalonians 5:24.

ERIC

Ever powerful ruler; Godly power

ॐ

Deuteronomy 28:13   *The Lord will make you the head, not the tail. If you pay attention to the commands of the Lord your God that I give you this day and carefully follow them, you will always be at the top, never at the bottom.*

Mark 10:43–45   *...Whoever wants to become great among you must be your servant, and whoever wants to be first must be slave of all. For even the Son of Man did not come to be served, but to serve, and to give His life as a ransom for many.*

You have been set apart with vision and perspective to reproduce the likeness of Christ in others by reflecting His image. You are guided by principles and values worth dying for. You know how to balance transparency with being an example. You are one who is secure enough to be vulnerable. You do not lead to gather followers; you lead to develop leaders. You lead by honoring God with authority, influence, direction, foresight, and skill. Your credible choices set a precedence for favor. You earn trust by your willingness to confront and bring discipline in a Godly manner. You are strong enough to let your "yes" be "yes" and your "no" be "no," with no compromise or jealousy. Your strength is determined by your submitted and teachable servant's heart. The more you mature, the more humble, gentle, and meek you will become. With integrity you communicate love, affirmation, nurturing, and spiritual care. If you as a shepherd ever forget what it is like to be a sheep, you will become a hireling. Your highest aim is to honor and glorify God.

ERICA

Ever powerful ruler; Godly power

৪৩

Deuteronomy 28:13 *The Lord will make you the head, not the tail. If you pay attention to the commands of the Lord your God that I give you this day and carefully follow them, you will always be at the top, never at the bottom.*

Mark 10:43–45 *...Whoever wants to become great among you must be your servant, and whoever wants to be first must be slave of all. For even the Son of Man did not come to be served, but to serve, and to give His life as a ransom for many.*

You have been set apart with vision and perspective to reproduce the likeness of Christ in others by reflecting His image. You are guided by principles and values worth dying for. You know how to balance transparency with being an example. You are one who is secure enough to be vulnerable. You do not lead to gather followers; you lead to develop leaders. You lead by honoring God with authority, influence, direction, foresight, and skill. Your credible choices set a precedence for favor. You earn trust by your willingness to confront and bring discipline in a Godly manner. You are strong enough to let your "yes" be "yes" and your "no" be "no," with no compromise or jealousy. Your strength is determined by your submitted and teachable servant's heart. The more you mature, the more humble, gentle, and meek you will become. With integrity you communicate love, affirmation, nurturing, and spiritual care. If you as a shepherd ever forget what it is like to be a sheep, you will become a hireling. Your highest aim is to honor and glorify God.

ERIN

Peace; deliverer of peace

ℰℰ

Isaiah 26:3 *You will keep in perfect peace him whose mind is steadfast, because he trusts in You.*

Philippians 4:7 *And the peace of God, which transcends all understanding, will guard your hearts and your minds in Christ Jesus.*

Your life defines peace. You will have a content and calm composure in the midst of distress, disturbance, or agitation. As you follow the Prince of Peace, you will be secure in who you are in Christ. The discipline of keeping your mind on Christ, loving God's law, and being controlled by the Holy Spirit will keep you in perfect peace. God's peace will serve as an umpire to determine whether you are safe or out of God's will (Colossians 3:15). Do not think it strange when you are in battles, fights, and quarrels, because God wants to use you to bring harmony, order, unity, agreement, quietness, and calmness to the adverse situation. You are one whose intimate friendship with the Lord brings reconciliation to the offended, distressed, and troubled. "In repentance and rest is your salvation, in quietness and trust is your strength," Isaiah 30:15. Your refreshing comes as you renew your mind daily in the Word of God. "Great peace have they who love Your law, and nothing can make them stumble," Psalm 119:165.

ERNEST

Earnest one; vigorous spirit

෨

Psalm 63:1, 5, 8   *My soul thirsts for You. My soul will be satisfied. My soul clings to you.*

I Corinthians 15:58   *Therefore, my dear brothers, stand firm. Let nothing move you. Always give yourselves fully to the work of the Lord, because you know that your labor is not in vain.*

Your very being lives to be in constant harmony with your Creator; that both of your hearts beat as one. Therefore, you are continually yielding every area to the likeness of Christ with strong discipline. You have a devoted allegiance to Christ and his teachings. Your character is one of devotion, dedication, consecration, loyalty, and faithfulness. You are called to help the fallen take a stand, and to remove shame and fear. You dispel division by bringing the very unity of God. As you seek and trust in Him with all your heart, leaning not to your own understanding, He will protect you from being blind-sided by the enemy of your soul. Be known as one who loves God with all your heart, soul, mind, and strength.

ESTHER

A star; humility of spirit

&

Micah 6:8 *He has showed you, O man, what is good. And what does the Lord require of you? To act justly and to love mercy and to walk humbly with your God.*

I Peter 5:6 *Humble yourselves, therefore, under God's mighty hand, that He may lift you up in due time.*

Prove to be trustworthy over little and God will make you ruler over much (Luke 19:17). The higher you lift the Lord, the more dependent you will be on Him. He increases; you decrease (John 3:30). Being exalted only comes from God—not from you or anyone else. It is for the purpose of enlarging His kingdom. Take no credit for the enormous favor God will give you. It is His grace that will give entrance to these doors of favor, as you choose His approval over man's. Philippians 2:3 says, "Do nothing out of selfish ambition or vain conceit, but in humility consider others better than yourselves." Humility and the fear of the Lord bring wealth, honor, and life (Proverbs 22:4).

ETHAN

Firm; steadfast heart

❧

Job 23:11 *My feet have closely followed His steps; I have kept to His way without turning aside.*

James 1:12 *Blessed is the man who perseveres under trial, because when he has stood the test, he will receive the crown of life that God has promised to those who love Him.*

You stand firm without fear. You lift up your face without shame. Your uncompromised commitment to Jesus Christ makes you firmly fixed on His promises. Your mind is steadfast and you are kept in peace because you trust God (Isaiah 26:3). You prepare your mind for action, are self-controlled, and set your hope fully on the grace to be given you when Jesus Christ is revealed (I Peter 1:13). Through you, God brings His stability to the wavering. Your message is, "Finish well, endure hardship, persevere to the end, and reach your goal!"

EUGENE

Well-born; noble

❧

Isaiah 32:8 *But the noble man makes noble plans, and by noble deeds he stands.*

Luke 8:15 *But the seed on good soil stands for those with a noble and good heart, who hear the word, retain it, and by persevering produce a crop.*

Proverbs 18:12 says, "Before his downfall a man's heart is proud, but humility comes before honor." You are one who has a humble confidence in recognizing and expressing reverence, worship, adoration, trust, deference, tribute, admiration, and respect. This is the result of being secure in the truth of who you are in the Lord. Through humility, King Jesus made a way for you to be engrafted into His royalty. He made of Himself no reputation and took on the nature of a servant (Philippians 2:7) to affirm your value. Through self-denial, you prioritize excellence in virtue, truthfulness, and faithfulness. Because of the respect you have earned, you dismantle inferiority, disgrace, shame, and offenses. No one feels second-rate in your presence. The deeper that the Lord is your object of reverence, the greater your confidence will be in giving approval and worth. Because you are tall in spirit, your face is always turned upward.

EVA

Life; full of life

ॐ

John 14:6 *Jesus answered, I am the way and the truth and the life. No one comes to the Father except through Me.*

Deuteronomy 30:19–20 *This day I call heaven and earth as witnesses against you that I have set before you life and death, blessings and curses. Now choose life, so that you and your children may live and that you may love the Lord your God, listen to His voice, and hold fast to Him. For the Lord is your life, and He will give you many years in the land He swore to give to your fathers, Abraham, Isaac, and Jacob.*

Your life's purpose is to serve God, seek His kingdom, do the Father's will, finish the divine task, complete the course joyfully, and attain Christ-likeness. You throw a life-line to those with a death sentence—those who are weary, disgusted, bitter, empty, barren, oppressed, and isolated. With your focus kept on eternal rather than temporal values, you will bring Christ's resurrection power to hearts in the grave. The very gates of hell cannot prevail and be strong enough to stand up under the direct attack of the church. Colossians 3:1–4 says, "Since, then, you have been raised with Christ, set your hearts on things above, not on earthly things. For you died, and your life is now hidden with Christ in God. When Christ, who is your life, appears, then you also will appear with Him in glory." I Samuel 25:29 says, "Your life will be bound securely in the bundle of the living by the Lord your God. But the lives of your enemies He will hurl away as from the pocket of a sling." Psalm 27:1 says, "The Lord is the stronghold of your life—of whom shall you be afraid?" Enjoy life to the fullest! (John 10:10)

EVAN

God is gracious; God's gift

৪১

Romans 8:32   *He who did not spare His own Son, but gave Him up for us all—how will He not also, along with Him, graciously give us all things?*

I Corinthians 15:10   *But by the grace of God I am what I am, and His grace to me was not without effect.*

Ephesians 2:8 says, "For it is by grace you have been saved, through faith—and this is not from yourselves, it is the gift of God." You are one who brings about balance and harmony through mercy, forgiveness, approval, kindness, and patience—all with a grateful heart. This attitude of gratitude will rule in the midst of inconsiderate behavior. Your nature defies the law of the Pharisees, and is against being self-reliant, prejudice, and selfish. Being full of grace is devotion built through faithfulness and a willingness to quickly pardon. You are blessed with creativity in expressing God's greatest gift of grace—the life of His only Son, Jesus Christ. God says to you through Jeremiah 24:7, "I will give them a heart to know Me, that I am the Lord. They will be My people, and I will be their God, for they will return to Me with all their heart." Ezekiel 11:19 says, "I will give them an undivided heart and put a new spirit in them; I will remove from them their heart of stone and give them a heart of flesh." Accountability will keep your report accurate and your integrity irreproachable.

EVANGELINE

Bearer of good news; messenger of truth

Psalm 89:1–2   *I will sing of the Lord's great love forever; with my mouth I will make Your faithfulness known through all generations. I will declare that Your love stands firm forever, that You established Your faithfulness in heaven itself.*

Psalm 51:6   *Surely You desire truth in the inner parts; You teach me wisdom in the inmost place.*

John 14:6   *Jesus answered, "I am the way and the truth and the life. No one comes to the Father except through Me."*

"You know the truth and the truth has set you free," John 8:32. You are one who is aggressive toward lies and deception. Your purpose is to bring about truth through openness, revelation, authenticity, accuracy, and honesty. As God's messenger, you will have firmness in keeping and executing His promises and also your own. Your God-given wisdom will be based on God's Word alone. Zechariah 8:16 says, "These are the things you are to do: Speak the truth to each other, and render true and sound judgment in your courts." May true instruction be in your mouth and nothing false be found on your lips (Malachi 2:6).

EZRA

Helper; a strong supporter

❧

Deuteronomy 33:27 *The eternal God is your refuge, and underneath are the everlasting arms. He will drive out your enemy before you, saying, "Destroy him!"*

Isaiah 46:4 *Even to your old age and gray hairs I am He, I am He who will sustain you. I have made you and I will carry you; I will sustain you and I will rescue you.*

A support holds up a structure with a firm foundation. God gives you help and approval through blessing, comfort, encouragement, friendship, loyalty, and protection. When you face tough times, God will carry you on eagles' wings and hold you close to Himself (Exodus 19:4). He will stoop to whatever level you are to make you great (Psalm 18:35). Not only are you upheld by His righteous right hand (Isaiah 41:10), but you uphold others. You serve as a mainstay to strengthen and uphold; to build up and reinforce. This endurance brings wholeness to all those you touch. II Timothy 2:19 says, "Nevertheless, God's solid foundation stands firm, sealed with this inscription: 'The Lord knows those who are His,'" and, "Everyone who confesses the name of the Lord must turn away from wickedness."

FAITH

Belief and faith in God; loyalty, fidelity, trustful

&

Proverbs 2:7–8   *He holds victory in store for the upright, He is a shield to those whose walk is blameless, for He guards the course of the just and protects the way of His faithful ones.*

Hebrews 11:1   *Now faith is being sure of what we hope for and certain of what we do not see.*

Because you believe in Jesus Christ, you have eternal life (John 3:15). Faith must be accompanied by action in order to bring life (James 2:17). You are one who has made a commitment to God to be loyal, true, dependable, enduring, and steadfast. Your ultimate purpose is to please God in all you do, for you know without faith it is impossible (Hebrews 11:6). Everything is possible for him who believes (Mark 9:23). You are confident that every one of His promises to you will be fulfilled. Your loyalty is shown by a steadfast devotion of an unquestioning kind. This is why you are especially sensitive to betrayal. This allows God to restore hope, security, purpose, and His faithfulness in those whom He has given you to serve. Your commitment is with singleness of heart and ready obedience. You are kept in perfect peace because your mind is steadfast and you trust in your God (Isaiah 26:3).

FAY

Belief and faith in God; loyalty, fidelity, trustful

∾

Proverbs 2:7–8 *He holds victory in store for the upright, He is a shield to those whose walk is blameless, for He guards the course of the just and protects the way of His faithful ones.*

Hebrews 11:1 *Now faith is being sure of what we hope for and certain of what we do not see.*

Because you believe in Jesus Christ, you have eternal life (John 3:15). Faith must be accompanied by action in order to bring life (James 2:17). You are one who has made a commitment to God to be loyal, true, dependable, enduring, and steadfast. Your ultimate purpose is to please God in all you do, for you know without faith it is impossible (Hebrews 11:6). Everything is possible for him who believes (Mark 9:23). You are confident that every one of His promises to you will be fulfilled. Your loyalty is shown by a steadfast devotion of an unquestioning kind. This is why you are especially sensitive to betrayal. This allows God to restore hope, security, purpose, and His faithfulness in those whom He has given you to serve. Your commitment is with singleness of heart and ready obedience. You are kept in perfect peace because your mind is steadfast and you trust in your God (Isaiah 26:3).

FAYTH

Belief and faith in God; loyalty, fidelity, trustful

&

Proverbs 2:7–8 *He holds victory in store for the upright, He is a shield to those whose walk is blameless, for He guards the course of the just and protects the way of His faithful ones.*

Hebrews 11:1 *Now faith is being sure of what we hope for and certain of what we do not see.*

Because you believe in Jesus Christ, you have eternal life (John 3:15). Faith must be accompanied by action in order to bring life (James 2:17). You are one who has made a commitment to God to be loyal, true, dependable, enduring, and steadfast. Your ultimate purpose is to please God in all you do, for you know without faith it is impossible (Hebrews 11:6). Everything is possible for him who believes (Mark 9:23). You are confident that every one of His promises to you will be fulfilled. Your loyalty is shown by a steadfast devotion of an unquestioning kind. This is why you are especially sensitive to betrayal. This allows God to restore hope, security, purpose, and His faithfulness in those whom He has given you to serve. Your commitment is with singleness of heart and ready obedience. You are kept in perfect peace because your mind is steadfast and you trust in your God (Isaiah 26:3).

FORREST

Woodsman; strong, manly

ॐ

Proverbs 24:5 *A wise man has great power, and a man of knowledge increases strength.*

Ephesians 6:10 *Finally, be strong in the Lord and in His mighty power.*

You are one who has an un-compromised commitment to righteousness, respectability, honesty, character, excellence, value, worth, kindness, innocence, generosity, trustworthiness, faithfulness, justice, hope, and love. You can do everything through Him who gives you strength (Philippians 4:11–13). The Lord is the source of your strength because you turn back the battle at the gate (Isaiah 28:6). You renew your strength by your hope being in the Lord (Isaiah 40:31). Jesus says, "My grace is sufficient for you, for My power is made perfect in weaknesses. Therefore you will boast all the more gladly about your weaknesses, so that Christ's power may rest on you. That is why for Christ's sake, you delight in weaknesses, in insults, in hardships, in persecutions, and in difficulties. For when you are weak, then you are strong," II Corinthians 12:9–10. You are clothed with strength and dignity (Proverbs 31:25).

FOSTER

Forester; strong, manly

કળ

Proverbs 24:5 *A wise man has great power, and a man of knowledge increases strength.*

Ephesians 6:10 *Finally, be strong in the Lord and in His mighty power.*

You are one who has an un-compromised commitment to righteousness, respectability, honesty, character, excellence, value, worth, kindness, innocence, generosity, trustworthiness, faithfulness, justice, hope, and love. You can do everything through Him who gives you strength (Philippians 4:11–13). The Lord is the source of your strength because you turn back the battle at the gate (Isaiah 28:6). You renew your strength by your hope being in the Lord (Isaiah 40:31). Jesus says, "My grace is sufficient for you, for My power is made perfect in weaknesses. Therefore you will boast all the more gladly about your weaknesses, so that Christ's power may rest on you. That is why for Christ's sake, you delight in weaknesses, in insults, in hardships, in persecutions, and in difficulties. For when you are weak, then you are strong," II Corinthians 12:9–10. You are clothed with strength and dignity (Proverbs 31:25).

FRANCES

Free one; living in freedom

&

Isaiah 61:1 *The Spirit of the Sovereign Lord is on me, because the Lord has anointed me to preach good news to the poor. He has sent me to bind up the brokenhearted, to proclaim freedom for the captives and release from darkness for the prisoners.*

Galatians 5:1 *It is for freedom that Christ has set us free. Stand firm, then, and do not let yourselves be burdened again by a yoke of slavery.*

There are no restrictions on your abandoned commitment to the Lord Jesus Christ. Knowing God's truth frees you from the bondage and care of sin and oppression (John 8:32). The free gift of God— Jesus Christ—exchanges offense for God's grace, condemnation for justification, shame for holiness and the spirit of the world for the Spirit of God. You are fearless as you loose those in bondage and give pardon to the imprisoned—all because the law of the Spirit of life set you free from the law of sin and death. Do not use your freedom to indulge the sinful nature; rather, serve one another in love (Galatians 5:13). Freely you have received; freely give (Matthew 10:8).

FRANCIS

Free one; living in freedom

❧

Isaiah 61:1 *The Spirit of the Sovereign Lord is on me, because the Lord has anointed me to preach good news to the poor. He has sent me to bind up the brokenhearted, to proclaim freedom for the captives and release from darkness for the prisoners.*

Galatians 5:1 *It is for freedom that Christ has set us free. Stand firm, then, and do not let yourselves be burdened again by a yoke of slavery.*

There are no restrictions on your abandoned commitment to the Lord Jesus Christ. Knowing God's truth frees you from the bondage and care of sin and oppression (John 8:32). The free gift of God—Jesus Christ—exchanges offense for God's grace, condemnation for justification, shame for holiness and the spirit of the world for the Spirit of God. You are fearless as you loose those in bondage and give pardon to the imprisoned—all because the law of the Spirit of life set you free from the law of sin and death. Do not use your freedom to indulge the sinful nature; rather, serve one another in love (Galatians 5:13). Freely you have received; freely give (Matthew 10:8).

FRANK

Free one; living in freedom

❧

Isaiah 61:1 *The Spirit of the Sovereign Lord is on me, because the Lord has anointed me to preach good news to the poor. He has sent me to bind up the brokenhearted, to proclaim freedom for the captives and release from darkness for the prisoners.*

Galatians 5:1 *It is for freedom that Christ has set us free. Stand firm, then, and do not let yourselves be burdened again by a yoke of slavery.*

There are no restrictions on your abandoned commitment to the Lord Jesus Christ. Knowing God's truth frees you from the bondage and care of sin and oppression (John 8:32). The free gift of God—Jesus Christ—exchanges offense for God's grace, condemnation for justification, shame for holiness and the spirit of the world for the Spirit of God. You are fearless as you loose those in bondage and give pardon to the imprisoned—all because the law of the Spirit of life set you free from the law of sin and death. Do not use your freedom to indulge the sinful nature; rather, serve one another in love (Galatians 5:13). Freely you have received; freely give (Matthew 10:8).

FRANKLIN

Free one; living in freedom

Isaiah 61:1 *The Spirit of the Sovereign Lord is on me, because the Lord has anointed me to preach good news to the poor. He has sent me to bind up the brokenhearted, to proclaim freedom for the captives and release from darkness for the prisoners.*

Galatians 5:1 *It is for freedom that Christ has set us free. Stand firm, then, and do not let yourselves be burdened again by a yoke of slavery.*

There are no restrictions on your abandoned commitment to the Lord Jesus Christ. Knowing God's truth frees you from the bondage and care of sin and oppression (John 8:32). The free gift of God—Jesus Christ—exchanges offense for God's grace, condemnation for justification, shame for holiness and the spirit of the world for the Spirit of God. You are fearless as you loose those in bondage and give pardon to the imprisoned—all because the law of the Spirit of life set you free from the law of sin and death. Do not use your freedom to indulge the sinful nature; rather, serve one another in love (Galatians 5:13). Freely you have received; freely give (Matthew 10:8).

FRED

Peaceful ruler; peaceful

ಐ

Isaiah 26:3 *You will keep in perfect peace him whose mind is steadfast, because he trusts in You.*

Philippians 4:7 *And the peace of God, which transcends all understanding, will guard your hearts and your minds in Christ Jesus.*

Your life defines peace. You will have a content and calm composure in the midst of distress, disturbance, or agitation. As you follow the Prince of Peace, you will be secure in who you are in Christ. The discipline of keeping your mind on Christ, loving God's law, and being controlled by the Holy Spirit will keep you in perfect peace. God's peace will serve as an umpire to determine whether you are safe or out of God's will (Colossians 3:15). Do not think it strange when you are in battles, fights, and quarrels, because God wants to use you to bring harmony, order, unity, agreement, quietness, and calmness to the adverse situation. You are one whose intimate friendship with the Lord brings reconciliation to the offended, distressed, and troubled. "In repentance and rest is your salvation, in quietness and trust is your strength," Isaiah 30:15. Your refreshing comes as you renew your mind daily in the Word of God. "Great peace have they who love Your law, and nothing can make them stumble," Psalm 119:165.

FREDERICK

Peaceful ruler; peaceful

ℰ

Isaiah 26:3 *You will keep in perfect peace him whose mind is steadfast, because he trusts in You.*

Philippians 4:7 *And the peace of God, which transcends all understanding, will guard your hearts and your minds in Christ Jesus.*

Your life defines peace. You will have a content and calm composure in the midst of distress, disturbance, or agitation. As you follow the Prince of Peace, you will be secure in who you are in Christ. The discipline of keeping your mind on Christ, loving God's law, and being controlled by the Holy Spirit will keep you in perfect peace. God's peace will serve as an umpire to determine whether you are safe or out of God's will (Colossians 3:15). Do not think it strange when you are in battles, fights, and quarrels, because God wants to use you to bring harmony, order, unity, agreement, quietness, and calmness to the adverse situation. You are one whose intimate friendship with the Lord brings reconciliation to the offended, distressed, and troubled. "In repentance and rest is your salvation, in quietness and trust is your strength," Isaiah 30:15. Your refreshing comes as you renew your mind daily in the Word of God. "Great peace have they who love Your law, and nothing can make them stumble," Psalm 119:165.

GABE

Man of God; God is my strength

❧

Proverbs 24:5 *A wise man has great power, and a man of knowledge increases strength.*

Ephesians 6:10 *Finally, be strong in the Lord and in His mighty power.*

You are one who has an un-compromised commitment to righteousness, respectability, honesty, character, excellence, value, worth, kindness, innocence, generosity, trustworthiness, faithfulness, justice, hope, and love. You can do everything through Him who gives you strength (Philippians 4:11–13). The Lord is the source of your strength because you turn back the battle at the gate (Isaiah 28:6). You renew your strength by your hope being in the Lord (Isaiah 40:31). Jesus says, "My grace is sufficient for you, for My power is made perfect in weaknesses. Therefore you will boast all the more gladly about your weaknesses, so that Christ's power may rest on you. That is why for Christ's sake, you delight in weaknesses, in insults, in hardships, in persecutions, and in difficulties. For when you are weak, then you are strong," II Corinthians 12:9–10. You are clothed with strength and dignity (Proverbs 31:25).

GABRIEL

Man of God; God is my strength

ℰ

Proverbs 24:5 *A wise man has great power, and a man of knowledge increases strength.*

Ephesians 6:10 *Finally, be strong in the Lord and in His mighty power.*

You are one who has an un-compromised commitment to righteousness, respectability, honesty, character, excellence, value, worth, kindness, innocence, generosity, trustworthiness, faithfulness, justice, hope, and love. You can do everything through Him who gives you strength (Philippians 4:11–13). The Lord is the source of your strength because you turn back the battle at the gate (Isaiah 28:6). You renew your strength by your hope being in the Lord (Isaiah 40:31). Jesus says, "My grace is sufficient for you, for My power is made perfect in weaknesses. Therefore you will boast all the more gladly about your weaknesses, so that Christ's power may rest on you. That is why for Christ's sake, you delight in weaknesses, in insults, in hardships, in persecutions, and in difficulties. For when you are weak, then you are strong," II Corinthians 12:9–10. You are clothed with strength and dignity (Proverbs 31:25).

GAIL

Father rejoices; source of joy

ॐ

Psalm 149:4–5 *For the Lord takes delight in His people; He crowns the humble with salvation. Let the saints rejoice in this honor and sing for joy on their beds.*

Psalm 45:7 *You love righteousness and hate wickedness; therefore God, your God, has set you above your companions by anointing you with the oil of joy.*

Psalm 16:11 says, "You have made known to me the path of life; You will fill me with joy in Your presence, with eternal pleasures at Your right hand." Your heavenly Father has trusted you with a quality that releases healing, restores hope, and brings refreshing. You are one who takes the source of tears and defeat, and turns them into confident trust with rejoicing. As you experience and remain sensitive to the things that sorrow the heart of God, He will pour His oil of joy on and through you to restore hope to those who are mourning (Isaiah 61:1–3). Experiences of sorrow prepare and enlarge your capacity for joy. The joy of the Lord will be your strength to endure the cross He has called you to bear. You are to fix your eyes on Jesus, the author and perfecter of your faith, who for the joy set before Him endured the cross, scorning its shame, and sat down at the right hand of the throne of God (Hebrews 12:2). He will be faithful to give you a song in your "night" season (Psalm 42:8). God rejoices over you with gladness! (Zephaniah 3:17)

GALE

Father rejoices; source of joy

ଚ୍ଚ

Psalm 149:4–5 *For the Lord takes delight in His people; He crowns the humble with salvation. Let the saints rejoice in this honor and sing for joy on their beds.*

Psalm 45:7 *You love righteousness and hate wickedness; therefore God, your God, has set you above your companions by anointing you with the oil of joy.*

Psalm 16:11 says, "You have made known to me the path of life; You will fill me with joy in Your presence, with eternal pleasures at Your right hand." Your heavenly Father has trusted you with a quality that releases healing, restores hope, and brings refreshing. You are one who takes the source of tears and defeat, and turns them into confident trust with rejoicing. As you experience and remain sensitive to the things that sorrow the heart of God, He will pour His oil of joy on and through you to restore hope to those who are mourning (Isaiah 61:1–3). Experiences of sorrow prepare and enlarge your capacity for joy. The joy of the Lord will be your strength to endure the cross He has called you to bear. You are to fix your eyes on Jesus, the author and perfecter of your faith, who for the joy set before Him endured the cross, scorning its shame, and sat down at the right hand of the throne of God (Hebrews 12:2). He will be faithful to give you a song in your "night" season (Psalm 42:8). God rejoices over you with gladness! (Zephaniah 3:17)

GARRETT

Gentle; courteous spirit

Titus 3:4–5 *But when the kindness and love of God our Savior appeared, He saved us, not because of righteous things we had done, but because of His mercy.*

I Peter 3:8–9 *Finally, all of you, live in harmony with one another; be sympathetic, love as brothers, be compassionate and humble. Do not repay evil with evil or insult with insult, but with blessing, because to this you were called so that you may inherit a blessing.*

God first, others next, and you last. With a servant's heart and a humble mind, you extend the gracious approval of the Lord. This graciousness springs from an inherit thoughtfulness and consideration. Through you, God defines good manners and politeness. You are hospitable to the shipwrecked (Acts 28:7) and you bring divine connection for needs to be provided (Acts 27:3). Because you are attentive to details, the broken are dealt with gently. The rejected are shown kindness and the humble are given honor. Your conversation is always full of grace and seasoned with salt (Colossians 4:6). The behavior of the rude and impolite are corrected because you will not be misled. You know that bad company corrupts good character (I Corinthians 15:33). You show respect to all because of your willingness to value the opinion of another and overlook an offense (Proverbs 19:11). Like Jesus, you are a friend of the publicans and sinners (Luke 7:34).

GARY

Spear; man of loyalty

ᑌ

Romans 12:9–10 *Love must be sincere. Hate what is evil; cling to what is good. Be devoted to one another in brotherly love. Honor one another above yourselves.*

Proverbs 2:7–8 *He holds victory in store for the upright, He is a shield to those whose walk is blameless, for He guards the course of the just and protects the way of His faithful ones.*

As one with a loyal spirit, the Lord has called you to be faithful, devoted, obedient, dependable, and true. You are noble in disarming the enemy's attacks of fear, selfishness, failure, betrayal, dishonesty, and faithlessness. You are unyielding and have a resolute confidence in your commitment to God's Word. With it, you will help others overcome being cowards, losers, quitters, or betrayers. Knowing God's loyalty to you will strengthen your loyalty to others. Isaiah 1:17 says, "Learn to do right! Seek justice, encourage the oppressed. Defend the cause of the fatherless, plead the case of the widow."

GAVIN

White hawk; fully satisfied

ℰℐ

Proverbs 15:16 *Better a little with the fear of the Lord than great wealth with turmoil.*

Hebrews 13:5 *Keep your lives free from the love of money and be content with what you have, because God has said, "Never will I leave you; never will I forsake you."*

You have learned to be content whatever the circumstances. Your attitude is governed by God, not by outward situations. You know what it is to be in need and you know what it is to have plenty. You have learned the secret of being content in any and every situation, whether well fed or hungry, living in plenty or in want. You can do everything through Him who gives you strength (Philippians 4:11–13). The Lord is your source of strength because you turn back the battle at the gate (Isaiah 28:6). You renew your strength because your hope is in the Lord (Isaiah 40:31). Jesus says, "My grace is sufficient for you, for my power is made perfect in weakness. Therefore, you will boast all the more gladly about your weaknesses, so that Christ's power may rest on you. That is why, for Christ's sake, you delight in weaknesses, in insults, in hardships, in persecutions, and in difficulties. For when you are weak, then you are strong," II Corinthians 12:9–10. Contentment is God's guide to His will for you. You give rest to the weary, truth to those who murmur, peace to the dissatisfied, and quietness to the troubled.

GAY

Father rejoices; source of joy

ॐ

Psalm 149:4–5 *For the Lord takes delight in His people; He crowns the humble with salvation. Let the saints rejoice in this honor and sing for joy on their beds.*

Psalm 45:7 *You love righteousness and hate wickedness; therefore God, your God, has set you above your companions by anointing you with the oil of joy.*

Psalm 16:11 says, "You have made known to me the path of life; You will fill me with joy in Your presence, with eternal pleasures at Your right hand." Your heavenly Father has trusted you with a quality that releases healing, restores hope, and brings refreshing. You are one who takes the source of tears and defeat, and turns them into confident trust with rejoicing. As you experience and remain sensitive to the things that sorrow the heart of God, He will pour His oil of joy on and through you to restore hope to those who are mourning (Isaiah 61:1–3). Experiences of sorrow prepare and enlarge your capacity for joy. The joy of the Lord will be your strength to endure the cross He has called you to bear. You are to fix your eyes on Jesus, the author and perfecter of your faith, who for the joy set before Him endured the cross, scorning its shame, and sat down at the right hand of the throne of God (Hebrews 12:2). He will be faithful to give you a song in your "night" season (Psalm 42:8). God rejoices over you with gladness! (Zephaniah 3:17)

GAYLE

Father rejoices; source of joy

&

Psalm 149:4–5 For the Lord takes delight in His people; He crowns the humble with salvation. Let the saints rejoice in this honor and sing for joy on their beds.

Psalm 45:7 You love righteousness and hate wickedness; therefore God, your God, has set you above your companions by anointing you with the oil of joy.

Psalm 16:11 says, "You have made known to me the path of life; You will fill me with joy in Your presence, with eternal pleasures at Your right hand." Your heavenly Father has trusted you with a quality that releases healing, restores hope, and brings refreshing. You are one who takes the source of tears and defeat, and turns them into confident trust with rejoicing. As you experience and remain sensitive to the things that sorrow the heart of God, He will pour His oil of joy on and through you to restore hope to those who are mourning (Isaiah 61:1–3). Experiences of sorrow prepare and enlarge your capacity for joy. The joy of the Lord will be your strength to endure the cross He has called you to bear. You are to fix your eyes on Jesus, the author and perfecter of your faith, who for the joy set before Him endured the cross, scorning its shame, and sat down at the right hand of the throne of God (Hebrews 12:2). He will be faithful to give you a song in your "night" season (Psalm 42:8). God rejoices over you with gladness! (Zephaniah 3:17)

GENE

Well born; noble

ॐ

Isaiah 32:8 *But the noble man makes noble plans, and by noble deeds he stands.*

Luke 8:15 *But the seed on good soil stands for those with a noble and good heart, who hear the word, retain it, and by persevering produce a crop.*

Proverbs 18:12 says, "Before his downfall a man's heart is proud, but humility comes before honor." You are one who has a humble confidence in recognizing and expressing reverence, worship, adoration, trust, deference, tribute, admiration, and respect. This is the result of being secure in the truth of who you are in the Lord. Through humility, King Jesus made a way for you to be engrafted into His royalty. He made of Himself no reputation and took on the nature of a servant (Philippians 2:7) to affirm your value. Through self-denial, you prioritize excellence in virtue, truthfulness, and faithfulness. Because of the respect you have earned, you dismantle inferiority, disgrace, shame, and offenses. No one feels second-rate in your presence. The deeper that the Lord is your object of reverence, the greater your confidence will be in giving approval and worth. Because you are tall in spirit, your face is always turned upward.

GEORGE

Farmer; industrious

৪০

Colossians 1:16 *For by Him all things were created: things in heaven and on earth, visible and invisible, whether thrones or powers or rulers or authorities; all things were created by Him and for Him.*

Ephesians 2:10 *For we are God's workmanship, created in Christ Jesus to do good works, which God prepared in advance for us to do.*

To be industrious means to be skillful, hardworking, zealous, and diligent. By persevering, you give careful attention to detail. There is not a lazy bone in your body. Through you the Lord will originate. How you deal with the past determines your future. Regardless of the curses or blessings, the failures or successes, you are God's platform for a "new thing." You cannot lean on your own understanding or reasoning. God Almighty created the heavens, the earth, and you in His image. So the more completely dependent you become on your Creator, the more productive your life will be for Him! I Peter 4:19, "So then, those who suffer according to God's will should commit themselves to their Creator and continue to do good."

GEORGIA

Farmer; industrious

❧

Colossians 1:16 *For by Him all things were created: things in heaven and on earth, visible and invisible, whether thrones or powers or rulers or authorities; all things were created by Him and for Him.*

Ephesians 2:10 *For we are God's workmanship, created in Christ Jesus to do good works, which God prepared in advance for us to do.*

To be industrious means to be skillful, hardworking, zealous, and diligent. By persevering, you give careful attention to detail. There is not a lazy bone in your body. Through you the Lord will originate. How you deal with the past determines your future. Regardless of the curses or blessings, the failures or successes, you are God's platform for a "new thing." You cannot lean on your own understanding or reasoning. God Almighty created the heavens, the earth, and you in His image. So the more completely dependent you become on your Creator, the more productive your life will be for Him! I Peter 4:19, "So then, those who suffer according to God's will should commit themselves to their Creator and continue to do good."

GEORGIE

Farmer; industrious

ℰↄ

Colossians 1:16 *For by Him all things were created: things in heaven and on earth, visible and invisible, whether thrones or powers or rulers or authorities; all things were created by Him and for Him.*

Ephesians 2:10 *For we are God's workmanship, created in Christ Jesus to do good works, which God prepared in advance for us to do.*

To be industrious means to be skillful, hardworking, zealous, and diligent. By persevering, you give careful attention to detail. There is not a lazy bone in your body. Through you the Lord will originate. How you deal with the past determines your future. Regardless of the curses or blessings, the failures or successes, you are God's platform for a "new thing." You cannot lean on your own understanding or reasoning. God Almighty created the heavens, the earth, and you in His image. So the more completely dependent you become on your Creator, the more productive your life will be for Him! I Peter 4:19, "So then, those who suffer according to God's will should commit themselves to their Creator and continue to do good."

GERALD

Spear; God's warrior

❦

II Chronicles 32:7–8   *There is a greater power with us than with him. With him is only the arm of flesh, but with us is the Lord our God to help us and to fight our battles.*

II Timothy 2:3–4   *Endure hardship with us like a good soldier of Christ Jesus. No one serving as a soldier gets involved in civilian affairs - he wants to please his commanding officer.*

Exodus 14:14 says, "The Lord will fight for you; you need only be still." You are armed with the ability to handle the spear and shield—to stand on God's Word by faith, supporting the King of kings against His enemies. As God's defending warrior, you are His example of a brave champion, soldier, and hero. The ultimate war was a contest with death and when Christ said, "It is finished" on the cross, He declared victory over death, hell, and the grave. You are equipped to be used of God as one who protects by warding off attacks, calling for justice, and providing shelter. When God is all of this to you, you will be that vindication for others. Because of your faith in Jesus Christ, you will ever be aggressive towards the enemy's tools of defeat, failure, and victimization. Your ultimate purpose is to be one who stands in the gap (Ezekiel 22:30) as a defender of the weak. This includes those who are easily influenced, confused, quitters, faint, frail, fragile, and frightened. Your primary spiritual warfare will be that of brave intercession—reaching, meeting, and entreating God for His favor to set the captives free. Then you will "learn to do right! Seek justice, encourage the oppressed. Defend the cause of the fatherless, plead the case of the widow," Isaiah 1:17.

GERRY

Spear; God's warrior

&

II Chronicles 32:7–8 *There is a greater power with us than with him. With him is only the arm of flesh, but with us is the Lord our God to help us and to fight our battles.*

II Timothy 2:3–4 *Endure hardship with us like a good soldier of Christ Jesus. No one serving as a soldier gets involved in civilian affairs - he wants to please his commanding officer.*

Exodus 14:14 says, "The Lord will fight for you; you need only be still." You are armed with the ability to handle the spear and shield—to stand on God's Word by faith, supporting the King of kings against His enemies. As God's defending warrior, you are His example of a brave champion, soldier, and hero. The ultimate war was a contest with death and when Christ said, "It is finished" on the cross, He declared victory over death, hell, and the grave. You are equipped to be used of God as one who protects by warding off attacks, calling for justice, and providing shelter. When God is all of this to you, you will be that vindication for others. Because of your faith in Jesus Christ, you will ever be aggressive towards the enemy's tools of defeat, failure, and victimization. Your ultimate purpose is to be one who stands in the gap (Ezekiel 22:30) as a defender of the weak. This includes those who are easily influenced, confused, quitters, faint, frail, fragile, and frightened. Your primary spiritual warfare will be that of brave intercession—reaching, meeting, and entreating God for His favor to set the captives free. Then you will "learn to do right! Seek justice, encourage the oppressed. Defend the cause of the fatherless, plead the case of the widow," Isaiah 1:17.

GIANNA

God is gracious; God's gracious gift

Romans 8:32 *He who did not spare His own Son, but gave Him up for us all—how will He not also, along with Him, graciously give us all things?*

I Corinthians 15:10 *But by the grace of God I am what I am, and His grace to me was not without effect.*

Ephesians 2:8 says, "For it is by grace you have been saved, through faith—and this is not from yourselves, it is the gift of God." You are one who brings about balance and harmony through mercy, forgiveness, approval, kindness, and patience—all with a grateful heart. This attitude of gratitude will rule in the midst of inconsiderate behavior. Your nature defies the law of the Pharisees, and is against being self-reliant, prejudice, and selfish. Being full of grace is devotion built through faithfulness and a willingness to quickly pardon. You are blessed with creativity in expressing God's greatest gift of grace—the life of His only Son, Jesus Christ. God says to you through Jeremiah 24:7, "I will give them a heart to know Me, that I am the Lord. They will be My people, and I will be their God, for they will return to Me with all their heart." Ezekiel 11:19 says, "I will give them an undivided heart and put a new spirit in them; I will remove from them their heart of stone and give them a heart of flesh." Accountability will keep your report accurate and your integrity irreproachable.

GINA

A queen; of humble heart

Isaiah 32:8 *But the noble man makes noble plans, and by noble deeds he stands.*

Luke 8:15 *But the seed on good soil stands for those with a noble and good heart, who hear the word, retain it, and by persevering produce a crop.*

Proverbs 18:12 says, "Before his downfall a man's heart is proud, but humility comes before honor." You are one who has a humble confidence in recognizing and expressing reverence, worship, adoration, trust, deference, tribute, admiration, and respect. This is the result of being secure in the truth of who you are in the Lord. Through humility, King Jesus made a way for you to be engrafted into His royalty. He made of Himself no reputation and took on the nature of a servant (Philippians 2:7) to affirm your value. Through self-denial, you prioritize excellence in virtue, truthfulness, and faithfulness. Because of the respect you have earned, you dismantle inferiority, disgrace, shame, and offenses. No one feels second-rate in your presence. The deeper that the Lord is your object of reverence, the greater your confidence will be in giving approval and worth. Because you are tall in spirit, your face is always turned upward.

GINGER

Maidenly; pure one

I Timothy 5:22   *...do not share in the sins of others. Keep yourself pure.*

I Peter 1:22   *Now that you have purified yourselves by obeying the truth so that you have sincere love for your brothers, love one another deeply, from the heart.*

Through the process of heat, trials, and refinement, purity is established. Your nature defies being stubborn, judgmental, and haughty. The commandment of the Lord is clear—giving insight to life (Psalm 19:8). You bring wholeness to the dirty, defiled, contaminated, polluted, double-minded, and raped. Your willingness to be transparent is the venue through which He makes His Word clear, simple, and unadulterated. Your choice to be pure enables you to see God (Matthew 5:8) and to know Him as King and Friend (Proverbs 22:11). It also allows your words to be pleasant (Proverbs 15:26) and causes you to ascend to the holy place of the Lord, where you receive blessings and righteousness from the God of salvation (Psalm 24:3–5). Proverbs 20:11 says, "Even a child is known by his actions, by whether his conduct is pure and right."

GINNY

Maidenly; pure one

I Timothy 5:22 *...do not share in the sins of others. Keep yourself pure.*

I Peter 1:22 *Now that you have purified yourselves by obeying the truth so that you have sincere love for your brothers, love one another deeply, from the heart.*

Through the process of heat, trials, and refinement, purity is established. Your nature defies being stubborn, judgmental, and haughty. The commandment of the Lord is clear—giving insight to life (Psalm 19:8). You bring wholeness to the dirty, defiled, contaminated, polluted, double-minded, and raped. Your willingness to be transparent is the venue through which He makes His Word clear, simple, and unadulterated. Your choice to be pure enables you to see God (Matthew 5:8) and to know Him as King and Friend (Proverbs 22:11). It also allows your words to be pleasant (Proverbs 15:26) and causes you to ascend to the holy place of the Lord, where you receive blessings and righteousness from the God of salvation (Psalm 24:3–5). Proverbs 20:11 says, "Even a child is known by his actions, by whether his conduct is pure and right."

GLADYS

A princess; God's princess

ℰℐ

Exodus 19:5   *Now if you obey me fully and keep my covenant, then out of all nations you will be My treasured possession.*

I Corinthians 6:20   *You were bought at a price. Therefore honor God with your body.*

With a humble confidence, you recognize that your undeserved worth is based on the spotless Lamb sacrificed for you. No greater love will you experience than from the One who laid down His life for you. You pour back your love to Him lavishly with no thought of the cost to you or your reputation. In fact, you are willing to give up everything you have to be His disciple (Luke 14:25–33). This debt of love causes you to give forethought to all your investments as to whether Christ gets all the glory. You will not gamble or be bribed because you know the incredible price paid for you. Therefore you bring value to the insignificant, meaning to the absurd, and worth to the wasted. Your high standard of excellence will bear eternal fruit because of your commitment to please God more than man. As a child of the King, through you castaways will be restored to heirs.

GLENN

Dweller in a valley; prosperous one

ॐ

Psalm 1:1–3 *Blessed is the man who does not walk in the counsel of the wicked or stand in the way of sinners or sit in the seat of mockers. But his delight is in the law of the Lord, and on His law he meditates day and night. He is like a tree planted by the streams of water, which yields its fruit in season and whose leaf does not wither. Whatever he does prospers.*

Joshua 1:8 *Do not let this book of the law depart from your mouth; meditate on it day and night, so that you may be careful to do everything written in it. Then you will be prosperous and successful.*

You are one who knows that your success is not based on luck or good fortune. It is because you are willing to loose your life for Christ's sake in order to find it (Matthew 10:39). You let the word of Christ dwell in you richly (Colossians 3:16). You allow the Lord to stretch and strengthen you in order to enlarge your borders of influence and maturity (Isaiah 54:1–3). You welcome the cutting and pruning that makes way for increase to bear fruit, more fruit, and much fruit (John 15). You enter a covenant with the Lord of obedience, seeking Him diligently and wholeheartedly (II Chronicles 31:21), which causes you to prosper in everything you do (Deuteronomy 29:9). You are content in need and in plenty (Philippians 4:11–12) because prosperity is not a love of money (I Timothy 6:6–10), power, popularity, or possessions. In spite of failure, disappointment, loss, and defeat, you let nothing separate you from the love of God (Romans 8:37–39). Instead of being blind to the hungry, you will feed them. Instead of abhorring the naked, you will clothe them. Instead of ignoring the poor and fatherless, you will be God's hand of provision. You will offer provisions of hope, courage, and strength not to give up, but rather to start again and to make it to the finish line. You are a faithful steward helping them exchange their temporal for His eternal (Philippians 4:19). As your mantle is to build up, develop, and cause to succeed, know that "no weapon formed against you will prosper," Isaiah 54:17. Your goal is to hear the Master say, "Well done, good and faithful servant! You have been faithful with a few things, I will put you in charge of many things. Come share your Master's happiness!" (Matthew 25:21) May you prosper in all things and be in health, just as your soul prospers (3 John 2).

GLENNIS

Dweller in a valley; prosperous one

Psalm 1:1–3 *Blessed is the man who does not walk in the counsel of the wicked or stand in the way of sinners or sit in the seat of mockers. But his delight is in the law of the Lord, and on His law he meditates day and night. He is like a tree planted by the streams of water, which yields its fruit in season and whose leaf does not wither. Whatever he does prospers.*

Joshua 1:8 *Do not let this book of the law depart from your mouth; meditate on it day and night, so that you may be careful to do everything written in it. Then you will be prosperous and successful.*

You are one who knows that your success is not based on luck or good fortune. It is because you are willing to loose your life for Christ's sake in order to find it (Matthew 10:39). You let the word of Christ dwell in you richly (Colossians 3:16). You allow the Lord to stretch and strengthen you in order to enlarge your borders of influence and maturity (Isaiah 54:1–3). You welcome the cutting and pruning that makes way for increase to bear fruit, more fruit, and much fruit (John 15). You enter a covenant with the Lord of obedience, seeking Him diligently and wholeheartedly (II Chronicles 31:21), which causes you to prosper in everything you do (Deuteronomy 29:9). You are content in need and in plenty (Philippians 4:11–12) because prosperity is not a love of money (I Timothy 6:6–10), power, popularity, or possessions. In spite of failure, disappointment, loss, and defeat, you let nothing separate you from the love of God (Romans 8:37–39). Instead of being blind to the hungry, you will feed them. Instead of abhorring the naked, you will clothe them. Instead of ignoring the poor and fatherless, you will be God's hand of provision. You will offer provisions of hope, courage, and strength not to give up, but rather to start again and to make it to the finish line. You are a faithful steward helping them exchange their temporal for His eternal (Philippians 4:19). As your mantle is to build up, develop, and cause to succeed, know that "no weapon formed against you will prosper," Isaiah 54:17. Your goal is to hear the Master say, "Well done, good and faithful servant! You have been faithful with a few things, I will put you in charge of many things. Come share your Master's happiness!" (Matthew 25:21) May you prosper in all things and be in health, just as your soul prospers (3 John 2).

GLENYCE

Dweller in a valley; prosperous one

❧

Psalm 1:1–3 *Blessed is the man who does not walk in the counsel of the wicked or stand in the way of sinners or sit in the seat of mockers. But his delight is in the law of the Lord, and on His law he meditates day and night. He is like a tree planted by the streams of water, which yields its fruit in season and whose leaf does not wither. Whatever he does prospers.*

Joshua 1:8 *Do not let this book of the law depart from your mouth; meditate on it day and night, so that you may be careful to do everything written in it. Then you will be prosperous and successful.*

You are one who knows that your success is not based on luck or good fortune. It is because you are willing to loose your life for Christ's sake in order to find it (Matthew 10:39). You let the word of Christ dwell in you richly (Colossians 3:16). You allow the Lord to stretch and strengthen you in order to enlarge your borders of influence and maturity (Isaiah 54:1–3). You welcome the cutting and pruning that makes way for increase to bear fruit, more fruit, and much fruit (John 15). You enter a covenant with the Lord of obedience, seeking Him diligently and wholeheartedly (II Chronicles 31:21), which causes you to prosper in everything you do (Deuteronomy 29:9). You are content in need and in plenty (Philippians 4:11–12) because prosperity is not a love of money (I Timothy 6:6–10), power, popularity, or possessions. In spite of failure, disappointment, loss, and defeat, you let nothing separate you from the love of God (Romans 8:37–39). Instead of being blind to the hungry, you will feed them. Instead of abhorring the naked, you will clothe them. Instead of ignoring the poor and fatherless, you will be God's hand of provision. You will offer provisions of hope, courage, and strength not to give up, but rather to start again and to make it to the finish line. You are a faithful steward helping them exchange their temporal for His eternal (Philippians 4:19). As your mantle is to build up, develop, and cause to succeed, know that "no weapon formed against you will prosper," Isaiah 54:17. Your goal is to hear the Master say, "Well done, good and faithful servant! You have been faithful with a few things, I will put you in charge of many things. Come share your Master's happiness!" (Matthew 25:21) May you prosper in all things and be in health, just as your soul prospers (3 John 2).

GLORIA

Glory; glory of God

❧

Isaiah 58:8 *Then your light will break forth like the dawn, and your healing will quickly appear; then your righteousness will go before you, and the glory of the Lord will be your rear guard.*

Romans 8:17–18 *Now if we are children, then we are heirs—heirs of God and co-heirs with Christ, if indeed we share in His sufferings in order that we may also share in His glory. I consider that our present sufferings are not worth comparing with the glory that will be revealed in us.*

Isaiah 60:1 says, "Arise, shine, for your light has come, and the glory of the Lord rises upon you." You are God's consecrated, anointed one to show forth His brilliant beauty in your security of His creation of you. The current work of the Lord is revealed in and through you as you display His majesty, splendor, and honor in worship. Sharing in His glory results in the Holy Spirit ruling over the flesh. This equips you to confront shame, confusion, dishonor, and reproach (Psalm 4:2 and Philippians 3:19). You lift up heads that hang down (Psalm 3:3) and you defy spiritual deafness, pride, arrogance, idolatry, and self-righteousness. You are ever mindful of laying aside your reputation for His! Glory is God's character exhibited through His Son in grace, power, resurrection, and transfiguration. He is the source through which all splendor, perfection, and protection proceed. Your presence reveals His (I Chronicles 16:24–35).

GOLDIE

Golden; a heavenly viewpoint

&

Proverbs 3:13–14 *Blessed is the man who finds wisdom, the man who gains understanding, for she is more profitable than silver and yields better returns than gold.*

II Timothy 2:20–21 *In a large house there are articles not only of gold and silver, but also of wood and clay; some are for noble purposes and some for ignoble. If a man cleanses himself from the latter, he will be an instrument for noble purposes, made holy, useful to the Master and prepared to do any good work.*

The Lord knows the way that you take. When He has tested you, you will come forth as gold (Job 23:10). Trials have come so that your faith—of greater worth than gold, which perishes even though refined by fire—may be proved genuine and may result in praise, glory, and honor when Jesus Christ is revealed (I Peter 1:6–7). When the Refiner of your soul intensifies the heat, His purpose is to reveal the purity He sees in you. The dross is removed and His very likeness is revealed. The blood of Jesus acts as a filter to bring cleansing and clarity. Your pure heart sees God! (Matthew 5:8) Like Jesus, you see what your Heavenly Father is doing and you do it. You have resolved to know nothing except Jesus Christ and Him crucified (I Corinthians 2:2). You have your Father's eyes, seeing from His position and perspective. The more clearly you see that you are God's treasured possession (Deuteronomy 7:6), the more you will bring value, worth, and favor to those He has given you to serve. Because you love God's commands more than pure gold and you consider all His precepts right, you hate every wrong path (Psalm 119:127–128).

GORDON

From the gore-shaped hill; ascending one

ॐ

Psalm 24:3–4   *Who may ascend the hill of the Lord? Who may stand in His holy place? He who has clean hands and a pure heart, who does not lift up his soul to an idol or swear by what is false. He will receive blessings from the Lord and vindication from God his Savior.*

Ephesians 2:6   *And God raised us up with Christ and seated us with Him in the heavenly realms in Christ Jesus.*

Your constant prayer is Isaiah 54:2–3, "Enlarge the place of your tent, stretch your tent curtains wide, do not hold back; lengthen your cords, strengthen your stakes. For you will spread out to the right and to the left." You put no limits on God, for you know He will supply all your needs according to His riches and with Him all things are possible. The more you decrease, the greater He increases in you. As you increase in all the Christ-like qualities, they will keep you from being ineffective and unproductive in your knowledge of Him (II Peter 1:3–8). You do not settle for second-best, nor shrink from responsibility. There is not a lazy bone in your body. You are creative in moving forward, scaling new heights, and soaring as an eagle. Your message to the fallen is Proverbs 24:16, "Though a righteous man falls seven times, he rises again." As you exalt Him, He will exalt you. Promotion comes from God!

GRACE

Thanks; thankful spirit

ಕ್ರ

Romans 8:32 *He who did not spare His own Son, but gave Him up for us all—how will He not also, along with Him, graciously give us all things?*

I Corinthians 15:10 *But by the grace of God I am what I am, and His grace to me was not without effect.*

Ephesians 2:8 says, "For it is by grace you have been saved, through faith—and this is not from yourselves, it is the gift of God." You are one who brings about balance and harmony through mercy, forgiveness, approval, kindness, and patience—all with a grateful heart. This attitude of gratitude will rule in the midst of inconsiderate behavior. Your nature defies the law of the Pharisees, and is against being self-reliant, prejudice, and selfish. Being full of grace is devotion built through faithfulness and a willingness to quickly pardon. You are blessed with creativity in expressing God's greatest gift of grace—the life of His only Son, Jesus Christ. God says to you through Jeremiah 24:7, "I will give them a heart to know Me, that I am the Lord. They will be My people, and I will be their God, for they will return to Me with all their heart." Ezekiel 11:19 says, "I will give them an undivided heart and put a new spirit in them; I will remove from them their heart of stone and give them a heart of flesh." Accountability will keep your report accurate and your integrity irreproachable.

GRADY

Noble; full of honor

&

Isaiah 32:8 *But the noble man makes noble plans, and by noble deeds he stands.*

Luke 8:15 *But the seed on good soil stands for those with a noble and good heart, who hear the word, retain it, and by persevering produce a crop.*

Proverbs 18:12 says, "Before his downfall a man's heart is proud, but humility comes before honor." You are one who has a humble confidence in recognizing and expressing reverence, worship, adoration, trust, deference, tribute, admiration, and respect. This is the result of being secure in the truth of who you are in the Lord. Through humility, King Jesus made a way for you to be engrafted into His royalty. He made of Himself no reputation and took on the nature of a servant (Philippians 2:7) to affirm your value. Through self-denial, you prioritize excellence in virtue, truthfulness, and faithfulness. Because of the respect you have earned, you dismantle inferiority, disgrace, shame, and offenses. No one feels second-rate in your presence. The deeper that the Lord is your object of reverence, the greater your confidence will be in giving approval and worth. Because you are tall in spirit, your face is always turned upward.

GRANT

Great one; generous heart

∞

Deuteronomy 16:17 *Each of you must bring a gift in proportion to the way the Lord your God has blessed you.*

II Corinthians 9:6–8 *Remember this: Whoever sows sparingly will also reap sparingly, and whoever sows generously will also reap generously. Each man should give what he has decided in his heart to give, not reluctantly or under compulsion, for God loves a cheerful giver. And God is able to make all grace abound to you, so that in all things at all times, having all that you need, you will abound in every good work.*

You are bighearted, not selfish. You are generous, not stingy. You are unreserved, not tightfisted. Your life is earmarked by your liberal praise and worship to your Savior, Jesus Christ. Knowing Him as your Provider releases you to give, give, give! You reflect the kindness of the Lord with your pleasant servant's heart. You are inclined to do good by being courteous, helpful, and gentle. Through you, God will display His mighty hand of love and help. You will open your arms to the poor and extend your hands to the needy (Proverbs 31:20). "He who gives to the poor will lack nothing," Proverbs 28:27. When giving to the needy, never let your left hand know what your right hand is doing, so that your giving may be a secret. Then your Father, who sees what is done in secret, will reward you (Matthew 6:3–4). Luke 6:38 says, "Give, and it will be given to you. A good measure, pressed down, shaken together and running over, will be poured into your lap. For with the measure you use, it will be measured to you."

GRAY

Gray-haired; watchful one

ℰↄ

Isaiah 62:6 *I have posted watchmen on your walls, O Jerusalem; they will never be silent day or night. You who call on the Lord give yourselves no rest.*

I Corinthians 16:13–14 *Be on your guard; stand firm in the faith; be men of courage; be strong. Do everything in love.*

The Lord has appointed you as His watchman. You must hear His voice and give warning for Him (Ezekiel 3:17). You must be watchful, alert, prepared, actively observant, and on guard. You have quick intelligence and a readiness to take prompt action—whether alerting to danger or opportunities. You are spiritually wide awake and aware of all surrounding circumstances. This is accomplished by your devoted prayer life and your being watchful and thankful (Colossians 4:2). You are able to keep your head in all situations (II Timothy 4:5). You are self-controlled and alert, able to resist the devil and stand firm in your faith (I Peter 5:8–9). You exercise self-restraint that governs all passions and desires. This enables you to be conformed to the mind of Christ. You must stay ready for the Lord's return (Luke 12:35–40).

GRAYSON

Gray haired; watchful one

ℰℐ

Isaiah 62:6   *I have posted watchmen on your walls, O Jerusalem; they will never be silent day or night. You who call on the Lord give yourselves no rest.*

I Corinthians 16:13–14   *Be on your guard; stand firm in the faith; be men of courage; be strong. Do everything in love.*

The Lord has appointed you as His watchman. You must hear His voice and give warning for Him (Ezekiel 3:17). You must be watchful, alert, prepared, actively observant, and on guard. You have quick intelligence and a readiness to take prompt action—whether alerting to danger or opportunities. You are spiritually wide awake and aware of all surrounding circumstances. This is accomplished by your devoted prayer life and your being watchful and thankful (Colossians 4:2). You are able to keep your head in all situations (II Timothy 4:5). You are self-controlled and alert, able to resist the devil and stand firm in your faith (I Peter 5:8–9). You exercise self-restraint that governs all passions and desires. This enables you to be conformed to the mind of Christ. You must stay ready for the Lord's return (Luke 12:35–40).

GREG

Watchman; watchful one

&

Isaiah 62:6   *I have posted watchmen on your walls, O Jerusalem; they will never be silent day or night. You who call on the Lord give yourselves no rest.*

I Corinthians 16:13–14   *Be on your guard; stand firm in the faith; be men of courage; be strong. Do everything in love.*

The Lord has appointed you as His watchman. You must hear His voice and give warning for Him (Ezekiel 3:17). You must be watchful, alert, prepared, actively observant, and on guard. You have quick intelligence and a readiness to take prompt action—whether alerting to danger or opportunities. You are spiritually wide awake and aware of all surrounding circumstances. This is accomplished by your devoted prayer life and your being watchful and thankful (Colossians 4:2). You are able to keep your head in all situations (II Timothy 4:5). You are self-controlled and alert, able to resist the devil and stand firm in your faith (I Peter 5:8–9). You exercise self-restraint that governs all passions and desires. This enables you to be conformed to the mind of Christ. You must stay ready for the Lord's return (Luke 12:35–40).

GREGORY

Watchman; watchful one

෫

Isaiah 62:6   *I have posted watchmen on your walls, O Jerusalem; they will never be silent day or night. You who call on the Lord give yourselves no rest.*

I Corinthians 16:13–14   *Be on your guard; stand firm in the faith; be men of courage; be strong. Do everything in love.*

The Lord has appointed you as His watchman. You must hear His voice and give warning for Him (Ezekiel 3:17). You must be watchful, alert, prepared, actively observant, and on guard. You have quick intelligence and a readiness to take prompt action—whether alerting to danger or opportunities. You are spiritually wide awake and aware of all surrounding circumstances. This is accomplished by your devoted prayer life and your being watchful and thankful (Colossians 4:2). You are able to keep your head in all situations (II Timothy 4:5). You are self-controlled and alert, able to resist the devil and stand firm in your faith (I Peter 5:8–9). You exercise self-restraint that governs all passions and desires. This enables you to be conformed to the mind of Christ. You must stay ready for the Lord's return (Luke 12:35–40).

GWEN

White; blessed one

&

Exodus 23:25 *Worship the Lord your God, and His blessing will be on your food and water. I will take away sickness from among you.*

Proverbs 10:22 *The blessing of the Lord brings wealth, and He adds no trouble to it.*

God has resourced you in order to give you great influence and favor. He commands His blessings where you establish unity (Psalm 133). He will turn every curse into a blessing for you because He loves you (Deuteronomy 23:5). True abundance is giving out of your nothingness, with a total dependence on God. Wealth is not in the amount you have, but in the attitude in which you give it. Because of your standard of integrity and gratitude, you have an eye for value, fruitfulness, and generosity. Your heart is for the poor, barren, and destitute, but you resist the lazy and stingy. You transfer God's possessions, power, and pleasure to others. Make wise investments of your time, energy, and resources that will keep reproducing rather than insuring your own personal gratification. You are blessed to be a blessing. The greater your obedience to the Lord, the greater will be His blessings (Deuteronomy 28:1–14).

GWYNN

White; blessed one

ℰᴒ

Exodus 23:25 *Worship the Lord your God, and His blessing will be on your food and water. I will take away sickness from among you.*

Proverbs 10:22 *The blessing of the Lord brings wealth, and He adds no trouble to it.*

God has resourced you in order to give you great influence and favor. He commands His blessings where you establish unity (Psalm 133). He will turn every curse into a blessing for you because He loves you (Deuteronomy 23:5). True abundance is giving out of your nothingness, with a total dependence on God. Wealth is not in the amount you have, but in the attitude in which you give it. Because of your standard of integrity and gratitude, you have an eye for value, fruitfulness, and generosity. Your heart is for the poor, barren, and destitute, but you resist the lazy and stingy. You transfer God's possessions, power, and pleasure to others. Make wise investments of your time, energy, and resources that will keep reproducing rather than insuring your own personal gratification. You are blessed to be a blessing. The greater your obedience to the Lord, the greater will be His blessings (Deuteronomy 28:1–14).

HAILEY

Meadow of hay; industrious

ॐ

Colossians 1:16   *For by Him all things were created: things in heaven and on earth, visible and invisible, whether thrones or powers or rulers or authorities; all things were created by Him and for Him.*

Ephesians 2:10   *For we are God's workmanship, created in Christ Jesus to do good works, which God prepared in advance for us to do.*

To be industrious means to be skillful, hardworking, zealous, and diligent. By persevering, you give careful attention to detail. There is not a lazy bone in your body. Through you the Lord will originate. How you deal with the past determines your future. Regardless of the curses or blessings, the failures or successes, you are God's platform for a "new thing." You cannot lean on your own understanding or reasoning. God Almighty created the heavens, the earth, and you in His image. So the more completely dependent you become on your Creator, the more productive your life will be for Him! I Peter 4:19, "So then, those who suffer according to God's will should commit themselves to their Creator and continue to do good."

HANNAH

Grace; full of grace

&

Romans 8:32   *He who did not spare His own Son, but gave Him up for us all—how will He not also, along with Him, graciously give us all things?*

I Corinthians 15:10   *But by the grace of God I am what I am, and His grace to me was not without effect.*

Ephesians 2:8 says, "For it is by grace you have been saved, through faith—and this is not from yourselves, it is the gift of God." You are one who brings about balance and harmony through mercy, forgiveness, approval, kindness, and patience—all with a grateful heart. This attitude of gratitude will rule in the midst of inconsiderate behavior. Your nature defies the law of the Pharisees, and is against being self-reliant, prejudice, and selfish. Being full of grace is devotion built through faithfulness and a willingness to quickly pardon. You are blessed with creativity in expressing God's greatest gift of grace—the life of His only Son, Jesus Christ. God says to you through Jeremiah 24:7, "I will give them a heart to know Me, that I am the Lord. They will be My people, and I will be their God, for they will return to Me with all their heart." Ezekiel 11:19 says, "I will give them an undivided heart and put a new spirit in them; I will remove from them their heart of stone and give them a heart of flesh." Accountability will keep your report accurate and your integrity irreproachable.

HARLEY

Army-meadow; strong leader

❦

Deuteronomy 28:13   *The Lord will make you the head, not the tail. If you pay attention to the commands of the Lord your God that I give you this day and carefully follow them, you will always be at the top, never at the bottom.*

Mark 10:43–45   *...Whoever wants to become great among you must be your servant, and whoever wants to be first must be slave of all. For even the Son of Man did not come to be served, but to serve, and to give His life as a ransom for many.*

You have been set apart with vision and perspective to reproduce the likeness of Christ in others by reflecting His image. You are guided by principles and values worth dying for. You know how to balance transparency with being an example. You are one who is secure enough to be vulnerable. You do not lead to gather followers; you lead to develop leaders. You lead by honoring God with authority, influence, direction, foresight, and skill. Your credible choices set a precedence for favor. You earn trust by your willingness to confront and bring discipline in a Godly manner. You are strong enough to let your "yes" be "yes" and your "no" be "no," with no compromise or jealousy. Your strength is determined by your submitted and teachable servant's heart. The more you mature, the more humble, gentle, and meek you will become. With integrity you communicate love, affirmation, nurturing, and spiritual care. If you as a shepherd ever forget what it is like to be a sheep, you will become a hireling. Your highest aim is to honor and glorify God.

HAROLD

Ruler; strong leader

৪৩

Deuteronomy 28:13   *The Lord will make you the head, not the tail. If you pay attention to the commands of the Lord your God that I give you this day and carefully follow them, you will always be at the top, never at the bottom.*

Mark 10:43–45   *...Whoever wants to become great among you must be your servant, and whoever wants to be first must be slave of all. For even the Son of Man did not come to be served, but to serve, and to give His life as a ransom for many.*

You have been set apart with vision and perspective to reproduce the likeness of Christ in others by reflecting His image. You are guided by principles and values worth dying for. You know how to balance transparency with being an example. You are one who is secure enough to be vulnerable. You do not lead to gather followers; you lead to develop leaders. You lead by honoring God with authority, influence, direction, foresight, and skill. Your credible choices set a precedence for favor. You earn trust by your willingness to confront and bring discipline in a Godly manner. You are strong enough to let your "yes" be "yes" and your "no" be "no," with no compromise or jealousy. Your strength is determined by your submitted and teachable servant's heart. The more you mature, the more humble, gentle, and meek you will become. With integrity you communicate love, affirmation, nurturing, and spiritual care. If you as a shepherd ever forget what it is like to be a sheep, you will become a hireling. Your highest aim is to honor and glorify God.

HARRIET

Army-power; full of wisdom

※

James 3:17   *But the wisdom that comes from heaven is first of all pure; then peace-loving, considerate, submissive, full of mercy and good fruit, impartial and sincere.*

Proverbs 9:10   *The fear of the Lord is the beginning of wisdom, and knowledge of the Holy One is understanding.*

You are a person of moral excellence. You exemplify right living put into practice. The Lord has not only equipped you with skills for living correctly, but also the ability to impart that to others. The Spirit of truth will guide you into all truth, allowing you to have insight into the true nature of things (John 16:13). Out of your reverential respect for the Lord, you have wisdom to give guidance and direction. You are a safe sounding board who steers those who are hungry for knowledge of the Holy One in the right direction. You need only to ask for the wisdom you lack, and God will give it to you generously (James 1:5). Having spiritual discernment is having the ability to separate the difference between God's wisdom and the world's and the ability to make the right choice—regardless. Luke 21:15 says, "For I will give you words and wisdom that none of your adversaries will be able to resist or contradict."

HARRY

Ruler; strong leader

છ

Deuteronomy 28:13 *The Lord will make you the head, not the tail. If you pay attention to the commands of the Lord your God that I give you this day and carefully follow them, you will always be at the top, never at the bottom.*

Mark 10:43–45 *...Whoever wants to become great among you must be your servant, and whoever wants to be first must be slave of all. For even the Son of Man did not come to be served, but to serve, and to give His life as a ransom for many.*

You have been set apart with vision and perspective to reproduce the likeness of Christ in others by reflecting His image. You are guided by principles and values worth dying for. You know how to balance transparency with being an example. You are one who is secure enough to be vulnerable. You do not lead to gather followers; you lead to develop leaders. You lead by honoring God with authority, influence, direction, foresight, and skill. Your credible choices set a precedence for favor. You earn trust by your willingness to confront and bring discipline in a Godly manner. You are strong enough to let your "yes" be "yes" and your "no" be "no," with no compromise or jealousy. Your strength is determined by your submitted and teachable servant's heart. The more you mature, the more humble, gentle, and meek you will become. With integrity you communicate love, affirmation, nurturing, and spiritual care. If you as a shepherd ever forget what it is like to be a sheep, you will become a hireling. Your highest aim is to honor and glorify God.

HARVEY

Army-warrior; loyal

&

Romans 12:9–10 *Love must be sincere. Hate what is evil; cling to what is good. Be devoted to one another in brotherly love. Honor one another above yourselves.*

Proverbs 2:7–8 *He holds victory in store for the upright, He is a shield to those whose walk is blameless, for He guards the course of the just and protects the way of His faithful ones.*

As one with a loyal spirit, the Lord has called you to be faithful, devoted, obedient, dependable, and true. You are noble in disarming the enemy's attacks of fear, selfishness, failure, betrayal, dishonesty, and faithlessness. You are unyielding and have a resolute confidence in your commitment to God's Word. With it, you will help others overcome being cowards, losers, quitters, or betrayers. Knowing God's loyalty to you will strengthen your loyalty to others. Isaiah 1:17 says, "Learn to do right! Seek justice, encourage the oppressed. Defend the cause of the fatherless, plead the case of the widow."

HAYDEN

From the hedged hill; declaring victory

&

I John 5:4 *Everyone born of God overcomes the world. This is the victory that has overcome the world, even our faith.*

II Corinthians 2:14 *But thanks be to God, who always leads us in triumphal procession in Christ and through us spreads everywhere the fragrance of the knowledge of Him.*

Because of your faith in Jesus Christ, you will ever be aggressive towards the enemy's tools of defeat, failure, and victimization. You will push back Satan and overcome all his power. Jesus has given you authority to trample on snakes and scorpions and to overcome all the power of the enemy; nothing will harm you (Luke 10:19). Even in the severest of afflictions—such as hardship, persecution, famine, nakedness, danger, or sword—you are more than a conqueror through Christ who loves you (Romans 8:35–37). "Everyone born of God overcomes the world. This is the victory that has overcome the world, even our faith," I John 5:4. "Take heart, Jesus has overcome the world," John 16:33.

HAZEL

Hazelnut tree; quiet spirit

&

Isaiah 26:3 *You will keep in perfect peace him whose mind is steadfast, because he trusts in You.*

Philippians 4:7 *And the peace of God, which transcends all understanding, will guard your hearts and your minds in Christ Jesus.*

Your life defines peace. You will have a content and calm composure in the midst of distress, disturbance, or agitation. As you follow the Prince of Peace, you will be secure in who you are in Christ. The discipline of keeping your mind on Christ, loving God's law, and being controlled by the Holy Spirit will keep you in perfect peace. God's peace will serve as an umpire to determine whether you are safe or out of God's will (Colossians 3:15). Do not think it strange when you are in battles, fights, and quarrels, because God wants to use you to bring harmony, order, unity, agreement, quietness, and calmness to the adverse situation. You are one whose intimate friendship with the Lord brings reconciliation to the offended, distressed, and troubled. "In repentance and rest is your salvation, in quietness and trust is your strength," Isaiah 30:15. Your refreshing comes as you renew your mind daily in the Word of God. "Great peace have they who love Your law, and nothing can make them stumble," Psalm 119:165.

HEATHER

The heather flower; joyful spirit

ℬℭ

Psalm 149:4–5 *For the Lord takes delight in His people; He crowns the humble with salvation. Let the saints rejoice in this honor and sing for joy on their beds.*

Psalm 45:7 *You love righteousness and hate wickedness; therefore God, your God, has set you above your companions by anointing you with the oil of joy.*

Psalm 16:11 says, "You have made known to me the path of life; You will fill me with joy in Your presence, with eternal pleasures at Your right hand." Your heavenly Father has trusted you with a quality that releases healing, restores hope, and brings refreshing. You are one who takes the source of tears and defeat, and turns them into confident trust with rejoicing. As you experience and remain sensitive to the things that sorrow the heart of God, He will pour His oil of joy on and through you to restore hope to those who are mourning (Isaiah 61:1–3). Experiences of sorrow prepare and enlarge your capacity for joy. The joy of the Lord will be your strength to endure the cross He has called you to bear. You are to fix your eyes on Jesus, the author and perfecter of your faith, who for the joy set before Him endured the cross, scorning its shame, and sat down at the right hand of the throne of God (Hebrews 12:2). He will be faithful to give you a song in your "night" season (Psalm 42:8). God rejoices over you with gladness! (Zephaniah 3:17)

HEIDI

Nobleness; full of honor

Isaiah 32:8 *But the noble man makes noble plans, and by noble deeds he stands.*

Luke 8:15 *But the seed on good soil stands for those with a noble and good heart, who hear the word, retain it, and by persevering produce a crop.*

Proverbs 18:12 says, "Before his downfall a man's heart is proud, but humility comes before honor." You are one who has a humble confidence in recognizing and expressing reverence, worship, adoration, trust, deference, tribute, admiration, and respect. This is the result of being secure in the truth of who you are in the Lord. Through humility, King Jesus made a way for you to be engrafted into His royalty. He made of Himself no reputation and took on the nature of a servant (Philippians 2:7) to affirm your value. Through self-denial, you prioritize excellence in virtue, truthfulness, and faithfulness. Because of the respect you have earned, you dismantle inferiority, disgrace, shame, and offenses. No one feels second-rate in your presence. The deeper that the Lord is your object of reverence, the greater your confidence will be in giving approval and worth. Because you are tall in spirit, your face is always turned upward.

HELEN

Light; bright one

❧

Psalm 27:1 *The Lord is my light and my salvation—whom shall I fear? The Lord is the stronghold of my life; of whom shall I be afraid.*

Proverbs 4:18 *The path of the righteous is like the first gleam of dawn, shining ever brighter till the full light of day.*

You are one who reflects the shining brightness of the countenance of Jesus. You are aggressive toward the fruitless deeds of darkness from the evil one, by exposing them to the light of Jesus. Everything exposed by light becomes visible, for it is the light that makes everything visible (Ephesians 5:11–14). This radiance that God has given you serves as a beacon to give guidance to those yet in darkness. Your life's mission is found in the following two verses: Isaiah 60:1–3 says, "Arise, shine, for your light has come, and the glory of the Lord rises upon you. See, darkness covers the earth, and thick darkness is over the peoples, but the Lord rises upon you and His glory appears over you. Nations will come to your light, and kings to the brightness of your dawn." And in Acts 13:47, "For this is what the Lord has commanded us: 'I have made you a light for the Gentiles, that you may bring salvation to the ends of the earth.'" Continue to shine as His star, leading many to righteousness (Daniel 12:3 and Philippians 2:15).

HELENA

Light; bright one

&

Psalm 27:1   *The Lord is my light and my salvation—whom shall I fear? The Lord is the stronghold of my life; of whom shall I be afraid.*

Proverbs 4:18   *The path of the righteous is like the first gleam of dawn, shining ever brighter till the full light of day.*

You are one who reflects the shining brightness of the countenance of Jesus. You are aggressive toward the fruitless deeds of darkness from the evil one, by exposing them to the light of Jesus. Everything exposed by light becomes visible, for it is the light that makes everything visible (Ephesians 5:11–14). This radiance that God has given you serves as a beacon to give guidance to those yet in darkness. Your life's mission is found in the following two verses: Isaiah 60:1–3 says, "Arise, shine, for your light has come, and the glory of the Lord rises upon you. See, darkness covers the earth, and thick darkness is over the peoples, but the Lord rises upon you and His glory appears over you. Nations will come to your light, and kings to the brightness of your dawn." And in Acts 13:47, "For this is what the Lord has commanded us: 'I have made you a light for the Gentiles, that you may bring salvation to the ends of the earth.'" Continue to shine as His star, leading many to righteousness (Daniel 12:3 and Philippians 2:15).

HENRY

Ruler of an estate; industrious

ℰℬ

Colossians 1:16 *For by Him all things were created: things in heaven and on earth, visible and invisible, whether thrones or powers or rulers or authorities; all things were created by Him and for Him.*

Ephesians 2:10 *For we are God's workmanship, created in Christ Jesus to do good works, which God prepared in advance for us to do.*

To be industrious means to be skillful, hardworking, zealous, and diligent. By persevering, you give careful attention to detail. There is not a lazy bone in your body. Through you the Lord will originate. How you deal with the past determines your future. Regardless of the curses or blessings, the failures or successes, you are God's platform for a "new thing." You cannot lean on your own understanding or reasoning. God Almighty created the heavens, the earth, and you in His image. So the more completely dependent you become on your Creator, the more productive your life will be for Him! I Peter 4:19, "So then, those who suffer according to God's will should commit themselves to their Creator and continue to do good."

HERB

Glorious warrior; God's warrior

ॐ

II Chronicles 32:7–8   *There is a greater power with us than with him. With him is only the arm of flesh, but with us is the Lord our God to help us and to fight our battles.*

II Timothy 2:3–4   *Endure hardship with us like a good soldier of Christ Jesus. No one serving as a soldier gets involved in civilian affairs - he wants to please his commanding officer.*

Exodus 14:14 says, "The Lord will fight for you; you need only be still." You are armed with the ability to handle the spear and shield—to stand on God's Word by faith, supporting the King of kings against His enemies. As God's defending warrior, you are His example of a brave champion, soldier, and hero. The ultimate war was a contest with death and when Christ said, "It is finished" on the cross, He declared victory over death, hell, and the grave. You are equipped to be used of God as one who protects by warding off attacks, calling for justice, and providing shelter. When God is all of this to you, you will be that vindication for others. Because of your faith in Jesus Christ, you will ever be aggressive towards the enemy's tools of defeat, failure, and victimization. Your ultimate purpose is to be one who stands in the gap (Ezekiel 22:30) as a defender of the weak. This includes those who are easily influenced, confused, quitters, faint, frail, fragile, and frightened. Your primary spiritual warfare will be that of brave intercession—reaching, meeting, and entreating God for His favor to set the captives free. Then you will "learn to do right! Seek justice, encourage the oppressed. Defend the cause of the fatherless, plead the case of the widow," Isaiah 1:17.

HERBERT

Glorious warrior; God's warrior

&

II Chronicles 32:7–8 *There is a greater power with us than with him. With him is only the arm of flesh, but with us is the Lord our God to help us and to fight our battles.*

II Timothy 2:3–4 *Endure hardship with us like a good soldier of Christ Jesus. No one serving as a soldier gets involved in civilian affairs - he wants to please his commanding officer.*

Exodus 14:14 says, "The Lord will fight for you; you need only be still." You are armed with the ability to handle the spear and shield—to stand on God's Word by faith, supporting the King of kings against His enemies. As God's defending warrior, you are His example of a brave champion, soldier, and hero. The ultimate war was a contest with death and when Christ said, "It is finished" on the cross, He declared victory over death, hell, and the grave. You are equipped to be used of God as one who protects by warding off attacks, calling for justice, and providing shelter. When God is all of this to you, you will be that vindication for others. Because of your faith in Jesus Christ, you will ever be aggressive towards the enemy's tools of defeat, failure, and victimization. Your ultimate purpose is to be one who stands in the gap (Ezekiel 22:30) as a defender of the weak. This includes those who are easily influenced, confused, quitters, faint, frail, fragile, and frightened. Your primary spiritual warfare will be that of brave intercession—reaching, meeting, and entreating God for His favor to set the captives free. Then you will "learn to do right! Seek justice, encourage the oppressed. Defend the cause of the fatherless, plead the case of the widow," Isaiah 1:17.

HILLARIE

Cheerful; full of joy

☙

Psalm 149:4–5 *For the Lord takes delight in His people; He crowns the humble with salvation. Let the saints rejoice in this honor and sing for joy on their beds.*

Psalm 45:7 *You love righteousness and hate wickedness; therefore God, your God, has set you above your companions by anointing you with the oil of joy.*

Psalm 16:11 says, "You have made known to me the path of life; You will fill me with joy in Your presence, with eternal pleasures at Your right hand." Your heavenly Father has trusted you with a quality that releases healing, restores hope, and brings refreshing. You are one who takes the source of tears and defeat, and turns them into confident trust with rejoicing. As you experience and remain sensitive to the things that sorrow the heart of God, He will pour His oil of joy on and through you to restore hope to those who are mourning (Isaiah 61:1–3). Experiences of sorrow prepare and enlarge your capacity for joy. The joy of the Lord will be your strength to endure the cross He has called you to bear. You are to fix your eyes on Jesus, the author and perfecter of your faith, who for the joy set before Him endured the cross, scorning its shame, and sat down at the right hand of the throne of God (Hebrews 12:2). He will be faithful to give you a song in your "night" season (Psalm 42:8). God rejoices over you with gladness! (Zephaniah 3:17)

HILLARY

Cheerful; full of joy

෨

Psalm 149:4–5 *For the Lord takes delight in His people; He crowns the humble with salvation. Let the saints rejoice in this honor and sing for joy on their beds.*

Psalm 45:7 *You love righteousness and hate wickedness; therefore God, your God, has set you above your companions by anointing you with the oil of joy.*

Psalm 16:11 says, "You have made known to me the path of life; You will fill me with joy in Your presence, with eternal pleasures at Your right hand." Your heavenly Father has trusted you with a quality that releases healing, restores hope, and brings refreshing. You are one who takes the source of tears and defeat, and turns them into confident trust with rejoicing. As you experience and remain sensitive to the things that sorrow the heart of God, He will pour His oil of joy on and through you to restore hope to those who are mourning (Isaiah 61:1–3). Experiences of sorrow prepare and enlarge your capacity for joy. The joy of the Lord will be your strength to endure the cross He has called you to bear. You are to fix your eyes on Jesus, the author and perfecter of your faith, who for the joy set before Him endured the cross, scorning its shame, and sat down at the right hand of the throne of God (Hebrews 12:2). He will be faithful to give you a song in your "night" season (Psalm 42:8). God rejoices over you with gladness! (Zephaniah 3:17)

HOLLY

Holly tree; calming peace

ℰↃ

Isaiah 26:3 *You will keep in perfect peace him whose mind is steadfast, because he trusts in You.*

Philippians 4:7 *And the peace of God, which transcends all understanding, will guard your hearts and your minds in Christ Jesus.*

Your life defines peace. You will have a content and calm composure in the midst of distress, disturbance, or agitation. As you follow the Prince of Peace, you will be secure in who you are in Christ. The discipline of keeping your mind on Christ, loving God's law, and being controlled by the Holy Spirit will keep you in perfect peace. God's peace will serve as an umpire to determine whether you are safe or out of God's will (Colossians 3:15). Do not think it strange when you are in battles, fights, and quarrels, because God wants to use you to bring harmony, order, unity, agreement, quietness, and calmness to the adverse situation. You are one whose intimate friendship with the Lord brings reconciliation to the offended, distressed, and troubled. "In repentance and rest is your salvation, in quietness and trust is your strength," Isaiah 30:15. Your refreshing comes as you renew your mind daily in the Word of God. "Great peace have they who love Your law, and nothing can make them stumble," Psalm 119:165.

HOPE

Expectation, desire; trustful

&

Isaiah 40:31 *Those who hope in the Lord will renew their strength. They will soar on wings like eagles; they will run and not grow weary, they will walk and not be faint.*

Hebrews 6:18–20 *God did this so that, by two unchangeable things in which it is impossible for God to lie, we who have fled to take hold of the hope offered to us may be greatly encouraged. We have this hope as an anchor for the soul, firm and secure. It enters the inner sanctuary behind the curtain, where Jesus, who went before us, has entered on our behalf.*

Hope is the rope you hang on to when you have only seen God's promise inside your heart. You have a holy tenacity that God will fulfill His word. Your faith and hope are established in God because you believe in the resurrection of His Son, Jesus Christ (1 Peter 1:21). Hope is dependent on how strong God, His word, and His name are in you. This expectation energizes you to endure under trial, equipping you to wait patiently. You must tell your soul to find its rest in God alone, for your hope comes from Him (Psalm 62:5). You are blessed because your trust and confidence are in Him (Jeremiah 17:7). You are confident that He who began a good work in you will carry it on to completion until the day of Christ Jesus (Philippians 1:6). Restoration flows through you as a door of hope for the valley of trouble (Hosea 2:15). The apathetic are given purpose, the depressed are given encouragement, and the desperate are given expectation. You look forward—not backward. You are prepared for the future and not governed by the past. "Delight yourself in the Lord and He will give you the desires of your heart," Psalm 37:4. Earth has nothing you desire besides the Lord (Psalm 73:25).

HOWARD

Chief, guardian; bold

❧

Deuteronomy 31:6 *Be strong and courageous. Do not be afraid or terrified because of them, for the Lord your God goes with you; He will never leave you nor forsake you.*

Joshua 1:7 *Be strong and very courageous. Be careful to obey all the law My servant Moses gave you; do not turn from it to the right or to the left, that you may be successful wherever you go.*

You are equipped with mental and moral strength to venture, persevere, and withstand danger, fear, and difficulty. You have the firmness of mind to take a firm stand. You meet strain with fortitude and resilience, even when opposed or threatened. You have firm determination to achieve God's purpose in your life. With stubborn persistence and unwillingness to admit defeat, you base all victory on the finished work of the cross of Jesus. The Victor will use you to remove obstacles and invade darkness and death in order to bring the lost to a decision for Jesus. God's divine presence in and through you will bind fear and lead people to their God-given inheritance.

HOWIE

Chief, guardian; bold

❧

Deuteronomy 31:6   *Be strong and courageous. Do not be afraid or terrified because of them, for the Lord your God goes with you; He will never leave you nor forsake you.*

Joshua 1:7   *Be strong and very courageous. Be careful to obey all the law My servant Moses gave you; do not turn from it to the right or to the left, that you may be successful wherever you go.*

You are equipped with mental and moral strength to venture, persevere, and withstand danger, fear, and difficulty. You have the firmness of mind to take a firm stand. You meet strain with fortitude and resilience, even when opposed or threatened. You have firm determination to achieve God's purpose in your life. With stubborn persistence and unwillingness to admit defeat, you base all victory on the finished work of the cross of Jesus. The Victor will use you to remove obstacles and invade darkness and death in order to bring the lost to a decision for Jesus. God's divine presence in and through you will bind fear and lead people to their God-given inheritance.

HUDSON

Son of Hugh; intelligent, wise

৪৩

James 3:17 *But the wisdom that comes from heaven is first of all pure; then peace-loving, considerate, submissive, full of mercy and good fruit, impartial and sincere.*

Proverbs 9:10 *The fear of the Lord is the beginning of wisdom, and knowledge of the Holy One is understanding.*

You are a person of moral excellence. You exemplify right living put into practice. The Lord has not only equipped you with skills for living correctly, but also the ability to impart that to others. The Spirit of truth will guide you into all truth, allowing you to have insight into the true nature of things (John 16:13). Out of your reverential respect for the Lord, you have wisdom to give guidance and direction. You are a safe sounding board who steers those who are hungry for knowledge of the Holy One in the right direction. You need only to ask for the wisdom you lack, and God will give it to you generously (James 1:5). Having spiritual discernment is having the ability to separate the difference between God's wisdom and the world's and the ability to make the right choice—regardless. Luke 21:15 says, "For I will give you words and wisdom that none of your adversaries will be able to resist or contradict."

HUNTER

Hunter; one who pursues truth

ॐ

Psalm 89:1–2   *I will sing of the Lord's great love forever; with my mouth I will make Your faithfulness known through all generations. I will declare that Your love stands firm forever, that You established Your faithfulness in heaven itself.*

Psalm 51:6   *Surely You desire truth in the inner parts; You teach me wisdom in the inmost place.*

John 14:6   *Jesus answered, "I am the way and the truth and the life. No one comes to the Father except through Me."*

"You know the truth and the truth has set you free," John 8:32. You are one who is aggressive toward lies and deception. Your purpose is to bring about truth through openness, revelation, authenticity, accuracy, and honesty. As God's messenger, you will have firmness in keeping and executing His promises and also your own. Your God-given wisdom will be based on God's Word alone. Zechariah 8:16 says, "These are the things you are to do: Speak the truth to each other, and render true and sound judgment in your courts." May true instruction be in your mouth and nothing false be found on your lips (Malachi 2:6).

IAN

God's gracious gift; gracious one

ဥ

Romans 8:32 *He who did not spare His own Son, but gave Him up for us all—how will He not also, along with Him, graciously give us all things?*

I Corinthians 15:10 *But by the grace of God I am what I am, and His grace to me was not without effect.*

Ephesians 2:8 says, "For it is by grace you have been saved, through faith—and this is not from yourselves, it is the gift of God." You are one who brings about balance and harmony through mercy, forgiveness, approval, kindness, and patience—all with a grateful heart. This attitude of gratitude will rule in the midst of inconsiderate behavior. Your nature defies the law of the Pharisees, and is against being self-reliant, prejudice, and selfish. Being full of grace is devotion built through faithfulness and a willingness to quickly pardon. You are blessed with creativity in expressing God's greatest gift of grace—the life of His only Son, Jesus Christ. God says to you through Jeremiah 24:7, "I will give them a heart to know Me, that I am the Lord. They will be My people, and I will be their God, for they will return to Me with all their heart." Ezekiel 11:19 says, "I will give them an undivided heart and put a new spirit in them; I will remove from them their heart of stone and give them a heart of flesh." Accountability will keep your report accurate and your integrity irreproachable.

IKE

Laughter; cheerful faith

❦

Psalm 91:15   *He will call upon me, and I will answer Him; I will be with him in trouble, I will deliver him and honor him.*

II Peter 3:9   *The Lord is not slow in keeping His promise, as some understand slowness. He is patient with you, not wanting anyone to perish, but everyone to come to repentance.*

You, like Isaac, are a child of promise (Galatians 4:28). Hebrews 11:17–19 says, "By faith Abraham, when God tested him, offered Isaac as a sacrifice. He who had received the promises was about to sacrifice his one and only son, even though God had said to him, 'It is through Isaac that your offspring will be reckoned.' Abraham reasoned that God could raise the dead, and figuratively speaking, he did receive Isaac back from death." "If you belong to Christ, then you are Abraham's seed, and heirs according to the promise," Galatians 3:29. Abraham was fully persuaded that God had power to do what He had promised (Romans 4:21). You have inherited this same strong faith as you stay committed to God's Word and love Him (James 2:5). As God's fulfilled promise, you will not choose deception, denial, or to break any covenant you make. God will answer you because your motives are pure—without secret sin, indifference, stubbornness, instability, self-indulgence, and disobedience. You want God's will more than yours, regardless of the cost. Being given God's great and precious promises releases you to participate in His divine nature (II Peter 1:4).

IMMANUEL

God with us; God's faithfulness

&

Proverbs 2:7–8   *He holds victory in store for the upright, He is a shield to those whose walk is blameless, for He guards the course of the just and protects the way of His faithful ones.*

Psalm 15:1–5   *Lord, who may dwell in Your sanctuary? Who may live on Your holy hill? He whose walk is blameless and who does what is righteous, who speaks the truth from his heart and has no slander on his tongue, who does his neighbor no wrong and casts no slur on his fellow man, who despises a vile man but honors those who fear the Lord, who keeps his oath even when it hurts, who lends his money without usury and does not accept a bribe against the innocent. He who does these things will never be shaken.*

You are one who has made a commitment to God to be loyal, true, dependable, enduring, and steadfast. You unmask anything fake with the reality of God's Word. You are aggressive towards lies and deception to bring about truth. You are especially sensitive to betrayal, so that God can restore hope, security, purpose, and His faithfulness in those whom He has given you to serve. "Be faithful, even to the point of death, and I will give you a crown of life," Revelation 2:10. Anticipate the Master saying to you, "Well done, good and faithful servant! You have been faithful with a few things; I will put you in charge of many things. Come and share your Master's happiness!" (Matthew 25:21) "The one who calls you is faithful and he will do it," I Thessalonians 5:24.

IMOGENE

Innocent; pure one

ಸು

I Timothy 5:22 *...do not share in the sins of others. Keep yourself pure.*

I Peter 1:22 *Now that you have purified yourselves by obeying the truth so that you have sincere love for your brothers, love one another deeply, from the heart.*

Through the process of heat, trials, and refinement, purity is established. Your nature defies being stubborn, judgmental, and haughty. The commandment of the Lord is clear—giving insight to life (Psalm 19:8). You bring wholeness to the dirty, defiled, contaminated, polluted, double-minded, and raped. Your willingness to be transparent is the venue through which He makes His Word clear, simple, and unadulterated. Your choice to be pure enables you to see God (Matthew 5:8) and to know Him as King and Friend (Proverbs 22:11). It also allows your words to be pleasant (Proverbs 15:26) and causes you to ascend to the holy place of the Lord, where you receive blessings and righteousness from the God of salvation (Psalm 24:3–5). Proverbs 20:11 says, "Even a child is known by his actions, by whether his conduct is pure and right."

IRENE

Peace; peaceful spirit

Isaiah 26:3   *You will keep in perfect peace him whose mind is steadfast, because he trusts in You.*

Philippians 4:7   *And the peace of God, which transcends all understanding, will guard your hearts and your minds in Christ Jesus.*

Your life defines peace. You will have a content and calm composure in the midst of distress, disturbance, or agitation. As you follow the Prince of Peace, you will be secure in who you are in Christ. The discipline of keeping your mind on Christ, loving God's law, and being controlled by the Holy Spirit will keep you in perfect peace. God's peace will serve as an umpire to determine whether you are safe or out of God's will (Colossians 3:15). Do not think it strange when you are in battles, fights, and quarrels, because God wants to use you to bring harmony, order, unity, agreement, quietness, and calmness to the adverse situation. You are one whose intimate friendship with the Lord brings reconciliation to the offended, distressed, and troubled. "In repentance and rest is your salvation, in quietness and trust is your strength," Isaiah 30:15. Your refreshing comes as you renew your mind daily in the Word of God. "Great peace have they who love Your law, and nothing can make them stumble," Psalm 119:165.

ISAAC

Laughter; cheerful faith

❧

Psalm 91:15   *He will call upon me, and I will answer Him; I will be with him in trouble, I will deliver him and honor him.*

II Peter 3:9   *The Lord is not slow in keeping His promise, as some understand slowness. He is patient with you, not wanting anyone to perish, but everyone to come to repentance.*

You, like Isaac, are a child of promise (Galatians 4:28). Hebrews 11:17–19 says, "By faith Abraham, when God tested him, offered Isaac as a sacrifice. He who had received the promises was about to sacrifice his one and only son, even though God had said to him, 'It is through Isaac that your offspring will be reckoned.' Abraham reasoned that God could raise the dead, and figuratively speaking, he did receive Isaac back from death." "If you belong to Christ, then you are Abraham's seed, and heirs according to the promise," Galatians 3:29. Abraham was fully persuaded that God had power to do what He had promised (Romans 4:21). You have inherited this same strong faith as you stay committed to God's Word and love Him (James 2:5). As God's fulfilled promise, you will not choose deception, denial, or to break any covenant you make. God will answer you because your motives are pure—without secret sin, indifference, stubbornness, instability, self-indulgence, and disobedience. You want God's will more than yours, regardless of the cost. Being given God's great and precious promises releases you to participate in His divine nature (II Peter 1:4).

ISABELLA

Consecrated to God; consecrated one

&

Romans 12:1 *Therefore, I urge you brothers, in view of God's mercy, to offer your bodies as living sacrifices, holy and pleasing to God—this is your spiritual act of worship.*

Philippians 3:7–8 *But whatever was to my profit I now consider loss for the sake of Christ. What is more, I consider everything a loss compared to the surpassing greatness of knowing Christ Jesus my Lord, for whose sake I have lost all things. I consider them rubbish, that I may gain Christ.*

Before you were born, God set you apart and appointed you as a prophet to the nations (Jeremiah 1:5). You are to be devoted irrevocably to the worship of God. He will pour out His anointing upon you as you are faithful to follow Him wholeheartedly (Psalm 119:34). You are one who has made a commitment to be loyal, true, dependable, enduring, and steadfast. You unmask anything fake with the reality of God's Word. You are aggressive towards lies and deception in order to bring about truth. You are especially sensitive to betrayal, so that God can restore hope, security, purpose, and His faithfulness in those whom He has given you to serve. Let your eyes keep to God's ways (Proverbs 23:26).

ISABELLE

Consecrated to God; consecrated one

ℬↄ

Romans 12:1 *Therefore, I urge you brothers, in view of God's mercy, to offer your bodies as living sacrifices, holy and pleasing to God—this is your spiritual act of worship.*

Philippians 3:7–8 *But whatever was to my profit I now consider loss for the sake of Christ. What is more, I consider everything a loss compared to the surpassing greatness of knowing Christ Jesus my Lord, for whose sake I have lost all things. I consider them rubbish, that I may gain Christ.*

Before you were born, God set you apart and appointed you as a prophet to the nations (Jeremiah 1:5). You are to be devoted irrevocably to the worship of God. He will pour out His anointing upon you as you are faithful to follow Him wholeheartedly (Psalm 119:34). You are one who has made a commitment to be loyal, true, dependable, enduring, and steadfast. You unmask anything fake with the reality of God's Word. You are aggressive towards lies and deception in order to bring about truth. You are especially sensitive to betrayal, so that God can restore hope, security, purpose, and His faithfulness in those whom He has given you to serve. Let your eyes keep to God's ways (Proverbs 23:26).

ISAIAH

Deliverance of Jehovah; God is Savior

ॐ

Isaiah 12:2 *Surely God is my salvation; I will trust and not be afraid. The Lord, the Lord, is my strength and my song; He has become my salvation.*

Ephesians 2:8–9 *For it is by grace you have been saved, through faith—and this not from yourselves, it is a gift of God—not by works, so that no one can boast.*

The salvation of God is the light of His Son revealed in every crevice of your life. Where you are vulnerable, insecure, unstable, and weak, the Lord will rescue, deliver, and protect. The Lord desires to preserve you from being false, deceptive, misleading, and exaggerating. With your dependence on God for your salvation, you will ever want to be real and honest, with nothing to hide. You are not ashamed of the gospel, because it is the power of God for the salvation of everyone who believes (Romans 1:6). You have been chosen to deliver the truth of God's salvation to the lost and condemned. His work of grace, pardon, and forgiveness of sin will be experienced through you by Jesus Christ. Thanks be to God for His indescribable gift! (II Corinthians 9:15)

ISRAEL

World mighty; overcomer

&

Revelation 2:7   *To him who overcomes, I will give the right to eat from the tree of life, which is in the paradise of God.*

Romans 8:37   *No, in all these things we are more than conquerors through Him who loved us.*

An overcomer is a winner, champion, and victor who subdues, triumphs, and prevails. That which is intended to overwhelm, overthrow, defeat, humiliate, and manipulate is placed in your hands to gain and acquire by force. You win by overcoming obstacles and opposition. You overthrow by bringing down the destructive power of the enemy. The domineering control intended to thwart one's destiny is brought in subjection to the Victor's power. As you age, so shall you be equipped with increased strength to subdue the enemy's strongholds (Deuteronomy 33:25). You will reverse the curse in everyone you touch by releasing the surpassing victory enabled only by the One who loves you. God uses you to raise the standard, go over and above the mark, seize the Promised Land, and to be more than a conqueror.

IVY

Ivy plant; faithfulness

❧

Proverbs 2:7–8   *He holds victory in store for the upright, He is a shield to those whose walk is blameless, for He guards the course of the just and protects the way of His faithful ones.*

Psalm 15:1–5   *Lord, who may dwell in Your sanctuary? Who may live on Your holy hill? He whose walk is blameless and who does what is righteous, who speaks the truth from his heart and has no slander on his tongue, who does his neighbor no wrong and casts no slur on his fellow man, who despises a vile man but honors those who fear the Lord, who keeps his oath even when it hurts, who lends his money without usury and does not accept a bribe against the innocent. He who does these things will never be shaken.*

You are one who has made a commitment to God to be loyal, true, dependable, enduring, and steadfast. You unmask anything fake with the reality of God's Word. You are aggressive towards lies and deception to bring about truth. You are especially sensitive to betrayal, so that God can restore hope, security, purpose, and His faithfulness in those whom He has given you to serve. "Be faithful, even to the point of death, and I will give you a crown of life," Revelation 2:10. Anticipate the Master saying to you, "Well done, good and faithful servant! You have been faithful with a few things; I will put you in charge of many things. Come and share your Master's happiness!" (Matthew 25:21) "The one who calls you is faithful and he will do it," I Thessalonians 5:24.

JACK

Supplanter; truthful

❧

Psalm 89:1–2 *I will sing of the Lord's great love forever; with my mouth I will make Your faithfulness known through all generations. I will declare that Your love stands firm forever, that You established Your faithfulness in heaven itself.*

Psalm 51:6 *Surely You desire truth in the inner parts; You teach me wisdom in the inmost place.*

John 14:6 *Jesus answered, "I am the way and the truth and the life. No one comes to the Father except through Me."*

"You know the truth and the truth has set you free," John 8:32. You are one who is aggressive toward lies and deception. Your purpose is to bring about truth through openness, revelation, authenticity, accuracy, and honesty. As God's messenger, you will have firmness in keeping and executing His promises and also your own. Your God-given wisdom will be based on God's Word alone. Zechariah 8:16 says, "These are the things you are to do: Speak the truth to each other, and render true and sound judgment in your courts." May true instruction be in your mouth and nothing false be found on your lips (Malachi 2:6).

JACKIE

Supplanter; truthful

⃝

Psalm 89:1–2 *I will sing of the Lord's great love forever; with my mouth I will make Your faithfulness known through all generations. I will declare that Your love stands firm forever, that You established Your faithfulness in heaven itself.*

Psalm 51:6 *Surely You desire truth in the inner parts; You teach me wisdom in the inmost place.*

John 14:6 *Jesus answered, "I am the way and the truth and the life. No one comes to the Father except through Me."*

"You know the truth and the truth has set you free," John 8:32. You are one who is aggressive toward lies and deception. Your purpose is to bring about truth through openness, revelation, authenticity, accuracy, and honesty. As God's messenger, you will have firmness in keeping and executing His promises and also your own. Your God-given wisdom will be based on God's Word alone. Zechariah 8:16 says, "These are the things you are to do: Speak the truth to each other, and render true and sound judgment in your courts." May true instruction be in your mouth and nothing false be found on your lips (Malachi 2:6).

JACKSON

Supplanter; truthful

ℰ

Psalm 89:1–2 *I will sing of the Lord's great love forever; with my mouth I will make Your faithfulness known through all generations. I will declare that Your love stands firm forever, that You established Your faithfulness in heaven itself.*

Psalm 51:6 *Surely You desire truth in the inner parts; You teach me wisdom in the inmost place.*

John 14:6 *Jesus answered, "I am the way and the truth and the life. No one comes to the Father except through Me."*

"You know the truth and the truth has set you free," John 8:32. You are one who is aggressive toward lies and deception. Your purpose is to bring about truth through openness, revelation, authenticity, accuracy, and honesty. As God's messenger, you will have firmness in keeping and executing His promises and also your own. Your God-given wisdom will be based on God's Word alone. Zechariah 8:16 says, "These are the things you are to do: Speak the truth to each other, and render true and sound judgment in your courts." May true instruction be in your mouth and nothing false be found on your lips. (Malachi 2:6).

JACOB

Supplanter; truthful

&

Psalm 89:1–2 *I will sing of the Lord's great love forever; with my mouth I will make Your faithfulness known through all generations. I will declare that Your love stands firm forever, that You established Your faithfulness in heaven itself.*

Psalm 51:6 *Surely You desire truth in the inner parts; You teach me wisdom in the inmost place.*

John 14:6 *Jesus answered, "I am the way and the truth and the life. No one comes to the Father except through Me."*

"You know the truth and the truth has set you free," John 8:32. You are one who is aggressive toward lies and deception. Your purpose is to bring about truth through openness, revelation, authenticity, accuracy, and honesty. As God's messenger, you will have firmness in keeping and executing His promises and also your own. Your God-given wisdom will be based on God's Word alone. Zechariah 8:16 says, "These are the things you are to do: Speak the truth to each other, and render true and sound judgment in your courts." May true instruction be in your mouth and nothing false be found on your lips (Malachi 2:6).

JADA

Jade stone; wise

❧

James 3:17 *But the wisdom that comes from heaven is first of all pure; then peace-loving, considerate, submissive, full of mercy and good fruit, impartial and sincere.*

Proverbs 9:10 *The fear of the Lord is the beginning of wisdom, and knowledge of the Holy One is understanding.*

You are a person of moral excellence. You exemplify right living put into practice. The Lord has not only equipped you with skills for living correctly, but also the ability to impart that to others. The Spirit of truth will guide you into all truth, allowing you to have insight into the true nature of things (John 16:13). Out of your reverential respect for the Lord, you have wisdom to give guidance and direction. You are a safe sounding board who steers those who are hungry for knowledge of the Holy One in the right direction. You need only to ask for the wisdom you lack, and God will give it to you generously (James 1:5). Having spiritual discernment is having the ability to separate the difference between God's wisdom and the world's and the ability to make the right choice—regardless. Luke 21:15 says, "For I will give you words and wisdom that none of your adversaries will be able to resist or contradict."

JADE

Jade stone; wise

ॐ

James 3:17 *But the wisdom that comes from heaven is first of all pure; then peace-loving, considerate, submissive, full of mercy and good fruit, impartial and sincere.*

Proverbs 9:10 *The fear of the Lord is the beginning of wisdom, and knowledge of the Holy One is understanding.*

You are a person of moral excellence. You exemplify right living put into practice. The Lord has not only equipped you with skills for living correctly, but also the ability to impart that to others. The Spirit of truth will guide you into all truth, allowing you to have insight into the true nature of things (John 16:13). Out of your reverential respect for the Lord, you have wisdom to give guidance and direction. You are a safe sounding board who steers those who are hungry for knowledge of the Holy One in the right direction. You need only to ask for the wisdom you lack, and God will give it to you generously (James 1:5). Having spiritual discernment is having the ability to separate the difference between God's wisdom and the world's and the ability to make the right choice—regardless. Luke 21:15 says, "For I will give you words and wisdom that none of your adversaries will be able to resist or contradict."

JADEN

God has heard; integrity

&

Psalm 41:12 *In my integrity You uphold me and set me in Your presence forever.*

Proverbs 11:3 *The integrity of the upright guides them, but the unfaithful are destroyed by their duplicity.*

Spiritual deafness results from unheeded warnings, calloused hearts, rebellious disobedience, and stubborn unfaithfulness. This is prevented by being quick to hear, teachable, and having faith in God's Word. Security comes from knowing God's ears are attentive to your cry—before you call, He answers. Discernment and righteous judgment produce integrity. Integrity results in yielding weakness to God's power, based on a blameless walk. Proverbs 10:9 says, "The man of integrity walks securely, but he who takes crooked paths will be found out." You are one who has an uncompromised commitment to righteousness, respectability, honesty, character, excellence, innocence, generosity, trustworthiness, faithfulness, justice, hope, and love. Be truthful with others, as well as yourself. Be the same in public as you are in private. Titus 2:7–8 says, "In everything set them an example by doing what is good. In your teaching show integrity, seriousness and soundness of speech that cannot be condemned, so that those who oppose you may be ashamed because they have nothing bad to say about us."

JAKE

Supplanter; truthful

ℰℭ

Psalm 89:1–2 *I will sing of the Lord's great love forever; with my mouth I will make Your faithfulness known through all generations. I will declare that Your love stands firm forever, that You established Your faithfulness in heaven itself.*

Psalm 51:6 *Surely You desire truth in the inner parts; You teach me wisdom in the inmost place.*

John 14:6 *Jesus answered, "I am the way and the truth and the life. No one comes to the Father except through Me."*

"You know the truth and the truth has set you free," John 8:32. You are one who is aggressive toward lies and deception. Your purpose is to bring about truth through openness, revelation, authenticity, accuracy, and honesty. As God's messenger, you will have firmness in keeping and executing His promises and also your own. Your God-given wisdom will be based on God's Word alone. Zechariah 8:16 says, "These are the things you are to do: Speak the truth to each other, and render true and sound judgment in your courts." May true instruction be in your mouth and nothing false be found on your lips (Malachi 2:6).

JAMES

Supplanter; truthful

&

Psalm 89:1–2 *I will sing of the Lord's great love forever; with my mouth I will make Your faithfulness known through all generations. I will declare that Your love stands firm forever, that You established Your faithfulness in heaven itself.*

Psalm 51:6 *Surely You desire truth in the inner parts; You teach me wisdom in the inmost place.*

John 14:6 *Jesus answered, "I am the way and the truth and the life. No one comes to the Father except through Me."*

"You know the truth and the truth has set you free," John 8:32. You are one who is aggressive toward lies and deception. Your purpose is to bring about truth through openness, revelation, authenticity, accuracy, and honesty. As God's messenger, you will have firmness in keeping and executing His promises and also your own. Your God-given wisdom will be based on God's Word alone. Zechariah 8:16 says, "These are the things you are to do: Speak the truth to each other, and render true and sound judgment in your courts." May true instruction be in your mouth and nothing false be found on your lips (Malachi 2:6).

JAMEY

Supplanter; truthful

ဢ

Psalm 89:1–2 *I will sing of the Lord's great love forever; with my mouth I will make Your faithfulness known through all generations. I will declare that Your love stands firm forever, that You established Your faithfulness in heaven itself.*

Psalm 51:6 *Surely You desire truth in the inner parts; You teach me wisdom in the inmost place.*

John 14:6 *Jesus answered, "I am the way and the truth and the life. No one comes to the Father except through Me."*

"You know the truth and the truth has set you free," John 8:32. You are one who is aggressive toward lies and deception. Your purpose is to bring about truth through openness, revelation, authenticity, accuracy, and honesty. As God's messenger, you will have firmness in keeping and executing His promises and also your own. Your God-given wisdom will be based on God's Word alone. Zechariah 8:16 says, "These are the things you are to do: Speak the truth to each other, and render true and sound judgment in your courts." May true instruction be in your mouth and nothing false be found on your lips (Malachi 2:6).

JAMIE

Supplanter; truthful

❧

Psalm 89:1–2 *I will sing of the Lord's great love forever; with my mouth I will make Your faithfulness known through all generations. I will declare that Your love stands firm forever, that You established Your faithfulness in heaven itself.*

Psalm 51:6 *Surely You desire truth in the inner parts; You teach me wisdom in the inmost place.*

John 14:6 *Jesus answered, "I am the way and the truth and the life. No one comes to the Father except through Me."*

"You know the truth and the truth has set you free," John 8:32. You are one who is aggressive toward lies and deception. Your purpose is to bring about truth through openness, revelation, authenticity, accuracy, and honesty. As God's messenger, you will have firmness in keeping and executing His promises and also your own. Your God-given wisdom will be based on God's Word alone. Zechariah 8:16 says, "These are the things you are to do: Speak the truth to each other, and render true and sound judgment in your courts." May true instruction be in your mouth and nothing false be found on your lips (Malachi 2:6).

JAN

God is gracious; God's gracious gift

Romans 8:32 *He who did not spare His own Son, but gave Him up for us all—how will He not also, along with Him, graciously give us all things?*

I Corinthians 15:10 *But by the grace of God I am what I am, and His grace to me was not without effect.*

Ephesians 2:8 says, "For it is by grace you have been saved, through faith—and this is not from yourselves, it is the gift of God." You are one who brings about balance and harmony through mercy, forgiveness, approval, kindness, and patience—all with a grateful heart. This attitude of gratitude will rule in the midst of inconsiderate behavior. Your nature defies the law of the Pharisees, and is against being self-reliant, prejudice, and selfish. Being full of grace is devotion built through faithfulness and a willingness to quickly pardon. You are blessed with creativity in expressing God's greatest gift of grace—the life of His only Son, Jesus Christ. God says to you through Jeremiah 24:7, "I will give them a heart to know Me, that I am the Lord. They will be My people, and I will be their God, for they will return to Me with all their heart." Ezekiel 11:19 says, "I will give them an undivided heart and put a new spirit in them; I will remove from them their heart of stone and give them a heart of flesh." Accountability will keep your report accurate and your integrity irreproachable.

JANE

God is gracious; God's gracious gift

Romans 8:32   *He who did not spare His own Son, but gave Him up for us all—how will He not also, along with Him, graciously give us all things?*

I Corinthians 15:10   *But by the grace of God I am what I am, and His grace to me was not without effect.*

Ephesians 2:8 says, "For it is by grace you have been saved, through faith—and this is not from yourselves, it is the gift of God." You are one who brings about balance and harmony through mercy, forgiveness, approval, kindness, and patience—all with a grateful heart. This attitude of gratitude will rule in the midst of inconsiderate behavior. Your nature defies the law of the Pharisees, and is against being self-reliant, prejudice, and selfish. Being full of grace is devotion built through faithfulness and a willingness to quickly pardon. You are blessed with creativity in expressing God's greatest gift of grace—the life of His only Son, Jesus Christ. God says to you through Jeremiah 24:7, "I will give them a heart to know Me, that I am the Lord. They will be My people, and I will be their God, for they will return to Me with all their heart." Ezekiel 11:19 says, "I will give them an undivided heart and put a new spirit in them; I will remove from them their heart of stone and give them a heart of flesh." Accountability will keep your report accurate and your integrity irreproachable.

JANET

God is gracious; God's gracious gift

ॐ

Romans 8:32 *He who did not spare His own Son, but gave Him up for us all—how will He not also, along with Him, graciously give us all things?*

I Corinthians 15:10 *But by the grace of God I am what I am, and His grace to me was not without effect.*

Ephesians 2:8 says, "For it is by grace you have been saved, through faith—and this is not from yourselves, it is the gift of God." You are one who brings about balance and harmony through mercy, forgiveness, approval, kindness, and patience—all with a grateful heart. This attitude of gratitude will rule in the midst of inconsiderate behavior. Your nature defies the law of the Pharisees, and is against being self-reliant, prejudice, and selfish. Being full of grace is devotion built through faithfulness and a willingness to quickly pardon. You are blessed with creativity in expressing God's greatest gift of grace—the life of His only Son, Jesus Christ. God says to you through Jeremiah 24:7, "I will give them a heart to know Me, that I am the Lord. They will be My people, and I will be their God, for they will return to Me with all their heart." Ezekiel 11:19 says, "I will give them an undivided heart and put a new spirit in them; I will remove from them their heart of stone and give them a heart of flesh." Accountability will keep your report accurate and your integrity irreproachable.

JANICE

God is gracious; God's gracious gift

&

Romans 8:32 *He who did not spare His own Son, but gave Him up for us all—how will He not also, along with Him, graciously give us all things?*

I Corinthians 15:10 *But by the grace of God I am what I am, and His grace to me was not without effect.*

Ephesians 2:8 says, "For it is by grace you have been saved, through faith—and this is not from yourselves, it is the gift of God." You are one who brings about balance and harmony through mercy, forgiveness, approval, kindness, and patience—all with a grateful heart. This attitude of gratitude will rule in the midst of inconsiderate behavior. Your nature defies the law of the Pharisees, and is against being self-reliant, prejudice, and selfish. Being full of grace is devotion built through faithfulness and a willingness to quickly pardon. You are blessed with creativity in expressing God's greatest gift of grace—the life of His only Son, Jesus Christ. God says to you through Jeremiah 24:7, "I will give them a heart to know Me, that I am the Lord. They will be My people, and I will be their God, for they will return to Me with all their heart." Ezekiel 11:19 says, "I will give them an undivided heart and put a new spirit in them; I will remove from them their heart of stone and give them a heart of flesh." Accountability will keep your report accurate and your integrity irreproachable.

JASMINE

Jasmine flower; living fragrance

❧

II Corinthians 2:14–15 *But thanks be to God, who always leads us in triumphal procession in Christ and through us spreads everywhere the fragrance of the knowledge of Him. For we are to God the aroma of Christ among those who are being saved and those who are perishing.*

Ephesians 5:1–2 *Be imitators of God, therefore, as dearly loved children and live a life of love, just as Christ loved us and gave Himself up for us as a fragrant offering and sacrifice to God.*

Myrrh is a fragrant oil used as part of anointing oil that is produced from the wounds or injuries made in the bark of a tree. In Bible days, it was also used as incense in the worship of God. The way you process the wounds and injuries He allows to happen to you brings Him pleasure. You join with David's words in Psalm 119:50, "My comfort in my suffering is this: Your promise preserves my life." You are secure that nothing can touch your life without passing through your Sovereign Father's hands. Much like the woman who poured her expensive perfume from her alabaster box upon Jesus, you risk being poured out and wasted for your Savior's sake. He has chosen you to be pure worship to Him. It is at that point that the stench of this world will be invaded by the sweet fragrance of Christ through your life.

JASON

Healer; one who heals

∞

Isaiah 53:5 *But He was pierced for our transgressions, He was crushed for our iniquities; the punishment that brought us peace was upon Him, and by His stripes we are healed.*

Exodus 15:26 *If you listen carefully to the voice of the Lord your God and do what is right in His eyes, if you pay attention to His commands and keep all His decrees, I will not bring on you any of the diseases I brought on the Egyptians, for I am the Lord, who heals you.*

Your soul praises the Lord because you will not forget all His benefits—the forgiveness of your sins and healing of all your diseases (Psalm 103:2–3). As one who heals, you must know the Great Physician, Jesus Christ. The stripes He bore on His back have and shall take care of every ailment that would come your way. God has anointed you with divine compassion to care for the sick. He uses you to minister to all forms of disease. Through you he will restore others to health, soundness, and their original purity and integrity. Healing involves being therapeutic as you renew, reconstruct, and rebuild. This will require you to be ever attentive to the voice of the Lord, with the ability to see as He sees. Fear will not restrict you as you stand in faith believing for His healing touch. Mend the broken-hearted and the breach. Eliminate disease, distress, and evil as you allow His Word to operate through you.

JAY

Blue jay; integrity

ॐ

Psalm 41:12 *In my integrity You uphold me and set me in Your presence forever.*

Proverbs 11:3 *The integrity of the upright guides them, but the unfaithful are destroyed by their duplicity.*

Spiritual deafness results from unheeded warnings, calloused hearts, rebellious disobedience, and stubborn unfaithfulness. This is prevented by being quick to hear, teachable, and having faith in God's Word. Security comes from knowing God's ears are attentive to your cry—before you call, He answers. Discernment and righteous judgment produce integrity. Integrity results in yielding weakness to God's power, based on a blameless walk. Proverbs 10:9 says, "The man of integrity walks securely, but he who takes crooked paths will be found out." You are one who has an uncompromised commitment to righteousness, respectability, honesty, character, excellence, innocence, generosity, trustworthiness, faithfulness, justice, hope, and love. Be truthful with others, as well as yourself. Be the same in public as you are in private. Titus 2:7–8 says, "In everything set them an example by doing what is good. In your teaching show integrity, seriousness and soundness of speech that cannot be condemned, so that those who oppose you may be ashamed because they have nothing bad to say about us."

JAYDEN

God has heard; integrity

❦

Psalm 41:12   *In my integrity You uphold me and set me in Your presence forever.*

Proverbs 11:3   *The integrity of the upright guides them, but the unfaithful are destroyed by their duplicity.*

Spiritual deafness results from unheeded warnings, calloused hearts, rebellious disobedience, and stubborn unfaithfulness. This is prevented by being quick to hear, teachable, and having faith in God's Word. Security comes from knowing God's ears are attentive to your cry—before you call, He answers. Discernment and righteous judgment produce integrity. Integrity results in yielding weakness to God's power, based on a blameless walk. Proverbs 10:9 says, "The man of integrity walks securely, but he who takes crooked paths will be found out." You are one who has an uncompromised commitment to righteousness, respectability, honesty, character, excellence, innocence, generosity, trustworthiness, faithfulness, justice, hope, and love. Be truthful with others, as well as yourself. Be the same in public as you are in private. Titus 2:7–8 says, "In everything set them an example by doing what is good. In your teaching show integrity, seriousness and soundness of speech that cannot be condemned, so that those who oppose you may be ashamed because they have nothing bad to say about us."

JAYNE

God is gracious; God's gracious gift

ℭ

Romans 8:32 *He who did not spare His own Son, but gave Him up for us all—how will He not also, along with Him, graciously give us all things?*

I Corinthians 15:10 *But by the grace of God I am what I am, and His grace to me was not without effect.*

Ephesians 2:8 says, "For it is by grace you have been saved, through faith—and this is not from yourselves, it is the gift of God." You are one who brings about balance and harmony through mercy, forgiveness, approval, kindness, and patience—all with a grateful heart. This attitude of gratitude will rule in the midst of inconsiderate behavior. Your nature defies the law of the Pharisees, and is against being self-reliant, prejudice, and selfish. Being full of grace is devotion built through faithfulness and a willingness to quickly pardon. You are blessed with creativity in expressing God's greatest gift of grace—the life of His only Son, Jesus Christ. God says to you through Jeremiah 24:7, "I will give them a heart to know Me, that I am the Lord. They will be My people, and I will be their God, for they will return to Me with all their heart." Ezekiel 11:19 says, "I will give them an undivided heart and put a new spirit in them; I will remove from them their heart of stone and give them a heart of flesh." Accountability will keep your report accurate and your integrity irreproachable.

JEAN

God is gracious; God's gracious gift

℘

Romans 8:32 *He who did not spare His own Son, but gave Him up for us all—how will He not also, along with Him, graciously give us all things?*

I Corinthians 15:10 *But by the grace of God I am what I am, and His grace to me was not without effect.*

Ephesians 2:8 says, "For it is by grace you have been saved, through faith—and this is not from yourselves, it is the gift of God." You are one who brings about balance and harmony through mercy, forgiveness, approval, kindness, and patience—all with a grateful heart. This attitude of gratitude will rule in the midst of inconsiderate behavior. Your nature defies the law of the Pharisees, and is against being self-reliant, prejudice, and selfish. Being full of grace is devotion built through faithfulness and a willingness to quickly pardon. You are blessed with creativity in expressing God's greatest gift of grace—the life of His only Son, Jesus Christ. God says to you through Jeremiah 24:7, "I will give them a heart to know Me, that I am the Lord. They will be My people, and I will be their God, for they will return to Me with all their heart." Ezekiel 11:19 says, "I will give them an undivided heart and put a new spirit in them; I will remove from them their heart of stone and give them a heart of flesh." Accountability will keep your report accurate and your integrity irreproachable.

JEANETTE

God is gracious; God's gracious gift

જી

Romans 8:32 *He who did not spare His own Son, but gave Him up for us all—how will He not also, along with Him, graciously give us all things?*

I Corinthians 15:10 *But by the grace of God I am what I am, and His grace to me was not without effect.*

Ephesians 2:8 says, "For it is by grace you have been saved, through faith—and this is not from yourselves, it is the gift of God." You are one who brings about balance and harmony through mercy, forgiveness, approval, kindness, and patience—all with a grateful heart. This attitude of gratitude will rule in the midst of inconsiderate behavior. Your nature defies the law of the Pharisees, and is against being self-reliant, prejudice, and selfish. Being full of grace is devotion built through faithfulness and a willingness to quickly pardon. You are blessed with creativity in expressing God's greatest gift of grace—the life of His only Son, Jesus Christ. God says to you through Jeremiah 24:7, "I will give them a heart to know Me, that I am the Lord. They will be My people, and I will be their God, for they will return to Me with all their heart." Ezekiel 11:19 says, "I will give them an undivided heart and put a new spirit in them; I will remove from them their heart of stone and give them a heart of flesh." Accountability will keep your report accurate and your integrity irreproachable.

JEFF

Peaceful pledge; peaceful

&

Isaiah 26:3 *You will keep in perfect peace him whose mind is steadfast, because he trusts in You.*

Philippians 4:7 *And the peace of God, which transcends all understanding, will guard your hearts and your minds in Christ Jesus.*

Your life defines peace. You will have a content and calm composure in the midst of distress, disturbance, or agitation. As you follow the Prince of Peace, you will be secure in who you are in Christ. The discipline of keeping your mind on Christ, loving God's law, and being controlled by the Holy Spirit will keep you in perfect peace. God's peace will serve as an umpire to determine whether you are safe or out of God's will (Colossians 3:15). Do not think it strange when you are in battles, fights, and quarrels, because God wants to use you to bring harmony, order, unity, agreement, quietness, and calmness to the adverse situation. You are one whose intimate friendship with the Lord brings reconciliation to the offended, distressed, and troubled. "In repentance and rest is your salvation, in quietness and trust is your strength," Isaiah 30:15. Your refreshing comes as you renew your mind daily in the Word of God. "Great peace have they who love Your law, and nothing can make them stumble," Psalm 119:165.

JEFFREY

Divinely; peaceful

Isaiah 26:3 *You will keep in perfect peace him whose mind is steadfast, because he trusts in You.*

Philippians 4:7 *And the peace of God, which transcends all understanding, will guard your hearts and your minds in Christ Jesus.*

Your life defines peace. You will have a content and calm composure in the midst of distress, disturbance, or agitation. As you follow the Prince of Peace, you will be secure in who you are in Christ. The discipline of keeping your mind on Christ, loving God's law, and being controlled by the Holy Spirit will keep you in perfect peace. God's peace will serve as an umpire to determine whether you are safe or out of God's will (Colossians 3:15). Do not think it strange when you are in battles, fights, and quarrels, because God wants to use you to bring harmony, order, unity, agreement, quietness, and calmness to the adverse situation. You are one whose intimate friendship with the Lord brings reconciliation to the offended, distressed, and troubled. "In repentance and rest is your salvation, in quietness and trust is your strength," Isaiah 30:15. Your refreshing comes as you renew your mind daily in the Word of God. "Great peace have they who love Your law, and nothing can make them stumble," Psalm 119:165.

JENNA

White wave; fair lady

ৰ্জ

Psalm 27:4   *One thing I ask of the Lord, this is what I seek: that I may dwell in the house of the Lord all the days of my life, to gaze upon the beauty of the Lord and to seek Him in His temple.*

Philippians 4:5   *Let your gentleness be evident to all. The Lord is near.*

You are one who radiates the beauty of the Lord with calm assurance of being pleasing, flawless, clean, and pure before Him. As one who is marked by honesty, you have no prejudice or impartiality. You are able to minister to the victim as well as the victimizer. This is accomplished by the cleansing power of the blood of the Lamb, Jesus Christ. Your dignity is shown as you give honor to the undeserved, show kindness to the harsh, and remain calm in the face of violence. God exchanges the consuming ashes of your life for a crown of beauty (Isaiah 61:3). God rewards you with His righteous hand.

JENNIFER

White wave; fair lady

ॐ

Psalm 27:4   *One thing I ask of the Lord, this is what I seek: that I may dwell in the house of the Lord all the days of my life, to gaze upon the beauty of the Lord and to seek Him in His temple.*

Philippians 4:5   *Let your gentleness be evident to all. The Lord is near.*

You are one who radiates the beauty of the Lord with calm assurance of being pleasing, flawless, clean, and pure before Him. As one who is marked by honesty, you have no prejudice or impartiality. You are able to minister to the victim as well as the victimizer. This is accomplished by the cleansing power of the blood of the Lamb, Jesus Christ. Your dignity is shown as you give honor to the undeserved, show kindness to the harsh, and remain calm in the face of violence. God exchanges the consuming ashes of your life for a crown of beauty (Isaiah 61:3). God rewards you with His righteous hand.

JENNY

White wave; fair lady

❧

Psalm 27:4 *One thing I ask of the Lord, this is what I seek: that I may dwell in the house of the Lord all the days of my life, to gaze upon the beauty of the Lord and to seek Him in His temple.*

Philippians 4:5 *Let your gentleness be evident to all. The Lord is near.*

You are one who radiates the beauty of the Lord with calm assurance of being pleasing, flawless, clean, and pure before Him. As one who is marked by honesty, you have no prejudice or impartiality. You are able to minister to the victim as well as the victimizer. This is accomplished by the cleansing power of the blood of the Lamb, Jesus Christ. Your dignity is shown as you give honor to the undeserved, show kindness to the harsh, and remain calm in the face of violence. God exchanges the consuming ashes of your life for a crown of beauty (Isaiah 61:3). God rewards you with His righteous hand.

JEREMIAH

Appointed by Jehovah; appointed by God

ॐ

Jeremiah 1:5   *Before I formed you in the womb, I knew you, before you were born I set you apart; I appointed you as a prophet to the nations.*

John 15:16   *You did not choose Me, but I chose you and appointed you to go and bear fruit—fruit that will last. Then the Father will give you whatever you ask in My name.*

You hear the voice of the Lord saying, "Whom shall I send? And who will go for us?" And you say, "Here am I. Send me!" (Isaiah 6:8) The Lord has appointed you as a servant and witness of what you have seen of Him and what He shows you (Acts 26:16). You were chosen in Him before the creation of the world to be holy and blameless in His sight (Ephesians 1:4). God has placed His trust in you by giving you His authority and ordained you to reflect His character and thoughts. As one favored by God, you are His representative sent on His mission. Knowing He chooses the weak and foolish things to confound the wise requires humility, gratitude, and surrender. God's approval is upon you and His assignment is in you to accomplish His purposes. Make your calling sure and live a life worthy of the calling you have received. Be completely humble, gentle, patient, and bearing with one another in love (Ephesians 4:1–2). You refuse a maintenance mode, but rather fix your thoughts and destination on Jesus. You are equipped to fulfill the great commission (Matthew 28:18–20).

JEREMY

Appointed by Jehovah; appointed by God

ॐ

Jeremiah 1:5   *Before I formed you in the womb, I knew you, before you were born I set you apart; I appointed you as a prophet to the nations.*

John 15:16   *You did not choose Me, but I chose you and appointed you to go and bear fruit—fruit that will last. Then the Father will give you whatever you ask in My name.*

You hear the voice of the Lord saying, "Whom shall I send? And who will go for us?" And you say, "Here am I. Send me!" (Isaiah 6:8) The Lord has appointed you as a servant and witness of what you have seen of Him and what He shows you (Acts 26:16). You were chosen in Him before the creation of the world to be holy and blameless in His sight (Ephesians 1:4). God has placed His trust in you by giving you His authority and ordained you to reflect His character and thoughts. As one favored by God, you are His representative sent on His mission. Knowing He chooses the weak and foolish things to confound the wise requires humility, gratitude, and surrender. God's approval is upon you and His assignment is in you to accomplish His purposes. Make your calling sure and live a life worthy of the calling you have received. Be completely humble, gentle, patient, and bearing with one another in love (Ephesians 4:1–2). You refuse a maintenance mode, but rather fix your thoughts and destination on Jesus. You are equipped to fulfill the great commission (Matthew 28:18–20).

JERRY

Appointed by Jehovah; appointed by God

Jeremiah 1:5   *Before I formed you in the womb, I knew you, before you were born I set you apart; I appointed you as a prophet to the nations.*

John 15:16   *You did not choose Me, but I chose you and appointed you to go and bear fruit—fruit that will last. Then the Father will give you whatever you ask in My name.*

You hear the voice of the Lord saying, "Whom shall I send? And who will go for us?" And you say, "Here am I. Send me!" (Isaiah 6:8) The Lord has appointed you as a servant and witness of what you have seen of Him and what He shows you (Acts 26:16). You were chosen in Him before the creation of the world to be holy and blameless in His sight (Ephesians 1:4). God has placed His trust in you by giving you His authority and ordained you to reflect His character and thoughts. As one favored by God, you are His representative sent on His mission. Knowing He chooses the weak and foolish things to confound the wise requires humility, gratitude, and surrender. God's approval is upon you and His assignment is in you to accomplish His purposes. Make your calling sure and live a life worthy of the calling you have received. Be completely humble, gentle, patient, and bearing with one another in love (Ephesians 4:1–2). You refuse a maintenance mode, but rather fix your thoughts and destination on Jesus. You are equipped to fulfill the great commission (Matthew 28:18–20).

JESSE

Gift of Jehovah; gift of the Lord

৪১

James 1:17 *Every good and perfect gift is from above, coming down from the Father of the heavenly lights, who does not change like shifting shadows.*

I Samuel 16:7 *But the Lord said to Samuel, "Do not consider his appearance or his height, for I have rejected him. The Lord does not look at the things man looks at. Man looks at the outward appearance, but the Lord looks at the heart."*

You are God's tribute to Himself, His personal reward. Your life defines God's manners, with priorities on giving rather than receiving. You are to fan into flame the gift of God (II Timothy 1:6). Through you He will display His favor, encouragement and kindness even to the undeserved and hated. As you look beyond faults and see needs, you are God's channel through which His unselfish love flows and is revealed. Discipline your attention to the Giver, not to the gift, nor its wrappings. Give diligence to preserving a humble, submitted heart in full surrender to the Lord. Proverbs 18:16 says, "A gift opens the way for the giver and ushers him into the presence of the great."

JESSICA

Wealthy one; blessed one

Exodus 23:25 *Worship the Lord your God, and His blessing will be on your food and water. I will take away sickness from among you.*

Proverbs 10:22 *The blessing of the Lord brings wealth, and He adds no trouble to it.*

God has resourced you in order to give you great influence and favor. He commands His blessings where you establish unity (Psalm 133). He will turn every curse into a blessing for you because He loves you (Deuteronomy 23:5). True abundance is giving out of your nothingness, with a total dependence on God. Wealth is not in the amount you have, but in the attitude in which you give it. Because of your standard of integrity and gratitude, you have an eye for value, fruitfulness, and generosity. Your heart is for the poor, barren, and destitute, but you resist the lazy and stingy. You transfer God's possessions, power, and pleasure to others. Make wise investments of your time, energy, and resources that will keep reproducing rather than insuring your own personal gratification. You are blessed to be a blessing. The greater your obedience to the Lord, the greater will be His blessings (Deuteronomy 28:1–14).

JESSIE

God exists; gift of God

&

James 1:17 *Every good and perfect gift is from above, coming down from the Father of the heavenly lights, who does not change like shifting shadows.*

I Samuel 16:7 *But the Lord said to Samuel, "Do not consider his appearance or his height, for I have rejected him. The Lord does not look at the things man looks at. Man looks at the outward appearance, but the Lord looks at the heart."*

You are God's tribute to Himself, His personal reward. Your life defines God's manners, with priorities on giving rather than receiving. You are to fan into flame the gift of God (II Timothy 1:6). Through you He will display His favor, encouragement and kindness even to the undeserved and hated. As you look beyond faults and see needs, you are God's channel through which His unselfish love flows and is revealed. Discipline your attention to the Giver, not to the gift, nor its wrappings. Give diligence to preserving a humble, submitted heart in full surrender to the Lord. Proverbs 18:16 says, "A gift opens the way for the giver and ushers him into the presence of the great."

JILL

Youthful one; youthful heart

❧

Psalm 71:5, 17   *For You have been my hope, O Sovereign Lord, my confidence since my youth. Since my youth, O God, You have taught me, and to this day I declare Your marvelous deeds.*

I Timothy 4:12   *Don't let anyone look down on you because you are young, but set an example for the believers in speech, in life, in love, in faith and in purity.*

You are God's expression of childlikeness, refreshment, and vigor. You will undergo little erosion, not to your own credit but to the faithfulness of God. Your pursuit of a pure heart, which is God's innocence, will release His protection over you from all that would rob His youthfulness in you. Think it not strange when God would cross your path with those who are aged in spirit by weariness, shame, or fear. You are His ambassador to restore His strength, refreshment, and vigor. See yourself constantly as that child—full of faith and adoration for your Heavenly Father—on the Lord's lap: accepted, cuddled, and with strong arms around you. He will equip you to wait hopefully—to not be anxious or consumed with worry. Your childlike dependency on the Lord will keep you trusting, full of faith, and renewed.

JIM

Supplanter; truthful

☙

Psalm 89:1–2 *I will sing of the Lord's great love forever; with my mouth I will make Your faithfulness known through all generations. I will declare that Your love stands firm forever, that You established Your faithfulness in heaven itself.*

Psalm 51:6 *Surely You desire truth in the inner parts; You teach me wisdom in the inmost place.*

John 14:6 *Jesus answered, "I am the way and the truth and the life. No one comes to the Father except through Me."*

"You know the truth and the truth has set you free," John 8:32. You are one who is aggressive toward lies and deception. Your purpose is to bring about truth through openness, revelation, authenticity, accuracy, and honesty. As God's messenger, you will have firmness in keeping and executing His promises and also your own. Your God-given wisdom will be based on God's Word alone. Zechariah 8:16 says, "These are the things you are to do: Speak the truth to each other, and render true and sound judgment in your courts." May true instruction be in your mouth and nothing false be found on your lips (Malachi 2:6).

JIMMY

Supplanter; truthful

Psalm 89:1–2 *I will sing of the Lord's great love forever; with my mouth I will make Your faithfulness known through all generations. I will declare that Your love stands firm forever, that You established Your faithfulness in heaven itself.*

Psalm 51:6 *Surely You desire truth in the inner parts; You teach me wisdom in the inmost place.*

John 14:6 *Jesus answered, "I am the way and the truth and the life. No one comes to the Father except through Me."*

"You know the truth and the truth has set you free," John 8:32. You are one who is aggressive toward lies and deception. Your purpose is to bring about truth through openness, revelation, authenticity, accuracy, and honesty. As God's messenger, you will have firmness in keeping and executing His promises and also your own. Your God-given wisdom will be based on God's Word alone. Zechariah 8:16 says, "These are the things you are to do: Speak the truth to each other, and render true and sound judgment in your courts." May true instruction be in your mouth and nothing false be found on your lips (Malachi 2:6).

JOAN

God is gracious; God's gracious gift

Romans 8:32 *He who did not spare His own Son, but gave Him up for us all—how will He not also, along with Him, graciously give us all things?*

I Corinthians 15:10   *But by the grace of God I am what I am, and His grace to me was not without effect.*

Ephesians 2:8 says, "For it is by grace you have been saved, through faith—and this is not from yourselves, it is the gift of God." You are one who brings about balance and harmony through mercy, forgiveness, approval, kindness, and patience—all with a grateful heart. This attitude of gratitude will rule in the midst of inconsiderate behavior. Your nature defies the law of the Pharisees, and is against being self-reliant, prejudice, and selfish. Being full of grace is devotion built through faithfulness and a willingness to quickly pardon. You are blessed with creativity in expressing God's greatest gift of grace—the life of His only Son, Jesus Christ. God says to you through Jeremiah 24:7, "I will give them a heart to know Me, that I am the Lord. They will be My people, and I will be their God, for they will return to Me with all their heart." Ezekiel 11:19 says, "I will give them an undivided heart and put a new spirit in them; I will remove from them their heart of stone and give them a heart of flesh." Accountability will keep your report accurate and your integrity irreproachable.

JOANNE

Graceful one; gracious one

❧

Romans 8:32 *He who did not spare His own Son, but gave Him up for us all—how will He not also, along with Him, graciously give us all things?*

I Corinthians 15:10 *But by the grace of God I am what I am, and His grace to me was not without effect.*

Ephesians 2:8 says, "For it is by grace you have been saved, through faith—and this is not from yourselves, it is the gift of God." You are one who brings about balance and harmony through mercy, forgiveness, approval, kindness, and patience—all with a grateful heart. This attitude of gratitude will rule in the midst of inconsiderate behavior. Your nature defies the law of the Pharisees, and is against being self-reliant, prejudice, and selfish. Being full of grace is devotion built through faithfulness and a willingness to quickly pardon. You are blessed with creativity in expressing God's greatest gift of grace—the life of His only Son, Jesus Christ. God says to you through Jeremiah 24:7, "I will give them a heart to know Me, that I am the Lord. They will be My people, and I will be their God, for they will return to Me with all their heart." Ezekiel 11:19 says, "I will give them an undivided heart and put a new spirit in them; I will remove from them their heart of stone and give them a heart of flesh." Accountability will keep your report accurate and your integrity irreproachable.

JODY

Praised; praised of God

❧

Exodus 19:5   *Now if you obey me fully and keep my covenant, then out of all nations you will be My treasured possession.*

I Corinthians 6:20   *You were bought at a price. Therefore honor God with your body.*

With a humble confidence, you recognize that your undeserved worth is based on the spotless Lamb sacrificed for you. No greater love will you experience than from the One who laid down His life for you. You pour back your love to Him lavishly with no thought of the cost to you or your reputation. In fact, you are willing to give up everything you have to be His disciple (Luke 14:25–33). This debt of love causes you to give forethought to all your investments as to whether Christ gets all the glory. You will not gamble or be bribed because you know the incredible price paid for you. Therefore you bring value to the insignificant, meaning to the absurd, and worth to the wasted. Your high standard of excellence will bear eternal fruit because of your commitment to please God more than man. As a child of the King, through you castaways will be restored to heirs.

JOE

He shall add; increasing faithfulness

❧

Proverbs 2:7–8 *He holds victory in store for the upright, He is a shield to those whose walk is blameless, for He guards the course of the just and protects the way of His faithful ones.*

Psalm 15:1–5 *Lord, who may dwell in Your sanctuary? Who may live on Your holy hill? He whose walk is blameless and who does what is righteous, who speaks the truth from his heart and has no slander on his tongue, who does his neighbor no wrong and casts no slur on his fellow man, who despises a vile man but honors those who fear the Lord, who keeps his oath even when it hurts, who lends his money without usury and does not accept a bribe against the innocent. He who does these things will never be shaken.*

You are one who has made a commitment to God to be loyal, true, dependable, enduring, and steadfast. You unmask anything fake with the reality of God's Word. You are aggressive towards lies and deception to bring about truth. You are especially sensitive to betrayal, so that God can restore hope, security, purpose, and His faithfulness in those whom He has given you to serve. "Be faithful, even to the point of death, and I will give you a crown of life," Revelation 2:10. Anticipate the Master saying to you, "Well done, good and faithful servant! You have been faithful with a few things; I will put you in charge of many things. Come and share your Master's happiness!" (Matthew 25:21) "The one who calls you is faithful and he will do it," I Thessalonians 5:24.

JOEL

The Lord is God; declarer of God

&

Psalm 96:3 *Declare His glory among the nations, His marvelous deeds among all peoples.*

I John 1:5 *This is the message we have heard from Him and declare to you: God is light; in Him there is no darkness at all.*

You have a passionate hunger to know Christ, the power of His resurrection, and the fellowship of sharing in His sufferings (Philippians 3:10). This intimacy gives you direct access to the very heart of God, who shares His secrets with you. You are one who shows the mind of the Lord to the people by rightly dividing the word of truth. You spread out God's Word on the table for hungry souls who are seeking Him. This proclamation will come by your testimony, talents, and resources. You serve as a forerunner to advance the gospel. You are a herald, God's messenger of His revelation (Habakkuk 2:2–3). Those in hiding will be given light and those in denial will be set free as you reveal the true character and identity of God. Make clear what you publish and report. Your mouth is filled with God's praise, declaring His splendor all day long (Psalm 71:8).

JOHN

God is gracious; God's gracious gift

Romans 8:32 *He who did not spare His own Son, but gave Him up for us all—how will He not also, along with Him, graciously give us all things?*

I Corinthians 15:10 *But by the grace of God I am what I am, and His grace to me was not without effect.*

Ephesians 2:8 says, "For it is by grace you have been saved, through faith—and this is not from yourselves, it is the gift of God." You are one who brings about balance and harmony through mercy, forgiveness, approval, kindness, and patience—all with a grateful heart. This attitude of gratitude will rule in the midst of inconsiderate behavior. Your nature defies the law of the Pharisees, and is against being self-reliant, prejudice, and selfish. Being full of grace is devotion built through faithfulness and a willingness to quickly pardon. You are blessed with creativity in expressing God's greatest gift of grace—the life of His only Son, Jesus Christ. God says to you through Jeremiah 24:7, "I will give them a heart to know Me, that I am the Lord. They will be My people, and I will be their God, for they will return to Me with all their heart." Ezekiel 11:19 says, "I will give them an undivided heart and put a new spirit in them; I will remove from them their heart of stone and give them a heart of flesh." Accountability will keep your report accurate and your integrity irreproachable.

JONAH

Dove; peaceful

Isaiah 26:3 *You will keep in perfect peace him whose mind is steadfast, because he trusts in You.*

Philippians 4:7 *And the peace of God, which transcends all understanding, will guard your hearts and your minds in Christ Jesus.*

Your life defines peace. You will have a content and calm composure in the midst of distress, disturbance, or agitation. As you follow the Prince of Peace, you will be secure in who you are in Christ. The discipline of keeping your mind on Christ, loving God's law, and being controlled by the Holy Spirit will keep you in perfect peace. God's peace will serve as an umpire to determine whether you are safe or out of God's will (Colossians 3:15). Do not think it strange when you are in battles, fights, and quarrels, because God wants to use you to bring harmony, order, unity, agreement, quietness, and calmness to the adverse situation. You are one whose intimate friendship with the Lord brings reconciliation to the offended, distressed, and troubled. "In repentance and rest is your salvation, in quietness and trust is your strength," Isaiah 30:15. Your refreshing comes as you renew your mind daily in the Word of God. "Great peace have they who love Your law, and nothing can make them stumble," Psalm 119:165.

JONAS

Dove; peaceful

&

Isaiah 26:3 *You will keep in perfect peace him whose mind is steadfast, because he trusts in You.*

Philippians 4:7 *And the peace of God, which transcends all understanding, will guard your hearts and your minds in Christ Jesus.*

Your life defines peace. You will have a content and calm composure in the midst of distress, disturbance, or agitation. As you follow the Prince of Peace, you will be secure in who you are in Christ. The discipline of keeping your mind on Christ, loving God's law, and being controlled by the Holy Spirit will keep you in perfect peace. God's peace will serve as an umpire to determine whether you are safe or out of God's will (Colossians 3:15). Do not think it strange when you are in battles, fights, and quarrels, because God wants to use you to bring harmony, order, unity, agreement, quietness, and calmness to the adverse situation. You are one whose intimate friendship with the Lord brings reconciliation to the offended, distressed, and troubled. "In repentance and rest is your salvation, in quietness and trust is your strength," Isaiah 30:15. Your refreshing comes as you renew your mind daily in the Word of God. "Great peace have they who love Your law, and nothing can make them stumble," Psalm 119:165.

JONATHAN

God is gracious; God's gracious gift

༄

Romans 8:32   *He who did not spare His own Son, but gave Him up for us all—how will He not also, along with Him, graciously give us all things?*

I Corinthians 15:10   *But by the grace of God I am what I am, and His grace to me was not without effect.*

Ephesians 2:8 says, "For it is by grace you have been saved, through faith—and this is not from yourselves, it is the gift of God." You are one who brings about balance and harmony through mercy, forgiveness, approval, kindness, and patience—all with a grateful heart. This attitude of gratitude will rule in the midst of inconsiderate behavior. Your nature defies the law of the Pharisees, and is against being self-reliant, prejudice, and selfish. Being full of grace is devotion built through faithfulness and a willingness to quickly pardon. You are blessed with creativity in expressing God's greatest gift of grace—the life of His only Son, Jesus Christ. God says to you through Jeremiah 24:7, "I will give them a heart to know Me, that I am the Lord. They will be My people, and I will be their God, for they will return to Me with all their heart." Ezekiel 11:19 says, "I will give them an undivided heart and put a new spirit in them; I will remove from them their heart of stone and give them a heart of flesh." Accountability will keep your report accurate and your integrity irreproachable.

JORDAN

Descender; walking in humility

ß

Micah 6:8 *He has showed you, O man, what is good. And what does the Lord require of you? To act justly and to love mercy and to walk humbly with your God.*

I Peter 5:6 *Humble yourselves, therefore, under God's mighty hand, that He may lift you up in due time.*

Prove to be trustworthy over little and God will make you ruler over much (Luke 19:17). The higher you lift the Lord, the more dependent you will be on Him. He increases; you decrease (John 3:30). Being exalted only comes from God—not from you or anyone else. It is for the purpose of enlarging His kingdom. Take no credit for the enormous favor God will give you. It is His grace that will give entrance to these doors of favor, as you choose His approval over man's. Philippians 2:3 says, "Do nothing out of selfish ambition or vain conceit, but in humility consider others better than yourselves." Humility and the fear of the Lord bring wealth, honor, and life (Proverbs 22:4).

JOSEPH

He shall add; increasing faithfulness

ℰↃ

Proverbs 2:7–8 *He holds victory in store for the upright, He is a shield to those whose walk is blameless, for He guards the course of the just and protects the way of His faithful ones.*

Psalm 15:1–5 *Lord, who may dwell in Your sanctuary? Who may live on Your holy hill? He whose walk is blameless and who does what is righteous, who speaks the truth from his heart and has no slander on his tongue, who does his neighbor no wrong and casts no slur on his fellow man, who despises a vile man but honors those who fear the Lord, who keeps his oath even when it hurts, who lends his money without usury and does not accept a bribe against the innocent. He who does these things will never be shaken.*

You are one who has made a commitment to God to be loyal, true, dependable, enduring, and steadfast. You unmask anything fake with the reality of God's Word. You are aggressive towards lies and deception to bring about truth. You are especially sensitive to betrayal, so that God can restore hope, security, purpose, and His faithfulness in those whom He has given you to serve. "Be faithful, even to the point of death, and I will give you a crown of life," Revelation 2:10. Anticipate the Master saying to you, "Well done, good and faithful servant! You have been faithful with a few things; I will put you in charge of many things. Come and share your Master's happiness!" (Matthew 25:21) "The one who calls you is faithful and he will do it," I Thessalonians 5:24.

JOSHUA

God of salvation; God is Savior

Isaiah 12:2 *Surely God is my salvation; I will trust and not be afraid. The Lord, the Lord, is my strength and my song; He has become my salvation.*

Ephesians 2:8–9 *For it is by grace you have been saved, through faith—and this not from yourselves, it is a gift of God—not by works, so that no one can boast.*

The salvation of God is the light of His Son revealed in every crevice of your life. Where you are vulnerable, insecure, unstable, and weak, the Lord will rescue, deliver, and protect. The Lord desires to preserve you from being false, deceptive, misleading, and exaggerating. With your dependence on God for your salvation, you will ever want to be real and honest, with nothing to hide. You are not ashamed of the gospel, because it is the power of God for the salvation of everyone who believes (Romans 1:6). You have been chosen to deliver the truth of God's salvation to the lost and condemned. His work of grace, pardon, and forgiveness of sin will be experienced through you by Jesus Christ. Thanks be to God for His indescribable gift! (II Corinthians 9:15)

JOSIAH

Jehovah supports; strong supporter

&

Deuteronomy 33:27 *The eternal God is your refuge, and underneath are the everlasting arms. He will drive out your enemy before you, saying, "Destroy him!"*

Isaiah 46:4 *Even to your old age and gray hairs I am He, I am He who will sustain you. I have made you and I will carry you; I will sustain you and I will rescue you.*

A support holds up a structure with a firm foundation. God gives you help and approval through blessing, comfort, encouragement, friendship, loyalty, and protection. When you face tough times, God will carry you on eagles' wings and hold you close to Himself (Exodus 19:4). He will stoop to whatever level you are to make you great (Psalm 18:35). Not only are you upheld by His righteous right hand (Isaiah 41:10), but you uphold others. You serve as a mainstay to strengthen and uphold; to build up and reinforce. This endurance brings wholeness to all those you touch. II Timothy 2:19 says, "Nevertheless, God's solid foundation stands firm, sealed with this inscription: 'The Lord knows those who are His,'" and, "Everyone who confesses the name of the Lord must turn away from wickedness."

JOY

Joyful one; joyful

❧

Psalm 149:4–5 *For the Lord takes delight in His people; He crowns the humble with salvation. Let the saints rejoice in this honor and sing for joy on their beds.*

Psalm 45:7 *You love righteousness and hate wickedness; therefore God, your God, has set you above your companions by anointing you with the oil of joy.*

Psalm 16:11 says, "You have made known to me the path of life; You will fill me with joy in Your presence, with eternal pleasures at Your right hand." Your heavenly Father has trusted you with a quality that releases healing, restores hope, and brings refreshing. You are one who takes the source of tears and defeat, and turns them into confident trust with rejoicing. As you experience and remain sensitive to the things that sorrow the heart of God, He will pour His oil of joy on and through you to restore hope to those who are mourning (Isaiah 61:1–3). Experiences of sorrow prepare and enlarge your capacity for joy. The joy of the Lord will be your strength to endure the cross He has called you to bear. You are to fix your eyes on Jesus, the author and perfecter of your faith, who for the joy set before Him endured the cross, scorning its shame, and sat down at the right hand of the throne of God (Hebrews 12:2). He will be faithful to give you a song in your "night" season (Psalm 42:8). God rejoices over you with gladness! (Zephaniah 3:17)

JOYCE

Joyful one; joyful

ॐ

Psalm 149:4–5   *For the Lord takes delight in His people; He crowns the humble with salvation. Let the saints rejoice in this honor and sing for joy on their beds.*

Psalm 45:7   *You love righteousness and hate wickedness; therefore God, your God, has set you above your companions by anointing you with the oil of joy.*

Psalm 16:11 says, "You have made known to me the path of life; You will fill me with joy in Your presence, with eternal pleasures at Your right hand." Your heavenly Father has trusted you with a quality that releases healing, restores hope, and brings refreshing. You are one who takes the source of tears and defeat, and turns them into confident trust with rejoicing. As you experience and remain sensitive to the things that sorrow the heart of God, He will pour His oil of joy on and through you to restore hope to those who are mourning (Isaiah 61:1–3). Experiences of sorrow prepare and enlarge your capacity for joy. The joy of the Lord will be your strength to endure the cross He has called you to bear. You are to fix your eyes on Jesus, the author and perfecter of your faith, who for the joy set before Him endured the cross, scorning its shame, and sat down at the right hand of the throne of God (Hebrews 12:2). He will be faithful to give you a song in your "night" season (Psalm 42:8). God rejoices over you with gladness! (Zephaniah 3:17)

JUANITA

God's gracious gift; gracious one

☙

Romans 8:32 *He who did not spare His own Son, but gave Him up for us all—how will He not also, along with Him, graciously give us all things?*

I Corinthians 15:10 *But by the grace of God I am what I am, and His grace to me was not without effect.*

Ephesians 2:8 says, "For it is by grace you have been saved, through faith—and this is not from yourselves, it is the gift of God." You are one who brings about balance and harmony through mercy, forgiveness, approval, kindness, and patience—all with a grateful heart. This attitude of gratitude will rule in the midst of inconsiderate behavior. Your nature defies the law of the Pharisees, and is against being self-reliant, prejudice, and selfish. Being full of grace is devotion built through faithfulness and a willingness to quickly pardon. You are blessed with creativity in expressing God's greatest gift of grace—the life of His only Son, Jesus Christ. God says to you through Jeremiah 24:7, "I will give them a heart to know Me, that I am the Lord. They will be My people, and I will be their God, for they will return to Me with all their heart." Ezekiel 11:19 says, "I will give them an undivided heart and put a new spirit in them; I will remove from them their heart of stone and give them a heart of flesh." Accountability will keep your report accurate and your integrity irreproachable.

JUDY

Praised; praised of God

℘

Exodus 19:5   *Now if you obey me fully and keep my covenant, then out of all nations you will be My treasured possession.*

I Corinthians 6:20   *You were bought at a price. Therefore honor God with your body.*

With a humble confidence, you recognize that your undeserved worth is based on the spotless Lamb sacrificed for you. No greater love will you experience than from the One who laid down His life for you. You pour back your love to Him lavishly with no thought of the cost to you or your reputation. In fact, you are willing to give up everything you have to be His disciple (Luke 14:25–33). This debt of love causes you to give forethought to all your investments as to whether Christ gets all the glory. You will not gamble or be bribed because you know the incredible price paid for you. Therefore you bring value to the insignificant, meaning to the absurd, and worth to the wasted. Your high standard of excellence will bear eternal fruit because of your commitment to please God more than man. As a child of the King, through you castaways will be restored to heirs.

JULIA

Youthful one

&

Psalm 71:5, 17   *For You have been my hope, O Sovereign Lord, my confidence since my youth. Since my youth, O God, You have taught me, and to this day I declare Your marvelous deeds.*

I Timothy 4:12   *Don't let anyone look down on you because you are young, but set an example for the believers in speech, in life, in love, in faith and in purity.*

You are God's expression of childlikeness, refreshment, and vigor. You will undergo little erosion, not to your own credit but to the faithfulness of God. Your pursuit of a pure heart, which is God's innocence, will release His protection over you from all that would rob His youthfulness in you. Think it not strange when God would cross your path with those who are aged in spirit by weariness, shame, or fear. You are His ambassador to restore His strength, refreshment, and vigor. See yourself constantly as that child—full of faith and adoration for your Heavenly Father—on the Lord's lap: accepted, cuddled, and with strong arms around you. He will equip you to wait hopefully—to not be anxious or consumed with worry. Your childlike dependency on the Lord will keep you trusting, full of faith, and renewed.

JULIAN

Youthful one; youthful heart

଼ରୁ

Psalm 71:5, 17   *For You have been my hope, O Sovereign Lord, my confidence since my youth. Since my youth, O God, You have taught me, and to this day I declare Your marvelous deeds.*

I Timothy 4:12   *Don't let anyone look down on you because you are young, but set an example for the believers in speech, in life, in love, in faith and in purity.*

You are God's expression of childlikeness, refreshment, and vigor. You will undergo little erosion, not to your own credit but to the faithfulness of God. Your pursuit of a pure heart, which is God's innocence, will release His protection over you from all that would rob His youthfulness in you. Think it not strange when God would cross your path with those who are aged in spirit by weariness, shame, or fear. You are His ambassador to restore His strength, refreshment, and vigor. See yourself constantly as that child—full of faith and adoration for your Heavenly Father—on the Lord's lap: accepted, cuddled, and with strong arms around you. He will equip you to wait hopefully—to not be anxious or consumed with worry. Your childlike dependency on the Lord will keep you trusting, full of faith, and renewed.

JULIE

Youthful one

Psalm 71:5, 17   *For You have been my hope, O Sovereign Lord, my confidence since my youth. Since my youth, O God, You have taught me, and to this day I declare Your marvelous deeds.*

I Timothy 4:12   *Don't let anyone look down on you because you are young, but set an example for the believers in speech, in life, in love, in faith and in purity.*

You are God's expression of childlikeness, refreshment, and vigor. You will undergo little erosion, not to your own credit but to the faithfulness of God. Your pursuit of a pure heart, which is God's innocence, will release His protection over you from all that would rob His youthfulness in you. Think it not strange when God would cross your path with those who are aged in spirit by weariness, shame, or fear. You are His ambassador to restore His strength, refreshment, and vigor. See yourself constantly as that child—full of faith and adoration for your Heavenly Father—on the Lord's lap: accepted, cuddled, and with strong arms around you. He will equip you to wait hopefully—to not be anxious or consumed with worry. Your childlike dependency on the Lord will keep you trusting, full of faith, and renewed.

JUNE

Born in June; benevolent love

Deuteronomy 16:17 *Each of you must bring a gift in proportion to the way the Lord your God has blessed you.*

II Corinthians 9:6–8 *Remember this: Whoever sows sparingly will also reap sparingly, and whoever sows generously will also reap generously. Each man should give what he has decided in his heart to give, not reluctantly or under compulsion, for God loves a cheerful giver. And God is able to make all grace abound to you, so that in all things at all times, having all that you need, you will abound in every good work.*

You are bighearted, not selfish. You are generous, not stingy. You are unreserved, not tightfisted. Your life is earmarked by your liberal praise and worship to your Savior, Jesus Christ. Knowing Him as your Provider releases you to give, give, give! You reflect the kindness of the Lord with your pleasant servant's heart. You are inclined to do good by being courteous, helpful, and gentle. Through you, God will display His mighty hand of love and help. You will open your arms to the poor and extend your hands to the needy (Proverbs 31:20). "He who gives to the poor will lack nothing," Proverbs 28:27. When giving to the needy, never let your left hand know what your right hand is doing, so that your giving may be a secret. Then your Father, who sees what is done in secret, will reward you (Matthew 6:3–4). Luke 6:38 says, "Give, and it will be given to you. A good measure, pressed down, shaken together and running over, will be poured into your lap. For with the measure you use, it will be measured to you."

JUSTICE

Just, upright; God is judge

❧

Psalm 96:10–13 *Say among the nations, "The Lord reigns." The world is firmly established, it cannot be moved; He will judge the peoples with equity. Let the heavens rejoice, let the earth be glad; let the sea resound, and all that is in it; let the fields be jubilant, and everything in them. Then all the trees of the forest will sing for joy; they will sing before the Lord, for He comes, He comes to judge the earth. He will judge the world in righteousness and the peoples in His truth.*

II Timothy 4:1–5 *In the presence of God and of Christ Jesus, who will judge the living and the dead, and in view of His appearing and His kingdom, I give you this charge: Preach the Word; be prepared in season and out of season; correct, rebuke and encourage—with great patience and great instructions. For the time will come when men will not put up with sound doctrine. Instead, to suit their own desires, they will gather around them a great number of teachers to say what their itching ears want to hear. They will turn their ears away from the truth and turn aside to myths. But you, keep your head in all situations, endure hardship, do the work of an evangelist, discharge all the duties of your ministry.*

God Almighty is your Governor, Ruler, and Authority. He has the first and last word. He calls the shots, makes the decisions, and pronounces the sentence. He gives you discernment to know what His purpose is for your life. By his Word, you will know right from wrong and guilt from innocence. You will not yield to distrust, dishonesty, compromise, or to pleasing man more than God. He will be Supreme. Job 27:2–6 defines the stand you will take should God ever need to vindicate your integrity. Judges 2:18 says, "Whenever the Lord raised up a judge for them, He was with the judge and saved them out of the hands of their enemies as long as the judge lived; for the Lord had compassion on them as they groaned under those who oppressed and afflicted them." God gives deliverance and freedom from injustice. He will use you to do the same.

JUSTIN

Just; full of justice

&

Psalm 96:10–13   *Say among the nations, "The Lord reigns." The world is firmly established, it cannot be moved; He will judge the peoples with equity. Let the heavens rejoice, let the earth be glad; let the sea resound, and all that is in it; let the fields be jubilant, and everything in them. Then all the trees of the forest will sing for joy; they will sing before the Lord, for He comes, He comes to judge the earth. He will judge the world in righteousness and the peoples in His truth.*

II Timothy 4:1–5   *In the presence of God and of Christ Jesus, who will judge the living and the dead, and in view of His appearing and His kingdom, I give you this charge: Preach the Word; be prepared in season and out of season; correct, rebuke and encourage—with great patience and great instructions. For the time will come when men will not put up with sound doctrine. Instead, to suit their own desires, they will gather around them a great number of teachers to say what their itching ears want to hear. They will turn their ears away from the truth and turn aside to myths. But you, keep your head in all situations, endure hardship, do the work of an evangelist, discharge all the duties of your ministry.*

God Almighty is your Governor, Ruler, and Authority. He has the first and last word. He calls the shots, makes the decisions, and pronounces the sentence. He gives you discernment to know what His purpose is for your life. By his Word, you will know right from wrong and guilt from innocence. You will not yield to distrust, dishonesty, compromise, or to pleasing man more than God. He will be Supreme. Job 27:2–6 defines the stand you will take should God ever need to vindicate your integrity. Judges 2:18 says, "Whenever the Lord raised up a judge for them, He was with the judge and saved them out of the hands of their enemies as long as the judge lived; for the Lord had compassion on them as they groaned under those who oppressed and afflicted them." God gives deliverance and freedom from injustice. He will use you to do the same.

KADIN

Companion; friend

୫ର

Proverbs 17:17 *A friend loves at all times, and a brother is born for adversity.*

Ecclesiastes 4:9–10 *Two are better than one, because they have a good return for their work: if one falls down his friend can help him up. But pity the man who falls and has no one to help him up!*

Christ was the preeminent example of friendship. John 15:13–14 says, "Greater love has no man than this, that he lay down his life for his friends. You are my friends if you do what I command." With open arms, He gave all. Your mantle is to be God's man of peace. This is achieved by being understanding, loyal, faithful, and true. Proverbs 18:24 says, "A man of many companions may come to ruin, but there is a friend who sticks closer than a brother." It comes natural for you to be hospitable, generous, helpful, and good-humored. Your influence is based on your ability to be approachable, trusted, and respectful. Strangers who are lonely, outcast, or abandoned will find refuge with your "welcome" sign written on your heart. You are loving, as well as being loved—everyone's neighbor; everyone's buddy. Psalm 119:63 says, "I am a friend to all who fear You, to all who follow Your precepts." Proverbs 22:11 says, "He who loves a pure heart and whose speech is gracious will have the King for his friend."

KAITLYN

Pure; pure one

I Timothy 5:22 *...do not share in the sins of others. Keep yourself pure.*

I Peter 1:22 *Now that you have purified yourselves by obeying the truth so that you have sincere love for your brothers, love one another deeply, from the heart.*

Through the process of heat, trials, and refinement, purity is established. Your nature defies being stubborn, judgmental, and haughty. The commandment of the Lord is clear—giving insight to life (Psalm 19:8). You bring wholeness to the dirty, defiled, contaminated, polluted, double-minded, and raped. Your willingness to be transparent is the venue through which He makes His Word clear, simple, and unadulterated. Your choice to be pure enables you to see God (Matthew 5:8) and to know Him as King and Friend (Proverbs 22:11). It also allows your words to be pleasant (Proverbs 15:26) and causes you to ascend to the holy place of the Lord, where you receive blessings and righteousness from the God of salvation (Psalm 24:3–5). Proverbs 20:11 says, "Even a child is known by his actions, by whether his conduct is pure and right."

KALENA

Chaste; pure

✂

I Timothy 5:22 *...do not share in the sins of others. Keep yourself pure.*

I Peter 1:22 *Now that you have purified yourselves by obeying the truth so that you have sincere love for your brothers, love one another deeply, from the heart.*

Through the process of heat, trials, and refinement, purity is established. Your nature defies being stubborn, judgmental, and haughty. The commandment of the Lord is clear—giving insight to life (Psalm 19:8). You bring wholeness to the dirty, defiled, contaminated, polluted, double-minded, and raped. Your willingness to be transparent is the venue through which He makes His Word clear, simple, and unadulterated. Your choice to be pure enables you to see God (Matthew 5:8) and to know Him as King and Friend (Proverbs 22:11). It also allows your words to be pleasant (Proverbs 15:26) and causes you to ascend to the holy place of the Lord, where you receive blessings and righteousness from the God of salvation (Psalm 24:3–5). Proverbs 20:11 says, "Even a child is known by his actions, by whether his conduct is pure and right."

KALLIE

Singing lark; cheerful one

&

Proverbs 15:13 *A happy heart makes the face cheerful, but heartache crushes the spirit.*

Proverbs 17:22 *A cheerful heart is good medicine, but a crushed spirit dries up the bones.*

Your cheerful heart has a continual feast (Proverbs 15:15) and your cheerful look brings joy to the heart (Proverbs 15:30). Out of your deep love for God's Word, you are equipped to give approval, encouragement, and inspiration to the rejected, hopeless, and reluctant. You are very aware that Jesus Christ has overcome the world through His death and resurrection. In every situation you improve the outlook on the future. You cheer the despondent, downcast, and discouraged to victory. With the sorrows you allow God to heal in your own life, you are anointed to provide the oil of gladness to those who mourn (Isaiah 61:1–3). Your presence brings healing to the ugliest, most confused settings. God loves what a cheerful giver you are! (II Corinthians 9:7)

KARA

Beloved one; purity

&

I Timothy 5:22   *...do not share in the sins of others. Keep yourself pure.*

I Peter 1:22   *Now that you have purified yourselves by obeying the truth so that you have sincere love for your brothers, love one another deeply, from the heart.*

Through the process of heat, trials, and refinement, purity is established. Your nature defies being stubborn, judgmental, and haughty. The commandment of the Lord is clear—giving insight to life (Psalm 19:8). You bring wholeness to the dirty, defiled, contaminated, polluted, double-minded, and raped. Your willingness to be transparent is the venue through which He makes His Word clear, simple, and unadulterated. Your choice to be pure enables you to see God (Matthew 5:8) and to know Him as King and Friend (Proverbs 22:11). It also allows your words to be pleasant (Proverbs 15:26) and causes you to ascend to the holy place of the Lord, where you receive blessings and righteousness from the God of salvation (Psalm 24:3–5). Proverbs 20:11 says, "Even a child is known by his actions, by whether his conduct is pure and right."

KAREN

Pure; pure one

౭

I Timothy 5:22 *...do not share in the sins of others. Keep yourself pure.*

I Peter 1:22 *Now that you have purified yourselves by obeying the truth so that you have sincere love for your brothers, love one another deeply, from the heart.*

Through the process of heat, trials, and refinement, purity is established. Your nature defies being stubborn, judgmental, and haughty. The commandment of the Lord is clear—giving insight to life (Psalm 19:8). You bring wholeness to the dirty, defiled, contaminated, polluted, double-minded, and raped. Your willingness to be transparent is the venue through which He makes His Word clear, simple, and unadulterated. Your choice to be pure enables you to see God (Matthew 5:8) and to know Him as King and Friend (Proverbs 22:11). It also allows your words to be pleasant (Proverbs 15:26) and causes you to ascend to the holy place of the Lord, where you receive blessings and righteousness from the God of salvation (Psalm 24:3–5). Proverbs 20:11 says, "Even a child is known by his actions, by whether his conduct is pure and right."

KARI

Pure one

I Timothy 5:22 *...do not share in the sins of others. Keep yourself pure.*

I Peter 1:22 *Now that you have purified yourselves by obeying the truth so that you have sincere love for your brothers, love one another deeply, from the heart.*

Through the process of heat, trials, and refinement, purity is established. Your nature defies being stubborn, judgmental, and haughty. The commandment of the Lord is clear—giving insight to life (Psalm 19:8). You bring wholeness to the dirty, defiled, contaminated, polluted, double-minded, and raped. Your willingness to be transparent is the venue through which He makes His Word clear, simple, and unadulterated. Your choice to be pure enables you to see God (Matthew 5:8) and to know Him as King and Friend (Proverbs 22:11). It also allows your words to be pleasant (Proverbs 15:26) and causes you to ascend to the holy place of the Lord, where you receive blessings and righteousness from the God of salvation (Psalm 24:3–5). Proverbs 20:11 says, "Even a child is known by his actions, by whether his conduct is pure and right."

KATHERINE

Pure; pure one

I Timothy 5:22 *...do not share in the sins of others. Keep yourself pure.*

I Peter 1:22 *Now that you have purified yourselves by obeying the truth so that you have sincere love for your brothers, love one another deeply, from the heart.*

Through the process of heat, trials, and refinement, purity is established. Your nature defies being stubborn, judgmental, and haughty. The commandment of the Lord is clear—giving insight to life (Psalm 19:8). You bring wholeness to the dirty, defiled, contaminated, polluted, double-minded, and raped. Your willingness to be transparent is the venue through which He makes His Word clear, simple, and unadulterated. Your choice to be pure enables you to see God (Matthew 5:8) and to know Him as King and Friend (Proverbs 22:11). It also allows your words to be pleasant (Proverbs 15:26) and causes you to ascend to the holy place of the Lord, where you receive blessings and righteousness from the God of salvation (Psalm 24:3–5). Proverbs 20:11 says, "Even a child is known by his actions, by whether his conduct is pure and right."

KATHLEEN

Pure; pure one

&

I Timothy 5:22 *...do not share in the sins of others. Keep yourself pure.*

I Peter 1:22 *Now that you have purified yourselves by obeying the truth so that you have sincere love for your brothers, love one another deeply, from the heart.*

Through the process of heat, trials, and refinement, purity is established. Your nature defies being stubborn, judgmental, and haughty. The commandment of the Lord is clear—giving insight to life (Psalm 19:8). You bring wholeness to the dirty, defiled, contaminated, polluted, double-minded, and raped. Your willingness to be transparent is the venue through which He makes His Word clear, simple, and unadulterated. Your choice to be pure enables you to see God (Matthew 5:8) and to know Him as King and Friend (Proverbs 22:11). It also allows your words to be pleasant (Proverbs 15:26) and causes you to ascend to the holy place of the Lord, where you receive blessings and righteousness from the God of salvation (Psalm 24:3–5). Proverbs 20:11 says, "Even a child is known by his actions, by whether his conduct is pure and right."

KATHY

Pure; pure one

I Timothy 5:22 *...do not share in the sins of others. Keep yourself pure.*

I Peter 1:22 *Now that you have purified yourselves by obeying the truth so that you have sincere love for your brothers, love one another deeply, from the heart.*

Through the process of heat, trials, and refinement, purity is established. Your nature defies being stubborn, judgmental, and haughty. The commandment of the Lord is clear—giving insight to life (Psalm 19:8). You bring wholeness to the dirty, defiled, contaminated, polluted, double-minded, and raped. Your willingness to be transparent is the venue through which He makes His Word clear, simple, and unadulterated. Your choice to be pure enables you to see God (Matthew 5:8) and to know Him as King and Friend (Proverbs 22:11). It also allows your words to be pleasant (Proverbs 15:26) and causes you to ascend to the holy place of the Lord, where you receive blessings and righteousness from the God of salvation (Psalm 24:3–5). Proverbs 20:11 says, "Even a child is known by his actions, by whether his conduct is pure and right."

KATIE

Pure; pure one

&

I Timothy 5:22   *...do not share in the sins of others. Keep yourself pure.*

I Peter 1:22   *Now that you have purified yourselves by obeying the truth so that you have sincere love for your brothers, love one another deeply, from the heart.*

Through the process of heat, trials, and refinement, purity is established. Your nature defies being stubborn, judgmental, and haughty. The commandment of the Lord is clear—giving insight to life (Psalm 19:8). You bring wholeness to the dirty, defiled, contaminated, polluted, double-minded, and raped. Your willingness to be transparent is the venue through which He makes His Word clear, simple, and unadulterated. Your choice to be pure enables you to see God (Matthew 5:8) and to know Him as King and Friend (Proverbs 22:11). It also allows your words to be pleasant (Proverbs 15:26) and causes you to ascend to the holy place of the Lord, where you receive blessings and righteousness from the God of salvation (Psalm 24:3–5). Proverbs 20:11 says, "Even a child is known by his actions, by whether his conduct is pure and right."

KATRINA

Pure; purity

I Timothy 5:22   *...do not share in the sins of others. Keep yourself pure.*

I Peter 1:22   *Now that you have purified yourselves by obeying the truth so that you have sincere love for your brothers, love one another deeply, from the heart.*

Through the process of heat, trials, and refinement, purity is established. Your nature defies being stubborn, judgmental, and haughty. The commandment of the Lord is clear—giving insight to life (Psalm 19:8). You bring wholeness to the dirty, defiled, contaminated, polluted, double-minded, and raped. Your willingness to be transparent is the venue through which He makes His Word clear, simple, and unadulterated. Your choice to be pure enables you to see God (Matthew 5:8) and to know Him as King and Friend (Proverbs 22:11). It also allows your words to be pleasant (Proverbs 15:26) and causes you to ascend to the holy place of the Lord, where you receive blessings and righteousness from the God of salvation (Psalm 24:3–5). Proverbs 20:11 says, "Even a child is known by his actions, by whether his conduct is pure and right."

KAY

Pure; pure one

I Timothy 5:22 *...do not share in the sins of others. Keep yourself pure.*

I Peter 1:22 *Now that you have purified yourselves by obeying the truth so that you have sincere love for your brothers, love one another deeply, from the heart.*

Through the process of heat, trials, and refinement, purity is established. Your nature defies being stubborn, judgmental, and haughty. The commandment of the Lord is clear—giving insight to life (Psalm 19:8). You bring wholeness to the dirty, defiled, contaminated, polluted, double-minded, and raped. Your willingness to be transparent is the venue through which He makes His Word clear, simple, and unadulterated. Your choice to be pure enables you to see God (Matthew 5:8) and to know Him as King and Friend (Proverbs 22:11). It also allows your words to be pleasant (Proverbs 15:26) and causes you to ascend to the holy place of the Lord, where you receive blessings and righteousness from the God of salvation (Psalm 24:3–5). Proverbs 20:11 says, "Even a child is known by his actions, by whether his conduct is pure and right."

KAYLA

Pure; pure one

∞

I Timothy 5:22 ...*do not share in the sins of others. Keep yourself pure.*

I Peter 1:22 *Now that you have purified yourselves by obeying the truth so that you have sincere love for your brothers, love one another deeply, from the heart.*

Through the process of heat, trials, and refinement, purity is established. Your nature defies being stubborn, judgmental, and haughty. The commandment of the Lord is clear—giving insight to life (Psalm 19:8). You bring wholeness to the dirty, defiled, contaminated, polluted, double-minded, and raped. Your willingness to be transparent is the venue through which He makes His Word clear, simple, and unadulterated. Your choice to be pure enables you to see God (Matthew 5:8) and to know Him as King and Friend (Proverbs 22:11). It also allows your words to be pleasant (Proverbs 15:26) and causes you to ascend to the holy place of the Lord, where you receive blessings and righteousness from the God of salvation (Psalm 24:3–5). Proverbs 20:11 says, "Even a child is known by his actions, by whether his conduct is pure and right."

KAYLEE

Pure; pure one

I Timothy 5:22   *...do not share in the sins of others. Keep yourself pure.*

I Peter 1:22   *Now that you have purified yourselves by obeying the truth so that you have sincere love for your brothers, love one another deeply, from the heart.*

Through the process of heat, trials, and refinement, purity is established. Your nature defies being stubborn, judgmental, and haughty. The commandment of the Lord is clear—giving insight to life (Psalm 19:8). You bring wholeness to the dirty, defiled, contaminated, polluted, double-minded, and raped. Your willingness to be transparent is the venue through which He makes His Word clear, simple, and unadulterated. Your choice to be pure enables you to see God (Matthew 5:8) and to know Him as King and Friend (Proverbs 22:11). It also allows your words to be pleasant (Proverbs 15:26) and causes you to ascend to the holy place of the Lord, where you receive blessings and righteousness from the God of salvation (Psalm 24:3–5). Proverbs 20:11 says, "Even a child is known by his actions, by whether his conduct is pure and right."

KEIRA

Dark; seeker of light

&

Psalm 27:1 *The Lord is my light and my salvation—whom shall I fear? The Lord is the stronghold of my life; of whom shall I be afraid.*

Proverbs 4:18 *The path of the righteous is like the first gleam of dawn, shining ever brighter till the full light of day.*

You are one who reflects the shining brightness of the countenance of Jesus. You are aggressive toward the fruitless deeds of darkness from the evil one, by exposing them to the light of Jesus. Everything exposed by light becomes visible, for it is the light that makes everything visible (Ephesians 5:11–14). This radiance that God has given you serves as a beacon to give guidance to those yet in darkness. Your life's mission is found in the following two verses: Isaiah 60:1–3 says, "Arise, shine, for your light has come, and the glory of the Lord rises upon you. See, darkness covers the earth, and thick darkness is over the peoples, but the Lord rises upon you and His glory appears over you. Nations will come to your light, and kings to the brightness of your dawn." And in Acts 13:47, "For this is what the Lord has commanded us: 'I have made you a light for the Gentiles, that you may bring salvation to the ends of the earth.'" Continue to shine as His star, leading many to righteousness (Daniel 12:3 and Philippians 2:15).

KEITH

From the battle place; secure one

&

Deuteronomy 33:12 *Let the beloved of the Lord rest secure in Him, for He shields him all day long, and the one the Lord loves rests between His shoulders.*

Job 11:18 *You will be secure, because there is hope; you will look about you and take your rest in safety.*

Your life is bound securely in the bundle of the living by the Lord your God (I Samuel 25:29). You will not fear the terror of night, nor the arrow that flies by day (Psalm 91:5). You will have no fear of bad news; your heart is steadfast, trusting in the Lord (Psalm 112:7). You say with confidence that the Lord is your helper. God's sovereign protection frees you from doubt and harm. Because you find your shelter, assurance, stability, and strength in your personal relationship with the Lord, you are kept in a safe place. Lay with compassionate humility a firm foundation for others, providing them with solid security. As you stay hidden in the shadow of His wings (Psalm 61:4), you direct deliverance for the weak, insecure, unsheltered, and frail. You are to help others to become overcomers, victorious, confident, and secure—regardless of the risk and cost to you.

KEKE

Chaste; pure one

ß

I Timothy 5:22 *...do not share in the sins of others. Keep yourself pure.*

I Peter 1:22 *Now that you have purified yourselves by obeying the truth so that you have sincere love for your brothers, love one another deeply, from the heart.*

Through the process of heat, trials, and refinement, purity is established. Your nature defies being stubborn, judgmental, and haughty. The commandment of the Lord is clear—giving insight to life (Psalm 19:8). You bring wholeness to the dirty, defiled, contaminated, polluted, double-minded, and raped. Your willingness to be transparent is the venue through which He makes His Word clear, simple, and unadulterated. Your choice to be pure enables you to see God (Matthew 5:8) and to know Him as King and Friend (Proverbs 22:11). It also allows your words to be pleasant (Proverbs 15:26) and causes you to ascend to the holy place of the Lord, where you receive blessings and righteousness from the God of salvation (Psalm 24:3–5). Proverbs 20:11 says, "Even a child is known by his actions, by whether his conduct is pure and right."

KELLY

Warrior; excellent virtue

II Chronicles 32:7–8 *There is a greater power with us than with him. With him is only the arm of flesh, but with us is the Lord our God to help us and to fight our battles.*

II Timothy 2:3–4 *Endure hardship with us like a good soldier of Christ Jesus. No one serving as a soldier gets involved in civilian affairs - he wants to please his commanding officer.*

Exodus 14:14 says, "The Lord will fight for you; you need only be still." You are armed with the ability to handle the spear and shield—to stand on God's Word by faith, supporting the King of kings against His enemies. As God's defending warrior, you are His example of a brave champion, soldier, and hero. The ultimate war was a contest with death and when Christ said, "It is finished" on the cross, He declared victory over death, hell, and the grave. You are equipped to be used of God as one who protects by warding off attacks, calling for justice, and providing shelter. When God is all of this to you, you will be that vindication for others. Because of your faith in Jesus Christ, you will ever be aggressive towards the enemy's tools of defeat, failure, and victimization. Your ultimate purpose is to be one who stands in the gap (Ezekiel 22:30) as a defender of the weak. This includes those who are easily influenced, confused, quitters, faint, frail, fragile, and frightened. Your primary spiritual warfare will be that of brave intercession—reaching, meeting, and entreating God for His favor to set the captives free. Then you will "learn to do right! Seek justice, encourage the oppressed. Defend the cause of the fatherless, plead the case of the widow," Isaiah 1:17.

KELSEY

Seaport; protector of mankind

&

Deuteronomy 33:12 *Let the beloved of the Lord rest secure in Him, for He shields him all day long, and the one the Lord loves rests between His shoulders.*

Job 11:18 *You will be secure, because there is hope; you will look about you and take your rest in safety.*

Your life is bound securely in the bundle of the living by the Lord your God (I Samuel 25:29). You will not fear the terror of night, nor the arrow that flies by day (Psalm 91:5). You will have no fear of bad news; your heart is steadfast, trusting in the Lord (Psalm 112:7). You say with confidence that the Lord is your helper. God's sovereign protection frees you from doubt and harm. Because you find your shelter, assurance, stability, and strength in your personal relationship with the Lord, you are kept in a safe place. Lay with compassionate humility a firm foundation for others, providing them with solid security. As you stay hidden in the shadow of His wings (Psalm 61:4), you direct deliverance for the weak, insecure, unsheltered, and frail. You are to help others to become overcomers, victorious, confident, and secure—regardless of the risk and cost to you.

KEN

Handsome one; gracious, manly

&

Proverbs 24:5 *A wise man has great power, and a man of knowledge increases strength.*

Ephesians 6:10 *Finally, be strong in the Lord and in His mighty power.*

You are one who has an un-compromised commitment to righteousness, respectability, honesty, character, excellence, value, worth, kindness, innocence, generosity, trustworthiness, faithfulness, justice, hope, and love. You can do everything through Him who gives you strength (Philippians 4:11-13). The Lord is the source of your strength because you turn back the battle at the gate (Isaiah 28:6). You renew your strength by your hope being in the Lord (Isaiah 40:31). Jesus says, "My grace is sufficient for you, for My power is made perfect in weaknesses. Therefore you will boast all the more gladly about your weaknesses, so that Christ's power may rest on you. That is why for Christ's sake, you delight in weaknesses, in insults, in hardships, in persecutions, and in difficulties. For when you are weak, then you are strong," II Corinthians 12:9-10. You are clothed with strength and dignity (Proverbs 31:25).

KENNEDY

Helmet head; strong leader

∞

Deuteronomy 28:13 *The Lord will make you the head, not the tail. If you pay attention to the commands of the Lord your God that I give you this day and carefully follow them, you will always be at the top, never at the bottom.*

Mark 10:43–45 *...Whoever wants to become great among you must be your servant, and whoever wants to be first must be slave of all. For even the Son of Man did not come to be served, but to serve, and to give His life as a ransom for many.*

You have been set apart with vision and perspective to reproduce the likeness of Christ in others by reflecting His image. You are guided by principles and values worth dying for. You know how to balance transparency with being an example. You are one who is secure enough to be vulnerable. You do not lead to gather followers; you lead to develop leaders. You lead by honoring God with authority, influence, direction, foresight, and skill. Your credible choices set a precedence for favor. You earn trust by your willingness to confront and bring discipline in a Godly manner. You are strong enough to let your "yes" be "yes" and your "no" be "no," with no compromise or jealousy. Your strength is determined by your submitted and teachable servant's heart. The more you mature, the more humble, gentle, and meek you will become. With integrity you communicate love, affirmation, nurturing, and spiritual care. If you as a shepherd ever forget what it is like to be a sheep, you will become a hireling. Your highest aim is to honor and glorify God.

KENNETH

Handsome one; gracious, manly

ℰℴ

Proverbs 24:5 *A wise man has great power, and a man of knowledge increases strength.*

Ephesians 6:10 *Finally, be strong in the Lord and in His mighty power.*

You are one who has an un-compromised commitment to righteousness, respectability, honesty, character, excellence, value, worth, kindness, innocence, generosity, trustworthiness, faithfulness, justice, hope, and love. You can do everything through Him who gives you strength (Philippians 4:11–13). The Lord is the source of your strength because you turn back the battle at the gate (Isaiah 28:6). You renew your strength by your hope being in the Lord (Isaiah 40:31). Jesus says, "My grace is sufficient for you, for My power is made perfect in weaknesses. Therefore you will boast all the more gladly about your weaknesses, so that Christ's power may rest on you. That is why for Christ's sake, you delight in weaknesses, in insults, in hardships, in persecutions, and in difficulties. For when you are weak, then you are strong," II Corinthians 12:9–10. You are clothed with strength and dignity (Proverbs 31:25).

KERI

Dark one; seeker of light

૪ა

Psalm 27:1 *The Lord is my light and my salvation—whom shall I fear? The Lord is the stronghold of my life; of whom shall I be afraid.*

Proverbs 4:18 *The path of the righteous is like the first gleam of dawn, shining ever brighter till the full light of day.*

You are one who reflects the shining brightness of the countenance of Jesus. You are aggressive toward the fruitless deeds of darkness from the evil one, by exposing them to the light of Jesus. Everything exposed by light becomes visible, for it is the light that makes everything visible (Ephesians 5:11–14). This radiance that God has given you serves as a beacon to give guidance to those yet in darkness. Your life's mission is found in the following two verses: Isaiah 60:1–3 says, "Arise, shine, for your light has come, and the glory of the Lord rises upon you. See, darkness covers the earth, and thick darkness is over the peoples, but the Lord rises upon you and His glory appears over you. Nations will come to your light, and kings to the brightness of your dawn." And in Acts 13:47, "For this is what the Lord has commanded us: 'I have made you a light for the Gentiles, that you may bring salvation to the ends of the earth.'" Continue to shine as His star, leading many to righteousness (Daniel 12:3 and Philippians 2:15).

KERRY

Dark one; seeker of light

❧

Psalm 27:1 *The Lord is my light and my salvation—whom shall I fear? The Lord is the stronghold of my life; of whom shall I be afraid.*

Proverbs 4:18 *The path of the righteous is like the first gleam of dawn, shining ever brighter till the full light of day.*

You are one who reflects the shining brightness of the countenance of Jesus. You are aggressive toward the fruitless deeds of darkness from the evil one, by exposing them to the light of Jesus. Everything exposed by light becomes visible, for it is the light that makes everything visible (Ephesians 5:11–14). This radiance that God has given you serves as a beacon to give guidance to those yet in darkness. Your life's mission is found in the following two verses: Isaiah 60:1–3 says, "Arise, shine, for your light has come, and the glory of the Lord rises upon you. See, darkness covers the earth, and thick darkness is over the peoples, but the Lord rises upon you and His glory appears over you. Nations will come to your light, and kings to the brightness of your dawn." And in Acts 13:47, "For this is what the Lord has commanded us: 'I have made you a light for the Gentiles, that you may bring salvation to the ends of the earth.'" Continue to shine as His star, leading many to righteousness (Daniel 12:3 and Philippians 2:15).

KEVIN

Gentle, lovable; kind one

Titus 3:4–5 *But when the kindness and love of God our Savior appeared, He saved us, not because of righteous things we had done, but because of His mercy.*

I Peter 3:8–9 *Finally, all of you, live in harmony with one another; be sympathetic, love as brothers, be compassionate and humble. Do not repay evil with evil or insult with insult, but with blessing, because to this you were called so that you may inherit a blessing.*

God first, others next, and you last. With a servant's heart and a humble mind, you extend the gracious approval of the Lord. This graciousness springs from an inherit thoughtfulness and consideration. Through you, God defines good manners and politeness. You are hospitable to the shipwrecked (Acts 28:7) and you bring divine connection for needs to be provided (Acts 27:3). Because you are attentive to details, the broken are dealt with gently. The rejected are shown kindness and the humble are given honor. Your conversation is always full of grace and seasoned with salt (Colossians 4:6). The behavior of the rude and impolite are corrected because you will not be misled. You know that bad company corrupts good character (I Corinthians 15:33). You show respect to all because of your willingness to value the opinion of another and overlook an offense (Proverbs 19:11). Like Jesus, you are a friend of the publicans and sinners (Luke 7:34).

KIM

From the royal fortress meadow; noble one

ॐ

Isaiah 32:8   *But the noble man makes noble plans, and by noble deeds he stands.*

Luke 8:15   *But the seed on good soil stands for those with a noble and good heart, who hear the word, retain it, and by persevering produce a crop.*

Proverbs 18:12 says, "Before his downfall a man's heart is proud, but humility comes before honor." You are one who has a humble confidence in recognizing and expressing reverence, worship, adoration, trust, deference, tribute, admiration, and respect. This is the result of being secure in the truth of who you are in the Lord. Through humility, King Jesus made a way for you to be engrafted into His royalty. He made of Himself no reputation and took on the nature of a servant (Philippians 2:7) to affirm your value. Through self-denial, you prioritize excellence in virtue, truthfulness, and faithfulness. Because of the respect you have earned, you dismantle inferiority, disgrace, shame, and offenses. No one feels second-rate in your presence. The deeper that the Lord is your object of reverence, the greater your confidence will be in giving approval and worth. Because you are tall in spirit, your face is always turned upward.

KIMBERLY

From the royal fortress meadow; noble one

Isaiah 32:8 *But the noble man makes noble plans, and by noble deeds he stands.*

Luke 8:15 *But the seed on good soil stands for those with a noble and good heart, who hear the word, retain it, and by persevering produce a crop.*

Proverbs 18:12 says, "Before his downfall a man's heart is proud, but humility comes before honor." You are one who has a humble confidence in recognizing and expressing reverence, worship, adoration, trust, deference, tribute, admiration, and respect. This is the result of being secure in the truth of who you are in the Lord. Through humility, King Jesus made a way for you to be engrafted into His royalty. He made of Himself no reputation and took on the nature of a servant (Philippians 2:7) to affirm your value. Through self-denial, you prioritize excellence in virtue, truthfulness, and faithfulness. Because of the respect you have earned, you dismantle inferiority, disgrace, shame, and offenses. No one feels second-rate in your presence. The deeper that the Lord is your object of reverence, the greater your confidence will be in giving approval and worth. Because you are tall in spirit, your face is always turned upward.

KIRBY

Church town; worshipful spirit

◈

Psalm 27:4 *One thing I ask of the Lord, this is what I seek: that I may dwell in the house of the Lord all the days of my life, to gaze upon the beauty of the Lord and to seek Him in His temple.*

Psalm 132:7–8 *Let us go to His dwelling place; let us worship at His footstool—arise, O Lord, and come to Your resting place, You and the ark of Your might.*

You have been chosen of God to be His private cheerleader to bring Him pleasure, celebration, reverence, honor, and glory. You serve as His example of always putting Him first, with no competition in comparing Him with anyone or anything. It's all about Him, not you; His way, not yours; His timing, not yours; His control, not yours. Your love for the church—God's people—is in direct proportion to your intimacy with Him. You prioritize undistracted devotion in order to mirror His likeness. Offering your body as a living sacrifice, holy and pleasing to God, is your spiritual act of worship (Romans 12:1). There is no shame in expressing your extravagant love for your Lord—whether in bowing at His feet and washing them with your tears or allowing your heart to sing in extreme adversity. Worship keeps the focus on His fame and your self denial. It bridges the cross to the crown and your weaknesses to His strength.

KIRK

Dweller at the church; worshipful spirit

&

Psalm 27:4   *One thing I ask of the Lord, this is what I seek: that I may dwell in the house of the Lord all the days of my life, to gaze upon the beauty of the Lord and to seek Him in His temple.*

Psalm 132:7–8   *Let us go to His dwelling place; let us worship at His footstool—arise, O Lord, and come to Your resting place, You and the ark of Your might.*

You have been chosen of God to be His private cheerleader to bring Him pleasure, celebration, reverence, honor, and glory. You serve as His example of always putting Him first, with no competition in comparing Him with anyone or anything. It's all about Him, not you; His way, not yours; His timing, not yours; His control, not yours. Your love for the church—God's people—is in direct proportion to your intimacy with Him. You prioritize undistracted devotion in order to mirror His likeness. Offering your body as a living sacrifice, holy and pleasing to God, is your spiritual act of worship (Romans 12:1). There is no shame in expressing your extravagant love for your Lord—whether in bowing at His feet and washing them with your tears or allowing your heart to sing in extreme adversity. Worship keeps the focus on His fame and your self denial. It bridges the cross to the crown and your weaknesses to His strength.

KRISTEN

Christian; follower of Christ

I Chronicles 28:9   *And you, my son Solomon, acknowledge the God of your father, and serve Him with wholehearted devotion and with a willing mind, for the Lord searches every heart and understands every motive behind the thoughts. If you seek Him, He will be found by you; but if you forsake Him, He will reject you forever.*

I Corinthians 15:58   *Therefore, my dear brothers, stand firm. Let nothing move you. Always give yourselves fully to the work of the Lord, because you know that your labor is not in vain.*

Your very being lives to be in constant harmony with your Creator—that the both of your hearts beat as one. Therefore, you are continually yielding every area to the likeness of Christ with strong discipline as you follow Him. You have a devoted allegiance to Christ and His teachings. Your character is one of devotion, dedication, consecration, loyalty, and faithfulness. You are called to help the fallen take a stand and to remove shame and fear. You dispel division by bringing the very unity of God. As you seek and trust in Him with all your heart, leaning not to your own understanding, He will protect you from being blind-sided by the enemy of your soul. Be known as one who loves God with all your heart, soul, mind, and strength. You are one whom God has chosen to be an example of His Son, Jesus Christ.

KRISTI

Christian; follower of Christ

I Chronicles 28:9   *And you, my son Solomon, acknowledge the God of your father, and serve Him with wholehearted devotion and with a willing mind, for the Lord searches every heart and understands every motive behind the thoughts. If you seek Him, He will be found by you; but if you forsake Him, He will reject you forever.*

I Corinthians 15:58   *Therefore, my dear brothers, stand firm. Let nothing move you. Always give yourselves fully to the work of the Lord, because you know that your labor is not in vain.*

Your very being lives to be in constant harmony with your Creator—that the both of your hearts beat as one. Therefore, you are continually yielding every area to the likeness of Christ with strong discipline as you follow Him. You have a devoted allegiance to Christ and His teachings. Your character is one of devotion, dedication, consecration, loyalty, and faithfulness. You are called to help the fallen take a stand and to remove shame and fear. You dispel division by bringing the very unity of God. As you seek and trust in Him with all your heart, leaning not to your own understanding, He will protect you from being blind-sided by the enemy of your soul. Be known as one who loves God with all your heart, soul, mind, and strength. You are one whom God has chosen to be an example of His Son, Jesus Christ.

KURT

Bold counselor; able to counsel

℘

James 3:17 *But the wisdom that comes from heaven is first of all pure; then peace-loving, considerate, submissive, full of mercy and good fruit, impartial and sincere.*

Proverbs 9:10 *The fear of the Lord is the beginning of wisdom, and knowledge of the Holy One is understanding.*

You are a person of moral excellence. You exemplify right living put into practice. The Lord has not only equipped you with skills for living correctly, but also the ability to impart that to others. The Spirit of truth will guide you into all truth, allowing you to have insight into the true nature of things (John 16:13). Out of your reverential respect for the Lord, you have wisdom to give guidance and direction. You are a safe sounding board who steers those who are hungry for knowledge of the Holy One in the right direction. You need only to ask for the wisdom you lack, and God will give it to you generously (James 1:5). Having spiritual discernment is having the ability to separate the difference between God's wisdom and the world's and the ability to make the right choice—regardless. Luke 21:15 says, "For I will give you words and wisdom that none of your adversaries will be able to resist or contradict."

KYLE

From the straight; integrity

&

Psalm 41:12   *In my integrity You uphold me and set me in Your presence forever.*

Proverbs 11:3   *The integrity of the upright guides them, but the unfaithful are destroyed by their duplicity.*

Spiritual deafness results from unheeded warnings, calloused hearts, rebellious disobedience, and stubborn unfaithfulness. This is prevented by being quick to hear, teachable, and having faith in God's Word. Security comes from knowing God's ears are attentive to your cry—before you call, He answers. Discernment and righteous judgment produce integrity. Integrity results in yielding weakness to God's power, based on a blameless walk. Proverbs 10:9 says, "The man of integrity walks securely, but he who takes crooked paths will be found out." You are one who has an uncompromised commitment to righteousness, respectability, honesty, character, excellence, innocence, generosity, trustworthiness, faithfulness, justice, hope, and love. Be truthful with others, as well as yourself. Be the same in public as you are in private. Titus 2:7–8 says, "In everything set them an example by doing what is good. In your teaching show integrity, seriousness and soundness of speech that cannot be condemned, so that those who oppose you may be ashamed because they have nothing bad to say about us."

KYLEE

From the straight; integrity

∞

Psalm 41:12 *In my integrity You uphold me and set me in Your presence forever.*

Proverbs 11:3 *The integrity of the upright guides them, but the unfaithful are destroyed by their duplicity.*

Spiritual deafness results from unheeded warnings, calloused hearts, rebellious disobedience, and stubborn unfaithfulness. This is prevented by being quick to hear, teachable, and having faith in God's Word. Security comes from knowing God's ears are attentive to your cry—before you call, He answers. Discernment and righteous judgment produce integrity. Integrity results in yielding weakness to God's power, based on a blameless walk. Proverbs 10:9 says, "The man of integrity walks securely, but he who takes crooked paths will be found out." You are one who has an uncompromised commitment to righteousness, respectability, honesty, character, excellence, innocence, generosity, trustworthiness, faithfulness, justice, hope, and love. Be truthful with others, as well as yourself. Be the same in public as you are in private. Titus 2:7–8 says, "In everything set them an example by doing what is good. In your teaching show integrity, seriousness and soundness of speech that cannot be condemned, so that those who oppose you may be ashamed because they have nothing bad to say about us."

KYLIE

From the straight; integrity

ဆ

Psalm 41:12 *In my integrity You uphold me and set me in Your presence forever.*

Proverbs 11:3 *The integrity of the upright guides them, but the unfaithful are destroyed by their duplicity.*

Spiritual deafness results from unheeded warnings, calloused hearts, rebellious disobedience, and stubborn unfaithfulness. This is prevented by being quick to hear, teachable, and having faith in God's Word. Security comes from knowing God's ears are attentive to your cry—before you call, He answers. Discernment and righteous judgment produce integrity. Integrity results in yielding weakness to God's power, based on a blameless walk. Proverbs 10:9 says, "The man of integrity walks securely, but he who takes crooked paths will be found out." You are one who has an uncompromised commitment to righteousness, respectability, honesty, character, excellence, innocence, generosity, trustworthiness, faithfulness, justice, hope, and love. Be truthful with others, as well as yourself. Be the same in public as you are in private. Titus 2:7–8 says, "In everything set them an example by doing what is good. In your teaching show integrity, seriousness and soundness of speech that cannot be condemned, so that those who oppose you may be ashamed because they have nothing bad to say about us."

LANAE

Attractive; peaceful

✁

Isaiah 26:3 *You will keep in perfect peace him whose mind is steadfast, because he trusts in You.*

Philippians 4:7 *And the peace of God, which transcends all understanding, will guard your hearts and your minds in Christ Jesus.*

Your life defines peace. You will have a content and calm composure in the midst of distress, disturbance, or agitation. As you follow the Prince of Peace, you will be secure in who you are in Christ. The discipline of keeping your mind on Christ, loving God's law, and being controlled by the Holy Spirit will keep you in perfect peace. God's peace will serve as an umpire to determine whether you are safe or out of God's will (Colossians 3:15). Do not think it strange when you are in battles, fights, and quarrels, because God wants to use you to bring harmony, order, unity, agreement, quietness, and calmness to the adverse situation. You are one whose intimate friendship with the Lord brings reconciliation to the offended, distressed, and troubled. "In repentance and rest is your salvation, in quietness and trust is your strength," Isaiah 30:15. Your refreshing comes as you renew your mind daily in the Word of God. "Great peace have they who love Your law, and nothing can make them stumble," Psalm 119:165.

LANDON

Grassy meadow; refuge

ℰℒ

Deuteronomy 33:27   *The eternal God is your refuge, and underneath are the everlasting arms. He will drive out your enemy before you, saying, "Destroy him!"*

Psalm 27:5   *For in the day of trouble He will keep me safe in His dwelling; He will hide me in the shelter of His tabernacle and set me high upon a rock.*

God is your place of protection. Your heart is His home. As you hide in the shelter of His presence, the Lord protects you from those who conspire against you; those with accusing tongues (Psalm 31:19–20). The Lord uses you to be His refuge for the poor and needy in distress, His shelter from the storm, and a shade from the heat (Isaiah 25:4). You release security and confidence (Proverbs 14:26). You declare deliverance to the prisoners and you give hope that God will restore twice as much to them (Zechariah 9:12).

LANEY

God has answered my prayers; promises accomplished

∞

Psalm 91:15 *He will call upon me, and I will answer Him; I will be with him in trouble, I will deliver him and honor him.*

II Peter 3:9 *The Lord is not slow in keeping His promise, as some understand slowness. He is patient with you, not wanting anyone to perish, but everyone to come to repentance.*

You, like Isaac, are a child of promise (Galatians 4:28). Hebrews 11:17–19 says, "By faith Abraham, when God tested him, offered Isaac as a sacrifice. He who had received the promises was about to sacrifice his one and only son, even though God had said to him, 'It is through Isaac that your offspring will be reckoned.' Abraham reasoned that God could raise the dead, and figuratively speaking, he did receive Isaac back from death." "If you belong to Christ, then you are Abraham's seed, and heirs according to the promise," Galatians 3:29. Abraham was fully persuaded that God had power to do what He had promised (Romans 4:21). You have inherited this same strong faith as you stay committed to God's Word and love Him (James 2:5). As God's fulfilled promise, you will not choose deception, denial, or to break any covenant you make. God will answer you because your motives are pure—without secret sin, indifference, stubbornness, instability, self-indulgence, and disobedience. You want God's will more than yours, regardless of the cost. Being given God's great and precious promises releases you to participate in His divine nature (II Peter 1:4).

LARRY

Laurel-crowned one; victor

∾

I John 5:4   *Everyone born of God overcomes the world. This is the victory that has overcome the world, even our faith.*

II Corinthians 2:14   *But thanks be to God, who always leads us in triumphal procession in Christ and through us spreads everywhere the fragrance of the knowledge of Him.*

Because of your faith in Jesus Christ, you will ever be aggressive towards the enemy's tools of defeat, failure, and victimization. You will push back Satan and overcome all his power. Jesus has given you authority to trample on snakes and scorpions and to overcome all the power of the enemy; nothing will harm you (Luke 10:19). Even in the severest of afflictions—such as hardship, persecution, famine, nakedness, danger, or sword—you are more than a conqueror through Christ who loves you (Romans 8:35–37). "Everyone born of God overcomes the world. This is the victory that has overcome the world, even our faith," I John 5:4. "Take heart, Jesus has overcome the world," John 16:33.

LAURA

A crown of laurel leaves; victorious spirit

ℰℬ

I John 5:4   *Everyone born of God overcomes the world. This is the victory that has overcome the world, even our faith.*

II Corinthians 2:14   *But thanks be to God, who always leads us in triumphal procession in Christ and through us spreads everywhere the fragrance of the knowledge of Him.*

Because of your faith in Jesus Christ, you will ever be aggressive towards the enemy's tools of defeat, failure, and victimization. You will push back Satan and overcome all his power. Jesus has given you authority to trample on snakes and scorpions and to overcome all the power of the enemy; nothing will harm you (Luke 10:19). Even in the severest of afflictions—such as hardship, persecution, famine, nakedness, danger, or sword—you are more than a conqueror through Christ who loves you (Romans 8:35–37). "Everyone born of God overcomes the world. This is the victory that has overcome the world, even our faith," I John 5:4. "Take heart, Jesus has overcome the world," John 16:33.

LAUREN

A crown of laurel leaves; victorious spirit

❧

I John 5:4   *Everyone born of God overcomes the world. This is the victory that has overcome the world, even our faith.*

II Corinthians 2:14   *But thanks be to God, who always leads us in triumphal procession in Christ and through us spreads everywhere the fragrance of the knowledge of Him.*

Because of your faith in Jesus Christ, you will ever be aggressive towards the enemy's tools of defeat, failure, and victimization. You will push back Satan and overcome all his power. Jesus has given you authority to trample on snakes and scorpions and to overcome all the power of the enemy; nothing will harm you (Luke 10:19). Even in the severest of afflictions—such as hardship, persecution, famine, nakedness, danger, or sword—you are more than a conqueror through Christ who loves you (Romans 8:35–37). "Everyone born of God overcomes the world. This is the victory that has overcome the world, even our faith," I John 5:4. "Take heart, Jesus has overcome the world," John 16:33.

LAYLA

Dark as night; peaceful and quiet

꩜

Isaiah 26:3 *You will keep in perfect peace him whose mind is steadfast, because he trusts in You.*

Philippians 4:7 *And the peace of God, which transcends all understanding, will guard your hearts and your minds in Christ Jesus.*

Your life defines peace. You will have a content and calm composure in the midst of distress, disturbance, or agitation. As you follow the Prince of Peace, you will be secure in who you are in Christ. The discipline of keeping your mind on Christ, loving God's law, and being controlled by the Holy Spirit will keep you in perfect peace. God's peace will serve as an umpire to determine whether you are safe or out of God's will (Colossians 3:15). Do not think it strange when you are in battles, fights, and quarrels, because God wants to use you to bring harmony, order, unity, agreement, quietness, and calmness to the adverse situation. You are one whose intimate friendship with the Lord brings reconciliation to the offended, distressed, and troubled. "In repentance and rest is your salvation, in quietness and trust is your strength," Isaiah 30:15. Your refreshing comes as you renew your mind daily in the Word of God. "Great peace have they who love Your law, and nothing can make them stumble," Psalm 119:165.

LEAH

Weary one; contented one

&

Proverbs 15:16   *Better a little with the fear of the Lord than great wealth with turmoil.*

Hebrews 13:5   *Keep your lives free from the love of money and be content with what you have, because God has said, "Never will I leave you; never will I forsake you."*

You have learned to be content whatever the circumstances. Your attitude is governed by God, not by outward situations. You know what it is to be in need and you know what it is to have plenty. You have learned the secret of being content in any and every situation, whether well fed or hungry, living in plenty or in want. You can do everything through Him who gives you strength (Philippians 4:11–13). The Lord is your source of strength because you turn back the battle at the gate (Isaiah 28:6). You renew your strength because your hope is in the Lord (Isaiah 40:31). Jesus says, "My grace is sufficient for you, for my power is made perfect in weakness. Therefore, you will boast all the more gladly about your weaknesses, so that Christ's power may rest on you. That is why, for Christ's sake, you delight in weaknesses, in insults, in hardships, in persecutions, and in difficulties. For when you are weak, then you are strong," II Corinthians 12:9–10. Contentment is God's guide to His will for you. You give rest to the weary, truth to those who murmur, peace to the dissatisfied, and quietness to the troubled.

LEE

From the pasture meadow; prosperous one

&

Psalm 1:1–3 *Blessed is the man who does not walk in the counsel of the wicked or stand in the way of sinners or sit in the seat of mockers. But his delight is in the law of the Lord, and on His law he meditates day and night. He is like a tree planted by the streams of water, which yields its fruit in season and whose leaf does not wither. Whatever he does prospers.*

Joshua 1:8 *Do not let this book of the law depart from your mouth; meditate on it day and night, so that you may be careful to do everything written in it. Then you will be prosperous and successful.*

You are one who knows that your success is not based on luck or good fortune. It is because you are willing to loose your life for Christ's sake in order to find it (Matthew 10:39). You let the word of Christ dwell in you richly (Colossians 3:16). You allow the Lord to stretch and strengthen you in order to enlarge your borders of influence and maturity (Isaiah 54:1–3). You welcome the cutting and pruning that makes way for increase to bear fruit, more fruit, and much fruit (John 15). You enter a covenant with the Lord of obedience, seeking Him diligently and wholeheartedly (II Chronicles 31:21), which causes you to prosper in everything you do (Deuteronomy 29:9). You are content in need and in plenty (Philippians 4:11–12) because prosperity is not a love of money (I Timothy 6:6–10), power, popularity, or possessions. In spite of failure, disappointment, loss, and defeat, you let nothing separate you from the love of God (Romans 8:37–39). Instead of being blind to the hungry, you will feed them. Instead of abhorring the naked, you will clothe them. Instead of ignoring the poor and fatherless, you will be God's hand of provision. You will offer provisions of hope, courage, and strength not to give up, but rather to start again and to make it to the finish line. You are a faithful steward helping them exchange their temporal for His eternal (Philippians 4:19). As your mantle is to build up, develop, and cause to succeed, know that "no weapon formed against you will prosper," Isaiah 54:17. Your goal is to hear the Master say, "Well done, good and faithful servant! You have been faithful with a few things, I will put you in charge of many things. Come share your Master's happiness!" (Matthew 25:21) May you prosper in all things and be in health, just as your soul prospers (3 John 2).

LEIGH

Weary one; contented one

Proverbs 15:16 *Better a little with the fear of the Lord than great wealth with turmoil.*

Hebrews 13:5 *Keep your lives free from the love of money and be content with what you have, because God has said, "Never will I leave you; never will I forsake you."*

You have learned to be content whatever the circumstances. Your attitude is governed by God, not by outward situations. You know what it is to be in need and you know what it is to have plenty. You have learned the secret of being content in any and every situation, whether well fed or hungry, living in plenty or in want. You can do everything through Him who gives you strength (Philippians 4:11–13). The Lord is your source of strength because you turn back the battle at the gate (Isaiah 28:6). You renew your strength because your hope is in the Lord (Isaiah 40:31). Jesus says, "My grace is sufficient for you, for my power is made perfect in weakness. Therefore, you will boast all the more gladly about your weaknesses, so that Christ's power may rest on you. That is why, for Christ's sake, you delight in weaknesses, in insults, in hardships, in persecutions, and in difficulties. For when you are weak, then you are strong," II Corinthians 12:9–10. Contentment is God's guide to His will for you. You give rest to the weary, truth to those who murmur, peace to the dissatisfied, and quietness to the troubled.

LEILA

Dark as night; peaceful and quiet

&

Isaiah 26:3 *You will keep in perfect peace him whose mind is steadfast, because he trusts in You.*

Philippians 4:7 *And the peace of God, which transcends all understanding, will guard your hearts and your minds in Christ Jesus.*

Your life defines peace. You will have a content and calm composure in the midst of distress, disturbance, or agitation. As you follow the Prince of Peace, you will be secure in who you are in Christ. The discipline of keeping your mind on Christ, loving God's law, and being controlled by the Holy Spirit will keep you in perfect peace. God's peace will serve as an umpire to determine whether you are safe or out of God's will (Colossians 3:15). Do not think it strange when you are in battles, fights, and quarrels, because God wants to use you to bring harmony, order, unity, agreement, quietness, and calmness to the adverse situation. You are one whose intimate friendship with the Lord brings reconciliation to the offended, distressed, and troubled. "In repentance and rest is your salvation, in quietness and trust is your strength," Isaiah 30:15. Your refreshing comes as you renew your mind daily in the Word of God. "Great peace have they who love Your law, and nothing can make them stumble," Psalm 119:165.

LESLEY

Dweller at the gray fortress; calm spirit

৪১

Isaiah 26:3 *You will keep in perfect peace him whose mind is steadfast, because he trusts in You.*

Philippians 4:7 *And the peace of God, which transcends all understanding, will guard your hearts and your minds in Christ Jesus.*

Your life defines peace. You will have a content and calm composure in the midst of distress, disturbance, or agitation. As you follow the Prince of Peace, you will be secure in who you are in Christ. The discipline of keeping your mind on Christ, loving God's law, and being controlled by the Holy Spirit will keep you in perfect peace. God's peace will serve as an umpire to determine whether you are safe or out of God's will (Colossians 3:15). Do not think it strange when you are in battles, fights, and quarrels, because God wants to use you to bring harmony, order, unity, agreement, quietness, and calmness to the adverse situation. You are one whose intimate friendship with the Lord brings reconciliation to the offended, distressed, and troubled. "In repentance and rest is your salvation, in quietness and trust is your strength," Isaiah 30:15. Your refreshing comes as you renew your mind daily in the Word of God. "Great peace have they who love Your law, and nothing can make them stumble," Psalm 119:165.

LESLIE

Dweller at the gray fortress; calm spirit

Isaiah 26:3 *You will keep in perfect peace him whose mind is steadfast, because he trusts in You.*

Philippians 4:7 *And the peace of God, which transcends all understanding, will guard your hearts and your minds in Christ Jesus.*

Your life defines peace. You will have a content and calm composure in the midst of distress, disturbance, or agitation. As you follow the Prince of Peace, you will be secure in who you are in Christ. The discipline of keeping your mind on Christ, loving God's law, and being controlled by the Holy Spirit will keep you in perfect peace. God's peace will serve as an umpire to determine whether you are safe or out of God's will (Colossians 3:15). Do not think it strange when you are in battles, fights, and quarrels, because God wants to use you to bring harmony, order, unity, agreement, quietness, and calmness to the adverse situation. You are one whose intimate friendship with the Lord brings reconciliation to the offended, distressed, and troubled. "In repentance and rest is your salvation, in quietness and trust is your strength," Isaiah 30:15. Your refreshing comes as you renew your mind daily in the Word of God. "Great peace have they who love Your law, and nothing can make them stumble," Psalm 119:165.

LEVI

Joined; union

❧

Ecclesiastes 4:12 *Though one may be overpowered, two can defend themselves. A cord of three strands is not quickly broken.*

I Corinthians 1:10 *I appeal to you, brothers, in the name of our Lord Jesus Christ, that all of you agree with one another so that there may be no divisions among you and that you may be perfectly united in mind and thought.*

You are one who has chosen to separate yourself from wickedness, darkness, unbelief, idolatry, and uncleanness in order to be yoked together with your Heavenly Father. He will live and walk with you. He will be your God and you will be His son (II Corinthians 6:14–18). This inseparable union results in:

Psalm 133—anointing and God's blessings;

I Corinthians 12—no jealousy over different giftings in God's body;

Romans 6:5—identity with Christ's death and resurrection;

Philippians 2:1–5—having Christ's attitude—one in spirit and purpose;

Colossians 2:2–3—complete understanding of Christ's wisdom;

Ephesians 2:19–22—being a dwelling where God lives by His Spirit;

Ephesians 4:16—spiritual maturity.

You will have a greater sensitivity for ministry to relationships that are separated, severed, deserted, or abandoned. As Christ's team player, you will gladly take the risk to touch these types of people, in order that they may be one with Him in harmony. You will serve as a link to bring closeness.

LEWIS

Renowned warrior; victorious

❧

I John 5:4 *Everyone born of God overcomes the world. This is the victory that has overcome the world, even our faith.*

II Corinthians 2:14 *But thanks be to God, who always leads us in triumphal procession in Christ and through us spreads everywhere the fragrance of the knowledge of Him.*

Because of your faith in Jesus Christ, you will ever be aggressive towards the enemy's tools of defeat, failure, and victimization. You will push back Satan and overcome all his power. Jesus has given you authority to trample on snakes and scorpions and to overcome all the power of the enemy; nothing will harm you (Luke 10:19). Even in the severest of afflictions—such as hardship, persecution, famine, nakedness, danger, or sword—you are more than a conqueror through Christ who loves you (Romans 8:35–37). "Everyone born of God overcomes the world. This is the victory that has overcome the world, even our faith," I John 5:4. "Take heart, Jesus has overcome the world," John 16:33.

LIAM

Resolute protector; great protector

෪

Job 11:18   *You will be secure, because there is hope; you will look about you and take your rest in safety.*

Psalm 32:7   *You are my hiding place; You will protect me from trouble and surround me with songs of deliverance.*

Psalm 27:5   *For in the day of trouble He will keep me safe in His dwelling; He will hide me in the shelter of His tabernacle and set me high upon a rock.*

You are securely wrapped up and protected by Jesus Christ, who frees you from doubt and harm. Because you find your shelter, assurance, stability, and strength in your personal relationship with the Lord, you are kept in a safe place. You are confident that the Lord will fight for you; you need only be still (Exodus 14:14). As you stand firm on God's solid foundation (II Timothy 2:19) and stay hidden in the shadow of His wings (Psalm 61:4), you will provide deliverance for the weak, insecure, unsheltered, and frail. Instead of being defensive, you are a defender of injustice done to all mankind. You let discretion protect you (Proverbs 2:11). You will shield others from the enemy's destruction with love (I Corinthians 13:7) and the power of God's name (John 17:11). You display God's compassion through your humility. What you let him be in you, you will be to others.

LILA

Dark as night; peaceful and quiet

ℬ

Isaiah 26:3 *You will keep in perfect peace him whose mind is steadfast, because he trusts in You.*

Philippians 4:7 *And the peace of God, which transcends all understanding, will guard your hearts and your minds in Christ Jesus.*

Your life defines peace. You will have a content and calm composure in the midst of distress, disturbance, or agitation. As you follow the Prince of Peace, you will be secure in who you are in Christ. The discipline of keeping your mind on Christ, loving God's law, and being controlled by the Holy Spirit will keep you in perfect peace. God's peace will serve as an umpire to determine whether you are safe or out of God's will (Colossians 3:15). Do not think it strange when you are in battles, fights, and quarrels, because God wants to use you to bring harmony, order, unity, agreement, quietness, and calmness to the adverse situation. You are one whose intimate friendship with the Lord brings reconciliation to the offended, distressed, and troubled. "In repentance and rest is your salvation, in quietness and trust is your strength," Isaiah 30:15. Your refreshing comes as you renew your mind daily in the Word of God. "Great peace have they who love Your law, and nothing can make them stumble," Psalm 119:165.

LILLIAN

The lily; pure heart

ℰↄ

I Timothy 5:22   *...do not share in the sins of others. Keep yourself pure.*

I Peter 1:22   *Now that you have purified yourselves by obeying the truth so that you have sincere love for your brothers, love one another deeply, from the heart.*

Through the process of heat, trials, and refinement, purity is established. Your nature defies being stubborn, judgmental, and haughty. The commandment of the Lord is clear—giving insight to life (Psalm 19:8). You bring wholeness to the dirty, defiled, contaminated, polluted, double-minded, and raped. Your willingness to be transparent is the venue through which He makes His Word clear, simple, and unadulterated. Your choice to be pure enables you to see God (Matthew 5:8) and to know Him as King and Friend (Proverbs 22:11). It also allows your words to be pleasant (Proverbs 15:26) and causes you to ascend to the holy place of the Lord, where you receive blessings and righteousness from the God of salvation (Psalm 24:3–5). Proverbs 20:11 says, "Even a child is known by his actions, by whether his conduct is pure and right."

LILLIE

The lily; pure heart

I Timothy 5:22 *...do not share in the sins of others. Keep yourself pure.*

I Peter 1:22 *Now that you have purified yourselves by obeying the truth so that you have sincere love for your brothers, love one another deeply, from the heart.*

Through the process of heat, trials, and refinement, purity is established. Your nature defies being stubborn, judgmental, and haughty. The commandment of the Lord is clear—giving insight to life (Psalm 19:8). You bring wholeness to the dirty, defiled, contaminated, polluted, double-minded, and raped. Your willingness to be transparent is the venue through which He makes His Word clear, simple, and unadulterated. Your choice to be pure enables you to see God (Matthew 5:8) and to know Him as King and Friend (Proverbs 22:11). It also allows your words to be pleasant (Proverbs 15:26) and causes you to ascend to the holy place of the Lord, where you receive blessings and righteousness from the God of salvation (Psalm 24:3–5). Proverbs 20:11 says, "Even a child is known by his actions, by whether his conduct is pure and right."

LILY

The lily; pure heart

❧

I Timothy 5:22   *...do not share in the sins of others. Keep yourself pure.*

I Peter 1:22   *Now that you have purified yourselves by obeying the truth so that you have sincere love for your brothers, love one another deeply, from the heart.*

Through the process of heat, trials, and refinement, purity is established. Your nature defies being stubborn, judgmental, and haughty. The commandment of the Lord is clear—giving insight to life (Psalm 19:8). You bring wholeness to the dirty, defiled, contaminated, polluted, double-minded, and raped. Your willingness to be transparent is the venue through which He makes His Word clear, simple, and unadulterated. Your choice to be pure enables you to see God (Matthew 5:8) and to know Him as King and Friend (Proverbs 22:11). It also allows your words to be pleasant (Proverbs 15:26) and causes you to ascend to the holy place of the Lord, where you receive blessings and righteousness from the God of salvation (Psalm 24:3–5). Proverbs 20:11 says, "Even a child is known by his actions, by whether his conduct is pure and right."

LINDA

Pretty one; beauty

ℰᏅ

Isaiah 61:1–3   *The Spirit of the Sovereign Lord is on me, because the Lord has anointed me to preach good news to the poor. He has sent me to bind up the brokenhearted, to proclaim freedom for the captives and release from darkness for the prisoners, to proclaim the year of the Lord's favor and the day of vengeance of our God, to comfort all who mourn, and provide for those who grieve in Zion—to bestow on them a crown of beauty instead of ashes, the oil of gladness instead of mourning, and a garment of praise instead of a spirit of despair. They will be called oaks of righteousness, a planting of the Lord for the display of His splendor.*

Psalm 27:4   *One thing I ask of the Lord, this is what I seek: that I may dwell in the house of the Lord all the days of my life, to gaze upon the beauty of the Lord and to seek Him in His temple.*

The Lord desires to give you a private audience with Himself. This intimacy will allow you to reflect Him in all you are, all you do, and in all you say. You are one who radiates the beauty of the Lord with calm assurance of being pleasing, flawless, clean, and pure before Him. You are one who is marked by honesty without being prejudice or impartial. You are able to minister to the victim as well as the victimizer. You are not offended at the ashes of people's lives because you know how God turns them to His beauty. This is accomplished by the cleansing power of the blood of the Lamb—Jesus Christ. Because you prioritize eternal over temporal, you are not side-tracked on the external, whether it be ugly or beautiful. God has gifted you with the ability to see His beauty—regardless.

LINDSAY

Island of Linden trees; calming

&

Isaiah 26:3 *You will keep in perfect peace him whose mind is steadfast, because he trusts in You.*

Philippians 4:7 *And the peace of God, which transcends all understanding, will guard your hearts and your minds in Christ Jesus.*

Your life defines peace. You will have a content and calm composure in the midst of distress, disturbance, or agitation. As you follow the Prince of Peace, you will be secure in who you are in Christ. The discipline of keeping your mind on Christ, loving God's law, and being controlled by the Holy Spirit will keep you in perfect peace. God's peace will serve as an umpire to determine whether you are safe or out of God's will (Colossians 3:15). Do not think it strange when you are in battles, fights, and quarrels, because God wants to use you to bring harmony, order, unity, agreement, quietness, and calmness to the adverse situation. You are one whose intimate friendship with the Lord brings reconciliation to the offended, distressed, and troubled. "In repentance and rest is your salvation, in quietness and trust is your strength," Isaiah 30:15. Your refreshing comes as you renew your mind daily in the Word of God. "Great peace have they who love Your law, and nothing can make them stumble," Psalm 119:165.

LISA

Consecrated to God; consecrated one

&

Romans 12:1 *Therefore, I urge you brothers, in view of God's mercy, to offer your bodies as living sacrifices, holy and pleasing to God—this is your spiritual act of worship.*

Philippians 3:7–8 *But whatever was to my profit I now consider loss for the sake of Christ. What is more, I consider everything a loss compared to the surpassing greatness of knowing Christ Jesus my Lord, for whose sake I have lost all things. I consider them rubbish, that I may gain Christ.*

Before you were born, God set you apart and appointed you as a prophet to the nations (Jeremiah 1:5). You are to be devoted irrevocably to the worship of God. He will pour out His anointing upon you as you are faithful to follow Him wholeheartedly (Psalm 119:34). You are one who has made a commitment to be loyal, true, dependable, enduring, and steadfast. You unmask anything fake with the reality of God's Word. You are aggressive towards lies and deception in order to bring about truth. You are especially sensitive to betrayal, so that God can restore hope, security, purpose, and His faithfulness in those whom He has given you to serve. Let your eyes keep to God's ways (Proverbs 23:26).

LIZ

Consecrated to God; consecrated one

ॐ

Romans 12:1 *Therefore, I urge you brothers, in view of God's mercy, to offer your bodies as living sacrifices, holy and pleasing to God—this is your spiritual act of worship.*

Philippians 3:7–8 *But whatever was to my profit I now consider loss for the sake of Christ. What is more, I consider everything a loss compared to the surpassing greatness of knowing Christ Jesus my Lord, for whose sake I have lost all things. I consider them rubbish, that I may gain Christ.*

Before you were born, God set you apart and appointed you as a prophet to the nations (Jeremiah 1:5). You are to be devoted irrevocably to the worship of God. He will pour out His anointing upon you as you are faithful to follow Him wholeheartedly (Psalm 119:34). You are one who has made a commitment to be loyal, true, dependable, enduring, and steadfast. You unmask anything fake with the reality of God's Word. You are aggressive towards lies and deception in order to bring about truth. You are especially sensitive to betrayal, so that God can restore hope, security, purpose, and His faithfulness in those whom He has given you to serve. Let your eyes keep to God's ways (Proverbs 23:26).

LIZZIE

Consecrated to God; consecrated one

❧

Romans 12:1   *Therefore, I urge you brothers, in view of God's mercy, to offer your bodies as living sacrifices, holy and pleasing to God—this is your spiritual act of worship.*

Philippians 3:7–8   *But whatever was to my profit I now consider loss for the sake of Christ. What is more, I consider everything a loss compared to the surpassing greatness of knowing Christ Jesus my Lord, for whose sake I have lost all things. I consider them rubbish, that I may gain Christ.*

Before you were born, God set you apart and appointed you as a prophet to the nations (Jeremiah 1:5). You are to be devoted irrevocably to the worship of God. He will pour out His anointing upon you as you are faithful to follow Him wholeheartedly (Psalm 119:34). You are one who has made a commitment to be loyal, true, dependable, enduring, and steadfast. You unmask anything fake with the reality of God's Word. You are aggressive towards lies and deception in order to bring about truth. You are especially sensitive to betrayal, so that God can restore hope, security, purpose, and His faithfulness in those whom He has given you to serve. Let your eyes keep to God's ways (Proverbs 23:26).

LLOYD

Gray-haired one; wise one

&

James 3:17 *But the wisdom that comes from heaven is first of all pure; then peace-loving, considerate, submissive, full of mercy and good fruit, impartial and sincere.*

Proverbs 9:10 *The fear of the Lord is the beginning of wisdom, and knowledge of the Holy One is understanding.*

You are a person of moral excellence. You exemplify right living put into practice. The Lord has not only equipped you with skills for living correctly, but also the ability to impart that to others. The Spirit of truth will guide you into all truth, allowing you to have insight into the true nature of things (John 16:13). Out of your reverential respect for the Lord, you have wisdom to give guidance and direction. You are a safe sounding board who steers those who are hungry for knowledge of the Holy One in the right direction. You need only to ask for the wisdom you lack, and God will give it to you generously (James 1:5). Having spiritual discernment is having the ability to separate the difference between God's wisdom and the world's and the ability to make the right choice—regardless. Luke 21:15 says, "For I will give you words and wisdom that none of your adversaries will be able to resist or contradict."

LOGAN

Hollow in a meadow; devoted to God

&

I Chronicles 28:9   *And you, my son Solomon, acknowledge the God of your father, and serve Him with wholehearted devotion and with a willing mind, for the Lord searches every heart and understands every motive behind the thoughts. If you seek Him, He will be found by you; but if you forsake Him, He will reject you forever.*

I Corinthians 15:58   *Therefore, my dear brothers, stand firm. Let nothing move you. Always give yourselves fully to the work of the Lord, because you know that your labor is not in vain.*

Your very being lives to be in constant harmony with your Creator—that the both of your hearts beat as one. Therefore, you are continually yielding every area to the likeness of Christ with strong discipline as you follow Him. You have a devoted allegiance to Christ and His teachings. Your character is one of devotion, dedication, consecration, loyalty, and faithfulness. You are called to help the fallen take a stand and to remove shame and fear. You dispel division by bringing the very unity of God. As you seek and trust in Him with all your heart, leaning not to your own understanding, He will protect you from being blind-sided by the enemy of your soul. Be known as one who loves God with all your heart, soul, mind, and strength. You are one whom God has chosen to be an example of His Son, Jesus Christ.

LOIS

Famous warrior-maid; victorious

ℰℐ

I John 5:4 *Everyone born of God overcomes the world. This is the victory that has overcome the world, even our faith.*

II Corinthians 2:14 *But thanks be to God, who always leads us in triumphal procession in Christ and through us spreads everywhere the fragrance of the knowledge of Him.*

Because of your faith in Jesus Christ, you will ever be aggressive towards the enemy's tools of defeat, failure, and victimization. You will push back Satan and overcome all his power. Jesus has given you authority to trample on snakes and scorpions and to overcome all the power of the enemy; nothing will harm you (Luke 10:19). Even in the severest of afflictions—such as hardship, persecution, famine, nakedness, danger, or sword—you are more than a conqueror through Christ who loves you (Romans 8:35–37). "Everyone born of God overcomes the world. This is the victory that has overcome the world, even our faith," I John 5:4. "Take heart, Jesus has overcome the world," John 16:33.

LORENE

A crown of laurel leaves; victorious spirit

৪৩

I John 5:4 *Everyone born of God overcomes the world. This is the victory that has overcome the world, even our faith.*

II Corinthians 2:14 *But thanks be to God, who always leads us in triumphal procession in Christ and through us spreads everywhere the fragrance of the knowledge of Him.*

Because of your faith in Jesus Christ, you will ever be aggressive towards the enemy's tools of defeat, failure, and victimization. You will push back Satan and overcome all his power. Jesus has given you authority to trample on snakes and scorpions and to overcome all the power of the enemy; nothing will harm you (Luke 10:19). Even in the severest of afflictions—such as hardship, persecution, famine, nakedness, danger, or sword—you are more than a conqueror through Christ who loves you (Romans 8:35–37). "Everyone born of God overcomes the world. This is the victory that has overcome the world, even our faith," I John 5:4. "Take heart, Jesus has overcome the world," John 16:33.

LORIE

Crown of laurel leaves; victorious spirit

ᏻ

I John 5:4   *Everyone born of God overcomes the world. This is the victory that has overcome the world, even our faith.*

II Corinthians 2:14   *But thanks be to God, who always leads us in triumphal procession in Christ and through us spreads everywhere the fragrance of the knowledge of Him.*

Because of your faith in Jesus Christ, you will ever be aggressive towards the enemy's tools of defeat, failure, and victimization. You will push back Satan and overcome all his power. Jesus has given you authority to trample on snakes and scorpions and to overcome all the power of the enemy; nothing will harm you (Luke 10:19). Even in the severest of afflictions—such as hardship, persecution, famine, nakedness, danger, or sword—you are more than a conqueror through Christ who loves you (Romans 8:35–37). "Everyone born of God overcomes the world. This is the victory that has overcome the world, even our faith," I John 5:4. "Take heart, Jesus has overcome the world," John 16:33.

LOUIS

Renowned warrior; victorious

I John 5:4   *Everyone born of God overcomes the world. This is the victory that has overcome the world, even our faith.*

II Corinthians 2:14   *But thanks be to God, who always leads us in triumphal procession in Christ and through us spreads everywhere the fragrance of the knowledge of Him.*

Because of your faith in Jesus Christ, you will ever be aggressive towards the enemy's tools of defeat, failure, and victimization. You will push back Satan and overcome all his power. Jesus has given you authority to trample on snakes and scorpions and to overcome all the power of the enemy; nothing will harm you (Luke 10:19). Even in the severest of afflictions—such as hardship, persecution, famine, nakedness, danger, or sword—you are more than a conqueror through Christ who loves you (Romans 8:35–37). "Everyone born of God overcomes the world. This is the victory that has overcome the world, even our faith," I John 5:4. "Take heart, Jesus has overcome the world," John 16:33.

LOUISE

Famous warrior-maid; victorious

✆

I John 5:4 *Everyone born of God overcomes the world. This is the victory that has overcome the world, even our faith.*

II Corinthians 2:14 *But thanks be to God, who always leads us in triumphal procession in Christ and through us spreads everywhere the fragrance of the knowledge of Him.*

Because of your faith in Jesus Christ, you will ever be aggressive towards the enemy's tools of defeat, failure, and victimization. You will push back Satan and overcome all his power. Jesus has given you authority to trample on snakes and scorpions and to overcome all the power of the enemy; nothing will harm you (Luke 10:19). Even in the severest of afflictions—such as hardship, persecution, famine, nakedness, danger, or sword—you are more than a conqueror through Christ who loves you (Romans 8:35–37). "Everyone born of God overcomes the world. This is the victory that has overcome the world, even our faith," I John 5:4. "Take heart, Jesus has overcome the world," John 16:33.

LUANN

Graceful battle-maid; victorious spirit

❧

I John 5:4 *Everyone born of God overcomes the world. This is the victory that has overcome the world, even our faith.*

II Corinthians 2:14 *But thanks be to God, who always leads us in triumphal procession in Christ and through us spreads everywhere the fragrance of the knowledge of Him.*

Because of your faith in Jesus Christ, you will ever be aggressive towards the enemy's tools of defeat, failure, and victimization. You will push back Satan and overcome all his power. Jesus has given you authority to trample on snakes and scorpions and to overcome all the power of the enemy; nothing will harm you (Luke 10:19). Even in the severest of afflictions—such as hardship, persecution, famine, nakedness, danger, or sword—you are more than a conqueror through Christ who loves you (Romans 8:35–37). "Everyone born of God overcomes the world. This is the victory that has overcome the world, even our faith," I John 5:4. "Take heart, Jesus has overcome the world," John 16:33.

LUCAS

Light; enlightened one

&

Psalm 27:1 *The Lord is my light and my salvation—whom shall I fear? The Lord is the stronghold of my life; of whom shall I be afraid.*

Proverbs 4:18 *The path of the righteous is like the first gleam of dawn, shining ever brighter till the full light of day.*

You are one who reflects the shining brightness of the countenance of Jesus. You are aggressive toward the fruitless deeds of darkness from the evil one, by exposing them to the light of Jesus. Everything exposed by light becomes visible, for it is the light that makes everything visible (Ephesians 5:11–14). This radiance that God has given you serves as a beacon to give guidance to those yet in darkness. Your life's mission is found in the following two verses: Isaiah 60:1–3 says, "Arise, shine, for your light has come, and the glory of the Lord rises upon you. See, darkness covers the earth, and thick darkness is over the peoples, but the Lord rises upon you and His glory appears over you. Nations will come to your light, and kings to the brightness of your dawn." And in Acts 13:47, "For this is what the Lord has commanded us: 'I have made you a light for the Gentiles, that you may bring salvation to the ends of the earth.'" Continue to shine as His star, leading many to righteousness (Daniel 12:3 and Philippians 2:15).

LUCILLE

Light; bringer of light

❧

Psalm 27:1 *The Lord is my light and my salvation—whom shall I fear? The Lord is the stronghold of my life; of whom shall I be afraid.*

Proverbs 4:18 *The path of the righteous is like the first gleam of dawn, shining ever brighter till the full light of day.*

You are one who reflects the shining brightness of the countenance of Jesus. You are aggressive toward the fruitless deeds of darkness from the evil one, by exposing them to the light of Jesus. Everything exposed by light becomes visible, for it is the light that makes everything visible (Ephesians 5:11–14). This radiance that God has given you serves as a beacon to give guidance to those yet in darkness. Your life's mission is found in the following two verses: Isaiah 60:1–3 says, "Arise, shine, for your light has come, and the glory of the Lord rises upon you. See, darkness covers the earth, and thick darkness is over the peoples, but the Lord rises upon you and His glory appears over you. Nations will come to your light, and kings to the brightness of your dawn." And in Acts 13:47, "For this is what the Lord has commanded us: 'I have made you a light for the Gentiles, that you may bring salvation to the ends of the earth.'" Continue to shine as His star, leading many to righteousness (Daniel 12:3 and Philippians 2:15).

LUCY

Light; bringer of light

&

Psalm 27:1 *The Lord is my light and my salvation—whom shall I fear? The Lord is the stronghold of my life; of whom shall I be afraid.*

Proverbs 4:18 *The path of the righteous is like the first gleam of dawn, shining ever brighter till the full light of day.*

You are one who reflects the shining brightness of the countenance of Jesus. You are aggressive toward the fruitless deeds of darkness from the evil one, by exposing them to the light of Jesus. Everything exposed by light becomes visible, for it is the light that makes everything visible (Ephesians 5:11–14). This radiance that God has given you serves as a beacon to give guidance to those yet in darkness. Your life's mission is found in the following two verses: Isaiah 60:1–3 says, "Arise, shine, for your light has come, and the glory of the Lord rises upon you. See, darkness covers the earth, and thick darkness is over the peoples, but the Lord rises upon you and His glory appears over you. Nations will come to your light, and kings to the brightness of your dawn." And in Acts 13:47, "For this is what the Lord has commanded us: 'I have made you a light for the Gentiles, that you may bring salvation to the ends of the earth.'" Continue to shine as His star, leading many to righteousness (Daniel 12:3 and Philippians 2:15).

LUKE

Light; enlightened one

ॐ

Psalm 27:1 *The Lord is my light and my salvation—whom shall I fear? The Lord is the stronghold of my life; of whom shall I be afraid.*

Proverbs 4:18 *The path of the righteous is like the first gleam of dawn, shining ever brighter till the full light of day.*

You are one who reflects the shining brightness of the countenance of Jesus. You are aggressive toward the fruitless deeds of darkness from the evil one, by exposing them to the light of Jesus. Everything exposed by light becomes visible, for it is the light that makes everything visible (Ephesians 5:11–14). This radiance that God has given you serves as a beacon to give guidance to those yet in darkness. Your life's mission is found in the following two verses: Isaiah 60:1–3 says, "Arise, shine, for your light has come, and the glory of the Lord rises upon you. See, darkness covers the earth, and thick darkness is over the peoples, but the Lord rises upon you and His glory appears over you. Nations will come to your light, and kings to the brightness of your dawn." And in Acts 13:47, "For this is what the Lord has commanded us: 'I have made you a light for the Gentiles, that you may bring salvation to the ends of the earth.'" Continue to shine as His star, leading many to righteousness (Daniel 12:3 and Philippians 2:15).

LYLE

From the island; sojourner

ॐ

Isaiah 42:4, 12   *He will not falter or be discouraged till He establishes justice on earth. In His law the islands will put their hope. Let them give glory to the Lord and proclaim His praise in the islands.*

Hebrews 11:8–10   *By faith Abraham, when called to go to a place he would later receive as his inheritance, obeyed and went, even though he did not know where he was going. By faith he made his home in the promised land like a stranger in a foreign country; he lived in tents, as did Isaac and Jacob, who were heirs with him of the same promise. For he was looking forward to the city with foundations whose architect and builder is God.*

An island is a tract of land surrounded by the water of the Word, serving as a safety zone. You are constantly aware that life on earth is a temporary stay; you reside as a foreigner, a resident alien. As your focus remains heavenward, this world will have no hold on you with its cravings, lusts, and boastings because the love of the Father is in you (I John 2:15–17). You are one whose priorities are on eternal values rather than temporal. This releases you to discern the will of God without compromise—with a ready obedient heart. As you surround yourself with the water of the Word, you will stand in awe of Him. Hebrews 13:14 says, "For here we do not have an enduring city, but we are looking for the city that is to come."

LYNETTE

From the pool; refreshing one

Acts 3:19 *Repent, then, and turn to God, so that your sins may be wiped out, that times of refreshing may come from the Lord.*

II Timothy 1:16 *May the Lord show mercy to the household of Onesiphorus, because he often refreshed me and was not ashamed of my chains.*

You are one who restores strength because of knowing your own weakness. One who revives life because of dying to self. One who renews supply because of being emptied of self. One who reconciles offenses because your wisdom is from Christ. To bring this refreshing, you must know the all-sufficient one—El-Shaddai—in all your insufficiencies. As you learn to rest in His presence (Exodus 33:14), you will be a channel for His revival. Psalm 42:1–2 says, "As the deer pants for streams of water, so my soul pants for you, O God. My soul thirsts for God, for the living God. When can I go and meet with God?" To be His brook or His stream you must dwell in His stream. Stay thirsty for God's living water (John 7:37–38) .

LYNN

From the pool; refreshing one

ℰↃ

Acts 3:19 *Repent, then, and turn to God, so that your sins may be wiped out, that times of refreshing may come from the Lord.*

II Timothy 1:16 *May the Lord show mercy to the household of Onesiphorus, because he often refreshed me and was not ashamed of my chains.*

You are one who restores strength because of knowing your own weakness. One who revives life because of dying to self. One who renews supply because of being emptied of self. One who reconciles offenses because your wisdom is from Christ. To bring this refreshing, you must know the all-sufficient one—El-Shaddai—in all your insufficiencies. As you learn to rest in His presence (Exodus 33:14), you will be a channel for His revival. Psalm 42:1–2 says, "As the deer pants for streams of water, so my soul pants for you, O God. My soul thirsts for God, for the living God. When can I go and meet with God?" To be His brook or His stream you must dwell in His stream. Stay thirsty for God's living water (John 7:37–38).

MACK

Son of a wise leader; full of wisdom

୫୬

James 3:17 *But the wisdom that comes from heaven is first of all pure; then peace-loving, considerate, submissive, full of mercy and good fruit, impartial and sincere.*

Proverbs 9:10 *The fear of the Lord is the beginning of wisdom, and knowledge of the Holy One is understanding.*

You are a person of moral excellence. You exemplify right living put into practice. The Lord has not only equipped you with skills for living correctly, but also the ability to impart that to others. The Spirit of truth will guide you into all truth, allowing you to have insight into the true nature of things (John 16:13). Out of your reverential respect for the Lord, you have wisdom to give guidance and direction. You are a safe sounding board who steers those who are hungry for knowledge of the Holy One in the right direction. You need only to ask for the wisdom you lack, and God will give it to you generously (James 1:5). Having spiritual discernment is having the ability to separate the difference between God's wisdom and the world's and the ability to make the right choice—regardless. Luke 21:15 says, "For I will give you words and wisdom that none of your adversaries will be able to resist or contradict."

MACKENZIE

Son of a wise leader; full of wisdom

❦

James 3:17 *But the wisdom that comes from heaven is first of all pure; then peace-loving, considerate, submissive, full of mercy and good fruit, impartial and sincere.*

Proverbs 9:10 *The fear of the Lord is the beginning of wisdom, and knowledge of the Holy One is understanding.*

You are a person of moral excellence. You exemplify right living put into practice. The Lord has not only equipped you with skills for living correctly, but also the ability to impart that to others. The Spirit of truth will guide you into all truth, allowing you to have insight into the true nature of things (John 16:13). Out of your reverential respect for the Lord, you have wisdom to give guidance and direction. You are a safe sounding board who steers those who are hungry for knowledge of the Holy One in the right direction. You need only to ask for the wisdom you lack, and God will give it to you generously (James 1:5). Having spiritual discernment is having the ability to separate the difference between God's wisdom and the world's and the ability to make the right choice—regardless. Luke 21:15 says, "For I will give you words and wisdom that none of your adversaries will be able to resist or contradict."

MADELINE
Woman of Magdala; transformed heart

Ezekiel 36:26–27 *I will give you a new heart and put a new spirit in you; I will remove from you your heart of stone and give you a heart of flesh. And I will put My spirit in you and move you to follow My decrees and be careful to keep My laws.*

Romans 12:2 *Do not conform any longer to the pattern of this world, but be transformed by the renewing of your mind. Then you will be able to test and approve what God's will is—His good, pleasing and perfect will.*

The cross of Jesus Christ is your ultimate source of transformation. He exchanged your sin for His righteousness, your death for His life, your darkness for His light, your earthly for His eternal, and your past for His future. You were lost, but now you are found. You were blind, but now you see. The old has now become new. II Corinthians 5:17 says, "Therefore, if anyone is in Christ, he is a new creation; the old has gone, the new has come!" A metamorphosis is your transformation from God through Christ. Your conversion by the blood of Jesus is the greatest miracle you will ever experience. This changeless God has traded your sorrow for His joy, your pain for His healing, your emptiness for His fullness, and your rejection for His forgiveness. He adopts, accepts, and loves you. Put to death what belongs to your earthly nature and be clothed with the likeness of Christ (Colossians 3:1–14). As you align your will with His and are continually renewed in the knowledge of God's Word, He will transform many lives through yours. For those living a lie you bring truth, for the dying you bring life, for the rejected you bring acceptance, and for the trapped you bring freedom. His resurrection power flows in and through you. You will continually be transformed into the Lord's likeness with ever-increasing glory (II Corinthians 3:18).

MADISON

Good; honorable

Isaiah 32:8 *But the noble man makes noble plans, and by noble deeds he stands.*

Luke 8:15 *But the seed on good soil stands for those with a noble and good heart, who hear the word, retain it, and by persevering produce a crop.*

Proverbs 18:12 says, "Before his downfall a man's heart is proud, but humility comes before honor." You are one who has a humble confidence in recognizing and expressing reverence, worship, adoration, trust, deference, tribute, admiration, and respect. This is the result of being secure in the truth of who you are in the Lord. Through humility, King Jesus made a way for you to be engrafted into His royalty. He made of Himself no reputation and took on the nature of a servant (Philippians 2:7) to affirm your value. Through self-denial, you prioritize excellence in virtue, truthfulness, and faithfulness. Because of the respect you have earned, you dismantle inferiority, disgrace, shame, and offenses. No one feels second-rate in your presence. The deeper that the Lord is your object of reverence, the greater your confidence will be in giving approval and worth. Because you are tall in spirit, your face is always turned upward.

MADOLIA

Woman of Magdala; transformed heart

⚭

Ezekiel 36:26–27 *I will give you a new heart and put a new spirit in you; I will remove from you your heart of stone and give you a heart of flesh. And I will put My spirit in you and move you to follow My decrees and be careful to keep My laws.*

Romans 12:2 *Do not conform any longer to the pattern of this world, but be transformed by the renewing of your mind. Then you will be able to test and approve what God's will is—His good, pleasing and perfect will.*

The cross of Jesus Christ is your ultimate source of transformation. He exchanged your sin for His righteousness, your death for His life, your darkness for His light, your earthly for His eternal, and your past for His future. You were lost, but now you are found. You were blind, but now you see. The old has now become new. II Corinthians 5:17 says, "Therefore, if anyone is in Christ, he is a new creation; the old has gone, the new has come!" A metamorphosis is your transformation from God through Christ. Your conversion by the blood of Jesus is the greatest miracle you will ever experience. This changeless God has traded your sorrow for His joy, your pain for His healing, your emptiness for His fullness, and your rejection for His forgiveness. He adopts, accepts, and loves you. Put to death what belongs to your earthly nature and be clothed with the likeness of Christ (Colossians 3:1–14). As you align your will with His and are continually renewed in the knowledge of God's Word, He will transform many lives through yours. For those living a lie you bring truth, for the dying you bring life, for the rejected you bring acceptance, and for the trapped you bring freedom. His resurrection power flows in and through you. You will continually be transformed into the Lord's likeness with ever-increasing glory (II Corinthians 3:18).

MAE

Great one; esteemed one

Proverbs 22:1 *A good name is more desirable than great riches; to be esteemed is better than silver or gold.*

Hebrews 11:26 *He regarded disgrace for the sake of Christ as of greater value than the treasures of Egypt, because he was looking ahead to his reward.*

Your life is to reflect the very nature of God. It is holy, righteous, just, pure, spotless, faithful, and divine. Out of a humble, reverent heart you will ever be esteemed and prized by the Lord as you show Him respect, adoration, and praise. You will have no reason to be insecure in who you are in the Lord. Nor will you ever place blame on God or disapprove of His will for your life. You hold in highest regard and love those who minister to you (I Thessalonians 4:12–13). You do nothing out of selfish ambition or vain conceit, but in humility consider others better than yourself (Philippians 2:3).

MAGGIE

A pearl

❧

I Timothy 5:22   *...do not share in the sins of others. Keep yourself pure.*

I Peter 1:22   *Now that you have purified yourselves by obeying the truth so that you have sincere love for your brothers, love one another deeply, from the heart.*

Through the process of heat, trials, and refinement, purity is established. Your nature defies being stubborn, judgmental, and haughty. The commandment of the Lord is clear—giving insight to life (Psalm 19:8). You bring wholeness to the dirty, defiled, contaminated, polluted, double-minded, and raped. Your willingness to be transparent is the venue through which He makes His Word clear, simple, and unadulterated. Your choice to be pure enables you to see God (Matthew 5:8) and to know Him as King and Friend (Proverbs 22:11). It also allows your words to be pleasant (Proverbs 15:26) and causes you to ascend to the holy place of the Lord, where you receive blessings and righteousness from the God of salvation (Psalm 24:3–5). Proverbs 20:11 says, "Even a child is known by his actions, by whether his conduct is pure and right."

MAKAYLA

Who is like God; godliness

રજ

Exodus 15:11 *Who among the gods is like you, O Lord? Who is like You—majestic in holiness, awesome in glory, working wonders?*

I Timothy 4:8 *Godliness has value for all things, holding promise for both the present life and the life to come.*

Godliness with contentment is great gain (I Timothy 6:6). You are to pursue godliness (I Timothy 6:11). Your life is to reflect the very nature of God, which is holy, righteous, just, pure, spotless, faithful, and divine. The choices you make and the life you live are to define God's standard for living. As you follow the Lord, He desires for others to pattern their lives after you. Out of a humble, reverent heart and as you show Him respect, adoration, and praise, you will ever be esteemed and prized by the Lord. You will have no reason to be insecure in who you are, or to place blame on God, or to disapprove of His will for your life. He celebrates how He made you!

MALORIE

Counselor; full of wisdom

બ

James 3:17   *But the wisdom that comes from heaven is first of all pure; then peace-loving, considerate, submissive, full of mercy and good fruit, impartial and sincere.*

Proverbs 9:10   *The fear of the Lord is the beginning of wisdom, and knowledge of the Holy One is understanding.*

You are a person of moral excellence. You exemplify right living put into practice. The Lord has not only equipped you with skills for living correctly, but also the ability to impart that to others. The Spirit of truth will guide you into all truth, allowing you to have insight into the true nature of things (John 16:13). Out of your reverential respect for the Lord, you have wisdom to give guidance and direction. You are a safe sounding board who steers those who are hungry for knowledge of the Holy One in the right direction. You need only to ask for the wisdom you lack, and God will give it to you generously (James 1:5). Having spiritual discernment is having the ability to separate the difference between God's wisdom and the world's and the ability to make the right choice—regardless. Luke 21:15 says, "For I will give you words and wisdom that none of your adversaries will be able to resist or contradict."

MANDY

Worthy of love; beloved

Deuteronomy 33:12   *Let the beloved of the Lord rest secure in Him, for He shields him all day long, and the one the Lord loves rests between His shoulders.*

I John 4:7   *Dear friends, let us love one another, for love comes from God. Everyone who loves has been born of God and knows God.*

You are highly valued, treasured, and precious to the Lord. You are an eye-witness of the very majesty of Jesus Christ. He received glory and honor from God the Father when the voice came to Him from the Majestic Glory, saying, "This is my Son, whom I love; with Him I am well pleased," II Peter 1:16–17. As you stay committed to Him, one day you will also hear those words. "We know and rely on the love of God for us. God is love, whoever lives in love lives in God and God in him," I John 4:16. You are expressive in worship because you are near to the heart of God. As you give respect, pleasure, and adoration to the Lord, He will give it back to you. You are aggressive to show the love of God to those who are disliked, abhorred, and hated. Rest secure in Him!

MANNING

Heroic; honorable

Isaiah 32:8 *But the noble man makes noble plans, and by noble deeds he stands.*

Luke 8:15 *But the seed on good soil stands for those with a noble and good heart, who hear the word, retain it, and by persevering produce a crop.*

Proverbs 18:12 says, "Before his downfall a man's heart is proud, but humility comes before honor." You are one who has a humble confidence in recognizing and expressing reverence, worship, adoration, trust, deference, tribute, admiration, and respect. This is the result of being secure in the truth of who you are in the Lord. Through humility, King Jesus made a way for you to be engrafted into His royalty. He made of Himself no reputation and took on the nature of a servant (Philippians 2:7) to affirm your value. Through self-denial, you prioritize excellence in virtue, truthfulness, and faithfulness. Because of the respect you have earned, you dismantle inferiority, disgrace, shame, and offenses. No one feels second-rate in your presence. The deeper that the Lord is your object of reverence, the greater your confidence will be in giving approval and worth. Because you are tall in spirit, your face is always turned upward.

MARCIA

God of war; a brave heart

❦

Joshua 1:7 *Be strong and very courageous. Be careful to obey all the law My servant Moses gave you; do not turn from it to the right or to the left, that you may be successful wherever you go.*

Philippians 1:27b–28 *I will know that you stand firm in one spirit, contending as one man for the faith of the gospel without being frightened in any way by those who oppose you. This is a sign to them that they will be destroyed, but that you will be saved—and that by God.*

The brave are courageous, heroic, resolute, without dread, and bold. Cowards are fearful, timid, and fainthearted. They see victory in size rather than in faith. Running, hiding, escape mechanisms, and desertion are their game plan. They are dominated by the fear of man. You are dominated by your respectful fear of God. In stubborn faith, you say, "Nothing can hinder the Lord, nothing is impossible with Him." Your confidence lies in God's abiding presence and His great strength. God has mantled you as His encourager, invading strongholds of doubt and fear. Speak the Word of God boldly (Acts 4:31). The Lord trusts you to champion His cause by advancing the kingdom of heaven in all that you do.

MARCUS

Warlike one; mighty warrior

∽

II Chronicles 32:7–8 *There is a greater power with us than with him. With him is only the arm of flesh, but with us is the Lord our God to help us and to fight our battles.*

II Timothy 2:3–4 *Endure hardship with us like a good soldier of Christ Jesus. No one serving as a soldier gets involved in civilian affairs - he wants to please his commanding officer.*

Exodus 14:14 says, "The Lord will fight for you; you need only be still." You are armed with the ability to handle the spear and shield—to stand on God's Word by faith, supporting the King of kings against His enemies. As God's defending warrior, you are His example of a brave champion, soldier, and hero. The ultimate war was a contest with death and when Christ said, "It is finished" on the cross, He declared victory over death, hell, and the grave. You are equipped to be used of God as one who protects by warding off attacks, calling for justice, and providing shelter. When God is all of this to you, you will be that vindication for others. Because of your faith in Jesus Christ, you will ever be aggressive towards the enemy's tools of defeat, failure, and victimization. Your ultimate purpose is to be one who stands in the gap (Ezekiel 22:30) as a defender of the weak. This includes those who are easily influenced, confused, quitters, faint, frail, fragile, and frightened. Your primary spiritual warfare will be that of brave intercession—reaching, meeting, and entreating God for His favor to set the captives free. Then you will "learn to do right! Seek justice, encourage the oppressed. Defend the cause of the fatherless, plead the case of the widow," Isaiah 1:17.

MARGARET

A pearl

&

I Timothy 5:22   *...do not share in the sins of others. Keep yourself pure.*

I Peter 1:22   *Now that you have purified yourselves by obeying the truth so that you have sincere love for your brothers, love one another deeply, from the heart.*

Through the process of heat, trials, and refinement, purity is established. Your nature defies being stubborn, judgmental, and haughty. The commandment of the Lord is clear—giving insight to life (Psalm 19:8). You bring wholeness to the dirty, defiled, contaminated, polluted, double-minded, and raped. Your willingness to be transparent is the venue through which He makes His Word clear, simple, and unadulterated. Your choice to be pure enables you to see God (Matthew 5:8) and to know Him as King and Friend (Proverbs 22:11). It also allows your words to be pleasant (Proverbs 15:26) and causes you to ascend to the holy place of the Lord, where you receive blessings and righteousness from the God of salvation (Psalm 24:3–5). Proverbs 20:11 says, "Even a child is known by his actions, by whether his conduct is pure and right."

MARGE

A pearl

℘

I Timothy 5:22   *...do not share in the sins of others. Keep yourself pure.*

I Peter 1:22   *Now that you have purified yourselves by obeying the truth so that you have sincere love for your brothers, love one another deeply, from the heart.*

Through the process of heat, trials, and refinement, purity is established. Your nature defies being stubborn, judgmental, and haughty. The commandment of the Lord is clear—giving insight to life (Psalm 19:8). You bring wholeness to the dirty, defiled, contaminated, polluted, double-minded, and raped. Your willingness to be transparent is the venue through which He makes His Word clear, simple, and unadulterated. Your choice to be pure enables you to see God (Matthew 5:8) and to know Him as King and Friend (Proverbs 22:11). It also allows your words to be pleasant (Proverbs 15:26) and causes you to ascend to the holy place of the Lord, where you receive blessings and righteousness from the God of salvation (Psalm 24:3–5). Proverbs 20:11 says, "Even a child is known by his actions, by whether his conduct is pure and right."

MARIA

Myrrh; living fragrance

II Corinthians 2:14–15 *But thanks be to God, who always leads us in triumphal procession in Christ and through us spreads everywhere the fragrance of the knowledge of Him. For we are to God the aroma of Christ among those who are being saved and those who are perishing.*

Ephesians 5:1–2 *Be imitators of God, therefore, as dearly loved children and live a life of love, just as Christ loved us and gave Himself up for us as a fragrant offering and sacrifice to God.*

Myrrh is a fragrant oil used as part of anointing oil that is produced from the wounds or injuries made in the bark of a tree. In Bible days, it was also used as incense in the worship of God. The way you process the wounds and injuries He allows to happen to you brings Him pleasure. You join with David's words in Psalm 119:50, "My comfort in my suffering is this: Your promise preserves my life." You are secure that nothing can touch your life without passing through your Sovereign Father's hands. Much like the woman who poured her expensive perfume from her alabaster box upon Jesus, you risk being poured out and wasted for your Savior's sake. He has chosen you to be pure worship to Him. It is at that point that the stench of this world will be invaded by the sweet fragrance of Christ through your life.

MARIAH

Myrrh; living fragrance

ৰ্তৎ

II Corinthians 2:14–15 *But thanks be to God, who always leads us in triumphal procession in Christ and through us spreads everywhere the fragrance of the knowledge of Him. For we are to God the aroma of Christ among those who are being saved and those who are perishing.*

Ephesians 5:1–2 *Be imitators of God, therefore, as dearly loved children and live a life of love, just as Christ loved us and gave Himself up for us as a fragrant offering and sacrifice to God.*

Myrrh is a fragrant oil used as part of anointing oil that is produced from the wounds or injuries made in the bark of a tree. In Bible days, it was also used as incense in the worship of God. The way you process the wounds and injuries He allows to happen to you brings Him pleasure. You join with David's words in Psalm 119:50, "My comfort in my suffering is this: Your promise preserves my life." You are secure that nothing can touch your life without passing through your Sovereign Father's hands. Much like the woman who poured her expensive perfume from her alabaster box upon Jesus, you risk being poured out and wasted for your Savior's sake. He has chosen you to be pure worship to Him. It is at that point that the stench of this world will be invaded by the sweet fragrance of Christ through your life.

MARIE

Myrrh, living fragrance

છ૭

II Corinthians 2:14–15 *But thanks be to God, who always leads us in triumphal procession in Christ and through us spreads everywhere the fragrance of the knowledge of Him. For we are to God the aroma of Christ among those who are being saved and those who are perishing.*

Ephesians 5:1–2 *Be imitators of God, therefore, as dearly loved children and live a life of love, just as Christ loved us and gave Himself up for us as a fragrant offering and sacrifice to God.*

Myrrh is a fragrant oil used as part of anointing oil that is produced from the wounds or injuries made in the bark of a tree. In Bible days, it was also used as incense in the worship of God. The way you process the wounds and injuries He allows to happen to you brings Him pleasure. You join with David's words in Psalm 119:50, "My comfort in my suffering is this: Your promise preserves my life." You are secure that nothing can touch your life without passing through your Sovereign Father's hands. Much like the woman who poured her expensive perfume from her alabaster box upon Jesus, you risk being poured out and wasted for your Savior's sake. He has chosen you to be pure worship to Him. It is at that point that the stench of this world will be invaded by the sweet fragrance of Christ through your life.

MARILYN

Myrrh; living fragrance

❦

II Corinthians 2:14–15 *But thanks be to God, who always leads us in triumphal procession in Christ and through us spreads everywhere the fragrance of the knowledge of Him. For we are to God the aroma of Christ among those who are being saved and those who are perishing.*

Ephesians 5:1–2 *Be imitators of God, therefore, as dearly loved children and live a life of love, just as Christ loved us and gave Himself up for us as a fragrant offering and sacrifice to God.*

Myrrh is a fragrant oil used as part of anointing oil that is produced from the wounds or injuries made in the bark of a tree. In Bible days, it was also used as incense in the worship of God. The way you process the wounds and injuries He allows to happen to you brings Him pleasure. You join with David's words in Psalm 119:50, "My comfort in my suffering is this: Your promise preserves my life." You are secure that nothing can touch your life without passing through your Sovereign Father's hands. Much like the woman who poured her expensive perfume from her alabaster box upon Jesus, you risk being poured out and wasted for your Savior's sake. He has chosen you to be pure worship to Him. It is at that point that the stench of this world will be invaded by the sweet fragrance of Christ through your life.

MARK

Warlike one; mighty warrior

ℰ𝒪

II Chronicles 32:7–8   *There is a greater power with us than with him. With him is only the arm of flesh, but with us is the Lord our God to help us and to fight our battles.*

II Timothy 2:3–4   *Endure hardship with us like a good soldier of Christ Jesus. No one serving as a soldier gets involved in civilian affairs - he wants to please his commanding officer.*

Exodus 14:14 says, "The Lord will fight for you; you need only be still." You are armed with the ability to handle the spear and shield—to stand on God's Word by faith, supporting the King of kings against His enemies. As God's defending warrior, you are His example of a brave champion, soldier, and hero. The ultimate war was a contest with death and when Christ said, "It is finished" on the cross, He declared victory over death, hell, and the grave. You are equipped to be used of God as one who protects by warding off attacks, calling for justice, and providing shelter. When God is all of this to you, you will be that vindication for others. Because of your faith in Jesus Christ, you will ever be aggressive towards the enemy's tools of defeat, failure, and victimization. Your ultimate purpose is to be one who stands in the gap (Ezekiel 22:30) as a defender of the weak. This includes those who are easily influenced, confused, quitters, faint, frail, fragile, and frightened. Your primary spiritual warfare will be that of brave intercession—reaching, meeting, and entreating God for His favor to set the captives free. Then you will "learn to do right! Seek justice, encourage the oppressed. Defend the cause of the fatherless, plead the case of the widow," Isaiah 1:17.

MARSHA

God of war; a brave heart

❧

Joshua 1:7   *Be strong and very courageous. Be careful to obey all the law My servant Moses gave you; do not turn from it to the right or to the left, that you may be successful wherever you go.*

Philippians 1:27b–28   *I will know that you stand firm in one spirit, contending as one man for the faith of the gospel without being frightened in any way by those who oppose you. This is a sign to them that they will be destroyed, but that you will be saved—and that by God.*

The brave are courageous, heroic, resolute, without dread, and bold. Cowards are fearful, timid, and fainthearted. They see victory in size rather than in faith. Running, hiding, escape mechanisms, and desertion are their game plan. They are dominated by the fear of man. You are dominated by your respectful fear of God. In stubborn faith, you say, "Nothing can hinder the Lord, nothing is impossible with Him." Your confidence lies in God's abiding presence and His great strength. God has mantled you as His encourager, invading strongholds of doubt and fear. Speak the Word of God boldly (Acts 4:31). The Lord trusts you to champion His cause by advancing the kingdom of heaven in all that you do.

MARTHA

A lady; woman of discretion

෨

II Corinthians 8:7 *But just as you excel in everything—in faith, in speech, in knowledge, in complete earnestness and in your love for us—see that you also excel in this grace of giving.*

Philippians 4:8 *Finally, brothers, whatever is true, whatever is noble, whatever is right, whatever is pure, whatever is lovely, whatever is admirable—if anything is excellent or praiseworthy—think about such things.*

Excellent worth is comprised in your worship of God. Revelation 5:12 says, "Worthy is the Lamb, who was slain, to receive power and wealth and wisdom and strength and honor and glory and praise!" "All this also comes from the Lord Almighty, wonderful in counsel and magnificent in wisdom," Isaiah 28:29. God has given you an eye for quality, demonstrating His excellence of character and conduct. You go beyond human capacity with faith that transcends all understanding. Your faith is of greater worth than gold (I Peter 1:7). In quality, skill, and achievement, you go the extra mile. This is all about giving, not getting; serving, not controlling. Perfectionism leads to legalism. Excellence releases freedom. You are to show the insignificant and the wasted the more excellent way of God's love (I Corinthians 12:31 and chapter 13) and kindness (2 Peter 1:5–7). You are to excel in gifts that build up the church (I Corinthians 14:12). God uses you to restore genuine value, purpose, and productivity. Devoting yourself to doing what is good will lead to what is excellent and profitable for everyone (Titus 3:8). Your gentle and quiet spirit is of great worth in God's eyes (I Peter 3:4).

MARTIN

Warlike; loyal spirit

Romans 12:9–10   *Love must be sincere. Hate what is evil; cling to what is good. Be devoted to one another in brotherly love. Honor one another above yourselves.*

Proverbs 2:7–8   *He holds victory in store for the upright, He is a shield to those whose walk is blameless, for He guards the course of the just and protects the way of His faithful ones.*

As one with a loyal spirit, the Lord has called you to be faithful, devoted, obedient, dependable, and true. You are noble in disarming the enemy's attacks of fear, selfishness, failure, betrayal, dishonesty, and faithlessness. You are unyielding and have a resolute confidence in your commitment to God's Word. With it, you will help others overcome being cowards, losers, quitters, or betrayers. Knowing God's loyalty to you will strengthen your loyalty to others. Isaiah 1:17 says, "Learn to do right! Seek justice, encourage the oppressed. Defend the cause of the fatherless, plead the case of the widow."

MARTY

Warlike; loyal spirit

Romans 12:9–10   *Love must be sincere. Hate what is evil; cling to what is good. Be devoted to one another in brotherly love. Honor one another above yourselves.*

Proverbs 2:7–8   *He holds victory in store for the upright, He is a shield to those whose walk is blameless, for He guards the course of the just and protects the way of His faithful ones.*

As one with a loyal spirit, the Lord has called you to be faithful, devoted, obedient, dependable, and true. You are noble in disarming the enemy's attacks of fear, selfishness, failure, betrayal, dishonesty, and faithlessness. You are unyielding and have a resolute confidence in your commitment to God's Word. With it, you will help others overcome being cowards, losers, quitters, or betrayers. Knowing God's loyalty to you will strengthen your loyalty to others. Isaiah 1:17 says, "Learn to do right! Seek justice, encourage the oppressed. Defend the cause of the fatherless, plead the case of the widow."

MARVIN

Famous friend; friendly spirit

౭ඊ

Proverbs 17:17   *A friend loves at all times, and a brother is born for adversity.*

Ecclesiastes 4:9–10   *Two are better than one, because they have a good return for their work: if one falls down his friend can help him up. But pity the man who falls and has no one to help him up!*

Christ was the preeminent example of friendship. John 15:13–14 says, "Greater love has no man than this, that he lay down his life for his friends. You are my friends if you do what I command." With open arms, He gave all. Your mantle is to be God's man of peace. This is achieved by being understanding, loyal, faithful, and true. Proverbs 18:24 says, "A man of many companions may come to ruin, but there is a friend who sticks closer than a brother." It comes natural for you to be hospitable, generous, helpful, and good-humored. Your influence is based on your ability to be approachable, trusted, and respectful. Strangers who are lonely, outcast, or abandoned will find refuge with your "welcome" sign written on your heart. You are loving, as well as being loved—everyone's neighbor; everyone's buddy. Psalm 119:63 says, "I am a friend to all who fear You, to all who follow Your precepts." Proverbs 22:11 says, "He who loves a pure heart and whose speech is gracious will have the King for his friend."

MARY

Myrrh, living fragrance

ℰℭ

II Corinthians 2:14–15 *But thanks be to God, who always leads us in triumphal procession in Christ and through us spreads everywhere the fragrance of the knowledge of Him. For we are to God the aroma of Christ among those who are being saved and those who are perishing.*

Ephesians 5:1–2 *Be imitators of God, therefore, as dearly loved children and live a life of love, just as Christ loved us and gave Himself up for us as a fragrant offering and sacrifice to God.*

Myrrh is a fragrant oil used as part of anointing oil that is produced from the wounds or injuries made in the bark of a tree. In Bible days, it was also used as incense in the worship of God. The way you process the wounds and injuries He allows to happen to you brings Him pleasure. You join with David's words in Psalm 119:50, "My comfort in my suffering is this: Your promise preserves my life." You are secure that nothing can touch your life without passing through your Sovereign Father's hands. Much like the woman who poured her expensive perfume from her alabaster box upon Jesus, you risk being poured out and wasted for your Savior's sake. He has chosen you to be pure worship to Him. It is at that point that the stench of this world will be invaded by the sweet fragrance of Christ through your life.

MASON

Stone worker; reliable

❧

Psalm 32:1–2 *Blessed is he whose transgressions are forgiven, whose sins are covered. Blessed is the man whose sin the Lord does not count against him and in whose spirit is no deceit.*

Ephesians 4:32 *Be kind and compassionate to one another, forgiving each other, just as in Christ God forgave you.*

The conditions of forgiveness are confessing Jesus is Lord, believing God raised Him from the dead, and declaring His lordship over your life (Romans 10:9–10). Only God can pardon your sins and forgive your transgressions. He does not stay angry, but delights to show mercy and have compassion on you. He treads your inequities underfoot and hurls all of them into the depths of the sea (Micah 7:18–19). He never remembers them against you again! In Jesus alone you have redemption through His blood and the forgiveness of sins, in accordance with the riches of God's grace (Ephesians 1:7). The Lord has made you trustworthy, dependable, and loyal. He relies on you to express His forgiveness. This implies giving up all claim to punishment as well as any resentment or vengeful feelings. Cancel the debt because He cancelled yours. You do not blame or retaliate, but rather pardon with grace and mercy. Your life proclaims the Lord's forgiveness, liberty, and deliverance.

MATHIAS

Gift of Jehovah; gift of the Lord

෨

James 1:17 *Every good and perfect gift is from above, coming down from the Father of the heavenly lights, who does not change like shifting shadows.*

I Samuel 16:7 *But the Lord said to Samuel, "Do not consider his appearance or his height, for I have rejected him. The Lord does not look at the things man looks at. Man looks at the outward appearance, but the Lord looks at the heart."*

You are God's tribute to Himself, His personal reward. Your life defines God's manners, with priorities on giving rather than receiving. You are to fan into flame the gift of God (II Timothy 1:6). Through you He will display His favor, encouragement and kindness even to the undeserved and hated. As you look beyond faults and see needs, you are God's channel through which His unselfish love flows and is revealed. Discipline your attention to the Giver, not to the gift, nor its wrappings. Give diligence to preserving a humble, submitted heart in full surrender to the Lord. Proverbs 18:16 says, "A gift opens the way for the giver and ushers him into the presence of the great."

MATT

Gift of Jehovah; gift of the Lord

৪১

James 1:17 *Every good and perfect gift is from above, coming down from the Father of the heavenly lights, who does not change like shifting shadows.*

I Samuel 16:7 *But the Lord said to Samuel, "Do not consider his appearance or his height, for I have rejected him. The Lord does not look at the things man looks at. Man looks at the outward appearance, but the Lord looks at the heart."*

You are God's tribute to Himself, His personal reward. Your life defines God's manners, with priorities on giving rather than receiving. You are to fan into flame the gift of God (II Timothy 1:6). Through you He will display His favor, encouragement and kindness even to the undeserved and hated. As you look beyond faults and see needs, you are God's channel through which His unselfish love flows and is revealed. Discipline your attention to the Giver, not to the gift, nor its wrappings. Give diligence to preserving a humble, submitted heart in full surrender to the Lord. Proverbs 18:16 says, "A gift opens the way for the giver and ushers him into the presence of the great."

MATTHEW

Gift of Jehovah; gift of the Lord

ॐ

James 1:17 *Every good and perfect gift is from above, coming down from the Father of the heavenly lights, who does not change like shifting shadows.*

I Samuel 16:7 *But the Lord said to Samuel, "Do not consider his appearance or his height, for I have rejected him. The Lord does not look at the things man looks at. Man looks at the outward appearance, but the Lord looks at the heart."*

You are God's tribute to Himself, His personal reward. Your life defines God's manners, with priorities on giving rather than receiving. You are to fan into flame the gift of God (II Timothy 1:6). Through you He will display His favor, encouragement and kindness even to the undeserved and hated. As you look beyond faults and see needs, you are God's channel through which His unselfish love flows and is revealed. Discipline your attention to the Giver, not to the gift, nor its wrappings. Give diligence to preserving a humble, submitted heart in full surrender to the Lord. Proverbs 18:16 says, "A gift opens the way for the giver and ushers him into the presence of the great."

MATTIE

Gift of Jehovah; gift of the Lord

ᴈᴐ

James 1:17 *Every good and perfect gift is from above, coming down from the Father of the heavenly lights, who does not change like shifting shadows.*

I Samuel 16:7 *But the Lord said to Samuel, "Do not consider his appearance or his height, for I have rejected him. The Lord does not look at the things man looks at. Man looks at the outward appearance, but the Lord looks at the heart."*

You are God's tribute to Himself, His personal reward. Your life defines God's manners, with priorities on giving rather than receiving. You are to fan into flame the gift of God (II Timothy 1:6). Through you He will display His favor, encouragement and kindness even to the undeserved and hated. As you look beyond faults and see needs, you are God's channel through which His unselfish love flows and is revealed. Discipline your attention to the Giver, not to the gift, nor its wrappings. Give diligence to preserving a humble, submitted heart in full surrender to the Lord. Proverbs 18:16 says, "A gift opens the way for the giver and ushers him into the presence of the great."

MAX

Great; full of honor

$\partial \! \! \! \! \infty$

Isaiah 32:8 *But the noble man makes noble plans, and by noble deeds he stands.*

Luke 8:15 *But the seed on good soil stands for those with a noble and good heart, who hear the word, retain it, and by persevering produce a crop.*

Proverbs 18:12 says, "Before his downfall a man's heart is proud, but humility comes before honor." You are one who has a humble confidence in recognizing and expressing reverence, worship, adoration, trust, deference, tribute, admiration, and respect. This is the result of being secure in the truth of who you are in the Lord. Through humility, King Jesus made a way for you to be engrafted into His royalty. He made of Himself no reputation and took on the nature of a servant (Philippians 2:7) to affirm your value. Through self-denial, you prioritize excellence in virtue, truthfulness, and faithfulness. Because of the respect you have earned, you dismantle inferiority, disgrace, shame, and offenses. No one feels second-rate in your presence. The deeper that the Lord is your object of reverence, the greater your confidence will be in giving approval and worth. Because you are tall in spirit, your face is always turned upward.

MAY

Great one; esteemed one

&

Proverbs 22:1 *A good name is more desirable than great riches; to be esteemed is better than silver or gold.*

Hebrews 11:26 *He regarded disgrace for the sake of Christ as of greater value than the treasures of Egypt, because he was looking ahead to his reward.*

Your life is to reflect the very nature of God. It is holy, righteous, just, pure, spotless, faithful, and divine. Out of a humble, reverent heart you will ever be esteemed and prized by the Lord as you show Him respect, adoration, and praise. You will have no reason to be insecure in who you are in the Lord. Nor will you ever place blame on God or disapprove of His will for your life. You hold in highest regard and love those who minister to you (I Thessalonians 4:12–13). You do nothing out of selfish ambition or vain conceit, but in humility consider others better than yourself (Philippians 2:3).

MAYA

God's creative power; creative spirit

℘

Colossians 1:16 *For by Him all things were created: things in heaven and on earth, visible and invisible, whether thrones or powers or rulers or authorities; all things were created by Him and for Him.*

Ephesians 2:10 *For we are God's workmanship, created in Christ Jesus to do good works, which God prepared in advance for us to do.*

Through you the Lord will bring Himself into existence; He will originate. How you deal with the past determines your future. Regardless of curses or blessings, failures or successes, you are God's platform for a "new thing." You cannot lean to your own understanding or reasoning. God Almighty created the heavens, the earth, and you in His image. Isaiah 42:9, "See, the former things have taken place, and new things I declare; before they spring into being I announce them to you." Isaiah 43:18–19, "Forget the former things; do not dwell on the past. See, I am doing a new thing! Now it springs up; do you not perceive it? I am making a way in the desert and streams in the wasteland." Isaiah 48:6b, "From now on I will tell you of new things, of hidden things unknown to you." Isaiah 65:17–19, "Behold, I will create new heavens and a new earth. The former things will not be remembered, nor will they come to mind. But be glad and rejoice forever in what I will create, for I will create Jerusalem to be a delight and its people a joy. I will rejoice over Jerusalem and take delight in My people; the sound of weeping and of crying will be heard in it no more." Because of your passion for the eternal over the temporal, you are used of God to remove what can be shaken—the created things—so that what cannot be shaken may remain (Hebrews 12:27). The more completely dependent you become on your Creator, the more productive your life will be for Him! I Peter 4:19, "So then, those who suffer according to God's will should commit themselves to their Creator and continue to do good." As you stay yielded and surrendered to God, the clay of your heart will stay tender. Only then can He mold you into the image of His Son, Jesus Christ. God will work His approval through you to those who feel ugly, worthless, and to those who have no hope.

MCKENNA

Beautiful; strong one

Proverbs 24:5 *A wise man has great power, and a man of knowledge increases strength.*

Ephesians 6:10 *Finally, be strong in the Lord and in His mighty power.*

You are one who has an un-compromised commitment to righteousness, respectability, honesty, character, excellence, value, worth, kindness, innocence, generosity, trustworthiness, faithfulness, justice, hope, and love. You can do everything through Him who gives you strength (Philippians 4:11–13). The Lord is the source of your strength because you turn back the battle at the gate (Isaiah 28:6). You renew your strength by your hope being in the Lord (Isaiah 40:31). Jesus says, "My grace is sufficient for you, for My power is made perfect in weaknesses. Therefore you will boast all the more gladly about your weaknesses, so that Christ's power may rest on you. That is why for Christ's sake, you delight in weaknesses, in insults, in hardships, in persecutions, and in difficulties. For when you are weak, then you are strong," II Corinthians 12:9–10. You are clothed with strength and dignity (Proverbs 31:25).

MEGAN

A pearl; a gem of purity

ℰℛ

I Timothy 5:22   *...do not share in the sins of others. Keep yourself pure.*

I Peter 1:22   *Now that you have purified yourselves by obeying the truth so that you have sincere love for your brothers, love one another deeply, from the heart.*

Through the process of heat, trials, and refinement, purity is established. Your nature defies being stubborn, judgmental, and haughty. The commandment of the Lord is clear—giving insight to life (Psalm 19:8). You bring wholeness to the dirty, defiled, contaminated, polluted, double-minded, and raped. Your willingness to be transparent is the venue through which He makes His Word clear, simple, and unadulterated. Your choice to be pure enables you to see God (Matthew 5:8) and to know Him as King and Friend (Proverbs 22:11). It also allows your words to be pleasant (Proverbs 15:26) and causes you to ascend to the holy place of the Lord, where you receive blessings and righteousness from the God of salvation (Psalm 24:3–5). Proverbs 20:11 says, "Even a child is known by his actions, by whether his conduct is pure and right."

MELEEZA

Honey bee; skillful

&

Hosea 10:12   *Sow for yourselves righteousness, reap the fruit of unfailing love, and break up your unplowed ground; for it is time to seek the Lord, until He comes and showers righteousness on you.*

Deuteronomy 4:29   *But if from there you seek the Lord your God, you will find Him if you look for Him with all your heart and with all your soul.*

The Lord has divine attraction for you. He captures you with His love. He delights in you seeking His face. As the bee feeds on pollen and nectar, you feed on God's Word. The bees carry pollen from blossom to blossom, enabling flowering plants to produce seeds. You perform the same tasks through prayer and intercession. They perform a dance to give direction for rich food; you do that through worship. In self-denial, you keep your hands clean and your heart pure (Proverbs 24:3–6). With your diligent pursuit of the Lord, you bring order and have the ability to cause others to search for that same intimacy with Him. To the aimless, you give direction to stay the course. To the complacent, you ignite hunger through prayer and worship. Honey is the byproduct of your life!

MELISSA

Honey bee; skillful

৪০

Hosea 10:12 *Sow for yourselves righteousness, reap the fruit of unfailing love, and break up your unplowed ground; for it is time to seek the Lord, until He comes and showers righteousness on you.*

Deuteronomy 4:29 *But if from there you seek the Lord your God, you will find Him if you look for Him with all your heart and with all your soul.*

The Lord has divine attraction for you. He captures you with His love. He delights in you seeking His face. As the bee feeds on pollen and nectar, you feed on God's Word. The bees carry pollen from blossom to blossom, enabling flowering plants to produce seeds. You perform the same tasks through prayer and intercession. They perform a dance to give direction for rich food; you do that through worship. In self-denial, you keep your hands clean and your heart pure (Proverbs 24:3–6). With your diligent pursuit of the Lord, you bring order and have the ability to cause others to search for that same intimacy with Him. To the aimless, you give direction to stay the course. To the complacent, you ignite hunger through prayer and worship. Honey is the byproduct of your life!

MERCY

One who shows kindness; merciful

Matthew 5:7 *Blessed are the merciful, for they will be shown mercy.*

Hebrews 4:16 *Let us then approach the throne of grace with confidence, so that we may receive mercy and find grace to help us in our time of need.*

Micah 6:8 says, "He has showed you, O man, what is good. And what does the Lord require of you? To act justly and to love mercy and to walk humbly with your God." God has engrafted His heart of compassion in you in order to display it through you. You have a willingness to spare others from deserved punishment. You feel sympathy for those in distress. You endure with the intolerant, show tenderness to the indifferent, and forgive the cruel. God's wisdom has given you a kindly understanding and tolerance in judging others. Your soft heart will need daily renewal in God's Word in order to protect you from becoming angry and embittered. Romans 12:1 says, "Therefore, I urge you, brothers, in view of God's mercy, to offer your bodies as living sacrifices, holy and pleasing to God—this is your spiritual act of worship." James 2:13b says, "Mercy triumphs over judgment."

MERLE

Free spirit

❧

Isaiah 61:1 *The Spirit of the Sovereign Lord is on me, because the Lord has anointed me to preach good news to the poor. He has sent me to bind up the brokenhearted, to proclaim freedom for the captives and release from darkness for the prisoners.*

Galatians 5:1 *It is for freedom that Christ has set us free. Stand firm, then, and do not let yourselves be burdened again by a yoke of slavery.*

There are no restrictions on your abandoned commitment to the Lord Jesus Christ. Knowing God's truth frees you from the bondage and care of sin and oppression (John 8:32). The free gift of God—Jesus Christ—exchanges offense for God's grace, condemnation for justification, shame for holiness and the spirit of the world for the Spirit of God. You are fearless as you loose those in bondage and give pardon to the imprisoned—all because the law of the Spirit of life set you free from the law of sin and death. Do not use your freedom to indulge the sinful nature; rather, serve one another in love (Galatians 5:13). Freely you have received; freely give (Matthew 10:8).

MERLENE

Free spirit

Isaiah 61:1 *The Spirit of the Sovereign Lord is on me, because the Lord has anointed me to preach good news to the poor. He has sent me to bind up the brokenhearted, to proclaim freedom for the captives and release from darkness for the prisoners.*

Galatians 5:1 *It is for freedom that Christ has set us free. Stand firm, then, and do not let yourselves be burdened again by a yoke of slavery.*

There are no restrictions on your abandoned commitment to the Lord Jesus Christ. Knowing God's truth frees you from the bondage and care of sin and oppression (John 8:32). The free gift of God—Jesus Christ—exchanges offense for God's grace, condemnation for justification, shame for holiness and the spirit of the world for the Spirit of God. You are fearless as you loose those in bondage and give pardon to the imprisoned—all because the law of the Spirit of life set you free from the law of sin and death. Do not use your freedom to indulge the sinful nature; rather, serve one another in love (Galatians 5:13). Freely you have received; freely give (Matthew 10:8).

MERRILL

Famous; full of honor

❧

Isaiah 32:8 *But the noble man makes noble plans, and by noble deeds he stands.*

Luke 8:15 *But the seed on good soil stands for those with a noble and good heart, who hear the word, retain it, and by persevering produce a crop.*

Proverbs 18:12 says, "Before his downfall a man's heart is proud, but humility comes before honor." You are one who has a humble confidence in recognizing and expressing reverence, worship, adoration, trust, deference, tribute, admiration, and respect. This is the result of being secure in the truth of who you are in the Lord. Through humility, King Jesus made a way for you to be engrafted into His royalty. He made of Himself no reputation and took on the nature of a servant (Philippians 2:7) to affirm your value. Through self-denial, you prioritize excellence in virtue, truthfulness, and faithfulness. Because of the respect you have earned, you dismantle inferiority, disgrace, shame, and offenses. No one feels second-rate in your presence. The deeper that the Lord is your object of reverence, the greater your confidence will be in giving approval and worth. Because you are tall in spirit, your face is always turned upward.

MERRILLYN

Famous; full of honor

❧

Isaiah 32:8 *But the noble man makes noble plans, and by noble deeds he stands.*

Luke 8:15 *But the seed on good soil stands for those with a noble and good heart, who hear the word, retain it, and by persevering produce a crop.*

Proverbs 18:12 says, "Before his downfall a man's heart is proud, but humility comes before honor." You are one who has a humble confidence in recognizing and expressing reverence, worship, adoration, trust, deference, tribute, admiration, and respect. This is the result of being secure in the truth of who you are in the Lord. Through humility, King Jesus made a way for you to be engrafted into His royalty. He made of Himself no reputation and took on the nature of a servant (Philippians 2:7) to affirm your value. Through self-denial, you prioritize excellence in virtue, truthfulness, and faithfulness. Because of the respect you have earned, you dismantle inferiority, disgrace, shame, and offenses. No one feels second-rate in your presence. The deeper that the Lord is your object of reverence, the greater your confidence will be in giving approval and worth. Because you are tall in spirit, your face is always turned upward.

MIA

Mine; belonging to God

❧

Deuteronomy 33:27 *The eternal God is your refuge, and underneath are the everlasting arms. He will drive out your enemy before you, saying, "Destroy him!"*

Isaiah 46:4 *Even to your old age and gray hairs I am He, I am He who will sustain you. I have made you and I will carry you; I will sustain you and I will rescue you.*

A support holds up a structure with a firm foundation. God gives you help and approval through blessing, comfort, encouragement, friendship, loyalty, and protection. When you face tough times, God will carry you on eagles' wings and hold you close to Himself (Exodus 19:4). He will stoop to whatever level you are to make you great (Psalm 18:35). Not only are you upheld by His righteous right hand (Isaiah 41:10), but you uphold others. You serve as a mainstay to strengthen and uphold; to build up and reinforce. This endurance brings wholeness to all those you touch. II Timothy 2:19 says, "Nevertheless, God's solid foundation stands firm, sealed with this inscription: 'The Lord knows those who are His,'" and, "Everyone who confesses the name of the Lord must turn away from wickedness."

MICHAEL

Who is like God; Godliness

Exodus 15:11   *Who among the gods is like you, O Lord? Who is like You—majestic in holiness, awesome in glory, working wonders?*

I Timothy 4:8   *Godliness has value for all things, holding promise for both the present life and the life to come.*

Godliness with contentment is great gain (I Timothy 6:6). You are to pursue godliness (I Timothy 6:11). Your life is to reflect the very nature of God, which is holy, righteous, just, pure, spotless, faithful, and divine. The choices you make and the life you live are to define God's standard for living. As you follow the Lord, He desires for others to pattern their lives after you. Out of a humble, reverent heart and as you show Him respect, adoration, and praise, you will ever be esteemed and prized by the Lord. You will have no reason to be insecure in who you are, or to place blame on God, or to disapprove of His will for your life. He celebrates how He made you!

MICAH

Who is like God; Godliness

❧

Exodus 15:11 *Who among the gods is like you, O Lord? Who is like You— majestic in holiness, awesome in glory, working wonders?*

I Timothy 4:8 *Godliness has value for all things, holding promise for both the present life and the life to come.*

Godliness with contentment is great gain (I Timothy 6:6). You are to pursue godliness (I Timothy 6:11). Your life is to reflect the very nature of God, which is holy, righteous, just, pure, spotless, faithful, and divine. The choices you make and the life you live are to define God's standard for living. As you follow the Lord, He desires for others to pattern their lives after you. Out of a humble, reverent heart and as you show Him respect, adoration, and praise, you will ever be esteemed and prized by the Lord. You will have no reason to be insecure in who you are, or to place blame on God, or to disapprove of His will for your life. He celebrates how He made you!

MICHAIL

Who is like God; Godliness

⳾

Exodus 15:11   *Who among the gods is like you, O Lord? Who is like You— majestic in holiness, awesome in glory, working wonders?*

I Timothy 4:8   *Godliness has value for all things, holding promise for both the present life and the life to come.*

Godliness with contentment is great gain (I Timothy 6:6). You are to pursue godliness (I Timothy 6:11). Your life is to reflect the very nature of God, which is holy, righteous, just, pure, spotless, faithful, and divine. The choices you make and the life you live are to define God's standard for living. As you follow the Lord, He desires for others to pattern their lives after you. Out of a humble, reverent heart and as you show Him respect, adoration, and praise, you will ever be esteemed and prized by the Lord. You will have no reason to be insecure in who you are, or to place blame on God, or to disapprove of His will for your life. He celebrates how He made you!

MICHELLE

Who is like God; godliness

ℰℐ

Exodus 15:11   *Who among the gods is like you, O Lord? Who is like You—majestic in holiness, awesome in glory, working wonders?*

I Timothy 4:8   *Godliness has value for all things, holding promise for both the present life and the life to come.*

Godliness with contentment is great gain (I Timothy 6:6). You are to pursue godliness (I Timothy 6:11). Your life is to reflect the very nature of God, which is holy, righteous, just, pure, spotless, faithful, and divine. The choices you make and the life you live are to define God's standard for living. As you follow the Lord, He desires for others to pattern their lives after you. Out of a humble, reverent heart and as you show Him respect, adoration, and praise, you will ever be esteemed and prized by the Lord. You will have no reason to be insecure in who you are, or to place blame on God, or to disapprove of His will for your life. He celebrates how He made you!

MIKAELA

Who is like God; godliness

⚭

Exodus 15:11 *Who among the gods is like you, O Lord? Who is like You—majestic in holiness, awesome in glory, working wonders?*

I Timothy 4:8 *Godliness has value for all things, holding promise for both the present life and the life to come.*

Godliness with contentment is great gain (I Timothy 6:6). You are to pursue godliness (I Timothy 6:11). Your life is to reflect the very nature of God, which is holy, righteous, just, pure, spotless, faithful, and divine. The choices you make and the life you live are to define God's standard for living. As you follow the Lord, He desires for others to pattern their lives after you. Out of a humble, reverent heart and as you show Him respect, adoration, and praise, you will ever be esteemed and prized by the Lord. You will have no reason to be insecure in who you are, or to place blame on God, or to disapprove of His will for your life. He celebrates how He made you!

MIKE

Who is like God; godliness

❧

Exodus 15:11   *Who among the gods is like you, O Lord? Who is like You—majestic in holiness, awesome in glory, working wonders?*

I Timothy 4:8   *Godliness has value for all things, holding promise for both the present life and the life to come.*

Godliness with contentment is great gain (I Timothy 6:6). You are to pursue godliness (I Timothy 6:11). Your life is to reflect the very nature of God, which is holy, righteous, just, pure, spotless, faithful, and divine. The choices you make and the life you live are to define God's standard for living. As you follow the Lord, He desires for others to pattern their lives after you. Out of a humble, reverent heart and as you show Him respect, adoration, and praise, you will ever be esteemed and prized by the Lord. You will have no reason to be insecure in who you are, or to place blame on God, or to disapprove of His will for your life. He celebrates how He made you!

MILDRED

Gentle counselor; gentle

Titus 3:4–5 *But when the kindness and love of God our Savior appeared, He saved us, not because of righteous things we had done, but because of His mercy.*

I Peter 3:8–9 *Finally, all of you, live in harmony with one another; be sympathetic, love as brothers, be compassionate and humble. Do not repay evil with evil or insult with insult, but with blessing, because to this you were called so that you may inherit a blessing.*

God first, others next, and you last. With a servant's heart and a humble mind, you extend the gracious approval of the Lord. This graciousness springs from an inherit thoughtfulness and consideration. Through you, God defines good manners and politeness. You are hospitable to the shipwrecked (Acts 28:7) and you bring divine connection for needs to be provided (Acts 27:3). Because you are attentive to details, the broken are dealt with gently. The rejected are shown kindness and the humble are given honor. Your conversation is always full of grace and seasoned with salt (Colossians 4:6). The behavior of the rude and impolite are corrected because you will not be misled. You know that bad company corrupts good character (I Corinthians 15:33). You show respect to all because of your willingness to value the opinion of another and overlook an offense (Proverbs 19:11). Like Jesus, you are a friend of the publicans and sinners (Luke 7:34).

MILES

Soldier; God's warrior

❧

II Chronicles 32:7-8 *There is a greater power with us than with him. With him is only the arm of flesh, but with us is the Lord our God to help us and to fight our battles.*

II Timothy 2:3-4 *Endure hardship with us like a good soldier of Christ Jesus. No one serving as a soldier gets involved in civilian affairs - he wants to please his commanding officer.*

Exodus 14:14 says, "The Lord will fight for you; you need only be still." You are armed with the ability to handle the spear and shield—to stand on God's Word by faith, supporting the King of kings against His enemies. As God's defending warrior, you are His example of a brave champion, soldier, and hero. The ultimate war was a contest with death and when Christ said, "It is finished" on the cross, He declared victory over death, hell, and the grave. You are equipped to be used of God as one who protects by warding off attacks, calling for justice, and providing shelter. When God is all of this to you, you will be that vindication for others. Because of your faith in Jesus Christ, you will ever be aggressive towards the enemy's tools of defeat, failure, and victimization. Your ultimate purpose is to be one who stands in the gap (Ezekiel 22:30) as a defender of the weak. This includes those who are easily influenced, confused, quitters, faint, frail, fragile, and frightened. Your primary spiritual warfare will be that of brave intercession—reaching, meeting, and entreating God for His favor to set the captives free. Then you will "learn to do right! Seek justice, encourage the oppressed. Defend the cause of the fatherless, plead the case of the widow," Isaiah 1:17.

MILEY

Reliable; forgiving

❧

Psalm 32:1–2   *Blessed is he whose transgressions are forgiven, whose sins are covered. Blessed is the man whose sin the Lord does not count against him and in whose spirit is no deceit.*

Ephesians 4:32   *Be kind and compassionate to one another, forgiving each other, just as in Christ God forgave you.*

The conditions of forgiveness are confessing Jesus is Lord, believing God raised Him from the dead, and declaring His lordship over your life (Romans 10:9–10). Only God can pardon your sins and forgive your transgressions. He does not stay angry, but delights to show mercy and have compassion on you. He treads your inequities underfoot and hurls all of them into the depths of the sea (Micah 7:18–19). He never remembers them against you again! In Jesus alone you have redemption through His blood and the forgiveness of sins, in accordance with the riches of God's grace (Ephesians 1:7). The Lord has made you trustworthy, dependable, and loyal. He relies on you to express His forgiveness. This implies giving up all claim to punishment as well as any resentment or vengeful feelings. Cancel the debt because He cancelled yours. You do not blame or retaliate, but rather pardon with grace and mercy. Your life proclaims the Lord's forgiveness, liberty, and deliverance.

MILLIE

Gentle counselor; gentle

ℰↃ

Titus 3:4–5 *But when the kindness and love of God our Savior appeared, He saved us, not because of righteous things we had done, but because of His mercy.*

I Peter 3:8–9 *Finally, all of you, live in harmony with one another; be sympathetic, love as brothers, be compassionate and humble. Do not repay evil with evil or insult with insult, but with blessing, because to this you were called so that you may inherit a blessing.*

God first, others next, and you last. With a servant's heart and a humble mind, you extend the gracious approval of the Lord. This graciousness springs from an inherit thoughtfulness and consideration. Through you, God defines good manners and politeness. You are hospitable to the shipwrecked (Acts 28:7) and you bring divine connection for needs to be provided (Acts 27:3). Because you are attentive to details, the broken are dealt with gently. The rejected are shown kindness and the humble are given honor. Your conversation is always full of grace and seasoned with salt (Colossians 4:6). The behavior of the rude and impolite are corrected because you will not be misled. You know that bad company corrupts good character (I Corinthians 15:33). You show respect to all because of your willingness to value the opinion of another and overlook an offense (Proverbs 19:11). Like Jesus, you are a friend of the publicans and sinners (Luke 7:34).

MINDY

Honey; sweet spirit

℘

Proverbs 16:24   *Pleasant words are a honeycomb, sweet to the soul and healing to the bones.*

Psalm 119:103   *How sweet are Your words to my taste, sweeter than honey to my mouth!*

The Word of God is described as being "sweeter than honey from the honeycomb" in Psalm 19:10. It is symbolic of wisdom that is sweet to the soul, giving you a future hope that will not be cut off (Proverbs 24:13–14). Proverbs 27:7 says, "He who is full loathes honey, but to the hungry even what is bitter tastes sweet." The Lord has blessed you with the ability to see the good in everything. Even when bitter things come into your life, you are able to allow Him to turn it for His good because you hunger for more of Him. His fruit, the fruit of the Spirit, is sweet to your taste (Song of Solomon 2:3). As you are saturated with God's Word, your own words will be welcoming, agreeable, and pleasing. You are anointed to bring approval to those drinking the "bitter cup," giving them hope that will not be cut off. Because you have "tasted that the Lord is good," you will nurture spiritual hunger in new believers for the Word of God.

MINNIE

Resolute protector; great protector

Job 11:18   *You will be secure, because there is hope; you will look about you and take your rest in safety.*

Psalm 32:7   *You are my hiding place; You will protect me from trouble and surround me with songs of deliverance.*

Psalm 27:5   *For in the day of trouble He will keep me safe in His dwelling; He will hide me in the shelter of His tabernacle and set me high upon a rock.*

You are securely wrapped up and protected by Jesus Christ, who frees you from doubt and harm. Because you find your shelter, assurance, stability, and strength in your personal relationship with the Lord, you are kept in a safe place. You are confident that the Lord will fight for you; you need only be still (Exodus 14:14). As you stand firm on God's solid foundation (II Timothy 2:19) and stay hidden in the shadow of His wings (Psalm 61:4), you will provide deliverance for the weak, insecure, unsheltered, and frail. Instead of being defensive, you are a defender of injustice done to all mankind. You let discretion protect you (Proverbs 2:11). You will shield others from the enemy's destruction with love (I Corinthians 13:7) and the power of God's name (John 17:11). You display God's compassion through your humility. What you let him be in you, you will be to others.

MISSY

Honey bee; skillful

ଓ

Hosea 10:12 *Sow for yourselves righteousness, reap the fruit of unfailing love, and break up your unplowed ground; for it is time to seek the Lord, until He comes and showers righteousness on you.*

Deuteronomy 4:29 *But if from there you seek the Lord your God, you will find Him if you look for Him with all your heart and with all your soul.*

The Lord has divine attraction for you. He captures you with His love. He delights in you seeking His face. As the bee feeds on pollen and nectar, you feed on God's Word. The bees carry pollen from blossom to blossom, enabling flowering plants to produce seeds. You perform the same tasks through prayer and intercession. They perform a dance to give direction for rich food; you do that through worship. In self-denial, you keep your hands clean and your heart pure (Proverbs 24:3–6). With your diligent pursuit of the Lord, you bring order and have the ability to cause others to search for that same intimacy with Him. To the aimless, you give direction to stay the course. To the complacent, you ignite hunger through prayer and worship. Honey is the byproduct of your life!

MITCHELL

Who is like God; godliness

❧

Exodus 15:11 *Who among the gods is like you, O Lord? Who is like You—majestic in holiness, awesome in glory, working wonders?*

I Timothy 4:8 *Godliness has value for all things, holding promise for both the present life and the life to come.*

Godliness with contentment is great gain (I Timothy 6:6). You are to pursue godliness (I Timothy 6:11). Your life is to reflect the very nature of God, which is holy, righteous, just, pure, spotless, faithful, and divine. The choices you make and the life you live are to define God's standard for living. As you follow the Lord, He desires for others to pattern their lives after you. Out of a humble, reverent heart and as you show Him respect, adoration, and praise, you will ever be esteemed and prized by the Lord. You will have no reason to be insecure in who you are, or to place blame on God, or to disapprove of His will for your life. He celebrates how He made you!

MOLLY

Myrrh; living fragrance

∞

II Corinthians 2:14–15 *But thanks be to God, who always leads us in triumphal procession in Christ and through us spreads everywhere the fragrance of the knowledge of Him. For we are to God the aroma of Christ among those who are being saved and those who are perishing.*

Ephesians 5:1–2 *Be imitators of God, therefore, as dearly loved children and live a life of love, just as Christ loved us and gave Himself up for us as a fragrant offering and sacrifice to God.*

Myrrh is a fragrant oil used as part of anointing oil that is produced from the wounds or injuries made in the bark of a tree. In Bible days, it was also used as incense in the worship of God. The way you process the wounds and injuries He allows to happen to you brings Him pleasure. You join with David's words in Psalm 119:50, "My comfort in my suffering is this: Your promise preserves my life." You are secure that nothing can touch your life without passing through your Sovereign Father's hands. Much like the woman who poured her expensive perfume from her alabaster box upon Jesus, you risk being poured out and wasted for your Savior's sake. He has chosen you to be pure worship to Him. It is at that point that the stench of this world will be invaded by the sweet fragrance of Christ through your life.

MONA

Advice; woman of wisdom

❧

James 3:17 *But the wisdom that comes from heaven is first of all pure; then peace-loving, considerate, submissive, full of mercy and good fruit, impartial and sincere.*

Proverbs 9:10 *The fear of the Lord is the beginning of wisdom, and knowledge of the Holy One is understanding.*

You are a person of moral excellence. You exemplify right living put into practice. The Lord has not only equipped you with skills for living correctly, but also the ability to impart that to others. The Spirit of truth will guide you into all truth, allowing you to have insight into the true nature of things (John 16:13). Out of your reverential respect for the Lord, you have wisdom to give guidance and direction. You are a safe sounding board who steers those who are hungry for knowledge of the Holy One in the right direction. You need only to ask for the wisdom you lack, and God will give it to you generously (James 1:5). Having spiritual discernment is having the ability to separate the difference between God's wisdom and the world's and the ability to make the right choice—regardless. Luke 21:15 says, "For I will give you words and wisdom that none of your adversaries will be able to resist or contradict."

MONICA

Advice; woman of wisdom

❧

James 3:17 *But the wisdom that comes from heaven is first of all pure; then peace-loving, considerate, submissive, full of mercy and good fruit, impartial and sincere.*

Proverbs 9:10 *The fear of the Lord is the beginning of wisdom, and knowledge of the Holy One is understanding.*

You are a person of moral excellence. You exemplify right living put into practice. The Lord has not only equipped you with skills for living correctly, but also the ability to impart that to others. The Spirit of truth will guide you into all truth, allowing you to have insight into the true nature of things (John 16:13). Out of your reverential respect for the Lord, you have wisdom to give guidance and direction. You are a safe sounding board who steers those who are hungry for knowledge of the Holy One in the right direction. You need only to ask for the wisdom you lack, and God will give it to you generously (James 1:5). Having spiritual discernment is having the ability to separate the difference between God's wisdom and the world's and the ability to make the right choice—regardless. Luke 21:15 says, "For I will give you words and wisdom that none of your adversaries will be able to resist or contradict."

MONTGOMERY

Rich man's mountain; prosperity

ॐ

Psalm 1:1–3   Blessed is the man who does not walk in the counsel of the wicked or stand in the way of sinners or sit in the seat of mockers. But his delight is in the law of the Lord, and on His law he meditates day and night. He is like a tree planted by the streams of water, which yields its fruit in season and whose leaf does not wither. Whatever he does prospers.

Joshua 1:8   Do not let this book of the law depart from your mouth; meditate on it day and night, so that you may be careful to do everything written in it. Then you will be prosperous and successful.

You are one who knows that your success is not based on luck or good fortune. It is because you are willing to loose your life for Christ's sake in order to find it (Matthew 10:39). You let the word of Christ dwell in you richly (Colossians 3:16). You allow the Lord to stretch and strengthen you in order to enlarge your borders of influence and maturity (Isaiah 54:1–3). You welcome the cutting and pruning that makes way for increase to bear fruit, more fruit, and much fruit (John 15). You enter a covenant with the Lord of obedience, seeking Him diligently and wholeheartedly (II Chronicles 31:21), which causes you to prosper in everything you do (Deuteronomy 29:9). You are content in need and in plenty (Philippians 4:11–12) because prosperity is not a love of money (I Timothy 6:6–10), power, popularity, or possessions. In spite of failure, disappointment, loss, and defeat, you let nothing separate you from the love of God (Romans 8:37–39). Instead of being blind to the hungry, you will feed them. Instead of abhorring the naked, you will clothe them. Instead of ignoring the poor and fatherless, you will be God's hand of provision. You will offer provisions of hope, courage, and strength not to give up, but rather to start again and to make it to the finish line. You are a faithful steward helping them exchange their temporal for His eternal (Philippians 4:19). As your mantle is to build up, develop, and cause to succeed, know that "no weapon formed against you will prosper," Isaiah 54:17. Your goal is to hear the Master say, "Well done, good and faithful servant! You have been faithful with a few things, I will put you in charge of many things. Come share your Master's happiness!" (Matthew 25:21) May you prosper in all things and be in health, just as your soul prospers (3 John 2).

MONTY

Rich man's mountain; prosperity

❧

Psalm 1:1–3   *Blessed is the man who does not walk in the counsel of the wicked or stand in the way of sinners or sit in the seat of mockers. But his delight is in the law of the Lord, and on His law he meditates day and night. He is like a tree planted by the streams of water, which yields its fruit in season and whose leaf does not wither. Whatever he does prospers.*

Joshua 1:8   *Do not let this book of the law depart from your mouth; meditate on it day and night, so that you may be careful to do everything written in it. Then you will be prosperous and successful.*

You are one who knows that your success is not based on luck or good fortune. It is because you are willing to loose your life for Christ's sake in order to find it (Matthew 10:39). You let the word of Christ dwell in you richly (Colossians 3:16). You allow the Lord to stretch and strengthen you in order to enlarge your borders of influence and maturity (Isaiah 54:1–3). You welcome the cutting and pruning that makes way for increase to bear fruit, more fruit, and much fruit (John 15). You enter a covenant with the Lord of obedience, seeking Him diligently and wholeheartedly (II Chronicles 31:21), which causes you to prosper in everything you do (Deuteronomy 29:9). You are content in need and in plenty (Philippians 4:11–12) because prosperity is not a love of money (I Timothy 6:6–10), power, popularity, or possessions. In spite of failure, disappointment, loss, and defeat, you let nothing separate you from the love of God (Romans 8:37–39). Instead of being blind to the hungry, you will feed them. Instead of abhorring the naked, you will clothe them. Instead of ignoring the poor and fatherless, you will be God's hand of provision. You will offer provisions of hope, courage, and strength not to give up, but rather to start again and to make it to the finish line. You are a faithful steward helping them exchange their temporal for His eternal (Philippians 4:19). As your mantle is to build up, develop, and cause to succeed, know that "no weapon formed against you will prosper," Isaiah 54:17. Your goal is to hear the Master say, "Well done, good and faithful servant! You have been faithful with a few things, I will put you in charge of many things. Come share your Master's happiness!" (Matthew 25:21) May you prosper in all things and be in health, just as your soul prospers (3 John 2).

MORGAN

Bright seashore; great and bright

৪১

Psalm 27:1 *The Lord is my light and my salvation—whom shall I fear? The Lord is the stronghold of my life; of whom shall I be afraid.*

Proverbs 4:18 *The path of the righteous is like the first gleam of dawn, shining ever brighter till the full light of day.*

You are one who reflects the shining brightness of the countenance of Jesus. You are aggressive toward the fruitless deeds of darkness from the evil one, by exposing them to the light of Jesus. Everything exposed by light becomes visible, for it is the light that makes everything visible (Ephesians 5:11–14). This radiance that God has given you serves as a beacon to give guidance to those yet in darkness. Your life's mission is found in the following two verses: Isaiah 60:1–3 says, "Arise, shine, for your light has come, and the glory of the Lord rises upon you. See, darkness covers the earth, and thick darkness is over the peoples, but the Lord rises upon you and His glory appears over you. Nations will come to your light, and kings to the brightness of your dawn." And in Acts 13:47, "For this is what the Lord has commanded us: 'I have made you a light for the Gentiles, that you may bring salvation to the ends of the earth.'" Continue to shine as His star, leading many to righteousness (Daniel 12:3 and Philippians 2:15).

MYRA

Fragrant ointment; fresh aroma

❧

II Corinthians 2:14–15 *But thanks be to God, who always leads us in triumphal procession in Christ and through us spreads everywhere the fragrance of the knowledge of Him. For we are to God the aroma of Christ among those who are being saved and those who are perishing.*

Ephesians 5:1–2 *Be imitators of God, therefore, as dearly loved children and live a life of love, just as Christ loved us and gave Himself up for us as a fragrant offering and sacrifice to God.*

Myrrh is a fragrant oil used as part of anointing oil that is produced from the wounds or injuries made in the bark of a tree. In Bible days, it was also used as incense in the worship of God. The way you process the wounds and injuries He allows to happen to you brings Him pleasure. You join with David's words in Psalm 119:50, "My comfort in my suffering is this: Your promise preserves my life." You are secure that nothing can touch your life without passing through your Sovereign Father's hands. Much like the woman who poured her expensive perfume from her alabaster box upon Jesus, you risk being poured out and wasted for your Savior's sake. He has chosen you to be pure worship to Him. It is at that point that the stench of this world will be invaded by the sweet fragrance of Christ through your life.

NANCY

Grace; gracious one

&

Romans 8:32 *He who did not spare His own Son, but gave Him up for us all—how will He not also, along with Him, graciously give us all things?*

I Corinthians 15:10 *But by the grace of God I am what I am, and His grace to me was not without effect.*

Ephesians 2:8 says, "For it is by grace you have been saved, through faith—and this is not from yourselves, it is the gift of God." You are one who brings about balance and harmony through mercy, forgiveness, approval, kindness, and patience—all with a grateful heart. This attitude of gratitude will rule in the midst of inconsiderate behavior. Your nature defies the law of the Pharisees, and is against being self-reliant, prejudice, and selfish. Being full of grace is devotion built through faithfulness and a willingness to quickly pardon. You are blessed with creativity in expressing God's greatest gift of grace—the life of His only Son, Jesus Christ. God says to you through Jeremiah 24:7, "I will give them a heart to know Me, that I am the Lord. They will be My people, and I will be their God, for they will return to Me with all their heart." Ezekiel 11:19 says, "I will give them an undivided heart and put a new spirit in them; I will remove from them their heart of stone and give them a heart of flesh." Accountability will keep your report accurate and your integrity irreproachable.

NAOMI

The pleasant one; pleasant spirit

છે

Psalm 133:1 *How good and pleasant it is when brothers live together in unity!*

Psalm 147:1 *Praise the Lord. How good it is to sing praises to our God, how pleasant and fitting to praise Him!*

You bring great delight and pleasure to the Lord. Your faith pleases Him (Hebrews 11:6) and He is pleased to give you the kingdom (Luke 12:32). You prioritize worship (Psalm 135:3) and the knowledge and wisdom of God (Proverbs 2:10). You have chosen to stay within His boundary lines (Psalm 16:6). You welcome God's discipline. Even though it is painful and not pleasant at the time, it produces a harvest of righteousness and peace (Hebrews 12:11). You know that to the hungry even what is bitter tastes sweet (Proverbs 27:7). You have the ability to see the beauty of the Lord in the ugliest of circumstances (Song of Solomon 7:6). You are agreeable, refreshing, mild mannered, good natured, friendly, gracious, and kind. You desire to give enjoyment and satisfaction to those who are sad, discouraged, grieved, and crushed. Your life's message is Romans 12:1, "Therefore, I urge you, brothers, in view of God's mercy, to offer your bodies as living sacrifices, holy and pleasing to God—this is your spiritual act of worship."

NATALIE

Birthday of Christ; joyous spirit

❧

Psalm 149:4–5 *For the Lord takes delight in His people; He crowns the humble with salvation. Let the saints rejoice in this honor and sing for joy on their beds.*

Psalm 45:7 *You love righteousness and hate wickedness; therefore God, your God, has set you above your companions by anointing you with the oil of joy.*

Psalm 16:11 says, "You have made known to me the path of life; You will fill me with joy in Your presence, with eternal pleasures at Your right hand." Your heavenly Father has trusted you with a quality that releases healing, restores hope, and brings refreshing. You are one who takes the source of tears and defeat, and turns them into confident trust with rejoicing. As you experience and remain sensitive to the things that sorrow the heart of God, He will pour His oil of joy on and through you to restore hope to those who are mourning (Isaiah 61:1–3). Experiences of sorrow prepare and enlarge your capacity for joy. The joy of the Lord will be your strength to endure the cross He has called you to bear. You are to fix your eyes on Jesus, the author and perfecter of your faith, who for the joy set before Him endured the cross, scorning its shame, and sat down at the right hand of the throne of God (Hebrews 12:2). He will be faithful to give you a song in your "night" season (Psalm 42:8). God rejoices over you with gladness! (Zephaniah 3:17)

NATHAN

A gift; given of God

James 1:17 *Every good and perfect gift is from above, coming down from the Father of the heavenly lights, who does not change like shifting shadows.*

I Samuel 16:7 *But the Lord said to Samuel, "Do not consider his appearance or his height, for I have rejected him. The Lord does not look at the things man looks at. Man looks at the outward appearance, but the Lord looks at the heart."*

You are God's tribute to Himself, His personal reward. Your life defines God's manners, with priorities on giving rather than receiving. You are to fan into flame the gift of God (II Timothy 1:6). Through you He will display His favor, encouragement and kindness even to the undeserved and hated. As you look beyond faults and see needs, you are God's channel through which His unselfish love flows and is revealed. Discipline your attention to the Giver, not to the gift, nor its wrappings. Give diligence to preserving a humble, submitted heart in full surrender to the Lord. Proverbs 18:16 says, "A gift opens the way for the giver and ushers him into the presence of the great."

NATHANIEL

A gift; given of God

ॐ

James 1:17 *Every good and perfect gift is from above, coming down from the Father of the heavenly lights, who does not change like shifting shadows.*

I Samuel 16:7 *But the Lord said to Samuel, "Do not consider his appearance or his height, for I have rejected him. The Lord does not look at the things man looks at. Man looks at the outward appearance, but the Lord looks at the heart."*

You are God's tribute to Himself, His personal reward. Your life defines God's manners, with priorities on giving rather than receiving. You are to fan into flame the gift of God (II Timothy 1:6). Through you He will display His favor, encouragement and kindness even to the undeserved and hated. As you look beyond faults and see needs, you are God's channel through which His unselfish love flows and is revealed. Discipline your attention to the Giver, not to the gift, nor its wrappings. Give diligence to preserving a humble, submitted heart in full surrender to the Lord. Proverbs 18:16 says, "A gift opens the way for the giver and ushers him into the presence of the great."

NEAL

Champion

℞

Exodus 14:14   *The Lord will fight for you; you need only to be still.*

Philippians 3:14   *I press on toward the goal to win the prize for which God has called me heavenward in Christ Jesus.*

Your Lord Jesus Christ has disarmed the powers and authorities and made a public spectacle of them; triumphing over them by the cross (Colossians 2:15). The Lamb of God will overcome the enemy because He is Lord of lords and King of kings. With Him you will be His called, chosen, and faithful follower (Revelation 17:14). As you take refuge in Him, He spreads His protection over you (Psalm 5:11). You win, not by the sword of your strength, but by the Lord's right arm and the light of His face; for He loves you (Psalm 44:3). He has given you authority to overcome all the power of the enemy (Luke 10:19) and nothing will harm you. You lead truth, grace, and justice to victory. You defend the helpless, hopeless, and the honor of others. You are God's role model of courage, victory, and protection. Your daily life will win the respect of outsiders (I Thessalonians 4:12).

NEIL

Champion

℘

Exodus 14:14 *The Lord will fight for you; you need only to be still.*

Philippians 3:14 *I press on toward the goal to win the prize for which God has called me heavenward in Christ Jesus.*

Your Lord Jesus Christ has disarmed the powers and authorities and made a public spectacle of them; triumphing over them by the cross (Colossians 2:15). The Lamb of God will overcome the enemy because He is Lord of lords and King of kings. With Him you will be His called, chosen, and faithful follower (Revelation 17:14). As you take refuge in Him, He spreads His protection over you (Psalm 5:11). You win, not by the sword of your strength, but by the Lord's right arm and the light of His face; for He loves you (Psalm 44:3). He has given you authority to overcome all the power of the enemy (Luke 10:19) and nothing will harm you. You lead truth, grace, and justice to victory. You defend the helpless, hopeless, and the honor of others. You are God's role model of courage, victory, and protection. Your daily life will win the respect of outsiders (I Thessalonians 4:12).

NEVEAH

Forecaster; declarer of God

⤫

Psalm 96:3 *Declare His glory among the nations, His marvelous deeds among all peoples.*

I John 1:5 *This is the message we have heard from Him and declare to you: God is light; in Him there is no darkness at all.*

You have a passionate hunger to know Christ, the power of His resurrection, and the fellowship of sharing in His sufferings (Philippians 3:10). This intimacy gives you direct access to the very heart of God, who shares His secrets with you. You are one who shows the mind of the Lord to the people by rightly dividing the word of truth. You spread out God's Word on the table for hungry souls who are seeking Him. This proclamation will come by your testimony, talents, and resources. You serve as a forerunner to advance the gospel. You are a herald, God's messenger of His revelation (Habakkuk 2:2–3). Those in hiding will be given light and those in denial will be set free as you reveal the true character and identity of God. Make clear what you publish and report. Your mouth is filled with God's praise, declaring His splendor all day long (Psalm 71:8).

NICHOLAS

Victory of the people; victorious spirit

❧

I John 5:4 *Everyone born of God overcomes the world. This is the victory that has overcome the world, even our faith.*

II Corinthians 2:14 *But thanks be to God, who always leads us in triumphal procession in Christ and through us spreads everywhere the fragrance of the knowledge of Him.*

Because of your faith in Jesus Christ, you will ever be aggressive towards the enemy's tools of defeat, failure, and victimization. You will push back Satan and overcome all his power. Jesus has given you authority to trample on snakes and scorpions and to overcome all the power of the enemy; nothing will harm you (Luke 10:19). Even in the severest of afflictions—such as hardship, persecution, famine, nakedness, danger, or sword—you are more than a conqueror through Christ who loves you (Romans 8:35–37). "Everyone born of God overcomes the world. This is the victory that has overcome the world, even our faith," I John 5:4. "Take heart, Jesus has overcome the world," John 16:33.

NICHOLE

Victory of the people; victorious spirit

❧

I John 5:4 *Everyone born of God overcomes the world. This is the victory that has overcome the world, even our faith.*

II Corinthians 2:14 *But thanks be to God, who always leads us in triumphal procession in Christ and through us spreads everywhere the fragrance of the knowledge of Him.*

Because of your faith in Jesus Christ, you will ever be aggressive towards the enemy's tools of defeat, failure, and victimization. You will push back Satan and overcome all his power. Jesus has given you authority to trample on snakes and scorpions and to overcome all the power of the enemy; nothing will harm you (Luke 10:19). Even in the severest of afflictions—such as hardship, persecution, famine, nakedness, danger, or sword—you are more than a conqueror through Christ who loves you (Romans 8:35–37). "Everyone born of God overcomes the world. This is the victory that has overcome the world, even our faith," I John 5:4. "Take heart, Jesus has overcome the world," John 16:33.

NICIA

Peoples' victory; victorious one

൫

I John 5:4 *Everyone born of God overcomes the world. This is the victory that has overcome the world, even our faith.*

II Corinthians 2:14 *But thanks be to God, who always leads us in triumphal procession in Christ and through us spreads everywhere the fragrance of the knowledge of Him.*

Because of your faith in Jesus Christ, you will ever be aggressive towards the enemy's tools of defeat, failure, and victimization. You will push back Satan and overcome all his power. Jesus has given you authority to trample on snakes and scorpions and to overcome all the power of the enemy; nothing will harm you (Luke 10:19). Even in the severest of afflictions—such as hardship, persecution, famine, nakedness, danger, or sword—you are more than a conqueror through Christ who loves you (Romans 8:35–37). "Everyone born of God overcomes the world. This is the victory that has overcome the world, even our faith," I John 5:4. "Take heart, Jesus has overcome the world," John 16:33.

NICK

Victory of the people; victorious spirit

I John 5:4 *Everyone born of God overcomes the world. This is the victory that has overcome the world, even our faith.*

II Corinthians 2:14 *But thanks be to God, who always leads us in triumphal procession in Christ and through us spreads everywhere the fragrance of the knowledge of Him.*

Because of your faith in Jesus Christ, you will ever be aggressive towards the enemy's tools of defeat, failure, and victimization. You will push back Satan and overcome all his power. Jesus has given you authority to trample on snakes and scorpions and to overcome all the power of the enemy; nothing will harm you (Luke 10:19). Even in the severest of afflictions—such as hardship, persecution, famine, nakedness, danger, or sword—you are more than a conqueror through Christ who loves you (Romans 8:35–37). "Everyone born of God overcomes the world. This is the victory that has overcome the world, even our faith," I John 5:4. "Take heart, Jesus has overcome the world," John 16:33.

NICOLE

Victory of the people; victorious spirit

I John 5:4 *Everyone born of God overcomes the world. This is the victory that has overcome the world, even our faith.*

II Corinthians 2:14 *But thanks be to God, who always leads us in triumphal procession in Christ and through us spreads everywhere the fragrance of the knowledge of Him.*

Because of your faith in Jesus Christ, you will ever be aggressive towards the enemy's tools of defeat, failure, and victimization. You will push back Satan and overcome all his power. Jesus has given you authority to trample on snakes and scorpions and to overcome all the power of the enemy; nothing will harm you (Luke 10:19). Even in the severest of afflictions—such as hardship, persecution, famine, nakedness, danger, or sword—you are more than a conqueror through Christ who loves you (Romans 8:35–37). "Everyone born of God overcomes the world. This is the victory that has overcome the world, even our faith," I John 5:4. "Take heart, Jesus has overcome the world," John 16:33.

NIKKI

Victory of the people; victorious spirit

❧

I John 5:4 *Everyone born of God overcomes the world. This is the victory that has overcome the world, even our faith.*

II Corinthians 2:14 *But thanks be to God, who always leads us in triumphal procession in Christ and through us spreads everywhere the fragrance of the knowledge of Him.*

Because of your faith in Jesus Christ, you will ever be aggressive towards the enemy's tools of defeat, failure, and victimization. You will push back Satan and overcome all his power. Jesus has given you authority to trample on snakes and scorpions and to overcome all the power of the enemy; nothing will harm you (Luke 10:19). Even in the severest of afflictions—such as hardship, persecution, famine, nakedness, danger, or sword—you are more than a conqueror through Christ who loves you (Romans 8:35–37). "Everyone born of God overcomes the world. This is the victory that has overcome the world, even our faith," I John 5:4. "Take heart, Jesus has overcome the world," John 16:33.

NINA

Favor; grace

ℰℒ

Romans 8:32 *He who did not spare His own Son, but gave Him up for us all—how will He not also, along with Him, graciously give us all things?*

I Corinthians 15:10 *But by the grace of God I am what I am, and His grace to me was not without effect.*

Ephesians 2:8 says, "For it is by grace you have been saved, through faith—and this is not from yourselves, it is the gift of God." You are one who brings about balance and harmony through mercy, forgiveness, approval, kindness, and patience—all with a grateful heart. This attitude of gratitude will rule in the midst of inconsiderate behavior. Your nature defies the law of the Pharisees, and is against being self-reliant, prejudice, and selfish. Being full of grace is devotion built through faithfulness and a willingness to quickly pardon. You are blessed with creativity in expressing God's greatest gift of grace—the life of His only Son, Jesus Christ. God says to you through Jeremiah 24:7, "I will give them a heart to know Me, that I am the Lord. They will be My people, and I will be their God, for they will return to Me with all their heart." Ezekiel 11:19 says, "I will give them an undivided heart and put a new spirit in them; I will remove from them their heart of stone and give them a heart of flesh." Accountability will keep your report accurate and your integrity irreproachable.

NITA

God's gracious gift; gracious one

ৎ৩

Romans 8:32 *He who did not spare His own Son, but gave Him up for us all—how will He not also, along with Him, graciously give us all things?*

I Corinthians 15:10 *But by the grace of God I am what I am, and His grace to me was not without effect.*

Ephesians 2:8 says, "For it is by grace you have been saved, through faith—and this is not from yourselves, it is the gift of God." You are one who brings about balance and harmony through mercy, forgiveness, approval, kindness, and patience—all with a grateful heart. This attitude of gratitude will rule in the midst of inconsiderate behavior. Your nature defies the law of the Pharisees, and is against being self-reliant, prejudice, and selfish. Being full of grace is devotion built through faithfulness and a willingness to quickly pardon. You are blessed with creativity in expressing God's greatest gift of grace—the life of His only Son, Jesus Christ. God says to you through Jeremiah 24:7, "I will give them a heart to know Me, that I am the Lord. They will be My people, and I will be their God, for they will return to Me with all their heart." Ezekiel 11:19 says, "I will give them an undivided heart and put a new spirit in them; I will remove from them their heart of stone and give them a heart of flesh." Accountability will keep your report accurate and your integrity irreproachable.

NOAH

Comfort; refuge

❧

Deuteronomy 33:27   *The eternal God is your refuge, and underneath are the everlasting arms. He will drive out your enemy before you, saying, Destroy him!'*

Psalm 27:5   *For in the day of trouble He will keep me safe in His dwelling; He will hide me in the shelter of His tabernacle and set me high upon a rock.*

God is your place of protection. Your heart is His home. As you hide in the shelter of His presence, the Lord protects you from those who conspire against you; those with accusing tongues (Psalm 31:19–20). The Lord uses you to be His refuge for the poor and needy in distress, His shelter from the storm, and a shade from the heat (Isaiah 25:4). You release security and confidence (Proverbs 14:26). You declare deliverance to the prisoners and you give hope that God will restore twice as much to them (Zechariah 9:12).

NOEL

Birthday of Christ; joyous spirit

୪୬

Psalm 149:4–5 *For the Lord takes delight in His people; He crowns the humble with salvation. Let the saints rejoice in this honor and sing for joy on their beds.*

Psalm 45:7 *You love righteousness and hate wickedness; therefore God, your God, has set you above your companions by anointing you with the oil of joy.*

Psalm 16:11 says, "You have made known to me the path of life; You will fill me with joy in Your presence, with eternal pleasures at Your right hand." Your heavenly Father has trusted you with a quality that releases healing, restores hope, and brings refreshing. You are one who takes the source of tears and defeat, and turns them into confident trust with rejoicing. As you experience and remain sensitive to the things that sorrow the heart of God, He will pour His oil of joy on and through you to restore hope to those who are mourning (Isaiah 61:1–3). Experiences of sorrow prepare and enlarge your capacity for joy. The joy of the Lord will be your strength to endure the cross He has called you to bear. You are to fix your eyes on Jesus, the author and perfecter of your faith, who for the joy set before Him endured the cross, scorning its shame, and sat down at the right hand of the throne of God (Hebrews 12:2). He will be faithful to give you a song in your "night" season (Psalm 42:8). God rejoices over you with gladness! (Zephaniah 3:17)

NOLAN

Famous; noble one

Isaiah 32:8   *But the noble man makes noble plans, and by noble deeds he stands.*

Luke 8:15   *But the seed on good soil stands for those with a noble and good heart, who hear the word, retain it, and by persevering produce a crop.*

Proverbs 18:12 says, "Before his downfall a man's heart is proud, but humility comes before honor." You are one who has a humble confidence in recognizing and expressing reverence, worship, adoration, trust, deference, tribute, admiration, and respect. This is the result of being secure in the truth of who you are in the Lord. Through humility, King Jesus made a way for you to be engrafted into His royalty. He made of Himself no reputation and took on the nature of a servant (Philippians 2:7) to affirm your value. Through self-denial, you prioritize excellence in virtue, truthfulness, and faithfulness. Because of the respect you have earned, you dismantle inferiority, disgrace, shame, and offenses. No one feels second-rate in your presence. The deeper that the Lord is your object of reverence, the greater your confidence will be in giving approval and worth. Because you are tall in spirit, your face is always turned upward.

NORA

Noble; full of honor

∞

Isaiah 32:8 *But the noble man makes noble plans, and by noble deeds he stands.*

Luke 8:15 *But the seed on good soil stands for those with a noble and good heart, who hear the word, retain it, and by persevering produce a crop.*

Proverbs 18:12 says, "Before his downfall a man's heart is proud, but humility comes before honor." You are one who has a humble confidence in recognizing and expressing reverence, worship, adoration, trust, deference, tribute, admiration, and respect. This is the result of being secure in the truth of who you are in the Lord. Through humility, King Jesus made a way for you to be engrafted into His royalty. He made of Himself no reputation and took on the nature of a servant (Philippians 2:7) to affirm your value. Through self-denial, you prioritize excellence in virtue, truthfulness, and faithfulness. Because of the respect you have earned, you dismantle inferiority, disgrace, shame, and offenses. No one feels second-rate in your presence. The deeper that the Lord is your object of reverence, the greater your confidence will be in giving approval and worth. Because you are tall in spirit, your face is always turned upward.

NORMA

A rule, pattern or precept; example of godliness

Exodus 15:11   *Who among the gods is like you, O Lord? Who is like You—majestic in holiness, awesome in glory, working wonders?*

I Timothy 4:8   *Godliness has value for all things, holding promise for both the present life and the life to come.*

Godliness with contentment is great gain (I Timothy 6:6). You are to pursue godliness (I Timothy 6:11). Your life is to reflect the very nature of God, which is holy, righteous, just, pure, spotless, faithful, and divine. The choices you make and the life you live are to define God's standard for living. As you follow the Lord, He desires for others to pattern their lives after you. Out of a humble, reverent heart and as you show Him respect, adoration, and praise, you will ever be esteemed and prized by the Lord. You will have no reason to be insecure in who you are, or to place blame on God, or to disapprove of His will for your life. He celebrates how He made you!

NORRIS

Nurse; helpful spirit

❧

Isaiah 41:10 *So do not fear, for I am with you; do not be dismayed, for I am your God. I will strength you and help you; I will uphold you with My righteous right hand.*

I Corinthians 15:58 *Therefore, my dear brothers, stand firm. Let nothing move you. Always give yourselves fully to the work of the Lord, because you know that your labor in the Lord is not in vain.*

You say with confidence that the Lord is your helper. You are not afraid. What can man do to you (Hebrews 13:6)? This trust allows you the important role of being God's hands extended to your world. You serve with the strength He provides so that He gets all the credit (I Peter 4:11). Like the good Samaritan, you are moved with compassion to give practical help, providing sacrifice and kindness with unselfishness (Luke 10:25–37). You are eyes to the blind, feet to the lame, and the father to the needy (Job 29:15–16). You make the most of every opportunity to do good to all people (Galatians 6:10). As a caring one, you are cautious in avoiding mistakes and very attentive to details. His compassion flowing to and through you equips you to show concern for the neglected and indifferent. The complacent will be challenged to release their burdens and worries to the burden bearer, Jesus Christ. The Good Shepherd will continue to nurture you as you nurture others. Because you are devoted to the service of the Lord, you will hear, "Well done, good and faithful servant! You have been faithful with a few things; I will put you in charge of many things. Come and share your master's happiness!" (Matthew 25:23)

OLIVER

Olive tree; peaceful heart

&

Isaiah 26:3 *You will keep in perfect peace him whose mind is steadfast, because he trusts in You.*

Philippians 4:7 *And the peace of God, which transcends all understanding, will guard your hearts and your minds in Christ Jesus.*

Your life defines peace. You will have a content and calm composure in the midst of distress, disturbance, or agitation. As you follow the Prince of Peace, you will be secure in who you are in Christ. The discipline of keeping your mind on Christ, loving God's law, and being controlled by the Holy Spirit will keep you in perfect peace. God's peace will serve as an umpire to determine whether you are safe or out of God's will (Colossians 3:15). Do not think it strange when you are in battles, fights, and quarrels, because God wants to use you to bring harmony, order, unity, agreement, quietness, and calmness to the adverse situation. You are one whose intimate friendship with the Lord brings reconciliation to the offended, distressed, and troubled. "In repentance and rest is your salvation, in quietness and trust is your strength," Isaiah 30:15. Your refreshing comes as you renew your mind daily in the Word of God. "Great peace have they who love Your law, and nothing can make them stumble," Psalm 119:165.

OLIVIA

Olive tree; peaceful heart

℀

Isaiah 26:3 *You will keep in perfect peace him whose mind is steadfast, because he trusts in You.*

Philippians 4:7 *And the peace of God, which transcends all understanding, will guard your hearts and your minds in Christ Jesus.*

Your life defines peace. You will have a content and calm composure in the midst of distress, disturbance, or agitation. As you follow the Prince of Peace, you will be secure in who you are in Christ. The discipline of keeping your mind on Christ, loving God's law, and being controlled by the Holy Spirit will keep you in perfect peace. God's peace will serve as an umpire to determine whether you are safe or out of God's will (Colossians 3:15). Do not think it strange when you are in battles, fights, and quarrels, because God wants to use you to bring harmony, order, unity, agreement, quietness, and calmness to the adverse situation. You are one whose intimate friendship with the Lord brings reconciliation to the offended, distressed, and troubled. "In repentance and rest is your salvation, in quietness and trust is your strength," Isaiah 30:15. Your refreshing comes as you renew your mind daily in the Word of God. "Great peace have they who love Your law, and nothing can make them stumble," Psalm 119:165.

OPRAH

A fawn; free

෫ා

Isaiah 61:1 *The Spirit of the Sovereign Lord is on me, because the Lord has anointed me to preach good news to the poor. He has sent me to bind up the brokenhearted, to proclaim freedom for the captives and release from darkness for the prisoners.*

Galatians 5:1 *It is for freedom that Christ has set us free. Stand firm, then, and do not let yourselves be burdened again by a yoke of slavery.*

There are no restrictions on your abandoned commitment to the Lord Jesus Christ. Knowing God's truth frees you from the bondage and care of sin and oppression (John 8:32). The free gift of God—Jesus Christ—exchanges offense for God's grace, condemnation for justification, shame for holiness and the spirit of the world for the Spirit of God. You are fearless as you loose those in bondage and give pardon to the imprisoned—all because the law of the Spirit of life set you free from the law of sin and death. Do not use your freedom to indulge the sinful nature; rather, serve one another in love (Galatians 5:13). Freely you have received; freely give (Matthew 10:8).

ORPAH

A fawn; free

❧

Isaiah 61:1 *The Spirit of the Sovereign Lord is on me, because the Lord has anointed me to preach good news to the poor. He has sent me to bind up the brokenhearted, to proclaim freedom for the captives and release from darkness for the prisoners.*

Galatians 5:1 *It is for freedom that Christ has set us free. Stand firm, then, and do not let yourselves be burdened again by a yoke of slavery.*

There are no restrictions on your abandoned commitment to the Lord Jesus Christ. Knowing God's truth frees you from the bondage and care of sin and oppression (John 8:32). The free gift of God—Jesus Christ—exchanges offense for God's grace, condemnation for justification, shame for holiness and the spirit of the world for the Spirit of God. You are fearless as you loose those in bondage and give pardon to the imprisoned—all because the law of the Spirit of life set you free from the law of sin and death. Do not use your freedom to indulge the sinful nature; rather, serve one another in love (Galatians 5:13). Freely you have received; freely give. (Matthew 10:8).

OSCAR

Divine spear; appointed of God

❧

Jeremiah 1:5 *Before I formed you in the womb, I knew you, before you were born I set you apart; I appointed you as a prophet to the nations.*

John 15:16 *You did not choose Me, but I chose you and appointed you to go and bear fruit—fruit that will last. Then the Father will give you whatever you ask in My name.*

You hear the voice of the Lord saying, "Whom shall I send? And who will go for us?" And you say, "Here am I. Send me!" (Isaiah 6:8) The Lord has appointed you as a servant and witness of what you have seen of Him and what He shows you (Acts 26:16). You were chosen in Him before the creation of the world to be holy and blameless in His sight (Ephesians 1:4). God has placed His trust in you by giving you His authority and ordained you to reflect His character and thoughts. As one favored by God, you are His representative sent on His mission. Knowing He chooses the weak and foolish things to confound the wise requires humility, gratitude, and surrender. God's approval is upon you and His assignment is in you to accomplish His purposes. Make your calling sure and live a life worthy of the calling you have received. Be completely humble, gentle, patient, and bearing with one another in love (Ephesians 4:1–2). You refuse a maintenance mode, but rather fix your thoughts and destination on Jesus. You are equipped to fulfill the great commission (Matthew 28:18–20).

OWEN

Youth; youthful heart

&

Psalm 71:5, 17   *For You have been my hope, O Sovereign Lord, my confidence since my youth. Since my youth, O God, You have taught me, and to this day I declare Your marvelous deeds.*

I Timothy 4:12   *Don't let anyone look down on you because you are young, but set an example for the believers in speech, in life, in love, in faith and in purity.*

You are God's expression of childlikeness, refreshment, and vigor. You will undergo little erosion, not to your own credit but to the faithfulness of God. Your pursuit of a pure heart, which is God's innocence, will release His protection over you from all that would rob His youthfulness in you. Think it not strange when God would cross your path with those who are aged in spirit by weariness, shame, or fear. You are His ambassador to restore His strength, refreshment, and vigor. See yourself constantly as that child—full of faith and adoration for your Heavenly Father—on the Lord's lap: accepted, cuddled, and with strong arms around you. He will equip you to wait hopefully—to not be anxious or consumed with worry. Your childlike dependency on the Lord will keep you trusting, full of faith, and renewed.

PAIGE

Attendant; obedient spirit

Deuteronomy 11:26–28 *See, I am setting before you today a blessing and a curse—the blessing if you obey the commands of the Lord your God that I am giving you today; the curse if you disobey the commands of the Lord your God and turn from the way that I command you today by following other gods, which you have not known.*

I Samuel 15:22–23 *But Samuel replied: "Does the Lord delight in burnt offerings and sacrifices as much as in obeying the voice of the Lord? To obey is better than sacrifice, and to heed is better than the fat of rams. For rebellion is like the sin of divination, and arrogance like the evil of idolatry."*

Every one of your thoughts is to be taken captive to make them obedient to Christ. Once your obedience is complete, you are to be ready to punish every act of disobedience (II Corinthians 10:5–6). Over and over in scripture obedience is linked with hearing the voice of God. This requires attentive listening with agreement. You choose to submit to the control of your heavenly Father, willingly yielding to His commands. To hear God's Word and not practice it is to reject it. Therefore you will be instrumental in turning the hearts of the rebellious and stubborn who oppose Him. This will restore character that permits one to be easily handled or managed. "Now that you have purified yourselves by obeying the truth so that you have sincere love for your brothers, love one another deeply, from the heart," I Peter 1:22.

PAM

All honey; sweet spirit

Proverbs 16:24 *Pleasant words are a honeycomb, sweet to the soul and healing to the bones.*

Psalm 119:103 *How sweet are Your words to my taste, sweeter than honey to my mouth!*

The Word of God is described as being "sweeter than honey from the honeycomb" in Psalm 19:10. It is symbolic of wisdom that is sweet to the soul, giving you a future hope that will not be cut off (Proverbs 24:13–14). Proverbs 27:7 says, "He who is full loathes honey, but to the hungry even what is bitter tastes sweet." The Lord has blessed you with the ability to see the good in everything. Even when bitter things come into your life, you are able to allow Him to turn it for His good because you hunger for more of Him. His fruit, the fruit of the Spirit, is sweet to your taste (Song of Solomon 2:3). As you are saturated with God's Word, your own words will be welcoming, agreeable, and pleasing. You are anointed to bring approval to those drinking the "bitter cup," giving them hope that will not be cut off. Because you have "tasted that the Lord is good," you will nurture spiritual hunger in new believers for the Word of God.

PAMELA

All honey; sweet spirit

Proverbs 16:24 *Pleasant words are a honeycomb, sweet to the soul and healing to the bones.*

Psalm 119:103 *How sweet are Your words to my taste, sweeter than honey to my mouth!*

The Word of God is described as being "sweeter than honey from the honeycomb" in Psalm 19:10. It is symbolic of wisdom that is sweet to the soul, giving you a future hope that will not be cut off (Proverbs 24:13–14). Proverbs 27:7 says, "He who is full loathes honey, but to the hungry even what is bitter tastes sweet." The Lord has blessed you with the ability to see the good in everything. Even when bitter things come into your life, you are able to allow Him to turn it for His good because you hunger for more of Him. His fruit, the fruit of the Spirit, is sweet to your taste (Song of Solomon 2:3). As you are saturated with God's Word, your own words will be welcoming, agreeable, and pleasing. You are anointed to bring approval to those drinking the "bitter cup," giving them hope that will not be cut off. Because you have "tasted that the Lord is good," you will nurture spiritual hunger in new believers for the Word of God.

PARKER

Park keeper; stewardship

∞

Matthew 25:21 *His master replied, "Well done, good and faithful servant! You have been faithful with a few things; I will put you in charge of many things. Come and share your master's happiness!"*

Titus 1:3 *And at His appointed season He brought His word to light through the preaching entrusted to me by the command of God our Savior.*

You have a clear understanding that everything you are and all you possess are from God and belong to God. He has loaned everything to you and made you responsible to care for and use it for His glory. God has entrusted you to manage His affairs with accountability and integrity—without hiding anything and without manipulation. Obeying His commands allows you to give direction and oversight to those without goals and to show order to those in confusion. The Bible will be your greatest possession of stewardship. You are a servant to the body of Christ—the church—by the commission God gave you to present His Word in its fullness (Colossians 1:25). Your goal is not to please men, but God, who tests your heart (I Thessalonians 2:4). You are regarded as a servant of Christ, entrusted with the secret things of God. This trust requires you to prove yourself faithful (I Corinthians 4:1–2). You should use whatever gift you have received to serve others, faithfully administering God's grace in its various forms (I Peter 4:10). As you allow God to govern, coach, and guide your life, He will authorize you to be that for others.

PAT

Noble one; full of honor

❧

Isaiah 32:8   *But the noble man makes noble plans, and by noble deeds he stands.*

Luke 8:15   *But the seed on good soil stands for those with a noble and good heart, who hear the word, retain it, and by persevering produce a crop.*

Proverbs 18:12 says, "Before his downfall a man's heart is proud, but humility comes before honor." You are one who has a humble confidence in recognizing and expressing reverence, worship, adoration, trust, deference, tribute, admiration, and respect. This is the result of being secure in the truth of who you are in the Lord. Through humility, King Jesus made a way for you to be engrafted into His royalty. He made of Himself no reputation and took on the nature of a servant (Philippians 2:7) to affirm your value. Through self-denial, you prioritize excellence in virtue, truthfulness, and faithfulness. Because of the respect you have earned, you dismantle inferiority, disgrace, shame, and offenses. No one feels second-rate in your presence. The deeper that the Lord is your object of reverence, the greater your confidence will be in giving approval and worth. Because you are tall in spirit, your face is always turned upward.

PATRICIA

Noble one; full of honor

໒ઃ

Isaiah 32:8 *But the noble man makes noble plans, and by noble deeds he stands.*

Luke 8:15 *But the seed on good soil stands for those with a noble and good heart, who hear the word, retain it, and by persevering produce a crop.*

Proverbs 18:12 says, "Before his downfall a man's heart is proud, but humility comes before honor." You are one who has a humble confidence in recognizing and expressing reverence, worship, adoration, trust, deference, tribute, admiration, and respect. This is the result of being secure in the truth of who you are in the Lord. Through humility, King Jesus made a way for you to be engrafted into His royalty. He made of Himself no reputation and took on the nature of a servant (Philippians 2:7) to affirm your value. Through self-denial, you prioritize excellence in virtue, truthfulness, and faithfulness. Because of the respect you have earned, you dismantle inferiority, disgrace, shame, and offenses. No one feels second-rate in your presence. The deeper that the Lord is your object of reverence, the greater your confidence will be in giving approval and worth. Because you are tall in spirit, your face is always turned upward.

PATRICK

Noble one; full of honor

ೲ

Isaiah 32:8   *But the noble man makes noble plans, and by noble deeds he stands.*

Luke 8:15   *But the seed on good soil stands for those with a noble and good heart, who hear the word, retain it, and by persevering produce a crop.*

Proverbs 18:12 says, "Before his downfall a man's heart is proud, but humility comes before honor." You are one who has a humble confidence in recognizing and expressing reverence, worship, adoration, trust, deference, tribute, admiration, and respect. This is the result of being secure in the truth of who you are in the Lord. Through humility, King Jesus made a way for you to be engrafted into His royalty. He made of Himself no reputation and took on the nature of a servant (Philippians 2:7) to affirm your value. Through self-denial, you prioritize excellence in virtue, truthfulness, and faithfulness. Because of the respect you have earned, you dismantle inferiority, disgrace, shame, and offenses. No one feels second-rate in your presence. The deeper that the Lord is your object of reverence, the greater your confidence will be in giving approval and worth. Because you are tall in spirit, your face is always turned upward.

PATSY

Noble one; full of honor

༄

Isaiah 32:8 *But the noble man makes noble plans, and by noble deeds he stands.*

Luke 8:15 *But the seed on good soil stands for those with a noble and good heart, who hear the word, retain it, and by persevering produce a crop.*

Proverbs 18:12 says, "Before his downfall a man's heart is proud, but humility comes before honor." You are one who has a humble confidence in recognizing and expressing reverence, worship, adoration, trust, deference, tribute, admiration, and respect. This is the result of being secure in the truth of who you are in the Lord. Through humility, King Jesus made a way for you to be engrafted into His royalty. He made of Himself no reputation and took on the nature of a servant (Philippians 2:7) to affirm your value. Through self-denial, you prioritize excellence in virtue, truthfulness, and faithfulness. Because of the respect you have earned, you dismantle inferiority, disgrace, shame, and offenses. No one feels second-rate in your presence. The deeper that the Lord is your object of reverence, the greater your confidence will be in giving approval and worth. Because you are tall in spirit, your face is always turned upward.

PAUL

Little; dependent on God

ℭℭ

Isaiah 60:22   *The least of you will become a thousand, the smallest a mighty nation. I am the Lord; in its time I will do this swiftly.*

II Corinthians 3:5   *Not that we are competent in ourselves to claim anything for ourselves, but our competence comes from God.*

The word "little" here has nothing to do with size, insignificance, unimportance, or narrow-mindedness. It does mean you are totally dependent on God, for without Him you can do nothing (John 15:5). This is expressed by relying and trusting in His control. As God increases and you decrease, God will use you to touch the lives of the helpless, immature, and weak. II Corinthians 12:9–10 says, "My grace is sufficient for you, for My power is made perfect in weakness. Therefore I will boast all the more gladly about my weaknesses, so that Christ's power may rest on me. That is why, for Christ's sake, I delight in weaknesses, in insults, in hardships, in persecutions, in difficulties. For when I am weak, then I am strong." Your humility admits weaknesses and releases strengths. As you are faithful over a little, God will make you ruler over much (Luke 19:17).

PAULA

Little; dependent on God

೮೨

Isaiah 60:22   *The least of you will become a thousand, the smallest a mighty nation. I am the Lord; in its time I will do this swiftly.*

II Corinthians 3:5   *Not that we are competent in ourselves to claim anything for ourselves, but our competence comes from God.*

The word "little" here has nothing to do with size, insignificance, unimportance, or narrow-mindedness. It does mean you are totally dependent on God, for without Him you can do nothing (John 15:5). This is expressed by relying and trusting in His control. As God increases and you decrease, God will use you to touch the lives of the helpless, immature, and weak. II Corinthians 12:9–10 says, "My grace is sufficient for you, for My power is made perfect in weakness. Therefore I will boast all the more gladly about my weaknesses, so that Christ's power may rest on me. That is why, for Christ's sake, I delight in weaknesses, in insults, in hardships, in persecutions, in difficulties. For when I am weak, then I am strong." Your humility admits weaknesses and releases strengths. As you are faithful over a little, God will make you ruler over much (Luke 19:17).

PAULINE

Little; dependent on God

๛

Isaiah 60:22   *The least of you will become a thousand, the smallest a mighty nation. I am the Lord; in its time I will do this swiftly.*

II Corinthians 3:5   *Not that we are competent in ourselves to claim anything for ourselves, but our competence comes from God.*

The word "little" here has nothing to do with size, insignificance, unimportance, or narrow-mindedness. It does mean you are totally dependent on God, for without Him you can do nothing (John 15:5). This is expressed by relying and trusting in His control. As God increases and you decrease, God will use you to touch the lives of the helpless, immature, and weak. II Corinthians 12:9–10 says, "My grace is sufficient for you, for My power is made perfect in weakness. Therefore I will boast all the more gladly about my weaknesses, so that Christ's power may rest on me. That is why, for Christ's sake, I delight in weaknesses, in insults, in hardships, in persecutions, in difficulties. For when I am weak, then I am strong." Your humility admits weaknesses and releases strengths. As you are faithful over a little, God will make you ruler over much (Luke 19:17).

PEARL

A jewel; pure heart

❧

I Timothy 5:22   *...do not share in the sins of others. Keep yourself pure.*

I Peter 1:22   *Now that you have purified yourselves by obeying the truth so that you have sincere love for your brothers, love one another deeply, from the heart.*

Through the process of heat, trials, and refinement, purity is established. Your nature defies being stubborn, judgmental, and haughty. The commandment of the Lord is clear—giving insight to life (Psalm 19:8). You bring wholeness to the dirty, defiled, contaminated, polluted, double-minded, and raped. Your willingness to be transparent is the venue through which He makes His Word clear, simple, and unadulterated. Your choice to be pure enables you to see God (Matthew 5:8) and to know Him as King and Friend (Proverbs 22:11). It also allows your words to be pleasant (Proverbs 15:26) and causes you to ascend to the holy place of the Lord, where you receive blessings and righteousness from the God of salvation (Psalm 24:3–5). Proverbs 20:11 says, "Even a child is known by his actions, by whether his conduct is pure and right."

PEGGY

Pearl; gem of purity

❧

I Timothy 5:22   *...do not share in the sins of others. Keep yourself pure.*

I Peter 1:22   *Now that you have purified yourselves by obeying the truth so that you have sincere love for your brothers, love one another deeply, from the heart.*

Through the process of heat, trials, and refinement, purity is established. Your nature defies being stubborn, judgmental, and haughty. The commandment of the Lord is clear—giving insight to life (Psalm 19:8). You bring wholeness to the dirty, defiled, contaminated, polluted, double-minded, and raped. Your willingness to be transparent is the venue through which He makes His Word clear, simple, and unadulterated. Your choice to be pure enables you to see God (Matthew 5:8) and to know Him as King and Friend (Proverbs 22:11). It also allows your words to be pleasant (Proverbs 15:26) and causes you to ascend to the holy place of the Lord, where you receive blessings and righteousness from the God of salvation (Psalm 24:3–5). Proverbs 20:11 says, "Even a child is known by his actions, by whether his conduct is pure and right."

PENNY

A weaver; creative spirit

୫୦

Colossians 1:16 *For by Him all things were created: things in heaven and on earth, visible and invisible, whether thrones or powers or rulers or authorities; all things were created by Him and for Him.*

Ephesians 2:10 *For we are God's workmanship, created in Christ Jesus to do good works, which God prepared in advance for us to do.*

Through you the Lord will bring Himself into existence; He will originate. How you deal with the past determines your future. Regardless of curses or blessings, failures or successes, you are God's platform for a "new thing." You cannot lean to your own understanding or reasoning. God Almighty created the heavens, the earth, and you in His image. Isaiah 42:9, "See, the former things have taken place, and new things I declare; before they spring into being I announce them to you." Isaiah 43:18–19, "Forget the former things; do not dwell on the past. See, I am doing a new thing! Now it springs up; do you not perceive it? I am making a way in the desert and streams in the wasteland." Isaiah 48:6b, "From now on I will tell you of new things, of hidden things unknown to you." Isaiah 65:17–19, "Behold, I will create new heavens and a new earth. The former things will not be remembered, nor will they come to mind. But be glad and rejoice forever in what I will create, for I will create Jerusalem to be a delight and its people a joy. I will rejoice over Jerusalem and take delight in My people; the sound of weeping and of crying will be heard in it no more." Because of your passion for the eternal over the temporal, you are used of God to remove what can be shaken—the created things—so that what cannot be shaken may remain (Hebrews 12:27). The more completely dependent you become on your Creator, the more productive your life will be for Him! I Peter 4:19, "So then, those who suffer according to God's will should commit themselves to their Creator and continue to do good." As you stay yielded and surrendered to God, the clay of your heart will stay tender. Only then can He mold you into the image of His Son, Jesus Christ. God will work His approval through you to those who feel ugly, worthless, and to those who have no hope.

PERCY

Pierce the vale; freedom

&

Isaiah 61:1 *The Spirit of the Sovereign Lord is on me, because the Lord has anointed me to preach good news to the poor. He has sent me to bind up the brokenhearted, to proclaim freedom for the captives and release from darkness for the prisoners.*

Galatians 5:1 *It is for freedom that Christ has set us free. Stand firm, then, and do not let yourselves be burdened again by a yoke of slavery.*

There are no restrictions on your abandoned commitment to the Lord Jesus Christ. Knowing God's truth frees you from the bondage and care of sin and oppression (John 8:32). The free gift of God—Jesus Christ—exchanges offense for God's grace, condemnation for justification, shame for holiness and the spirit of the world for the Spirit of God. You are fearless as you loose those in bondage and give pardon to the imprisoned—all because the law of the Spirit of life set you free from the law of sin and death. Do not use your freedom to indulge the sinful nature; rather, serve one another in love (Galatians 5:13). Freely you have received; freely give (Matthew 10:8).

PERRY

Son of the leader; strong leader

℘

Deuteronomy 28:13   *The Lord will make you the head, not the tail. If you pay attention to the commands of the Lord your God that I give you this day and carefully follow them, you will always be at the top, never at the bottom.*

Mark 10:43–45   *...Whoever wants to become great among you must be your servant, and whoever wants to be first must be slave of all. For even the Son of Man did not come to be served, but to serve, and to give His life as a ransom for many.*

You have been set apart with vision and perspective to reproduce the likeness of Christ in others by reflecting His image. You are guided by principles and values worth dying for. You know how to balance transparency with being an example. You are one who is secure enough to be vulnerable. You do not lead to gather followers; you lead to develop leaders. You lead by honoring God with authority, influence, direction, foresight, and skill. Your credible choices set a precedence for favor. You earn trust by your willingness to confront and bring discipline in a Godly manner. You are strong enough to let your "yes" be "yes" and your "no" be "no," with no compromise or jealousy. Your strength is determined by your submitted and teachable servant's heart. The more you mature, the more humble, gentle, and meek you will become. With integrity you communicate love, affirmation, nurturing, and spiritual care. If you as a shepherd ever forget what it is like to be a sheep, you will become a hireling. Your highest aim is to honor and glorify God.

PETE

Rock; strong in spirit

❧

Matthew 16:18 *And I tell you that you are Peter, and on this rock I will build My church, and the gates of Hades will not overcome it.*

Proverbs 24:5 *A wise man has great power, and a man of knowledge increases strength.*

You are one who has an uncompromised commitment to righteousness, respectability, honesty, character, excellence, value, worth, kindness, innocence, generosity, trustworthiness, faithfulness, justice, hope, and love. You can do everything through Him who gives you strength (Philippians 4:11–13). The Lord is the source of your strength because you turn back the battle at the gate (Isaiah 28:6). You renew your strength through your hope being in the Lord (Isaiah 40:31). Jesus says, "My grace is sufficient for you, for My power is made perfect in weaknesses. Therefore you will boast all the more gladly about your weaknesses, so that Christ's power may rest on you. That is why for Christ's sake, you delight in weaknesses, in insults, in hardships, in persecutions, and in difficulties. For when you are weak, then you are strong," II Corinthians 12:9–10. You are clothed with strength and dignity (Proverbs 31:25). The Lord alone is your rock, salvation, and your fortress. You will never be shaken (Psalm 62:2).

PETER

Rock; strong in spirit

&

Matthew 16:18   *And I tell you that you are Peter, and on this rock I will build My church, and the gates of Hades will not overcome it.*

Proverbs 24:5   *A wise man has great power, and a man of knowledge increases strength.*

You are one who has an uncompromised commitment to righteousness, respectability, honesty, character, excellence, value, worth, kindness, innocence, generosity, trustworthiness, faithfulness, justice, hope, and love. You can do everything through Him who gives you strength (Philippians 4:11–13). The Lord is the source of your strength because you turn back the battle at the gate (Isaiah 28:6). You renew your strength through your hope being in the Lord (Isaiah 40:31). Jesus says, "My grace is sufficient for you, for My power is made perfect in weaknesses. Therefore you will boast all the more gladly about your weaknesses, so that Christ's power may rest on you. That is why for Christ's sake, you delight in weaknesses, in insults, in hardships, in persecutions, and in difficulties. For when you are weak, then you are strong," II Corinthians 12:9–10. You are clothed with strength and dignity (Proverbs 31:25). The Lord alone is your rock, salvation, and your fortress. You will never be shaken (Psalm 62:2).

PEYTON

Warrior's estate; God's warrior

଼ଔ

II Chronicles 32:7–8   *There is a greater power with us than with him. With him is only the arm of flesh, but with us is the Lord our God to help us and to fight our battles.*

II Timothy 2:3–4   *Endure hardship with us like a good soldier of Christ Jesus. No one serving as a soldier gets involved in civilian affairs - he wants to please his commanding officer.*

Exodus 14:14 says, "The Lord will fight for you; you need only be still." You are armed with the ability to handle the spear and shield—to stand on God's Word by faith, supporting the King of kings against His enemies. As God's defending warrior, you are His example of a brave champion, soldier, and hero. The ultimate war was a contest with death and when Christ said, "It is finished" on the cross, He declared victory over death, hell, and the grave. You are equipped to be used of God as one who protects by warding off attacks, calling for justice, and providing shelter. When God is all of this to you, you will be that vindication for others. Because of your faith in Jesus Christ, you will ever be aggressive towards the enemy's tools of defeat, failure, and victimization. Your ultimate purpose is to be one who stands in the gap (Ezekiel 22:30) as a defender of the weak. This includes those who are easily influenced, confused, quitters, faint, frail, fragile, and frightened. Your primary spiritual warfare will be that of brave intercession—reaching, meeting, and entreating God for His favor to set the captives free. Then you will "learn to do right! Seek justice, encourage the oppressed. Defend the cause of the fatherless, plead the case of the widow," Isaiah 1:17.

PHIL

Lover of horses; strong in spirit

Proverbs 24:5 *A wise man has great power, and a man of knowledge increases strength.*

Ephesians 6:10 *Finally, be strong in the Lord and in His mighty power.*

You are one who has an un-compromised commitment to righteousness, respectability, honesty, character, excellence, value, worth, kindness, innocence, generosity, trustworthiness, faithfulness, justice, hope, and love. You can do everything through Him who gives you strength (Philippians 4:11–13). The Lord is the source of your strength because you turn back the battle at the gate (Isaiah 28:6). You renew your strength by your hope being in the Lord (Isaiah 40:31). Jesus says, "My grace is sufficient for you, for My power is made perfect in weaknesses. Therefore you will boast all the more gladly about your weaknesses, so that Christ's power may rest on you. That is why for Christ's sake, you delight in weaknesses, in insults, in hardships, in persecutions, and in difficulties. For when you are weak, then you are strong," II Corinthians 12:9–10. You are clothed with strength and dignity (Proverbs 31:25).

PHILLIP

Lover of horses; strong in spirit

℘

Proverbs 24:5   *A wise man has great power, and a man of knowledge increases strength.*

Ephesians 6:10   *Finally, be strong in the Lord and in His mighty power.*

You are one who has an un-compromised commitment to righteousness, respectability, honesty, character, excellence, value, worth, kindness, innocence, generosity, trustworthiness, faithfulness, justice, hope, and love. You can do everything through Him who gives you strength (Philippians 4:11–13). The Lord is the source of your strength because you turn back the battle at the gate (Isaiah 28:6). You renew your strength by your hope being in the Lord (Isaiah 40:31). Jesus says, "My grace is sufficient for you, for My power is made perfect in weaknesses. Therefore you will boast all the more gladly about your weaknesses, so that Christ's power may rest on you. That is why for Christ's sake, you delight in weaknesses, in insults, in hardships, in persecutions, and in difficulties. For when you are weak, then you are strong," II Corinthians 12:9–10. You are clothed with strength and dignity (Proverbs 31:25).

PHYLLIS

Leaf; tenderhearted

ॐ

Job 14:7–9 *At least there is hope for a tree: if it is cut down, it will sprout again, and its new shoots will not fail. Its roots may grow old in the ground and its stump die in the soil, yet at the scent of water it will bud and put forth shoots like a plant.*

Ephesians 4:32 *Be kind and compassionate to one another, forgiving each other, just as in Christ God forgave you.*

The Lord has redeemed your life from the pit and has crowned you with love and compassion (Psalm 103:4). Like Christ, your root grew out of dry ground and into a tender shoot (Isaiah 53:2). Knowing the Lord is full of compassion and mercy energizes you to persevere to see what the Lord will bring to completion (James 5:11). This is accomplished through your tender heart of intercession (Psalm 51:1 and Psalm 79:8). You are the link between God as forgiver and the rejected, God as healer and the broken, and God as the tenderhearted responder and the hard-hearted. As God's "leaf," you represent when the flood is over (Genesis 8:11); the heart of obedience leading to prosperity (Psalm 1:3); a trust that never fears, worries, or fails to bear fruit (Jeremiah 17:8); healing for nations as you receive water from the sanctuary (Ezekiel 47:12 and Revelation 22:1–2). You are God's hand that delicately touches the hypersensitive areas of pain in the ruthless, bringing abundant life.

PIA

Devout; faithful

∾

Proverbs 2:7–8   *He holds victory in store for the upright, He is a shield to those whose walk is blameless, for He guards the course of the just and protects the way of His faithful ones.*

Psalm 15:1–5   *Lord, who may dwell in Your sanctuary? Who may live on Your holy hill? He whose walk is blameless and who does what is righteous, who speaks the truth from his heart and has no slander on his tongue, who does his neighbor no wrong and casts no slur on his fellow man, who despises a vile man but honors those who fear the Lord, who keeps his oath even when it hurts, who lends his money without usury and does not accept a bribe against the innocent. He who does these things will never be shaken.*

You are one who has made a commitment to God to be loyal, true, dependable, enduring, and steadfast. You unmask anything fake with the reality of God's Word. You are aggressive towards lies and deception to bring about truth. You are especially sensitive to betrayal, so that God can restore hope, security, purpose, and His faithfulness in those whom He has given you to serve. "Be faithful, even to the point of death, and I will give you a crown of life," Revelation 2:10. Anticipate the Master saying to you, "Well done, good and faithful servant! You have been faithful with a few things; I will put you in charge of many things. Come and share your Master's happiness!" (Matthew 25:21) "The one who calls you is faithful and he will do it," I Thessalonians 5:24.

POLLY

Little; dependent on God

&

Isaiah 60:22 *The least of you will become a thousand, the smallest a mighty nation. I am the Lord; in its time I will do this swiftly.*

II Corinthians 3:5 *Not that we are competent in ourselves to claim anything for ourselves, but our competence comes from God.*

The word "little" here has nothing to do with size, insignificance, unimportance, or narrow-mindedness. It does mean you are totally dependent on God, for without Him you can do nothing (John 15:5). This is expressed by relying and trusting in His control. As God increases and you decrease, God will use you to touch the lives of the helpless, immature, and weak. II Corinthians 12:9–10 says, "My grace is sufficient for you, for My power is made perfect in weakness. Therefore I will boast all the more gladly about my weaknesses, so that Christ's power may rest on me. That is why, for Christ's sake, I delight in weaknesses, in insults, in hardships, in persecutions, in difficulties. For when I am weak, then I am strong." Your humility admits weaknesses and releases strengths. As you are faithful over a little, God will make you ruler over much (Luke 19:17).

PRESTON

Priest's estate; consecrated one

❧

Romans 12:1   *Therefore, I urge you brothers, in view of God's mercy, to offer your bodies as living sacrifices, holy and pleasing to God—this is your spiritual act of worship.*

Philippians 3:7–8   *But whatever was to my profit I now consider loss for the sake of Christ. What is more, I consider everything a loss compared to the surpassing greatness of knowing Christ Jesus my Lord, for whose sake I have lost all things. I consider them rubbish, that I may gain Christ.*

Before you were born, God set you apart and appointed you as a prophet to the nations (Jeremiah 1:5). You are to be devoted irrevocably to the worship of God. He will pour out His anointing upon you as you are faithful to follow Him wholeheartedly (Psalm 119:34). You are one who has made a commitment to be loyal, true, dependable, enduring, and steadfast. You unmask anything fake with the reality of God's Word. You are aggressive towards lies and deception in order to bring about truth. You are especially sensitive to betrayal, so that God can restore hope, security, purpose, and His faithfulness in those whom He has given you to serve. Let your eyes keep to God's ways (Proverbs 23:26).

QUENTIN

Fifth; a manly heart

ℰℴ

Joshua 1:7 *Be strong and very courageous. Be careful to obey all the law My servant Moses gave you; do not turn from it to the right or to the left, that you may be successful wherever you go.*

Philippians 1:27b–28 *I will know that you stand firm in one spirit, contending as one man for the faith of the gospel without being frightened in any way by those who oppose you. This is a sign to them that they will be destroyed, but that you will be saved—and that by God.*

The brave are courageous, heroic, resolute, without dread, and bold. Cowards are fearful, timid, and fainthearted. They see victory in size rather than in faith. Running, hiding, escape mechanisms, and desertion are their game plan. They are dominated by the fear of man. You are dominated by your respectful fear of God. In stubborn faith, you say, "Nothing can hinder the Lord, nothing is impossible with Him." Your confidence lies in God's abiding presence and His great strength. God has mantled you as His encourager, invading strongholds of doubt and fear. Speak the Word of God boldly (Acts 4:31). The Lord trusts you to champion His cause by advancing the kingdom of heaven in all that you do.

QUINCY

Fifth; a manly heart

Joshua 1:7 *Be strong and very courageous. Be careful to obey all the law My servant Moses gave you; do not turn from it to the right or to the left, that you may be successful wherever you go.*

Philippians 1:27b–28 *I will know that you stand firm in one spirit, contending as one man for the faith of the gospel without being frightened in any way by those who oppose you. This is a sign to them that they will be destroyed, but that you will be saved—and that by God.*

The brave are courageous, heroic, resolute, without dread, and bold. Cowards are fearful, timid, and fainthearted. They see victory in size rather than in faith. Running, hiding, escape mechanisms, and desertion are their game plan. They are dominated by the fear of man. You are dominated by your respectful fear of God. In stubborn faith, you say, "Nothing can hinder the Lord, nothing is impossible with Him." Your confidence lies in God's abiding presence and His great strength. God has mantled you as His encourager, invading strongholds of doubt and fear. Speak the Word of God boldly (Acts 4:31). The Lord trusts you to champion His cause by advancing the kingdom of heaven in all that you do.

QUINN

Wise counselor; full of wisdom

ം

James 3:17 *But the wisdom that comes from heaven is first of all pure; then peace-loving, considerate, submissive, full of mercy and good fruit, impartial and sincere.*

Proverbs 9:10 *The fear of the Lord is the beginning of wisdom, and knowledge of the Holy One is understanding.*

You are a person of moral excellence. You exemplify right living put into practice. The Lord has not only equipped you with skills for living correctly, but also the ability to impart that to others. The Spirit of truth will guide you into all truth, allowing you to have insight into the true nature of things (John 16:13). Out of your reverential respect for the Lord, you have wisdom to give guidance and direction. You are a safe sounding board who steers those who are hungry for knowledge of the Holy One in the right direction. You need only to ask for the wisdom you lack, and God will give it to you generously (James 1:5). Having spiritual discernment is having the ability to separate the difference between God's wisdom and the world's and the ability to make the right choice—regardless. Luke 21:15 says, "For I will give you words and wisdom that none of your adversaries will be able to resist or contradict."

RACHEL

Little lamb; refreshing one

❧

Acts 3:19 *Repent, then, and turn to God, so that your sins may be wiped out, that times of refreshing may come from the Lord.*

II Timothy 1:16 *May the Lord show mercy to the household of Onesiphorus, because he often refreshed me and was not ashamed of my chains.*

You are one who restores strength because of knowing your own weakness. One who revives life because of dying to self. One who renews supply because of being emptied of self. One who reconciles offenses because your wisdom is from Christ. To bring this refreshing, you must know the all-sufficient one—El-Shaddai—in all your insufficiencies. As you learn to rest in His presence (Exodus 33:14), you will be a channel for His revival. Psalm 42:1–2 says, "As the deer pants for streams of water, so my soul pants for you, O God. My soul thirsts for God, for the living God. When can I go and meet with God?" To be His brook or His stream you must dwell in His stream. Stay thirsty for God's living water (John 7:37–38).

RAE

Wise; wise protector

&

Job 11:18   *You will be secure, because there is hope; you will look about you and take your rest in safety.*

Psalm 32:7   *You are my hiding place; You will protect me from trouble and surround me with songs of deliverance.*

Psalm 27:5   *For in the day of trouble He will keep me safe in His dwelling; He will hide me in the shelter of His tabernacle and set me high upon a rock.*

You are securely wrapped up and protected by Jesus Christ, who frees you from doubt and harm. Because you find your shelter, assurance, stability, and strength in your personal relationship with the Lord, you are kept in a safe place. You are confident that the Lord will fight for you; you need only be still (Exodus 14:14). As you stand firm on God's solid foundation (II Timothy 2:19) and stay hidden in the shadow of His wings (Psalm 61:4), you will provide deliverance for the weak, insecure, unsheltered, and frail. Instead of being defensive, you are a defender of injustice done to all mankind. You let discretion protect you (Proverbs 2:11). You will shield others from the enemy's destruction with love (I Corinthians 13:7) and the power of God's name (John 17:11). You display God's compassion through your humility. What you let him be in you, you will be to others.

RAILYN

Little lamb; refreshing one

&

Acts 3:19 *Repent, then, and turn to God, so that your sins may be wiped out, that times of refreshing may come from the Lord.*

II Timothy 1:16 *May the Lord show mercy to the household of Onesiphorus, because he often refreshed me and was not ashamed of my chains.*

You are one who restores strength because of knowing your own weakness. One who revives life because of dying to self. One who renews supply because of being emptied of self. One who reconciles offenses because your wisdom is from Christ. To bring this refreshing, you must know the all-sufficient one—El-Shaddai—in all your insufficiencies. As you learn to rest in His presence (Exodus 33:14), you will be a channel for His revival. Psalm 42:1–2 says, "As the deer pants for streams of water, so my soul pants for you, O God. My soul thirsts for God, for the living God. When can I go and meet with God?" To be His brook or His stream you must dwell in His stream. Stay thirsty for God's living water (John 7:37–38).

RALPH

Valiant; brave

Joshua 1:7 *Be strong and very courageous. Be careful to obey all the law My servant Moses gave you; do not turn from it to the right or to the left, that you may be successful wherever you go.*

Philippians 1:27b–28 *I will know that you stand firm in one spirit, contending as one man for the faith of the gospel without being frightened in any way by those who oppose you. This is a sign to them that they will be destroyed, but that you will be saved—and that by God.*

The brave are courageous, heroic, resolute, without dread, and bold. Cowards are fearful, timid, and fainthearted. They see victory in size rather than in faith. Running, hiding, escape mechanisms, and desertion are their game plan. They are dominated by the fear of man. You are dominated by your respectful fear of God. In stubborn faith, you say, "Nothing can hinder the Lord, nothing is impossible with Him." Your confidence lies in God's abiding presence and His great strength. God has mantled you as His encourager, invading strongholds of doubt and fear. Speak the Word of God boldly (Acts 4:31). The Lord trusts you to champion His cause by advancing the kingdom of heaven in all that you do.

RAMONA

Wise; wise protector

❧

Job 11:18 *You will be secure, because there is hope; you will look about you and take your rest in safety.*

Psalm 32:7 *You are my hiding place; You will protect me from trouble and surround me with songs of deliverance.*

Psalm 27:5 *For in the day of trouble He will keep me safe in His dwelling; He will hide me in the shelter of His tabernacle and set me high upon a rock.*

You are securely wrapped up and protected by Jesus Christ, who frees you from doubt and harm. Because you find your shelter, assurance, stability, and strength in your personal relationship with the Lord, you are kept in a safe place. You are confident that the Lord will fight for you; you need only be still (Exodus 14:14). As you stand firm on God's solid foundation (II Timothy 2:19) and stay hidden in the shadow of His wings (Psalm 61:4), you will provide deliverance for the weak, insecure, unsheltered, and frail. Instead of being defensive, you are a defender of injustice done to all mankind. You let discretion protect you (Proverbs 2:11). You will shield others from the enemy's destruction with love (I Corinthians 13:7) and the power of God's name (John 17:11). You display God's compassion through your humility. What you let him be in you, you will be to others.

RANDY

Shield-wolf; loyal one

❧

Romans 12:9–10 *Love must be sincere. Hate what is evil; cling to what is good. Be devoted to one another in brotherly love. Honor one another above yourselves.*

Proverbs 2:7–8 *He holds victory in store for the upright, He is a shield to those whose walk is blameless, for He guards the course of the just and protects the way of His faithful ones.*

As one with a loyal spirit, the Lord has called you to be faithful, devoted, obedient, dependable, and true. You are noble in disarming the enemy's attacks of fear, selfishness, failure, betrayal, dishonesty, and faithlessness. You are unyielding and have a resolute confidence in your commitment to God's Word. With it, you will help others overcome being cowards, losers, quitters, or betrayers. Knowing God's loyalty to you will strengthen your loyalty to others. Isaiah 1:17 says, "Learn to do right! Seek justice, encourage the oppressed. Defend the cause of the fatherless, plead the case of the widow."

RANGFU

Taking blessings to others; one who blesses

❧

Exodus 23:25 *Worship the Lord your God, and His blessing will be on your food and water. I will take away sickness from among you.*

Proverbs 10:22 *The blessing of the Lord brings wealth, and He adds no trouble to it.*

God has resourced you in order to give you great influence and favor. He commands His blessings where you establish unity (Psalm 133). He will turn every curse into a blessing for you because He loves you (Deuteronomy 23:5). True abundance is giving out of your nothingness, with a total dependence on God. Wealth is not in the amount you have, but in the attitude in which you give it. Because of your standard of integrity and gratitude, you have an eye for value, fruitfulness, and generosity. Your heart is for the poor, barren, and destitute, but you resist the lazy and stingy. You transfer God's possessions, power, and pleasure to others. Make wise investments of your time, energy, and resources that will keep reproducing rather than insuring your own personal gratification. You are blessed to be a blessing. The greater your obedience to the Lord, the greater will be His blessings (Deuteronomy 28:1–14).

RAQUEL

Little lamb; refreshing one

ℰℐ

Acts 3:19 *Repent, then, and turn to God, so that your sins may be wiped out, that times of refreshing may come from the Lord.*

II Timothy 1:16 *May the Lord show mercy to the household of Onesiphorus, because he often refreshed me and was not ashamed of my chains.*

You are one who restores strength because of knowing your own weakness. One who revives life because of dying to self. One who renews supply because of being emptied of self. One who reconciles offenses because your wisdom is from Christ. To bring this refreshing, you must know the all-sufficient one—El-Shaddai—in all your insufficiencies. As you learn to rest in His presence (Exodus 33:14), you will be a channel for His revival. Psalm 42:1–2 says, "As the deer pants for streams of water, so my soul pants for you, O God. My soul thirsts for God, for the living God. When can I go and meet with God?" To be His brook or His stream you must dwell in His stream. Stay thirsty for God's living water (John 7:37–38).

RAY

Wise; wise protector

❧

Job 11:18   *You will be secure, because there is hope; you will look about you and take your rest in safety.*

Psalm 32:7   *You are my hiding place; You will protect me from trouble and surround me with songs of deliverance.*

Psalm 27:5   *For in the day of trouble He will keep me safe in His dwelling; He will hide me in the shelter of His tabernacle and set me high upon a rock.*

You are securely wrapped up and protected by Jesus Christ, who frees you from doubt and harm. Because you find your shelter, assurance, stability, and strength in your personal relationship with the Lord, you are kept in a safe place. You are confident that the Lord will fight for you; you need only be still (Exodus 14:14). As you stand firm on God's solid foundation (II Timothy 2:19) and stay hidden in the shadow of His wings (Psalm 61:4), you will provide deliverance for the weak, insecure, unsheltered, and frail. Instead of being defensive, you are a defender of injustice done to all mankind. You let discretion protect you (Proverbs 2:11). You will shield others from the enemy's destruction with love (I Corinthians 13:7) and the power of God's name (John 17:11). You display God's compassion through your humility. What you let him be in you, you will be to others.

RAYMOND

Wise; wise protector

Job 11:18   *You will be secure, because there is hope; you will look about you and take your rest in safety.*

Psalm 32:7   *You are my hiding place; You will protect me from trouble and surround me with songs of deliverance.*

Psalm 27:5   *For in the day of trouble He will keep me safe in His dwelling; He will hide me in the shelter of His tabernacle and set me high upon a rock.*

You are securely wrapped up and protected by Jesus Christ, who frees you from doubt and harm. Because you find your shelter, assurance, stability, and strength in your personal relationship with the Lord, you are kept in a safe place. You are confident that the Lord will fight for you; you need only be still (Exodus 14:14). As you stand firm on God's solid foundation (II Timothy 2:19) and stay hidden in the shadow of His wings (Psalm 61:4), you will provide deliverance for the weak, insecure, unsheltered, and frail. Instead of being defensive, you are a defender of injustice done to all mankind. You let discretion protect you (Proverbs 2:11). You will shield others from the enemy's destruction with love (I Corinthians 13:7) and the power of God's name (John 17:11). You display God's compassion through your humility. What you let him be in you, you will be to others.

REAGAN

Little king; man of distinction

&

I Kings 3:9 *So give Your servant a discerning heart to govern Your people and to distinguish between right and wrong. For who is able to govern this great people of Yours?*

Hebrews 5:14 *But solid food is for the mature, who by constant use have trained themselves to distinguish good from evil.*

The sense of smell is the strongest of the five senses. In scripture it is equaled to discernment. It is marked by perception, justice, and insight, along with the ability to investigate and examine based on the absolute truth of scripture. Distinction is defined by the act of noticing differences, discretion, sensitivity, and the ability to distinguish good from evil. You are one who takes the crooked, dishonest corruptions of life and gives clear direction on God's straight path, from pollution to purpose. God has equipped you to remove the obstacles of dullness, indifference, and insignificance. He uses you as His shelter from the wind, His refuge from the storm, His streams of water in the desert, and His great rock in a thirsty land (Isaiah 32:1–8). This brings hearing to the deaf, sight to the blind, and understanding to the mind. This discernment will require disciplining your mind to be set on what the Spirit desires, which is justice and freedom. Stay away from what the carnal nature desires, which is judgment and criticism. You live His life, not yours. You think His thoughts, not yours. You speak His words, not yours. Intimacy with the Lord in His Word and in prayer will prevent you from being offended by the "crooked," so that your focus will be on how He discerns. He is the ultimate man of distinction.

REBA

Yoke; earnest devotee

༄

Psalm 63:1, 5, 8 *My soul thirsts for You. My soul will be satisfied. My soul clings to you.*

I Corinthians 15:58 *Therefore, my dear brothers, stand firm. Let nothing move you. Always give yourselves fully to the work of the Lord, because you know that your labor is not in vain.*

Your very being lives to be in constant harmony with your Creator; that both of your hearts beat as one. Therefore, you are continually yielding every area to the likeness of Christ with strong discipline. You have a devoted allegiance to Christ and his teachings. Your character is one of devotion, dedication, consecration, loyalty, and faithfulness. You are called to help the fallen take a stand, and to remove shame and fear. You dispel division by bringing the very unity of God. As you seek and trust in Him with all your heart, leaning not to your own understanding, He will protect you from being blind-sided by the enemy of your soul. Be known as one who loves God with all your heart, soul, mind, and strength.

REBECCA

Yoke; earnest devotee

ॐ

Psalm 63:1, 5, 8   *My soul thirsts for You. My soul will be satisfied. My soul clings to you.*

I Corinthians 15:58   *Therefore, my dear brothers, stand firm. Let nothing move you. Always give yourselves fully to the work of the Lord, because you know that your labor is not in vain.*

Your very being lives to be in constant harmony with your Creator; that both of your hearts beat as one. Therefore, you are continually yielding every area to the likeness of Christ with strong discipline. You have a devoted allegiance to Christ and his teachings. Your character is one of devotion, dedication, consecration, loyalty, and faithfulness. You are called to help the fallen take a stand, and to remove shame and fear. You dispel division by bringing the very unity of God. As you seek and trust in Him with all your heart, leaning not to your own understanding, He will protect you from being blindsided by the enemy of your soul. Be known as one who loves God with all your heart, soul, mind, and strength.

REBEKAH

Yoke; earnest devotee

Psalm 63:1, 5, 8   *My soul thirsts for You. My soul will be satisfied. My soul clings to you.*

I Corinthians 15:58   *Therefore, my dear brothers, stand firm. Let nothing move you. Always give yourselves fully to the work of the Lord, because you know that your labor is not in vain.*

Your very being lives to be in constant harmony with your Creator; that both of your hearts beat as one. Therefore, you are continually yielding every area to the likeness of Christ with strong discipline. You have a devoted allegiance to Christ and his teachings. Your character is one of devotion, dedication, consecration, loyalty, and faithfulness. You are called to help the fallen take a stand, and to remove shame and fear. You dispel division by bringing the very unity of God. As you seek and trust in Him with all your heart, leaning not to your own understanding, He will protect you from being blindsided by the enemy of your soul. Be known as one who loves God with all your heart, soul, mind, and strength.

REED

Red; courageous

๛

Deuteronomy 31:6 *Be strong and courageous. Do not be afraid or terrified because of them, for the Lord your God goes with you; He will never leave you nor forsake you.*

Joshua 1:7 *Be strong and very courageous. Be careful to obey all the law My servant Moses gave you; do not turn from it to the right or to the left, that you may be successful wherever you go.*

You are equipped with mental and moral strength to venture, persevere, and withstand danger, fear, and difficulty. You have the firmness of mind to take a firm stand. You meet strain with fortitude and resilience, even when opposed or threatened. You have firm determination to achieve God's purpose in your life. With stubborn persistence and unwillingness to admit defeat, you base all victory on the finished work of the cross of Jesus. The Victor will use you to remove obstacles and invade darkness and death in order to bring the lost to a decision for Jesus. God's divine presence in and through you will bind fear and lead people to their God-given inheritance.

REGGIE

Mighty advisor; wisdom

❧

James 3:17 *But the wisdom that comes from heaven is first of all pure; then peace-loving, considerate, submissive, full of mercy and good fruit, impartial and sincere.*

Proverbs 9:10 *The fear of the Lord is the beginning of wisdom, and knowledge of the Holy One is understanding.*

You are a person of moral excellence. You exemplify right living put into practice. The Lord has not only equipped you with skills for living correctly, but also the ability to impart that to others. The Spirit of truth will guide you into all truth, allowing you to have insight into the true nature of things (John 16:13). Out of your reverential respect for the Lord, you have wisdom to give guidance and direction. You are a safe sounding board who steers those who are hungry for knowledge of the Holy One in the right direction. You need only to ask for the wisdom you lack, and God will give it to you generously (James 1:5). Having spiritual discernment is having the ability to separate the difference between God's wisdom and the world's and the ability to make the right choice—regardless. Luke 21:15 says, "For I will give you words and wisdom that none of your adversaries will be able to resist or contradict."

REGINA

Might advisor; wisdom

✌

James 3:17   *But the wisdom that comes from heaven is first of all pure; then peace-loving, considerate, submissive, full of mercy and good fruit, impartial and sincere.*

Proverbs 9:10   *The fear of the Lord is the beginning of wisdom, and knowledge of the Holy One is understanding.*

You are a person of moral excellence. You exemplify right living put into practice. The Lord has not only equipped you with skills for living correctly, but also the ability to impart that to others. The Spirit of truth will guide you into all truth, allowing you to have insight into the true nature of things (John 16:13). Out of your reverential respect for the Lord, you have wisdom to give guidance and direction. You are a safe sounding board who steers those who are hungry for knowledge of the Holy One in the right direction. You need only to ask for the wisdom you lack, and God will give it to you generously (James 1:5). Having spiritual discernment is having the ability to separate the difference between God's wisdom and the world's and the ability to make the right choice—regardless. Luke 21:15 says, "For I will give you words and wisdom that none of your adversaries will be able to resist or contradict."

REID

Red; courageous

৶

Deuteronomy 31:6 *Be strong and courageous. Do not be afraid or terrified because of them, for the Lord your God goes with you; He will never leave you nor forsake you.*

Joshua 1:7 *Be strong and very courageous. Be careful to obey all the law My servant Moses gave you; do not turn from it to the right or to the left, that you may be successful wherever you go.*

You are equipped with mental and moral strength to venture, persevere, and withstand danger, fear, and difficulty. You have the firmness of mind to take a firm stand. You meet strain with fortitude and resilience, even when opposed or threatened. You have firm determination to achieve God's purpose in your life. With stubborn persistence and unwillingness to admit defeat, you base all victory on the finished work of the cross of Jesus. The Victor will use you to remove obstacles and invade darkness and death in order to bring the lost to a decision for Jesus. God's divine presence in and through you will bind fear and lead people to their God-given inheritance.

RENEE

Born again; born anew

∞

John 3:3 *In reply Jesus declared, "I tell you the truth, no one can see the kingdom of God unless he is born again".*

I Peter 1:23 *For you have been born again, not of perishable seed, but of imperishable, through the living and enduring word of God.*

By faith you have confessed with your mouth that Jesus is Lord and that God raised Him from the dead (Romans 10:9–10). You have chosen to get rid of sin and live in God's forgiveness, get rid of filth and live in His holiness, to say no to ungodliness and worldly passions and to say yes to righteous living (Titus 2:12). Your heart is set on things above because you have been raised with Christ in newness of life (Colossians 3:1). The way you know that you have passed from death to life is that you love unconditionally (I John 4:7). There is no pit so deep that you would not reach to bridge those dying in sin to God's grace. You release forgiveness for condemnation, light for darkness, sight for blindness, life for death, redemption for offenses, and pardon for sin. The same Spirit who raised Jesus from the dead lives in you. He releases through you His resurrection power to win the lost (Romans 8:11). Through your testimony, they will renounce the ways of the world and put on their new self, which is created to be like God (Ephesians 4:22–24 and Colossians 3:10). You are to teach everyone how to call on the name of the Lord so that they will be saved (Acts 2:21). The promise in your name extends to your whole family (Acts 16:31). May you never boast except in the cross of your Lord Jesus Christ, through which the world has been crucified to you and you to the world (Galatians 6:14–15). What really counts is being a new creation.

RESSIE

Reaper; industrious

Colossians 1:16 *For by Him all things were created: things in heaven and on earth, visible and invisible, whether thrones or powers or rulers or authorities; all things were created by Him and for Him.*

Ephesians 2:10 *For we are God's workmanship, created in Christ Jesus to do good works, which God prepared in advance for us to do.*

To be industrious means to be skillful, hardworking, zealous, and diligent. By persevering, you give careful attention to detail. There is not a lazy bone in your body. Through you the Lord will originate. How you deal with the past determines your future. Regardless of the curses or blessings, the failures or successes, you are God's platform for a "new thing." You cannot lean on your own understanding or reasoning. God Almighty created the heavens, the earth, and you in His image. So the more completely dependent you become on your Creator, the more productive your life will be for Him! I Peter 4:19, "So then, those who suffer according to God's will should commit themselves to their Creator and continue to do good."

REUBEN

Behold a son; favored son

∞

Exodus 33:13 *If you are pleased with me, teach me Your ways so I may know You and continue to find favor with You. Remember that this nation is Your people.*

Proverbs 3:3–4 *Let love and faithfulness never leave you; bind them around your neck, write them on the tablet of your heart. Then you win favor and a good name in the sight of God and man.*

Proverbs 16:15 says, "When a king's face brightens, it means life; his favor is like a rain cloud in spring." The key to favor is your commitment to God's love and faithfulness—always being aware that you are nothing without Him. But with Him, you are everything. As you daily wait on Him, abundant life is yours (Proverbs 8:34–35). As with Esther, you will have entrance to those in authority over you to be endued with power and resources. As your ways please the Lord, He will make even your enemies live at peace with you (Proverbs 16:7). The knowledge of God's approval keeps you focused on speaking the Word of God with authority, wherein you are not pleasing man, but God (I Thessalonians 2:4). You are energized and strengthened in your affirming of others—in doing good (Hebrews 13:16). The security you have as God's child gives you a willingness to contribute to the success and welfare of others, with no jealousy or partiality, but with humility, meekness, and gentleness.

RHONDA

Grand; strength of character

Proverbs 24:5 *A wise man has great power, and a man of knowledge increases strength.*

Ephesians 6:10 *Finally, be strong in the Lord and in His mighty power.*

You are one who has an un-compromised commitment to righteousness, respectability, honesty, character, excellence, value, worth, kindness, innocence, generosity, trustworthiness, faithfulness, justice, hope, and love. You can do everything through Him who gives you strength (Philippians 4:11–13). The Lord is the source of your strength because you turn back the battle at the gate (Isaiah 28:6). You renew your strength by your hope being in the Lord (Isaiah 40:31). Jesus says, "My grace is sufficient for you, for My power is made perfect in weaknesses. Therefore you will boast all the more gladly about your weaknesses, so that Christ's power may rest on you. That is why for Christ's sake, you delight in weaknesses, in insults, in hardships, in persecutions, and in difficulties. For when you are weak, then you are strong," II Corinthians 12:9–10. You are clothed with strength and dignity (Proverbs 31:25).

RICHARD

Powerful ruler; brave

∞

Deuteronomy 28:13 *The Lord will make you the head, not the tail. If you pay attention to the commands of the Lord your God that I give you this day and carefully follow them, you will always be at the top, never at the bottom.*

Mark 10:43–45 *...Whoever wants to become great among you must be your servant, and whoever wants to be first must be slave of all. For even the Son of Man did not come to be served, but to serve, and to give His life as a ransom for many.*

You have been set apart with vision and perspective to reproduce the likeness of Christ in others by reflecting His image. You are guided by principles and values worth dying for. You know how to balance transparency with being an example. You are one who is secure enough to be vulnerable. You do not lead to gather followers; you lead to develop leaders. You lead by honoring God with authority, influence, direction, foresight, and skill. Your credible choices set a precedence for favor. You earn trust by your willingness to confront and bring discipline in a Godly manner. You are strong enough to let your "yes" be "yes" and your "no" be "no," with no compromise or jealousy. Your strength is determined by your submitted and teachable servant's heart. The more you mature, the more humble, gentle, and meek you will become. With integrity you communicate love, affirmation, nurturing, and spiritual care. If you as a shepherd ever forget what it is like to be a sheep, you will become a hireling. Your highest aim is to honor and glorify God.

RICHARDSON

Powerful ruler; brave

&

Deuteronomy 28:13 *The Lord will make you the head, not the tail. If you pay attention to the commands of the Lord your God that I give you this day and carefully follow them, you will always be at the top, never at the bottom.*

Mark 10:43–45 *...Whoever wants to become great among you must be your servant, and whoever wants to be first must be slave of all. For even the Son of Man did not come to be served, but to serve, and to give His life as a ransom for many.*

You have been set apart with vision and perspective to reproduce the likeness of Christ in others by reflecting His image. You are guided by principles and values worth dying for. You know how to balance transparency with being an example. You are one who is secure enough to be vulnerable. You do not lead to gather followers; you lead to develop leaders. You lead by honoring God with authority, influence, direction, foresight, and skill. Your credible choices set a precedence for favor. You earn trust by your willingness to confront and bring discipline in a Godly manner. You are strong enough to let your "yes" be "yes" and your "no" be "no," with no compromise or jealousy. Your strength is determined by your submitted and teachable servant's heart. The more you mature, the more humble, gentle, and meek you will become. With integrity you communicate love, affirmation, nurturing, and spiritual care. If you as a shepherd ever forget what it is like to be a sheep, you will become a hireling. Your highest aim is to honor and glorify God.

RICHIE

Powerful ruler; brave

Deuteronomy 28:13 *The Lord will make you the head, not the tail. If you pay attention to the commands of the Lord your God that I give you this day and carefully follow them, you will always be at the top, never at the bottom.*

Mark 10:43–45 *...Whoever wants to become great among you must be your servant, and whoever wants to be first must be slave of all. For even the Son of Man did not come to be served, but to serve, and to give His life as a ransom for many.*

You have been set apart with vision and perspective to reproduce the likeness of Christ in others by reflecting His image. You are guided by principles and values worth dying for. You know how to balance transparency with being an example. You are one who is secure enough to be vulnerable. You do not lead to gather followers; you lead to develop leaders. You lead by honoring God with authority, influence, direction, foresight, and skill. Your credible choices set a precedence for favor. You earn trust by your willingness to confront and bring discipline in a Godly manner. You are strong enough to let your "yes" be "yes" and your "no" be "no," with no compromise or jealousy. Your strength is determined by your submitted and teachable servant's heart. The more you mature, the more humble, gentle, and meek you will become. With integrity you communicate love, affirmation, nurturing, and spiritual care. If you as a shepherd ever forget what it is like to be a sheep, you will become a hireling. Your highest aim is to honor and glorify God.

RICK

Powerful ruler; brave

❧

Deuteronomy 28:13 *The Lord will make you the head, not the tail. If you pay attention to the commands of the Lord your God that I give you this day and carefully follow them, you will always be at the top, never at the bottom.*

Mark 10:43–45 *...Whoever wants to become great among you must be your servant, and whoever wants to be first must be slave of all. For even the Son of Man did not come to be served, but to serve, and to give His life as a ransom for many.*

You have been set apart with vision and perspective to reproduce the likeness of Christ in others by reflecting His image. You are guided by principles and values worth dying for. You know how to balance transparency with being an example. You are one who is secure enough to be vulnerable. You do not lead to gather followers; you lead to develop leaders. You lead by honoring God with authority, influence, direction, foresight, and skill. Your credible choices set a precedence for favor. You earn trust by your willingness to confront and bring discipline in a Godly manner. You are strong enough to let your "yes" be "yes" and your "no" be "no," with no compromise or jealousy. Your strength is determined by your submitted and teachable servant's heart. The more you mature, the more humble, gentle, and meek you will become. With integrity you communicate love, affirmation, nurturing, and spiritual care. If you as a shepherd ever forget what it is like to be a sheep, you will become a hireling. Your highest aim is to honor and glorify God.

RILEY

Valiant; brave

⟪⟫

Joshua 1:7 *Be strong and very courageous. Be careful to obey all the law My servant Moses gave you; do not turn from it to the right or to the left, that you may be successful wherever you go.*

Philippians 1:27b–28 *I will know that you stand firm in one spirit, contending as one man for the faith of the gospel without being frightened in any way by those who oppose you. This is a sign to them that they will be destroyed, but that you will be saved—and that by God.*

The brave are courageous, heroic, resolute, without dread, and bold. Cowards are fearful, timid, and fainthearted. They see victory in size rather than in faith. Running, hiding, escape mechanisms, and desertion are their game plan. They are dominated by the fear of man. You are dominated by your respectful fear of God. In stubborn faith, you say, "Nothing can hinder the Lord, nothing is impossible with Him." Your confidence lies in God's abiding presence and His great strength. God has mantled you as His encourager, invading strongholds of doubt and fear. Speak the Word of God boldly (Acts 4:31). The Lord trusts you to champion His cause by advancing the kingdom of heaven in all that you do.

RITA

Pearl; gem of purity

I Timothy 5:22 *...do not share in the sins of others. Keep yourself pure.*

I Peter 1:22 *Now that you have purified yourselves by obeying the truth so that you have sincere love for your brothers, love one another deeply, from the heart.*

Through the process of heat, trials, and refinement, purity is established. Your nature defies being stubborn, judgmental, and haughty. The commandment of the Lord is clear—giving insight to life (Psalm 19:8). You bring wholeness to the dirty, defiled, contaminated, polluted, double-minded, and raped. Your willingness to be transparent is the venue through which He makes His Word clear, simple, and unadulterated. Your choice to be pure enables you to see God (Matthew 5:8) and to know Him as King and Friend (Proverbs 22:11). It also allows your words to be pleasant (Proverbs 15:26) and causes you to ascend to the holy place of the Lord, where you receive blessings and righteousness from the God of salvation (Psalm 24:3–5). Proverbs 20:11 says, "Even a child is known by his actions, by whether his conduct is pure and right."

ROB

Shining with fame; excellent worth

❧

II Corinthians 8:7 *But just as you excel in everything—in faith, in speech, in knowledge, in complete earnestness and in your love for us—see that you also excel in this grace of giving.*

Philippians 4:8 *Finally, brothers, whatever is true, whatever is noble, whatever is right, whatever is pure, whatever is lovely, whatever is admirable—if anything is excellent or praiseworthy—think about such things.*

Excellent worth is comprised in your worship of God. Revelation 5:12 says, "Worthy is the Lamb, who was slain, to receive power and wealth and wisdom and strength and honor and glory and praise!" "All this also comes from the Lord Almighty, wonderful in counsel and magnificent in wisdom," Isaiah 28:29. God has given you an eye for quality, demonstrating His excellence of character and conduct. You go beyond human capacity with faith that transcends all understanding. Your faith is of greater worth than gold (I Peter 1:7). In quality, skill, and achievement, you go the extra mile. This is all about giving, not getting; serving, not controlling. Perfectionism leads to legalism. Excellence releases freedom. You are to show the insignificant and the wasted the more excellent way of God's love (I Corinthians 12:31 and chapter 13) and kindness (2 Peter 1:5–7). You are to excel in gifts that build up the church (I Corinthians 14:12). God uses you to restore genuine value, purpose, and productivity. Devoting yourself to doing what is good will lead to what is excellent and profitable for everyone (Titus 3:8). Your gentle and quiet spirit is of great worth in God's eyes (I Peter 3:4).

ROBERT

Shining with fame; excellent worth

&

II Corinthians 8:7 *But just as you excel in everything—in faith, in speech, in knowledge, in complete earnestness and in your love for us—see that you also excel in this grace of giving.*

Philippians 4:8 *Finally, brothers, whatever is true, whatever is noble, whatever is right, whatever is pure, whatever is lovely, whatever is admirable—if anything is excellent or praiseworthy—think about such things.*

Excellent worth is comprised in your worship of God. Revelation 5:12 says, "Worthy is the Lamb, who was slain, to receive power and wealth and wisdom and strength and honor and glory and praise!" "All this also comes from the Lord Almighty, wonderful in counsel and magnificent in wisdom," Isaiah 28:29. God has given you an eye for quality, demonstrating His excellence of character and conduct. You go beyond human capacity with faith that transcends all understanding. Your faith is of greater worth than gold (I Peter 1:7). In quality, skill, and achievement, you go the extra mile. This is all about giving, not getting; serving, not controlling. Perfectionism leads to legalism. Excellence releases freedom. You are to show the insignificant and the wasted the more excellent way of God's love (I Corinthians 12:31 and chapter 13) and kindness (2 Peter 1:5-7). You are to excel in gifts that build up the church (I Corinthians 14:12). God uses you to restore genuine value, purpose, and productivity. Devoting yourself to doing what is good will lead to what is excellent and profitable for everyone (Titus 3:8). Your gentle and quiet spirit is of great worth in God's eyes (I Peter 3:4).

ROBERTA

Shining with fame; excellent worth

&

II Corinthians 8:7 *But just as you excel in everything—in faith, in speech, in knowledge, in complete earnestness and in your love for us—see that you also excel in this grace of giving.*

Philippians 4:8 *Finally, brothers, whatever is true, whatever is noble, whatever is right, whatever is pure, whatever is lovely, whatever is admirable—if anything is excellent or praiseworthy—think about such things.*

Excellent worth is comprised in your worship of God. Revelation 5:12 says, "Worthy is the Lamb, who was slain, to receive power and wealth and wisdom and strength and honor and glory and praise!" "All this also comes from the Lord Almighty, wonderful in counsel and magnificent in wisdom," Isaiah 28:29. God has given you an eye for quality, demonstrating His excellence of character and conduct. You go beyond human capacity with faith that transcends all understanding. Your faith is of greater worth than gold (I Peter 1:7). In quality, skill, and achievement, you go the extra mile. This is all about giving, not getting; serving, not controlling. Perfectionism leads to legalism. Excellence releases freedom. You are to show the insignificant and the wasted the more excellent way of God's love (I Corinthians 12:31 and chapter 13) and kindness (2 Peter 1:5–7). You are to excel in gifts that build up the church (I Corinthians 14:12). God uses you to restore genuine value, purpose, and productivity. Devoting yourself to doing what is good will lead to what is excellent and profitable for everyone (Titus 3:8). Your gentle and quiet spirit is of great worth in God's eyes (I Peter 3:4).

ROBIN

Shining with fame; strength of character

❦

II Corinthians 8:7 *But just as you excel in everything—in faith, in speech, in knowledge, in complete earnestness and in your love for us—see that you also excel in this grace of giving.*

Philippians 4:8 *Finally, brothers, whatever is true, whatever is noble, whatever is right, whatever is pure, whatever is lovely, whatever is admirable—if anything is excellent or praiseworthy—think about such things.*

Excellent worth is comprised in your worship of God. Revelation 5:12 says, "Worthy is the Lamb, who was slain, to receive power and wealth and wisdom and strength and honor and glory and praise!" "All this also comes from the Lord Almighty, wonderful in counsel and magnificent in wisdom," Isaiah 28:29. God has given you an eye for quality, demonstrating His excellence of character and conduct. You go beyond human capacity with faith that transcends all understanding. Your faith is of greater worth than gold (I Peter 1:7). In quality, skill, and achievement, you go the extra mile. This is all about giving, not getting; serving, not controlling. Perfectionism leads to legalism. Excellence releases freedom. You are to show the insignificant and the wasted the more excellent way of God's love (I Corinthians 12:31 and chapter 13) and kindness (2 Peter 1:5-7). You are to excel in gifts that build up the church (I Corinthians 14:12). God uses you to restore genuine value, purpose, and productivity. Devoting yourself to doing what is good will lead to what is excellent and profitable for everyone (Titus 3:8). Your gentle and quiet spirit is of great worth in God's eyes (I Peter 3:4).

ROD

Famous ruler; esteemed one

&

Proverbs 22:1 *A good name is more desirable than great riches; to be esteemed is better than silver or gold.*

Hebrews 11:26 *He regarded disgrace for the sake of Christ as of greater value than the treasures of Egypt, because he was looking ahead to his reward.*

Your life is to reflect the very nature of God. It is holy, righteous, just, pure, spotless, faithful, and divine. Out of a humble, reverent heart you will ever be esteemed and prized by the Lord as you show Him respect, adoration, and praise. You will have no reason to be insecure in who you are in the Lord. Nor will you ever place blame on God or disapprove of His will for your life. You hold in highest regard and love those who minister to you (I Thessalonians 4:12–13). You do nothing out of selfish ambition or vain conceit, but in humility consider others better than yourself (Philippians 2:3).

RODNEY

Famous ruler; esteemed one

ℰ℈

Proverbs 22:1 *A good name is more desirable than great riches; to be esteemed is better than silver or gold.*

Hebrews 11:26 *He regarded disgrace for the sake of Christ as of greater value than the treasures of Egypt, because he was looking ahead to his reward.*

Your life is to reflect the very nature of God. It is holy, righteous, just, pure, spotless, faithful, and divine. Out of a humble, reverent heart you will ever be esteemed and prized by the Lord as you show Him respect, adoration, and praise. You will have no reason to be insecure in who you are in the Lord. Nor will you ever place blame on God or disapprove of His will for your life. You hold in highest regard and love those who minister to you (I Thessalonians 4:12–13). You do nothing out of selfish ambition or vain conceit, but in humility consider others better than yourself (Philippians 2:3).

ROGER

Famous spear man; God's warrior

დ

II Chronicles 32:7-8 *There is a greater power with us than with him. With him is only the arm of flesh, but with us is the Lord our God to help us and to fight our battles.*

II Timothy 2:3-4 *Endure hardship with us like a good soldier of Christ Jesus. No one serving as a soldier gets involved in civilian affairs - he wants to please his commanding officer.*

Exodus 14:14 says, "The Lord will fight for you; you need only be still." You are armed with the ability to handle the spear and shield—to stand on God's Word by faith, supporting the King of kings against His enemies. As God's defending warrior, you are His example of a brave champion, soldier, and hero. The ultimate war was a contest with death and when Christ said, "It is finished" on the cross, He declared victory over death, hell, and the grave. You are equipped to be used of God as one who protects by warding off attacks, calling for justice, and providing shelter. When God is all of this to you, you will be that vindication for others. Because of your faith in Jesus Christ, you will ever be aggressive towards the enemy's tools of defeat, failure, and victimization. Your ultimate purpose is to be one who stands in the gap (Ezekiel 22:30) as a defender of the weak. This includes those who are easily influenced, confused, quitters, faint, frail, fragile, and frightened. Your primary spiritual warfare will be that of brave intercession—reaching, meeting, and entreating God for His favor to set the captives free. Then you will "learn to do right! Seek justice, encourage the oppressed. Defend the cause of the fatherless, plead the case of the widow," Isaiah 1:17.

ROLF

Fame-wolf; strong, manly

&

Proverbs 24:5 *A wise man has great power, and a man of knowledge increases strength.*

Ephesians 6:10 *Finally, be strong in the Lord and in His mighty power.*

You are one who has an un-compromised commitment to righteousness, respectability, honesty, character, excellence, value, worth, kindness, innocence, generosity, trustworthiness, faithfulness, justice, hope, and love. You can do everything through Him who gives you strength (Philippians 4:11–13). The Lord is the source of your strength because you turn back the battle at the gate (Isaiah 28:6). You renew your strength by your hope being in the Lord (Isaiah 40:31). Jesus says, "My grace is sufficient for you, for My power is made perfect in weaknesses. Therefore you will boast all the more gladly about your weaknesses, so that Christ's power may rest on you. That is why for Christ's sake, you delight in weaknesses, in insults, in hardships, in persecutions, and in difficulties. For when you are weak, then you are strong," II Corinthians 12:9–10. You are clothed with strength and dignity (Proverbs 31:25).

RON

Mighty power; strong one

൬

Proverbs 24:5 *A wise man has great power, and a man of knowledge increases strength.*

Ephesians 6:10 *Finally, be strong in the Lord and in His mighty power.*

You are one who has an un-compromised commitment to righteousness, respectability, honesty, character, excellence, value, worth, kindness, innocence, generosity, trustworthiness, faithfulness, justice, hope, and love. You can do everything through Him who gives you strength (Philippians 4:11–13). The Lord is the source of your strength because you turn back the battle at the gate (Isaiah 28:6). You renew your strength by your hope being in the Lord (Isaiah 40:31). Jesus says, "My grace is sufficient for you, for My power is made perfect in weaknesses. Therefore you will boast all the more gladly about your weaknesses, so that Christ's power may rest on you. That is why for Christ's sake, you delight in weaknesses, in insults, in hardships, in persecutions, and in difficulties. For when you are weak, then you are strong," II Corinthians 12:9–10. You are clothed with strength and dignity (Proverbs 31:25).

RONALD

Mighty power; strong one

❧

Proverbs 24:5 *A wise man has great power, and a man of knowledge increases strength.*

Ephesians 6:10 *Finally, be strong in the Lord and in His mighty power.*

You are one who has an un-compromised commitment to righteousness, respectability, honesty, character, excellence, value, worth, kindness, innocence, generosity, trustworthiness, faithfulness, justice, hope, and love. You can do everything through Him who gives you strength (Philippians 4:11–13). The Lord is the source of your strength because you turn back the battle at the gate (Isaiah 28:6). You renew your strength by your hope being in the Lord (Isaiah 40:31). Jesus says, "My grace is sufficient for you, for My power is made perfect in weaknesses. Therefore you will boast all the more gladly about your weaknesses, so that Christ's power may rest on you. That is why for Christ's sake, you delight in weaknesses, in insults, in hardships, in persecutions, and in difficulties. For when you are weak, then you are strong," II Corinthians 12:9–10. You are clothed with strength and dignity (Proverbs 31:25).

RONDA

Grand; strength of character

℘

Proverbs 24:5 *A wise man has great power, and a man of knowledge increases strength.*

Ephesians 6:10 *Finally, be strong in the Lord and in His mighty power.*

You are one who has an un-compromised commitment to righteousness, respectability, honesty, character, excellence, value, worth, kindness, innocence, generosity, trustworthiness, faithfulness, justice, hope, and love. You can do everything through Him who gives you strength (Philippians 4:11–13). The Lord is the source of your strength because you turn back the battle at the gate (Isaiah 28:6). You renew your strength by your hope being in the Lord (Isaiah 40:31). Jesus says, "My grace is sufficient for you, for My power is made perfect in weaknesses. Therefore you will boast all the more gladly about your weaknesses, so that Christ's power may rest on you. That is why for Christ's sake, you delight in weaknesses, in insults, in hardships, in persecutions, and in difficulties. For when you are weak, then you are strong," II Corinthians 12:9–10. You are clothed with strength and dignity (Proverbs 31:25).

RONNI

Mighty power; strong one

&

Proverbs 24:5 *A wise man has great power, and a man of knowledge increases strength.*

Ephesians 6:10 *Finally, be strong in the Lord and in His mighty power.*

You are one who has an un-compromised commitment to righteousness, respectability, honesty, character, excellence, value, worth, kindness, innocence, generosity, trustworthiness, faithfulness, justice, hope, and love. You can do everything through Him who gives you strength (Philippians 4:11–13). The Lord is the source of your strength because you turn back the battle at the gate (Isaiah 28:6). You renew your strength by your hope being in the Lord (Isaiah 40:31). Jesus says, "My grace is sufficient for you, for My power is made perfect in weaknesses. Therefore you will boast all the more gladly about your weaknesses, so that Christ's power may rest on you. That is why for Christ's sake, you delight in weaknesses, in insults, in hardships, in persecutions, and in difficulties. For when you are weak, then you are strong," II Corinthians 12:9–10. You are clothed with strength and dignity (Proverbs 31:25).

RONNIE

Mighty power; strong one

ಐ

Proverbs 24:5 *A wise man has great power, and a man of knowledge increases strength.*

Ephesians 6:10 *Finally, be strong in the Lord and in His mighty power.*

You are one who has an un-compromised commitment to righteousness, respectability, honesty, character, excellence, value, worth, kindness, innocence, generosity, trustworthiness, faithfulness, justice, hope, and love. You can do everything through Him who gives you strength (Philippians 4:11–13). The Lord is the source of your strength because you turn back the battle at the gate (Isaiah 28:6). You renew your strength by your hope being in the Lord (Isaiah 40:31). Jesus says, "My grace is sufficient for you, for My power is made perfect in weaknesses. Therefore you will boast all the more gladly about your weaknesses, so that Christ's power may rest on you. That is why for Christ's sake, you delight in weaknesses, in insults, in hardships, in persecutions, and in difficulties. For when you are weak, then you are strong," II Corinthians 12:9–10. You are clothed with strength and dignity (Proverbs 31:25).

ROSANNE

A rose; giver of love

༒

John 3:16   *For God so loved the world that He gave His one and only Son, that whoever believes in Him shall not perish but have everlasting life.*

Ephesians 3:17–19   *I pray that you, being rooted and established in love, may have power, together with all the saints, to grasp how wide and long and deep is the love of Christ, and to know this love that surpasses knowledge— that you may be filled to the measure of all the fullness of God.*

A giver is one who yields without restraint or control. You set apart people or things for a particular purpose or use. You put things into the possession of another for his use, by a commitment of trust. You attribute, ascribe, distribute, and communicate. The opposite of a giver of love is one who withholds, takes back, yields under pressure, retreats, resists, remains rigid, and betrays. This person holds resentment, rejection, avoidance, disapproval, bitterness, prejudice, selfishness, and hatred.

Love is devotion, affection, and involvement, which is based on admiration, respect, and appreciation. Love attaches, cleaves to, and sticks fast to anyone in order to build up and please. Love has an unselfish concern that freely accepts another in loyalty and seeks his good. When love is given, it becomes the channel through which God can befriend a person. The supreme expression of love is the self-sacrifice of our Lord on Calvary. I John 4:10 says, "This is love: not that we loved God, but that He loved us and sent His Son an atoning sacrifice for our sins." The character of love is expressed in patience and kindness—not envy, boasting, pride, rudeness, self-seeking, is not easily angered, keeps no records of wrongs, does not delight in evil, but rejoices in the truth. It always perseveres. Love never fails (I Corinthians 13:4–8).

ROSE

A rose; giver of love

⤲

John 3:16 *For God so loved the world that He gave His one and only Son, that whoever believes in Him shall not perish but have everlasting life.*

Ephesians 3:17–19 *I pray that you, being rooted and established in love, may have power, together with all the saints, to grasp how wide and long and deep is the love of Christ, and to know this love that surpasses knowledge— that you may be filled to the measure of all the fullness of God.*

A giver is one who yields without restraint or control. You set apart people or things for a particular purpose or use. You put things into the possession of another for his use, by a commitment of trust. You attribute, ascribe, distribute, and communicate. The opposite of a giver of love is one who withholds, takes back, yields under pressure, retreats, resists, remains rigid, and betrays. This person holds resentment, rejection, avoidance, disapproval, bitterness, prejudice, selfishness, and hatred.

Love is devotion, affection, and involvement, which is based on admiration, respect, and appreciation. Love attaches, cleaves to, and sticks fast to anyone in order to build up and please. Love has an unselfish concern that freely accepts another in loyalty and seeks his good. When love is given, it becomes the channel through which God can befriend a person. The supreme expression of love is the self-sacrifice of our Lord on Calvary. I John 4:10 says, "This is love: not that we loved God, but that He loved us and sent His Son an atoning sacrifice for our sins." The character of love is expressed in patience and kindness—not envy, boasting, pride, rudeness, self-seeking, is not easily angered, keeps no records of wrongs, does not delight in evil, but rejoices in the truth. It always perseveres. Love never fails (I Corinthians 13:4–8).

ROSETTA

A rose; giver of love

৪৩

John 3:16 *For God so loved the world that He gave His one and only Son, that whoever believes in Him shall not perish but have everlasting life.*

Ephesians 3:17–19 *I pray that you, being rooted and established in love, may have power, together with all the saints, to grasp how wide and long and deep is the love of Christ, and to know this love that surpasses knowledge— that you may be filled to the measure of all the fullness of God.*

A giver is one who yields without restraint or control. You set apart people or things for a particular purpose or use. You put things into the possession of another for his use, by a commitment of trust. You attribute, ascribe, distribute, and communicate. The opposite of a giver of love is one who withholds, takes back, yields under pressure, retreats, resists, remains rigid, and betrays. This person holds resentment, rejection, avoidance, disapproval, bitterness, prejudice, selfishness, and hatred.

Love is devotion, affection, and involvement, which is based on admiration, respect, and appreciation. Love attaches, cleaves to, and sticks fast to anyone in order to build up and please. Love has an unselfish concern that freely accepts another in loyalty and seeks his good. When love is given, it becomes the channel through which God can befriend a person. The supreme expression of love is the self-sacrifice of our Lord on Calvary. I John 4:10 says, "This is love: not that we loved God, but that He loved us and sent His Son an atoning sacrifice for our sins." The character of love is expressed in patience and kindness—not envy, boasting, pride, rudeness, self-seeking, is not easily angered, keeps no records of wrongs, does not delight in evil, but rejoices in the truth. It always perseveres. Love never fails (I Corinthians 13:4–8).

ROSIE

Rose; giver of love

❧

John 3:16 *For God so loved the world that He gave His one and only Son, that whoever believes in Him shall not perish but have everlasting life.*

Ephesians 3:17–19 *I pray that you, being rooted and established in love, may have power, together with all the saints, to grasp how wide and long and deep is the love of Christ, and to know this love that surpasses knowledge—that you may be filled to the measure of all the fullness of God.*

A giver is one who yields without restraint or control. You set apart people or things for a particular purpose or use. You put things into the possession of another for his use, by a commitment of trust. You attribute, ascribe, distribute, and communicate. The opposite of a giver of love is one who withholds, takes back, yields under pressure, retreats, resists, remains rigid, and betrays. This person holds resentment, rejection, avoidance, disapproval, bitterness, prejudice, selfishness, and hatred.

Love is devotion, affection, and involvement, which is based on admiration, respect, and appreciation. Love attaches, cleaves to, and sticks fast to anyone in order to build up and please. Love has an unselfish concern that freely accepts another in loyalty and seeks his good. When love is given, it becomes the channel through which God can befriend a person. The supreme expression of love is the self-sacrifice of our Lord on Calvary. I John 4:10 says, "This is love: not that we loved God, but that He loved us and sent His Son an atoning sacrifice for our sins." The character of love is expressed in patience and kindness—not envy, boasting, pride, rudeness, self-seeking, is not easily angered, keeps no records of wrongs, does not delight in evil, but rejoices in the truth. It always perseveres. Love never fails (I Corinthians 13:4–8).

ROY

Kingly; gracious, manly

❧

I Kings 3:9 *So give Your servant a discerning heart to govern Your people and to distinguish between right and wrong. For who is able to govern this great people of Yours?*

Hebrews 5:14 *But solid food is for the mature, who by constant use have trained themselves to distinguish good from evil.*

The sense of smell is the strongest of the five senses. In scripture it is equaled to discernment. It is marked by perception, justice, and insight, along with the ability to investigate and examine based on the absolute truth of scripture. Distinction is defined by the act of noticing differences, discretion, sensitivity, and the ability to distinguish good from evil. You are one who takes the crooked, dishonest corruptions of life and gives clear direction on God's straight path, from pollution to purpose. God has equipped you to remove the obstacles of dullness, indifference, and insignificance. He uses you as His shelter from the wind, His refuge from the storm, His streams of water in the desert, and His great rock in a thirsty land (Isaiah 32:1–8). This brings hearing to the deaf, sight to the blind, and understanding to the mind. This discernment will require disciplining your mind to be set on what the Spirit desires, which is justice and freedom. Stay away from what the carnal nature desires, which is judgment and criticism. You live His life, not yours. You think His thoughts, not yours. You speak His words, not yours. Intimacy with the Lord in His Word and in prayer will prevent you from being offended by the "crooked," so that your focus will be on how He discerns. He is the ultimate man of distinction.

RUBY

Red jewel; excellent spirit

✺

II Corinthians 8:7   *But just as you excel in everything—in faith, in speech, in knowledge, in complete earnestness and in your love for us—see that you also excel in this grace of giving.*

Philippians 4:8   *Finally, brothers, whatever is true, whatever is noble, whatever is right, whatever is pure, whatever is lovely, whatever is admirable—if anything is excellent or praiseworthy—think about such things.*

Excellent worth is comprised in your worship of God. Revelation 5:12 says, "Worthy is the Lamb, who was slain, to receive power and wealth and wisdom and strength and honor and glory and praise!" "All this also comes from the Lord Almighty, wonderful in counsel and magnificent in wisdom," Isaiah 28:29. God has given you an eye for quality, demonstrating His excellence of character and conduct. You go beyond human capacity with faith that transcends all understanding. Your faith is of greater worth than gold (I Peter 1:7). In quality, skill, and achievement, you go the extra mile. This is all about giving, not getting; serving, not controlling. Perfectionism leads to legalism. Excellence releases freedom. You are to show the insignificant and the wasted the more excellent way of God's love (I Corinthians 12:31 and chapter 13) and kindness (2 Peter 1:5–7). You are to excel in gifts that build up the church (I Corinthians 14:12). God uses you to restore genuine value, purpose, and productivity. Devoting yourself to doing what is good will lead to what is excellent and profitable for everyone (Titus 3:8). Your gentle and quiet spirit is of great worth in God's eyes (I Peter 3:4).

RUSSELL

Red-haired one; wise discretion

ᴈᴐ

James 3:17 *But the wisdom that comes from heaven is first of all pure; then peace-loving, considerate, submissive, full of mercy and good fruit, impartial and sincere.*

Proverbs 9:10 *The fear of the Lord is the beginning of wisdom, and knowledge of the Holy One is understanding.*

You are a person of moral excellence. You exemplify right living put into practice. The Lord has not only equipped you with skills for living correctly, but also the ability to impart that to others. The Spirit of truth will guide you into all truth, allowing you to have insight into the true nature of things (John 16:13). Out of your reverential respect for the Lord, you have wisdom to give guidance and direction. You are a safe sounding board who steers those who are hungry for knowledge of the Holy One in the right direction. You need only to ask for the wisdom you lack, and God will give it to you generously (James 1:5). Having spiritual discernment is having the ability to separate the difference between God's wisdom and the world's and the ability to make the right choice—regardless. Luke 21:15 says, "For I will give you words and wisdom that none of your adversaries will be able to resist or contradict."

RUTH

Compassionate; beautiful; companion

ℰℭ

Proverbs 17:17 *A friend loves at all times, and a brother is born for adversity.*

Ecclesiastes 4:9–10 *Two are better than one, because they have a good return for their work: if one falls down his friend can help him up. But pity the man who falls and has no one to help him up!*

Christ was the preeminent example of friendship. John 15:13–14 says, "Greater love has no man than this, that he lay down his life for his friends. You are my friends if you do what I command." With open arms, He gave all. Your mantle is to be God's man of peace. This is achieved by being understanding, loyal, faithful, and true. Proverbs 18:24 says, "A man of many companions may come to ruin, but there is a friend who sticks closer than a brother." It comes natural for you to be hospitable, generous, helpful, and good-humored. Your influence is based on your ability to be approachable, trusted, and respectful. Strangers who are lonely, outcast, or abandoned will find refuge with your "welcome" sign written on your heart. You are loving, as well as being loved—everyone's neighbor; everyone's buddy. Psalm 119:63 says, "I am a friend to all who fear You, to all who follow Your precepts." Proverbs 22:11 says, "He who loves a pure heart and whose speech is gracious will have the King for his friend."

RYAN

Little king; man of distinction

৪৩

I Kings 3:9   *So give Your servant a discerning heart to govern Your people and to distinguish between right and wrong. For who is able to govern this great people of Yours?*

Hebrews 5:14   *But solid food is for the mature, who by constant use have trained themselves to distinguish good from evil.*

The sense of smell is the strongest of the five senses. In scripture it is equaled to discernment. It is marked by perception, justice, and insight, along with the ability to investigate and examine based on the absolute truth of scripture. Distinction is defined by the act of noticing differences, discretion, sensitivity, and the ability to distinguish good from evil. You are one who takes the crooked, dishonest corruptions of life and gives clear direction on God's straight path, from pollution to purpose. God has equipped you to remove the obstacles of dullness, indifference, and insignificance. He uses you as His shelter from the wind, His refuge from the storm, His streams of water in the desert, and His great rock in a thirsty land (Isaiah 32:1–8). This brings hearing to the deaf, sight to the blind, and understanding to the mind. This discernment will require disciplining your mind to be set on what the Spirit desires, which is justice and freedom. Stay away from what the carnal nature desires, which is judgment and criticism. You live His life, not yours. You think His thoughts, not yours. You speak His words, not yours. Intimacy with the Lord in His Word and in prayer will prevent you from being offended by the "crooked," so that your focus will be on how He discerns. He is the ultimate man of distinction.

SABRINA

Passionate; passionate one

౭ఎ

Isaiah 62:1 *For Zion's sake I will not keep silent, for Jerusalem's sake I will not remain quiet, till her righteousness shines out like the dawn, her salvation like a blazing torch.*

II Timothy 1:6 *For this reason I remind you to fan into flame the gift of God, which is in you through the laying on of my hands.*

The way Jesus Christ served His heavenly Father is your only example to follow. The word "enthusiastic" means "possessed by God." Zeal for God's house consumed Jesus (John 2:17). Even to His parents He said, "Didn't you know I had to be in my Father's house?" Luke 2:49. "He put on righteousness as His breastplate, and the helmet of salvation on His head; He put on the garments of vengeance and wrapped Himself in zeal as in a cloak," Isaiah 59:17. Just as Jesus was determined and passionate, so are you. As you fervently worship God as the all-consuming fire (Hebrews 12:29), you will invade the strongholds of weariness in spirit, soul, and body. You bring balance to those dominated by their emotions. God's Word and His presence will keep His fire ignited in and through you. Guard against always putting out fires, but keep in mind that you must always start them! May you have an infusion of spiritual adrenaline.

SADIE

Princess; God's Princess

Exodus 19:5   *Now if you obey me fully and keep my covenant, then out of all nations you will be My treasured possession.*

I Corinthians 6:20   *You were bought at a price. Therefore honor God with your body.*

With a humble confidence, you recognize that your undeserved worth is based on the spotless Lamb sacrificed for you. No greater love will you experience than from the One who laid down His life for you. You pour back your love to Him lavishly with no thought of the cost to you or your reputation. In fact, you are willing to give up everything you have to be His disciple (Luke 14:25–33). This debt of love causes you to give forethought to all your investments as to whether Christ gets all the glory. You will not gamble or be bribed because you know the incredible price paid for you. Therefore you bring value to the insignificant, meaning to the absurd, and worth to the wasted. Your high standard of excellence will bear eternal fruit because of your commitment to please God more than man. As a child of the King, through you castaways will be restored to heirs.

SALLY

Princess; God's princess

ಹಿ

Exodus 19:5 *Now if you obey me fully and keep my covenant, then out of all nations you will be My treasured possession.*

I Corinthians 6:20 *You were bought at a price. Therefore honor God with your body.*

With a humble confidence, you recognize that your undeserved worth is based on the spotless Lamb sacrificed for you. No greater love will you experience than from the One who laid down His life for you. You pour back your love to Him lavishly with no thought of the cost to you or your reputation. In fact, you are willing to give up everything you have to be His disciple (Luke 14:25–33). This debt of love causes you to give forethought to all your investments as to whether Christ gets all the glory. You will not gamble or be bribed because you know the incredible price paid for you. Therefore you bring value to the insignificant, meaning to the absurd, and worth to the wasted. Your high standard of excellence will bear eternal fruit because of your commitment to please God more than man. As a child of the King, through you castaways will be restored to heirs.

SAM

Heard or asked of God; integrity

☙

Psalm 41:12 *In my integrity You uphold me and set me in Your presence forever.*

Proverbs 11:3 *The integrity of the upright guides them, but the unfaithful are destroyed by their duplicity.*

Spiritual deafness results from unheeded warnings, calloused hearts, rebellious disobedience, and stubborn unfaithfulness. This is prevented by being quick to hear, teachable, and having faith in God's Word. Security comes from knowing God's ears are attentive to your cry—before you call, He answers. Discernment and righteous judgment produce integrity. Integrity results in yielding weakness to God's power, based on a blameless walk. Proverbs 10:9 says, "The man of integrity walks securely, but he who takes crooked paths will be found out." You are one who has an uncompromised commitment to righteousness, respectability, honesty, character, excellence, innocence, generosity, trustworthiness, faithfulness, justice, hope, and love. Be truthful with others, as well as yourself. Be the same in public as you are in private. Titus 2:7–8 says, "In everything set them an example by doing what is good. In your teaching show integrity, seriousness and soundness of speech that cannot be condemned, so that those who oppose you may be ashamed because they have nothing bad to say about us."

SAMANTHA

Heard or asked of God; integrity

&

Psalm 41:12 *In my integrity You uphold me and set me in Your presence forever.*

Proverbs 11:3 *The integrity of the upright guides them, but the unfaithful are destroyed by their duplicity.*

Spiritual deafness results from unheeded warnings, calloused hearts, rebellious disobedience, and stubborn unfaithfulness. This is prevented by being quick to hear, teachable, and having faith in God's Word. Security comes from knowing God's ears are attentive to your cry—before you call, He answers. Discernment and righteous judgment produce integrity. Integrity results in yielding weakness to God's power, based on a blameless walk. Proverbs 10:9 says, "The man of integrity walks securely, but he who takes crooked paths will be found out." You are one who has an uncompromised commitment to righteousness, respectability, honesty, character, excellence, innocence, generosity, trustworthiness, faithfulness, justice, hope, and love. Be truthful with others, as well as yourself. Be the same in public as you are in private. Titus 2:7–8 says, "In everything set them an example by doing what is good. In your teaching show integrity, seriousness and soundness of speech that cannot be condemned, so that those who oppose you may be ashamed because they have nothing bad to say about us."

SAMUEL

Heard or asked of God; integrity

ॐ

Psalm 41:12 *In my integrity You uphold me and set me in Your presence forever.*

Proverbs 11:3 *The integrity of the upright guides them, but the unfaithful are destroyed by their duplicity.*

Spiritual deafness results from unheeded warnings, calloused hearts, rebellious disobedience, and stubborn unfaithfulness. This is prevented by being quick to hear, teachable, and having faith in God's Word. Security comes from knowing God's ears are attentive to your cry—before you call, He answers. Discernment and righteous judgment produce integrity. Integrity results in yielding weakness to God's power, based on a blameless walk. Proverbs 10:9 says, "The man of integrity walks securely, but he who takes crooked paths will be found out." You are one who has an uncompromised commitment to righteousness, respectability, honesty, character, excellence, innocence, generosity, trustworthiness, faithfulness, justice, hope, and love. Be truthful with others, as well as yourself. Be the same in public as you are in private. Titus 2:7–8 says, "In everything set them an example by doing what is good. In your teaching show integrity, seriousness and soundness of speech that cannot be condemned, so that those who oppose you may be ashamed because they have nothing bad to say about us."

SANDI

Helper, defender of mankind; compassion with humility

∞

Hosea 11:4 *I led them with cords of human kindness, with ties of love; I lifted the yoke from their neck and bent down to feed them.*

Matthew 9:36 *When He saw the crowds, He had compassion on them, because they were harassed and helpless, like sheep without a shepherd.*

You are obedient, respectful, faithful, and bring pleasure to those whom you serve. Even with inconsiderate behavior, you are patient (I Peter 2:18). You are tender with the harsh, merciful with the intolerant, and sympathetic with the suffering. Because you cast your cares on the Lord, you are able to lift the burdens of others (Psalm 55:22). The reason you are so easily trusted is because of your humble nature. All glory and credit belong to God, not you. Your passion to help energizes you to meet the need regardless of what it is—guidance, relief, encouragement, or support. God allows you to see the root of the need rather than being sidetracked by all the symptoms. Sickness is healed, the hungry are fed, sight is restored, the unlovely are touched and the afflicted are delivered. You defend rather than offend, forgive rather than accuse, and you protect rather than abandon. You can depend on God's fresh supply daily. "Because of the Lord's great love we are not consumed, for His compassions never fail. They are new every morning; great is your faithfulness," Lamentations 3:22–23. Your compassion connects the heart of God to the heart of man.

SANDRA

Helper, defender of mankind; compassion with humility

೪

Hosea 11:4   *I led them with cords of human kindness, with ties of love; I lifted the yoke from their neck and bent down to feed them.*

Matthew 9:36   *When He saw the crowds, He had compassion on them, because they were harassed and helpless, like sheep without a shepherd.*

You are obedient, respectful, faithful, and bring pleasure to those whom you serve. Even with inconsiderate behavior, you are patient (I Peter 2:18). You are tender with the harsh, merciful with the intolerant, and sympathetic with the suffering. Because you cast your cares on the Lord, you are able to lift the burdens of others (Psalm 55:22). The reason you are so easily trusted is because of your humble nature. All glory and credit belong to God, not you. Your passion to help energizes you to meet the need regardless of what it is—guidance, relief, encouragement, or support. God allows you to see the root of the need rather than being sidetracked by all the symptoms. Sickness is healed, the hungry are fed, sight is restored, the unlovely are touched and the afflicted are delivered. You defend rather than offend, forgive rather than accuse, and you protect rather than abandon. You can depend on God's fresh supply daily. "Because of the Lord's great love we are not consumed, for His compassions never fail. They are new every morning; great is your faithfulness," Lamentations 3:22–23. Your compassion connects the heart of God to the heart of man.

SANDY

Helper, defender of mankind; compassion with humility

Hosea 11:4 *I led them with cords of human kindness, with ties of love; I lifted the yoke from their neck and bent down to feed them.*

Matthew 9:36 *When He saw the crowds, He had compassion on them, because they were harassed and helpless, like sheep without a shepherd.*

You are obedient, respectful, faithful, and bring pleasure to those whom you serve. Even with inconsiderate behavior, you are patient (I Peter 2:18). You are tender with the harsh, merciful with the intolerant, and sympathetic with the suffering. Because you cast your cares on the Lord, you are able to lift the burdens of others (Psalm 55:22). The reason you are so easily trusted is because of your humble nature. All glory and credit belong to God, not you. Your passion to help energizes you to meet the need regardless of what it is—guidance, relief, encouragement, or support. God allows you to see the root of the need rather than being sidetracked by all the symptoms. Sickness is healed, the hungry are fed, sight is restored, the unlovely are touched and the afflicted are delivered. You defend rather than offend, forgive rather than accuse, and you protect rather than abandon. You can depend on God's fresh supply daily. "Because of the Lord's great love we are not consumed, for His compassions never fail. They are new every morning; great is your faithfulness," Lamentations 3:22–23. Your compassion connects the heart of God to the heart of man.

SARA

Princess; God's princess

ॐ

Exodus 19:5 *Now if you obey me fully and keep my covenant, then out of all nations you will be My treasured possession.*

I Corinthians 6:20 *You were bought at a price. Therefore honor God with your body.*

With a humble confidence, you recognize that your undeserved worth is based on the spotless Lamb sacrificed for you. No greater love will you experience than from the One who laid down His life for you. You pour back your love to Him lavishly with no thought of the cost to you or your reputation. In fact, you are willing to give up everything you have to be His disciple (Luke 14:25–33). This debt of love causes you to give forethought to all your investments as to whether Christ gets all the glory. You will not gamble or be bribed because you know the incredible price paid for you. Therefore you bring value to the insignificant, meaning to the absurd, and worth to the wasted. Your high standard of excellence will bear eternal fruit because of your commitment to please God more than man. As a child of the King, through you castaways will be restored to heirs.

SARAH

Princess; God's princess

❧

Exodus 19:5 *Now if you obey me fully and keep my covenant, then out of all nations you will be My treasured possession.*

I Corinthians 6:20   *You were bought at a price. Therefore honor God with your body.*

With a humble confidence, you recognize that your undeserved worth is based on the spotless Lamb sacrificed for you. No greater love will you experience than from the One who laid down His life for you. You pour back your love to Him lavishly with no thought of the cost to you or your reputation. In fact, you are willing to give up everything you have to be His disciple (Luke 14:25–33). This debt of love causes you to give forethought to all your investments as to whether Christ gets all the glory. You will not gamble or be bribed because you know the incredible price paid for you. Therefore you bring value to the insignificant, meaning to the absurd, and worth to the wasted. Your high standard of excellence will bear eternal fruit because of your commitment to please God more than man. As a child of the King, through you castaways will be restored to heirs.

SAVANNAH

Treeless plain; open heart

ॐ

Ezekiel 36:26–27   I will give you a new heart and put a new spirit in you; I will remove from you your heart of stone and give you a heart of flesh. And I will put My spirit in you and move you to follow My decrees and be careful to keep My laws.

Romans 12:2   Do not conform any longer to the pattern of this world, but be transformed by the renewing of your mind. Then you will be able to test and approve what God's will is—His good, pleasing and perfect will.

The cross of Jesus Christ is your ultimate source of transformation. He exchanged your sin for His righteousness, your death for His life, your darkness for His light, your earthly for His eternal, and your past for His future. You were lost, but now you are found. You were blind, but now you see. The old has now become new. II Corinthians 5:17 says, "Therefore, if anyone is in Christ, he is a new creation; the old has gone, the new has come!" A metamorphosis is your transformation from God through Christ. Your conversion by the blood of Jesus is the greatest miracle you will ever experience. This changeless God has traded your sorrow for His joy, your pain for His healing, your emptiness for His fullness, and your rejection for His forgiveness. He adopts, accepts, and loves you. Put to death what belongs to your earthly nature and be clothed with the likeness of Christ (Colossians 3:1–14). As you align your will with His and are continually renewed in the knowledge of God's Word, He will transform many lives through yours. For those living a lie you bring truth, for the dying you bring life, for the rejected you bring acceptance, and for the trapped you bring freedom. His resurrection power flows in and through you. You will continually be transformed into the Lord's likeness with ever-increasing glory (II Corinthians 3:18).

SCHYLOR

A shelter; a refuge

෨

Deuteronomy 33:27 *The eternal God is your refuge, and underneath are the everlasting arms. He will drive out your enemy before you, saying, "Destroy him!"*

Psalm 27:5 *For in the day of trouble He will keep me safe in His dwelling; He will hide me in the shelter of His tabernacle and set me high upon a rock.*

God is your place of protection. Your heart is His home. As you hide in the shelter of His presence, the Lord protects you from those who conspire against you; those with accusing tongues (Psalm 31:19–20). The Lord uses you to be His refuge for the poor and needy in distress, His shelter from the storm, and a shade from the heat (Isaiah 25:4). You release security and confidence (Proverbs 14:26). You declare deliverance to the prisoners and you give hope that God will restore twice as much to them (Zechariah 9:12).

SCOTT

From Scotland; loyal

Romans 12:9–10 *Love must be sincere. Hate what is evil; cling to what is good. Be devoted to one another in brotherly love. Honor one another above yourselves.*

Proverbs 2:7–8 *He holds victory in store for the upright, He is a shield to those whose walk is blameless, for He guards the course of the just and protects the way of His faithful ones.*

As one with a loyal spirit, the Lord has called you to be faithful, devoted, obedient, dependable, and true. You are noble in disarming the enemy's attacks of fear, selfishness, failure, betrayal, dishonesty, and faithlessness. You are unyielding and have a resolute confidence in your commitment to God's Word. With it, you will help others overcome being cowards, losers, quitters, or betrayers. Knowing God's loyalty to you will strengthen your loyalty to others. Isaiah 1:17 says, "Learn to do right! Seek justice, encourage the oppressed. Defend the cause of the fatherless, plead the case of the widow."

SCOTTIE

From Scotland; loyal

Romans 12:9–10 *Love must be sincere. Hate what is evil; cling to what is good. Be devoted to one another in brotherly love. Honor one another above yourselves.*

Proverbs 2:7–8 *He holds victory in store for the upright, He is a shield to those whose walk is blameless, for He guards the course of the just and protects the way of His faithful ones.*

As one with a loyal spirit, the Lord has called you to be faithful, devoted, obedient, dependable, and true. You are noble in disarming the enemy's attacks of fear, selfishness, failure, betrayal, dishonesty, and faithlessness. You are unyielding and have a resolute confidence in your commitment to God's Word. With it, you will help others overcome being cowards, losers, quitters, or betrayers. Knowing God's loyalty to you will strengthen your loyalty to others. Isaiah 1:17 says, "Learn to do right! Seek justice, encourage the oppressed. Defend the cause of the fatherless, plead the case of the widow."

SEAN

God is gracious; God's gift

ε&

Romans 8:32 *He who did not spare His own Son, but gave Him up for us all—how will He not also, along with Him, graciously give us all things?*

I Corinthians 15:10 *But by the grace of God I am what I am, and His grace to me was not without effect.*

Ephesians 2:8 says, "For it is by grace you have been saved, through faith—and this is not from yourselves, it is the gift of God." You are one who brings about balance and harmony through mercy, forgiveness, approval, kindness, and patience—all with a grateful heart. This attitude of gratitude will rule in the midst of inconsiderate behavior. Your nature defies the law of the Pharisees, and is against being self-reliant, prejudice, and selfish. Being full of grace is devotion built through faithfulness and a willingness to quickly pardon. You are blessed with creativity in expressing God's greatest gift of grace—the life of His only Son, Jesus Christ. God says to you through Jeremiah 24:7, "I will give them a heart to know Me, that I am the Lord. They will be My people, and I will be their God, for they will return to Me with all their heart." Ezekiel 11:19 says, "I will give them an undivided heart and put a new spirit in them; I will remove from them their heart of stone and give them a heart of flesh." Accountability will keep your report accurate and your integrity irreproachable.

SELINA

Peaceful; where God dwells

☙

Isaiah 26:3 *You will keep in perfect peace him whose mind is steadfast, because he trusts in You.*

Philippians 4:7 *And the peace of God, which transcends all understanding, will guard your hearts and your minds in Christ Jesus.*

Your life defines peace. You will have a content and calm composure in the midst of distress, disturbance, or agitation. As you follow the Prince of Peace, you will be secure in who you are in Christ. The discipline of keeping your mind on Christ, loving God's law, and being controlled by the Holy Spirit will keep you in perfect peace. God's peace will serve as an umpire to determine whether you are safe or out of God's will (Colossians 3:15). Do not think it strange when you are in battles, fights, and quarrels, because God wants to use you to bring harmony, order, unity, agreement, quietness, and calmness to the adverse situation. You are one whose intimate friendship with the Lord brings reconciliation to the offended, distressed, and troubled. "In repentance and rest is your salvation, in quietness and trust is your strength," Isaiah 30:15. Your refreshing comes as you renew your mind daily in the Word of God. "Great peace have they who love Your law, and nothing can make them stumble," Psalm 119:165.

SETH

Appointed; God's chosen one

&

Jeremiah 1:5   *Before I formed you in the womb, I knew you, before you were born I set you apart; I appointed you as a prophet to the nations.*

John 15:16   *You did not choose Me, but I chose you and appointed you to go and bear fruit—fruit that will last. Then the Father will give you whatever you ask in My name.*

You hear the voice of the Lord saying, "Whom shall I send? And who will go for us?" And you say, "Here am I. Send me!" (Isaiah 6:8) The Lord has appointed you as a servant and witness of what you have seen of Him and what He shows you (Acts 26:16). You were chosen in Him before the creation of the world to be holy and blameless in His sight (Ephesians 1:4). God has placed His trust in you by giving you His authority and ordained you to reflect His character and thoughts. As one favored by God, you are His representative sent on His mission. Knowing He chooses the weak and foolish things to confound the wise requires humility, gratitude, and surrender. God's approval is upon you and His assignment is in you to accomplish His purposes. Make your calling sure and live a life worthy of the calling you have received. Be completely humble, gentle, patient, and bearing with one another in love (Ephesians 4:1–2). You refuse a maintenance mode, but rather fix your thoughts and destination on Jesus. You are equipped to fulfill the great commission (Matthew 28:18–20).

SHANA

Little wise one; gracious spirit

৪১

Romans 8:32 *He who did not spare His own Son, but gave Him up for us all—how will He not also, along with Him, graciously give us all things?*

I Corinthians 15:10 *But by the grace of God I am what I am, and His grace to me was not without effect.*

Ephesians 2:8 says, "For it is by grace you have been saved, through faith—and this is not from yourselves, it is the gift of God." You are one who brings about balance and harmony through mercy, forgiveness, approval, kindness, and patience—all with a grateful heart. This attitude of gratitude will rule in the midst of inconsiderate behavior. Your nature defies the law of the Pharisees, and is against being self-reliant, prejudice, and selfish. Being full of grace is devotion built through faithfulness and a willingness to quickly pardon. You are blessed with creativity in expressing God's greatest gift of grace—the life of His only Son, Jesus Christ. God says to you through Jeremiah 24:7, "I will give them a heart to know Me, that I am the Lord. They will be My people, and I will be their God, for they will return to Me with all their heart." Ezekiel 11:19 says, "I will give them an undivided heart and put a new spirit in them; I will remove from them their heart of stone and give them a heart of flesh." Accountability will keep your report accurate and your integrity irreproachable.

SHANIA

Newly created; God's creation

❦

Ephesians 2:10   *For we are God's workmanship, created in Christ Jesus to do good works, which God prepared in advance for us to do.*

II Corinthians 5:17   *Therefore, if anyone is in Christ, he is a new creation; the old has gone, the new has come!*

Through you the Lord will bring Himself into existence: He will originate. How you deal with the past determines your future. Regardless of curses or blessings, failures or successes, you are God's platform for a "new thing." You cannot lean to your own understanding or reasoning. God Almighty created the heavens, the earth, and you in His image. Isaiah 42:9, "See, the former things have taken place, and new things I declare; before they spring into being I announce them to you." Isaiah 43:18–19, "Forget the former things; do not dwell on the past. See, I am doing a new thing! Now it springs up; do you not perceive it? I am making a way in the desert and streams in the wasteland." Isaiah 48:6b, "From now on I will tell you of new things, of hidden things unknown to you." Isaiah 65:17–19, "Behold, I will create new heavens and a new earth. The former things will not be remembered, nor will they come to mind. But be glad and rejoice forever in what I will create, for I will create Jerusalem to be a delight and its people a joy. I will rejoice over Jerusalem and take delight in My people; the sound of weeping and of crying will be heard in it no more." Because of your passion for the eternal over the temporal, you are used of God to remove what can be shaken—the created things—so that what cannot be shaken may remain (Hebrews 12:27). The more completely dependent you become on your Creator, the more productive your life will be for Him! I Peter 4:19, "So then, those who suffer according to God's will should commit themselves to their Creator and continue to do good." As you stay yielded and surrendered to God, the clay of your heart will stay tender. Only then can He mold you into the image of His Son, Jesus Christ. God will work His approval through you to those who feel ugly, worthless, and to those who have no hope.

SHANNON

Little wise one; gracious spirit

Romans 8:32   *He who did not spare His own Son, but gave Him up for us all—how will He not also, along with Him, graciously give us all things?*

I Corinthians 15:10   *But by the grace of God I am what I am, and His grace to me was not without effect.*

Ephesians 2:8 says, "For it is by grace you have been saved, through faith—and this is not from yourselves, it is the gift of God." You are one who brings about balance and harmony through mercy, forgiveness, approval, kindness, and patience—all with a grateful heart. This attitude of gratitude will rule in the midst of inconsiderate behavior. Your nature defies the law of the Pharisees, and is against being self-reliant, prejudice, and selfish. Being full of grace is devotion built through faithfulness and a willingness to quickly pardon. You are blessed with creativity in expressing God's greatest gift of grace—the life of His only Son, Jesus Christ. God says to you through Jeremiah 24:7, "I will give them a heart to know Me, that I am the Lord. They will be My people, and I will be their God, for they will return to Me with all their heart." Ezekiel 11:19 says, "I will give them an undivided heart and put a new spirit in them; I will remove from them their heart of stone and give them a heart of flesh." Accountability will keep your report accurate and your integrity irreproachable.

SHARLAY

Womanly; cherished one

❧

Zephaniah 3:17 *The Lord your God is with you, He is mighty to save. He will take great delight in you, He will quiet you with His love, He will rejoice over you with singing.*

Ephesians 5:28–30 *In this same way, husbands ought to love their wives as their own bodies. He who loves his wife loves himself. After all, no one ever hated His own body, but he feeds and cares for it, just as Christ does the church - for we are members of His body.*

You are God's "treasured possession" (Deuteronomy 7:6). By giving the very life of His Son, God has committed to highly value you and take good care of you. He will treat you tenderly in tough times. You are to relate to others as Jesus relates to the Father and to us. Paul served as an example for you. I Thessalonians 2:7–8 says, "We were gentle among you, like a mother caring for her little children. We loved you so much that we were delighted to share with you not only the gospel of God but our lives as well, because you had become so dear to us." The warmth you experience being held close to His heart will enable you to melt the ice in others—the rejected and the castaways. Be free to be intimate with your Maker with trust and selfless submission.

SHARLENE

Little womanly one; womanly

Zephaniah 3:17 *The Lord your God is with you, He is mighty to save. He will take great delight in you, He will quiet you with His love, He will rejoice over you with singing.*

Ephesians 5:28–30 *In this same way, husbands ought to love their wives as their own bodies. He who loves his wife loves himself. After all, no one ever hated His own body, but he feeds and cares for it, just as Christ does the church - for we are members of His body.*

You are God's "treasured possession" (Deuteronomy 7:6). By giving the very life of His Son, God has committed to highly value you and take good care of you. He will treat you tenderly in tough times. You are to relate to others as Jesus relates to the Father and to us. Paul served as an example for you. I Thessalonians 2:7–8 says, "We were gentle among you, like a mother caring for her little children. We loved you so much that we were delighted to share with you not only the gospel of God but our lives as well, because you had become so dear to us." The warmth you experience being held close to His heart will enable you to melt the ice in others—the rejected and the castaways. Be free to be intimate with your Maker with trust and selfless submission.

SHARON

A princess; a princess

Exodus 19:5 *Now if you obey me fully and keep my covenant, then out of all nations you will be My treasured possession.*

I Corinthians 6:20 *You were bought at a price. Therefore honor God with your body.*

With a humble confidence, you recognize that your undeserved worth is based on the spotless Lamb sacrificed for you. No greater love will you experience than from the One who laid down His life for you. You pour back your love to Him lavishly with no thought of the cost to you or your reputation. In fact, you are willing to give up everything you have to be His disciple (Luke 14:25–33). This debt of love causes you to give forethought to all your investments as to whether Christ gets all the glory. You will not gamble or be bribed because you know the incredible price paid for you. Therefore you bring value to the insignificant, meaning to the absurd, and worth to the wasted. Your high standard of excellence will bear eternal fruit because of your commitment to please God more than man. As a child of the King, through you castaways will be restored to heirs.

SHAWN

God is gracious; God's gracious gift

&

Romans 8:32 *He who did not spare His own Son, but gave Him up for us all—how will He not also, along with Him, graciously give us all things?*

I Corinthians 15:10 *But by the grace of God I am what I am, and His grace to me was not without effect.*

Ephesians 2:8 says, "For it is by grace you have been saved, through faith—and this is not from yourselves, it is the gift of God." You are one who brings about balance and harmony through mercy, forgiveness, approval, kindness, and patience—all with a grateful heart. This attitude of gratitude will rule in the midst of inconsiderate behavior. Your nature defies the law of the Pharisees, and is against being self-reliant, prejudice, and selfish. Being full of grace is devotion built through faithfulness and a willingness to quickly pardon. You are blessed with creativity in expressing God's greatest gift of grace—the life of His only Son, Jesus Christ. God says to you through Jeremiah 24:7, "I will give them a heart to know Me, that I am the Lord. They will be My people, and I will be their God, for they will return to Me with all their heart." Ezekiel 11:19 says, "I will give them an undivided heart and put a new spirit in them; I will remove from them their heart of stone and give them a heart of flesh." Accountability will keep your report accurate and your integrity irreproachable.

SHEILA

Irish heavenly; contented heart

℘

Proverbs 15:16   *Better a little with the fear of the Lord than great wealth with turmoil.*

Hebrews 13:5   *Keep your lives free from the love of money and be content with what you have, because God has said, "Never will I leave you; never will I forsake you."*

You have learned to be content whatever the circumstances. Your attitude is governed by God, not by outward situations. You know what it is to be in need and you know what it is to have plenty. You have learned the secret of being content in any and every situation, whether well fed or hungry, living in plenty or in want. You can do everything through Him who gives you strength (Philippians 4:11–13). The Lord is your source of strength because you turn back the battle at the gate (Isaiah 28:6). You renew your strength because your hope is in the Lord (Isaiah 40:31). Jesus says, "My grace is sufficient for you, for my power is made perfect in weakness. Therefore, you will boast all the more gladly about your weaknesses, so that Christ's power may rest on you. That is why, for Christ's sake, you delight in weaknesses, in insults, in hardships, in persecutions, and in difficulties. For when you are weak, then you are strong," II Corinthians 12:9–10. Contentment is God's guide to His will for you. You give rest to the weary, truth to those who murmur, peace to the dissatisfied, and quietness to the troubled.

SHELBY

From the ledge estate; where God dwells

Psalm 23:6 *Surely goodness and love will follow me all the days of my life, and I will dwell in the house of the Lord forever.*

Psalm 16:8 *I have set the Lord always before me. Because He is at my right hand, I will not be shaken.*

Psalm 63:7 *I sing in the shadow of Thy wings.*

Abide means to stay, dwell, submit, and to endure. The Lord has promised to strengthen your heart because you are fully committed to Him (II Chronicles 16:9). Do not think it strange that the closer you get to Him, the darker it will become. It is like one focusing in the dark room of a photographer—you will be the first to see the by-products of the "negatives"—the good out of the bad! In the holy of holies, where He dwells, there is no natural form of light—just His glory. It is in that shadow where He will birth the songs and reveal the hidden treasures of His heart. You are one whose intimate friendship with the Lord will bring reconciliation to the offended, distressed, and troubled.

SHELLY

Shell island; peaceful spirit

လ

Isaiah 26:3 *You will keep in perfect peace him whose mind is steadfast, because he trusts in You.*

Philippians 4:7 *And the peace of God, which transcends all understanding, will guard your hearts and your minds in Christ Jesus.*

Your life defines peace. You will have a content and calm composure in the midst of distress, disturbance, or agitation. As you follow the Prince of Peace, you will be secure in who you are in Christ. The discipline of keeping your mind on Christ, loving God's law, and being controlled by the Holy Spirit will keep you in perfect peace. God's peace will serve as an umpire to determine whether you are safe or out of God's will (Colossians 3:15). Do not think it strange when you are in battles, fights, and quarrels, because God wants to use you to bring harmony, order, unity, agreement, quietness, and calmness to the adverse situation. You are one whose intimate friendship with the Lord brings reconciliation to the offended, distressed, and troubled. "In repentance and rest is your salvation, in quietness and trust is your strength," Isaiah 30:15. Your refreshing comes as you renew your mind daily in the Word of God. "Great peace have they who love Your law, and nothing can make them stumble," Psalm 119:165.

SHERI

Little womanly one; cherished one

∞

Zephaniah 3:17 *The Lord your God is with you, He is mighty to save. He will take great delight in you, He will quiet you with His love, He will rejoice over you with singing.*

Ephesians 5:28–30 *In this same way, husbands ought to love their wives as their own bodies. He who loves his wife loves himself. After all, no one ever hated His own body, but he feeds and cares for it, just as Christ does the church - for we are members of His body.*

You are God's "treasured possession" (Deuteronomy 7:6). By giving the very life of His Son, God has committed to highly value you and take good care of you. He will treat you tenderly in tough times. You are to relate to others as Jesus relates to the Father and to us. Paul served as an example for you. I Thessalonians 2:7–8 says, "We were gentle among you, like a mother caring for her little children. We loved you so much that we were delighted to share with you not only the gospel of God but our lives as well, because you had become so dear to us." The warmth you experience being held close to His heart will enable you to melt the ice in others—the rejected and the castaways. Be free to be intimate with your Maker with trust and selfless submission.

SHERRY

Little womanly one; cherished one

❧

Zephaniah 3:17 *The Lord your God is with you, He is mighty to save. He will take great delight in you, He will quiet you with His love, He will rejoice over you with singing.*

Ephesians 5:28–30 *In this same way, husbands ought to love their wives as their own bodies. He who loves his wife loves himself. After all, no one ever hated His own body, but he feeds and cares for it, just as Christ does the church - for we are members of His body.*

You are God's "treasured possession" (Deuteronomy 7:6). By giving the very life of His Son, God has committed to highly value you and take good care of you. He will treat you tenderly in tough times. You are to relate to others as Jesus relates to the Father and to us. Paul served as an example for you. I Thessalonians 2:7–8 says, "We were gentle among you, like a mother caring for her little children. We loved you so much that we were delighted to share with you not only the gospel of God but our lives as well, because you had become so dear to us." The warmth you experience being held close to His heart will enable you to melt the ice in others—the rejected and the castaways. Be free to be intimate with your Maker with trust and selfless submission.

SHIRLEY

From the bright meadow; restful spirit

໖৩

Psalm 116:7 *Be at rest once more, O my soul, for the Lord has been good to you.*

Matthew 11:28–30 *Come to Me, all you who are weary and burdened, and I will give you rest. Take My yoke upon you and learn from Me, for I am gentle and humble in heart, and you will find rest for your souls. For My yoke is easy and My burden is light.*

The Lord makes you lie down in green pastures, and leads you beside quiet waters (Psalm 23:2). It is in His presence where He quiets you with His love, stills your anxious heart, and brings refreshing to weariness. You not only have peace in the midst of the storm, but you bring it to others at any cost. Those who are faint are strengthened, the empty are filled, and the confused are given clarity. Don't allow disobedience to rob your rest, but rather allow faith to give entrance to it (Hebrews 4:1–11). Wait upon the Lord, be still before Him, and encourage yourself in His presence. "Then I heard a voice from heaven say, 'Write: Blessed are the dead who die in the Lord from now on.' 'Yes,' says the Spirit, 'they will rest from their labor, for their deeds will follow them,'" Revelation 14:13.

SIDNEY

Saint Denis; discerner of excellence

&

II Corinthians 8:7 *But just as you excel in everything—in faith, in speech, in knowledge, in complete earnestness and in your love for us—see that you also excel in this grace of giving.*

Philippians 4:8 *Finally, brothers, whatever is true, whatever is noble, whatever is right, whatever is pure, whatever is lovely, whatever is admirable—if anything is excellent or praiseworthy—think about such things.*

Excellent worth is comprised in your worship of God. Revelation 5:12 says, "Worthy is the Lamb, who was slain, to receive power and wealth and wisdom and strength and honor and glory and praise!" "All this also comes from the Lord Almighty, wonderful in counsel and magnificent in wisdom," Isaiah 28:29. God has given you an eye for quality, demonstrating His excellence of character and conduct. You go beyond human capacity with faith that transcends all understanding. Your faith is of greater worth than gold (I Peter 1:7). In quality, skill, and achievement, you go the extra mile. This is all about giving, not getting; serving, not controlling. Perfectionism leads to legalism. Excellence releases freedom. You are to show the insignificant and the wasted the more excellent way of God's love (I Corinthians 12:31 and chapter 13) and kindness (2 Peter 1:5-7). You are to excel in gifts that build up the church (I Corinthians 14:12). God uses you to restore genuine value, purpose, and productivity. Devoting yourself to doing what is good will lead to what is excellent and profitable for everyone (Titus 3:8). Your gentle and quiet spirit is of great worth in God's eyes (I Peter 3:4).

SIERRA

Black; pure one

&

I Timothy 5:22   *...do not share in the sins of others. Keep yourself pure.*

I Peter 1:22   *Now that you have purified yourselves by obeying the truth so that you have sincere love for your brothers, love one another deeply, from the heart.*

Through the process of heat, trials, and refinement, purity is established. Your nature defies being stubborn, judgmental, and haughty. The commandment of the Lord is clear—giving insight to life (Psalm 19:8). You bring wholeness to the dirty, defiled, contaminated, polluted, double-minded, and raped. Your willingness to be transparent is the venue through which He makes His Word clear, simple, and unadulterated. Your choice to be pure enables you to see God (Matthew 5:8) and to know Him as King and Friend (Proverbs 22:11). It also allows your words to be pleasant (Proverbs 15:26) and causes you to ascend to the holy place of the Lord, where you receive blessings and righteousness from the God of salvation (Psalm 24:3–5). Proverbs 20:11 says, "Even a child is known by his actions, by whether his conduct is pure and right."

SKYLER

A shelter; a refuge

ଙ୬

Deuteronomy 33:27 *The eternal God is your refuge, and underneath are the everlasting arms. He will drive out your enemy before you, saying, "Destroy him!"*

Psalm 27:5 *For in the day of trouble He will keep me safe in His dwelling; He will hide me in the shelter of His tabernacle and set me high upon a rock.*

God is your place of protection. Your heart is His home. As you hide in the shelter of His presence, the Lord protects you from those who conspire against you; those with accusing tongues (Psalm 31:19–20). The Lord uses you to be His refuge for the poor and needy in distress, His shelter from the storm, and a shade from the heat (Isaiah 25:4). You release security and confidence (Proverbs 14:26). You declare deliverance to the prisoners and you give hope that God will restore twice as much to them (Zechariah 9:12).

SOLOMON

Peaceable; peaceful

&

Isaiah 26:3 *You will keep in perfect peace him whose mind is steadfast, because he trusts in You.*

Philippians 4:7 *And the peace of God, which transcends all understanding, will guard your hearts and your minds in Christ Jesus.*

Your life defines peace. You will have a content and calm composure in the midst of distress, disturbance, or agitation. As you follow the Prince of Peace, you will be secure in who you are in Christ. The discipline of keeping your mind on Christ, loving God's law, and being controlled by the Holy Spirit will keep you in perfect peace. God's peace will serve as an umpire to determine whether you are safe or out of God's will (Colossians 3:15). Do not think it strange when you are in battles, fights, and quarrels, because God wants to use you to bring harmony, order, unity, agreement, quietness, and calmness to the adverse situation. You are one whose intimate friendship with the Lord brings reconciliation to the offended, distressed, and troubled. "In repentance and rest is your salvation, in quietness and trust is your strength," Isaiah 30:15. Your refreshing comes as you renew your mind daily in the Word of God. "Great peace have they who love Your law, and nothing can make them stumble," Psalm 119:165.

SOMMER

Warm; full of life

ॐ

John 14:6 *Jesus answered, I am the way and the truth and the life. No one comes to the Father except through Me.*

Deuteronomy 30:19–20 *This day I call heaven and earth as witnesses against you that I have set before you life and death, blessings and curses. Now choose life, so that you and your children may live and that you may love the Lord your God, listen to His voice, and hold fast to Him. For the Lord is your life, and He will give you many years in the land He swore to give to your fathers, Abraham, Isaac, and Jacob.*

Your life's purpose is to serve God, seek His kingdom, do the Father's will, finish the divine task, complete the course joyfully, and attain Christ-likeness. You throw a life-line to those with a death sentence—those who are weary, disgusted, bitter, empty, barren, oppressed, and isolated. With your focus kept on eternal rather than temporal values, you will bring Christ's resurrection power to hearts in the grave. The very gates of hell cannot prevail and be strong enough to stand up under the direct attack of the church. Colossians 3:1–4 says, "Since, then, you have been raised with Christ, set your hearts on things above, not on earthly things. For you died, and your life is now hidden with Christ in God. When Christ, who is your life, appears, then you also will appear with Him in glory." I Samuel 25:29 says, "Your life will be bound securely in the bundle of the living by the Lord your God. But the lives of your enemies He will hurl away as from the pocket of a sling." Psalm 27:1 says, "The Lord is the stronghold of your life—of whom shall you be afraid?" Enjoy life to the fullest! (John 10:10)

SONIA

Wisdom; woman of wisdom

❧

James 3:17 *But the wisdom that comes from heaven is first of all pure; then peace-loving, considerate, submissive, full of mercy and good fruit, impartial and sincere.*

Proverbs 9:10 *The fear of the Lord is the beginning of wisdom, and knowledge of the Holy One is understanding.*

You are a person of moral excellence. You exemplify right living put into practice. The Lord has not only equipped you with skills for living correctly, but also the ability to impart that to others. The Spirit of truth will guide you into all truth, allowing you to have insight into the true nature of things (John 16:13). Out of your reverential respect for the Lord, you have wisdom to give guidance and direction. You are a safe sounding board who steers those who are hungry for knowledge of the Holy One in the right direction. You need only to ask for the wisdom you lack, and God will give it to you generously (James 1:5). Having spiritual discernment is having the ability to separate the difference between God's wisdom and the world's and the ability to make the right choice—regardless. Luke 21:15 says, "For I will give you words and wisdom that none of your adversaries will be able to resist or contradict."

SONJA

Wisdom; woman of wisdom

໙

James 3:17 *But the wisdom that comes from heaven is first of all pure; then peace-loving, considerate, submissive, full of mercy and good fruit, impartial and sincere.*

Proverbs 9:10 *The fear of the Lord is the beginning of wisdom, and knowledge of the Holy One is understanding.*

You are a person of moral excellence. You exemplify right living put into practice. The Lord has not only equipped you with skills for living correctly, but also the ability to impart that to others. The Spirit of truth will guide you into all truth, allowing you to have insight into the true nature of things (John 16:13). Out of your reverential respect for the Lord, you have wisdom to give guidance and direction. You are a safe sounding board who steers those who are hungry for knowledge of the Holy One in the right direction. You need only to ask for the wisdom you lack, and God will give it to you generously (James 1:5). Having spiritual discernment is having the ability to separate the difference between God's wisdom and the world's and the ability to make the right choice—regardless. Luke 21:15 says, "For I will give you words and wisdom that none of your adversaries will be able to resist or contradict."

SONYA

Wisdom; woman of wisdom

&

James 3:17 *But the wisdom that comes from heaven is first of all pure; then peace-loving, considerate, submissive, full of mercy and good fruit, impartial and sincere.*

Proverbs 9:10 *The fear of the Lord is the beginning of wisdom, and knowledge of the Holy One is understanding.*

You are a person of moral excellence. You exemplify right living put into practice. The Lord has not only equipped you with skills for living correctly, but also the ability to impart that to others. The Spirit of truth will guide you into all truth, allowing you to have insight into the true nature of things (John 16:13). Out of your reverential respect for the Lord, you have wisdom to give guidance and direction. You are a safe sounding board who steers those who are hungry for knowledge of the Holy One in the right direction. You need only to ask for the wisdom you lack, and God will give it to you generously (James 1:5). Having spiritual discernment is having the ability to separate the difference between God's wisdom and the world's and the ability to make the right choice—regardless. Luke 21:15 says, "For I will give you words and wisdom that none of your adversaries will be able to resist or contradict."

SOPHIA

Wisdom; woman of wisdom

&

James 3:17 *But the wisdom that comes from heaven is first of all pure; then peace-loving, considerate, submissive, full of mercy and good fruit, impartial and sincere.*

Proverbs 9:10 *The fear of the Lord is the beginning of wisdom, and knowledge of the Holy One is understanding.*

You are a person of moral excellence. You exemplify right living put into practice. The Lord has not only equipped you with skills for living correctly, but also the ability to impart that to others. The Spirit of truth will guide you into all truth, allowing you to have insight into the true nature of things (John 16:13). Out of your reverential respect for the Lord, you have wisdom to give guidance and direction. You are a safe sounding board who steers those who are hungry for knowledge of the Holy One in the right direction. You need only to ask for the wisdom you lack, and God will give it to you generously (James 1:5). Having spiritual discernment is having the ability to separate the difference between God's wisdom and the world's and the ability to make the right choice—regardless. Luke 21:15 says, "For I will give you words and wisdom that none of your adversaries will be able to resist or contradict."

SPENCER

Dispenser of provisions; faithful steward

෮෬

Matthew 25:21 *His master replied, "Well done, good and faithful servant! You have been faithful with a few things; I will put you in charge of many things. Come and share your master's happiness!"*

Titus 1:3 *And at His appointed season He brought His word to light through the preaching entrusted to me by the command of God our Savior.*

You have a clear understanding that everything you are and all you possess are from God and belong to God. He has loaned everything to you and made you responsible to care for and use it for His glory. God has entrusted you to manage His affairs with accountability and integrity—without hiding anything and without manipulation. Obeying His commands allows you to give direction and oversight to those without goals and to show order to those in confusion. The Bible will be your greatest possession of stewardship. You are a servant to the body of Christ—the church—by the commission God gave you to present His Word in its fullness (Colossians 1:25). Your goal is not to please men, but God, who tests your heart (I Thessalonians 2:4). You are regarded as a servant of Christ, entrusted with the secret things of God. This trust requires you to prove yourself faithful (I Corinthians 4:1–2). You should use whatever gift you have received to serve others, faithfully administering God's grace in its various forms (I Peter 4:10). As you allow God to govern, coach, and guide your life, He will authorize you to be that for others.

STACY

Of the resurrection; transformed heart

❧

Ezekiel 36:26–27 *I will give you a new heart and put a new spirit in you; I will remove from you your heart of stone and give you a heart of flesh. And I will put My spirit in you and move you to follow My decrees and be careful to keep My laws.*

Romans 12:2 *Do not conform any longer to the pattern of this world, but be transformed by the renewing of your mind. Then you will be able to test and approve what God's will is—His good, pleasing and perfect will.*

The cross of Jesus Christ is your ultimate source of transformation. He exchanged your sin for His righteousness, your death for His life, your darkness for His light, your earthly for His eternal, and your past for His future. You were lost, but now you are found. You were blind, but now you see. The old has now become new. II Corinthians 5:17 says, "Therefore, if anyone is in Christ, he is a new creation; the old has gone, the new has come!" A metamorphosis is your transformation from God through Christ. Your conversion by the blood of Jesus is the greatest miracle you will ever experience. This changeless God has traded your sorrow for His joy, your pain for His healing, your emptiness for His fullness, and your rejection for His forgiveness. He adopts, accepts, and loves you. Put to death what belongs to your earthly nature and be clothed with the likeness of Christ (Colossians 3:1–14). As you align your will with His and are continually renewed in the knowledge of God's Word, He will transform many lives through yours. For those living a lie you bring truth, for the dying you bring life, for the rejected you bring acceptance, and for the trapped you bring freedom. His resurrection power flows in and through you. You will continually be transformed into the Lord's likeness with ever-increasing glory (II Corinthians 3:18).

STAN

Dweller at the rocky meadow; sturdy spirit

୫୬

Job 23:11 *My feet have closely followed His steps; I have kept to His way without turning aside.*

James 1:12 *Blessed is the man who perseveres under trial, because when he has stood the test, he will receive the crown of life that God has promised to those who love Him.*

You stand firm without fear. You lift up your face without shame. Your uncompromised commitment to Jesus Christ makes you firmly fixed on His promises. Your mind is steadfast and you are kept in peace because you trust God (Isaiah 26:3). You prepare your mind for action, are self-controlled, and set your hope fully on the grace to be given you when Jesus Christ is revealed (I Peter 1:13). Through you, God brings His stability to the wavering. Your message is, "Finish well, endure hardship, persevere to the end, and reach your goal!"

STANLEY

Dweller at the rocky meadow; sturdy spirit

❧

Job 23:11 *My feet have closely followed His steps; I have kept to His way without turning aside.*

James 1:12 *Blessed is the man who perseveres under trial, because when he has stood the test, he will receive the crown of life that God has promised to those who love Him.*

You stand firm without fear. You lift up your face without shame. Your uncompromised commitment to Jesus Christ makes you firmly fixed on His promises. Your mind is steadfast and you are kept in peace because you trust God (Isaiah 26:3). You prepare your mind for action, are self-controlled, and set your hope fully on the grace to be given you when Jesus Christ is revealed (I Peter 1:13). Through you, God brings His stability to the wavering. Your message is, "Finish well, endure hardship, persevere to the end, and reach your goal!"

STASY

Of the resurrection; transformed heart

Ezekiel 36:26–27 *I will give you a new heart and put a new spirit in you;
I will remove from you your heart of stone and give you a heart of flesh. And
I will put My spirit in you and move you to follow My decrees and be careful
to keep My laws.*

Romans 12:2 *Do not conform any longer to the pattern of this world, but
be transformed by the renewing of your mind. Then you will be able to test
and approve what God's will is—His good, pleasing and perfect will.*

The cross of Jesus Christ is your ultimate source of transformation.
He exchanged your sin for His righteousness, your death for His
life, your darkness for His light, your earthly for His eternal, and
your past for His future. You were lost, but now you are found.
You were blind, but now you see. The old has now become new. II
Corinthians 5:17 says, "Therefore, if anyone is in Christ, he is a new
creation; the old has gone, the new has come!" A metamorphosis is
your transformation from God through Christ. Your conversion by
the blood of Jesus is the greatest miracle you will ever experience.
This changeless God has traded your sorrow for His joy, your pain
for His healing, your emptiness for His fullness, and your rejection
for His forgiveness. He adopts, accepts, and loves you. Put to death
what belongs to your earthly nature and be clothed with the likeness
of Christ (Colossians 3:1–14). As you align your will with His and
are continually renewed in the knowledge of God's Word, He
will transform many lives through yours. For those living a lie you
bring truth, for the dying you bring life, for the rejected you bring
acceptance, and for the trapped you bring freedom. His resurrection
power flows in and through you. You will continually be transformed
into the Lord's likeness with ever-increasing glory (II Corinthians
3:18).

STEEN

Stone; strong in spirit

༄

Matthew 16:18 *And I tell you that you are Peter, and on this rock I will build My church, and the gates of Hades will not overcome it.*

Proverbs 24:5 *A wise man has great power, and a man of knowledge increases strength.*

You are one who has an uncompromised commitment to righteousness, respectability, honesty, character, excellence, value, worth, kindness, innocence, generosity, trustworthiness, faithfulness, justice, hope, and love. You can do everything through Him who gives you strength (Philippians 4:11–13). The Lord is the source of your strength because you turn back the battle at the gate (Isaiah 28:6). You renew your strength through your hope being in the Lord (Isaiah 40:31). Jesus says, "My grace is sufficient for you, for My power is made perfect in weaknesses. Therefore you will boast all the more gladly about your weaknesses, so that Christ's power may rest on you. That is why for Christ's sake, you delight in weaknesses, in insults, in hardships, in persecutions, and in difficulties. For when you are weak, then you are strong," II Corinthians 12:9–10. You are clothed with strength and dignity (Proverbs 31:25). The Lord alone is your rock, salvation, and your fortress. You will never be shaken (Psalm 62:2).

STELLA

A star; humility of spirit

ॐ

Micah 6:8 *He has showed you, O man, what is good. And what does the Lord require of you? To act justly and to love mercy and to walk humbly with your God.*

I Peter 5:6 *Humble yourselves, therefore, under God's mighty hand, that He may lift you up in due time.*

Prove to be trustworthy over little and God will make you ruler over much (Luke 19:17). The higher you lift the Lord, the more dependent you will be on Him. He increases; you decrease (John 3:30). Being exalted only comes from God—not from you or anyone else. It is for the purpose of enlarging His kingdom. Take no credit for the enormous favor God will give you. It is His grace that will give entrance to these doors of favor, as you choose His approval over man's. Philippians 2:3 says, "Do nothing out of selfish ambition or vain conceit, but in humility consider others better than yourselves." Humility and the fear of the Lord bring wealth, honor, and life (Proverbs 22:4).

STEPHANIE

Crowned one

୫୦

Hebrews 2:9   *But we see Jesus, who was made a little lower than the angels, now crowned with glory and honor because He suffered death, so that by the grace of God He might taste death for everyone.*

James 1:12   *Blessed is the man who perseveres under trial, because when he has stood the test, he will receive the crown of life that God has promised to those who love Him.*

Your testimony is recorded in Psalm 21:1–7. The blessings of salvation, joy, longevity, and favor are based on your trust of the Most High. In humility you will never forget the pit from which you were dug, because the Lord redeemed your life from the pit and crowned you with love and compassion (Psalm 103:4). His wisdom sets a garland of grace on your head and presents you with a crown of splendor (Proverbs 4:9). The greater you understand Christ's death, the brighter your crown will be. Honor, victory, power, and dominion will be given back to Him. When casting your crowns at His feet (Revelation 4:10), you will be secure in having stood the test and given Him all the glory. The Lord says to you in Revelation 3:11, "I am coming soon. Hold on to what you have, so that no one will take your crown."

STEPHEN

Crowned one

&

Hebrews 2:9   *But we see Jesus, who was made a little lower than the angels, now crowned with glory and honor because He suffered death, so that by the grace of God He might taste death for everyone.*

James 1:12   *Blessed is the man who perseveres under trial, because when he has stood the test, he will receive the crown of life that God has promised to those who love Him.*

Your testimony is recorded in Psalm 21:1–7. The blessings of salvation, joy, longevity, and favor are based on your trust of the Most High. In humility you will never forget the pit from which you were dug, because the Lord redeemed your life from the pit and crowned you with love and compassion (Psalm 103:4). His wisdom sets a garland of grace on your head and presents you with a crown of splendor (Proverbs 4:9). The greater you understand Christ's death, the brighter your crown will be. Honor, victory, power, and dominion will be given back to Him. When casting your crowns at His feet (Revelation 4:10), you will be secure in having stood the test and given Him all the glory. The Lord says to you in Revelation 3:11, "I am coming soon. Hold on to what you have, so that no one will take your crown."

STERLING

Standard of excellent quality; excellent worth

∂

II Corinthians 8:7 *But just as you excel in everything—in faith, in speech, in knowledge, in complete earnestness and in your love for us—see that you also excel in this grace of giving.*

Philippians 4:8 *Finally, brothers, whatever is true, whatever is noble, whatever is right, whatever is pure, whatever is lovely, whatever is admirable—if anything is excellent or praiseworthy—think about such things.*

Excellent worth is comprised in your worship of God. Revelation 5:12 says, "Worthy is the Lamb, who was slain, to receive power and wealth and wisdom and strength and honor and glory and praise!" "All this also comes from the Lord Almighty, wonderful in counsel and magnificent in wisdom," Isaiah 28:29. God has given you an eye for quality, demonstrating His excellence of character and conduct. You go beyond human capacity with faith that transcends all understanding. Your faith is of greater worth than gold (I Peter 1:7). In quality, skill, and achievement, you go the extra mile. This is all about giving, not getting; serving, not controlling. Perfectionism leads to legalism. Excellence releases freedom. You are to show the insignificant and the wasted the more excellent way of God's love (I Corinthians 12:31 and chapter 13) and kindness (2 Peter 1:5-7). You are to excel in gifts that build up the church (I Corinthians 14:12). God uses you to restore genuine value, purpose, and productivity. Devoting yourself to doing what is good will lead to what is excellent and profitable for everyone (Titus 3:8). Your gentle and quiet spirit is of great worth in God's eyes (I Peter 3:4).

STEVE

Crowned one

&

Hebrews 2:9   *But we see Jesus, who was made a little lower than the angels, now crowned with glory and honor because He suffered death, so that by the grace of God He might taste death for everyone.*

James 1:12   *Blessed is the man who perseveres under trial, because when he has stood the test, he will receive the crown of life that God has promised to those who love Him.*

Your testimony is recorded in Psalm 21:1–7. The blessings of salvation, joy, longevity, and favor are based on your trust of the Most High. In humility you will never forget the pit from which you were dug, because the Lord redeemed your life from the pit and crowned you with love and compassion (Psalm 103:4). His wisdom sets a garland of grace on your head and presents you with a crown of splendor (Proverbs 4:9). The greater you understand Christ's death, the brighter your crown will be. Honor, victory, power, and dominion will be given back to Him. When casting your crowns at His feet (Revelation 4:10), you will be secure in having stood the test and given Him all the glory. The Lord says to you in Revelation 3:11, "I am coming soon. Hold on to what you have, so that no one will take your crown."

STEVEN

Crowned one

&

Hebrews 2:9   *But we see Jesus, who was made a little lower than the angels, now crowned with glory and honor because He suffered death, so that by the grace of God He might taste death for everyone.*

James 1:12   *Blessed is the man who perseveres under trial, because when he has stood the test, he will receive the crown of life that God has promised to those who love Him.*

Your testimony is recorded in Psalm 21:1–7. The blessings of salvation, joy, longevity, and favor are based on your trust of the Most High. In humility you will never forget the pit from which you were dug, because the Lord redeemed your life from the pit and crowned you with love and compassion (Psalm 103:4). His wisdom sets a garland of grace on your head and presents you with a crown of splendor (Proverbs 4:9). The greater you understand Christ's death, the brighter your crown will be. Honor, victory, power, and dominion will be given back to Him. When casting your crowns at His feet (Revelation 4:10), you will be secure in having stood the test and given Him all the glory. The Lord says to you in Revelation 3:11, "I am coming soon. Hold on to what you have, so that no one will take your crown."

SUE

Graceful lily; full of grace

&

Romans 8:32 *He who did not spare His own Son, but gave Him up for us all—how will He not also, along with Him, graciously give us all things?*

I Corinthians 15:10 *But by the grace of God I am what I am, and His grace to me was not without effect.*

Ephesians 2:8 says, "For it is by grace you have been saved, through faith—and this is not from yourselves, it is the gift of God." You are one who brings about balance and harmony through mercy, forgiveness, approval, kindness, and patience—all with a grateful heart. This attitude of gratitude will rule in the midst of inconsiderate behavior. Your nature defies the law of the Pharisees, and is against being self-reliant, prejudice, and selfish. Being full of grace is devotion built through faithfulness and a willingness to quickly pardon. You are blessed with creativity in expressing God's greatest gift of grace—the life of His only Son, Jesus Christ. God says to you through Jeremiah 24:7, "I will give them a heart to know Me, that I am the Lord. They will be My people, and I will be their God, for they will return to Me with all their heart." Ezekiel 11:19 says, "I will give them an undivided heart and put a new spirit in them; I will remove from them their heart of stone and give them a heart of flesh." Accountability will keep your report accurate and your integrity irreproachable.

SUMMER

Warm; full of life

ଔ

John 14:6 *Jesus answered, I am the way and the truth and the life. No one comes to the Father except through Me.*

Deuteronomy 30:19–20 *This day I call heaven and earth as witnesses against you that I have set before you life and death, blessings and curses. Now choose life, so that you and your children may live and that you may love the Lord your God, listen to His voice, and hold fast to Him. For the Lord is your life, and He will give you many years in the land He swore to give to your fathers, Abraham, Isaac, and Jacob.*

Your life's purpose is to serve God, seek His kingdom, do the Father's will, finish the divine task, complete the course joyfully, and attain Christ-likeness. You throw a life-line to those with a death sentence—those who are weary, disgusted, bitter, empty, barren, oppressed, and isolated. With your focus kept on eternal rather than temporal values, you will bring Christ's resurrection power to hearts in the grave. The very gates of hell cannot prevail and be strong enough to stand up under the direct attack of the church. Colossians 3:1–4 says, "Since, then, you have been raised with Christ, set your hearts on things above, not on earthly things. For you died, and your life is now hidden with Christ in God. When Christ, who is your life, appears, then you also will appear with Him in glory." I Samuel 25:29 says, "Your life will be bound securely in the bundle of the living by the Lord your God. But the lives of your enemies He will hurl away as from the pocket of a sling." Psalm 27:1 says, "The Lord is the stronghold of your life—of whom shall you be afraid?" Enjoy life to the fullest! (John 10:10)

SUSAN

Graceful lily; full of grace

℘

Romans 8:32 *He who did not spare His own Son, but gave Him up for us all—how will He not also, along with Him, graciously give us all things?*

I Corinthians 15:10 *But by the grace of God I am what I am, and His grace to me was not without effect.*

Ephesians 2:8 says, "For it is by grace you have been saved, through faith—and this is not from yourselves, it is the gift of God." You are one who brings about balance and harmony through mercy, forgiveness, approval, kindness, and patience—all with a grateful heart. This attitude of gratitude will rule in the midst of inconsiderate behavior. Your nature defies the law of the Pharisees, and is against being self-reliant, prejudice, and selfish. Being full of grace is devotion built through faithfulness and a willingness to quickly pardon. You are blessed with creativity in expressing God's greatest gift of grace—the life of His only Son, Jesus Christ. God says to you through Jeremiah 24:7, "I will give them a heart to know Me, that I am the Lord. They will be My people, and I will be their God, for they will return to Me with all their heart." Ezekiel 11:19 says, "I will give them an undivided heart and put a new spirit in them; I will remove from them their heart of stone and give them a heart of flesh." Accountability will keep your report accurate and your integrity irreproachable.

SUZANNE

Graceful lily; full of grace

જી

Romans 8:32 *He who did not spare His own Son, but gave Him up for us all—how will He not also, along with Him, graciously give us all things?*

I Corinthians 15:10 *But by the grace of God I am what I am, and His grace to me was not without effect.*

Ephesians 2:8 says, "For it is by grace you have been saved, through faith—and this is not from yourselves, it is the gift of God." You are one who brings about balance and harmony through mercy, forgiveness, approval, kindness, and patience—all with a grateful heart. This attitude of gratitude will rule in the midst of inconsiderate behavior. Your nature defies the law of the Pharisees, and is against being self-reliant, prejudice, and selfish. Being full of grace is devotion built through faithfulness and a willingness to quickly pardon. You are blessed with creativity in expressing God's greatest gift of grace—the life of His only Son, Jesus Christ. God says to you through Jeremiah 24:7, "I will give them a heart to know Me, that I am the Lord. They will be My people, and I will be their God, for they will return to Me with all their heart." Ezekiel 11:19 says, "I will give them an undivided heart and put a new spirit in them; I will remove from them their heart of stone and give them a heart of flesh." Accountability will keep your report accurate and your integrity irreproachable.

SYBIL

Future gazing; prophetic

&

Isaiah 62:6 *I have posted watchmen on your walls, O Jerusalem; they will never be silent day or night. You who call on the Lord give yourselves no rest.*

I Corinthians 16:13–14 *Be on your guard; stand firm in the faith; be men of courage; be strong. Do everything in love.*

The Lord has appointed you as His watchman. You must hear His voice and give warning for Him (Ezekiel 3:17). You must be watchful, alert, prepared, actively observant, and on guard. You have quick intelligence and a readiness to take prompt action—whether alerting to danger or opportunities. You are spiritually wide awake and aware of all surrounding circumstances. This is accomplished by your devoted prayer life and your being watchful and thankful (Colossians 4:2). You are able to keep your head in all situations (II Timothy 4:5). You are self-controlled and alert, able to resist the devil and stand firm in your faith (I Peter 5:8–9). You exercise self-restraint that governs all passions and desires. This enables you to be conformed to the mind of Christ. You must stay ready for the Lord's return (Luke 12:35–40).

SYDNEY

Saint Denis; discerner of excellence

෮

II Corinthians 8:7 *But just as you excel in everything—in faith, in speech, in knowledge, in complete earnestness and in your love for us—see that you also excel in this grace of giving.*

Philippians 4:8 *Finally, brothers, whatever is true, whatever is noble, whatever is right, whatever is pure, whatever is lovely, whatever is admirable—if anything is excellent or praiseworthy—think about such things.*

Excellent worth is comprised in your worship of God. Revelation 5:12 says, "Worthy is the Lamb, who was slain, to receive power and wealth and wisdom and strength and honor and glory and praise!" "All this also comes from the Lord Almighty, wonderful in counsel and magnificent in wisdom," Isaiah 28:29. God has given you an eye for quality, demonstrating His excellence of character and conduct. You go beyond human capacity with faith that transcends all understanding. Your faith is of greater worth than gold (I Peter 1:7). In quality, skill, and achievement, you go the extra mile. This is all about giving, not getting; serving, not controlling. Perfectionism leads to legalism. Excellence releases freedom. You are to show the insignificant and the wasted the more excellent way of God's love (I Corinthians 12:31 and chapter 13) and kindness (2 Peter 1:5-7). You are to excel in gifts that build up the church (I Corinthians 14:12). God uses you to restore genuine value, purpose, and productivity. Devoting yourself to doing what is good will lead to what is excellent and profitable for everyone (Titus 3:8). Your gentle and quiet spirit is of great worth in God's eyes (I Peter 3:4).

SYLVIA

From the forest; secure one

୪୬

Deuteronomy 33:12 *Let the beloved of the Lord rest secure in Him, for He shields him all day long, and the one the Lord loves rests between His shoulders.*

Job 11:18 *You will be secure, because there is hope; you will look about you and take your rest in safety.*

Your life is bound securely in the bundle of the living by the Lord your God (I Samuel 25:29). You will not fear the terror of night, nor the arrow that flies by day (Psalm 91:5). You will have no fear of bad news; your heart is steadfast, trusting in the Lord (Psalm 112:7). You say with confidence that the Lord is your helper. God's sovereign protection frees you from doubt and harm. Because you find your shelter, assurance, stability, and strength in your personal relationship with the Lord, you are kept in a safe place. Lay with compassionate humility a firm foundation for others, providing them with solid security. As you stay hidden in the shadow of His wings (Psalm 61:4), you direct deliverance for the weak, insecure, unsheltered, and frail. You are to help others to become overcomers, victorious, confident, and secure—regardless of the risk and cost to you.

TALON

Claw; strength

❧

Proverbs 24:5 *A wise man has great power, and a man of knowledge increases strength.*

Ephesians 6:10 *Finally, be strong in the Lord and in His mighty power.*

You are one who has an un-compromised commitment to righteousness, respectability, honesty, character, excellence, value, worth, kindness, innocence, generosity, trustworthiness, faithfulness, justice, hope, and love. You can do everything through Him who gives you strength (Philippians 4:11–13). The Lord is the source of your strength because you turn back the battle at the gate (Isaiah 28:6). You renew your strength by your hope being in the Lord (Isaiah 40:31). Jesus says, "My grace is sufficient for you, for My power is made perfect in weaknesses. Therefore you will boast all the more gladly about your weaknesses, so that Christ's power may rest on you. That is why for Christ's sake, you delight in weaknesses, in insults, in hardships, in persecutions, and in difficulties. For when you are weak, then you are strong," II Corinthians 12:9–10. You are clothed with strength and dignity (Proverbs 31:25).

TAMMY

A twin; seeker of truth

ഔ

Psalm 89:1–2 *I will sing of the Lord's great love forever; with my mouth I will make Your faithfulness known through all generations. I will declare that Your love stands firm forever, that You established Your faithfulness in heaven itself.*

Psalm 51:6 *Surely You desire truth in the inner parts; You teach me wisdom in the inmost place.*

John 14:6 *Jesus answered, "I am the way and the truth and the life. No one comes to the Father except through Me."*

"You know the truth and the truth has set you free," John 8:32. You are one who is aggressive toward lies and deception. Your purpose is to bring about truth through openness, revelation, authenticity, accuracy, and honesty. As God's messenger, you will have firmness in keeping and executing His promises and also your own. Your God-given wisdom will be based on God's Word alone. Zechariah 8:16 says, "These are the things you are to do: Speak the truth to each other, and render true and sound judgment in your courts." May true instruction be in your mouth and nothing false be found on your lips (Malachi 2:6).

TANYA

A fair queen; noble spirit

ॐ

Isaiah 32:8 *But the noble man makes noble plans, and by noble deeds he stands.*

Luke 8:15 *But the seed on good soil stands for those with a noble and good heart, who hear the word, retain it, and by persevering produce a crop.*

Proverbs 18:12 says, "Before his downfall a man's heart is proud, but humility comes before honor." You are one who has a humble confidence in recognizing and expressing reverence, worship, adoration, trust, deference, tribute, admiration, and respect. This is the result of being secure in the truth of who you are in the Lord. Through humility, King Jesus made a way for you to be engrafted into His royalty. He made of Himself no reputation and took on the nature of a servant (Philippians 2:7) to affirm your value. Through self-denial, you prioritize excellence in virtue, truthfulness, and faithfulness. Because of the respect you have earned, you dismantle inferiority, disgrace, shame, and offenses. No one feels second-rate in your presence. The deeper that the Lord is your object of reverence, the greater your confidence will be in giving approval and worth. Because you are tall in spirit, your face is always turned upward.

TAYLOR

Tailor; industrious

❧

Colossians 1:16 *For by Him all things were created: things in heaven and on earth, visible and invisible, whether thrones or powers or rulers or authorities; all things were created by Him and for Him.*

Ephesians 2:10 *For we are God's workmanship, created in Christ Jesus to do good works, which God prepared in advance for us to do.*

To be industrious means to be skillful, hardworking, zealous, and diligent. By persevering, you give careful attention to detail. There is not a lazy bone in your body. Through you the Lord will originate. How you deal with the past determines your future. Regardless of the curses or blessings, the failures or successes, you are God's platform for a "new thing." You cannot lean on your own understanding or reasoning. God Almighty created the heavens, the earth, and you in His image. So the more completely dependent you become on your Creator, the more productive your life will be for Him! I Peter 4:19, "So then, those who suffer according to God's will should commit themselves to their Creator and continue to do good."

TED

Gift of God

❧

James 1:17 *Every good and perfect gift is from above, coming down from the Father of the heavenly lights, who does not change like shifting shadows.*

I Samuel 16:7 *But the Lord said to Samuel, "Do not consider his appearance or his height, for I have rejected him. The Lord does not look at the things man looks at. Man looks at the outward appearance, but the Lord looks at the heart."*

You are God's tribute to Himself, His personal reward. Your life defines God's manners, with priorities on giving rather than receiving. You are to fan into flame the gift of God (II Timothy 1:6). Through you He will display His favor, encouragement and kindness even to the undeserved and hated. As you look beyond faults and see needs, you are God's channel through which His unselfish love flows and is revealed. Discipline your attention to the Giver, not to the gift, nor its wrappings. Give diligence to preserving a humble, submitted heart in full surrender to the Lord. Proverbs 18:16 says, "A gift opens the way for the giver and ushers him into the presence of the great."

TERESA

Reaper; industrious

୫ଠ

Colossians 1:16   *For by Him all things were created: things in heaven and on earth, visible and invisible, whether thrones or powers or rulers or authorities; all things were created by Him and for Him.*

Ephesians 2:10   *For we are God's workmanship, created in Christ Jesus to do good works, which God prepared in advance for us to do.*

To be industrious means to be skillful, hardworking, zealous, and diligent. By persevering, you give careful attention to detail. There is not a lazy bone in your body. Through you the Lord will originate. How you deal with the past determines your future. Regardless of the curses or blessings, the failures or successes, you are God's platform for a "new thing." You cannot lean on your own understanding or reasoning. God Almighty created the heavens, the earth, and you in His image. So the more completely dependent you become on your Creator, the more productive your life will be for Him! I Peter 4:19, "So then, those who suffer according to God's will should commit themselves to their Creator and continue to do good."

TERI

Reaper; caring one

જી

Hosea 10:12 *Sow for yourselves righteousness, reap the fruit of unfailing love, and break up your unplowed ground; for it is time to seek the Lord, until He comes and showers righteousness on you.*

Galatians 6:8 *The one who sows to please his sinful nature will reap destruction; the one who sows to please the Spirit, from the Spirit will reap eternal life.*

The Lord would have you know that "the very hairs of your head are all numbered, so do not be afraid; you are worth more than many sparrows to Him" (Luke 12:7). "Cast all your anxieties on Him because He cares for you," I Peter 5:7. With this total dependence on the Lord, you will obtain a great harvest for His kingdom. Psalm 126:5–6 says, "Those who sow in tears will reap with songs of joy. He who goes out weeping, carrying seed to sow, will return with songs of joy, carrying sheaves with him." As a caring one, you are cautious in avoiding mistakes and very attentive to details. His compassion flowing to and through you equips you to show concern for the neglected and the indifferent. The complacent will be challenged to release their burdens and worries to the burden bearer, Jesus Christ. The Good Shepherd will continue to nurture you as you nurture others.

TERRENCE

Smooth-polished one

ಹ

Isaiah 42:16 I will lead the blind by ways they have not known, along unfamiliar paths I will guide them; I will turn the darkness into the light before them and make the rough places smooth. These are the things I will do; I will not forsake them.

Isaiah 45:2 I will go before you and will level the mountains; I will break down gates of bronze and cut through bars of iron.

You are level, gently-flowing, calm, steady in motion, and pleasant. You make rough places smooth; you calm storms and soothe pain. Your soft words and kind actions strip weapons of deception, flattery, and hypocrisy. You make places level by crushing Satan under your feet (Romans 16:18–20). Your presence brings equality to rank and degree. You will not tolerate self-promotion or any form of being prejudiced by yourself or by others. You also will not tolerate any form of superiority or inferiority. "Whether you turn to the right or to the left, your ears will hear a voice behind you, saying, 'This is the way; walk in it,'" Isaiah 30:21. This keen discernment to God's voice directs you to remove obstacles, hindrances, stumbling blocks, and offenses from the paths of those whom He has given you to serve in order to reveal God's glory (Isaiah 40:3–5). They will be changed from self-righteousness, pride, and other forms of evil to repentance, humility, and submission. "Make level paths for your feet, so that the lame may not be disabled, but rather healed," Hebrews 12:13.

TERRY

Smooth-polished one

&

Isaiah 42:16 *I will lead the blind by ways they have not known, along unfamiliar paths I will guide them; I will turn the darkness into the light before them and make the rough places smooth. These are the things I will do; I will not forsake them.*

Isaiah 45:2 *I will go before you and will level the mountains; I will break down gates of bronze and cut through bars of iron.*

You are level, gently-flowing, calm, steady in motion, and pleasant. You make rough places smooth; you calm storms and soothe pain. Your soft words and kind actions strip weapons of deception, flattery, and hypocrisy. You make places level by crushing Satan under your feet (Romans 16:18–20). Your presence brings equality to rank and degree. You will not tolerate self-promotion or any form of being prejudiced by yourself or by others. You also will not tolerate any form of superiority or inferiority. "Whether you turn to the right or to the left, your ears will hear a voice behind you, saying, 'This is the way; walk in it,'" Isaiah 30:21. This keen discernment to God's voice directs you to remove obstacles, hindrances, stumbling blocks, and offenses from the paths of those whom He has given you to serve in order to reveal God's glory (Isaiah 40:3–5). They will be changed from self-righteousness, pride, and other forms of evil to repentance, humility, and submission. "Make level paths for your feet, so that the lame may not be disabled, but rather healed," Hebrews 12:13.

TESSA

Reaper; industrious

८०

Colossians 1:16 *For by Him all things were created: things in heaven and on earth, visible and invisible, whether thrones or powers or rulers or authorities; all things were created by Him and for Him.*

Ephesians 2:10 *For we are God's workmanship, created in Christ Jesus to do good works, which God prepared in advance for us to do.*

To be industrious means to be skillful, hardworking, zealous, and diligent. By persevering, you give careful attention to detail. There is not a lazy bone in your body. Through you the Lord will originate. How you deal with the past determines your future. Regardless of the curses or blessings, the failures or successes, you are God's platform for a "new thing." You cannot lean on your own understanding or reasoning. God Almighty created the heavens, the earth, and you in His image. So the more completely dependent you become on your Creator, the more productive your life will be for Him! I Peter 4:19, "So then, those who suffer according to God's will should commit themselves to their Creator and continue to do good."

THELMA

Nurse; caring one

&

Isaiah 41:10 *So do not fear, for I am with you; do not be dismayed, for I am your God. I will strength you and help you; I will uphold you with My righteous right hand.*

I Corinthians 15:58 *Therefore, my dear brothers, stand firm. Let nothing move you. Always give yourselves fully to the work of the Lord, because you know that your labor in the Lord is not in vain.*

You say with confidence that the Lord is your helper. You are not afraid. What can man do to you (Hebrews 13:6)? This trust allows you the important role of being God's hands extended to your world. You serve with the strength He provides so that He gets all the credit (I Peter 4:11). Like the good Samaritan, you are moved with compassion to give practical help, providing sacrifice and kindness with unselfishness (Luke 10:25–37). You are eyes to the blind, feet to the lame, and the father to the needy (Job 29:15–16). You make the most of every opportunity to do good to all people (Galatians 6:10). As a caring one, you are cautious in avoiding mistakes and very attentive to details. His compassion flowing to and through you equips you to show concern for the neglected and indifferent. The complacent will be challenged to release their burdens and worries to the burden bearer, Jesus Christ. The Good Shepherd will continue to nurture you as you nurture others. Because you are devoted to the service of the Lord, you will hear, "Well done, good and faithful servant! You have been faithful with a few things; I will put you in charge of many things. Come and share your master's happiness!" (Matthew 25:23)

THERESA

Reaper; industrious

ॐ

Colossians 1:16 *For by Him all things were created: things in heaven and on earth, visible and invisible, whether thrones or powers or rulers or authorities; all things were created by Him and for Him.*

Ephesians 2:10 *For we are God's workmanship, created in Christ Jesus to do good works, which God prepared in advance for us to do.*

To be industrious means to be skillful, hardworking, zealous, and diligent. By persevering, you give careful attention to detail. There is not a lazy bone in your body. Through you the Lord will originate. How you deal with the past determines your future. Regardless of the curses or blessings, the failures or successes, you are God's platform for a "new thing." You cannot lean on your own understanding or reasoning. God Almighty created the heavens, the earth, and you in His image. So the more completely dependent you become on your Creator, the more productive your life will be for Him! I Peter 4:19, "So then, those who suffer according to God's will should commit themselves to their Creator and continue to do good."

THOMAS

Twin; seeker of truth

&

Psalm 89:1–2 *I will sing of the Lord's great love forever; with my mouth I will make Your faithfulness known through all generations. I will declare that Your love stands firm forever, that You established Your faithfulness in heaven itself.*

Psalm 51:6 *Surely You desire truth in the inner parts; You teach me wisdom in the inmost place.*

John 14:6 *Jesus answered, "I am the way and the truth and the life. No one comes to the Father except through Me."*

"You know the truth and the truth has set you free," John 8:32. You are one who is aggressive toward lies and deception. Your purpose is to bring about truth through openness, revelation, authenticity, accuracy, and honesty. As God's messenger, you will have firmness in keeping and executing His promises and also your own. Your God-given wisdom will be based on God's Word alone. Zechariah 8:16 says, "These are the things you are to do: Speak the truth to each other, and render true and sound judgment in your courts." May true instruction be in your mouth and nothing false be found on your lips (Malachi 2:6).

TIARA

Crowned; thankful

ॐ

Hebrews 2:9   *But we see Jesus, who was made a little lower than the angels, now crowned with glory and honor because He suffered death, so that by the grace of God He might taste death for everyone.*

James 1:12   *Blessed is the man who perseveres under trial, because when he has stood the test, he will receive the crown of life that God has promised to those who love Him.*

Your testimony is recorded in Psalm 21:1–7. The blessings of salvation, joy, longevity, and favor are based on your trust of the Most High. In humility you will never forget the pit from which you were dug, because the Lord redeemed your life from the pit and crowned you with love and compassion (Psalm 103:4). His wisdom sets a garland of grace on your head and presents you with a crown of splendor (Proverbs 4:9). The greater you understand Christ's death, the brighter your crown will be. Honor, victory, power, and dominion will be given back to Him. When casting your crowns at His feet (Revelation 4:10), you will be secure in having stood the test and given Him all the glory. The Lord says to you in Revelation 3:11, "I am coming soon. Hold on to what you have, so that no one will take your crown."

TIFFANY

Appearance of God; in God's image

Exodus 15:11 *Who among the gods is like you, O Lord? Who is like You—majestic in holiness, awesome in glory, working wonders?*

I Timothy 4:8 *Godliness has value for all things, holding promise for both the present life and the life to come.*

Godliness with contentment is great gain (I Timothy 6:6). You are to pursue godliness (I Timothy 6:11). Your life is to reflect the very nature of God, which is holy, righteous, just, pure, spotless, faithful, and divine. The choices you make and the life you live are to define God's standard for living. As you follow the Lord, He desires for others to pattern their lives after you. Out of a humble, reverent heart and as you show Him respect, adoration, and praise, you will ever be esteemed and prized by the Lord. You will have no reason to be insecure in who you are, or to place blame on God, or to disapprove of His will for your life. He celebrates how He made you!

TIM

Honoring God; blessed of God

✂

Exodus 23:25 *Worship the Lord your God, and His blessing will be on your food and water. I will take away sickness from among you.*

Proverbs 10:22 *The blessing of the Lord brings wealth, and He adds no trouble to it.*

God has resourced you in order to give you great influence and favor. He commands His blessings where you establish unity (Psalm 133). He will turn every curse into a blessing for you because He loves you (Deuteronomy 23:5). True abundance is giving out of your nothingness, with a total dependence on God. Wealth is not in the amount you have, but in the attitude in which you give it. Because of your standard of integrity and gratitude, you have an eye for value, fruitfulness, and generosity. Your heart is for the poor, barren, and destitute, but you resist the lazy and stingy. You transfer God's possessions, power, and pleasure to others. Make wise investments of your time, energy, and resources that will keep reproducing rather than insuring your own personal gratification. You are blessed to be a blessing. The greater your obedience to the Lord, the greater will be His blessings (Deuteronomy 28:1–14).

TIMOTHY

Honoring God; blessed of God

༄

Exodus 23:25 *Worship the Lord your God, and His blessing will be on your food and water. I will take away sickness from among you.*

Proverbs 10:22 *The blessing of the Lord brings wealth, and He adds no trouble to it.*

God has resourced you in order to give you great influence and favor. He commands His blessings where you establish unity (Psalm 133). He will turn every curse into a blessing for you because He loves you (Deuteronomy 23:5). True abundance is giving out of your nothingness, with a total dependence on God. Wealth is not in the amount you have, but in the attitude in which you give it. Because of your standard of integrity and gratitude, you have an eye for value, fruitfulness, and generosity. Your heart is for the poor, barren, and destitute, but you resist the lazy and stingy. You transfer God's possessions, power, and pleasure to others. Make wise investments of your time, energy, and resources that will keep reproducing rather than insuring your own personal gratification. You are blessed to be a blessing. The greater your obedience to the Lord, the greater will be His blessings (Deuteronomy 28:1–14).

TINA

Believer in Christ; follower of Christ

ॐ

I Chronicles 28:9 *And you, my son Solomon, acknowledge the God of your father, and serve Him with wholehearted devotion and with a willing mind, for the Lord searches every heart and understands every motive behind the thoughts. If you seek Him, He will be found by you; but if you forsake Him, He will reject you forever.*

I Corinthians 15:58 *Therefore, my dear brothers, stand firm. Let nothing move you. Always give yourselves fully to the work of the Lord, because you know that your labor is not in vain.*

Your very being lives to be in constant harmony with your Creator—that the both of your hearts beat as one. Therefore, you are continually yielding every area to the likeness of Christ with strong discipline as you follow Him. You have a devoted allegiance to Christ and His teachings. Your character is one of devotion, dedication, consecration, loyalty, and faithfulness. You are called to help the fallen take a stand and to remove shame and fear. You dispel division by bringing the very unity of God. As you seek and trust in Him with all your heart, leaning not to your own understanding, He will protect you from being blind-sided by the enemy of your soul. Be known as one who loves God with all your heart, soul, mind, and strength. You are one whom God has chosen to be an example of His Son, Jesus Christ.

TITUS

Heroic; honorable

❧

Isaiah 32:8 *But the noble man makes noble plans, and by noble deeds he stands.*

Luke 8:15 *But the seed on good soil stands for those with a noble and good heart, who hear the word, retain it, and by persevering produce a crop.*

Proverbs 18:12 says, "Before his downfall a man's heart is proud, but humility comes before honor." You are one who has a humble confidence in recognizing and expressing reverence, worship, adoration, trust, deference, tribute, admiration, and respect. This is the result of being secure in the truth of who you are in the Lord. Through humility, King Jesus made a way for you to be engrafted into His royalty. He made of Himself no reputation and took on the nature of a servant (Philippians 2:7) to affirm your value. Through self-denial, you prioritize excellence in virtue, truthfulness, and faithfulness. Because of the respect you have earned, you dismantle inferiority, disgrace, shame, and offenses. No one feels second-rate in your presence. The deeper that the Lord is your object of reverence, the greater your confidence will be in giving approval and worth. Because you are tall in spirit, your face is always turned upward.

TOBIAS

The Lord is good; believing the Lord is good

ജ

Psalm 34:8 *Taste and see that the Lord is good; blessed is the man who takes refuge in Him.*

Nahum 1:7 *The Lord is good, a refuge in times of trouble. He cares for those who trust in Him.*

The Lord looks upon you with His favor and approval. Because you trust in Him, He finds you suitable to fulfill His purpose. You express the kindness of God's heart. Through you, God extends His grace, tenderness, and compassion to those who have failed and feel worthless. Those whom the world would consider "trash" find God's goodness. Your presence contributes to the well-being and happiness of all those whom God has assigned to your life. You are to command them to do good and be rich in good deeds (I Timothy 6:18). God is fully complete—all you ever need is found in Him. His goodness in you brings Him pleasure. You overcome evil with good (Romans 12:21) by being honest, reliable, considerate, and generous. Your life's message is Romans 8:28, "And we know that in all things God works for the good of those who love Him, who have been called according to His purpose." God's will for you will always be good (Romans 12:2). Hold on to the good (I Thessalonians 5:21) and don't forget to do good and to share with others, for with such sacrifices God is pleased (Hebrews 13:16).

TOBY

The Lord is good; believing the Lord is good

৪৩

Psalm 34:8 *Taste and see that the Lord is good; blessed is the man who takes refuge in Him.*

Nahum 1:7 *The Lord is good, a refuge in times of trouble. He cares for those who trust in Him.*

The Lord looks upon you with His favor and approval. Because you trust in Him, He finds you suitable to fulfill His purpose. You express the kindness of God's heart. Through you, God extends His grace, tenderness, and compassion to those who have failed and feel worthless. Those whom the world would consider "trash" find God's goodness. Your presence contributes to the well-being and happiness of all those whom God has assigned to your life. You are to command them to do good and be rich in good deeds (I Timothy 6:18). God is fully complete—all you ever need is found in Him. His goodness in you brings Him pleasure. You overcome evil with good (Romans 12:21) by being honest, reliable, considerate, and generous. Your life's message is Romans 8:28, "And we know that in all things God works for the good of those who love Him, who have been called according to His purpose." God's will for you will always be good (Romans 12:2). Hold on to the good (I Thessalonians 5:21) and don't forget to do good and to share with others, for with such sacrifices God is pleased (Hebrews 13:16).

TODD

A fox; wise chooser

᛭

James 3:17   *But the wisdom that comes from heaven is first of all pure; then peace-loving, considerate, submissive, full of mercy and good fruit, impartial and sincere.*

Proverbs 9:10 *The fear of the Lord is the beginning of wisdom, and knowledge of the Holy One is understanding.*

You are a person of moral excellence. You exemplify right living put into practice. The Lord has not only equipped you with skills for living correctly, but also the ability to impart that to others. The Spirit of truth will guide you into all truth, allowing you to have insight into the true nature of things (John 16:13). Out of your reverential respect for the Lord, you have wisdom to give guidance and direction. You are a safe sounding board who steers those who are hungry for knowledge of the Holy One in the right direction. You need only to ask for the wisdom you lack, and God will give it to you generously (James 1:5). Having spiritual discernment is having the ability to separate the difference between God's wisdom and the world's and the ability to make the right choice—regardless. Luke 21:15 says, "For I will give you words and wisdom that none of your adversaries will be able to resist or contradict."

TOM

Twin; seeker of truth

❧

Psalm 89:1–2   *I will sing of the Lord's great love forever; with my mouth I will make Your faithfulness known through all generations. I will declare that Your love stands firm forever, that You established Your faithfulness in heaven itself.*

Psalm 51:6   *Surely You desire truth in the inner parts; You teach me wisdom in the inmost place.*

John 14:6   *Jesus answered, "I am the way and the truth and the life. No one comes to the Father except through Me."*

"You know the truth and the truth has set you free," John 8:32. You are one who is aggressive toward lies and deception. Your purpose is to bring about truth through openness, revelation, authenticity, accuracy, and honesty. As God's messenger, you will have firmness in keeping and executing His promises and also your own. Your God-given wisdom will be based on God's Word alone. Zechariah 8:16 says, "These are the things you are to do: Speak the truth to each other, and render true and sound judgment in your courts." May true instruction be in your mouth and nothing false be found on your lips (Malachi 2:6).

TONIA

A fair queen; noble spirit

Isaiah 32:8 *But the noble man makes noble plans, and by noble deeds he stands.*

Luke 8:15 *But the seed on good soil stands for those with a noble and good heart, who hear the word, retain it, and by persevering produce a crop.*

Proverbs 18:12 says, "Before his downfall a man's heart is proud, but humility comes before honor." You are one who has a humble confidence in recognizing and expressing reverence, worship, adoration, trust, deference, tribute, admiration, and respect. This is the result of being secure in the truth of who you are in the Lord. Through humility, King Jesus made a way for you to be engrafted into His royalty. He made of Himself no reputation and took on the nature of a servant (Philippians 2:7) to affirm your value. Through self-denial, you prioritize excellence in virtue, truthfulness, and faithfulness. Because of the respect you have earned, you dismantle inferiority, disgrace, shame, and offenses. No one feels second-rate in your presence. The deeper that the Lord is your object of reverence, the greater your confidence will be in giving approval and worth. Because you are tall in spirit, your face is always turned upward.

TONY

Inestimable; priceless one

ॐ

Exodus 19:5 *Now if you obey me fully and keep my covenant, then out of all nations you will be My treasured possession.*

I Corinthians 6:20 *You were bought at a price. Therefore honor God with your body.*

With a humble confidence, you recognize that your undeserved worth is based on the spotless Lamb sacrificed for you. No greater love will you experience than from the One who laid down His life for you. You pour back your love to Him lavishly with no thought of the cost to you or your reputation. In fact, you are willing to give up everything you have to be His disciple (Luke 14:25–33). This debt of love causes you to give forethought to all your investments as to whether Christ gets all the glory. You will not gamble or be bribed because you know the incredible price paid for you. Therefore you bring value to the insignificant, meaning to the absurd, and worth to the wasted. Your high standard of excellence will bear eternal fruit because of your commitment to please God more than man. As a child of the King, through you castaways will be restored to heirs.

TONYA

A fair queen; noble spirit

❧

Isaiah 32:8 *But the noble man makes noble plans, and by noble deeds he stands.*

Luke 8:15 *But the seed on good soil stands for those with a noble and good heart, who hear the word, retain it, and by persevering produce a crop.*

Proverbs 18:12 says, "Before his downfall a man's heart is proud, but humility comes before honor." You are one who has a humble confidence in recognizing and expressing reverence, worship, adoration, trust, deference, tribute, admiration, and respect. This is the result of being secure in the truth of who you are in the Lord. Through humility, King Jesus made a way for you to be engrafted into His royalty. He made of Himself no reputation and took on the nature of a servant (Philippians 2:7) to affirm your value. Through self-denial, you prioritize excellence in virtue, truthfulness, and faithfulness. Because of the respect you have earned, you dismantle inferiority, disgrace, shame, and offenses. No one feels second-rate in your presence. The deeper that the Lord is your object of reverence, the greater your confidence will be in giving approval and worth. Because you are tall in spirit, your face is always turned upward.

TORI

Laurel leaves; victorious spirit

I John 5:4   *Everyone born of God overcomes the world. This is the victory that has overcome the world, even our faith.*

II Corinthians 2:14   *But thanks be to God, who always leads us in triumphal procession in Christ and through us spreads everywhere the fragrance of the knowledge of Him.*

Because of your faith in Jesus Christ, you will ever be aggressive towards the enemy's tools of defeat, failure, and victimization. You will push back Satan and overcome all his power. Jesus has given you authority to trample on snakes and scorpions and to overcome all the power of the enemy; nothing will harm you (Luke 10:19). Even in the severest of afflictions—such as hardship, persecution, famine, nakedness, danger, or sword—you are more than a conqueror through Christ who loves you (Romans 8:35–37). "Everyone born of God overcomes the world. This is the victory that has overcome the world, even our faith," I John 5:4. "Take heart, Jesus has overcome the world," John 16:33.

TRACY

To reap; industrious

౮

Colossians 1:16 *For by Him all things were created: things in heaven and on earth, visible and invisible, whether thrones or powers or rulers or authorities; all things were created by Him and for Him.*

Ephesians 2:10 *For we are God's workmanship, created in Christ Jesus to do good works, which God prepared in advance for us to do.*

To be industrious means to be skillful, hardworking, zealous, and diligent. By persevering, you give careful attention to detail. There is not a lazy bone in your body. Through you the Lord will originate. How you deal with the past determines your future. Regardless of the curses or blessings, the failures or successes, you are God's platform for a "new thing." You cannot lean on your own understanding or reasoning. God Almighty created the heavens, the earth, and you in His image. So the more completely dependent you become on your Creator, the more productive your life will be for Him! I Peter 4:19, "So then, those who suffer according to God's will should commit themselves to their Creator and continue to do good."

TRAVIS

From the crossroads; diligent spirit

☙

Colossians 1:16 *For by Him all things were created: things in heaven and on earth, visible and invisible, whether thrones or powers or rulers or authorities; all things were created by Him and for Him.*

Ephesians 2:10 *For we are God's workmanship, created in Christ Jesus to do good works, which God prepared in advance for us to do.*

To be industrious means to be skillful, hardworking, zealous, and diligent. By persevering, you give careful attention to detail. There is not a lazy bone in your body. Through you the Lord will originate. How you deal with the past determines your future. Regardless of the curses or blessings, the failures or successes, you are God's platform for a "new thing." You cannot lean on your own understanding or reasoning. God Almighty created the heavens, the earth, and you in His image. So the more completely dependent you become on your Creator, the more productive your life will be for Him! I Peter 4:19, "So then, those who suffer according to God's will should commit themselves to their Creator and continue to do good."

TREY

Three; united

∽

Ecclesiastes 4:12 *Though one may be overpowered, two can defend themselves. A cord of three strands is not quickly broken.*

I Corinthians 1:10 *I appeal to you, brothers, in the name of our Lord Jesus Christ, that all of you agree with one another so that there may be no divisions among you and that you may be perfectly united in mind and thought.*

You are one who has chosen to separate yourself from wickedness, darkness, unbelief, idolatry, and uncleanness in order to be yoked together with your Heavenly Father. He will live and walk with you. He will be your God and you will be His son (II Corinthians 6:14–18). This inseparable union results in:

Psalm 133—anointing and God's blessings;

I Corinthians 12—no jealousy over different giftings in God's body;

Romans 6:5—identity with Christ's death and resurrection;

Philippians 2:1–5—having Christ's attitude – one in spirit and purpose;

Colossians 2:2–3—complete understanding of Christ's wisdom;

Ephesians 2:19–22—being a dwelling where God lives by His Spirit;

Ephesians 4:16—spiritual maturity.

You will have a greater sensitivity for ministry to relationships that are separated, severed, deserted, or abandoned. As Christ's team player, you will gladly take the risk to touch these types of people, in order that they may be one with Him in harmony. You will serve as a link to bring closeness.

TRICIA

Noble one; full of honor

৪৩

Isaiah 32:8 *But the noble man makes noble plans, and by noble deeds he stands.*

Luke 8:15 *But the seed on good soil stands for those with a noble and good heart, who hear the word, retain it, and by persevering produce a crop.*

Proverbs 18:12 says, "Before his downfall a man's heart is proud, but humility comes before honor." You are one who has a humble confidence in recognizing and expressing reverence, worship, adoration, trust, deference, tribute, admiration, and respect. This is the result of being secure in the truth of who you are in the Lord. Through humility, King Jesus made a way for you to be engrafted into His royalty. He made of Himself no reputation and took on the nature of a servant (Philippians 2:7) to affirm your value. Through self-denial, you prioritize excellence in virtue, truthfulness, and faithfulness. Because of the respect you have earned, you dismantle inferiority, disgrace, shame, and offenses. No one feels second-rate in your presence. The deeper that the Lord is your object of reverence, the greater your confidence will be in giving approval and worth. Because you are tall in spirit, your face is always turned upward.

TRINITY

Triad; united

&

Ecclesiastes 4:12 *Though one may be overpowered, two can defend themselves. A cord of three strands is not quickly broken.*

I Corinthians 1:10 *I appeal to you, brothers, in the name of our Lord Jesus Christ, that all of you agree with one another so that there may be no divisions among you and that you may be perfectly united in mind and thought.*

You are one who has chosen to separate yourself from wickedness, darkness, unbelief, idolatry, and uncleanness in order to be yoked together with your Heavenly Father. He will live and walk with you. He will be your God and you will be His son (II Corinthians 6:14–18). This inseparable union results in:

Psalm 133—anointing and God's blessings;

I Corinthians 12—no jealousy over different giftings in God's body;

Romans 6:5—identity with Christ's death and resurrection;

Philippians 2:1–5—having Christ's attitude - one in spirit and purpose;

Colossians 2:2–3—complete understanding of Christ's wisdom;

Ephesians 2:19-22—being a dwelling where God lives by His Spirit;

Ephesians 4:16—spiritual maturity.

You will have a greater sensitivity for ministry to relationships that are separated, severed, deserted, or abandoned. As Christ's team player, you will gladly take the risk to touch these types of people, in order that they may be one with Him in harmony. You will serve as a link to bring closeness.

TRIPP

Traveler; walks with God

౨౦

Psalm 56:13 *For you have delivered me from death and my feet from stumbling, that I may walk before God in the light of life.*

Psalm 26:2–3 *Test me, O Lord, and try me, examine my heart and my mind; for Your love is ever before me, and I walk continually in Your truth.*

"Enoch walked with God; then he was no more, because God took him away," Genesis 5:24. "Noah was a righteous man, blameless among the people of his time, and he walked with God," Genesis 6:9. Your fellowship with God reveals how you walk by faith, not by sight (II Corinthians 5:7). The courage you display as an unschooled, ordinary person will astonish people and cause them to take note that you have been with Jesus (Acts 4:13). This divine friendship is earmarked by drawing near to God with a sincere heart in full assurance of faith, having your heart sprinkled to cleanse you from a guilty conscience, and having your body washed with pure water (Hebrews 10:22). Think it not strange that your path will often cross with those who wander aimlessly with no direction or purpose. You are to show them God's example of walking in truth and in His light. As you allow Him to give you an undivided heart that fears His name, so you will train others (Psalm 86:11).

TRISHA

Noble one; full of honor

❧

Isaiah 32:8 *But the noble man makes noble plans, and by noble deeds he stands.*

Luke 8:15 *But the seed on good soil stands for those with a noble and good heart, who hear the word, retain it, and by persevering produce a crop.*

Proverbs 18:12 says, "Before his downfall a man's heart is proud, but humility comes before honor." You are one who has a humble confidence in recognizing and expressing reverence, worship, adoration, trust, deference, tribute, admiration, and respect. This is the result of being secure in the truth of who you are in the Lord. Through humility, King Jesus made a way for you to be engrafted into His royalty. He made of Himself no reputation and took on the nature of a servant (Philippians 2:7) to affirm your value. Through self-denial, you prioritize excellence in virtue, truthfulness, and faithfulness. Because of the respect you have earned, you dismantle inferiority, disgrace, shame, and offenses. No one feels second-rate in your presence. The deeper that the Lord is your object of reverence, the greater your confidence will be in giving approval and worth. Because you are tall in spirit, your face is always turned upward.

TRISTAN

Bold; courageous

&

Deuteronomy 31:6   *Be strong and courageous. Do not be afraid or terrified because of them, for the Lord your God goes with you; He will never leave you nor forsake you.*

Joshua 1:7   *Be strong and very courageous. Be careful to obey all the law My servant Moses gave you; do not turn from it to the right or to the left, that you may be successful wherever you go.*

You are equipped with mental and moral strength to venture, persevere, and withstand danger, fear, and difficulty. You have the firmness of mind to take a firm stand. You meet strain with fortitude and resilience, even when opposed or threatened. You have firm determination to achieve God's purpose in your life. With stubborn persistence and unwillingness to admit defeat, you base all victory on the finished work of the cross of Jesus. The Victor will use you to remove obstacles and invade darkness and death in order to bring the lost to a decision for Jesus. God's divine presence in and through you will bind fear and lead people to their God-given inheritance.

TROY

At the place of the curly-haired people; reliable

ৰ৩

Psalm 32:1–2 *Blessed is he whose transgressions are forgiven, whose sins are covered. Blessed is the man whose sin the Lord does not count against him and in whose spirit is no deceit.*

Ephesians 4:32 *Be kind and compassionate to one another, forgiving each other, just as in Christ God forgave you.*

The conditions of forgiveness are confessing Jesus is Lord, believing God raised Him from the dead, and declaring His lordship over your life (Romans 10:9–10). Only God can pardon your sins and forgive your transgressions. He does not stay angry, but delights to show mercy and have compassion on you. He treads your inequities underfoot and hurls all of them into the depths of the sea (Micah 7:18–19). He never remembers them against you again! In Jesus alone you have redemption through His blood and the forgiveness of sins, in accordance with the riches of God's grace (Ephesians 1:7). The Lord has made you trustworthy, dependable, and loyal. He relies on you to express His forgiveness. This implies giving up all claim to punishment as well as any resentment or vengeful feelings. Cancel the debt because He cancelled yours. You do not blame or retaliate, but rather pardon with grace and mercy. Your life proclaims the Lord's forgiveness, liberty, and deliverance.

TYLER

Tile maker; industrious one

ॐ

Colossians 1:16 *For by Him all things were created: things in heaven and on earth, visible and invisible, whether thrones or powers or rulers or authorities; all things were created by Him and for Him.*

Ephesians 2:10 *For we are God's workmanship, created in Christ Jesus to do good works, which God prepared in advance for us to do.*

To be industrious means to be skillful, hardworking, zealous, and diligent. By persevering, you give careful attention to detail. There is not a lazy bone in your body. Through you the Lord will originate. How you deal with the past determines your future. Regardless of the curses or blessings, the failures or successes, you are God's platform for a "new thing." You cannot lean on your own understanding or reasoning. God Almighty created the heavens, the earth, and you in His image. So the more completely dependent you become on your Creator, the more productive your life will be for Him! I Peter 4:19, "So then, those who suffer according to God's will should commit themselves to their Creator and continue to do good."

URIAH

Jehovah is my light; bright one

&

Psalm 27:1 *The Lord is my light and my salvation—whom shall I fear? The Lord is the stronghold of my life; of whom shall I be afraid.*

Proverbs 4:18 *The path of the righteous is like the first gleam of dawn, shining ever brighter till the full light of day.*

You are one who reflects the shining brightness of the countenance of Jesus. You are aggressive toward the fruitless deeds of darkness from the evil one, by exposing them to the light of Jesus. Everything exposed by light becomes visible, for it is the light that makes everything visible (Ephesians 5:11–14). This radiance that God has given you serves as a beacon to give guidance to those yet in darkness. Your life's mission is found in the following two verses: Isaiah 60:1–3 says, "Arise, shine, for your light has come, and the glory of the Lord rises upon you. See, darkness covers the earth, and thick darkness is over the peoples, but the Lord rises upon you and His glory appears over you. Nations will come to your light, and kings to the brightness of your dawn." And in Acts 13:47, "For this is what the Lord has commanded us: 'I have made you a light for the Gentiles, that you may bring salvation to the ends of the earth.'" Continue to shine as His star, leading many to righteousness (Daniel 12:3 and Philippians 2:15).

URSULA

Little she bear; strong endurance

Proverbs 24:5 *A wise man has great power, and a man of knowledge increases strength.*

Ephesians 6:10 *Finally, be strong in the Lord and in His mighty power.*

You are one who has an un-compromised commitment to righteousness, respectability, honesty, character, excellence, value, worth, kindness, innocence, generosity, trustworthiness, faithfulness, justice, hope, and love. You can do everything through Him who gives you strength (Philippians 4:11–13). The Lord is the source of your strength because you turn back the battle at the gate (Isaiah 28:6). You renew your strength by your hope being in the Lord (Isaiah 40:31). Jesus says, "My grace is sufficient for you, for My power is made perfect in weaknesses. Therefore you will boast all the more gladly about your weaknesses, so that Christ's power may rest on you. That is why for Christ's sake, you delight in weaknesses, in insults, in hardships, in persecutions, and in difficulties. For when you are weak, then you are strong," II Corinthians 12:9–10. You are clothed with strength and dignity (Proverbs 31:25).

VALERIE

Strong; of determined purpose

Proverbs 24:5 *A wise man has great power, and a man of knowledge increases strength.*

Ephesians 6:10 *Finally, be strong in the Lord and in His mighty power.*

You are one who has an un-compromised commitment to righteousness, respectability, honesty, character, excellence, value, worth, kindness, innocence, generosity, trustworthiness, faithfulness, justice, hope, and love. You can do everything through Him who gives you strength (Philippians 4:11–13). The Lord is the source of your strength because you turn back the battle at the gate (Isaiah 28:6). You renew your strength by your hope being in the Lord (Isaiah 40:31). Jesus says, "My grace is sufficient for you, for My power is made perfect in weaknesses. Therefore you will boast all the more gladly about your weaknesses, so that Christ's power may rest on you. That is why for Christ's sake, you delight in weaknesses, in insults, in hardships, in persecutions, and in difficulties. For when you are weak, then you are strong," II Corinthians 12:9–10. You are clothed with strength and dignity (Proverbs 31:25).

VAN

Thresher; industrious spirit

દ્ય

Colossians 1:16 *For by Him all things were created: things in heaven and on earth, visible and invisible, whether thrones or powers or rulers or authorities; all things were created by Him and for Him.*

Ephesians 2:10 *For we are God's workmanship, created in Christ Jesus to do good works, which God prepared in advance for us to do.*

To be industrious means to be skillful, hardworking, zealous, and diligent. By persevering, you give careful attention to detail. There is not a lazy bone in your body. Through you the Lord will originate. How you deal with the past determines your future. Regardless of the curses or blessings, the failures or successes, you are God's platform for a "new thing." You cannot lean on your own understanding or reasoning. God Almighty created the heavens, the earth, and you in His image. So the more completely dependent you become on your Creator, the more productive your life will be for Him! I Peter 4:19, "So then, those who suffer according to God's will should commit themselves to their Creator and continue to do good."

VAUGHN

Small; dependent on God

૭૦

Isaiah 60:22 *The least of you will become a thousand, the smallest a mighty nation. I am the Lord; in its time I will do this swiftly.*

II Corinthians 3:5 *Not that we are competent in ourselves to claim anything for ourselves, but our competence comes from God.*

The word "little" here has nothing to do with size, insignificance, unimportance, or narrow-mindedness. It does mean you are totally dependent on God, for without Him you can do nothing (John 15:5). This is expressed by relying and trusting in His control. As God increases and you decrease, God will use you to touch the lives of the helpless, immature, and weak. II Corinthians 12:9–10 says, "My grace is sufficient for you, for My power is made perfect in weakness. Therefore I will boast all the more gladly about my weaknesses, so that Christ's power may rest on me. That is why, for Christ's sake, I delight in weaknesses, in insults, in hardships, in persecutions, in difficulties. For when I am weak, then I am strong." Your humility admits weaknesses and releases strengths. As you are faithful over a little, God will make you ruler over much (Luke 19:17).

VELMA

Guardian; resolute protector

&

Job 11:18 *You will be secure, because there is hope; you will look about you and take your rest in safety.*

Psalm 32:7 *You are my hiding place; You will protect me from trouble and surround me with songs of deliverance.*

Psalm 27:5 *For in the day of trouble He will keep me safe in His dwelling; He will hide me in the shelter of His tabernacle and set me high upon a rock.*

You are securely wrapped up and protected by Jesus Christ, who frees you from doubt and harm. Because you find your shelter, assurance, stability, and strength in your personal relationship with the Lord, you are kept in a safe place. You are confident that the Lord will fight for you; you need only be still (Exodus 14:14). As you stand firm on God's solid foundation (II Timothy 2:19) and stay hidden in the shadow of His wings (Psalm 61:4), you will provide deliverance for the weak, insecure, unsheltered, and frail. Instead of being defensive, you are a defender of injustice done to all mankind. You let discretion protect you (Proverbs 2:11). You will shield others from the enemy's destruction with love (I Corinthians 13:7) and the power of God's name (John 17:11). You display God's compassion through your humility. What you let him be in you, you will be to others.

VERA

Faith, true; faithful spirit

∞

Proverbs 2:7–8 *He holds victory in store for the upright, He is a shield to those whose walk is blameless, for He guards the course of the just and protects the way of His faithful ones.*

Psalm 15:1–5 *Lord, who may dwell in Your sanctuary? Who may live on Your holy hill? He whose walk is blameless and who does what is righteous, who speaks the truth from his heart and has no slander on his tongue, who does his neighbor no wrong and casts no slur on his fellow man, who despises a vile man but honors those who fear the Lord, who keeps his oath even when it hurts, who lends his money without usury and does not accept a bribe against the innocent. He who does these things will never be shaken.*

You are one who has made a commitment to God to be loyal, true, dependable, enduring, and steadfast. You unmask anything fake with the reality of God's Word. You are aggressive towards lies and deception to bring about truth. You are especially sensitive to betrayal, so that God can restore hope, security, purpose, and His faithfulness in those whom He has given you to serve. "Be faithful, even to the point of death, and I will give you a crown of life," Revelation 2:10. Anticipate the Master saying to you, "Well done, good and faithful servant! You have been faithful with a few things; I will put you in charge of many things. Come and share your Master's happiness!" (Matthew 25:21) "The one who calls you is faithful and he will do it," I Thessalonians 5:24.

VERNA

Spring-like; abundant life

&

John 14:6 *Jesus answered, I am the way and the truth and the life. No one comes to the Father except through Me.*

Deuteronomy 30:19–20 *This day I call heaven and earth as witnesses against you that I have set before you life and death, blessings and curses. Now choose life, so that you and your children may live and that you may love the Lord your God, listen to His voice, and hold fast to Him. For the Lord is your life, and He will give you many years in the land He swore to give to your fathers, Abraham, Isaac, and Jacob.*

Your life's purpose is to serve God, seek His kingdom, do the Father's will, finish the divine task, complete the course joyfully, and attain Christ-likeness. You throw a life-line to those with a death sentence—those who are weary, disgusted, bitter, empty, barren, oppressed, and isolated. With your focus kept on eternal rather than temporal values, you will bring Christ's resurrection power to hearts in the grave. The very gates of hell cannot prevail and be strong enough to stand up under the direct attack of the church. Colossians 3:1–4 says, "Since, then, you have been raised with Christ, set your hearts on things above, not on earthly things. For you died, and your life is now hidden with Christ in God. When Christ, who is your life, appears, then you also will appear with Him in glory." I Samuel 25:29 says, "Your life will be bound securely in the bundle of the living by the Lord your God. But the lives of your enemies He will hurl away as from the pocket of a sling." Psalm 27:1 says, "The Lord is the stronghold of your life—of whom shall you be afraid?" Enjoy life to the fullest! (John 10:10)

VESTA

Keeper of the house; faithful one

ꝏ

Proverbs 2:7–8 *He holds victory in store for the upright, He is a shield to those whose walk is blameless, for He guards the course of the just and protects the way of His faithful ones.*

Psalm 15:1–5 *Lord, who may dwell in Your sanctuary? Who may live on Your holy hill? He whose walk is blameless and who does what is righteous, who speaks the truth from his heart and has no slander on his tongue, who does his neighbor no wrong and casts no slur on his fellow man, who despises a vile man but honors those who fear the Lord, who keeps his oath even when it hurts, who lends his money without usury and does not accept a bribe against the innocent. He who does these things will never be shaken.*

You are one who has made a commitment to God to be loyal, true, dependable, enduring, and steadfast. You unmask anything fake with the reality of God's Word. You are aggressive towards lies and deception to bring about truth. You are especially sensitive to betrayal, so that God can restore hope, security, purpose, and His faithfulness in those whom He has given you to serve. "Be faithful, even to the point of death, and I will give you a crown of life," Revelation 2:10. Anticipate the Master saying to you, "Well done, good and faithful servant! You have been faithful with a few things; I will put you in charge of many things. Come and share your Master's happiness!" (Matthew 25:21) "The one who calls you is faithful and he will do it," I Thessalonians 5:24.

VICK

Victory; victorious spirit

❧

I John 5:4 *Everyone born of God overcomes the world. This is the victory that has overcome the world, even our faith.*

II Corinthians 2:14 *But thanks be to God, who always leads us in triumphal procession in Christ and through us spreads everywhere the fragrance of the knowledge of Him.*

Because of your faith in Jesus Christ, you will ever be aggressive towards the enemy's tools of defeat, failure, and victimization. You will push back Satan and overcome all his power. Jesus has given you authority to trample on snakes and scorpions and to overcome all the power of the enemy; nothing will harm you (Luke 10:19). Even in the severest of afflictions—such as hardship, persecution, famine, nakedness, danger, or sword—you are more than a conqueror through Christ who loves you (Romans 8:35–37). "Everyone born of God overcomes the world. This is the victory that has overcome the world, even our faith," I John 5:4. "Take heart, Jesus has overcome the world," John 16:33.

VICKIE

Victory; victorious spirit

❧

I John 5:4 *Everyone born of God overcomes the world. This is the victory that has overcome the world, even our faith.*

II Corinthians 2:14 *But thanks be to God, who always leads us in triumphal procession in Christ and through us spreads everywhere the fragrance of the knowledge of Him.*

Because of your faith in Jesus Christ, you will ever be aggressive towards the enemy's tools of defeat, failure, and victimization. You will push back Satan and overcome all his power. Jesus has given you authority to trample on snakes and scorpions and to overcome all the power of the enemy; nothing will harm you (Luke 10:19). Even in the severest of afflictions—such as hardship, persecution, famine, nakedness, danger, or sword—you are more than a conqueror through Christ who loves you (Romans 8:35–37). "Everyone born of God overcomes the world. This is the victory that has overcome the world, even our faith," I John 5:4. "Take heart, Jesus has overcome the world," John 16:33.

VICTOR

Victory; victorious spirit

❧

I John 5:4   *Everyone born of God overcomes the world. This is the victory that has overcome the world, even our faith.*

II Corinthians 2:14   *But thanks be to God, who always leads us in triumphal procession in Christ and through us spreads everywhere the fragrance of the knowledge of Him.*

Because of your faith in Jesus Christ, you will ever be aggressive towards the enemy's tools of defeat, failure, and victimization. You will push back Satan and overcome all his power. Jesus has given you authority to trample on snakes and scorpions and to overcome all the power of the enemy; nothing will harm you (Luke 10:19). Even in the severest of afflictions—such as hardship, persecution, famine, nakedness, danger, or sword—you are more than a conqueror through Christ who loves you (Romans 8:35–37). "Everyone born of God overcomes the world. This is the victory that has overcome the world, even our faith," I John 5:4. "Take heart, Jesus has overcome the world," John 16:33.

VICTORIA

Victor; victorious spirit

&

I John 5:4 *Everyone born of God overcomes the world. This is the victory that has overcome the world, even our faith.*

II Corinthians 2:14 *But thanks be to God, who always leads us in triumphal procession in Christ and through us spreads everywhere the fragrance of the knowledge of Him.*

Because of your faith in Jesus Christ, you will ever be aggressive towards the enemy's tools of defeat, failure, and victimization. You will push back Satan and overcome all his power. Jesus has given you authority to trample on snakes and scorpions and to overcome all the power of the enemy; nothing will harm you (Luke 10:19). Even in the severest of afflictions—such as hardship, persecution, famine, nakedness, danger, or sword—you are more than a conqueror through Christ who loves you (Romans 8:35–37). "Everyone born of God overcomes the world. This is the victory that has overcome the world, even our faith," I John 5:4. "Take heart, Jesus has overcome the world," John 16:33.

VINCE

Conquering one; strong in victory

∞

I John 5:4   *Everyone born of God overcomes the world. This is the victory that has overcome the world, even our faith.*

II Corinthians 2:14   *But thanks be to God, who always leads us in triumphal procession in Christ and through us spreads everywhere the fragrance of the knowledge of Him.*

Because of your faith in Jesus Christ, you will ever be aggressive towards the enemy's tools of defeat, failure, and victimization. You will push back Satan and overcome all his power. Jesus has given you authority to trample on snakes and scorpions and to overcome all the power of the enemy; nothing will harm you (Luke 10:19). Even in the severest of afflictions—such as hardship, persecution, famine, nakedness, danger, or sword—you are more than a conqueror through Christ who loves you (Romans 8:35–37). "Everyone born of God overcomes the world. This is the victory that has overcome the world, even our faith," I John 5:4. "Take heart, Jesus has overcome the world," John 16:33.

VINCENT

Conquering one; strong in victory

ɬↄ

I John 5:4   *Everyone born of God overcomes the world. This is the victory that has overcome the world, even our faith.*

II Corinthians 2:14   *But thanks be to God, who always leads us in triumphal procession in Christ and through us spreads everywhere the fragrance of the knowledge of Him.*

Because of your faith in Jesus Christ, you will ever be aggressive towards the enemy's tools of defeat, failure, and victimization. You will push back Satan and overcome all his power. Jesus has given you authority to trample on snakes and scorpions and to overcome all the power of the enemy; nothing will harm you (Luke 10:19). Even in the severest of afflictions—such as hardship, persecution, famine, nakedness, danger, or sword—you are more than a conqueror through Christ who loves you (Romans 8:35–37). "Everyone born of God overcomes the world. This is the victory that has overcome the world, even our faith," I John 5:4. "Take heart, Jesus has overcome the world," John 16:33.

VIOLA

Violet; humble

❧

Micah 6:8 *He has showed you, O man, what is good. And what does the Lord require of you? To act justly and to love mercy and to walk humbly with your God.*

I Peter 5:6 *Humble yourselves, therefore, under God's mighty hand, that He may lift you up in due time.*

Prove to be trustworthy over little and God will make you ruler over much (Luke 19:17). The higher you lift the Lord, the more dependent you will be on Him. He increases; you decrease (John 3:30). Being exalted only comes from God—not from you or anyone else. It is for the purpose of enlarging His kingdom. Take no credit for the enormous favor God will give you. It is His grace that will give entrance to these doors of favor, as you choose His approval over man's. Philippians 2:3 says, "Do nothing out of selfish ambition or vain conceit, but in humility consider others better than yourselves." Humility and the fear of the Lord bring wealth, honor, and life (Proverbs 22:4).

VIOLET

A violet; humble

৪৩

Micah 6:8 *He has showed you, O man, what is good. And what does the Lord require of you? To act justly and to love mercy and to walk humbly with your God.*

I Peter 5:6 *Humble yourselves, therefore, under God's mighty hand, that He may lift you up in due time.*

Prove to be trustworthy over little and God will make you ruler over much (Luke 19:17). The higher you lift the Lord, the more dependent you will be on Him. He increases; you decrease (John 3:30). Being exalted only comes from God—not from you or anyone else. It is for the purpose of enlarging His kingdom. Take no credit for the enormous favor God will give you. It is His grace that will give entrance to these doors of favor, as you choose His approval over man's. Philippians 2:3 says, "Do nothing out of selfish ambition or vain conceit, but in humility consider others better than yourselves." Humility and the fear of the Lord bring wealth, honor, and life (Proverbs 22:4).

VIRGINIA

Maidenly; pure one

∞

I Timothy 5:22   *...do not share in the sins of others. Keep yourself pure.*

I Peter 1:22   *Now that you have purified yourselves by obeying the truth so that you have sincere love for your brothers, love one another deeply, from the heart.*

Through the process of heat, trials, and refinement, purity is established. Your nature defies being stubborn, judgmental, and haughty. The commandment of the Lord is clear—giving insight to life (Psalm 19:8). You bring wholeness to the dirty, defiled, contaminated, polluted, double-minded, and raped. Your willingness to be transparent is the venue through which He makes His Word clear, simple, and unadulterated. Your choice to be pure enables you to see God (Matthew 5:8) and to know Him as King and Friend (Proverbs 22:11). It also allows your words to be pleasant (Proverbs 15:26) and causes you to ascend to the holy place of the Lord, where you receive blessings and righteousness from the God of salvation (Psalm 24:3–5). Proverbs 20:11 says, "Even a child is known by his actions, by whether his conduct is pure and right."

VON

Small; dependent on God

❧

Isaiah 60:22   *The least of you will become a thousand, the smallest a mighty nation. I am the Lord; in its time I will do this swiftly.*

II Corinthians 3:5   *Not that we are competent in ourselves to claim anything for ourselves, but our competence comes from God.*

The word "little" here has nothing to do with size, insignificance, unimportance, or narrow-mindedness. It does mean you are totally dependent on God, for without Him you can do nothing (John 15:5). This is expressed by relying and trusting in His control. As God increases and you decrease, God will use you to touch the lives of the helpless, immature, and weak. II Corinthians 12:9–10 says, "My grace is sufficient for you, for My power is made perfect in weakness. Therefore I will boast all the more gladly about my weaknesses, so that Christ's power may rest on me. That is why, for Christ's sake, I delight in weaknesses, in insults, in hardships, in persecutions, in difficulties. For when I am weak, then I am strong." Your humility admits weaknesses and releases strengths. As you are faithful over a little, God will make you ruler over much (Luke 19:17).

WADE

The advancer; champion

Exodus 14:14   *The Lord will fight for you; you need only to be still.*

Philippians 3:14   *I press on toward the goal to win the prize for which God has called me heavenward in Christ Jesus.*

Your Lord Jesus Christ has disarmed the powers and authorities and made a public spectacle of them; triumphing over them by the cross (Colossians 2:15). The Lamb of God will overcome the enemy because He is Lord of lords and King of kings. With Him you will be His called, chosen, and faithful follower (Revelation 17:14). As you take refuge in Him, He spreads His protection over you (Psalm 5:11). You win, not by the sword of your strength, but by the Lord's right arm and the light of His face; for He loves you (Psalm 44:3). He has given you authority to overcome all the power of the enemy (Luke 10:19) and nothing will harm you. You lead truth, grace, and justice to victory. You defend the helpless, hopeless, and the honor of others. You are God's role model of courage, victory, and protection. Your daily life will win the respect of outsiders (I Thessalonians 4:12).

WALKER

Cloth cleaner; industrious

&

Colossians 1:16 *For by Him all things were created: things in heaven and on earth, visible and invisible, whether thrones or powers or rulers or authorities; all things were created by Him and for Him.*

Ephesians 2:10 *For we are God's workmanship, created in Christ Jesus to do good works, which God prepared in advance for us to do.*

To be industrious means to be skillful, hardworking, zealous, and diligent. By persevering, you give careful attention to detail. There is not a lazy bone in your body. Through you the Lord will originate. How you deal with the past determines your future. Regardless of the curses or blessings, the failures or successes, you are God's platform for a "new thing." You cannot lean on your own understanding or reasoning. God Almighty created the heavens, the earth, and you in His image. So the more completely dependent you become on your Creator, the more productive your life will be for Him! I Peter 4:19, "So then, those who suffer according to God's will should commit themselves to their Creator and continue to do good."

WALLACE

Man from Wales; man of peace

ॐ

Isaiah 26:3 *You will keep in perfect peace him whose mind is steadfast, because he trusts in You.*

Philippians 4:7 *And the peace of God, which transcends all understanding, will guard your hearts and your minds in Christ Jesus.*

Your life defines peace. You will have a content and calm composure in the midst of distress, disturbance, or agitation. As you follow the Prince of Peace, you will be secure in who you are in Christ. The discipline of keeping your mind on Christ, loving God's law, and being controlled by the Holy Spirit will keep you in perfect peace. God's peace will serve as an umpire to determine whether you are safe or out of God's will (Colossians 3:15). Do not think it strange when you are in battles, fights, and quarrels, because God wants to use you to bring harmony, order, unity, agreement, quietness, and calmness to the adverse situation. You are one whose intimate friendship with the Lord brings reconciliation to the offended, distressed, and troubled. "In repentance and rest is your salvation, in quietness and trust is your strength," Isaiah 30:15. Your refreshing comes as you renew your mind daily in the Word of God. "Great peace have they who love Your law, and nothing can make them stumble," Psalm 119:165.

WALT

Powerful warrior; army ruler; powerful

&

Deuteronomy 28:13 *The Lord will make you the head, not the tail. If you pay attention to the commands of the Lord your God that I give you this day and carefully follow them, you will always be at the top, never at the bottom.*

Mark 10:43–45 *...Whoever wants to become great among you must be your servant, and whoever wants to be first must be slave of all. For even the Son of Man did not come to be served, but to serve, and to give His life as a ransom for many.*

You have been set apart with vision and perspective to reproduce the likeness of Christ in others by reflecting His image. You are guided by principles and values worth dying for. You know how to balance transparency with being an example. You are one who is secure enough to be vulnerable. You do not lead to gather followers; you lead to develop leaders. You lead by honoring God with authority, influence, direction, foresight, and skill. Your credible choices set a precedence for favor. You earn trust by your willingness to confront and bring discipline in a Godly manner. You are strong enough to let your "yes" be "yes" and your "no" be "no," with no compromise or jealousy. Your strength is determined by your submitted and teachable servant's heart. The more you mature, the more humble, gentle, and meek you will become. With integrity you communicate love, affirmation, nurturing, and spiritual care. If you as a shepherd ever forget what it is like to be a sheep, you will become a hireling. Your highest aim is to honor and glorify God.

WALTER

Powerful warrior; army ruler; powerful

ɞ

Deuteronomy 28:13 *The Lord will make you the head, not the tail. If you pay attention to the commands of the Lord your God that I give you this day and carefully follow them, you will always be at the top, never at the bottom.*

Mark 10:43–45 *...Whoever wants to become great among you must be your servant, and whoever wants to be first must be slave of all. For even the Son of Man did not come to be served, but to serve, and to give His life as a ransom for many.*

You have been set apart with vision and perspective to reproduce the likeness of Christ in others by reflecting His image. You are guided by principles and values worth dying for. You know how to balance transparency with being an example. You are one who is secure enough to be vulnerable. You do not lead to gather followers; you lead to develop leaders. You lead by honoring God with authority, influence, direction, foresight, and skill. Your credible choices set a precedence for favor. You earn trust by your willingness to confront and bring discipline in a Godly manner. You are strong enough to let your "yes" be "yes" and your "no" be "no," with no compromise or jealousy. Your strength is determined by your submitted and teachable servant's heart. The more you mature, the more humble, gentle, and meek you will become. With integrity you communicate love, affirmation, nurturing, and spiritual care. If you as a shepherd ever forget what it is like to be a sheep, you will become a hireling. Your highest aim is to honor and glorify God.

WANDA

Wanderer; walks with God

℘

Psalm 56:13   *For you have delivered me from death and my feet from stumbling, that I may walk before God in the light of life.*

Psalm 26:2–3   *Test me, O Lord, and try me, examine my heart and my mind; for Your love is ever before me, and I walk continually in Your truth.*

"Enoch walked with God; then he was no more, because God took him away," Genesis 5:24. "Noah was a righteous man, blameless among the people of his time, and he walked with God," Genesis 6:9. Your fellowship with God reveals how you walk by faith, not by sight (II Corinthians 5:7). The courage you display as an unschooled, ordinary person will astonish people and cause them to take note that you have been with Jesus (Acts 4:13). This divine friendship is earmarked by drawing near to God with a sincere heart in full assurance of faith, having your heart sprinkled to cleanse you from a guilty conscience, and having your body washed with pure water (Hebrews 10:22). Think it not strange that your path will often cross with those who wander aimlessly with no direction or purpose. You are to show them God's example of walking in truth and in His light. As you allow Him to give you an undivided heart that fears His name, so you will train others (Psalm 86:11).

WANDEKA

Wanderer; walks with God

Psalm 56:13 *For you have delivered me from death and my feet from stumbling, that I may walk before God in the light of life.*

Psalm 26:2–3 *Test me, O Lord, and try me, examine my heart and my mind; for Your love is ever before me, and I walk continually in Your truth.*

"Enoch walked with God; then he was no more, because God took him away," Genesis 5:24. "Noah was a righteous man, blameless among the people of his time, and he walked with God," Genesis 6:9. Your fellowship with God reveals how you walk by faith, not by sight (II Corinthians 5:7). The courage you display as an unschooled, ordinary person will astonish people and cause them to take note that you have been with Jesus (Acts 4:13). This divine friendship is earmarked by drawing near to God with a sincere heart in full assurance of faith, having your heart sprinkled to cleanse you from a guilty conscience, and having your body washed with pure water (Hebrews 10:22). Think it not strange that your path will often cross with those who wander aimlessly with no direction or purpose. You are to show them God's example of walking in truth and in His light. As you allow Him to give you an undivided heart that fears His name, so you will train others (Psalm 86:11).

WARREN

Protecting friend; one who protects

ଚଠ

Job 11:18 *You will be secure, because there is hope; you will look about you and take your rest in safety.*

Psalm 32:7 *You are my hiding place; You will protect me from trouble and surround me with songs of deliverance.*

Psalm 27:5 *For in the day of trouble He will keep me safe in His dwelling; He will hide me in the shelter of His tabernacle and set me high upon a rock.*

You are securely wrapped up and protected by Jesus Christ, who frees you from doubt and harm. Because you find your shelter, assurance, stability, and strength in your personal relationship with the Lord, you are kept in a safe place. You are confident that the Lord will fight for you; you need only be still (Exodus 14:14). As you stand firm on God's solid foundation (II Timothy 2:19) and stay hidden in the shadow of His wings (Psalm 61:4), you will provide deliverance for the weak, insecure, unsheltered, and frail. Instead of being defensive, you are a defender of injustice done to all mankind. You let discretion protect you (Proverbs 2:11). You will shield others from the enemy's destruction with love (I Corinthians 13:7) and the power of God's name (John 17:11). You display God's compassion through your humility. What you let him be in you, you will be to others.

WASHINGTON

Town of smart men; wisdom

❧

James 3:17 *But the wisdom that comes from heaven is first of all pure; then peace-loving, considerate, submissive, full of mercy and good fruit, impartial and sincere.*

Proverbs 9:10 *The fear of the Lord is the beginning of wisdom, and knowledge of the Holy One is understanding.*

You are a person of moral excellence. You exemplify right living put into practice. The Lord has not only equipped you with skills for living correctly, but also the ability to impart that to others. The Spirit of truth will guide you into all truth, allowing you to have insight into the true nature of things (John 16:13). Out of your reverential respect for the Lord, you have wisdom to give guidance and direction. You are a safe sounding board who steers those who are hungry for knowledge of the Holy One in the right direction. You need only to ask for the wisdom you lack, and God will give it to you generously (James 1:5). Having spiritual discernment is having the ability to separate the difference between God's wisdom and the world's and the ability to make the right choice—regardless. Luke 21:15 says, "For I will give you words and wisdom that none of your adversaries will be able to resist or contradict."

WAYNE

Wagon maker; lifter of cares

ᏏᎤ

Hosea 11:4 *I led them with cords of human kindness, with ties of love; I lifted the yoke from their neck and bent down to feed them.*

Matthew 9:36 *When He saw the crowds, He had compassion on them, because they were harassed and helpless, like sheep without a shepherd.*

You are obedient, respectful, faithful, and bring pleasure to those whom you serve. Even with inconsiderate behavior, you are patient (I Peter 2:18). You are tender with the harsh, merciful with the intolerant, and sympathetic with the suffering. Because you cast your cares on the Lord, you are able to lift the burdens of others (Psalm 55:22). The reason you are so easily trusted is because of your humble nature. All glory and credit belong to God, not you. Your passion to help energizes you to meet the need regardless of what it is—guidance, relief, encouragement, or support. God allows you to see the root of the need rather than being sidetracked by all the symptoms. Sickness is healed, the hungry are fed, sight is restored, the unlovely are touched and the afflicted are delivered. You defend rather than offend, forgive rather than accuse, and you protect rather than abandon. You can depend on God's fresh supply daily. "Because of the Lord's great love we are not consumed, for His compassions never fail. They are new every morning; great is your faithfulness," Lamentations 3:22–23. Your compassion connects the heart of God to the heart of man.

WELFORD

A well near a river crossing; refreshing one

&

Acts 3:19 *Repent, then, and turn to God, so that your sins may be wiped out, that times of refreshing may come from the Lord.*

II Timothy 1:16 *May the Lord show mercy to the household of Onesiphorus, because he often refreshed me and was not ashamed of my chains.*

You are one who restores strength because of knowing your own weakness. One who revives life because of dying to self. One who renews supply because of being emptied of self. One who reconciles offenses because your wisdom is from Christ. To bring this refreshing, you must know the all-sufficient one—El-Shaddai—in all your insufficiencies. As you learn to rest in His presence (Exodus 33:14), you will be a channel for His revival. Psalm 42:1–2 says, "As the deer pants for streams of water, so my soul pants for you, O God. My soul thirsts for God, for the living God. When can I go and meet with God?" To be His brook or His stream you must dwell in His stream. Stay thirsty for God's living water (John 7:37–38).

WENDY

Wanderer; walks with God

℘

Psalm 56:13 *For you have delivered me from death and my feet from stumbling, that I may walk before God in the light of life.*

Psalm 26:2–3 *Test me, O Lord, and try me, examine my heart and my mind; for Your love is ever before me, and I walk continually in Your truth.*

"Enoch walked with God; then he was no more, because God took him away," Genesis 5:24. "Noah was a righteous man, blameless among the people of his time, and he walked with God," Genesis 6:9. Your fellowship with God reveals how you walk by faith, not by sight (II Corinthians 5:7). The courage you display as an unschooled, ordinary person will astonish people and cause them to take note that you have been with Jesus (Acts 4:13). This divine friendship is earmarked by drawing near to God with a sincere heart in full assurance of faith, having your heart sprinkled to cleanse you from a guilty conscience, and having your body washed with pure water (Hebrews 10:22). Think it not strange that your path will often cross with those who wander aimlessly with no direction or purpose. You are to show them God's example of walking in truth and in His light. As you allow Him to give you an undivided heart that fears His name, so you will train others (Psalm 86:11).

WHITNEY

White island; enlightened one

Psalm 27:1 *The Lord is my light and my salvation—whom shall I fear?*
The Lord is the stronghold of my life; of whom shall I be afraid.

Proverbs 4:18 *The path of the righteous is like the first gleam of dawn,*
shining ever brighter till the full light of day.

You are one who reflects the shining brightness of the countenance of Jesus. You are aggressive toward the fruitless deeds of darkness from the evil one, by exposing them to the light of Jesus. Everything exposed by light becomes visible, for it is the light that makes everything visible (Ephesians 5:11–14). This radiance that God has given you serves as a beacon to give guidance to those yet in darkness. Your life's mission is found in the following two verses: Isaiah 60:1–3 says, "Arise, shine, for your light has come, and the glory of the Lord rises upon you. See, darkness covers the earth, and thick darkness is over the peoples, but the Lord rises upon you and His glory appears over you. Nations will come to your light, and kings to the brightness of your dawn." And in Acts 13:47, "For this is what the Lord has commanded us: 'I have made you a light for the Gentiles, that you may bring salvation to the ends of the earth.'" Continue to shine as His star, leading many to righteousness (Daniel 12:3 and Philippians 2:15).

WILL

Resolute protector; great protector

❧

Job 11:18 *You will be secure, because there is hope; you will look about you and take your rest in safety.*

Psalm 32:7 *You are my hiding place; You will protect me from trouble and surround me with songs of deliverance.*

Psalm 27:5 *For in the day of trouble He will keep me safe in His dwelling; He will hide me in the shelter of His tabernacle and set me high upon a rock.*

You are securely wrapped up and protected by Jesus Christ, who frees you from doubt and harm. Because you find your shelter, assurance, stability, and strength in your personal relationship with the Lord, you are kept in a safe place. You are confident that the Lord will fight for you; you need only be still (Exodus 14:14). As you stand firm on God's solid foundation (II Timothy 2:19) and stay hidden in the shadow of His wings (Psalm 61:4), you will provide deliverance for the weak, insecure, unsheltered, and frail. Instead of being defensive, you are a defender of injustice done to all mankind. You let discretion protect you (Proverbs 2:11). You will shield others from the enemy's destruction with love (I Corinthians 13:7) and the power of God's name (John 17:11). You display God's compassion through your humility. What you let him be in you, you will be to others.

WILLIAM

Resolute protector; great protector

෫ර

Job 11:18 *You will be secure, because there is hope; you will look about you and take your rest in safety.*

Psalm 32:7 *You are my hiding place; You will protect me from trouble and surround me with songs of deliverance.*

Psalm 27:5 *For in the day of trouble He will keep me safe in His dwelling; He will hide me in the shelter of His tabernacle and set me high upon a rock.*

You are securely wrapped up and protected by Jesus Christ, who frees you from doubt and harm. Because you find your shelter, assurance, stability, and strength in your personal relationship with the Lord, you are kept in a safe place. You are confident that the Lord will fight for you; you need only be still (Exodus 14:14). As you stand firm on God's solid foundation (II Timothy 2:19) and stay hidden in the shadow of His wings (Psalm 61:4), you will provide deliverance for the weak, insecure, unsheltered, and frail. Instead of being defensive, you are a defender of injustice done to all mankind. You let discretion protect you (Proverbs 2:11). You will shield others from the enemy's destruction with love (I Corinthians 13:7) and the power of God's name (John 17:11). You display God's compassion through your humility. What you let him be in you, you will be to others.

WILSON

Son of Will; resolute protector

∞

Job 11:18 *You will be secure, because there is hope; you will look about you and take your rest in safety.*

Psalm 32:7 *You are my hiding place; You will protect me from trouble and surround me with songs of deliverance.*

Psalm 27:5 *For in the day of trouble He will keep me safe in His dwelling; He will hide me in the shelter of His tabernacle and set me high upon a rock.*

You are securely wrapped up and protected by Jesus Christ, who frees you from doubt and harm. Because you find your shelter, assurance, stability, and strength in your personal relationship with the Lord, you are kept in a safe place. You are confident that the Lord will fight for you; you need only be still (Exodus 14:14). As you stand firm on God's solid foundation (II Timothy 2:19) and stay hidden in the shadow of His wings (Psalm 61:4), you will provide deliverance for the weak, insecure, unsheltered, and frail. Instead of being defensive, you are a defender of injustice done to all mankind. You let discretion protect you (Proverbs 2:11). You will shield others from the enemy's destruction with love (I Corinthians 13:7) and the power of God's name (John 17:11). You display God's compassion through your humility. What you let him be in you, you will be to others.

WINFIELD

Stone marker of friendship; friend

ॐ

Proverbs 17:17 *A friend loves at all times, and a brother is born for adversity.*

Ecclesiastes 4:9–10 *Two are better than one, because they have a good return for their work: if one falls down his friend can help him up. But pity the man who falls and has no one to help him up!*

Christ was the preeminent example of friendship. John 15:13–14 says, "Greater love has no man than this, that he lay down his life for his friends. You are my friends if you do what I command." With open arms, He gave all. Your mantle is to be God's man of peace. This is achieved by being understanding, loyal, faithful, and true. Proverbs 18:24 says, "A man of many companions may come to ruin, but there is a friend who sticks closer than a brother." It comes natural for you to be hospitable, generous, helpful, and good-humored. Your influence is based on your ability to be approachable, trusted, and respectful. Strangers who are lonely, outcast, or abandoned will find refuge with your "welcome" sign written on your heart. You are loving, as well as being loved—everyone's neighbor; everyone's buddy. Psalm 119:63 says, "I am a friend to all who fear You, to all who follow Your precepts." Proverbs 22:11 says, "He who loves a pure heart and whose speech is gracious will have the King for his friend."

WINNIE

Winning; victorious

ℰᴥ

I John 5:4 *Everyone born of God overcomes the world. This is the victory that has overcome the world, even our faith.*

II Corinthians 2:14 *But thanks be to God, who always leads us in triumphal procession in Christ and through us spreads everywhere the fragrance of the knowledge of Him.*

Because of your faith in Jesus Christ, you will ever be aggressive towards the enemy's tools of defeat, failure, and victimization. You will push back Satan and overcome all his power. Jesus has given you authority to trample on snakes and scorpions and to overcome all the power of the enemy; nothing will harm you (Luke 10:19). Even in the severest of afflictions—such as hardship, persecution, famine, nakedness, danger, or sword—you are more than a conqueror through Christ who loves you (Romans 8:35–37). "Everyone born of God overcomes the world. This is the victory that has overcome the world, even our faith," I John 5:4. "Take heart, Jesus has overcome the world," John 16:33.

WINSTON

Friend; friendly spirit

&

Proverbs 17:17 *A friend loves at all times, and a brother is born for adversity.*

Ecclesiastes 4:9–10 *Two are better than one, because they have a good return for their work: if one falls down his friend can help him up. But pity the man who falls and has no one to help him up!*

Christ was the preeminent example of friendship. John 15:13–14 says, "Greater love has no man than this, that he lay down his life for his friends. You are my friends if you do what I command." With open arms, He gave all. Your mantle is to be God's man of peace. This is achieved by being understanding, loyal, faithful, and true. Proverbs 18:24 says, "A man of many companions may come to ruin, but there is a friend who sticks closer than a brother." It comes natural for you to be hospitable, generous, helpful, and good-humored. Your influence is based on your ability to be approachable, trusted, and respectful. Strangers who are lonely, outcast, or abandoned will find refuge with your "welcome" sign written on your heart. You are loving, as well as being loved—everyone's neighbor; everyone's buddy. Psalm 119:63 says, "I am a friend to all who fear You, to all who follow Your precepts." Proverbs 22:11 says, "He who loves a pure heart and whose speech is gracious will have the King for his friend."

WRIGHT

Wagon maker; lifter of cares

ও

Hosea 11:4 *I led them with cords of human kindness, with ties of love; I lifted the yoke from their neck and bent down to feed them.*

Matthew 9:36 *When He saw the crowds, He had compassion on them, because they were harassed and helpless, like sheep without a shepherd.*

You are obedient, respectful, faithful, and bring pleasure to those whom you serve. Even with inconsiderate behavior, you are patient (I Peter 2:18). You are tender with the harsh, merciful with the intolerant, and sympathetic with the suffering. Because you cast your cares on the Lord, you are able to lift the burdens of others (Psalm 55:22). The reason you are so easily trusted is because of your humble nature. All glory and credit belong to God, not you. Your passion to help energizes you to meet the need regardless of what it is—guidance, relief, encouragement, or support. God allows you to see the root of the need rather than being sidetracked by all the symptoms. Sickness is healed, the hungry are fed, sight is restored, the unlovely are touched and the afflicted are delivered. You defend rather than offend, forgive rather than accuse, and you protect rather than abandon. You can depend on God's fresh supply daily. "Because of the Lord's great love we are not consumed, for His compassions never fail. They are new every morning; great is your faithfulness," Lamentations 3:22–23. Your compassion connects the heart of God to the heart of man.

WYATT

Little warrior; God's warrior

৩

II Chronicles 32:7–8 *There is a greater power with us than with him. With him is only the arm of flesh, but with us is the Lord our God to help us and to fight our battles.*

II Timothy 2:3–4 *Endure hardship with us like a good soldier of Christ Jesus. No one serving as a soldier gets involved in civilian affairs - he wants to please his commanding officer.*

Exodus 14:14 says, "The Lord will fight for you; you need only be still." You are armed with the ability to handle the spear and shield—to stand on God's Word by faith, supporting the King of kings against His enemies. As God's defending warrior, you are His example of a brave champion, soldier, and hero. The ultimate war was a contest with death and when Christ said, "It is finished" on the cross, He declared victory over death, hell, and the grave. You are equipped to be used of God as one who protects by warding off attacks, calling for justice, and providing shelter. When God is all of this to you, you will be that vindication for others. Because of your faith in Jesus Christ, you will ever be aggressive towards the enemy's tools of defeat, failure, and victimization. Your ultimate purpose is to be one who stands in the gap (Ezekiel 22:30) as a defender of the weak. This includes those who are easily influenced, confused, quitters, faint, frail, fragile, and frightened. Your primary spiritual warfare will be that of brave intercession—reaching, meeting, and entreating God for His favor to set the captives free. Then you will "learn to do right! Seek justice, encourage the oppressed. Defend the cause of the fatherless, plead the case of the widow," Isaiah 1:17.

XAVIER

Brilliant; full of wisdom

❧

James 3:17 *But the wisdom that comes from heaven is first of all pure; then peace-loving, considerate, submissive, full of mercy and good fruit, impartial and sincere.*

Proverbs 9:10 *The fear of the Lord is the beginning of wisdom, and knowledge of the Holy One is understanding.*

You are a person of moral excellence. You exemplify right living put into practice. The Lord has not only equipped you with skills for living correctly, but also the ability to impart that to others. The Spirit of truth will guide you into all truth, allowing you to have insight into the true nature of things (John 16:13). Out of your reverential respect for the Lord, you have wisdom to give guidance and direction. You are a safe sounding board who steers those who are hungry for knowledge of the Holy One in the right direction. You need only to ask for the wisdom you lack, and God will give it to you generously (James 1:5). Having spiritual discernment is having the ability to separate the difference between God's wisdom and the world's and the ability to make the right choice—regardless. Luke 21:15 says, "For I will give you words and wisdom that none of your adversaries will be able to resist or contradict."

XERXES

Ruler; man of distinction

❧

I Kings 3:9 *So give Your servant a discerning heart to govern Your people and to distinguish between right and wrong. For who is able to govern this great people of Yours?*

Hebrews 5:14 *But solid food is for the mature, who by constant use have trained themselves to distinguish good from evil.*

The sense of smell is the strongest of the five senses. In scripture it is equaled to discernment. It is marked by perception, justice, and insight, along with the ability to investigate and examine based on the absolute truth of scripture. Distinction is defined by the act of noticing differences, discretion, sensitivity, and the ability to distinguish good from evil. You are one who takes the crooked, dishonest corruptions of life and gives clear direction on God's straight path, from pollution to purpose. God has equipped you to remove the obstacles of dullness, indifference, and insignificance. He uses you as His shelter from the wind, His refuge from the storm, His streams of water in the desert, and His great rock in a thirsty land (Isaiah 32:1–8). This brings hearing to the deaf, sight to the blind, and understanding to the mind. This discernment will require disciplining your mind to be set on what the Spirit desires, which is justice and freedom. Stay away from what the carnal nature desires, which is judgment and criticism. You live His life, not yours. You think His thoughts, not yours. You speak His words, not yours. Intimacy with the Lord in His Word and in prayer will prevent you from being offended by the "crooked," so that your focus will be on how He discerns. He is the ultimate man of distinction.

YOLANDA

A violet; humble

❧

Micah 6:8 *He has showed you, O man, what is good. And what does the Lord require of you? To act justly and to love mercy and to walk humbly with your God.*

I Peter 5:6 *Humble yourselves, therefore, under God's mighty hand, that He may lift you up in due time.*

Prove to be trustworthy over little and God will make you ruler over much (Luke 19:17). The higher you lift the Lord, the more dependent you will be on Him. He increases; you decrease (John 3:30). Being exalted only comes from God—not from you or anyone else. It is for the purpose of enlarging His kingdom. Take no credit for the enormous favor God will give you. It is His grace that will give entrance to these doors of favor, as you choose His approval over man's. Philippians 2:3 says, "Do nothing out of selfish ambition or vain conceit, but in humility consider others better than yourselves." Humility and the fear of the Lord bring wealth, honor, and life. (Proverbs 22:4).

YVONNE

Hero; courageous heart

Deuteronomy 31:6 *Be strong and courageous. Do not be afraid or terrified because of them, for the Lord your God goes with you; He will never leave you nor forsake you.*

Joshua 1:7 *Be strong and very courageous. Be careful to obey all the law My servant Moses gave you; do not turn from it to the right or to the left, that you may be successful wherever you go.*

You are equipped with mental and moral strength to venture, persevere, and withstand danger, fear, and difficulty. You have the firmness of mind to take a firm stand. You meet strain with fortitude and resilience, even when opposed or threatened. You have firm determination to achieve God's purpose in your life. With stubborn persistence and unwillingness to admit defeat, you base all victory on the finished work of the cross of Jesus. The Victor will use you to remove obstacles and invade darkness and death in order to bring the lost to a decision for Jesus. God's divine presence in and through you will bind fear and lead people to their God-given inheritance.

ZACH

Jehovah has remembered; the Lord remembers

❧

Psalm 98:3 *He has remembered His love and His faithfulness to the house of Israel; all the ends of the earth have seen the salvation of our God.*

Psalm 136:23 *To the One who remembered us in our low estate His love endures forever.*

God remembers that you are dust (Psalm 103:14), His covenant is forever (Psalm 111:5), and He remembers your sins no more (Isaiah 43:25). This requires of you that you forget not the Lord (Deuteronomy 6:12), nor all His benefits (Psalm 103:2). God uses you to awaken His life to the forgotten, selfish, neglected, and disregarded. "Can a mother forget the baby at her breast and have no compassion on the child she has borne? Though she may forget, I will not forget you! See, I have engraved you on the palm of My hands; your walls are ever before Me," Isaiah 49:15–16. "God is not unjust; He will not forget your work and the love you have shown Him as you have helped His people and continued to help them," Hebrews 6:10.

ZACHARIAH

Jehovah has remembered; the Lord remembers

ॐ

Psalm 98:3 *He has remembered His love and His faithfulness to the house of Israel; all the ends of the earth have seen the salvation of our God.*

Psalm 136:23 *To the One who remembered us in our low estate His love endures forever.*

God remembers that you are dust (Psalm 103:14), His covenant is forever (Psalm 111:5), and He remembers your sins no more (Isaiah 43:25). This requires of you that you forget not the Lord (Deuteronomy 6:12), nor all His benefits (Psalm 103:2). God uses you to awaken His life to the forgotten, selfish, neglected, and disregarded. "Can a mother forget the baby at her breast and have no compassion on the child she has borne? Though she may forget, I will not forget you! See, I have engraved you on the palm of My hands; your walls are ever before Me," Isaiah 49:15–16. "God is not unjust; He will not forget your work and the love you have shown Him as you have helped His people and continued to help them," Hebrews 6:10.

ZACHARY

Jehovah has remembered; the Lord remembers

❧

Psalm 98:3 *He has remembered His love and His faithfulness to the house of Israel; all the ends of the earth have seen the salvation of our God.*

Psalm 136:23 *To the One who remembered us in our low estate His love endures forever.*

God remembers that you are dust (Psalm 103:14), His covenant is forever (Psalm 111:5), and He remembers your sins no more (Isaiah 43:25). This requires of you that you forget not the Lord (Deuteronomy 6:12), nor all His benefits (Psalm 103:2). God uses you to awaken His life to the forgotten, selfish, neglected, and disregarded. "Can a mother forget the baby at her breast and have no compassion on the child she has borne? Though she may forget, I will not forget you! See, I have engraved you on the palm of My hands; your walls are ever before Me," Isaiah 49:15–16. "God is not unjust; He will not forget your work and the love you have shown Him as you have helped His people and continued to help them," Hebrews 6:10.

ZECHARIAH

Jehovah has remembered; the Lord remembers

❧

Psalm 98:3 *He has remembered His love and His faithfulness to the house of Israel; all the ends of the earth have seen the salvation of our God.*

Psalm 136:23 *To the One who remembered us in our low estate His love endures forever.*

God remembers that you are dust (Psalm 103:14), His covenant is forever (Psalm 111:5), and He remembers your sins no more (Isaiah 43:25). This requires of you that you forget not the Lord (Deuteronomy 6:12), nor all His benefits (Psalm 103:2). God uses you to awaken His life to the forgotten, selfish, neglected, and disregarded. "Can a mother forget the baby at her breast and have no compassion on the child she has borne? Though she may forget, I will not forget you! See, I have engraved you on the palm of My hands; your walls are ever before Me," Isaiah 49:15–16. "God is not unjust; He will not forget your work and the love you have shown Him as you have helped His people and continued to help them," Hebrews 6:10.

ZOE

Life; filled with life

🙰

John 14:6 *Jesus answered, I am the way and the truth and the life. No one comes to the Father except through Me.*

Deuteronomy 30:19–20 *This day I call heaven and earth as witnesses against you that I have set before you life and death, blessings and curses. Now choose life, so that you and your children may live and that you may love the Lord your God, listen to His voice, and hold fast to Him. For the Lord is your life, and He will give you many years in the land He swore to give to your fathers, Abraham, Isaac, and Jacob.*

Your life's purpose is to serve God, seek His kingdom, do the Father's will, finish the divine task, complete the course joyfully, and attain Christ-likeness. You throw a life-line to those with a death sentence—those who are weary, disgusted, bitter, empty, barren, oppressed, and isolated. With your focus kept on eternal rather than temporal values, you will bring Christ's resurrection power to hearts in the grave. The very gates of hell cannot prevail and be strong enough to stand up under the direct attack of the church. Colossians 3:1–4 says, "Since, then, you have been raised with Christ, set your hearts on things above, not on earthly things. For you died, and your life is now hidden with Christ in God. When Christ, who is your life, appears, then you also will appear with Him in glory." I Samuel 25:29 says, "Your life will be bound securely in the bundle of the living by the Lord your God. But the lives of your enemies He will hurl away as from the pocket of a sling." Psalm 27:1 says, "The Lord is the stronghold of your life—of whom shall you be afraid?" Enjoy life to the fullest! (John 10:10)

Conclusion

There is an ultimate name book being written called the Lamb's Book of Life. Whoever has sinned against the Lord will be blotted out of His book (Exodus 32:33). "He who overcomes will, like them, be dressed in white. I will never blot out his name from the book of life, but will acknowledge his name before my Father and His angels," Revelation 3:5. Our choices decide whether we are erased or sealed. We will be judged according to what we did as recorded in the books (Revelation 20:12). "Nothing impure will ever enter it, nor will anyone who does what is shameful or deceitful, but only those whose names are written in the Lamb's Book of Life," Revelation 21:27.

When we transition from this earth to our eternal home in heaven, we will be given an everlasting name (Isaiah 56:5); a new name that the mouth of the Lord will bestow (Isaiah 62:2). Revelation 3:12 says, "Him who overcomes I will make a pillar in the temple of my God. Never again will he leave it. I will write on him the name of my God and the name of the city of my God, the new Jerusalem, which is coming down out of heaven from my God; and I will also write on him My new name."

I wonder what my new name will be. Whatever God chooses, I believe it will be an extension of His own. I am looking forward to Him affirming you and me by saying, "Welcome home. This is my beloved son/daughter in whom I am well pleased."

Reference Books:

1. What's in a Name?
   Compiled by Linda Francis, John Hartzell, Al Palmquist
   Ark Products

2. The Everything Baby Names Book
   By Lisa Shaw
   Adams Media Corporation

3. 35,000+ Baby Names
   By Bruce Lansky
   Meadowbrook Press

4. 50,000 Best Baby Names
   By Diane Strafford
   Sourcebooks, Inc.

5. Big Book of Baby Names and Announcements
   By Sandra Buzbee Bailey
   HP Books

6. The Very Best of Baby Names
   By Barbara Kay Turner
   Berkley Books, NY

7. Baby Names for the New Century
   By Pamela Samuelson
   Harper Paperbooks

8. 20,000 Names for Baby
   By Carol McD. Wallace
   Avon Books

9. Strong's Exhaustive Concordance
   By James Strong
   Crusade Bible Publishers, Inc.

10. Vine's Expository Dictionary
    By W.E. Vine
    Fleming H. Revell Company

11. The Thompson Chain Reference Bible
    New International Version
    Compiled and edited by Frank Charles Thompson, D.D., Ph.D.
    B.B. Kirkbride Bible Co., Inc.

Index of Character Traits

Objects, places and occupations are included.

Consecrated: Bessie, Beth, Betty, Elizabeth, Isabella, Isabelle, Lisa, Liz, Lizzie, Preston

Constancy: Connie, Constance

Contented: Leah, Leigh, Sheila

Counsel: Avery, Connor, Conrad, Kurt

Counselor: Aubrey, Avery, Kurt, Malorie, Mildred, Millie, Quinn

Courageous: Ariel, Dale, Dean, Reed, Reid, Tristan, Yvonne

Courteous: Curtis, Garrett

Creation: Adam, Addison, Shania

Creative: Adrian, Adriana, Maya, Penny

Crossroads: Travis

Crown: Laura, Lauren, Lorene, Lorie

Crowned: Larry, Stephanie, Stephen, Steve, Steven, Tiara

Dane: Dana

Dark: Colby, Colton, Darcy, Doug, Douglas, Keira, Keri, Kerry, Layla, Leila, Lila

Day: Daisy

Dear: Cherise, Darla, Darlene

Declarer: Joel, Neveah

Decree: Dathan

Defender: Brynna, Chad, Sandi, Sandra, Sandy

Deliverance: Isaiah

Delivered: Braden, Brayden

Deliverer: Erin

Dependent: Paul, Paula, Pauline, Polly, Vaughn, Von

Descender: Jordan

Desire: Hope

Determined: Valerie

Devoted: Dorene, Landon

Devotee: Connie, Constance, Reba, Rebecca, Rebekah

Devout: Pia

Dignity: Donna

Diligent: Amelia, Bev, Beverly, Emily, Travis

Discerner: Denise, Dennis, Sidney, Sydney

Discretion: Martha, Russell

Dispenser: Spencer

Distinction: Cameron, Camron, Reagan, Ryan, Xerxes

Divine: Deva, Diana, Diane, Oscar

Divinely: Jeffrey

Dove: Jonah, Jonas

Dweller: Bev, Beverly, Carson, Cora, Corey, Corina, Corrie, Cory, Courtney, Dale, Dean, Dwight, Glenn, Glennis, Glenyce, Kirk, Lesley, Leslie, Stan, Stanley

Dwells: Celina, Celine, Selina, Shelby

Earnest: Connie, Constance, Ernest, Reba, Rebecca, Rebekah

Earth: Adam, Adrian, Adriana

Endurance: Ursula

Enduring: Craig

Enlightened: Lucas, Luke, Whitney

Enthusiastic: Aiden, Brenda

Established: Brody

Estate: Preston, Shelby

Esteemed: Mae, May, Rod, Rodney

Exalted: Aliyah

Excel: Brice, Bryce

Excellence: Sidney, Sydney

Excellent: Bob, Doris, Kelly, Rob, Robert, Roberta, Ruby, Sterling

Expectation: Hope

Fair: Tanya, Tonia, Tonya

Faith: April, Faith, Fay, Fayth, Ike, Isaac, Vera

Faithful: Arleen, Arlene, Arleta,, Caleb, Dillan, Dillon, Dylan, Pia, Spencer, Vera, Vesta

Faithfulness: Emmanuel, Immanuel, Ivy, Joe, Joseph

Fame: Bob, Rob, Robert, Roberta, Robin, Rolf

Famous: Buddy, Lois, Louise, Marvin, Merrill, Merrillyn, Nolan, Rod, Rodney, Roger

Farm: Colby

Farmer: George, Georgia, Georgie

Favor: Nina

Favored: Ben, Benjamin, Reuben

Fawn: Oprah, Orpah

Fidelity: Faith, Fay, Fayth
Fiery: Aiden, Brenda
Fifth: Quentin, Quincy
Fighter: Dustin
Firm: Carson, Ethan
Firmness: Connie, Constance
Flower: Heather, Jasmine
Follower: Chris, Christian, Christina,
    Christine, Christopher, Christy,
    Kristen, Kristi, Tina
Forest: Sylvia
Forester: Foster, Neveah
Forgiving: Miley
Fortress: Kim, Kimberly, Lesley, Leslie
Foundation: Carson
Fragrance: Jasmine, Maria, Mariah,
    Marie, Marilyn, Mary, Molly
Fragrant: Myra
Free: Alida, Dorsey, Frances, Francis,
    Frank, Franklin, Merle, Merlene,
    Oprah, Orpah
Freedom: Frances, Francis, Frank,
    Franklin, Percy
Fresh: Myra
Friend: Caden, Edwin, Kadin, Marvin,
    Warren, Winfield, Winston
Friendly: Buddy, Edwin, Marvin,
    Winston
Friendship: Winfield

Gazing: Cybil, Sybil
Gem: Megan, Peggy, Rita
Generous: Grant
Gentle: Garrett, Kevin, Mildred, Millie
Gift: Brett, Dorothy, Dot, Dottie, Evan,
    Gianna, Ian, Jan, Jane, Janet, Janice,
    Jayne, Jean, Jeanette, Jesse, Jessie,
    Joan, John, Jonathan, Juanita,
    Mathias, Matt, Matthew, Nathan,
    Nathaniel, Nita, Sean, Shawn, Ted
Giver: Courtney, Rosanne, Rose,
    Rosetta, Rosie
Glittering: Candice, Candy
Glorious: Herb, Herbert
Glory: Deva, Diana, Diane, Gloria
Glowing: Candice, Candy

God: Celina, Celine, Eli, Elijah, Joshua,
    Makayla, Marcia, Marsha, Mia,
    Michael, Micah, Michail, Michelle,
    Mikaela, Mike, Mitchell, Nathan,
    Nathaniel, Sadie, Sally, Sam,
    Samantha, Samuel, Sean, Selina,
    Seth, Shawn, Shelby, Ted, Tiffany,
    Tim, Timothy, Tripp, Vaughn, Von,
    Wanda, Wandeka, Wendy
Godliness: Makayla, Michael, Micah,
    Michail, Michelle, Mikaela, Mike,
    Mitchell, Norma, Tiffany
Golden: Goldie
Good: Bonnie, Clyde, Evangeline,
    Madison, Tobias, Toby
Good News: Ava
Grace: Hannah, Nancy, Nina, Sue,
    Susan, Suzanne
Graceful: Anita, Ann, Anna, Anne,
    Annette, Annie, Joanne, Luann,
    Sue, Susan, Suzanne
Gracious: Anita, Ann, Anna, Anne,
    Annette, Annie, Evan, Gianna,
    Ian, Jan, Jane, Janet, Janice, Jayne,
    Jean, Jeanette, Joan, Joanne, John,
    Jonathan, Juanita, Ken, Kenneth,
    Nancy, Nita, Roy, Sean, Shana,
    Shannon, Shawn
Grand: Rhonda, Ronda
Great: Bill, Billie, Billy, Grant, Liam,
    Mae, Max, May, Minnie, Morgan,
    Will, William
Guardian: Ed, Edward, Howard,
    Howie, Velma

Handsome: Allan, Allen, Ken, Kenneth
Happy: Blythe
Hawk: Gavin
Healer: Jason
Heard: Jayden, Sam, Samantha, Samuel
Heather: Heather
Heavenly: Goldie, Sheila
Helmet Head: Kennedy
Helper: Alec, Aleck, Alex, Alexander,
    Alexis, Cooper, Ezra, Sandi,
    Sandra, Sandy
Helpful: Norris

Hero: Yvonne
Heroic: Manning, Titus
Hill: Brent
Holly: Holly
Honey: Mindy, Pam, Pamela
Honey Bee: Meleeza, Melissa, Missy
Honor: Al, Albert, Brianna, Brianne, Earl, Grady, Heidi, Max, Merrill, Merrillyn, Nora, Pat, Patricia, Patrick, Patsy, Tricia, Trisha
Honorable: Madison, Manning, Titus
Honoring: Tim, Timothy
Horses: Phil, Phillip
Humble: Aliyah, Cecil, Celia, Gina, Viola, Violet, Yolanda
Humility: Claudette, Claudia, Esther, Jordan, Sandi, Sandra, Sandy, Stella
Hunter: Chase, Hunter

Illuminated: Allee, Allie
Image: Tiffany
Industrious: Amelia, Butch, Carter, Dana, Emily, George, Georgia, Georgie, Hailey, Henry, Ressie, Taylor, Teresa, Tessa, Theresa, Tracy, Tyler, Van, Walker
Inestimable: Anthony, Antonio, Tony
Innocent: Imogene
Integrity: Arthur, Artie, Clyde, Jaden, Jay, Jayden, Kyle, Kylee, Kylie, Sam, Samantha, Samuel
Intelligent: Hudson
Irish: Sheila
Island: Lindsay, Lyle, Shelly, Whitney
Ivy: Ivy

Jade: Jada, Jade
Jasmine: Jasmine
Jehovah: Eli, Elijah, Mathias, Matt, Matthew, Uriah, Zach, Zachariah, Zachary, Zechariah
Jewel: Amber, Pearl, Ruby
Joined: Levi
Joy: Abby, Abigail, Barbara, Barbie, Blythe, Carlene, Carmie, Carmen, Carol, Caroline, Carolyn, Charlotte, Charmay, Gail, Gale, Gay, Gayle, Hillarie, Hillary, Natalie, Noel
Joyful: Heather, Joy, Joyce
Judge: Dan, Daniel, Danielle, Justice
June: June
Just: Derek, Derrick, Justice, Justin
Justice: Justin

Keeper: Parker, Vesta
Kind: Kevin
Kindness: Mercy
King: Reagan, Ryan
Kingly: Roy

Lady: Donna, Jenna, Jennifer, Jenny, Martha
Lamb: Rachel, Railyn, Raquel
Lame: Claudette, Claudia
Laughter: Ike, Isaac
Laurel: Larry, Laura, Lauren, Lorene, Lorie, Tori
Law: Dathan
Leader: Derek, Derrick, Harley, Harold, Harry, Kennedy, Mack, Mackenzie, Perry
Leaf: Phyllis
Learned: Chance, Chancellor
Leaves: Laura, Lauren, Lorene, Lorie, Tori
Life: Chloe, Cloe, Daisy, Eva, Sommer, Summer, Verna, Zoe
Lifter: Wayne, Wright
Light: Aaron, Chandler, Cindy, Claire, Colton, Cynthia, Darcy, Doug, Douglas, Eleanor, Helen, Helena, Keira, Keri, Kerry, Lucas, Lucille, Lucy, Luke, Uriah
Lily: Elaine, Lillian, Lillie, Lily, Sue, Susan, Suzanne
Lion: Ariel
Little: Caroline, Charlene, Charlotte, Darla, Darlene, Paul, Paula, Pauline, Polly, Rachel, Railyn, Raquel, Reagan, Ryan, Shana, Shannon, Sharlene, Sheri, Sherry, Wyatt
Living: Frances, Francis, Frank, Franklin

Lofty: Alta
Love:, Amanda, Courtney, June, Mandy, Rosanne, Rose, Rosetta, Rosie
Loveable: Kevin
Loved: Darla, Darlene
Loyal: Dustin, Harvey, Marvin, Marty, Randy, Scott, Scottie
Loyalty: Faith, Fay, Fayth, Gary

Maidenly: Ginger, Ginny, Virginia
Maker: Cooper, Tyler
Man: Gabe, Gabriel, Gary, Wallace, Xerxes
Manly: Andrae, Andrew, Andy, Carl, Charles, Chuck, Drew, Forrest, Foster, Ken, Kenneth, Quentin, Quincy, Rolf, Roy
Meadow: Ashlee, Ashley, Ashlyn, Bev, Beverly, Brad, Braden, Bradley, Brady, Brayden, Hailey, Harley, Kim, Kimberly, Landon, Lee, Shirley, Stan, Stanley
Merciful: Mercy
Messenger: Angel, Angela, Angelina, Evangeline
Mighty: Don, Donald, Donovan, Israel, Marcus, Mark, Reggie, Regina, Ron, Ronald, Ronni, Ronnie
Mine: Mia
Mold: Clay
Mountain: Montgomery, Monty
Myrrh: Maria, Mariah, Marie, Marilyn, Mary, Molly

Night: Layla, Leila, Lila
Nobility: DeElla, Dutchess
Noble: Al, Albert, Alta, Arthur, Artie, Aubrey, Audrey, Austin, DeElla, Dutchess, Eugene, Gene, Grady, Heidi, Kim, Kimberly, Nolan, Nora, Pat, Patricia, Patrick, Patsy, Tanya, Tonia, Tonya, Tricia, Trisha
Nobleman: Earl
Nurse: Emma, Norris, Thelma

Obedient: Paige
Ointment: Myra
Open: Savannah

Overcomer: Don, Donald, Donovan, Israel

Park: Parker
Passionate: Brinleigh, Chonda, Sabrina
Pasture: Lee
Peace: Erin, Holly, Irene, Wallace
Peaceable: Solomon
Peaceful; Celina, Celine, Fred, Frederick, Irene, Jeff, Jeffrey, Jonah, Jonas, Lanae, Layla, Leila, Lila, Oliver, Olivia, Selina, Shelly, Solomon
Pearl: Maggie, Margaret, Marge, Megan, Peggy, Rita
Plain: Savannah
Plant: Ivy
Pleasant: Naomi
Pledge: Arleen, Arlene, Arleta, Jeff
Poet: Devin, Devon
Polished: Terrence, Terry
Pool: Lynette, Lynn
Possession: Dominic
Power: Bridget, Eric, Erica, Harriet, Maya, Ron, Ronald, Ronni, Ronnie
Powerful: Dick, Eric, Erica, Richard, Richardson, Richie, Rick, Walt, Walter
Praised: Jody, Judy
Prayers: Eliana, Laney
Precious: Amber
Pretty: Linda
Priceless: Anthony, Antonio, Tony
Priest: Preston
Princess: Gladys, Sadie, Sally, Sara, Sarah, Sharon
Promises: Eliana, Laney
Prophetic: Cybil, Sybil
Prosperity: Montgomery, Monty
Prosperous: Cora, Corey, Corina, Corrie, Cory, Ed, Edward, Glenn, Glennis, Glenyce, Lee
Protecting: Warren
Protector: Alec, Aleck, Alex, Alexander, Alexis, Bill, Billie, Billy, Chelsea, Chelsey, Kelsey, Liam, Minnie, Rae,

Ramona, Ray, Raymond, Velma, Will, William, Wilson
Provider: Brad, Bradley, Brady
Provisions: Spencer
Pure: Arianna, Catherine, Cathy, Ciara, Ginger, Ginny, Imogene, Jewel, Kaitlyn, Kalena, Karen, Kari, Katherine, Kathleen, Kathy, Katie, Katrina, Kay, Kayla, Kaylee, Keke, Lillian, Lillie, Lily, Pearl, Sierra, Virginia
Purity: Crystal, Kara, Megan, Peggy, Rita
Purpose: Valerie

Quality: Sterling
Queen: Gina, Tanya, Tonia, Tonya
Quick: Brice, Bryce
Quiet: Hazel, Layla, Leila, Lila

Raven: Brendan
Reap: Tracy
Reaper: Autumn, Ressie, Teresa, Teri, Tessa, Theresa
Red: Reed, Reid, Ruby, Russell
Reflector: Cindy, Claire, Cynthia
Refreshing: Brooke, Brooklyn, Carlene, Caroline, Lynette, Lynn, Rachel, Railyn, Raquel, Welford
Refuge, Landon, Noah, Schylor, Skyler
Rejoices: Gail, Gale, Gay, Gayle
Reliable: Mason, Miley, Troy
Remembered: Zach, Zachariah, Zachary, Zechariah
Renowned: Lewis, Louis
Report: Clyde
Resolute: Bill, Billie, Billy, Liam, Minnie, Velma, Will, William, Wilson
Restful: Shirley
Reverence: Austin
Rich: Edwin, Montgomery, Monty
Rising: Brent
River: Welford
Rock: Pete, Peter
Rose: Rosanne, Rose, Rosetta, Rosie
Royal: Kim, Kimberly
Rule: Norma

Ruler: Derek, Derrick, Dick, Eric, Erica, Fred, Frederick, Harold, Harry, Henry, Richard, Richardson, Richie, Rick, Rod, Rodney, Walt, Walter, Xerxes

Satisfied: Gavin
Savior: Isaiah, Joshua
Sea: Dillan, Dillon, Dylan
Seaport: Chelsea, Chelsey, Kelsey
Seashore: Morgan
Secretary: Chance, Chancellor
Secure: Alec, Aleck, Alex, Alexander, Alexis, Keith, Sylvia
Seeker: Doug, Douglas, Keira, Keri, Kerry, Tammy, Thomas, Tom
Seeking: Chase, Debbie, Debby, Deborah, Debra
Shelter: Schylor, Skyler
Shield: Randy
Shining: Bob, Rob, Robert, Roberta, Robin
Silver: Arianna
Singing: Callie, Kallie
Skillful: Meleeza, Melissa, Missy
Small: Vaughn, Von
Smart: Washington
Smooth: Terrence, Terry
Sojourner: Lyle
Soldier: Miles
Son: Ben, Benjamin, Hudson, Mack, Mackenzie, Perry, Reuben, Wilson
Song: Carmie, Carmen, Carol, Carolyn, Charmay
Spear: Gary, Gerald, Gerry, Oscar
Spring-like: Easter, Verna
Star: Esther, Stella
Steadfast: Ethan
Steep: Brent
Steward: Spencer
Stewardship: Bailey, Parker
Stone: Jada, Jade, Mason, Steen, Winfield
Straight: Kyle, Kylee, Kylie
Stranger: Barbara, Barbie
Strength: Audrey, Brian, Brianna, Brianne, Bridget, Bryan, Byron,

Gabe, Gabriel, Rhonda, Robin, Ronda, Talon

Strong: Andrae, Andrew, Andy, Audrey, Brandon, Brian, Brianna, Brianne, Bridget, Brittany, Brittney, Bryan, Carl, Carrie, Charles, Chuck, Craig, Dick, Drew, Ezra, Forrest, Foster, Harley, Harold, Harry, Josiah, Kennedy, McKenna, Perry, Pete, Peter, Phil, Phillip, Rolf, Ron, Ronald, Ronni, Ronnie, Steen, Ursula, Valerie, Vince, Vincent

Sturdy: Stan, Stanley

Supplanter: Jack, Jackie, Jackson, Jacob, Jake, James, Jamey, Jamie, Jim, Jimmy

Supporter: Ezra, Josiah

Sweet: Bonnie, Mindy, Pam, Pamela

Tailor: Taylor

Tenderhearted: Phyllis

Thankful: Grace, Tiara

Thanks: Grace

Three: Trey

Thresher: Van

Town: Washington

Transformed: Easter, Madeline, Madolia, Stacy, Stasy

Transparent: Crystal

Traveler: Tripp

Tree: Hazel, Holly, Lindsay, Oliver, Olivia

Treeless: Savannah

Triad: Trinity

True: Vera

Trustful: Faith, Fay, Fayth, Hope

Truth: Aleta, Angel, Angela, Angelina, Dwight, Evangeline, Hunter, Tammy, Thomas, Tom

Truthful: Alice, Alicia, Allison, Alyssa, Jack, Jackie, Jackson, Jacob, Jake, James, Jamey, Jamie, Jim, Jimmy

Twin: Tammy, Thomas, Tom

Union: Levi

United: Trey, Trinity

Upright: Justice

Vale: Percy

Valiant: Ralph, Riley

Victor: Larry

Victorious: Cole, Colin, Laura, Lauren, Lewis, Lois, Lorene, Lorie, Louis, Louise, Luann, Nicholas, Nichole, Nicia, Nick, Nicole, Nikki, Tori, Vick, Vickie, Victor, Victoria, Winnie

Victory: Brandon, Cole, Colin, Hayden, Nicholas, Nichole, Nicia, Nick, Nicole, Nikki, Vick, Vickie, Victor, Victoria, Vince, Vincent

Vigilant: Cliff, Clifford

Vigorous: Ernest

Violet: Viola, Violet, Yolanda

Virtue: Brian, Brianna, Brianne, Bryan, Doris, Kelly

Wagon maker: Wayne, Wright

Walks: Tripp, Wanda, Wandeka, Wendy

Wanderer: Wanda, Wandeka, Wendy

War: Marcia, Marsha

Warlike: Chad, Marcus, Mark, Martin, Marty

Warm: Sommer, Summer

Warrior: Gerald, Gerry, Harvey, Herb, Herbert, Kelly, Lewis, Lois, Louis, Louise, Marcus, Mark, Miles, Peyton, Roger, Walt, Walter, Wyatt

Watchful: Gray, Grayson, Greg, Gregory

Watchman: Greg, Gregory

Water: Doug, Douglas

Wave: Jenna, Jennifer, Jenny

Wealthy: Jessica

Weary: Leah, Leigh

Weaver: Penny

Well: Welford

Well-born: Eugene, Gene

White: Candice, Candy, Dwight, Gavin, Gwen, Gwynn, Jenna, Jennifer, Jenny, Whitney

Whole: Caleb

Will: Wilson

Winning: Winnie

Wisdom: Cassidy, Connor, Conrad, Dallas, Harriet, Mack, Mackenzie, Malorie, Mona, Monica, Quinn, Reggie, Regina, Sonia, Sonja, Sonya, Sophia, Washington, Xavier

Wise: Dallas, Denise, Dennis, Hudson, Jada, Jade, Lloyd, Mack, Mackenzie, Quinn, Rae, Ramona, Ray, Raymond, Russell, Shana, Shannon, Todd

Woman: Andrea, Madeline, Madolia, Martha, Mona, Monica, Sonia, Sonja, Sonya, Sophia

Womanly: Andrea, Carlene, Carol, Caroline, Carolyn, Carrie, Charlene, Charlotte, Sharlay, Sharlene, Sheri, Sherry

Woodsman: Forrest

Worker: Mason

Worshipful: Kirby, Kirk

Worth: Bob, Rob, Robert, Roberta, Sterling

Worthy: Austin

Writer: Devin, Devon

Young: Chloe, Cloe

Youth: Owen

Youthful: Jill, Julia, Julian, Julie, Owen